Bulletproofing Web Applications

Bulletproofing Web Applications

Adam Kolawa, Wendell Hicken, and Cynthia Dunlop

M&T Books

An imprint of Hungry Minds, Inc.

Best-Selling Books • Digital Downloads • e-Books • Answer Networks • e-Newsletters • Branded Web Sites • e-Learning

New York, NY • Cleveland, OH • Indianapolis, IN

Bulletproofing Web Applications

Published by
M&T Books
An imprint of Hungry Minds, Inc.
909 Third Avenue
New York, NY 10022
www.hungryminds.com

Copyright © 2002 Hungry Minds, Inc. All rights reserved. No part of this book, including interior design, cover design, and icons, may be reproduced or transmitted in any form, by any means (electronic, photocopying, recording, or otherwise) without the prior written permission of the publisher.

Library of Congress Control Number: 2001092904

ISBN: 0-7645-4866-2

Printed in the United States of America

10 9 8 7 6 5 4 3 2 1

1B/RU/RS/QR/IN

Distributed in the United States by Hungry Minds, Inc.

Distributed by CDG Books Canada Inc. for Canada; by Transworld Publishers Limited in the United Kingdom; by IDG Norge Books for Norway; by IDG Sweden Books for Sweden; by IDG Books Australia Publishing Corporation Pty. Ltd. for Australia and New Zealand; by TransQuest Publishers Pte Ltd. for Singapore, Malaysia, Thailand, Indonesia, and Hong Kong; by Gotop Information Inc. for Taiwan; by ICG Muse, Inc. for Japan; by Intersoft for South Africa; by Eyrolles for France; by International Thomson Publishing for Germany, Austria, and Switzerland; by Distribuidora Cuspide for Argentina; by LR International for Brazil; by Galileo Libros for Chile; by Ediciones ZETA S.C.R. Ltda. for Peru; by WS Computer Publishing Corporation, Inc., for the Philippines; by Contemporanea de Ediciones for Venezuela; by Express Computer Distributors for the Caribbean and West Indies; by Micronesia Media Distributor, Inc. for Micronesia; by Chips Computadoras S.A. de C.V. for Mexico; by Editorial Norma de Panama S.A. for Panama; by American Bookshops for Finland.

For general information on Hungry Minds' products and services please contact our Customer Care department within the U.S. at 800-762-2974, outside the U.S. at 317-572-3993 or fax 317-572-4002.

For sales inquiries and reseller information, including discounts, premium and bulk quantity sales, and foreign-language translations, please contact our Customer Care department at 800-434-3422, fax 317-572-4002 or write to Hungry Minds, Inc., Attn: Customer Care Department, 10475 Crosspoint Boulevard, Indianapolis, IN 46256.

For information on licensing foreign or domestic rights, please contact our Sub-Rights Customer Care department at 212-884-5000.

For information on using Hungry Minds' products and services in the classroom or for ordering examination copies, please contact our Educational Sales department at 800-434-2086 or fax 317-572-4005.

For press review copies, author interviews, or other publicity information, please contact our Public Relations department at 317-572-3168 or fax 317-572-4168.

For authorization to photocopy items for corporate, personal, or educational use, please contact Copyright Clearance Center, 222 Rosewood Drive, Danvers, MA 01923, or fax 978-750-4470.

LIMIT OF LIABILITY/DISCLAIMER OF WARRANTY: THE PUBLISHER AND AUTHOR HAVE USED THEIR BEST EFFORTS IN PREPARING THIS BOOK. THE PUBLISHER AND AUTHOR MAKE NO REPRESENTATIONS OR WARRANTIES WITH RESPECT TO THE ACCURACY OR COMPLETENESS OF THE CONTENTS OF THIS BOOK AND SPECIFICALLY DISCLAIM ANY IMPLIED WARRANTIES OF MERCHANTABILITY OR FITNESS FOR A PARTICULAR PURPOSE. THERE ARE NO WARRANTIES WHICH EXTEND BEYOND THE DESCRIPTIONS CONTAINED IN THIS PARAGRAPH. NO WARRANTY MAY BE CREATED OR EXTENDED BY SALES REPRESENTATIVES OR WRITTEN SALES MATERIALS. THE ACCURACY AND COMPLETENESS OF THE INFORMATION PROVIDED HEREIN AND THE OPINIONS STATED HEREIN ARE NOT GUARANTEED OR WARRANTED TO PRODUCE ANY PARTICULAR RESULTS, AND THE ADVICE AND STRATEGIES CONTAINED HEREIN MAY NOT BE SUITABLE FOR EVERY INDIVIDUAL. NEITHER THE PUBLISHER NOR AUTHOR SHALL BE LIABLE FOR ANY LOSS OF PROFIT OR ANY OTHER COMMERCIAL DAMAGES, INCLUDING BUT NOT LIMITED TO SPECIAL, INCIDENTAL, CONSEQUENTIAL, OR OTHER DAMAGES.

Trademarks: Hungry Minds, the Hungry Minds logo, M&T Books, the M&T Books logo, and Professional Mindware are trademarks or registered trademarks of Hungry Minds, Inc. in the United States and other countries and may not be used without written permission. All other trademarks are the property of their respective owners. Hungry Minds, Inc., is not associated with any product or vendor mentioned in this book.

Hungry Minds™ is a trademark of Hungry Minds, Inc.

is a trademark of Hungry Minds, Inc.

Credits

ACQUISITIONS MANAGER
Chris Webb

SENIOR PROJECT EDITOR
Jodi Jensen

TECHNICAL EDITORS
Matt Haughey
Matt Hamer

DEVELOPMENT EDITORS
Kezia Endsley
Susan Hobbs
Gus Miklos

COPY EDITOR
Kate Talbot

EDITORIAL MANAGER
Mary Beth Wakefield

SENIOR VICE PRESIDENT, TECHNICAL PUBLISHING
Richard Swadley

VICE PRESIDENT AND PUBLISHER
Joseph B. Wikert

PROJECT COORDINATOR
Dale White

GRAPHICS AND PRODUCTION SPECIALISTS
Sean Decker, Stephanie Jumper, Gabriele McCann, Laurie Petrone, Jill Piscitelli, Betty Schulte, Julie Trippetti, Jeremey Unger, Mary Virgin, Erin Zeltner

QUALITY CONTROL TECHNICIANS
David Faust, Susan Moritz, Carl Pierce

SENIOR PERMISSIONS EDITOR
Carmen Krikorian

MEDIA DEVELOPMENT SPECIALIST
Megan Decraene

PROOFREADING AND INDEXING
TECHBOOKS Production Services

COVER IMAGE
© Noma/Images.com

SPECIAL HELP
Sara Shlaer

About the Authors

Adam Kolawa is the CEO of ParaSoft Corporation, a leading provider of software productivity solutions. Kolawa came to the United States from Poland in 1983 to pursue a Ph.D. at the California Institute of Technology. In 1987, he and a group of fellow graduate students founded ParaSoft with the hopes of creating value-added products that could significantly improve the software development process. Kolawa's years of experience with various software development processes has resulted in his unique insight into the high-tech industry and his uncanny ability to successfully identify technology trends. As a result, he has orchestrated the development of several successful commercial software products to meet growing industry needs to improve software quality – often before the trends have been widely accepted. Kolawa has been granted seven patents for the technologies behind these innovative tools. In addition, Kolawa has contributed to and written commentary pieces and technical articles for various leading publications such as *Software Development, Java Report* and *SD Times*. He has also presented on software quality, trends, and development issues at industry conferences including JavaOne, Quality Week, Linux Expo, and Software Development. Kolawa holds a Ph.D. in theoretical physics from the California Institute of Technology. In 2001, Kolawa was awarded the Los Angeles Ernst & Young's Entrepreneur of the Year Award in the software category.

Wendell Hicken is the Vice President of Advanced Research and Development for ParaSoft Corporation. In his 12 years with the company, he has played a major role in all facets of product development – from the initial design phase, through development, and up to final product release. He has been essential to the conception, implementation, and continued development of products such as WebKing, RuleWizard, CodeWizard, Insure++, and the technologies that drive them. Hicken is also heavily involved in the development of many new Web-based innovations. Hicken holds a BS in Engineering and Applied Science from the California Institute of Technology.

Cynthia Dunlop is a Senior Technical Author for ParaSoft Corporation. Since 1998, Dunlop has been responsible for crafting ParaSoft product manuals and technical papers. Dunlop can also be credited with authoring numerous technical articles about issues related to software development. Prior to joining ParaSoft, Dunlop worked as a writing instructor at Washington State University. Dunlop holds an MA in English from Washington State University and a BA in English from UCLA.

Foreword

Testing and QA always get the short end of the stick – but they don't have to.

On a typical project (if such a thing exists), the software development lifecycle is expanded at the beginning and compressed at the end. Business requirements take longer to gather than anyone expects as developers, customers, and end users struggle to define their expectations. Planners underestimate the time necessary to translate those requirements into application models.

When the programmers finally begin coding, the project is already behind schedule. From the outset, the programmers rush through their work, under pressure from managers and customers to deliver the software according to the original schedule.

Through Herculean effort, the programmers accomplish their task; but under constant pressure, they're prone to cut corners. The one place this is most likely to happen is in the debugging process. When they hand over the project to a quality assurance (QA) team, shortcuts often happen there as well: Although it's rarely stated overtly, QA's job is to approve the code – not find fault with it, especially nontrivial design flaws that might require significant reworking of the application and delay its deployment.

This debugging/testing reality is especially true of server-side Web apps. Few developers understand how to test or troubleshoot Web apps effectively, and under the constant pressure to deliver, deliver, deliver, they don't have time to learn how to leverage this new paradigm. After all, the top brass says, the important job is to make the application live so that we can engage in competitive e-business – you can swat the bugs and improve performance later, right?

Wrong, and that's where *Bulletproofing Web Applications* offers a service to the software development community by providing techniques and best practices for integrating testing and QA into the complete Web development lifecycle – where they belong.

Alan Zeichick
Editor-in-Chief
BZ Media's SD Times

Preface

This book discusses strategies for bulletproofing Web applications. By *Web application,* we mean an enterprise system running on a server, accessed by a client that is typically a Web browser. These kinds of applications are usually associated with the HTTP protocol and use HTML for at least part of their interface. By *bulletproofing,* we mean making sure your application is robust, scalable, efficient, and reliable.

Many people viewed Web development as child's play during the early days of small static Web sites. It's now obvious, however, that Web development is as complex as traditional software development – if not more so. As a result of this complexity, it's almost impossible to produce a completely reliable Web application unless you implement (and continue to follow) a well-defined development process that incorporates a set of vital bulletproofing practices. That's where this book comes in.

We, the authors, have spent many years at ParaSoft Corporation working on technologies that help companies improve the reliability of their software. During this time, we have had the opportunity to observe many different companies' software development processes and gain a good understanding of what practices can be used to increase the reliability of many types of software products. Based on our extensive experience working with Web applications at several levels, we have developed what we feel is a useful approach to the challenge of developing bulletproof Web applications. This book describes that approach and suggests ways that you can apply it to your own development process and projects.

Intended Audience

This book is intended for people who are already familiar with Web applications, from developers to Quality Assurance testers to managers of Web development projects. Although we review the basic ideas, we don't show you everything you need to know to create Web applications. We do show you development and testing practices that you can apply to your application, and we give you ideas for improving the processes you use during development, including some tips on how to ensure that team members leverage one another's work (rather than step on each others' toes).

What You'll Learn

We describe and demonstrate a variety of bulletproofing practices that will help you predict and prevent potential problems, detect and remove existing problems, and construct your application in such a way that it can recover if an error occurs.

Many of these practices are based on practices that have proven successful for traditional software development and were extended to meet the unique needs and challenges of Web development. Although there is no "silver bullet" for reliable Web applications, there are a number of techniques and tools that can significantly improve application reliability.

Each time we introduce a general practice, we show you a variety of ways to perform that practice (including manual solutions, scripting solutions, and automatic tools). We emphasize automating your procedures whenever possible. We stress automation so strongly because we've seen how it can improve both reliability and efficiency, enabling team members to spend their time improving the application instead of putting out fires and performing tedious tasks. To keep our discussions concrete, we refer to specific languages and tools. Where we claim that you can write scripts to automate certain tasks, we usually give examples that you can actually run yourself. This is not intended to limit you to the scripts or tools we show but to provide illustrations of ideas we hope you can apply to improve your own application.

Beginning with Chapter 4, we develop a sample e-commerce site ("The Online Grocer") so that we can provide concrete examples in the discussions throughout the book. The primary version is developed using Java servlets and the Apache Web server. Additional versions using JSP, WML, XML, and other technologies are introduced in Part III. The implementation, however, is not the key point; the focus is on the methods for building and testing the application. Most of the ideas we discuss apply equally to applications developed using various technologies. Even the specific Java-centered approaches have analogous practices for other languages.

How This Book Is Organized

This book has been divided into three parts. If you are in a rush to find out more about a specific topic, jump right in to the chapter that seems most applicable. You can always go back to the introductory section later when you have more time.

Part I: Getting Started

Part I provides an overview of the development process and introduces the Online Grocer Web application that we refer to throughout the rest of the book. If you want to grasp the fundamental development strategies and issues we frequently touch on, we recommend that you read Chapters 1 through 3 before diving into the rest of the book. For details about the Online Grocer application, you can read Chapters 4 through 6. These details are particularly useful if you're having trouble following the examples mentioned in later chapters.

Part II: Bulletproofing Practices

Part II provides detailed information about challenges and practices relevant to most Web applications. It includes discussions of strategies such as defensive programming, coding standards, unit testing, functionality testing, content verification, and load testing. Generally speaking, these topics are introduced in the order in which you would encounter them during the development of your application. For the most part, these chapters can be read in any order, although they occasionally reference one another.

Part III: Other Technologies

Part III discusses "specialty" bulletproofing practices that are primarily applicable to applications using the relevant technology. We start by covering issues related to using databases in Web applications, move to XML and the related technologies of SOAP and Web services, and conclude by discussing components such as EJBs and server-side scripting technologies such as JSP.

Appendixes

In the appendixes, you'll find a summary of the key points from our sample programs, procedures, and tools, along with a list of additional resources. Some of these resources provide more information on topics we discuss in depth, whereas others offer a starting point for learning about topics that we touch on but don't cover in detail.

CD-ROM

The CD-ROM that accompanies this book includes the sample files referenced in the book – often with more detail than you'll find in the chapters. We encourage you to use these examples to see our practices in action and to experiment with ways of bringing these practices into your own development process. The CD also contains evaluation versions of many of ParaSoft's tools, as well as versions of freely available Web development tools.

Conventions

Throughout the book we use simple conventions common to most technical books. Code examples, or text you would type are entered in a fixed font as follows:

```
sample code
```

We use *italic type* to indicate a new term that we're defining, and we use shaded sidebars when we want to provide more detail about concepts mentioned in the text.

Icons Used in This Book

Icons appear in the text to indicate important or especially helpful items. Here's a list of the icons and their functions:

Notes provide additional or critical information and technical data on the current topic.

Cross-Reference icons point you to someplace else in the book where you can find more information on a particular topic.

The Tip icon points you to useful techniques and helpful hints.

The Caution icon is your warning of a potential problem or pitfall.

The On the CD-ROM icon points out a related sample file or additional information that you can find on the CD accompanying this book.

Feedback

We welcome your feedback on any aspect of this book. You can send e-mail to us at `bulletproof@parasoft.com`. We've also set up a Web page at `www.parasoft.com/bulletproof` where you can find any errata, along with additional examples.

Acknowledgments

This book is the product of many people's effort and help. We would like to thank the following people for their direct contributions:

Sierra Roberts, for making this project a reality and managing the entire process.

Jim Clune, for writing Chapters 17 and 18 and reviewing numerous other sections.

Marek Kucharski, for writing Chapters 16 and 20.

Dr. Roman Salvador, for writing Chapter 19 and contributing to Chapters 7, 8, and 9.

Arthur Hicken, for contributing to Chapter 16.

Alan Zeichick, for writing the Foreword.

Everyone at Hungry Minds who helped us mold our ideas into a presentable book, including Chris Webb for helping us get this book published, Jodi Jensen, for getting this project on track and coordinating its many facets; Susan Hobbs, Kate Talbot, Gus Miklos, Matthew Haughey, Matthew Hamer, and Kezia Endsley for their suggestions and editorial improvements; Carmen Krikorian for obtaining the necessary permissions for the CD; Megan Decraene for her work building and testing the CD; and the graphics and production staffs.

We also want to extend a special thanks to everyone at ParaSoft who has played a "behind the scenes" role in the development and quality of this book and the programs on the CD. This includes everyone in our development, quality assurance, marketing, sales, and corporate departments – especially Jenny Ahn, our invaluable Vice President. Last, but certainly not least, we would like to thank our customers for providing the feedback that has shaped our ideas and products.

Contents at a Glance

Contents

Part I

Getting Started

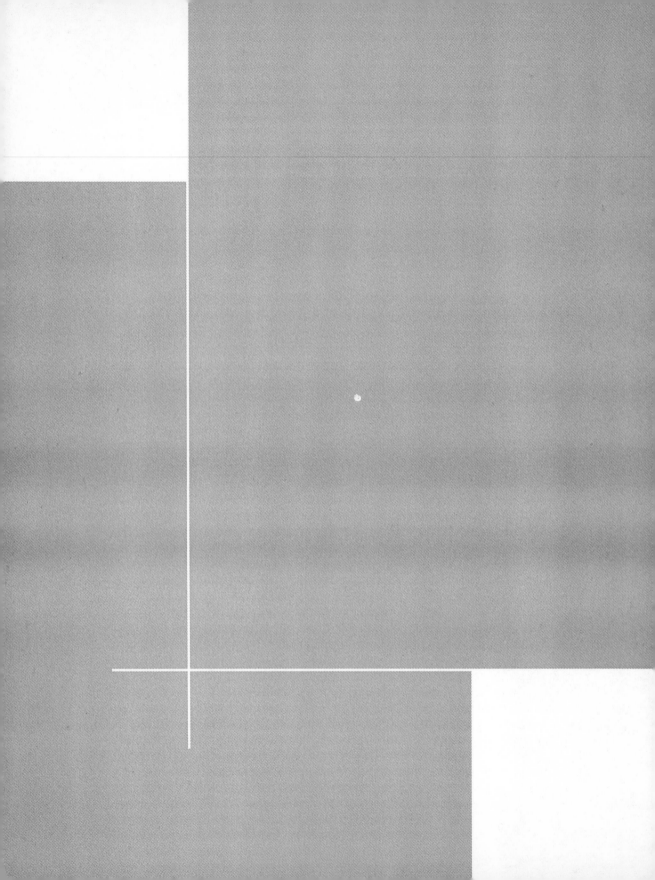

Chapter 1

Laying the Foundation for Reliable Web Applications

IN THIS CHAPTER

- Improving the development process
- Examining development process models
- Controlling errors during development
- Automating the development process
- Implementing a bug-hostile development process

EVEN THE MOST EXPERIENCED DEVELOPERS have difficulty producing reliable dynamic Web applications. The pages of these multitiered applications with Web interfaces constantly change, depending on user, time, and other variables. As a result, it's a challenge to ensure that different paths through the application don't contain errors and to verify that the application meets specifications under all possible conditions.

Because Web development can be so complicated, a well-defined, efficient development process is critical. Before you learn about the specific methods that bulletproof a Web application, take a closer look at the development process and explore ways to create a development process that effectively reduces the number of errors in the final product.

Improving the Development Process

Everyone in the development community is concerned about errors in his or her Web applications or software products. However, most people take the wrong approach to solving the problem of errors: They try to remove errors *after* they are introduced, by testing the software toward the end of the development cycle. Sometimes this strategy is effective, but most often it is not. In fact, more than half of all software projects fail because this type of testing strategy does not allow the company to ship an acceptable product within the project's deadlines and budget.

These problems can be solved by focusing on error prevention from the earliest stages of the software development process. Study after study has shown that error prevention is much more effective than error detection. When you consistently take steps to prevent errors rather than try to clean them up at the last minute, you end up releasing a more reliable product in less time. This book helps you create and implement a development process with built-in practices for preventing errors from being introduced and for removing errors as early as possible, before they have a chance to build upon one another and lead to more errors. Implementing such a development process is the key to bulletproofing your Web application. If you don't have a well-defined development process and everything is done randomly, ad hoc, with a lot of caffeine, the software you produce will inevitably have many bugs. If you have an orderly process, your software will have fewer bugs, and your development team will be working fewer late nights.

The first step in improving your Web development process is to take a quick overview of the general practices that compose any effective development process. After all, it is now clear that Web development is a type of software development – not an entirely different endeavor, as many thought in the early years of Web development. At first, Web development was not considered software development, but rather a hobby. This was largely due to the simple, static nature of most Web sites developed at the time. High-level executives figured that if their grandson could create a Web site in school, their developers could develop a corporate Web site in an afternoon. As Web sites grew increasingly complex, people realized that developing Web sites is as complicated as – if not more complicated than – building n-tier, complex client/server applications. As a result, developers started applying more and more traditional software development practices to their Web development projects. Since then, most developers and development managers have recognized that dynamic Web sites are very complicated software development projects that need to be approached and managed like any other software development project.

Because Web development projects are, indeed, software development projects, you can benefit from applying traditional software development practices to your Web development process. After we define the software development process and look at two types of software development processes, we explore the general bug-control practices that can be built into any software development process.

Examining Development Process Models

A *software development process* is a set of procedures that, when performed successfully, convert user requirements into deliverable software products. Ideally, the process is flexible and scalable enough so that it can successfully create many products of various types.

Considering the variations in training, expertise, projects, tools, and so on, it is not surprising that different development teams have different development processes. This variety of processes is beneficial: Certain processes are better suited for certain projects than others, and the more processes that are available, the easier it is to find one that perfectly suits the needs of the project at hand. However, despite this variety, most effective development processes share the following fundamental phases:

- Design
- Implementation
- Integration
- Testing

The position and length of these four phases distinguish one development process from another. Viewed in these terms, every software development process is similar to either the *waterfall* model or the *iterative* model.

The waterfall development model

The waterfall model contains lengthy design, implementation, integration, and testing phases. It is named after a waterfall because, as Figure 1-1 illustrates, its progression is steady and irreversible toward the destination. Just as a waterfall flows toward a river, stream, or lake, a waterfall software development process always moves toward the next phase and, ultimately, the release.

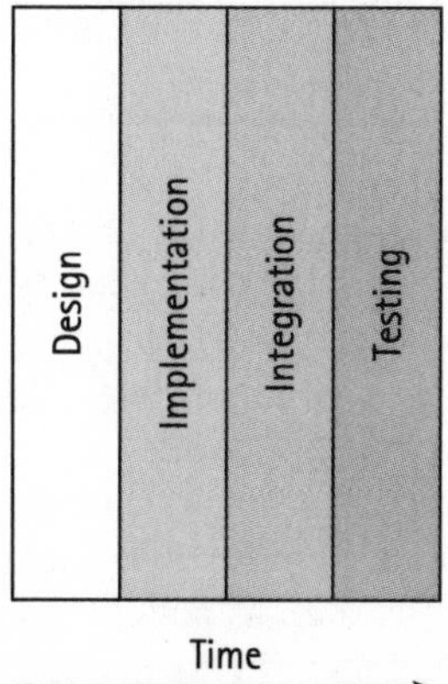

Figure 1-1: The waterfall development process moves through each phase of development until final release.

The waterfall model is better suited for stable projects because a significant change introduced in integration or testing can require much costly redesign, reimplementation, and recoding. With this comes increased expenses, a much longer development process, and an increased likelihood of introducing errors. Because of this model's inability to accommodate late changes, it works best for well-known, well-defined projects. For example, a waterfall model would be a wise choice if you were developing an accounting application and had definite plans to include all the traditional accounting features. Projects with vague or rapidly changing requirements generally should not be developed using a waterfall model.

The iterative development model

If you have a project with vague or rapidly changing requirements, the iterative model is a better solution than the waterfall model. In this model, an application is developed in a series of many brief design-implementation-integration-testing iterations, each of which implements the features critical for one release. Releases occur not only after the entire application is finished but also after you successfully implement the features requested for the current iteration. Releases are thus more frequent in this model than in the waterfall model, and the difference from version to version is probably less noticeable.

It is interesting to note that the series of iterations resembles one waterfall-like process if you look at the process from a distance, as shown in Figure 1-2. Much design is performed before a single iteration starts, the series of small iterations themselves resemble an implementation and integration phase, and a large amount of testing is performed after the completion of all iterations, when the application is truly complete.

The iterative model's many small iterations enable it to accommodate the sort of frequent and late changes that cause a project in the waterfall model to overshoot its release date and budget. This accommodation of change makes the iterative model particularly well-suited to situations in which it is difficult – or even impossible – to have a clear idea of the project's scope, for example, when you are developing a unique, ground-breaking application or an application that targets a rapidly changing market such as the Internet market. This model's series of frequent iterations makes it possible to release a working version of the product as soon as possible so that customers can use the product and decide which additional features are needed.

These two models exemplify vastly different philosophies on what constitutes process. Other models fall somewhere in between the one long iteration of the waterfall model and the numerous cycles of the iterative model. No matter which type of development process you use, you can ensure its success by integrating the following practices into it:

- Focus your work on necessary, important features.
- Keep bugs under control and prevent them from increasing exponentially.
- Automate as much of the development process as possible.

The remainder of this chapter discusses general strategies for integrating these practices into the four fundamental phases that development processes share. First, you learn about the purpose and benefits of controlling bugs and automating your development process. Then, you are introduced to the specific bug-control and automation practices discussed throughout this book. You can integrate these practices into various development processes by adjusting the associated tasks' position and length as needed.

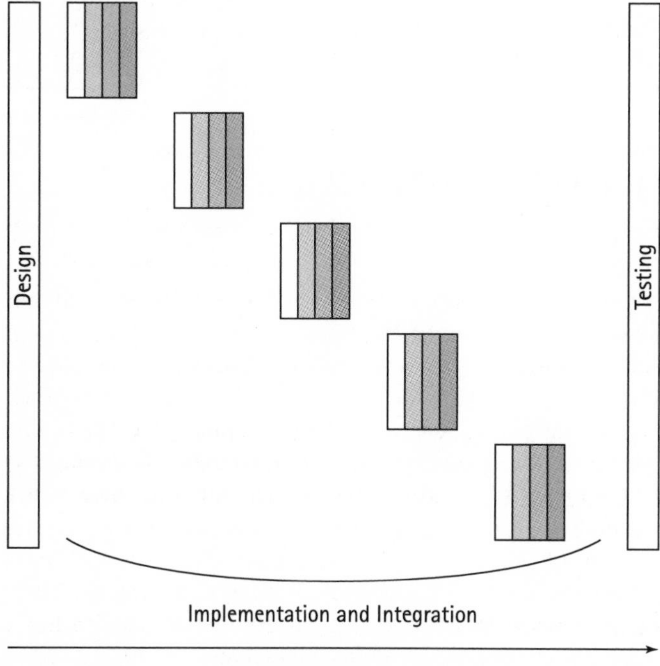

Figure 1-2: An iterative development process contains many frequent design/implementation/integration/testing cycles.

Focusing on the Important Features

Regardless of whether you are developing a product for internal use or external customers, you must elicit some degree of outside feedback to discover which features customers want and to ensure that these features are implemented in a way customers deem both usable and valuable.

The type and degree of feedback you need depends on the completeness and stability of your project's specification. If you are developing a stable product, you aim for specific customer feedback. If you are developing a new, breakthrough product, you first try to elicit market feedback and later aim for customer feedback.

The best way to elicit feedback depends on your company and targeted market, which lies beyond the scope of this book. The only advice we offer on this matter is that if you are serious about receiving a substantial amount of feedback on feature after feature, you should consider using an iterative development process. This process facilitates feedback because it enables you to deliver early betas and deliver releases incrementally.

In Chapter 10, you learn how to set up a staging server on which you can deploy a beta version of the application and elicit feedback before the official release.

Controlling Errors during Development

In the least effective development processes, bugs are not controlled. Rather, all but the most serious problems are ignored until the final stages of the development process. This is more dangerous than most people realize. When you allow bugs to enter and remain in your code, the bugs build on and interact with one another. This interaction usually has the critical effect of their increasing exponentially, rather than linearly, with time and the number of code lines. When bugs increase exponentially, you end up with significantly more bugs per code line than with a linear increase – so many more that often the project is cancelled.

There are, naturally, many kinds of errors. Some errors demand immediate attention, even with relatively crude development processes. This class of errors includes compilation errors in source code and crashes in core functionality. Other errors are visible but do not seem to require immediate fixing: this includes an incorrectly updated element on the Web site that is visible but does not affect other core functionality. A more insidious error is one that cannot be found without more thorough testing. Such errors can affect core functionality, but along paths developers do not commonly exercise.

One measure of the effectiveness of your development process is your group's attitude toward these kinds of errors. If any visible error is marked for immediate fixing, your group will be regarded as bug-hostile. If your group tends to tolerate errors, especially under the guise of "Well, that's not likely to happen anyway," you are headed for trouble.

The key to avoiding an exponential increase of bugs is error prevention, as well as finding and fixing existing bugs as early as possible. As Figure 1-3 demonstrates, one way to do this is to integrate error-prevention and error-detection measures into your development process. The specific error-prevention and error-detection techniques shown in this figure are introduced in the section "Controlling bugs during implementation" and discussed throughout this book.

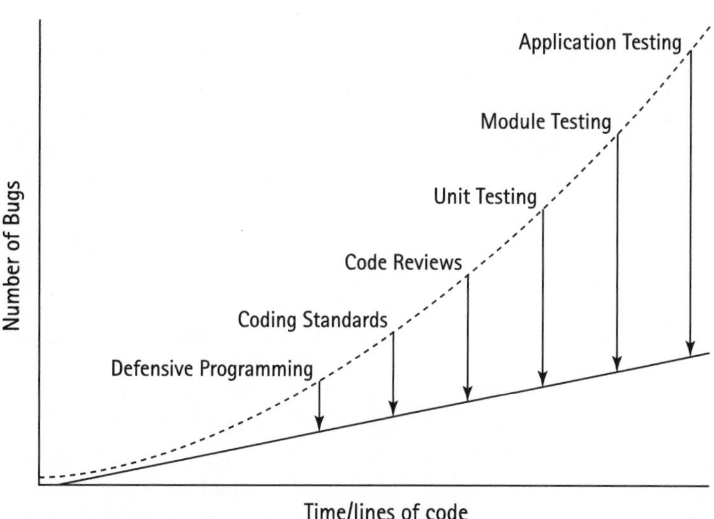

Figure 1-3: Bug control practices prevent the number of bugs from increasing exponentially.

Before you start looking at specific error control techniques, it's important to acknowledge that bugs can, indeed, be prevented. One of the greatest hurdles in keeping bugs under control is the widely held belief that bugs are inevitable. This is completely false. Errors don't just occur; every error in code exists because there was a possibility for error (for example, in the language or development process) and a developer made a mistake. The more error-prone the language and development process, the more errors are introduced. Thus, the key to preventing errors is to minimize the possibility of introducing errors.

Throughout this book, we discuss strategies for reducing the possibility of error. One of the best ways to do this is to implement and enforce coding standards for all developers, in all languages, every day, as described in Chapter 8.

When you acknowledge that errors can be prevented, you can start taking steps toward controlling them. To control errors best, ask yourself two questions each time you find an error:

- How could I have automatically detected this error?
- How could I have prevented this error?

Routinely answering these questions every time you find an error helps you prevent similar errors from occurring. It also improves your ability to detect as many bugs as possible. Because bugs build on one another, each bug prevented or detected early in the process usually means finding and fixing not just one bug fewer, but many bugs fewer later on.

Many developers and managers claim that they do not have the time or money to spend on such bug-control efforts. The fact is that those who are most concerned about releasing products on time and on budget are most in need of such practices. Study after study has confirmed that

- Focusing on error prevention results in shorter development schedules and higher productivity.
- The longer a defect remains in the system, the more expensive and difficult its removal becomes.

Automating the Development Process

Although bug control can and should reduce development time and cost, it does not always do so. Its great potential is often unrealized because inefficiencies of the development process do not make bug control a feasible and efficient strategy. Specifically, if the development process and bug-control measures are not as automatic as possible, they end up consuming almost as much time, money, and effort as they could potentially save, and your project quality does not improve as much as it would if you automated your development and bug-control efforts. For a development process to control bugs successfully and – at the same time – reduce development time, effort, and cost, it should have the following elements built in to it:

- A source code repository and version control system
- Automated regular builds
- A bug-tracking system
- Automatic development tools

A source code repository and version control system

A *source code repository* establishes a central place where the entire source base can be stored and accessed When you use a source code repository, you can not only track the history of the code but also improve efficiency by ensuring that revisions are not carelessly overwritten. The ability to revert back to archived versions also enables you to take risks with your revisions and to start over again when so many bugs have been introduced that recoding is easier than debugging.

Version control systems that can be used to establish and manage a source code repository include RCS, CVS, Microsoft Visual SourceSafe, and Rational ClearCase. You can use these tools as is or customize them to your team's specific needs by wrapping them with your own scripts.

Automated regular builds

Regularly scheduled builds that automatically reconstruct the entire application are a very effective way to prevent an application's components from evolving in incompatible directions. For example, inconsistencies can creep into standard form interfaces, or the different developers can inadvertently add inconsistencies in GUI components. Such builds should be scheduled to occur as frequently as is practical – preferably on a nightly basis. For maximal effectiveness, regularly scheduled builds should start with a clean slate by pulling all necessary code from the source code repository into an empty directory, then compiling the necessary components, and building the application. Upon success, the procedure should also run all available test cases and report any failures that occur.

A well-planned build process offers the following benefits:

- Provides early detection of incompatible changes in the application components
- Ensures that the application continues to run as expected and detects any errors introduced by newly integrated code
- Helps you assess the project's status quickly, which, in turn, enables you to respond quickly to the market
- Helps the development team work together more efficiently and encourages team members to work more carefully

A bug-tracking system

A bug-tracking system, such as GNATS or Bugzilla, has two main uses. The first and most important use is to record and track all errors not detected by your test suite. Careful recording of every bug report into the system facilitates problem tracking and provides valuable data about the types of errors teams or developers tend to make – data that can be used to hone error-prevention and error-detection efforts. Ideally, the system ensures that the appropriate people are automatically notified about the problem, and it correlates bugs to source versions.

The second use of a bug-tracking system is to record feature requests not yet being implemented. A reliable method for storing features facilitates the design phase of the next iteration. If recorded in this way, feature ideas can be easily and quickly recalled when it is time to debate the next feature set.

Automatic development tools

Automatic development tools come in many flavors. For bug-control purposes, you want automatic development tools that

- Prevent and detect errors at the unit level.
- Detect application-level errors.
- Perform regression testing.

The time you spend evaluating multiple tools and finding the best solution pays off in the long run. The time spent evaluating a tool is easily regained if you find a tool that automates more processes than other tools or enables you to find and prevent more bugs than other tools. The development tools that help you control errors most effectively are those that

- **Contain the most effective technology:** The tools with the best technology find and prevent the most errors. If an error-prevention or error-detection tool does not effectively prevent or find errors, all of its other features are irrelevant.
- **Require minimal user interaction:** Compare how much user interaction each tool requires. Look for features such as automatic creation of test cases, harnesses, and stubs, easy ways to enter user-defined test cases, and so on.
- **Are customizable:** The better you can tailor the tool to your specific team and project needs, the more efficiently you can control bugs.
- **Have interactive and batch modes:** Look for a tool you can run interactively and in batch mode. Use interactive mode as you are testing newly developed code and fixing errors. Use batch mode during the automated regular build to perform regression testing.

- **Integrate with other infrastructure components:** Many development tools can be integrated into the compilation and building process. Such integration is helpful in ensuring that no new errors are introduced and in catching new errors as soon as possible – when the code is fresh in your mind and before the new error spurs additional errors.

Implementing a Bug-Hostile Development Process

When you have all the elements critical for an effective development process, you can start implementing them in a way that controls bugs.

As you implement a new development process (or refine an existing one), you must make sure that all your team members understand how each practice of the process relates to them and why it is being implemented. The best process in the world is of no use if your team members regularly circumvent its requirements because they view them as a nuisance.

If your organization is not accustomed to following many procedures, you will find resistance to implementing anything that adds significant overhead to your development process. We have found that the best solution to this problem is to find the simplest process with the lowest implementation cost, which provides immediate benefits. Although this seems a self-evident truth, many people read a book such as this one and immediately introduce so much overhead to their development process that the changes, even though sound in spirit, fail to take root.

Many people are now promoting lightweight, or *agile*, methodologies. You can find more detail on agile methodologies at `http://martinfowler.com/articles/newMethodology.html`, `www.sdmagazine.com/documents/s=844/sdm0108a/0108a.htm`, and `www.agileAlliance.org`.

You can do two main things to increase the chances of team members' buying into a new development process:

- Use automation to ensure that the benefit of performing each required practice clearly compensates for the resources necessary to perform it.
- Tailor the development process to the team's current projects, strengths, and weaknesses. Blindly pushing every possible practice into an existing project is a sure recipe for disaster.

After you decide which practices are the most critical in your development process, use your automatic testing tools to establish gates for ensuring that critical practices are not overlooked. *Gates* are quality checks that prevent you from moving to the next development stage until you have prevented and/or detected as many errors as possible at the current development stage. By using gates, you can

- Prevent code from becoming error-prone.
- Prevent error-prone code from causing errors.
- Prevent existing errors from spawning more errors.
- Ensure that existing errors are found and fixed as easily, quickly, and cheaply as possible.
- Ensure that the same errors are not repeatedly introduced into the code.

Controlling bugs during design

Bug control should be an issue as early as the design phase. The first step in the design phase is to determine which features to implement in the current iteration (either one of many brief iterations or a long waterfall iteration). To do this, developers and managers make a master list of all possible feature candidates (including those entered in the bug-tracking system) and select features, with the help of customer and/or market feedback. Chosen features are assigned to specific team members. The remaining features are recorded in the bug-tracking system so that they can be easily accessed when it is time to design subsequent iterations.

After the feature set is selected and specific tasks are assigned, you determine how to lay out the new code. In doing so, strive for flexibility. Flexibility is especially critical if you are working within an iterative development process, because you will undoubtedly have to extend the design in later iterations. The design that is the simplest, most readable, and most flexible will foster the fewest errors as the application is modified. This process can be automated with the use of CAD tools such as Rational Rose or graphics tools such as Visio, which help you map the page flow through your Web application.

Ideally, the design phase concludes with a design review in which developers explain their designs to one another. Simply explaining the design sometimes exposes complexity and ambiguity that can lead to errors during the initial implementation or during modification.

Controlling bugs during implementation

Because implementation is the phase in which most bugs are introduced, it is the prime phase for performing bug control. The main methods of controlling bugs during implementation are

- Practice defensive programming
- Enforce coding standards

- Perform code reviews
- Perform unit testing
- Use test suites as gates

The methods discussed here are the ones introduced earlier in Figure 1-3.

PRACTICING DEFENSIVE PROGRAMMING

One way to control bugs during implementation is to enlist the help of the ultimate authority on your code's status: the application itself. You detect subtle, difficult-to-find bugs by designing and implementing code sections to monitor and validate the internal state of an application.

When you program defensively, you anticipate where failures might occur and then create an infrastructure that

- Tests for errors.
- Notifies you when anticipated failures occur.
- Performs any damage-control actions you have specified (such as stopping program execution, redirecting users to a backup server, turning on debugging information you can use to diagnose the problem, and so on).

Effective defensive programming techniques include

- Validating user input
- Embedding debugging support
- Software firewalls
- Design by Contract

These defensive programming techniques are discussed in detail in Chapter 7.

ENFORCING CODING STANDARDS

Coding standards are language-specific rules that, if followed, significantly reduce the opportunities for developers to introduce errors into an application. Coding standards do not uncover existing problems; rather, they prevent errors from occurring.

Generally, two types of coding standards help you prevent errors:

- **Industrywide coding standards:** Rules that are accepted as best practices by experts in the given language (for example, the C++ coding standard "Write `delete` if you write `new`" or the Java coding standard "Use `StringBuffer` instead of `String` for nonconstant strings").
- **Custom coding standards:** Rules that are specific to a certain development team, project, or developer. There are three types of custom coding standards: company, project-specific, and personal:

- *Company coding standards* are rules specific to your company or development team, for example, a rule that enforces a naming convention unique to your company.
- *Project-specific coding standards* are rules designed especially for a particular project.
- *Personal coding standards* are rules that help you prevent your most common errors.

Because coding standards are designed to prevent bugs rather than detect them, you should use coding standards all the time, in all languages, to reduce the possibility of errors.

In some companies, coding standards are enforced during code review. We have found that you can optimize both coding standard enforcement and code review if you enforce coding standards automatically before the code review. Enforcing them automatically is faster, more precise, and more objective than enforcing them manually. Moreover, when you enforce coding standards automatically before the code review, you remove the most tedious part of the code review and also ensure that the code to be reviewed is already written in the style the team members have agreed on and can readily understand.

Coding standard enforcement is discussed in detail in Chapter 8.

PERFORMING CODE REVIEWS

After code is written and coding standards are enforced automatically, developers get together and perform a code review. This review is similar to the design review; the developers verbally explain their code. As in the design review, problems that could later lead to errors are often exposed.

PERFORMING UNIT TESTING

Unit testing involves testing the smallest possible unit of an application or system (for example, a servlet in a Web application or a class in a C++ application). Unit testing is universally recognized as an essential component of the software development process. Practitioners of unit testing enjoy benefits such as easier error detection, which has the very desirable outcome of increasing software quality at the same time that it reduces development time and cost.

The first way that unit testing facilitates error detection is by making it easier for you to reach the errors. As Figure 1-4 illustrates, when you test at the unit level, you are much closer to the errors and have a much greater chance of designing inputs that reach errors. You also have a greater chance of achieving 100-percent coverage.

The second way that unit testing facilitates error detection is by preventing bugs from spawning more bugs, which relieves you from having to wade through problem after problem to remedy what began as a single, simple error. Because bugs build upon and interact with one another, if you leave a bug in your code, chances are it will lead to additional bugs. If you delay testing until the later stages of development, you will probably have to fix more bugs, spend more time finding and fixing each bug, and change more code in order to remove each bug. If you test as you go, it is easier to find and fix each bug, and you minimize the chances of bugs spawning more bugs. The result: a significant reduction in debugging time and cost.

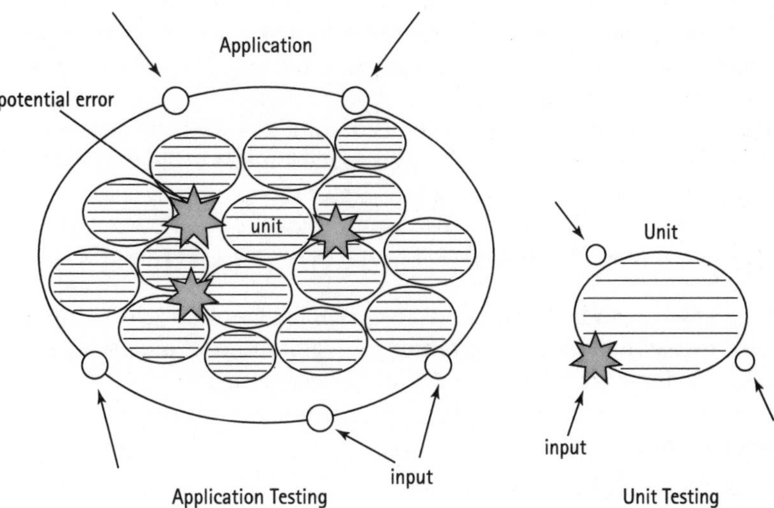

Figure 1-4: When you perform unit testing, reaching (and thus detecting) errors is easier.

However, unit testing can be difficult to perform. Just making a unit testable is often difficult. Making a C++ or Java class testable usually requires the creation of scaffolding and stubs. Making a dynamic Web application's servlet fully testable requires the deployment of the program, as well as the invocation of specific instances of the related output pages. In addition, unit testing involves several complex types of testing:

- **White box testing:** Ensures that the unit is constructed properly and does not contain any hidden weaknesses.
- **Black box testing:** Ensures that the unit functions in the way it is intended to function.
- **Regression testing:** Ensures that modifications do not introduce errors into a previously correct unit.

Fortunately, there are ways of integrating unit testing into your development process so that it not only improves quality but also saves you significantly more time and resources than it consumes.

The concept of unit testing is discussed in detail in Chapter 9. Additional testing strategies that can be applied to Web applications at the unit or application level are discussed in Chapters 11–14.

USING TEST SUITES AS GATES

Before you proceed from implementation to integration and testing, you enforce coding standards, perform a code review, perform unit testing, and correct all problems and errors. In addition, start performing automated regular builds. These builds should begin as soon as you write your first chunk of code. At this phase in the development process, your build should compile and build the code and then have your unit-testing tool(s) run your entire test suite to ensure that changes have not introduced errors (that is, you perform regression testing). The test cases run at this point should be the same test cases you used when performing unit testing. You should not move to the next phase of development until you pass all of these tests.

The logistics of building (or deploying) a Web application, as well as information on establishing gates, is discussed in detail in Chapter 10.

Controlling bugs during integration and testing

When you are ready to start building the complete application, add integration into your automated regular builds. After performing integration, your automated regular builds should perform the following tests in the background:

- Module testing
- Application-level black box testing
- Application-level white box testing
- Application-level regression testing

These measures ensure that any errors related to the interaction between units are detected as soon as possible. They find problems (such as memory corruption) that cannot be detected until integration and ensure that modifications do not introduce new errors into previously clean, functional code.

Module and application testing are discussed in Chapter 15.

PERFORMING MODULE TESTING

After you verify that your units are constructed strongly and work as expected, perform module testing to verify that each module works correctly and that modules interact as expected. A *module* is a collection of units. For example, each component of a Web application (such as a database, a legacy system, a fully functional EJB, an ERP system, or any levels of the tiered diagram in Figure 2-1 in Chapter 2) is a module. Another example of a module is a compiled program.

One way to verify a module's functionality is to connect the module to a testing tool that emulates the behavior of other system elements. For example, to perform module testing on a database, you could hook it up to one of these testing tools and see how it responds to different types and loads of requests.

After you verify that each module works okay on its own, check how the modules interact with one another. This process often involves verifying whether high-level requirements are implemented. For example, if you had a meal-planning application, you would want to verify that the main dishes it suggests each week are varied. Not only do you want the main ingredients to vary, but you also want the types of main ingredients to vary so that the system does not recommend four types of fish entrees within five days.

In most cases, you verify this type of high-level functionality by writing testing routines that run in the appropriate situation and verify whether the functionality works as expected. You can start adding such routines at the module level and then extend them to check application-level functionality.

It is important to note that you often need to write code and understand code in order to test code. That's why it is best for developers to test their own code thoroughly before passing it off to QA. This is the standard for all industries in which quality is critical. Would you want to fly on an airplane that was never tested by someone familiar with its operation, design, and potential weaknesses?

PERFORMING APPLICATION-LEVEL BLACK BOX TESTING

Application-level black box testing checks whether the entire application performs according to specification. If you perform unit and module testing, you can be confident that each unit and module works as expected, but you must wait until the integration phase to determine whether all the units and modules interact according to specification. As soon as you start to build the application, start building an application-level black box testing suite. This suite should include a test case for every aspect of the program's application-level functionality and for every error detected.

Application-level functionality testing also involves extending the set of high-level testing routines introduced in the discussion of module testing. Creating these routines is often the only feasible way to check the high-level design requirements most critical to your application's functionality.

PERFORMING APPLICATION-LEVEL WHITE BOX TESTING

Application-level white box testing examines the construction and performance of the entire application. For traditional software applications, this type of testing involves running the application and checking for memory problems and logical/algorithmic errors. For Web applications, this involves flushing and testing as many paths through the application as possible and checking whether each path contains critical problems.

Because complete coverage is often difficult to achieve at this level, you must be vigilant about monitoring these tests' coverage. An incredible difference exists between uncovering ten errors when your test suite has covered the majority of your application and discovering ten errors when your test suite has covered only 2 percent of the application. Without coverage data, error-found information is a useless metric. More importantly, without coverage data, you never know how many serious problems might be lurking in the untested parts of your code. You should not consider this phase of testing complete until you have covered 70–80 percent of the full-featured application's code and all the application's critical paths.

PERFORMING APPLICATION-LEVEL REGRESSION TESTING

An application-level regression test suite is composed of all the test cases you develop as you build units and integrate units into an application. Creating a comprehensive, well thought-out test suite helps you control errors in two ways. First, simply running the test cases detects errors. Second, this test suite can be used a gate. You should not work on other features or move to other iterations until this test suite is passed cleanly.

COMPLETING APPLICATION TESTING

As you find errors throughout this testing phase, remember to determine their causes and to write coding standards that prevent them. Also, each time you discover an error that your tools or test cases did not detect, do the following:

1. Enter the error in your bug-tracking system.
2. Create a test case for it.
3. Determine why the error was not detected and adjust your test suite, tool settings, and practices accordingly.

Finally, when you have a working, presentable product, perform usability testing so that you can receive valuable user feedback before placing the product on the market. As mentioned in the "Focusing Work on Important Features" sidebar at the beginning of this chapter, the best way to elicit valuable user feedback is to adopt an iterative development process and request feedback after each short iteration. This way, you never go too long without hearing from users, and you dramatically reduce the risk of investing too much time and effort into a design that does not meet customers' needs.

After you perform all these steps, achieve 70–80 percent coverage of your full-featured build, cover all your critical paths, and pass most, if not all, of your test cases, you are ready to move on to the next iteration or project.

Summary

In this chapter, we review basic elements that increase the efficiency and effectiveness of any development process. We discuss the importance of a well-defined development process and how you configure such a process so that it controls bugs throughout development. Along the way, we introduce general components that are critical to the success of a development process. We also introduce many bug-control practices, such as coding standard enforcement, unit testing, module testing, and application-level testing. These are expanded upon later in this book.

In the next chapter, we dissect the anatomy of Web applications, explain how Web applications are typically assembled, and offer tips on assembling reliable Web applications in the most efficient way possible.

Chapter 2

The Anatomy of a Web Application

IN THIS CHAPTER

- The definition of *Web application structure*
- The basics of building a Web application
- The Web development team

CHAPTER 1 PROVIDES A BASIC OVERVIEW of what an effective software development process looks like. The process is independent of the type of product you are developing and can be applied to any application, including Web applications. This chapter describes the structure of a typical Web application and looks at how an application is assembled.

Having an efficient method for assembling a Web application is a key factor in developing a successful Web application. Web applications must always be reliable and often have to be produced and updated on very tight development schedules. However, these applications' complex architecture and unique challenges make them considerably more difficult to build and test than traditional applications. Just assembling a functional Web application out of the disparate files, components, and hardware that are its building blocks can be a complex feat. Rapidly assembling a Web application in such a way that the parts work together as expected is an even greater challenge. Nevertheless, if this is not done, the application fails to be as reliable or timely as the market demands.

Another common requirement for many Web applications is the capability to support frequent design changes. Because the application is stored in a central location, you can support such changes without requiring customers to go through any kind of upgrade process. Maintaining customer interest generally requires the constant addition of new content and features. As new technologies or designs become popular, you want your application to support different ways of doing things. Your business model might also require rapid changes. For instance, as ad clickthroughs taper off, many Web sites are redesigning how they present and deliver ads, in an attempt to maintain advertiser support. This means that your application has to be more flexible than a typical non-Web application.

Defining Web Application Structure

When we use the term *Web application*, we mean a complex n-tier Web application consisting mainly of *dynamic* elements – elements that change, based on user, time, inputs, and so on. Generally, the components of Web applications are organized into three tiers:

- The Web client (the user's machine)
- The front network of Web servers
- The back network of middleware, databases, legacy systems, and the like

Tier architecture

A *tier architecture* is one in which the application is divided into multiple distinct modules. Each module is designed to handle a well-defined subtask, such as managing a database, implementing a business logic layer, or handling the user interface. From this perspective, tier architecture is much like modular programming.

The distinguishing aspect of a tier architecture is that the layers are independent components that might not even be running on the same machine. They work together but are not merged together into a single executable application. Generally, lower levels have no specific knowledge about what higher levels are doing. Each layer of a tier can run on different or multiple machines, and the various tiers are often implemented by different parties, in different languages, or using different standards. One advantage of a well-designed tier architecture is that you can often replace components at one level with different, equivalent components, making no changes to the rest of your architecture.

For instance, a Web application could have a Web browser (say, Internet Explorer running on Windows) talking to a Web server (say, Apache running on Linux) using HTTP. The Web server could handle the request by starting a Perl script. This script could connect to a Web service implemented on another machine, using Simplified Object Access Protocol (SOAP), and process the results to return data to the original Web browser. In the world of Web applications, this is a trivial example!

Figure 2-1 shows one possible structure of a Web application. As the figure's general structure illustrates, all the application's tiers communicate with each other to produce the pages that appear on the user's browser. When a client makes a request, the Web application's front and back networks work with each other to fulfill the request, and the data is sent back to the client.

Don't worry about the specific components of Figure 2-1. These vary from application to application and change as technology evolves. Instead, focus on the overall architecture, and note how complex Web application structures can be.

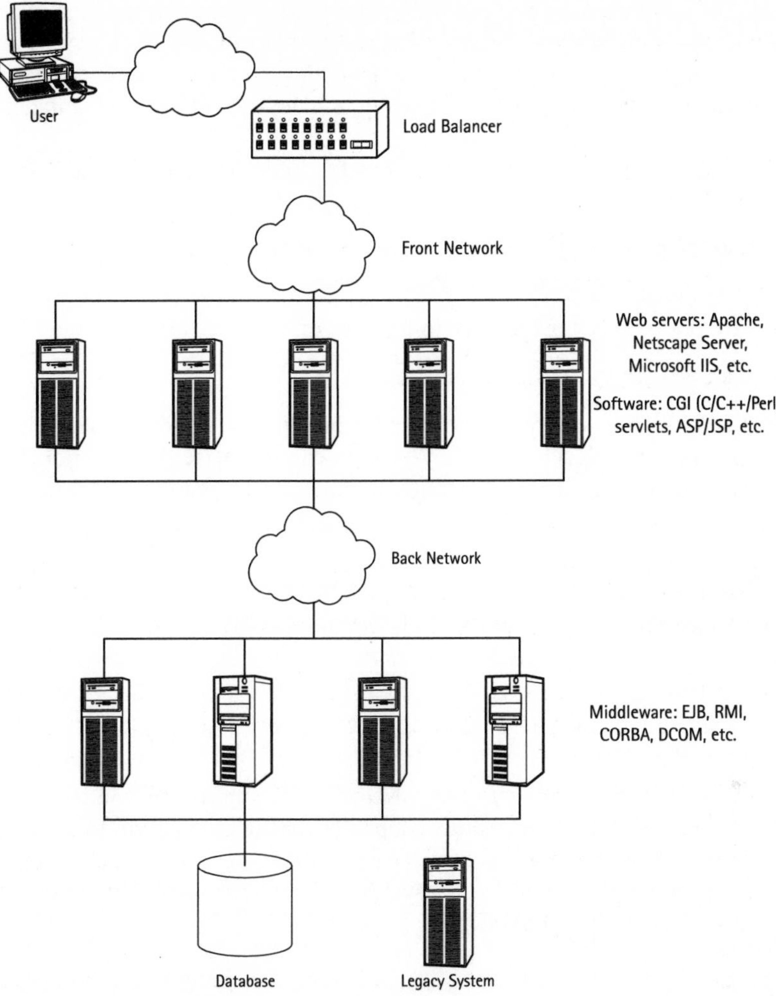

Figure 2-1: The structure of a Web application.

Web services

Often, the tiers of Web applications include Web services. *Web services* are self-contained units of business logic that can be accessed programmatically over the Internet by another software system. As these services continue to grow in popularity, many developers will be creating them or working on Web applications that plug in to Web services. Web services enhance functionality by providing an additional layer to a traditional Web application. These services plug in to traditional Web applications at the business logic tier and communicate with the existing application using Simple Object Access Protocol (SOAP), Web Services Description Language (WSDL), or other Internet-friendly protocols.

An example of a Web service is a unit of business logic that creates a meal plan by working with an online grocer's business logic. Another example is a service that helps a user find the lowest price on an item by searching multiple e-commerce sites and reporting the best available prices. Web services have several main advantages:

- They allow you to provide a new layer of functionality that can use data from multiple Web sites.
- They can be plugged in to multiple applications with minimal effort because they use Internet-friendly protocols.
- They are reasonably inexpensive to implement.
- They can be sold to multiple Web sites.
- When a good Web service for a particular functionality is developed (for example, a map service), multiple Web sites can purchase this functionality, which saves them from constantly having to reinvent the wheel.

We discuss Web services in greater detail in Chapter 18.

Now that you have had a bird's-eye view of how a Web application can be structured and how many building blocks must cooperate for the application to work, it should be clear why assembling a functional Web application is such a challenging task. In the next section, you will learn several general strategies that make the assembly process as smooth and painless as possible.

The logistics of the assembly process are discussed in Chapter 10.

Building Web Applications

To learn how these applications are built, you will begin with the most basic overview and progress to the tasks each Web team member performs on a day-to-day basis. The processes and practices described are based on those adopted by development teams with a history of producing reliable applications efficiently and economically.

Before examining the mechanical process involved in constructing a Web application, we're going to give you a closer look at its building blocks.

Application building blocks

Referring to Figure 2-1, you can see that a Web application can span multiple machines and different architectures. Each of these machines and architectures can have a different set of scripts, programs, and components. These building blocks might include

- The Web server (Apache, Microsoft IIS)
- Application servers (IBM WebSphere, BEA WebLogic)
- Custom code (DLLs, Java servlets, EJB, CORBA, scripts)
- Databases
- Static files (HTML, images, style sheets)

Several distinctions can be made between components of a Web application. Building blocks might remain on the servers or be sent to the client's browser. They might be static, or might be generated dynamically. They might be composed of data, algorithms, or both. The point to keep in mind is that the building blocks comprising Web applications are diverse. Understanding Web applications requires at least a basic knowledge of how these components work together.

The construction process

Assembling an operational, reliable application out of these disparate building blocks can be a nightmare. Often, for lack of a better method, people try to assemble an application by manually entering commands and running scripts on the various machines. However, this method has its share of problems:

- It is very prone to error.
- It is time-consuming.
- It is difficult to repeat.

This means that if you assemble your application manually, you will likely invest much time and effort trying to get all facets of your application in place. Chances are that every time you perform a complex process, you will forget something or do something incorrectly. Moreover, after you finally get everything in the correct place, you have no easy way to repeat your actions and will have to start from scratch again the next time you need to update, back up, move, or reconstruct the application. You must perform almost as much work as you did the first time you assembled the application.

However, if you automate this process as described in Chapter 10, you have to identify and correct each mistake only once, as long as each time you find an error, you fix the part of the process that caused that error. By the time you go through the process several times, you have ironed out most of the possible problems and established a solid, repeatable assembly process.

The major components required for establishing a repeatable assembly process include

- Specific source code repositories
- Staging areas
- Other components of the Web infrastructure
- Automated deployment technology

SPECIFIC SOURCE CODE REPOSITORIES

As mentioned in Chapter 1, a *source code repository* (source control) establishes a central place where the entire source base can be stored and accessed. With Web applications, the source code repository contains and manages access to all source code, scripts, executables, image files, and other files involved in building the Web application infrastructure, as well as any static files sent to users' browsers. Managing source code access is critical in Web development. The number of people from different departments working on the same source base creates much greater potential for error and confusion than a single group of developers sharing one source base.

Depending on your organization, you can have a single, central source code repository or different source code repositories divided according to groups or application modules. One common scenario is to use different source repositories for developers and writers. You need to analyze your organization to decide which setup is most appropriate for streamlining your development.

Whichever configuration you choose, the key to using source control is to ensure that everyone knows where his files belong and has access to necessary files. People who will be making modifications should have appropriate access to modify the files under control. If everyone does not have appropriate access, you are likely to end up with different versions of the same file spread across your system. This inevitably leads to added work and/or errors.

Because source control systems record the changes made each time a file is modified, they provide you with a history of modifications and help to identify who is responsible for various changes, should questions arise about what was done. These systems also allow you to undo changes you want to reverse, for whatever reason, and to track the growth or evolution of a project over time.

Another added benefit of using source code repositories is the capability to make frequent backups and snapshots of the work in progress. As long as all the important parts of your application are checked in, you can get a complete snapshot of the project in development just by backing up your source code repository. This is also useful in case you ever want to revert to an older version of the application.

STAGING AREAS

A *staging area* is a private version of the complete Web application. The purpose of a staging area is to provide a safe zone where application modifications can be tested before they are made live. This way, errors can be found and fixed before they reach the public. Some files (such as images and static pages) can be thoroughly tested without a staging area, but dynamic functionality (such as programs, database connections, and the like) cannot.

The staging area should look like the actual Web application but should contain copies of the same components used in the actual Web application. If the staging area does not contain similar databases, legacy systems, application servers, and so on, you cannot use it to determine how your application will perform. However, if you use the actual Web application components in the staging area (for example, if your staging area contains staging Web servers that interface with your database), you risk changing or possibly corrupting parts of your live application as you test your staging area. If you do need to mix live components into your staging area, be aware of the risks, and actively work to prevent potential problems.

The terms *test system* and *production system* are sometimes used to describe what we call the *staging area* and *live application,* respectively.

Often, development teams establish two staging area levels: a *personal staging area* (a private Web server containing all application components related to the application areas on which a developer is working) and a projectwide *shared staging area* (a directory that is essentially an internal-use-only Web server shared by all developers and Quality Assurance [QA]). The personal staging area lets developers start testing their work as early as possible so that they can find and fix problems before they check code into the common source code repository or have QA start testing their updates. When the entire application has to meet certain standards before it is deployed, the addition of just one bad file to the source code repository and/or shared staging area can prevent everyone's changes from being applied to the publicly available application.

For a discussion of how you can establish and maintain staging areas as efficiently as possible, see Chapter 10.

OTHER WEB BUILDING BLOCKS

Virtually all Web applications have dependencies on outside systems. The most common outside dependency is on the Web server itself. Part of your application includes configuring the Web server to deliver your files in the appropriate fashion. This requires you to consider who will have access to your files and to determine whether you want to set up domains and require authentication. If you are transmitting sensitive information, you should consider using HTTPS, which necessitates extra setup for the server and requires you to get appropriate certificates from the necessary security providers.

Some Web applications are tightly coupled to the Web server. For example, if you are using Apache, you can implement critical parts using FastCGI. This technique lets you bundle your application into dynamically loaded modules that execute as part of the browser rather than as separate processes.

If you are using servlets, you must make sure that your server is configured to support servlets and that the environment is properly set up to call your servlets.

All this information (which server, what changes were made, what the actual requirements of your application are) has to be well documented and stored in a central location so that other people can set up alternative staging areas without hunting for details vital to the site's execution.

Outside the server proper, there can also be databases, legacy systems, and anything else necessary to complete the Web application. In some cases, these resources are deployable (for instance, you can make a local copy of the database for testing), and in some cases they are not. A *nondeployable* resource is a module that cannot be moved, either for legal or technical reasons (for example, it might run only on certain hardware). In this case, you document how to access the resource and make sure that everyone understands whether the resource is available for testing purposes or needs special handling.

Throughout this book, we refer to different technologies used for building Web applications. Often, these are merely illustrative. Because so many technologies are available, we can only hope to cover a small portion in detail in a book of this size. We've included some references in Appendix E and hope that you will be able to find additional information on anything we mention that interests you. If you have questions, you can e-mail the authors at `bulletproof@parasoft.com`.

AUTOMATED DEPLOYMENT TECHNOLOGY

Automated deployment technology is any type of technology that automates the processes involved in taking the building blocks of a Web application and performing all compilations, initializations, transfers, and other operations necessary to assemble them into a functioning application.

THE DEPLOYMENT INFRASTRUCTURE AT WORK

In an efficient, repeatable development process, the parts of the Web construction infrastructure work together as follows (see Figure 2-2):

1. The source of the application is stored in the source code repository. A program or script retrieves the most recent versions of required files.
2. The staging area is cleaned. This helps you determine whether your deployment infrastructure can successfully create or re-create the application from scratch.
3. The deployment technology accesses the current files and then performs all operations (compiling files, setting values, and so on) necessary to assemble the files and other infrastructure components into a complete version of the application on a staging area.
4. The staging area is tested, away from the public eye.
5. After the staging area is deemed publishable, the staging area is cleared, and the application is deployed on the deployment area. In some cases, you can do an *incremental publish*, that is, modify only files that have changed. This is more efficient but requires a great confidence in the publishing procedure.

Different source code can live on the production servers and staging servers. For example, production servers can contain the current application at the same time that the staging servers contain the code for a completely reinvented version of the application.

CGI and FastCGI

CGI stands for the *Common Gateway Interface*. This protocol, developed in the early days of the Web, lets standard Web servers connect to programs (or scripts) written by developers to process certain URLs (especially form submissions). A program written to use CGI should work with any standard Web server. When a request comes in, the CGI program is invoked, processes the request, and sends a response back to the server. This is fine and dandy, but if your program is handling many requests, the overhead of starting and stopping the process becomes significant.

A more efficient solution is to keep the program in memory and always available to handle requests. You can extend most servers in this fashion if you write your code to their specific API. For instance, you can write dynamic libraries to be loaded as Apache modules. FastCGI is an open extension to CGI that lets you get this equivalent benefit without writing to a specific Web server API (although the server still needs to support FastCGI). You can learn more about FastCGI at `www.fastcgi.com`.

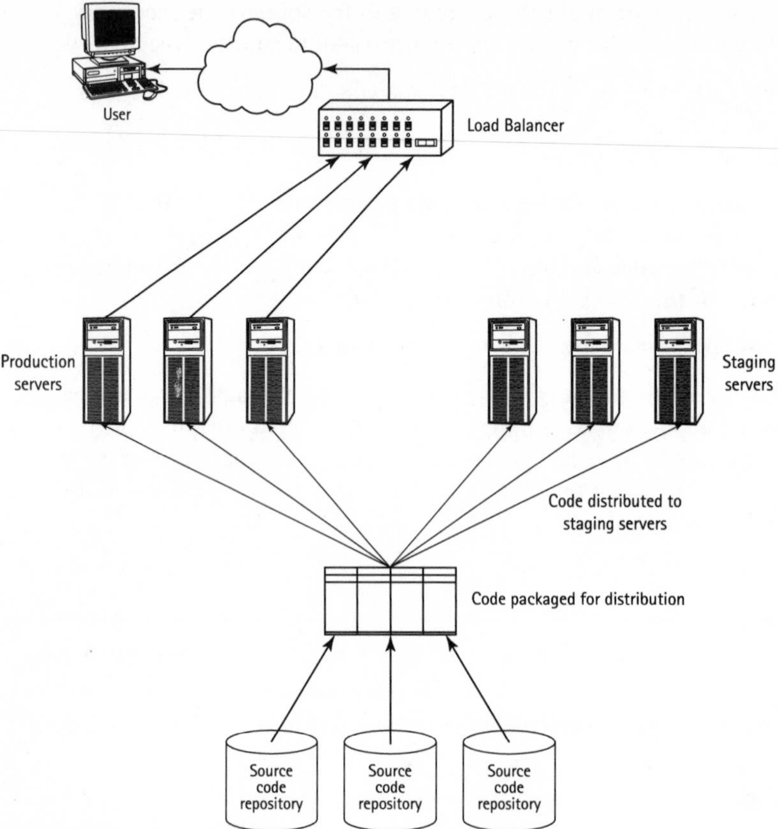

Figure 2-2: The process of assembling a Web application.

The final deployment can be performed in two ways. The first and more popular method is to transfer the files from the staging servers to the production servers. The second method is to repeat the complete deployment process used to assemble the staging area in order to reassemble the application on the production servers. This includes compiling files, performing initializations, and so on.

Although the second method might seem like more work than the first, it is easier and more accurate. When you use the first method, you have to develop and perfect a new repeatable deployment process that accurately transfers files from the staging area to the deployment area. When you modify the application, you have to modify and debug two processes: the process that assembles the application on the staging area and the process that transfers files from the staging area to the deployment area. If you have already developed and debugged a similar deployment procedure for the staging area, using the second method to deploy the actual application requires only that you change the destination directories from the staging area to the deployment area.

Before you can implement an assembly process, you need the necessary human resources: people to create the source code from which you can build the application, as well as people responsible for testing and assembling the application. That's where the Web team comes in. In the next section, you will learn about the team members, their roles, and how they can work together productively – without stepping on one another's toes.

Understanding the Web Development Team

Because Web applications are so complex, they typically require the collaboration of many groups of people. Examples of people who commonly work on a Web application include

- Artists
- Writers
- Designers
- Developers
- Quality Assurance team members
- Webmasters

In addition, the Web team often includes managers, database engineers, system administrators, consultants, and so on. We don't directly address how these team members fit into the development process, but you can apply the general principles discussed here to them as well.

These team members need to work not only independently but also together in such a way that their work adds up, instead of competing with one another's efforts.

The general workflow

Figure 2-3 displays a general overview of how Web team members can work together to build an application. As you can see, the source code repository is the heart of the system; it is what ties the team members together. The developers, artists, designers, and writers add and access files from the source code repository. Developers generally also add their *test suites* (sets of tests designed to verify the functionality and construction of the application segment they work with) and deployment infrastructure to this repository. QA accesses source code and developers' test cases from the repository and adds its own test cases to the repository. Similarly, Webmasters access source code and the developers' deployment infrastructure from the repository and add in their own modifications to the deployment infrastructure.

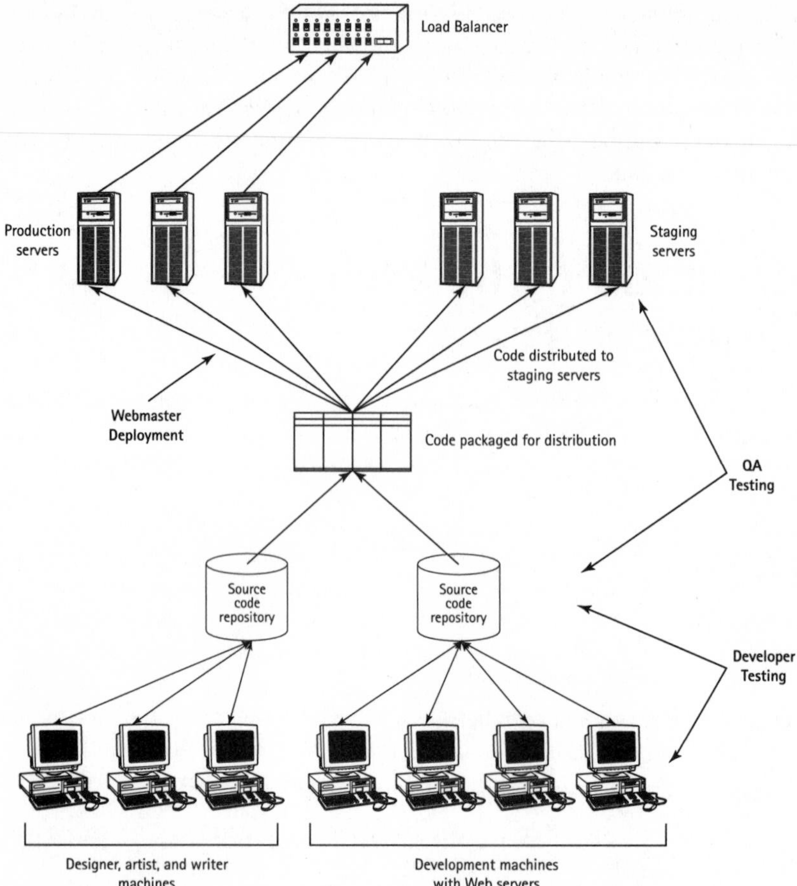

Figure 2-3: How team members fit in to the Web-building process.

Before a source file is added to the source code repository, whoever created it must test it as much as possible. Testing the files before checking them into the source code repository helps maintain the quality of the main repository. In turn, this leads to fewer errors being added to the code and increased efficiency for everyone working on the application.

Artists test their files by visually inspecting their images and sending them for the appropriate reviews. Depending on your target user, the artists will have additional restrictions regarding file sizes, image formats, and the number of available colors. If you want to support many clients, the artists will have many versions of key resources. For example, they can produce small black and white images for handheld devices and phones, simple color images for low-resolution monitors, and full-color images for high-bandwidth, high-end users. These requirements should be clearly communicated as early as possible so that the artists can produce the correct images with no wasted effort. When appropriate, provide tools to guarantee that artists produce images satisfying the necessary requirements. This is an appropriate *check-in* gate (that is, each file cannot be checked into the source code repository until it passes the requirements).

Writers and designers also test their work. Writers' testing includes editing, verifying, and proofreading their work and getting any necessary approvals. Designers test their static pages, template pages, style sheets, and the like, to check for coding errors.

Developers test all files related to the application units on which they are working. Each developer gathers her files – as well as the other images, style sheets, static pages, and files relating to those files – and deploys them on a personal staging area. Here, the developers use the practices discussed in Part II of this book to check how well each application unit is constructed and whether it functions according to specification. After each developer verifies the functionality and construction of the staging area, he or she deploys the application unit's files on a shared staging area and checks the files, test cases, and deployment infrastructure into the source code repository.

Ideally, QA starts testing the new or modified parts of the application as soon as they are checked into the source code repository. You significantly reduce development time and improve application reliability by involving QA as early in the process as possible. When QA starts testing earlier, it uncovers problems earlier. The earlier a problem is found, the faster and easier it is to fix, and the less of a chance it has to spawn more problems throughout the application.

After the files in the source code repository meet QA's standards, the Webmaster is in charge of assembling them into the publicly accessible Web application. The Webmaster is also responsible for troubleshooting deployment problems, creating mirror sites, and making emergency repairs to fix corrupted files. Basically, the Webmaster must be able to assemble a complex application quickly and, on demand, fix or reassemble it immediately.

Team member roles

Now that we have established what the general applicationwide workflow looks like, it's time to take a closer look at the actions each team member performs as the team builds a Web application.

One way to ensure that the project is completed as efficiently as possible is to have each team member work on one track and have all team members work on their interrelated tracks in parallel. Figure 2-4 illustrates how the work can be organized across the various tracks. We recommend that one iteration of the set of tracks correspond with the implementation of a small segment of the application (for example, a new "wish list" functionality) rather than with the implementation of the entire application. Study after study has confirmed that this iterative approach is an efficient way to develop a reliable Web application. Moreover, this type of development process is best suited to the rapidly changing nature of Web development. If you quickly develop and implement one new piece of functionality at a time, you can better respond to changing market and consumer demands.

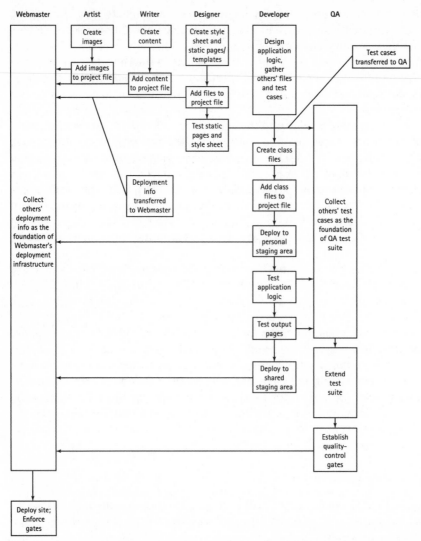

Figure 2-4: Web team members work on different yet related tracks to produce the final application.

For examples of the studies mentioned in the preceding paragraph, see "Building E-Business Apps Faster" by Roger Fournier in the December 18, 2000 issue of *InfoWorld* and "Build High-Quality E-Business Applications" by Phil Hollows in the November 2000 issue of *e-Business Advisor*.

Regardless of the scope of each set of tracks, one thing should unite the parallel tracks: a common file that contains all the information about how the application is assembled, tested, and deployed. We refer to this file as a *project file*. Before anyone starts working on the application, one person (often the Webmaster) creates the foundational project file. Each time someone working on the application adds to or modifies the application's contents, test cases, or deployment infrastructure, that person checks out the project file, adds his changes to it, and checks it back into the source code repository. In this way, each team member's work builds on the others' work. At the end of each iteration, the team has a single project file from which they can assemble, test, and deploy the most current incarnation of the application. In other words, nobody's efforts are lost. Rather, everyone's efforts accumulate, and team members who perform the bulk of their work during the latter end of the development process – such as QA and the Webmaster(s) – can easily access and build on all the other team members' efforts. As a result of this collaboration and sharing, the entire development process becomes much less error-prone and more efficient.

The following sections describe the actions each team member performs on his track.

ARTISTS

The artists' role is to design the application's images, logos, buttons, and so on. They can integrate design tools such as PhotoShop into their Web IDE so that they have a central workspace for all their Web-related projects. When the files are completed, they add the files to the source code repository; then they add information about how to access and organize these files into the project file. At this point, the project file contains information about how to gather and organize all the artists' files that will be used in the application.

WRITERS

The writers are responsible for researching and writing the application's content. After creating files that contain site content, they add information to the project file regarding how to access and organize these files. When these files are complete, the writers check them into source control.

At this point, the project file contains information about how to gather and organize

- Image files that will be used in the application
- Files that contain the application's content

DESIGNERS

Designers generally create templates and style sheets that determine the static and dynamic pages' look and feel. To create these files, designers usually integrate their favorite Web design tools (Dreamweaver, FrontPage, and so forth) into their Web IDEs and use their preferred tools to create template and Cascading Style Sheet (CSS) files. While creating templates, designers use the image files contributed by the artists to the source code repository and the project file; sometimes they also access the content provided by the writers. Before each designer checks a file into the source code repository, he or she tests the HTML code and CSS to check for invalid, nonportable, or error-prone code. After fixing any problems, the designer adds the files to the source code repository and then to the project file, adds test cases and instructions about how to access and organize these files. After the project file is checked into the source code repository, QA can use the designers' test cases as the beginning of its application-level test suite.

At this point, the project file contains information about how to gather and organize

- Image files that will be used on the application
- Files that contain the application's content
- A template and style sheet that establish the pages' look and feel

DEVELOPERS

In a nutshell, developers do all they can to place a high-quality application unit on the shared staging area. This involves a significant amount of testing; the testing practices that should be applied are discussed throughout this book. If all developers save their testing infrastructure into the project file, QA can easily access each new or modified test and perform testing in parallel with development. If the development and QA teams work together in this way, the developers' testing efforts are leveraged to help QA perform application-level testing as soon and efficiently as possible.

Throughout the development and testing process, the developers add information to the project file explaining how to access and organize the servlets and other files they develop. They also save their test and deployment infrastructure in the project file. After this information is saved, the developers (or other team members) can easily update it when part of the application is modified. When a developer is done working on a particular application unit, he or she checks the project file and all related source code into the source code repository. By the time the developers reach this stage of the development track, the project file contains, at least, the following:

- Information on how to gather and organize all files related to the application
- A repeatable deployment infrastructure (instructions on how to deploy each application unit to each developer's personal staging area and the shared staging area)
- The developers' test cases and testing infrastructure

QUALITY ASSURANCE

As we said before, QA ideally works in parallel with development so that tests are created as each part of the application is being developed. QA's first task is to take the developers' tests and make them the foundation for its own test suite. This way, QA can immediately tell when code fails tests that it passed previously. If the developers save their testing infrastructure into the shared project file, QA can easily access all of these test cases and the test parameters used. As Table 2-1 illustrates, QA inherits a very comprehensive testing foundation from the other team members.

TABLE 2-1 ELEMENTS OF THE QA MASTER TEST SUITE

Element	Based On
Details about how to access source files	Deployment information provided by developers, designers, writers, and artists
An application-level test suite	Developers' and designers' test suites
Gates that check all test cases	An application-level regression test suite

As soon as modified files are checked into the source code repository, QA starts its main job: extending the developers' test suite so that it tests the entire application, including the interactions between the various application units and modules. As tests are extended and created, they are saved into the project file. If problems are found, the developers can use the project file to easily re-create the problem and test whether their modifications solve the problem.

Another critical type of testing generally performed at this stage is automatic virtual user testing. In this type of testing, a master machine controls virtual users who test the staging area on multiple remote machines. These machines typically represent different types of users from different areas of the world so that QA can determine how the application will react to user traffic.

QA repeats all available tests nightly to ensure that it immediately spots any error introduced. These tests should not involve human intervention. You can set up an automatic process by creating a script that specifies the types of tests you want to perform and then configuring your system to run this script every night.

QA might also want to establish and enforce quality control gates to ensure that problematic files never reach the public. Gates prevent files with problems from progressing to the next logical stage. (If the file sits on a developer's personal staging area, the next logical stage is the shared staging area. If the file sits on the shared staging area, the next logical stage is the deployment area.) When a development team uses gates, every file is passed through the appropriate test cases whenever the application or application unit is deployed. If a single error is found, the deployment is aborted.

Gates might seem an unnecessary obstacle, but they are a valuable way to prevent small mistakes from having severe repercussions. Even when a team tests files methodically, there is always a chance that an error will somehow slip through.

Someone might modify code and forget to retest. Someone might make a minor one-line change and think that there's no need to retest. People are human, and mistakes happen. Sometimes, though, these little mistakes can result in a critical problem's being introduced into the application and made available to the world. By using gates to ensure that all files pass appropriate, thorough, carefully designed tests, development teams significantly reduce the chances of errors ever reaching the public. Such gates can be set up with scripts or automated with Web tools. If the developers set up similar gates to ensure that files are checked before reaching their personal staging areas, QA can simply modify the gates so that they apply to the entire application.

For more information on QA-level testing, see Chapter 15.

When QA is done adding tests, it checks the project file into the source code repository. At this point, the project file contains

- Information on how to gather and organize all files related to the application
- A repeatable deployment infrastructure (instructions on how to deploy each application unit to each developer's personal staging area and the shared staging area)
- The developers' test cases and testing infrastructure
- QA's test cases and testing infrastructure

WEBMASTERS

After QA determines that the application on the staging area does not contain problems, the Webmaster (or team of Webmasters) deploys the application. This is similar to the deployment procedures performed by the team's developers, but it can increase in difficulty with the number of application parts that must be deployed. As Table 2-2 shows, as long as the developers have been using the project file to save the deployment information they used to deploy their application units, the Webmaster should have to change only the target location to deploy the entire application.

If QA creates formal gates that prevent the deployment of the application if any of its files do not meet the specified criteria, the Webmaster is responsible for implementing these gates and notifying QA when the application does not meet the conditions required to pass the gate. QA then notifies the appropriate developers and asks them to fix the problem. After QA verifies that the problem is solved, it notifies the Webmaster, who then attempts to republish the application.

TABLE 2-2 WEBMASTER DEPLOYMENT INFRASTRUCTURE ELEMENTS

Element	Based On
Details on how to find the needed files	Project file information added by developers, designers, writers, and artists
Details on necessary file transformations (compilations and the like) and transfers	Developers' unit-level deployment infrastructure
Quality Assurance gates	QA's gates (based on development tests)

When the Webmaster is finished deploying the application, the project file contains

- Information on how to gather and organize all files related to the application
- A complete repeatable deployment infrastructure (instructions on how to deploy each application unit to each developer's personal staging area, the shared staging area, and the deployment area)
- The developers' test cases and testing infrastructure
- QA's test cases and testing infrastructure

This project file is the culmination of all the work performed on all the team members' tracks.

Summary

In this chapter, we cover the process of assembling a Web application. First, we look at the components that make up a Web application. Then we explore the mechanics involved in assembling a Web application out of these components. Finally, we look at how Web team members work together to assemble a reliable Web application as efficiently as possible.

The next chapter describes pitfalls unique to Web applications and offers tips on steering clear of these pitfalls as you build and modify your Web application.

Chapter 3

Identifying Web Development Pitfalls

IN THIS CHAPTER

- Tracing the history of Web development
- Compensating for decoupled state
- Giving up flow control
- Determining your client
- Planning for scalability

THE WEB HAS EVOLVED FROM A FORUM FOR SIMPLE, static information to a medium for complex dynamic applications. This transition involved introducing many features and concepts of traditional software development to Web development and adapting them to the unique needs of this new forum. As a result, when software developers move to Web development, they often encounter new problems with previously mastered issues, as well as challenges that have no precedent in non-Web development. This chapter describes general pitfalls that commonly trouble developers who have not yet mastered Web development.

A *static* site is a site on which everything is fixed. Regardless of how or when a page is accessed, you always get the same results. Static sites are composed solely of simple elements: HTML files, images, and the like. Static sites are relatively easy to test and maintain because the number of things that can go wrong is small. They are also easy to make scalable because you can use caching or multiple servers.

A *dynamic* site typically contains nonchanging HTML and images like those found on static sites. However, it also contains elements that change, depending on circumstances such as time, user, database contents, and so on. Dynamic sites require additional programs or scripts that need to be tested and supported and are therefore much trickier.

This book focuses on dynamic sites.

Tracing the History of Web Development

Although Web development is not a fundamentally different activity from traditional development, there are some important differences in how the applications are constructed. To understand some of the key pitfalls in Web development, it is helpful to have basic information about the events leading to the widespread adoption of Web applications. From this history lesson, you will learn why and how Web applications differ from traditional applications.

Figure 3-1 shows a traditional application. In a traditional application, more or less everything is under the developer's direct control (subject only to the constraints of the operating system and the user interface on the platform being used). This kind of environment has been the basis of a large, thriving software industry.

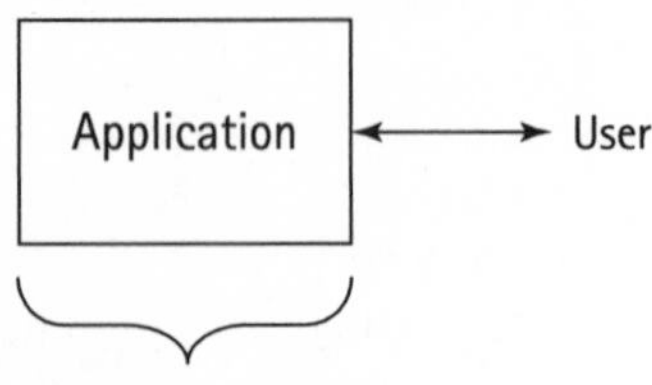

Figure 3-1: A traditional application.

Programs developed under this traditional paradigm have grown to be large, all-in-one behemoths. These are the normal programs you buy on a CD or DVD and install on your computer as a complete system, requiring sometimes more than a gigabyte of your personal disk space. Programming skills were developed to allow the construction of these kinds of programs, including popular object-oriented techniques, dynamic libraries for sharing code, and the like.

Tracing the evolution of client/server applications

As more machines became connected, forming networks and intranets, the inefficiencies of traditional development required new approaches. There was a move from storing a complete copy of an application on each machine to sharing programs stored on a single machine. People also began to have databases on one machine and place the software-handling requests on a specialized server rather than have each user (the client) handle them independently. This client/server model enabled larger organizations to deploy increasingly complicated programs.

In a typical client/server program, both the client and server are written to work together and are maintained by the same development organization (naturally, third-party contributions can play a significant role). Figure 3-2 shows a client/server application. The main difference between this application and a traditional application is that the developer's code is separated into two distinct pieces. Naturally, a more complicated application could involve multiple servers, but in all cases, the developer generally has control over how the application is constructed.

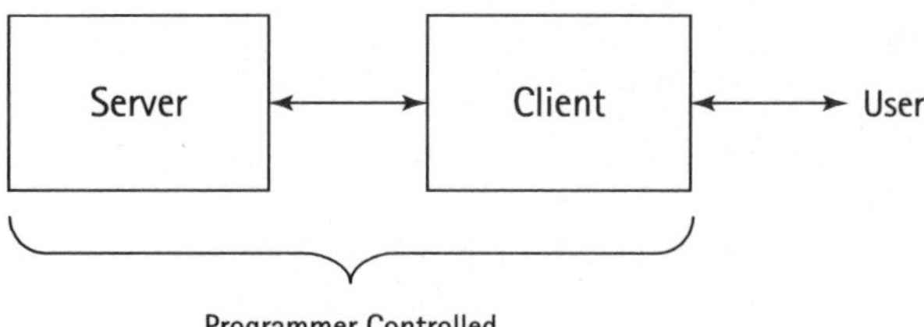

Figure 3-2: A client/server application.

The early Web server and browser incarnations are examples of client/server development. The Web (or *World Wide Web*, as it was originally called) was initially designed as a way of sharing *hypertext* (linked) documents. One key element was the creation of HTTP (*Hypertext Transfer Protocol*), which provides standard communication between conforming clients and servers. The early servers did nothing more than choose from a selection of static (or relatively static) pages, and the early clients were simple browsers capable only of displaying static pages and initiating requests for new pages.

Tracing the evolution of Web-based applications

When the Internet became a household item, the Web became a common platform for distributed computing. Web designers were not content with static information, and a growing audience wanted more dynamic, stimulating content.

When the industry first looked at dynamic Web development, it saw the HTML output and assumed that Web development was limited to providing changing text to users. Before long, however, developers realized the full potential of the technology: They could write applications that interact with databases at the back end and could use a Web browser as a standard GUI at the front end. The age-old problem of teaching people to use a GUI would disappear because any computer owner – and, therefore, any potential software purchaser – knows how to use a Web browser.

Figure 3-3 shows the design of one possible Web-based application. The Web server and Web browser are generally standard components that are not written by the developer (although developers can choose or customize the Web server and make requirements about which Web browsers they allow). The bulk of the application is written as plug-ins or add-ons to the basic server functionality (possibly including additional application servers such as BEA). On the client side, dynamic control is limited to whatever hooks the browser provides (typically JavaScript or browser plug-ins).

Is Client/Server Dead?

When Web applications started to become popular, it appeared to some that client/server was in trouble. After all, every client/server application has a learning curve, and often a very steep one, because people must learn to use a proprietary client before they can put the application to full use. When companies realized that they could deliver applications with a standard GUI everyone already knew how to use, they flocked to the Web. Web-based applications offer additional benefits: They give developers the ability to update software in one place — the server. This relieves companies from having to mail out updates and thus streamlines the maintenance process. Web-based applications also increase application portability. However, Web development isn't a silver bullet solution, and client/server still has a valuable place in software development.

Web proponents sometimes claim that client/server is dead; client/server users see glaring weaknesses in the Web paradigm. The answer to this debate lies somewhere between the two extremes. The Web paradigm is useful for certain types of applications, but its inherent shortcomings and difficulties will cause many client/server applications that migrated to the Web to return to the client/server paradigm or to move to a hybrid that draws on both.

Is client/server dead? The answer is definitely no. Dynamic Web development has much potential but is also fraught with problems. Client/server is more limited than Web development but can solve many problems inherent in the Web paradigm. We believe that the conclusion to this debate will not be the triumph of one approach over the other but rather a hybrid of the two paradigms (such as a customized thin-client browser) that merges them so that the advantages of each compensate for the drawbacks of the other.

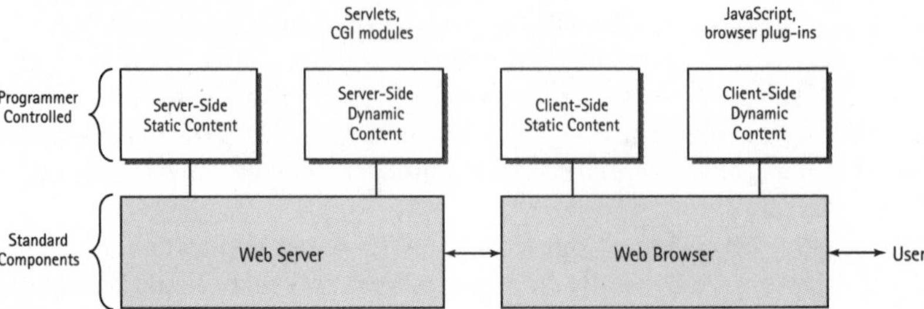

Figure 3-3: A Web application.

Understanding fundamental problems in Web applications

Fundamentally, the greatest pitfalls of Web development arise from the basic architecture design of Web servers and Web browsers. Decoupling the application into server and client pieces introduces complexities common to client/server applications. Further complications arise from being limited to HTTP for communication and HTML for display (you can do several things to get around this, but that is not the focus of this chapter). The desire to support a wide range of browsers, written by many groups, adds another layer of complexity. Finally, making the application publicly available over the Web so that a single server (or group of servers that make up an application) is essentially serving the global population imposes further demands on inhomogeneous environments and scalability.

In the rest of this chapter, you will learn about the following specific issues:

- **Decoupled state:** How to decide where to store information about the state of your application (a problem shared with client/server applications)
- **Web browsers:** How to cope with issues related to using standard third-party Web browsers as clients and how to deal with many conflicting browsers (a problem unique to Web development)
- **Scalability:** How to make sure that your application can support as many users as necessary (a problem common to Web and client/server applications but more problematic for Web applications)

The majority of this book explores practices that help you assemble and test your application in ways that prevent these issues from troubling your award-winning application.

The term *state* refers to information that depends on context. If users log in to your application, the knowledge that they are logged in is state information.

If your application does not have any *context* (in other words, responses to requests do not vary, regardless of any other factors), it is considered *stateless*.

Compensating for Decoupled State

To revisit the history of computing, the earliest traditional programs stored all the programs' required state in variables, local or global. As the number of variables skyrocketed and it became impossible to cleanly maintain correct code with global access to data, new programming languages and techniques were developed to divide programs into smaller, more manageable pieces. The earliest improvements were reusable functions with local variables. Later improvements added objects, which gave better control of data and discouraged global, universally (to the program) accessible data. In the new object-oriented paradigm, global variables are discouraged at best and, in many cases, completely forbidden.

When you switch to Web development, however, all bets are off. The client software doesn't know about your objects and is generally communicating only via HTTP (the basic communication protocol of the Web). When a Web browser communicates with a Web server, the request takes the form of a URL (*Uniform Resource Locator*), optional `POST` data (used with forms), and optional header request properties (which can include the referring page and cookies). The server is obligated to generate a response with no other information about what the user is doing.

Cookies provide a general mechanism for Web servers to store persistent information on the user's Web browser. As such, they are often used on dynamic sites to track all kinds of information. Basically, when the server sends a response to the client, it attaches a header that says, "Whenever you request pages from this server, send me back this information." From then on, the client sends the extra information with the request, as long as the cookie's requirements are met.

One important point to make about cookies is that not all users like cookies. Some users inevitably have browsers that refuse to acknowledge the passed-in cookie, or they delete the cookies prematurely. You must be aware of this possibility, even if you require cookies for your site. Chapter 13 provides an example of how to test for these kinds of situations.

You can find more details about cookies at `home.netscape.com/newsref/std/cookie_spec.html`. This information is old but does go into some detail about how cookies conceptually work. There is also an unofficial Cookie FAQ at `www.cookiecentral.com/fax/`.

The chief problem with Web applications – and the one issue that consistently troubles new Web developers – is that the Web server and Web browser are fully decoupled. The server sees the client's requests but otherwise does not know what the client is up to. Dynamic Web sites do not inherently carry state from page to page; each instance of each page is displayed independently of what happened in the past. This lack of coupling is intentional and beneficial (it improves scalability and encourages you to handle errors better) and needs to be handled, not ignored. It's critical that you make earnest efforts to understand state if you want your Web application to function as expected.

There are several ways you can introduce some degree of coupling by storing state information. If you are using servlets, for instance, a common way to handle decoupled state is to store the user's state inside a local object, which is indexed from a cookie. When the client request comes, the cookie is used to find the state object, and then an appropriate response can be generated. Alternatively, the associated state can be stored in a database or on disk. If you do not store any state, each interaction with a Web page has to be handled independently, without regard for what events occurred in the past.

Object-Oriented Programming (OOP) and Web Development

Because dynamic Web development can easily break the object-oriented paradigm, it keeps object-oriented developers on their toes. For object-oriented developers, a key part of making the switch to dynamic Web design is to keep track of which state their Web pages are in, rather than assume that the current state is always valid. In object-oriented programming, you always know what the state is because nothing changes without your knowledge. In dynamic Web development, however, many things change behind the scenes.

In principle, storing information in state variables breaks the object-oriented paradigm. A fundamental principle of OOP is that all necessary information is encapsulated inside objects. Objects have to carry state information throughout the application, and as the information is modified, the object is "morphed" accordingly. In Web development, though, objects don't carry from one page to the next. A page is created and represented by objects, but the objects die as the page disappears. The most important information from the objects can be stored in state variables and re-created. However, every time an object is re-created, it is inevitably a new, slightly different instance. This re-creation violates the fundamental object-oriented concept of flow throughout the application. Although the Web paradigm seems object-oriented on a small scale, the object-oriented paradigm is broken on a larger scale.

Developers trained in object-oriented programming often enter Web development with the assumption that if they have the variables stored in their objects, those variables will be ready to apply to the new page. It is surprising for them to find that the variables are not carried over. To master dynamic Web development, these developers must switch their thinking.

If your application has dynamic pages that depend on server state, you can be certain that you are viewing or testing the correct page only by ensuring that your state variables are properly configured for each page. Unfortunately, configuring state variables for Web pages is a tedious and time-consuming task. The best way to do this is to create paths, as we explain in Chapter 13.

In the next section, you will learn about options to store state and about their possible ramifications. Then you will become acquainted with several security issues related to storing state.

Storing state

State information can be stored in a variety of ways: by using the application or server, the client, or the delivery system. This section focuses on the most common methods. A variety of methods are available, but unfortunately, there are no silver bullets. Each method has its advantages and disadvantages; the best option for your application depends on the needs and goals of your project.

STORING STATE ON THE SERVER

If you want to store application state on the server, you use dynamic/short-term memory (such as servlet/FastCGI global variables), static/long-term storage (such as files or databases), or the server cache.

If you need to store critical data such as customer profiles or purchase information, your best bet is to store it in files or databases. Storing information in files and databases is slow because you have to access the file or database every time you need to record, update, or access state information. However, if you are working with critical data, sacrificing speed is usually worth the gain in security.

When you are less concerned about the state information you are storing, you can store it using dynamic/short-term memory or a server cache. Both these methods are faster than storing state in files or databases, but they are less reliable. When you store state in dynamic/short-term memory, the state is held as long as the program is alive. If the program whose global variables store the state terminates unexpectedly, the state information is lost, and there is no way to retrieve it. When you store state using the server cache, the main problem you encounter is that cache behavior varies from server to server, so your application can behave unpredictably.

If you store state on the server by using dynamic/short-term memory, you must carefully think about who owns the state and how long it will persist. If you store a large amount of information for each logged in user and never expire the state, you will certainly run out of memory eventually. If you do expire the information, you need a clear recovery path if the user accesses the application after you have timed out his data. You also need to account for the possibility of missing or corrupted data not letting you restore state and the server being reset between requests, and the like. If you have used a load balancer to use several Web servers, you do not want to store multiple (out-of-sync!) copies of user state across different Web servers.

STORING STATE ON THE CLIENT

State can be stored on the client by using browser-specific caches and cookies, using JavaScript state variables, or embedding state information in the HTML itself. These methods are fast but somewhat unreliable and unpredictable.

Browser-specific caches are dangerous for two reasons: They might or might not be shared between users, and they vary from browser to browser. The behavior of browser-specific cookies also varies from browser to browser. If you use cookies on the client, you have to make sure that they are configured properly, that they expire properly, and that your application works if the client doesn't support cookies (or that you make it clear to your users that your application requires cookie support).

Storing browser-specific state variables using JavaScript is especially dangerous if you are using frames. If the frame is moved, the variable disappears. If you store state using JavaScript variables, you must be careful that your application stays in sync with the server and that your code is portable enough not to lose information under various failure cases (more common in this type of solution than in the others).

Additional problems are caused by the browsers' varying degrees of JavaScript support. For more information on issues related to JavaScript portability, see Chapter 8.

If you store variables by embedding them in your HTML (for example, as hidden fields inside forms or extra arguments added to URLs), you entertain the greatest possibility of aged variables being introduced to your server. It's common in this case to introduce one or two variables, consider the problem solved, and forget about some other state information that is necessary. As the state information grows, the HTML pages become larger, more cluttered, more confusing, and more prone to nonintuitive bugs. Also, this can expose your internal variables to third parties and represents an additional source of possible security attacks.

As you can see, storing state on the client can lead to unpredictable results. This is probably not a problem if you are storing noncritical state information (such as what page the user visited last). However, if you are storing critical information such as key user records, you probably want to store the data in the most secure place possible: on the server, using a file or database.

Safeguarding security

Anytime you have state stored, you have to consider security issues. For instance, if you show one user a page containing personal credit card information and later someone comes to that browser and clicks the Back button a few times, that person will have access to the initial user's personal information (this is why browsers clear PASSWORD fields on forms when you click the Back button). Similarly, someone could write a program to dig through a browser's cache files, looking for credit cards, passwords, or other sensitive information.

If you make a habit of passing variables through URL arguments (for instance, `http://mysite.com/app.jsp?password=not-so-secure`), anyone going through the server log or the user's history will see the user's password as plain text. This same security problem occurs when forms are submitted using the `GET` protocol. W3C (The World Wide Web Consortium) recommends never using `GET` to submit forms, precisely for this reason.

Moreover, if you always use cookies to log users in to your site automatically, you are forcing users to have a secure machine. This isn't possible if, for instance, your user is running from a public library. If users are going to use your site securely, you have to ensure that they can log out completely and that no one else can reach their personal information without appropriate authorization. This issue also affects how you timeout your state data. If someone walks away from a machine and forgets to log out, it is helpful to invalidate her log in automatically from the server side after a certain amount of idle time has passed. However, if you do this, make sure that the user also has a clear and obvious way to log out, so that you do not rely solely on the timeout.

In addition, if you are handling personal information or implementing an e-commerce solution, you should support an encrypted version of HTTP: HTTPS. This keeps private information safe from Internet pirates. However, you have to make sure that your solution works with your target customers. In doing so, consider whether your protocol works through firewalls, proxies, and the like, and whether you have the appropriate certificates to allow trusted communication.

Because the Web uses a well-known protocol and generates an enormous amount of traffic, mostly business-related, it makes a particularly tempting target for security attacks. Even though you might never be subjected to such attacks, you should always plan as though you will be. Don't wait until your application is finished to think about security.

For more information on security issues, see the W3C hosted Web security FAQ at `www.w3.org/Security/Faq/`.

Perils Inherent in the Web's Decoupled State

We discovered the perils inherent in the Web's decoupled state while watching a team of developers new to Web development construct a dynamic Web site. They struggled to connect the pages into a consistent application but failed because they neglected to consider that each page has its own state. They would find a problem in one path through the application, fix that problem, and break something in another path. It didn't take long to see that the developers were chasing their tails trying to figure out how to connect the pages.

The code itself was complicated and convoluted – full of state variables for which nobody knew the values. Then came the biggest clue to the nature of the problem. When the developers ran the code for the back-end applications, they encountered bugs that arose from going through multiple paths and arriving at the same page from different directions. Because they couldn't control the state variables, the developers invariably ended up with the wrong versions of pages, making it impossible to debug the application. The best available solution was to rewrite the code for the entire project.

Now that you're aware of the problems inherent in storing state in Web applications, you can look at the related issue of flow. *Flow* describes the course that users take as they navigate through your application. This is essential to understanding state because your state has to be correct regardless of what paths your users follow. Your flow control (or lack thereof) is usually a key factor to consider while deciding how to store your application's state.

Giving Up Flow Control

A significant development problem with Web-based applications is the control of flow. As Figure 3-4 illustrates, the flow in traditional client/server applications can be well defined and controlled. This control is possible because when you write the client, you control user movement through menus. By providing certain menu items on certain pages, you restrict the way users can move through the application and ensure that they will take a logical path. Client/server applications act as finite state machines that have a limited number of states and always know what state the user is in.

As Figure 3-5 illustrates, paths are not nearly as well defined on the Web because the nature of Web development allows for a virtually infinite number of possible paths through the application. This problem occurs because by choosing to use standard Web browsers as clients, you are forced to accept their notion of acceptable paths.

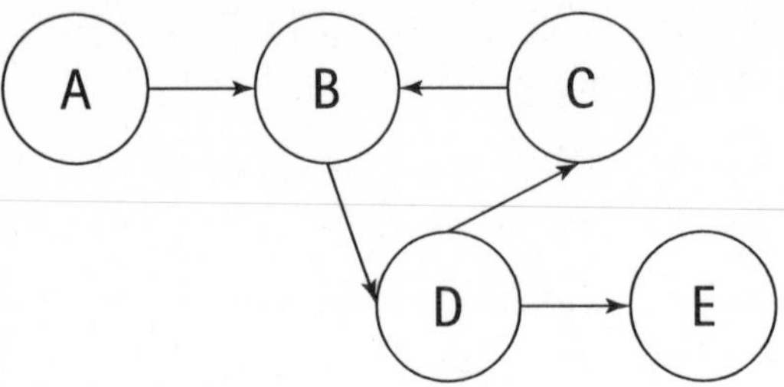

Figure 3-4: Possible flow through a client/server application.

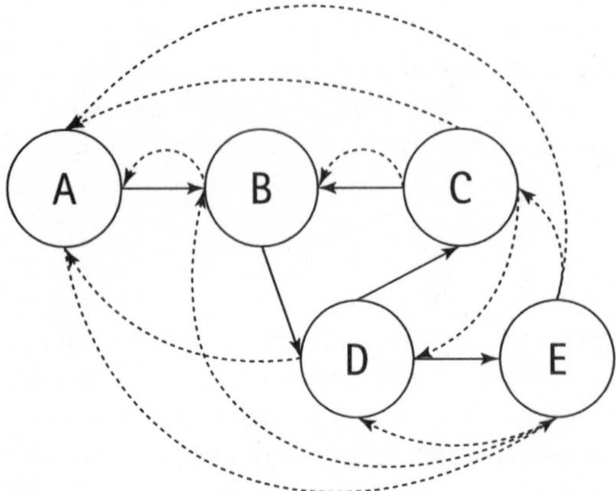

Figure 3-5: Possible flow through a Web application.

A number of factors contribute to the virtually infinite number of possible paths. Third-party sites can contain links to parts of your application that you did not intend to be entry points. Users can bookmark locations deep within your application. The same user can be logged in to your application from different browsers on the same computer or even completely different computers. A user can access old URLs by using the browser's history capabilities or might be looking at old HTML snapshots that were saved to disk and no longer match anything on the server (maybe the browser didn't save everything properly when the file was written to disk). Moreover, browsers' Back and Forward buttons allow users to move back and forth through the application in ways you might not have anticipated, and they become out of sync without your knowing it (developers have tried various methods to work around this obstacle, with little success). As a result of these and other complicating factors, it's virtually impossible for the server to determine what precise state the user is in.

In light of all this, it's clear that testing paths through your Web application can be a much more critical and complicated job than it appears at first blush. You need to consider atypical (jump) paths, including links to your site that don't go through the expected entry page and delays long enough to timeout state information that might be stored on the server.

Flow control problems exist by nature of choosing a Web browser as your client. In the next section, you will learn about problems related to dependencies on specific Web browsers.

Determining Your Client

Although you can control the Web server with which you are building your application, you cannot always require your users to stick to a single Web browser. Indeed, the point of abstracting the Web application from the browsers and clients is to allow different clients to work seamlessly.

As a result, your Web application will typically be designed to work with a variety of browsers; these browsers compose the set of clients you need to support. In some instances, you can restrict all your users to using a specific version of, for instance, Internet Explorer. Far more often, the goal is to reach as many potential users as possible, opening the space of all possible clients to include an ever-growing range of third-party browsers. Supporting all versions of all browsers is possible only if you drastically limit the possible functionality of your application. A better goal is to provide high functionality on a subset of the most common browsers and basic functionality for other provided browsers. In any case, if your application is publicly visible on the Web, you do not want it to be an embarrassment to your organization when it completely fails on certain browsers.

Even if you target only one browser, that browser might be running on many hardware configurations, with different screen resolutions and numbers of colors, and your application might be accessed by individuals with special needs (for example, people with visual impairments). Because you don't control these clients, there is no way to test them all exhaustively. The best you can do is to test the most important environments, simulate as many others as possible, and rely on coding standards to prevent most nonportable practices.

Chapter 8 provides a detailed discussion of how you can use coding standards to increase portability.

The advantage to surrendering control of the client is the opposite of the preceding problem: You can support platforms you've never heard of, work in situations wildly different from the ones for which you were originally planning, and reach new markets.

As the Web evolves, the types of clients you might target is growing from basic HTML-based browsers to hand-held or phone-based devices with special requirements and possibly special languages (HDML, WML, XML, and so on). You will learn about several challenges and strategies involved in developing for these devices in Chapter 17. To support different browsers, you must test whether your HTML and scripting are portable. For HTML or JavaScript to be deemed portable, the data has to display and function properly on all targeted browsers. Creating portable HTML is difficult because of browsers' varied support for HTML. Some HTML tags are optional with certain browsers and not others. For instance, the `<SCRIPT>` tag is not supported by older browsers without JavaScript support. You can get around this by using comments inside the script tags, like this:

```
<SCRIPT><!–
// here's the actual script
// --></SCRIPT>
```

Similarly, various browsers (and even different versions of the same browser) treat many attributes differently. Sorting through the mess to find out what's portable is complicated by the fact that Web standards lag behind the state-of-the-art browsers by years, so there are no entirely reliable documents.

Scripting support also varies from browser to browser. VBScript generally limits you to Internet Explorer. JavaScript is more widely supported, but different DOMs and different implementations of the language complicate the task of writing portable code. Luckily, you can write JavaScript code to detect the browser on which you are running and can try to modify the JavaScript as appropriate. Although this common solution works, it requires far more stringent testing than most organizations can provide. This explains why JavaScript portability errors are some of the most common flaws littering today's Web sites.

Even if your Web application seamlessly handles all the issues discussed so far for a single user, your project will be dead on arrival if you fail to address the issue of scalability.

Planning for Scalability

When your entire application lives on one computer (the user's), the only question of scalability is, How big or fast does the computer have to be to use this application? As you move to a distributed environment, you have to think ahead more. You must consider how many users you expect to access this application simultaneously, what resources they are going to require, and for how long. If multiple servers are required, you have to determine how you will switch among them. Perhaps most importantly, if you guess wrong and the application does become swamped, you must decide whether (and possibly how) to fail gracefully.

Even if all the other aspects of Web development are executed flawlessly, underestimating load or ignoring scalability issues altogether can lead to flaws that you might not be able to correct in time to save your application from an untimely demise. To prevent such disasters, you need to ensure that scalability concerns permeate your entire development process.

You will learn all about load-testing your application in Chapter 14.

Dealing with the delivery system

The delivery system lies between your server and the user's browser. (Referring to Figure 3-3, the delivery system is represented by the line between the Web server and the Web browser.) The delivery system includes things such as bandwidth, security, and caching.

The delivery system is important because its scalability affects your ability to guarantee certain performance expectations for your users. (For instance, 95 percent of all requests [clicks] should be processed within 30 seconds.) To make such promises, you need to know where your users are running their Web browsers. Just as you earlier decided which Web browsers to support, you need to decide where you are going to allow clients to run from.

In analyzing whether your delivery system meets your needs, consider whether the pipe to your server is large enough to handle the amount of data you expect to send out. Some users will have a high-bandwidth connection to your application, and others will be chugging along with antiquated modems. Which do you support? Do you support them equally, or can you adapt your site's content for the user's connection? For instance, you might want to send lower-resolution images (or no images at all!) to users who are logged in via a modem.

For an example of how you might deal with the delivery system, consider the efforts of a site that contains a list of recent news items on its home page. Many of these items are accompanied by large images. To accommodate users who do not want to wait for these images to download, the site allows users to specify the maximum number of images to be displayed on this page. The pictures are removed from the remaining news items so that the users can still read the information or click through to a detailed page containing any illustration in which they are interested.

Understanding the perils of caching

One common way to improve scalability is to take advantage of caching. By *caching*, we mean storing commonly accessed information (frequently accessed pages, results of common queries, and so forth) in such a way that it can be retrieved more efficiently than a normal access. Caching can be a very positive feature to improve the performance of your Web application, reduce bandwidth requirements, and improve scalability. You can cache at the server level, the delivery system level (via proxies), and the client level.

Note that you have more control over some aspects of caching than others. You generally have good control over how the Web server is caching data, because you choose and configure the Web server (unless you are deploying to a third-part hosting service). You can use your own proxies to do some caching at the delivery system level.

A common technique implemented by Web applications with many users is to direct user requests to a central location that routes them to various servers. This is a good technique for scalability and load balancing but is not caching. If the initial machine kept copies of the most frequently accessed pages in memory and returned those results immediately, as appropriate, instead of redirecting the request, that would be an instance of caching.

What you have less control over is how the user's browser caches your data and which proxies beyond your control sit between you and the user. In most client/server applications, the communication between the client and the server is relatively direct. The network is involved in routing packets and so forth, but every request the client sends is handled by the server, and every response the server makes goes to the client. Because HTTP introduces a standardized, high-usage protocol, various applications have taken to inserting themselves between the client and server to provide additional functionality. In general, these processes are called *proxies* and sit between the Web server and Web browser. For instance, some ISPs cache pages commonly accessed by their users. When users request a page, they get a copy from the ISP instead of you. If that page happens to have data stored in it, they get that old data instead of what you wanted them to have.

You cannot assume that all requests from the client will be handled by your server, and you must take this into account when deciding how to store state. It is easy to make the assumption that when the client requests a new URL, the server will always receive a request for a new page, which allows the server to properly update the client. However, in some cases, the client might be effectively unable to talk directly to your server because some proxy thinks that it knows better.

In the extreme case, you can try to disable caching by marking all your files as noncacheable, using HTTP headers. If you do so, you are dependent on any proxies and browsers correctly interpreting these headers. You will also have effectively disabled the Back button on most browsers because when old resources are immediately discarded, your application might not be able to move backwards in a meaningful way. This is another complication to the flow control issue discussed earlier.

Any kind of caching (and like it or not, there will be caching) complicates all the issues introduced in this chapter.

Avoiding refresh problems

A related method to improve scalability is to minimize the overall number of requests to your Web server and/or the size of the responses. Often, only a small section of each dynamic page is truly dynamic and has to be updated. As discussed earlier, browsers have minimal support for this notion by caching static images or scripts so that they do not need to be continually re-requested when the currently visible page is changed. Aside from this case, however, browsers are built to reload entire pages – no matter how much or how little of the page changes. As a result, page updates consume a large amount of bandwidth, traffic is created or worsened, and the application is perceived as being slow and unwieldy.

Ideally, only the truly dynamic portion of pages is updated with each update or change request. One way to improve bandwidth is to be careful refreshing dynamic Web site pages with updated information from the server. If you have small areas of the screen that are supposed to be interactive and are constantly changing, you face the challenge of providing the user with an updated display and connecting to the server. Some developers use HTML frames as a solution, but frames are restrictive in layout (nonoverlapping rectangles), have limited portability, and are quickly falling out of favored usage for many sites.

Another approach is to use JavaScript: Rather than connect to the server to get updated content, generate it locally with custom scripts. This has implications for portability and also increases the size of your delivered pages. The biggest problem, though, is that when the client is executed, its actions do not matter until the server connects to it. JavaScript seems to make the page dynamic. However, all it does is mimic dynamic interactivity, because if you don't have a reliable method of saving information from the page, whatever happens with the script is irrelevant. After users modify the page and everything looks correct, they need to click the Submit button, which tells the server to perform the actions they want. Without this functionality, all the information is lost.

A more promising, yet more demanding, option is to create custom technology that can perform such isolated updates tailored for the particular application. If you want quick client-side performance for your application, you can write a proprietary thin client that acts as a smart browser. This customized browser would improve performance by updating only the parts of the pages that need to interact with the back end. Because you control the connection between the client and server, users can immediately register to the server what they are doing. Even if the application dies, the server knows what the user has done up to the last moment. Client/server applications are therefore more intuitive to use because they provide a constant connection to the server.

The problem with this solution is that it requires a trade-off between the performance increase enabled by the proprietary browser and the usability of the general browser. Proprietary browsers can update pages much faster than general browsers, but if you use a proprietary browser, your users must learn how to use this specific type of browser. If the application has many repeat users, the performance benefit of the proprietary browser will likely outweigh the drawback of the initial learning curve. For example, users of online stock-trading applications would likely accept an initial learning curve in exchange for improved performance, but an application with a small percentage of repeat visitors should probably sacrifice performance for the instant usability associated with general browsers.

You can also create dynamic content by using *applets*, small Java programs that are embedded in HTML pages and execute on the client. However, applets impose extra restrictions on browser portability and can be slow to download.

For more information about applets, visit `java.sun.com/applets`.

Summary

In this chapter, we take a quick look at the evolution of Web development, introduce a variety of possible perils inherent in the nature of Web development, and offer tips on avoiding these perils. We explore pitfalls related to issues such as decoupled state, security, flow control, conflicting Web browsers, scalability, caching, delivery systems, and refreshing pages.

In the next chapter, we discuss the design phase in terms of the Online Grocer application we created to illustrate the practices we recommend for avoiding Web development perils and bulletproofing your Web application.

Chapter 4

Designing a Demo Web Application – The Online Grocer

IN THIS CHAPTER

- Creating a basic specification
- Extending the specification
- Choosing the architecture and technology

SO FAR, WE HAVE DESCRIBED THE DEVELOPMENT PROCESS, the structure of a Web application, the process of assembling a Web application, and general Web development pitfalls to avoid. Now, we will introduce a few issues to consider when you are in the design phase of the development process. To give you concrete examples of the practices discussed here and throughout the book, we developed and assembled a demo Web application, the Online Grocer, which is included on the CD-ROM. To illustrate a wide array of Web development practices, we implement different versions of this demo application throughout the book. All the versions share a common specification and design but vary in architecture and technology.

In this chapter, we use our specific design experiences and choices to illustrate general practices you can apply to your own application design. We offer you some general tips on what to do at each step of the design phase, as well as describe how we performed the recommended practices. First, we cover the creation and recording of application requirements, and then we look at issues to consider when translating the requirements to an actual application.

Creating a Basic Specification

Creating a specification is the process of deciding what your application is going to be. Your specification can be very informal (say, you want to make an exciting site to sell kid's toys), semiformal (more detail about what makes an exciting site for kids), or very formal (detailed descriptions of features, how they interact, and how they will be tested to make sure that kids think they're exciting). The sample specification here will fall in between informal and semiformal because this book is more concerned with bulletproofing Web applications than with producing detailed specifications.

The first step in designing an application is to specify the basic functionality. What is its general purpose, and what actions will it allow the user to perform?

The Online Grocer application's main purpose is to enable customers to choose and purchase various kinds of produce. The user should be able to

1. Log in.
2. Enter search criteria for the desired type of produce.
3. View a list of items that satisfy the search criteria.
4. View detailed information about a produce item.
5. Add items to the shopping cart.
6. View the contents of the shopping cart.
7. Modify the shopping cart.
8. Purchase the items in the shopping cart.
9. Log out.

As you can see, this Web application is very simple, but it will allow us to demonstrate the practices involved in bulletproofing your application.

General requirements specification

After you establish the main actions the user will perform on your application, create a specification that translates these user actions into pages (you use pages because they are the user interface for a Web application). Specifications describe each of an application's features from the user's perspective. They include information about what each element should do and what it should look like.

The typical specification process begins by describing in complete sentences and paragraphs what you expect each page to contain and how you expect it to function. For an example of such a specification, see the model specification in the following section. Next, you might want to create an abbreviated specification document, based on this specification information. The second specification document would contain all the information included in the paragraph-form specification but represent it in a brief outline format that developers can read at a glance while they are developing.

The demo specification

The Online Grocer application's general purpose is to provide an e-commerce application where customers can choose and purchase various kinds of produce. Here's a more detailed summary of the pages we hope to create.

SPLASH PAGE (PAGE 1)

The application's first page will be the Splash Page. It should have something to catch the users' attention and allow users to log in securely. It will contain

- A text field where a user can enter a username
- A text field where a user can enter a password
- A Log In button

If the log in succeeds, page 3 will be displayed. If it fails, page 2 will be displayed.

LOG IN FAILED (PAGE 2)

When a user does not log in successfully, the application will display the Log In Failed page. This page should explain why the log in failed and allow the user to re-enter the username and password.

MAIN SEARCH (PAGE 3)

The initial page after the log in will be the Main Search page. It should have a high-level description of the available produce. It should contain a form that allows the user to search for produce by type (fruit or vegetable) or by attribute (Red, Green, Yellow+Orange, Weird). The user should be able to select any combination of elements. A Submit button should be selectable if at least one choice is made. Default choices will be determined later. When the page is submitted, it should lead to page 4. This page and subsequent pages, except for page 6 and 7, should have a link to the Shopping Cart page. This page and all subsequent pages should also allow the user to log out.

SEARCH RESULTS (PAGE 4)

After the user searches for products, the application will display the Search Results page. This page should display items from the database that match the user's search criteria (or show a special page if no matches exist). An image from the database should be displayed for each product. If the user selects one of these images, he should be brought to page 5. The Search Results page (and all subsequent pages, except for page 7) should also contain a button that allows the user to begin a new search; this button should link to page 3.

DETAILED PRODUCT INFO (PAGE 5)

If the user clicks an individual product, the application will display the Detailed Product Info page. It should show detailed information about the product (large image, description, price). It should also contain a button that allows the user to submit the selected item to the shopping cart. When this button is clicked, the user should be brought to page 6, and server state should be updated to contain the contents of the new cart.

SHOPPING CART (PAGE 6)

Most pages will contain a link to the Shopping Cart page, which the user can select when she is done adding items to the shopping cart. This page should show the items in the shopping cart and list the cost and selected quantity of each item. The page should enable the user to change the quantity of each item, and it should contain an Update button that lets the user submit new quantities. When this button is clicked, the server state should be updated to contain the contents of the new cart. It should also contain a Purchase button that enables the user to purchase the item(s) and clear the shopping cart.

LOG OUT (PAGE 7)

Most pages will contain a link to the Log Out page. If the shopping cart is not empty, this page should ask the user to confirm whether he really wants to log out. If the user responds yes, he will be brought to page 1. If the response is no, the user will be brought to page 6.

Extending the Specification

When you have your basic requirements, you can start developing the specification in more detail. For Web applications, this commonly comes down to deciding which pages you are going to create and how the user will move between them. You can begin by writing your ideas for each page on a piece of paper and laying the pieces out on a table to find patterns of relationships. For a formal development process, you can introduce a flowcharting tool to track how the requirements interact between pages.

Mapping the requirements

The first step in extending the specification is to map the requirements. Mapping the requirements involves creating a basic flow diagram that illustrates how your listed requirements translate into a set of pages. This page map should describe how the pages relate to one another, providing a high-level visual representation of how the application is designed to work.

One useful technique for prototyping your application at the design stage is to create a notecard for each page and lay all notecards out on a table. Work through the application as though you were a user, and see how easy or difficult it is to accomplish the key activities your application offers. This helps you to anticipate user click paths (requirements) that you might otherwise overlook. Whether you create a flow diagram or simply determine how the flow should work, a little upfront work will pay off later.

A *path* is a specific sequence of pages that a user might take while using your Web application. You will get a more detailed definition in Chapter 13, where we discuss paths.

Remember, at this point, you are focusing on the logical flow through the application. The pages' look and feel is determined later by the development team's artists.

Figure 4-1 shows the basic flow through the Online Grocer application. Three of the pages (the Log Out page, the Main Search page, and the Shopping Cart page) are reachable from most of the pages after the log in. To simplify the flow, we labeled these three pages A, B, and C.

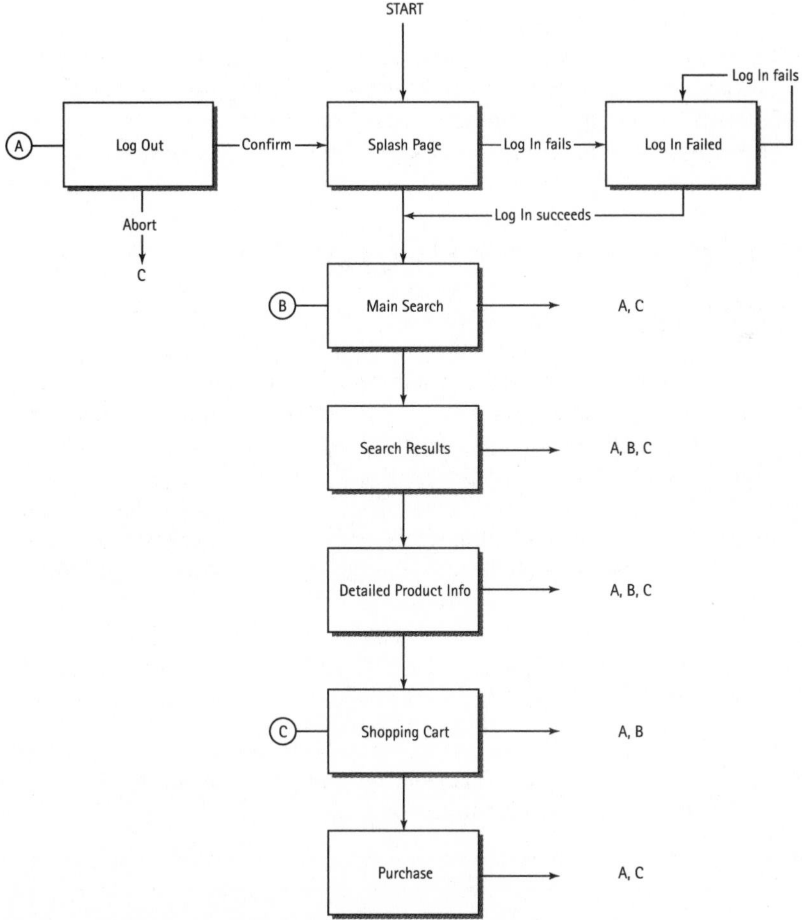

Figure 4-1: The Online Grocer application's preliminary design.

Test requirements

At this point, you know enough about your application to create some test requirements: basic tests that you can apply to your application to verify that the specification has been met. You do this by describing your *use cases*. Use cases are the click paths through the application that represent the user experience described in the specification. These use cases should represent the application's most fundamental functionality and should therefore always work.

If your use cases represent loops, make sure that you thoroughly test the functionality of these paths later and ensure that they can handle the expected amount and type of traffic.

For the Online Grocer application, the use cases include the two paths shown in Figure 4-2. The path on the left is the most basic possible path through the application that will result in a complete transaction. The path on the right represents the path of a user that searches for (and purchases) several produce items.

Choosing the Architecture and Technology

Because much effort would be required to change your architecture and technology in the middle of your development process, it's a good idea to think carefully about your situation and needs before you make any architecture or technology decisions. Ask yourself questions about logistical issues such as where to store state information (for example, information about whether the user is logged in), how to store content information, how the application works with existing systems, and so on. For example, if you were responsible for developing the Online Grocer application, you might want to address the following issues:

- How often should the shopping cart and product list access the database? Will users access the product list each time or use caches? Will the shopping cart be stored in the browser or in the database?

  (In answering these questions, consider the pros and cons of the various state storage options discussed in Chapter 3.)

- How many products will you have? If you have millions of products, you need to store them in a database. If you have thousands of products, though, how will you access them? Sending all the products to the browser would be too slow to be feasible. You need to divide the products into classes so that the application can search through them.

- Are you going to connect to an inventory control system that controls a brick and mortar store? If so, you must create a Web front end that works with this legacy system. If not, you will have more freedom in developing the Web application.
- When does user state expire?
- How many users and purchases do you want to support concurrently?
- What bandwidth will the images require?

Choosing an architecture

After you resolve these issues, you can start fleshing out your implementation and design a preliminary architecture. In the Online Grocer application's implementation, we will use a database and store all information in the database to ensure that data is not lost. User state will never expire; it will always be stored in the database. We will support as many users as the database allows.

Choosing fundamental technology

After you choose an architecture, you decide which technology to use to implement this architecture. Specific technology issues to consider include

- Which machine or machines will host the Web server? Are you going to use Windows, Linux, or some other solution? Will you be hosting the site or using a Web site hosting service (which will impose additional restrictions)? Your choice of an operating system can restrict your other options.
- Which Web server will you use? Microsoft's IIS? Apache? Another Web server?
- In which technologies or languages will your application be implemented? If you have client-side code, some options (for example, JavaScript, VBScript, and code requiring a specific plug-in) exist only for certain browser/OS combinations, and others are supported by a greater variety of platforms. Common Web application implementations are C/C++, Java servlets, ASP, JSP, PHP, ColdFusion, and so forth.

Our technology decisions regarding the Online Grocer application are determined by several factors. Because we're writing this book using Microsoft Windows machines, we will consider that the host platform. To keep the examples useful to Unix readers (and because it's freely available), we will use the Apache Web Server. The application logic will be implemented as a Java servlet.

Log In
Main Search
Search Results
Detailed Product Info
Shopping Cart
Log Out

Log In
Main Search
Search Results
Detailed Product Info
Shopping Cart
Log Out

Figure 4-2: Two of the main use cases for the Online Grocer application.

In Chapter 6, when you get into the actual implementation, we explain more about how the sample Java servlet works.

We will use a database that supports JDBC, the standard Java means of working with databases. Because most vendors support this protocol, we can write the servlet in a portable fashion and safely assume that we will be able to get the database going. Because we chose JDBC, we need to know at least some SQL (Structured Query Language), commonly used to interact with databases. We cover the database-specific issues in Chapter 16.

Because our demo is an e-commerce application, it has additional restrictions, based on who the suppliers are, which technologies handle the financial transactions, and how products are supplied to end users. We don't address these issues in this book because we're building a demo Web application, not a full-featured commercial site.

Any number of other implementations would have suited the book just as well, so don't feel excluded if you are using a different technology.

Choosing development tools

Now that we have covered application design, architecture, and fundamental technologies, we will introduce some of the tools that we will be using throughout the examples in this book and that you might want to use in your own development process. These tools cover many product categories necessary to develop bulletproof Web applications. Generally speaking, we are most familiar with and comfortable working with these tools. If you choose different tools, you can still apply the same principles and general techniques, as appropriate for your development environment.

To add some structure to the list of tools, we have divided them into three categories:

- Scripting languages
- Code construction tools
- General Web development tools

Many tools discussed here are available on the companion CD, and most of the development tools available on the CD are developed by ParaSoft Corporation. ParaSoft Corporation provides error-prevention and error-detection software tools that help developers significantly reduce errors in their software. For more information about ParaSoft and its products, see its Web site at `www.parasoft.com`.

SCRIPTING LANGUAGES

Scripting languages are programming languages that help you automate many simple tasks. In contrast to system programming languages such as C++ and Java, scripting languages generally use typeless variables for more rapid development and to enable you to express simple ideas more easily and in fewer lines of code. This is one of the reasons many Web applications contain modules that are implemented using scripting languages.

Some common scripting languages include Perl, Python, Ruby, and Tcl. In this book, we often refer to scripting languages when we are automating various tasks. Although we primarily refer to examples written in Python, the choice of language is arbitrary. You should feel free to use whatever scripting language or combinations thereof best suit your personal needs and preferences.

Python is an interpreted, interactive, object-oriented programming language. It has an elegant syntax and a small number of powerful, high-level data types built in. Python has recently grown in use. At the time of this writing, it is used by an estimated half a million people in companies around the world. We chose to use Python for scripting examples here because its increasing popularity means that it will be relevant to many readers and because Python's legibility allows you to focus on software engineering principles without becoming distracted by the syntax. For more information about Python, see `www.python.org`.

All our Python examples are available on the CD and were tested on a Windows 2000 machine, using Python 2.1. Most of them run without modification on any platform supported by Python 2.1. To run some examples, you might have to install extra modules on to your Python. Generally, such instances are pointed out in the text.

Another Python technology you might find useful is Jython. Jython is a Java-based Python implementation that can be embedded in any Java-based applications you have. For more information on Jython, see `www.jython.org`. You can also use Python to write applets or as your scripting language inside an ASP page.

CODE CONSTRUCTION TOOLS

Code construction tools are programs designed to test the code you have used to build various parts of your application. We concentrate primarily on Java in this section because the Online Grocer application uses Java.

JTEST Jtest is a Java unit-testing tool that automatically tests any Java software – servlets, JSP, Enterprise JavaBeans (EJBs), or applets – at the class level without requiring the developer to write a test case, harness, or stub. Jtest automatically tests code construction (white box testing), tests code functionality (black box testing), and maintains code integrity (regression testing). In addition, Jtest checks whether code follows more than 240 Java coding standards, and it allows the creation and checking of any number of custom coding standards.

We discuss Jtest in Chapters 7 through 9 and Chapter 19.

JCONTRACT Jcontract is a Java development tool that checks Design by Contract format-specification information at runtime; it can be run independently of Jtest, but the two tools are complementary. After you use Jtest to test your class or component thoroughly at the unit level, use Jcontract to instrument and compile the DbC-commented code. Jcontract will then monitor the application at runtime and perform the user-determined action if a contract is violated. Jcontract is particularly useful for determining whether an application misuses specific classes or components and for detecting system-level functionality problems.

We discuss Jcontract in Chapters 7 and 19.

GENERAL WEB DEVELOPMENT TOOLS

General Web development tools are any other tools you use to develop, test, or manage your Web application files. This broad category includes tools designed to test specialized technology and tools that test the application via an HTTP connection, text editors, HTML editors, and so forth. Of the many possible types of tools to discuss, we focus on

- Types of tools used to develop the Online Grocer application
- Types of tools we believe provide the greatest amount of bulletproofing potential for the largest number of readers

WEBKING WebKing is a comprehensive Web development, testing, and management tool that performs many of the practices involved in creating a bulletproof Web application. It exposes load, construction, functionality, presentation, content, and design problems by examining the application's dynamic and static pages. In addition, WebKing provides an infrastructure that can automatically compile, deploy, and test programs and scripts and verify the related output pages.

We discuss WebKing throughout the book.

SOAPTEST SOAPtest is a tool for testing Web services that use SOAP as a wire protocol and HTTP as a transport protocol. SOAPtest provides an easy interface for exercising Web services and testing their functionality. It can be used to confirm the responses to SOAP RPC calls with features such as fault detection, textual comparisons, and XML validation by DTDs or XML Schemas. It can also be used to express and flag complex patterns in XML. In addition, SOAPtest lets users validate responses that require application-specific verification (such as business logic validation) and performs regression testing of Web services.

We discuss SOAPtest in Chapter 18.

C/C++ Code Construction Tools

If your Web application's CGI programs, server add-ons, or other components are written in C/C++, you might want to explore the following C/C++ code construction tools, which are similar to the Java tools we discuss.

C++Test is a unit-testing tool that can test C/C++ programs at the class or function level. C++Test automatically tests any C/C++ class, function, or component without requiring the developer to write a test case, harness, or stub. C++Test tests code construction (white box testing), tests code functionality (black box testing), maintains code integrity (regression testing), and graphically monitors code coverage. It also performs static analysis and allows the creation and checking of customized coding standards.

CodeWizard is a coding standard verification tool for C/C++. CodeWizard statically analyzes code to check whether it follows a sophisticated set of more than 240 C/C++ coding rules designed to prevent errors. CodeWizard also can be used develop and check custom coding standards.

Insure++ is an automatic, runtime error-detection tool for C/C++. Insure++ uncovers problems such as memory corruption, memory leaks, pointer errors, and I/O errors.

DATARECON DataRecon is a database verification and monitoring tool that allows database design verification, data validation, structural verification, and regression testing. When you can use HTTP to reach the part of the application that accesses the databases, DataRecon can check whether the application writes the correct information to the database, reads the correct information from the database, and adds it to the Web page as expected.

We discuss DataRecon in Chapter 16.

RCS AND CVS RCS is a freely available tool that manages your source code repository, as discussed in Chapter 2. RCS can run on Windows or Unix. We won't go into much detail about using RCS, other than to show how to integrate it with WebKing to develop the Online Grocer application. For information on RCS, visit `www.cs.purdue.edu/homes/trinkle/RCS` or `www.gnu.org/software/rcs`.

Another commonly used package is CVS, the Concurrent Versions System. CVS is a tool built on top of RCS to provide more support for multiple users. The home page is `http://cvshome.org`.

Summary

This chapter describes the main steps in the design phase, demonstrates the design process for the Online Grocer application, and introduces several tools we used to develop the Online Grocer application and that we think you will find helpful. In the next chapter, we demonstrate how to build a prototype for an application and give you basic information on how WebKing works. This will help you work with the WebKing examples that appear throughout the book. In the chapter after that, we cover the coding of the Online Grocer application and show how bulletproofing practices are introduced at the code construction level.

Chapter 5

Prototyping the Online Grocer Application

IN THIS CHAPTER

- ◆ Understanding the advantages of prototyping
- ◆ Building a prototype
- ◆ Creating a project file
- ◆ Modifying a project file
- ◆ Creating a basic deployment infrastructure
- ◆ Creating a basic testing infrastructure

THIS CHAPTER DESCRIBES ONE WAY you can start building a bulletproof Web application. Here you will learn how and why to create a small, static prototype of your application. As with Chapter 4, we use our experience with the Online Grocer application to demonstrate general practices that will help you in your own prototyping efforts. In practice, you perform your prototyping as part of the design phase, but to keep this discussion simple, we are singling out the prototype.

This chapter also describes how the WebKing program provided on the CD can interact with your prototype. The prototype is small and straightforward, so you can get right down to the business of seeing how things work. Because we use WebKing in many examples throughout this book, this is a good place to get an idea of how it ties in to the development process. By working through the examples, you will have a better grasp of the recommended practices we describe, even if you use tools other than WebKing.

If you have not already done so, we recommend that you install WebKing before you proceed with this chapter. The WebKing installation program is located on the CD in the back of the book; you can find the installation instructions in Appendix C.

Understanding the Advantages of Prototyping

The main practices discussed in this chapter are

- **Building a prototype:** How to build a prototype that represents the page flow through your application and provides a foundation on which you can build your application
- **Creating a project file:** How to build a project file – like the project file discussed in Chapter 2 – that will eventually include all the deployment information and test cases developed by the team
- **Deploying the application:** How to build a skeletal deployment infrastructure that can be expanded incrementally as the application develops
- **Specifying and testing critical paths through the prototype:** How to test whether the prototype works correctly and build a skeletal test suite that can be expanded as the application develops

As you can probably tell, the practices described in this chapter help you build the foundation for your application's development, testing, and deployment. The purpose of building each element incrementally is twofold: It helps you create your application more efficiently and helps you keep your bugs under control.

Working in this way increases your efficiency because you always have a foundational application, project file, deployment infrastructure, and test infrastructure on which you can build. Each time you replace and expand part of the prototype application, you can quickly replace and/or add the necessary elements in the project file, deployment infrastructure, and test cases and then deploy and test it as early as possible. Essentially, this approach facilitates the critical unit-testing process we discuss in great detail in Part II.

This approach also keeps your bugs under control by helping you test your deployment process. The deployment process is difficult and needs to be debugged. Each time you add information about a file's source location to the shared project file and add or modify information about how and where an application needs to be deployed, a possibility for error is introduced. If you add file source and deployment information as soon as each file is added and then deploy and test the modified application to check whether that minor change introduced problems, it is much easier to pinpoint and fix your problems. If you wait until your entire application – with hundreds or thousands of files – is completed before you start establishing a deployment infrastructure, building the application, and testing the application, you are likely to end up with a myriad of problems after the initial deployment. Searching for the root of each problem will be like searching for a needle in a haystack.

This prototype approach is just one way to begin building your application. You can take many approaches. The best approach depends on your development process and your project. For example, if you practice Extreme Programming, you would probably build your prototype in an incremental fashion, starting with just a single page and immediately testing your application as a single page. Precisely how you build your prototype is not as important as establishing a regular procedure for early, consistent testing.

Extreme Programming, also known as *XP*, is a relatively new development process that focuses on small teams with rapid development cycles. Our discussion here is necessarily simplistic. For more information on Extreme Programming, refer to the books in Appendix E and at `www.xprogramming.com`.

Building a Prototype

In the prototype approach, the first step in building an application from a design is to create a very basic, limited-functionality prototype. The purpose of this prototype is to demonstrate application flow and provide your team with a framework from which to develop the application. The prototype serves as a constant reminder of what the application is supposed to do and how each element of the application is supposed to function. As you and your team develop the application, you gradually replace prototype pages with application files. For example, you can replace one prototype page with a servlet that connects to the database, another prototype page with XML and JavaBeans, and so on. In the earliest phases of the development process, the application is a mixture of actual pages and prototype pages. Eventually, most prototype files (except possibly image files) are replaced.

Because the prototype always provides at least a basic functionality, it also serves as a type of scaffolding for the parts of the application you add. That is, it provides you with a working structure that lets you access (and test) something that would not otherwise be accessible.

Creating your prototype

When you build the prototype, you create one static HTML page for each page included in the design page-flow specification discussed in Chapter 4 and connect the prototype pages so that they represent the flow described in your design. You can create your prototype pages using your favorite HTML design tool (Dreamweaver, FrontPage, and the like). You don't want to spend too much time fine-tuning your code or design at this point because these files probably will not be used in the actual application. If your application has dynamic elements such as forms, use static HTML (including static links) to mimic the expected functionality.

As you create these files, save them in the most logical and convenient place. You do not have to save them all in the same directory because your project file will contain instructions about how to gather and organize files from multiple locations.

After the complete prototype is built, add the files into the source code repository so that multiple team members can work on them throughout the prototyping phase and build on them during the development phase. Some files you use (such as static HTML pages) will never reach your application, but others (such as image files for logos, images, buttons, and so on) will. These files will probably change before the application is completed, but as long as the original image is checked in to the source code repository, you always have a placeholder for that image, and the file's name and location are established.

Creating the Online Grocer prototype

When we began developing the Online Grocer application introduced in Chapter 4, we reviewed the page flow design diagram created in the section "Mapping the Requirements" and then used Dreamweaver to design a prototype to represent the pages' general contents and flow. We represented each page as follows:

- Page 1 is the Splash page (see Figure 5-1). It is supposed to allow users to log in. We mimic the log in procedure by adding two text fields and two Log In buttons. The first Log In button represents a successful log in; this button has a static link to Page 3, the Main Search page. The second Log In button represents a failed log in; this button has a static link to Page 2, the Log In Failed page. These two buttons will eventually be replaced by a single Submit button that submits data entered into the user name and password text fields.

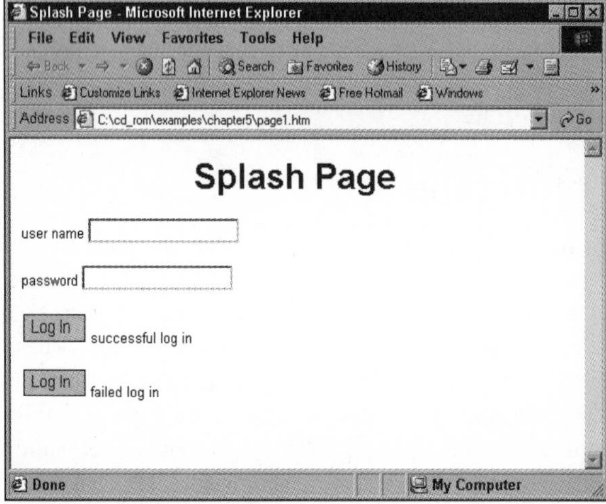

Figure 5-1: Page 1 prototype.

- Page 2 is the Log In Failed page (see Figure 5-2). It is designed to lead to the Main Search page upon successful log in. We mimic this functionality by creating two text fields and a Log In button with a static link to the Main Search page.

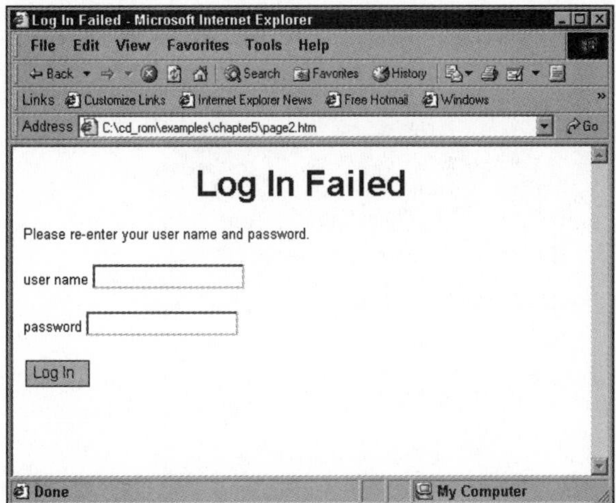

Figure 5-2: Page 2 prototype.

- Page 3 is the Main Search page (see Figure 5-3). It contains check boxes for available search criteria and a submit button labeled Search. The Search button has a static link to the Search Results prototype page. This page also contains a Log Out link that links to the Log Out page and a Go to Shopping Cart link that leads to the Shopping Cart page.

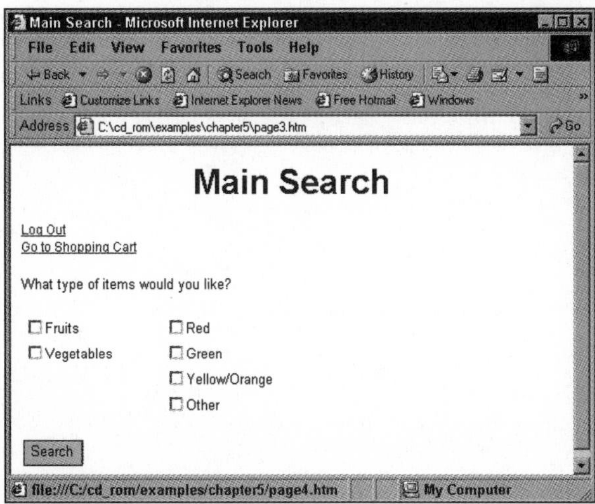

Figure 5-3: Page 3 prototype.

- Page 4 is the Search Results page (see Figure 5-4). In the final application, this page will contain a list of available produce that matches the search criteria specified in the form from Page 3. For the prototype, this page always contains the same images. To keep the prototype as simple as possible, only the first image on the page links to the Detailed Product Info page. This page also contains the standard links to the Main Search page, the Log Out page, and the Shopping Cart page.

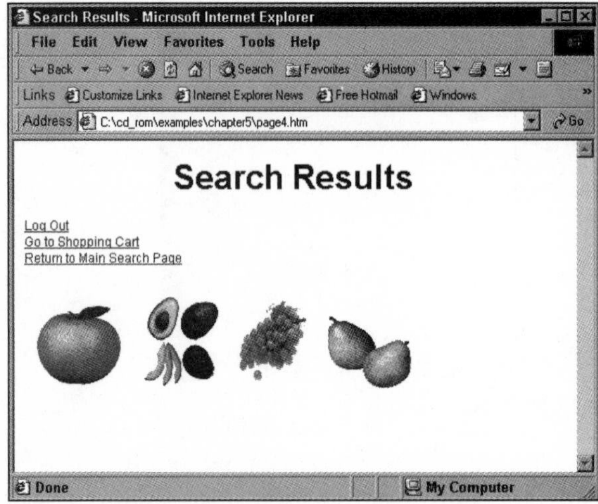

Figure 5-4: Page 4 prototype.

- Page 5 is the Detailed Product Info page (see Figure 5-5). This page will eventually contain information pulled from the database about whatever product is selected in Page 4. For the prototype, it is a static page with information about the one clickable item in the Page 4 prototype page. This page also contains the standard links to the Main Search page, the Log Out page, and the Shopping Cart page.

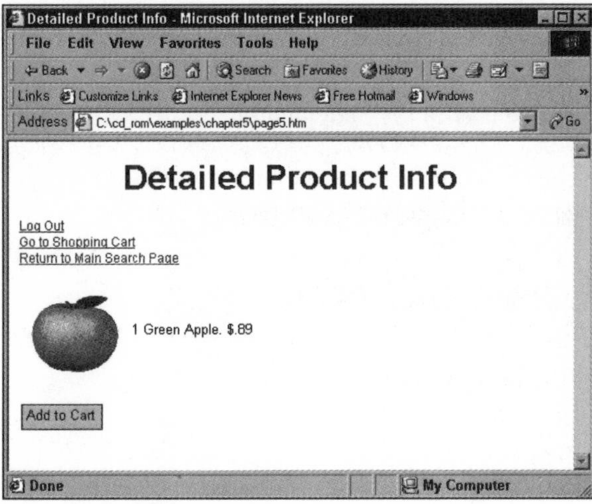

Figure 5-5: Page 5 prototype.

- Page 6 is the Shopping Cart page (see Figure 5-6). The prototype version is a static page that always has the same produce item in the shopping cart. It contains an Update button that reloads this page but does not change the number of items in the shopping cart. In addition, it has a Check Out button that does not link to anything for the time being, as well as the standard links to the Main Search page and the Log Out page.

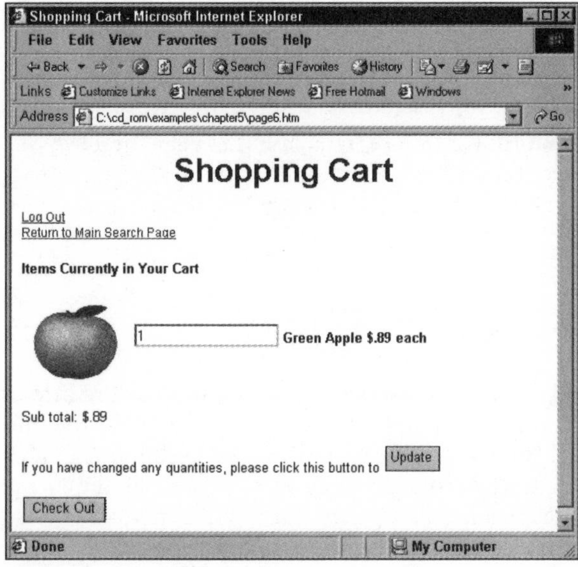

Figure 5-6: Page 6 prototype.

- Page 7 is the Log Out page (see Figure 5-7). It asks the user whether she really wants to log out, and it contains two buttons: a Yes button and a No button. The Yes button contains a link to Page 1, the Splash page. The No button returns the user to the Shopping Cart page.

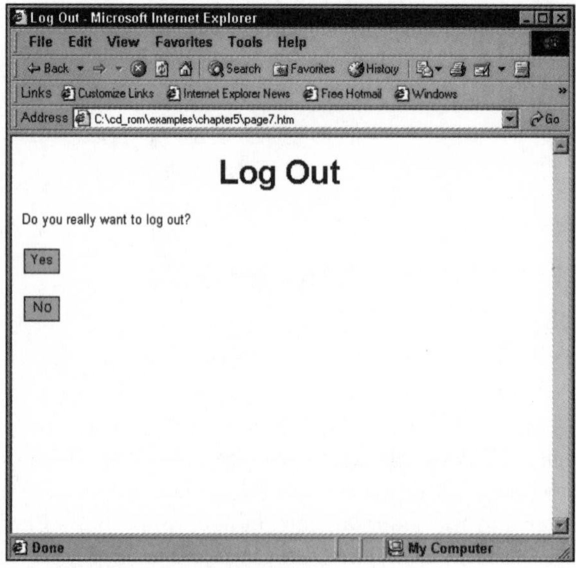

Figure 5-7: Page 7 prototype.

After we completed these pages, we added all related files to the source code repository.

These files are available on the CD at `examples/chapter5`.

Creating a Project File

The next step in creating a foundational development infrastructure is to create the shared project file described in Chapter 2. This is the file with all the information required to assemble and test your application. The most useful project files contain information about how to gather your source files, as well as the blueprints for your deployment and testing infrastructures. Ideally, the project file is updated every time the application is updated. For example, if you add a servlet to the application, in the project file you add information about where to find the servlet, how to deploy it, and how to test it. When you keep the project file in sync with the application, it is much easier to test each application part as soon as you add or modify it. If you work in this manner, assembling and deploying the final version of the application involve only a few minor modifications.

WebKing can automatically create project files and use the information stored in them to test and deploy an application automatically, with the click of a button or as part of the automated regular build process.

Creating a project file with WebKing

To create a project, do the following:

1. Start WebKing as described in Appendix C.
2. Choose Project → New Project.

You now have a project that can contain any number of related sites. WebKing represents this project and all the sites you add to it in the Project tab on the left side of the GUI. We refer to the tree of information that this tab will eventually contain as the *Project tree.*

The first step in adding source files to your project is to load them into WebKing:

1. Right-click the Project tree's New Project node, and choose Add New Site from the shortcut menu. The Add New Site to Project panel opens (see Figure 5-8).

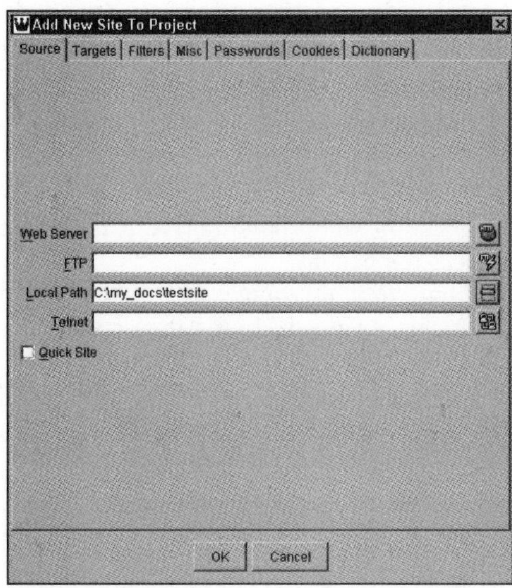

Figure 5-8: Specifying a source location in the Add New Site to Project panel.

2. If the directory containing the majority of your source files is available via a local path, use the button to the right of the Local Path field to browse to that main directory.

   If the directory containing the majority of your source files is available via an FTP connection, enter the name of the FTP server you use to access these files in the FTP field. Then configure additional options by clicking the button next to the FTP field. The FTP panel shown in Figure 5-9 opens (more detailed information is available in the WebKing User's Guide).

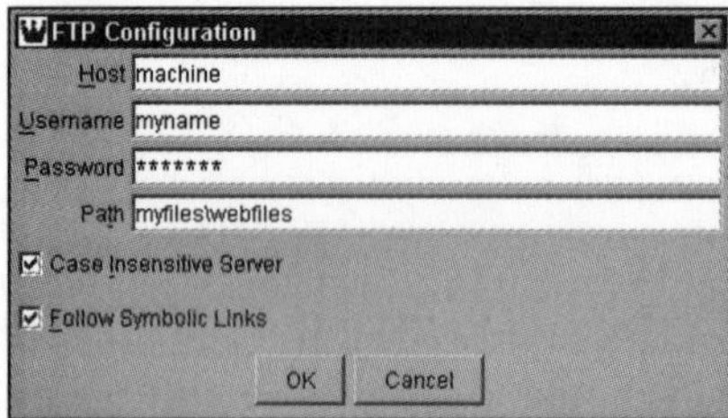

Figure 5-9: Specifying FTP connection parameters.

WebKing then loads the files in the indicated directory. These files are represented in the Project tree on the left side of the WebKing GUI. This tree represents the structure of the files and directories in your application.

If your source code is distributed across multiple non-nested directories, you can add the code in the additional directories by creating indirect links. For information on using indirect links, see the WebKing User's Guide.

Now WebKing knows where to find the files that make up your prototype. When you are ready to deploy your application with WebKing, WebKing automatically gathers all your files from the indicated locations.

To save the information about how to gather and organize the files that will compose the application, choose Project→Save. WebKing then creates the project file that will eventually contain all the relevant deployment information and test cases. Note that WebKing automatically prompts you to save the project file when you close the file or exit WebKing. If you prefer, you can wait until this point to save the project file.

Ideally, the next step is to add the project file to the source code repository in a location where all team members can access it.

Creating the Online Grocer project file

To give you an example of how to create and save a project file, we're going to walk you through the steps involved in creating the initial project file for the Online Grocer application.

The main goal at this point is to tell WebKing where to find all the files we are going to use for the prototype, as well as how to organize those files in the application.

These files are stored on the CD-ROM at `examples/chapter5`.

To tell WebKing how to gather the static HTML files, we created a new project and added our source files to that project. Figure 5-10 shows the values we entered to indicate the location of these files.

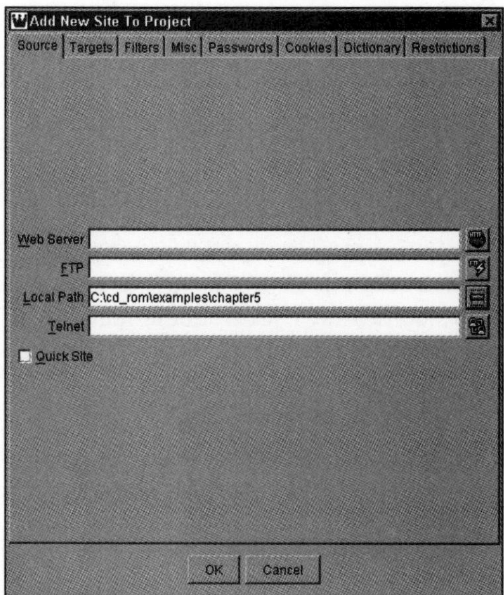

Figure 5-10: Specifying the source of the Online Grocer prototype files.

WebKing then added the specified files and directories to its Project tree. Figure 5-11 shows the Project tree WebKing created.

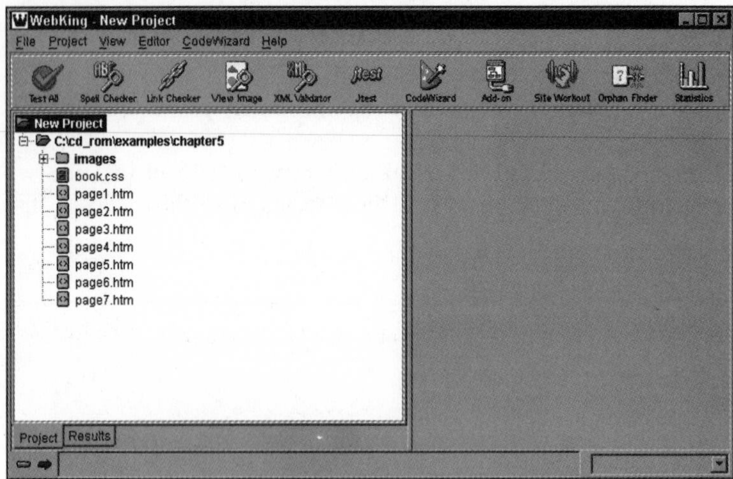

Figure 5-11: Online Grocer source files added to the Project tree.

At this point, the Project tree contained all the files in the prototype, so we decided to save this information. To do this, we chose Project → Save, and WebKing created a project file containing the information necessary to gather and organize the prototype's source files. Finally, we added the project file to our source code repository.

Modifying a Project File

When a team member wants to add to or modify a project file, he accesses the most recent version by checking it out of the source code repository, makes the necessary changes to the project file, and checks the modified file back in to the source code repository. Any time a team member wants to access the most recent version of the project file, he can retrieve it from the source code repository. If a team member wants to work on one of the application's files, she checks out the file through WebKing, edits it in any editor or design tool integrated into WebKing, and checks the file back in through WebKing. The following two sections show you how to integrate and use the RCS source control/version control system and third-party tools within WebKing.

Integrating and accessing source control

By default, WebKing is configured to work with RCS source control. RCS, introduced in Chapter 4, is one example of a tool that can be used to establish and maintain a source code repository (described in Chapters 1 and 2).

To integrate your RCS-based source control system into WebKing, do the following:

1. Choose File → Customize Preferences to open the WebKing Preferences panel.
2. In the preferences panel's RCS tab (see Figure 5-12), check the Enable RCS check box.
3. In the Check-Out Command field, enter the name (and full path, if necessary) of your check out (`co`) command.
4. In the Check-In Command field, enter the name (and full path, if necessary) of your check in (`ci`) command.
5. In the RCS Command field, enter the name (and full path, if necessary) of your `rcs` command.
6. In the File Extension field, enter the file extension of files in the source code repository. This value is usually `,v`, but some versions are configured to use other extensions (for example, `%v`).
7. (Optional) If you use RCS to store the archived files in a subdirectory, enter that name in the Directory field. Typically, the name is `RCS`.

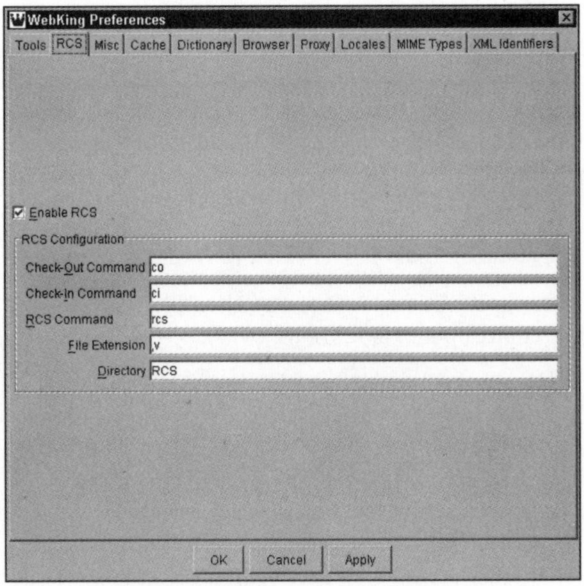

Figure 5-12: Entering RCS settings.

After you integrate your source control system into WebKing, you can check files in and out from within the WebKing environment.

If you configure WebKing in this way, you still must initially add files to the source code repository in the normal manner.

To check a file in or out of your source code repository via WebKing, do the following:

1. In the Project tree, right-click the file you want to check out or check in. A shortcut menu opens.
2. Choose either Check In or Check Out from the shortcut menu.

Integrating and accessing a third-party Web development tool

WebKing's extensible architecture lets you integrate all your Web-related tools into a single environment much like a traditional development IDE such as Microsoft's Visual Studio. You can integrate any third-party tool into WebKing. After you integrate a tool, you access it by simply clicking the toolbar button that WebKing creates for it. To integrate a third-party Web development tool such as Dreamweaver or FrontPage into WebKing, do the following:

1. Choose File → Customize Preferences to open the WebKing Preferences panel.
2. In the preferences panel's Tools tab, click New. A dialog box opens.
3. In the dialog box, choose External Tool and click OK. A new set of fields opens in the preferences panel (see Figure 5-13).
4. In the Tool's tab Name field, enter the tool's name.
5. In the Executable field, enter (or browse to) the name and path of the executable file associated with this tool.
6. (Optional) If you want WebKing to pass any arguments to the tool, enter those arguments in the Arguments field.

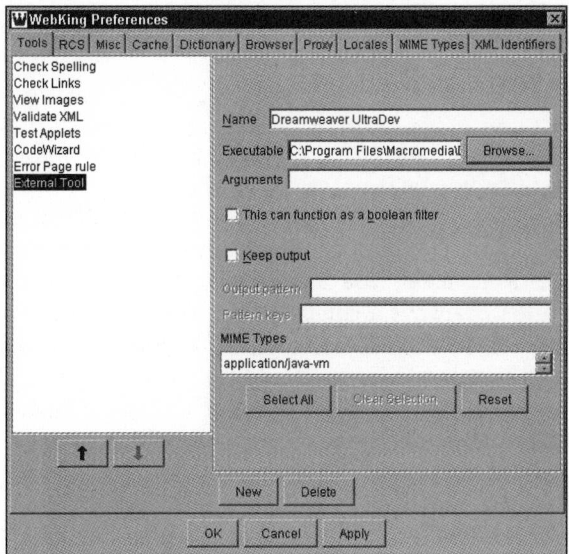

Figure 5-13: Integrating Dreamweaver UltraDev into WebKing.

WebKing integrates this tool into its environment and creates a toolbar button for it.

To use a third-party tool that you have integrated into WebKing, open the tool by clicking the toolbar button associated with that tool, and use the tool as usual. Alternatively, you can select the Project tree node that represents the file to which you want to apply the tool and then click the appropriate toolbar button.

If your source is accessed from a local directory, WebKing automatically recognizes any changes you make and save in the third-party tool. If your source is accessed from an FTP connection, you choose Project→Refresh to prompt WebKing to reload the modified files.

The same button icon is used for all third-party tools you integrate. To determine which tool a button is associated with, position your cursor over each button, and look at the label displayed in the pop-up window.

Creating a Basic Deployment Infrastructure

After creating a working prototype, you create a skeletal deployment infrastructure. Although deploying a static prototype is not necessary in order to view and test it, you must eventually deploy the developing application to test it. In other words, deployment is inevitable. If you wait until late in the development process before you start thinking about deployment, you are likely to end up with a disaster. Deploying a Web application is always a complex procedure. The longer you wait before you start deploying the application, the more problems you have to debug in the initial deployment, and the more difficult it is to isolate the root cause of each problem. The best way to avoid this situation is to start creating a minimal deployment infrastructure as soon as the prototype is ready and then update it each time you modify the prototype.

Establishing a functioning deployment infrastructure for a prototype is not difficult. After this basic infrastructure is established, you can modify it as your application evolves. For example, if you replace a static page with a servlet, you want to add information about how to compile the class files that are the servlet's source, as well as information about where to transfer the servlet. If you keep your deployment infrastructure in sync with your application, deploying each modified version of the application requires only one or two simple changes to the infrastructure.

If you continue modifying and saving the deployment infrastructure as you modify the application, you can always deploy a working application with the click of a button or as part of your automated regular builds. As we mentioned earlier in this chapter, this is a critical step in being able to quickly test whether your modifications function as expected and to fix any problems before they spread across the application, become embedded in the application, or spawn additional bugs in the application.

Creating a deployment infrastructure with WebKing

WebKing facilitates the creation of the deployment infrastructure by providing easy ways to enter deployment instructions. Also, WebKing automates the deployment process so that it can be performed as quickly and efficiently as possible. After the infrastructure is established and debugged, you can perform flawless deployments with the click of a button or overnight as part of your automated regular build.

The first step in establishing a skeletal deployment infrastructure is to tell WebKing where you want to deploy the application. You do this by setting up targets. At this point, you set up only one target – your staging area. A staging area is a critical element of the Web development process because it provides you with a place to test the application thoroughly and out of the public's sight.

Staging areas are introduced in Chapter 2, and discussed in detail in Chapter 10.

To configure WebKing to deploy the application to your staging area, do the following:

1. Right-click the root Project tree node of the site you are working with, and choose Site Properties from the shortcut menu. The Site Properties panel opens.
2. Enter your target (a directory in your staging Web server) in the Targets tab's Locations tab. Indicate a target that is accessible via a local path or an FTP connection.

   To deploy your application to a local path, enter the full path to your application's root (for example, `C:\Apache\htdocs\files`) in the Local Path field, or click the Local Path button and browse to this location.

   To deploy your application to a location that has to be accessed via an FTP connection, click the FTP button, and add the appropriate information to the FTP configuration dialog box.

If you want WebKing to perform any deployment operations, such as compilations, initializations, and so on, you enter them before you deploy the application. Here, you do not need to perform any operations because you are publishing only static files, so you can skip this step for now. As you start replacing the prototype files with application files, add information about each new or modified file's deployment operations when you add or update the file. Chapter 10 discusses this procedure in detail.

At this point, you should be ready to deploy the prototype application. When you deploy the application, WebKing transfers the files from your source(s) to your selected target and automatically performs any tests, operations, and transformations you have configured. Here, you will be performing a basic transfer: You ask WebKing simply to pull the files from the indicated source and transfer them to the indicated target.

To deploy your application to your staging area, do the following:

1. Choose Project→Publish. WebKing opens a dialog box that asks you to specify two things:

   - The sites you want to publish. (Because you've added files for only one site at this point, you don't need to worry about this option.)

- Whether you want to perform a full publish (transfer all files in the selected site[s] to the target) or update the application (transfer only modified files to the target).

2. In this dialog box, indicate your publishing preferences.

WebKing then transfers files from your source location(s) to the selected target.

Deploying the Online Grocer prototype

We set up the deployment infrastructure for the Online Grocer prototype as follows.

First, we specified where we wanted to deploy the prototype. We wanted to use a local Web server as our staging area, so we had to configure WebKing to deploy the files to `C:\Program Files\Apache Group\Apache\htdocs`. To do this, we opened the Site Properties panel, opened the Targets tab, and used the button to the right of the Local Path field to specify the location of our staging area. Figure 5-14 shows these settings.

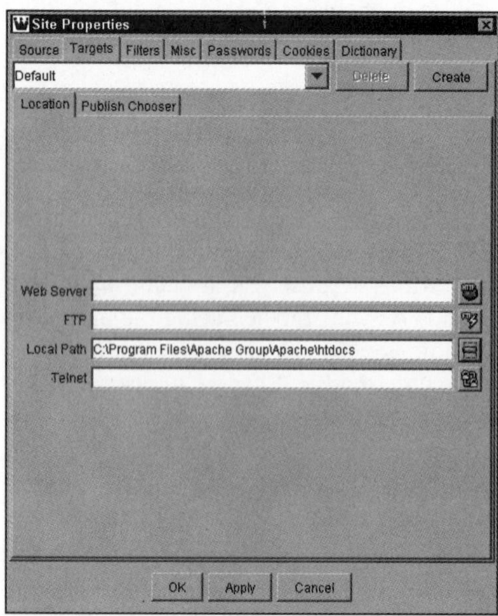

Figure 5-14: Indicating a staging area as a deployment target for the Online Grocer prototype.

We then saved this information. Next, we wanted to deploy the application immediately to test whether the deployment worked as expected. We deployed the application by choosing Project→Publish and then viewed the staging area in our browser to see whether the application deployed correctly. After we confirmed that the application deployed correctly, we saved this deployment information into the WebKing project file.

Creating a Basic Testing Infrastructure

You've created a prototype, created a file that can store all necessary information about that prototype, established an infrastructure that can automatically deploy it, and actually deployed it. Before you consider your prototype complete and start thinking about how to develop it into an application, test the prototype to ensure that it functions as expected. If a prototype does not work, it is not a good framework on which to design and build your application, and you might not be able to use it as scaffolding to help you reach and test each part of the actual application as soon as you develop it. Moreover, you can use your working prototype to perform usability testing and see how users react to your general design and application flow.

There are two ways to test whether this prototype works. The first way is to analyze all available HTML files statically to check for broken links and other critical problems. This method works with static HTML files but is difficult to apply to dynamically generated pages. The second way is to specify the most critical paths through the application, test whether the pages in each path flow as expected, and save the critical paths as test cases that can be repeated and revised throughout the application's lifecycle.

A *path* is a specific sequence of pages that a user might take while using your Web application. We provide a more detailed definition when we discuss paths in Chapter 13.

We recommend that you not limit yourself to the first method because when you specify and test a set of critical paths, you not only test the prototype but also create a basic set of test cases that can be adapted and re-used as the static pages are replaced by application files. To ensure that you create test cases that test the most vital aspects of your prototype's functionality and your application's functionality, create one test case that represents each path described in the application's major use cases (as contained in the application's design). As the application evolves, you can modify the test cases so that dynamically generated pages replace static pages in the paths. Then you can use the modified test cases to check the modified application's most basic functionality. Your paths should always test the same general flow through the application, and the application should always pass the tests that check this basic but critical functionality. Files that do not pass these basic tests should not be checked into the source code repository.

Testing paths in WebKing

We explain the path-creation procedure in detail in Chapter 13. Here, we're going to give you a quick overview of how to specify critical paths through a static prototype.

Before you specify paths in WebKing, you have to indicate a Web server source for your application. You cannot specify paths if your source code is available only in a local directory or via an FTP connection.

To indicate your Web server source, do the following:

1. Open the Site Properties panel by right-clicking the root Project tree node of the site you are working with and choosing Site Properties from the shortcut menu.
2. In the Web Server field of the Source tab, enter the name of your application's base URL (for example, `http://mymachine.parasoft.com`).

If you are working with a truly dynamic application, you follow a slightly different procedure. Instructions for loading a dynamic application are in Chapter 11.

Next, you use WebKing's Path tree to specify the paths you want to test. The Path tree graphically represents possible paths that users can take through your application.

To specify a simple static path in the Path tree, do the following:

1. Indicate which page is your application's main entry page by double-clicking its Project tree node and selecting the Anchor option in the Basic tab of the properties panel that opens (see Figure 5-15). If you do not specify the main entry page, WebKing will not know the page where it should start creating paths.

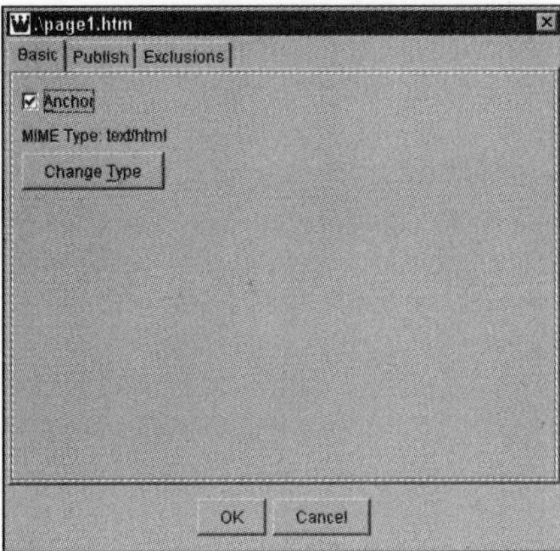

Figure 5-15: Indicating your application's main entry page.

2. Press F4 to have WebKing open the Path tab and generate a default set of paths in the Path tree. Each level of the tree represents one step in a possible path. Multiple branches can stem from a single page's node because multiple links can be followed from a single page. Because the same page (or multiple instances of the same page) can be accessed at various points in various paths, the same page can be represented multiple times in this tree.

3. In the Path tree, extend the default paths in one of the following ways:

   - **Expand links in a browser (Windows only):** Right-click the root Path tree node, and choose Expand Using Browser from the shortcut menu. The first page of your path opens in the WebKing Path Creator browser (see Figure 5-16). In the browser, specify your path by clicking links. When you are done indicating a path, close the browser window.

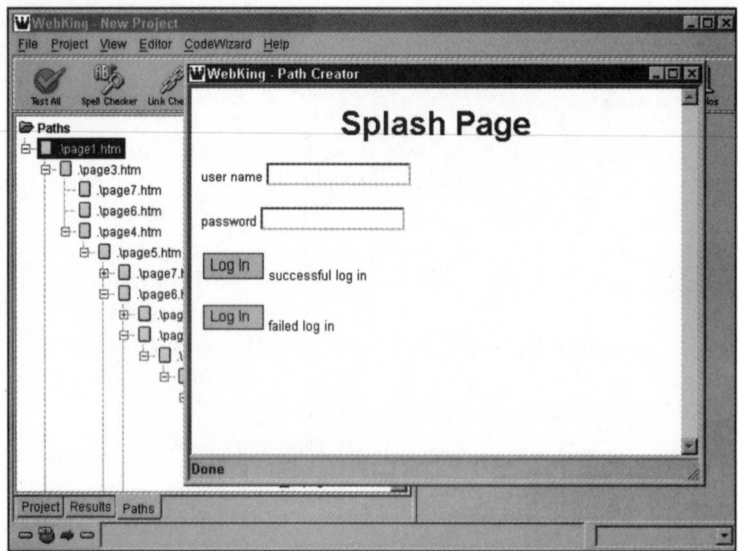

Figure 5-16: Extending a path using WebKing's Path Creator browser.

- **Expand links in the Path tree (Windows or Unix):** Right-click the Path tree node associated with the page whose links you want to expand. Choose Expand Links from the shortcut menu. In the Expand Links dialog box (see Figure 5-17), specify which links you want to expand, how deeply you want to expand those links, and whether you want to expand all links or new links. Continue adding links to the path by repeating these steps.

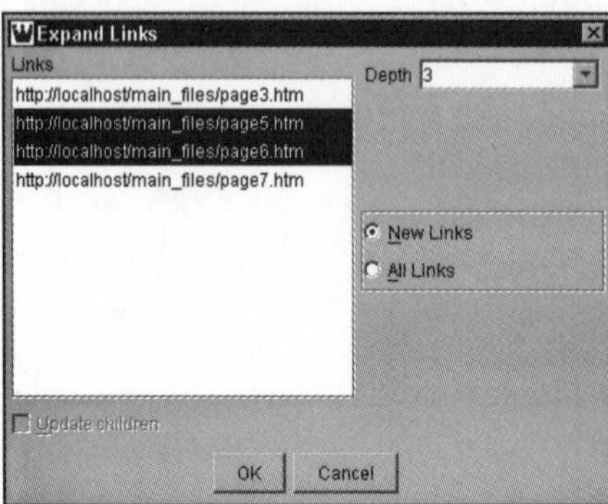

Figure 5-17: Extending a path by adding specific links from the Path tree.

More steps are required for specifying paths that include dynamic pages. For a discussion on specifying these more complex paths, see Chapter 13.

When you are done, the paths you specified are represented in the Path tree. You then can determine whether the pages flow as expected by looking at the icons used in the Path tree. If the pages flow as expected, all Path tree nodes are represented with one of the possible working link icons (the icons vary, depending on the nature of the page). If the pages do not flow as expected, WebKing uses the broken link icon to mark flow problems. Figure 5-18 displays one possible working link icon; the broken link icon is displayed in Figure 5-19.

Figure 5-18: A Path tree node with a working link icon.

.\page.htm

Figure 5-19: A Path tree node with the broken link icon.

After you fix any problems found, your prototype is complete and should be checked in to the source code repository. Before you close WebKing, be sure that you save your project file so that your work can be easily restored. The WebKing project file will then contain information about how to gather your source files, information about how to deploy your application, and a description of the most critical paths through your application.

Testing the Online Grocer prototype paths

To test the main paths through our Online Grocer prototype, we first set up WebKing to load the application from a Web server source (our staging area). To do this, we added the Web server source in the Site Properties panel by completing the Site Properties panel's Web Server field, shown in Figure 5-20.

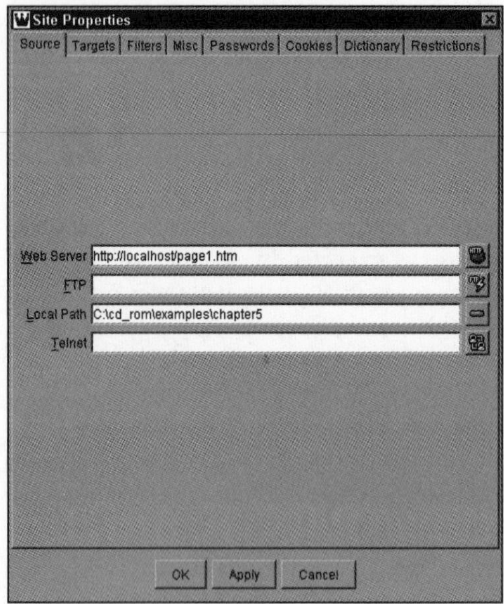

Figure 5-20: Specifying the Web server source for the Online Grocer prototype.

Next, we marked `page1.htm` as an anchor to indicate that it is the main entryway into the application. Then we prompted WebKing to create a base set of paths, by pressing F4. Figure 5-21 shows the paths WebKing created. Note that by default WebKing creates paths that are, at most, three levels deep.

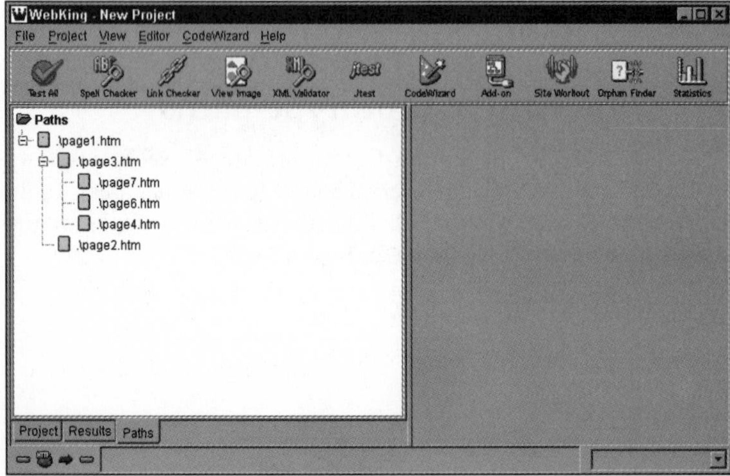

Figure 5-21: Automatically created paths for the Online Grocer prototype.

Next, we wanted to test whether the prototype successfully implements the use cases described in Chapter 4. Here's a shorthand notation using just the page numbers:

- **Path 1:** 1→3→4→5→6→7
- **Path 2:** 1→3→4→5→6→3→4→5→6→3→4→5→6→7

To demonstrate the two possible methods of specifying paths, we specified Path 1 using the shortcut menu options in the Path tree and specified Path 2 by clicking links in the WebKing Path Creator browser.

Specifying Path 1 was simple because the majority of the path was created automatically when WebKing created the default set of paths. To start extending this path so that it would represent the complete path we wanted to test, we chose to expand links from `page4.htm` by right-clicking that page's Project tree node and choosing Expand Links from the shortcut menu. In the dialog box that opened, we specified the links we wanted to add to our path. Because we wanted to add pages 5, 6, and 7 to our path, we chose to expand `page5.htm` and told WebKing to expand links to a depth of 3 (so that it would expands links three levels beyond the selected page). Our settings appear in Figure 5-22.

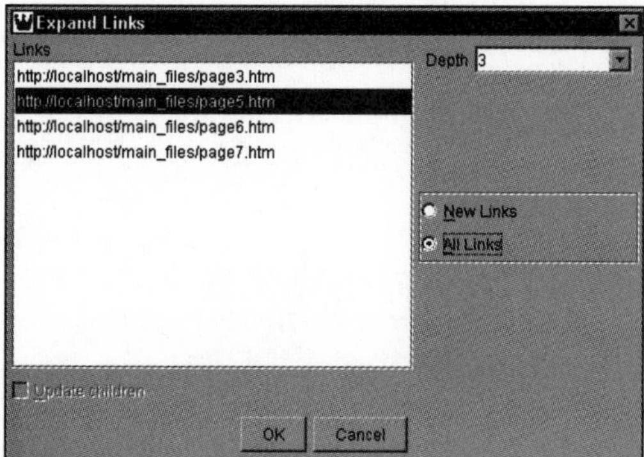

Figure 5-22: Specifying that we wanted to add Page 5 and related files to Path 1.

Pages 5, 6, and 7 (and additional files) were then added to our Path tree.

The paths added to the WebKing Path tree include a full representation of the first path we wanted to test (refer to Figure 5-21).

If WebKing adds pages that you do not want included in your set of paths, you can delete single pages or path segments by right-clicking the appropriate Path tree node(s) and choosing Delete Path from the shortcut menu.

If you look at the icon for the `checkout.htm` node in Figure 5-23, you will notice that it is different from the others. This is the broken link icon. In this case, the broken link does not involve files in our critical paths but does remind us that we have forgotten to create a checkout page.

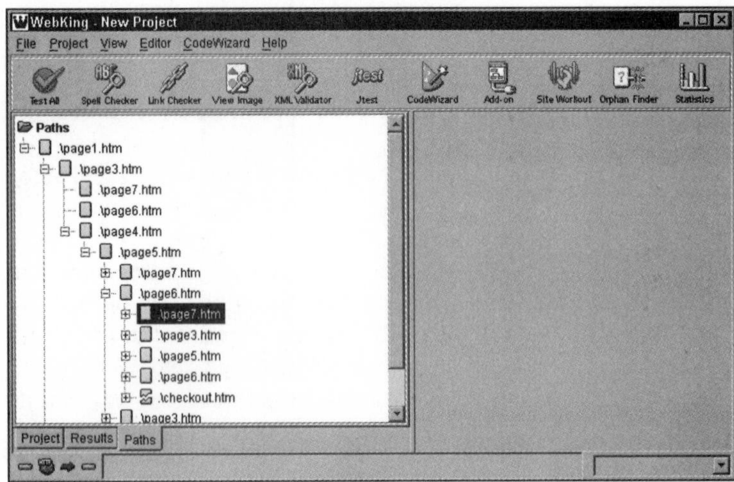

Figure 5-23: Path 1 (and additional paths) represented in WebKing.

Next, we added Path 2 to WebKing's Path tree by right-clicking the `page1.htm` node (the application's root node) and choosing Expand Using Browser from the shortcut menu.

WebKing then opened a special browser that displayed `page1.htm`. We specified Path 2 by clicking the appropriate links in this browser. Each time we clicked a link, the page that opened was added to WebKing's Path tree. Figure 5-24 shows how WebKing represented Path 2.

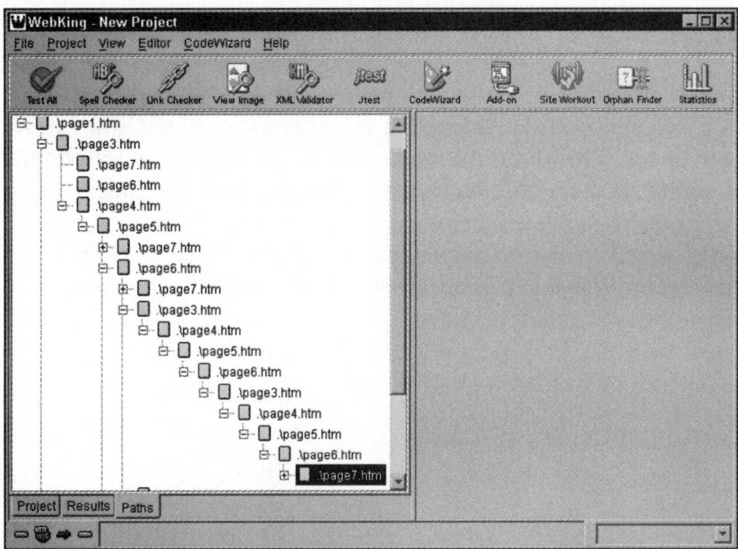

Figure 5-24: Path 2 (and additional paths) represented in WebKing.

At this point, both paths we wanted to test were represented, and by simply looking at the icons used in the Path tree, we could determine whether the pages in the paths flowed as expected. (When the pages flow as expected, all the nodes in the paths are represented with the working link icon. If the pages do not flow as expected, WebKing places a broken link icon next to nodes for files it could not find by following the specified links.) In this case, all pages in the two critical paths flowed as expected.

Finally, we added our path information to our WebKing project file by choosing Project → Save. Now, whenever we open this project file, WebKing contains all the information required to gather the application's source files, organize those files, deploy those files to our staging area, and test whether the prototype flows as expected. As the application develops, we will modify the necessary information accordingly and then redeploy and retest the application to ensure that its most basic functionality always works.

Completing the process

If you follow these recommended practices, you will have a functional prototype and a basic project file that can successfully deploy and test your prototype. Your next step is to plan how you will turn the prototype into the application. As you develop the application, be sure to update the project file's deployment and testing infrastructure each time you modify a part of the application. If you allow too wide a gap between the application and the project file, you will have a much more difficult time deploying the application, troubleshooting deployment problems, and using the modified prototype as scaffolding that lets you test otherwise unreachable parts of the application.

Summary

In this chapter, we explore and demonstrate one possible way to start converting your design into a Web application. We explain the advantages of the prototyping approach and how to apply it. Along the way, we describe how to build a prototype application, project file, skeletal deployment infrastructure, and basic testing infrastructure.

The next chapter describes how we implement the Online Grocer application in Java and contains tips for Web applications implemented in any language.

Chapter 6

Implementing the Online Grocer Application

IN THIS CHAPTER

- Working with Java servlets
- Developing the class hierarchy for the Online Grocer application
- Developing the dispatch framework
- Developing the shopping servlet
- Developing the data framework
- Putting it all together

THIS CHAPTER EXPLORES ISSUES that arise when setting up a Java servlet implementation of the Online Grocer application and explains how the goal of making it bulletproof is built into the code. The Online Grocer application is referred to repeatedly throughout the book, so a basic understanding of the code will help you gain the most from the examples.

There are several versions of the Online Grocer application; to illustrate concepts, we implement various components in different ways. This application is designed to be flexible so that we can apply different approaches and try different practices while discussing new technologies. You can make your own changes and see how this affects the application. Also, although this version is written using Java servlets, you can just as easily code a solution using C++, Perl, ASP, or many other Web technologies.

Because the main goal of the Online Grocer application is to provide an example, the code is designed for simplicity to illustrate the principles discussed. It is not meant as a fully featured, robust end application, but exploring methods to increase its robustness would be an excellent exercise.

The version created in this chapter has intentional that errors we will clean up as we proceed through the book. The initial version, as well as a clean version, can be found on the CD. Appendix B describes each of the bugs in the initial version and lists where in the book we discuss the methods used to detect and fix them.

When explaining the code in this chapter, we highlight key principles we believe are applicable to any implementation. If you get lost in the code, you can scan the text for these principles.

Working with Java Servlets

The main version of the Online Grocer application is implemented using *Java servlets,* a technology from Sun Microsystems that enables developers to extend Web servers with applications written in the Java programming language. The choice of an implementation language for the Online Grocer application is largely arbitrary. If we implemented this application using any number of other languages, most examples in this book would change very little.

Our choice of Java servlets is based primarily on the following:

- We like Java! Writing Web applications in a language with which you are comfortable increases your productivity and effectiveness.
- Java servlets are widely supported by Apache Web server, iPlanet Web server, Microsoft IIS, and many others. Also, when written using pure Java, servlets are portable across different architectures.
- Java servlets are scalable at the server level. You don't have to worry about micromanaging multiple instances of your servlet as long as you are careful about keeping your code thread-safe.

Of course, other solutions have their own benefits and drawbacks.

A related technology, Java Server Pages (JSP), is an extension of Java servlets designed to assist in creating HTML or XML pages. JSP is closely related in concept to Active Server Pages (ASP), which are used on many applications. These technologies make it easy to combine static templates and dynamic content.

To keep the example simpler, we do not use JSP in this implementation of the Online Grocer application, but we discuss this technology in Chapter 20.

Reviewing servlet programming

To write a Java servlet, you create a class that extends the `HttpServlet` class. This class is expected to override at least one of the following functions to make its functionality available to the server providing the HTTP connection:

```
public void doDelete(HttpServletRequest req, HttpServletResponse res)
public void doGet(HttpServletRequest req, HttpServletResponse res)
public void doPost(HttpServletRequest req, HttpServletResponse res)
public void doPut(HttpServletRequest req, HttpServletResponse res)
```

Each method corresponds to the similarly named HTTP request: `doGet()` is called whenever a `GET` request is made to a servlet, `doPost()` is called whenever a `POST` request (for example, a form submission) is made to a servlet, and so forth. The `req` parameter represents the request and any available information, and the `res` parameter represents the response that will be returned to the user. Any methods you do not override will simply not accept the corresponding HTTP request.

If your servlet needs special initialization or cleanup code, you can also override the following hooks:

```
public void init(ServletConfig config)
public void destroy()
```

The `ServletConfig` object lets you pass initialization options (for instance, the username and password to use when connecting to a database) to your servlet from a configuration file. Using this object relieves you from having to include those dependencies in your code.

The following is a minimal, functioning Web application that responds `Hello!` to any `GET` request. This isn't a particularly well-behaved servlet – it doesn't even have the courtesy to generate proper HTML. It does work, though.

```
import java.io.*;
import javax.servlet.http.*;

public class HelloServlet extends HttpServlet
{
    public void doGet(HttpServletRequest req,
                      HttpServletResponse res)
        throws IOException
    {
        PrintWriter out = res.getWriter();
        out.println("Hello!");
    }
}
```

To run this example, you need a Web server with support for Java servlets. Most of this book was written using Windows 2000 with the Apache Web server version 1.3.6; this version of the Apache Web server is available on the CD. For a servlet engine, we used both the Apache JServ servlet engine version 1.0 and Tomcat version 3.2.1 (Tomcat is also on the CD). We recommend using Tomcat because it is a more current engine and is being actively developed by the Jakarta project at

Creating an Infrastructure for Testing Early and Often

As the mantra goes, "Test early, test often." If you are going to test your code ruthlessly, you must be able to run tests with minimal effort. In the case of servlet development, this requires the ability to test your code *immediately* after you compile it.

We have seen some groups delay servlet testing until a fair amount of development has been completed because they implemented a process that required their servlets to be deployed to a common server before testing could occur. This is an inefficient practice that hampers productivity.

Code can be tested immediately if each developer has access to an individual Web server running on his or her own machine. This arrangement also provides developers the safety to test without the possibility of interfering with code others are working on.

When an application has dependencies on other components (for instance, databases), early testing is commonly resisted. In this case, you need to configure your environment appropriately by sharing a common database, giving developers their own databases, or stubbing out database access.

Another hindrance to immediate testing is having to move `.class` files after they are compiled. If you have to copy compiled class files to a different directory before you can test them, you will probably test less often than you would if you did not have to copy them. To avoid this, configure your build process so that you can run your servlets immediately after compilation with no extra steps. Doing so typically involves one of the following configurations:

- Configure your build process to place newly built class files into directories from which your servlet engine runs them.
- Configure your servlet engine to look into your development directory.

The best solution depends on your individual build procedure. In addition, your servlet engine should be configured to recognize updates and execute the current code automatically. This gives you the speediest testing turnaround cycle possible.

Naturally, testing early doesn't eliminate the need for testing a deployed application. It does, however, improve the overall efficiency of your development process and make the later phases of testing decidedly less painful. We discuss the benefits of early testing in greater detail in Chapter 9, when we cover unit testing.

apache.org. Naturally, you also need a Java development environment to compile the .java file into a .class file; the examples in this book were tested using JDK version 1.3.0.

Reviewing multithreaded programming

Servlets are typically run inside a *multithreaded* environment, where the server is capable of creating multiple threads to handle several HTTP requests simultaneously. All these requests are handled by the same instance of the servlet class. In general, this isn't difficult to account for, especially because Java has language support for synchronizing the behavior of multiple threads when necessary. However, it can introduce difficult-to-debug problems into the application if you are not properly prepared.

For a simple example of something that can go wrong, create an HTML page with the following form:

```
<FORM ACTION=/servlet/BuggyServlet METHOD=GET>
Your name: <INPUT TYPE=TEXT NAME=USER>
<INPUT TYPE=SUBMIT>
</FORM>
```

Then, create BuggyServlet as follows:

```
import java.io.*;
import javax.servlet.http.*;

public class BuggyServlet extends HttpServlet {
    String user;
    public void doGet(HttpServletRequest req,
                      HttpServletResponse res)
        throws IOException
    {
        user = req.getParameter("USER");
        try {
            Thread.sleep(2000); // Wait two seconds
        } catch (InterruptedException e) {
        }
        PrintWriter out = res.getWriter();
        out.println("Hello "+user);
    }
}
```

The Danger of Deadlocks

Multithreaded programming introduces many layers of complexity beyond those touched on so far. For instance, a common solution to race conditions in Java code is to use the `synchronized` keyword to protect a section of code from simultaneously being executed by different threads. This is often the correct solution. However, if you get carried away and mark most of your routines as synchronized, without thinking the issues through carefully, you are likely to end up with performance problems, or even worse, deadlocks. A *deadlock* occurs when two threads are unable to proceed because each is waiting for the other. These errors are very serious because your application is essentially dead in the water.

The following classes (available on the CD) illustrate how such a deadlock can occur simply by marking functions as synchronized:

```
class Lock {
    Lock lock;
    synchronized void func1() {
        try {
            Thread.sleep(1000);
        } catch (InterruptedException e) {
        }
        lock.func2();
    }
    synchronized void func2() {
    }
}

public class LockTest {
    public static void main(String[] args) {
        Lock lock1 = new Lock();
        final Lock lock2 = new Lock();
        lock1.lock = lock2;
        lock2.lock = lock1;
        new Thread() {
            public void run() {
                lock2.func1();
            }
        }.start();
        lock1.func1();

    }

}
```

In this code, the main thread gets a lock on the `lock1` instance, and the second thread, created by `Thread.start()`, gets a lock on the `lock2` instance. Now the main thread is waiting for `lock2`, and the second thread is waiting for `lock1`. Because both locks are being held, neither process can continue, and you have a deadlock.

One helpful resource on this subject is *Concurrent Programming in Java: Design Principles and Patterns* by Doug Lea, who has also created `util.concurrent`, a useful package for solving some concurrency issues. This package is available at `gee.cs.oswego.edu/dl/classes/EDU/oswego/cs/dl/util/concurrent/intro.html`.

Normally, the servlet responds `Hello user`, where `user` is the name entered in the original form. However, because we stored the name in a member variable instead of a local one, it is shared between multiple threads. As a result, if one thread assigns `user` to `Fred` and another thread assigns `user` to `Barney` before the first thread prints its message, both requests will return the same reply: `Hello Barney`. This kind of problem is referred to as a *race condition* because each thread is racing to complete its task before another thread interrupts it. Because the timing is very close, these problems do not occur often. However, when they do, determining their cause can be very difficult because such problems are very hard to reproduce. The `sleep()` has been added to make the race condition easier to observe; without it, the race is still present but will occur very rarely.

If you want to reproduce the race condition for yourself, these files are available on the CD.

The biggest implication of a multithreaded environment is that any member variables of the servlet class can be shared between several threads at once. If you want to modify this variable, you must use the `synchronized` keyword from Java to make a *lock*, which allows only one thread at a time to access that portion of the code.

Several resources (listed in the preceding sidebar) are available to help you work in a multithreaded environment. However, if you want to require that your servlet always run in a single thread, you can have your class implement the `SingleThreadModel` interface. This is an empty interface that simply tells the server that a single instance of your class should be handling only one request at a time. The server can still create multiple instances of the class to handle multiple requests simultaneously. In general, this is not as efficient as a multithreaded approach and is not recommended.

Developing the Class Hierarchy for the Online Grocer Application

Because Java is an object-oriented language, the Online Grocer application will be constructed of many types of objects. In Java, these types are referred to as *classes.* The source files will have the extension `.java`. The compiled files we will deploy as the application will have the `.class` extension. Multiple class files can be combined into a `.jar` file, much as C/C++ programs are compiled into `.o` or `.obj` files and `.a`, `.lib`, or `.exe` files.

Figure 6-1 shows the class hierarchy used for the Online Grocer application. Each bubble represents a class. Arrows pointing upwards denote inheritance; for instance, the `CustomerDatabaseJDBC` class extends `CustomerDatabase`. Dotted lines represent a usage relationship. In this case, `ProductDatabase` depends on the `Product` class to hold the actual information about any given product. The bubbles at the bottom have the same meaning but indicate a different pattern: Because `ShoppingServlet` is a `DispatchServlet` (by inheritance), it uses `DispatchContexts`. However, we always arrange it so that the instances of `DispatchContext` it uses are, in fact, `ShoppingContext` objects. We explain the reasons for this later in this chapter.

To keep this example simple, we placed all these classes in a single Java package named `fruits`. We discuss each of these classes in turn.

The major components include

- The `DispatchServlet` classes, which provide an abstraction layer on top of the raw servlet API
- The `ShoppingServlet` classes, which provide the application logic
- The data support classes, including connections to a database, which manage the data that the application displays and collects

The source files are located on the CD.

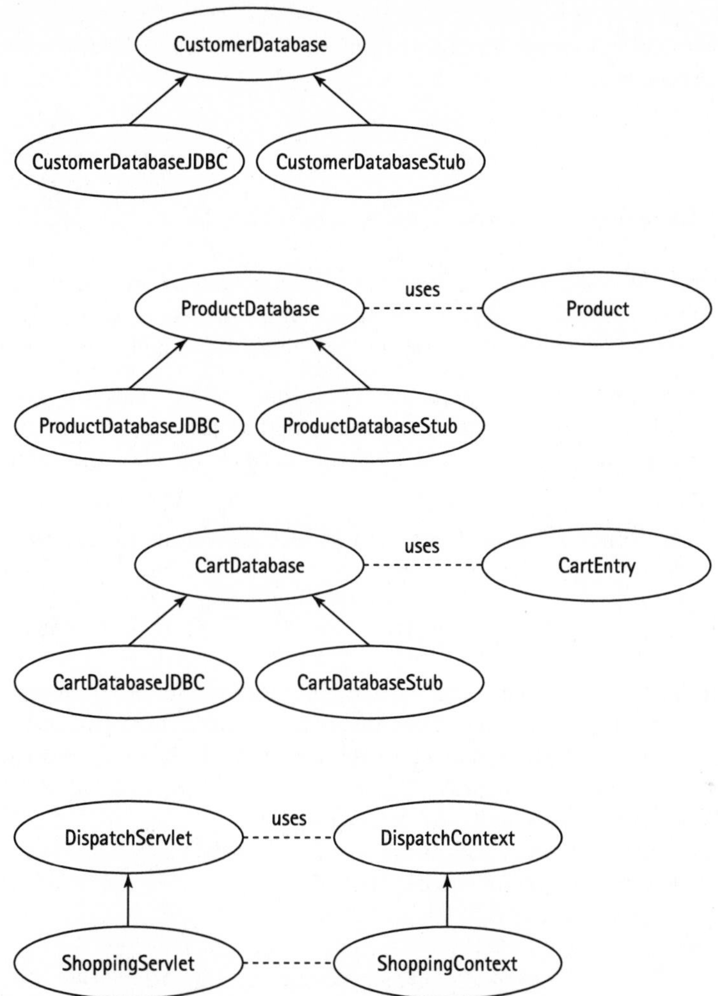

Figure 6-1: The relationships of the Online Grocer's classes.

Developing the Dispatch Framework

Although we could have implemented `ShoppingServlet` directly by extending `HttpServlet`, we chose to create a few small classes first to give us some extra basic functionality. By keeping these as separate classes, we can debug and maintain this logic more easily. This is the first principle for bulletproof code construction.

Small and easily maintained units are easiest to make robust. They are also easiest to test.

The specific functionality we want `DispatchServlet` to provide is

1. To combine `GET` and `POST` handling into a single routine and use Java's reflection mechanism to dispatch the actual call (this lets us easily invoke debugging routines without cluttering the application logic).
2. To combine the request and response into a single object. This also gives us a place to store application-specific data that applies to most routines but is not appropriate for a method variable because the class has to be thread-safe.
3. To put a protective wrapper around any servlet exceptions so that errors are reported in a quick and easy way.

Simplifying the servlet API

The first goal of `DispatchServlet` is to simplify the servlet API. Often, the `doGet()` routine inside a servlet becomes quite messy with logic to determine which routine to execute and what's actually being requested. Here's an example:

```
public void doGet(HttpServletRequest req,
                  HttpServletResponse res) {
    // Okay, time to figure out what the user wants!
    if (req.getParameter("BUY") != null) {
        // Looks like they filled out one of our buy forms
        int type = Integer.parseString(req.getParameter("TYPE"));
        switch(type) {
        case 1: // This means shoes!
            doShoeLogic(req, res);
            break;
        case 2: // This means shirts!
            doShirtLogic(req, res);
            break;
        default:
            // uh-oh - this doesn't mean anything?
            break;
        }
    } else if (req.getParameter("HISTORY")) {
        showHistory(req, res);
```

```
    }
    // and on and on...
}
```

Sometimes developers create many separate servlets to get around this problem, but that means ending up with more objects to understand and more instances to clutter memory. Instead, we standardize on a single selection mechanism. If there is a parameter named `METHOD`, that's the method that will handle the logic for this request. If not, we call a default method specified in the constructor. In this case, the preceding code simply disappears, with `doShoeLogic()`, `doShirtLogic()`, and `showHistory()` being handled automatically. Here's the code that does the trick:

```
protected String defaultMethod;
protected Class[] parms;

protected DispatchServlet(String defaultMethod) {
    this.defaultMethod = defaultMethod;

    parms = new Class[1];
    parms[0] = DispatchContext.class;
}
public void doGet(HttpServletRequest req,
                  HttpServletResponse res)
    throws ServletException, IOException {
    doInteraction(req, res);
}
public void doPost(HttpServletRequest req,
                   HttpServletResponse res)
    throws ServletException, IOException {
    doInteraction(req, res);
}
void doInteraction(HttpServletRequest req,
                   HttpServletResponse res)
    throws ServletException, IOException {
    DispatchContext context = null;
    res.setContentType("text/html");
    try {
        String method = req.getParameter("METHOD");
        if (method == null) {
            method = defaultMethod;
        }
        context = createContext(req, res);
        if (context != null) {
            Method m = getClass().getMethod(method, parms);
```

```
            Object[] passed_args = new Object[1];
            passed_args[0] = context;
            m.invoke(this, passed_args);
        } // else createContext handled it.
    } catch (InvocationTargetException e) {
        Throwable t = e.getTargetException();
        handleException(req, res, t);
    } catch (Throwable t) {
        handleException(req, res, t);
    } finally {
        if (context != null)
            context.destroy();
    }
}
```

The complete class is located on the CD.

The meat of the logic is buried inside `doInteraction()`:

```
Method m = getClass().getMethod(method, parms);
Object[] passed_args = new Object[1];
passed_args[0] = context;
m.invoke(this, passed_args);
```

This code uses the Java language feature known as ***reflection***. The `getMethod()` function says, "Look for a function whose name matches `method` and whose arguments match `parms`, and return the information necessary to invoke it." If we find such a function, we create the arguments and make the function call. If the function is not available, Java throws an exception that ends up calling the `handleException()` method (explained later in the section "Establishing uniform exception handling"). Because we are using reflection, there aren't any actual calls to the functions that implement the logic, as there would normally be. Instead, we generate URLs like this:

```
http://sample.com/servlet/MyServlet?METHOD=doShoeLogic
```

This now invokes the `doShoeLogic()` method without any additional coding. If we are implementing forms, we can pass the `METHOD` parameter as a hidden argument:

```
<INPUT TYPE=HIDDEN NAME=METHOD VALUE=doShoeLogic>
```

The reflection mechanism is also nice because it lets us create new methods solely for debugging. In normal use, these methods are never called. When we want to call them, we just enter an appropriate URL into the Web browser, and the function is invoked automatically – for example:

```
http://sample.com/servlet/MyServlet?METHOD=showDebugInformation
```

You can also easily test any routines by entering URLs into your browser. This does have a dark side, though. Malicious users can try to discover new strings you have used, call functions you didn't intend for them to call, or call your functions in the wrong order. You must always protect against these cases by performing validation in your servlet, requiring passwords, removing your debug routines in your final user-visible application, and so on.

Combining parameters

If you read through the previous examples in detail, you might have noticed that the manually implemented `doGet()` accepts two parameters (`request` and `response`), but the reflection-based routine accepts only one (`context`). This satisfies the second desired functionality and helps to simplify the API.

The `DispatchContext` class acts primarily as a wrapper around the `HttpServletRequest` and `HttpServletReponse` objects. Most of the methods just pass the call to the appropriate contained instance variable. In the design patterns way of thinking, this is called a *facade*. We have added a few higher-level helper functions that we think we can use later. There's also a hook for a cleanup method named `destroy()`. We guarantee that this is called, even in the presence of exceptions, so that we can manage resources cleanly and avoid leaks.

We developed a routine named `createContext()` that builds the wrapper, so children classes can override this method and specialize the `DispatchContext` class to provide more functionality, as well as have a place to store thread-specific state. In the next section, we describe how we used this when implementing the `ShoppingServlet` class.

```
protected DispatchContext createContext(HttpServletRequest req,
                                        HttpServletResponse res)
    throws ServletException {
    return new DispatchContext(req, res);
}
```

The complete `DispatchContext` class is on the CD. Here's the basic gist:

```
public class DispatchContext {
    protected HttpServletRequest req;
    protected HttpServletResponse res;
    public DispatchContext(HttpServletRequest req, HttpServletResponse res) {
        this.req = req;
        this.res = res;
    }
    public PrintWriter getWriter() throws IOException {
        return res.getWriter();
    }
    public String getRequiredParameter(String s) throws ServletException {
        String sValue = req.getParameter(s);
        if (sValue == null) {
            throw new ServletException("Parameter " + s + " missing");
        }
        return sValue;
    }
    ...
}
```

Design Patterns and Refactoring

Design Patterns refer to specific idioms or patterns that occur commonly in software development. By giving these recurring patterns names and definitions, you can create a common vocabulary that helps you describe your application. The classic reference for design patterns is the book *Design Patterns* by Gamma, Helm, Johnson, and Vlissides, which explains the concepts and contains a catalog of actual design patterns you can use. As more developers become acquainted with these terms and concepts, expect more books and literature to develop these concepts further.

A *facade* is one example of a design pattern. According to *Design Patterns,* a facade is an interface that is built on top of a subsystem, in order to provide a higher-level interface. The facade should make the subsystem easier to use.

This provides a tidy explanation of why we created `DispatchContext`. We believe that familiarity with these concepts helps you write clean, understandable code.

Another angle for approaching the `DispatchContext` class is *refactoring*: a set of techniques to clean up your code incrementally by rewriting it to improve the structural integrity of the code gradually. Here, we have made a small change to allow us to reuse a simple way of implementing servlets. By keeping it independent, we improve the clarity of our code. An excellent book on this subject is *Refactoring* by Martin Fowler.

The other detail not yet explained is the two mysterious lines from the constructor:

```
parms = new Class[1];
parms[0] = DispatchContext.class;
```

This is the function signature that the reflection uses when looking up the method to call. By storing this inside a member variable, descendant classes can specialize the signature they are using for their logic methods to be as specific as necessary. This lets us move from

```
public void doGet(HttpServletRequest req,
                  HttpServletResponse res)
```

to

```
public void login(ShoppingContext context)
```

We believe that this makes the code much more legible. Because we eliminated the application-specific `doGet()` method, there's no chance of application-specific bugs in this routine.

Readable code is more likely to be bug-free code.

The observant reader will note that we have merely moved the problem from the `doGet()` routine into the calling URL in each instance. We can still call the wrong method, but instead of a logic error in the code, this is now an error in the originating URL or form.

Establishing uniform exception handling

The final goal of the dispatch framework is to provide a last line of defense against unhandled exceptions, including I/O errors, coding errors that cause exceptions, insufficient resources, and so forth. In C++ you can also use exception handling for a last line of defense. All our exceptions are routed to the following method:

```
protected void handleException(HttpServletRequest req,
                               HttpServletResponse res,
                               Throwable t) {
     try {
         PrintWriter out = res.getWriter();
         out.println("<P>Caught " + t+"</P>");
         out.println("<PRE>");
         t.printStackTrace(out);
         out.println("</PRE>");
         out.close();
     } catch (IOException e) {
     }
}
```

If you are expecting errors in specific implementations of certain routines, they will probably implement their own exception handling. This routine is intended to handle anything for which we don't have a better default behavior or which we might have overlooked. The implementation here is one that is useful while debugging the application: Any time we reach an exception, the browser tells us what happened and where, so we don't have to analyze the log files or other information for this data. Note that if an exception occurs while we are already creating the response, this response becomes "glued" to the end of that response, instead of replacing it. This is something else that would need to be improved for a full production site.

For the final application, we will replace the debugging stack traces with something more user-friendly. We discuss the benefits of this approach in more detail in Chapter 11, when we also use this routine to automatically find problems with the Online Grocer application.

Adding support early for testing pays off in the long run.

Because we intend the dispatch framework to be generic code that we can reuse with many servlets, we want to make sure that it is correctly coded. We describe how to test the dispatch classes in Chapter 9, where we discuss unit testing.

Developing the Shopping Servlet

The `ShoppingServlet` class is the heart of the Online Grocer application – it contains the logic that implements the customer experience. In a larger application, we would likely have many servlets divided between tasks, but for such a small example, we don't need to go that far. Because we are using the `DispatchServlet` class created earlier, the first thing we do here is connect to that. The relevant parts of `ShoppingServlet` look like this:

```
public class ShoppingServlet extends DispatchServlet {
    public ShoppingServlet() {
        super("home");

        parms[0] = ShoppingContext.class;
        ...
    }
    protected DispatchContext createContext(HttpServletRequest req,
                                            HttpServletResponse res)
        throws ServletException {
        return new ShoppingContext(req, res);
    }
    ...
}
```

The complete class is on the CD.

As you can see, we set up the code to create `ShoppingContexts` instead of `DispatchContexts`. For this application, the primary goal of the contexts is to manage session information.

Creating sessions

In the abstract sense, a *session* consists of a completed user experience with your Web application. A session entails that a user sit down at his computer, connect to your application, and later walk away. If the user returns and uses your application again (and we hope that users do!), this is generally considered a new session.

Note the ambiguity in this definition: If someone takes a break while using your application, does that terminate the session? What if the user's computer crashes (because of a different application, you hope) and he or she reboots? The Online Grocer's servlet addresses these issues by using the Java Servlet API, which lets the servlet engine handle the details.

The Java Servlet API provides an `HttpSession` class that represents the session with the user. The main benefit of a session object is to provide a good place to store information about the connection. You can't store this information in the `Servlet` object because of the multithreading issues discussed earlier. The session also provides you with storage that will persist between multiple requests. For instance, if you require users to log in to your application (as we do), the session can store information about whether the current HTTP request comes from a user who is logged in. You can also store customization information about the current user, the user's identity from your database, or anything else relevant to your application.

Here's the code for the `ShoppingContext` object:

```
public class ShoppingContext extends DispatchContext {
    private HttpSession session;
    public ShoppingContext(HttpServletRequest req,
                           HttpServletResponse res) {
        super(req, res);
        session = req.getSession(true);
    }
    public void login(int user) {
        session.putValue("user", new Integer(user));
    }
    public void logout() {
        session.removeValue("user");
    }
    public int getUser() {
        Integer id = (Integer) session.getValue("user");
        if (id == null)
            return -1;
        return id.intValue();
    }
    public boolean hasUser() {
        return session.getValue("user") != null;
    }
}
```

We get an instance of the `HttpSession` class by calling the `getSession()` method from the `HttpServletRequest`:

```
session = req.getSession(true);
```

The parameter `true` tells the servlet engine to create a new session object if one does not already exist. Therefore, the first HTTP request instantiates a session object, and further requests reuse the same instance. Generally, the session object persists in memory until one of the following actions occurs:

- **The server is restarted.** This (you hope) will not happen frequently on the production site.
- **The session is closed.** You can do this programmatically by calling the `invalidate()` method on the `HttpSession` object. In the preceding code, we could add a `session.invalidate()` call at the end of the `logout()` method. Because we didn't, the same session object is available if the same user makes another request.
- **The session times out.** If enough time passes and a session is not used, the session is automatically invalidated and garbage collected. This is essential to proper resource management. If resources accumulate for each session and are never destroyed, the servlet engine is guaranteed to run out of memory eventually. How long it takes a session to time out depends on the servlet engine, but it is typically a long time, relative to the frequency of requests (for instance, 30 minutes). That way, you don't get timeouts during a normal session – only at the end.

The only information that `ShoppingServlet` stores in the session is the user ID. If we have a user ID, we know that we are talking to a logged in user. If there is no user ID, we are talking to someone who is not logged in (or has just logged out). We show you what the user ID means when we showcase the database in Chapter 16.

Store data in the appropriate place to prevent errors.

Depending on the application, the appropriate place is not always the same. Session objects and databases represent two common locations to store user- and session-dependent information. We discuss these issues in Chapter 3 in the context of Web application pitfalls.

Adding functionality

Now that the framework is set up, all we have to do is add methods for whatever functionality we want. We will start with the default method, `home()`, which displays the Log In page:

```
public void home(ShoppingContext context)
    throws IOException
{
    // Log out any users who might have been left over
    context.logout();
    showLoginPage(context, false, null);
}
```

First, we log out anyone recorded in the current session because showing the Log In page to someone who is already logged in doesn't make sense. This can occur if someone uses the application, walks away, and someone else sits down and connects to the same application before the session times out. Even though we use the same instance of the `HttpSession` object, we don't want to reuse the log in information.

There's no other logic for this routine. All we have to do is display the actual Log In page. Rather than place the display logic in the same routine as the application logic, we move it (and all the display routines) into a separate method. This particular method takes a few parameters, so we can reuse the display code in several contexts.

```
void showLoginPage(ShoppingContext context, boolean complain, String error)
    throws IOException
{
    PrintWriter out = context.getWriter();

    header(out, "Login");
    out.println("<!-- FORM must have METHOD attribute set: POST or GET -->");
    out.println("<FORM NAME=login ACTION=\""+SERVLET+"\">");
    out.println("<TABLE BORDER=0 CELLPADDING=0 CELLSPACING=0>");
    out.println(
        "\n<!-- CENTER: Illegal VALIGN attribute value: should be MIDDLE -->");
    out.println("<TR><TD ALIGN=CENTER VALIGN=CENTER HEIGHT=164 WIDTH=207 " +
        "BACKGROUND=\"/tomato.gif\">");
    out.println("<INPUT TYPE=TEXT NAME=USER SIZE=8><BR>");
    out.println("<INPUT TYPE=PASSWORD NAME=PASSWORD SIZE=8><BR>");
    out.println("<INPUT TYPE=HIDDEN NAME=METHOD VALUE=login>");
    out.println("<INPUT TYPE=HIDDEN NAME=FRUITS VALUE=on>");
    out.println("<INPUT TYPE=HIDDEN NAME=RED VALUE=red>");
```

```
    out.println("<INPUT TYPE=HIDDEN NAME=YELLOW VALUE=yellow>");
    out.println("</TD></TR><TR><TD ALIGN=CENTER>");
    out.println("<INPUT TYPE=IMAGE SRC=\"/login.gif\" BORDER=0 NAME=Login><BR>");
    out.println("</TD></TR></TABLE>");
    out.println("</FORM>");
    if (complain) {
        out.println("<P><B>Please re-enter your username and password.</B></P>");
    }
    // Mark the page as improper, so we can detect site errors!
    if (error != null) {
        out.println("<!-- Error: " + error + " -->");
    }
    footer(out);
}
```

You can see some of the errors we left in the code to show you debugging techniques later on.

The `complain` parameter is set to `true` if we are showing the Log In page a second time as a response to an invalid log in. In this case, we add an additional message so that the user knows why we threw him or her back to the same page.

The `error` parameter is used to help debug the application. Any time we encounter an unexpected flow condition, we take users back to the Log In page to start over. If this happens, we add a special message inside an HTML comment. Then we can set up tools to detect these kinds of flow errors automatically. This is explained in more detail in Chapter 11 and is another illustration of how adding support for testing early in the development process can pay off later.

Note that although we advocate separation of application logic from display logic, this isn't necessarily the best way to do so. As you can see, the HTML is messy, and it's unlikely that you want your content developers and graphic designers writing Java code to add content to your application. A real application would probably use JSPs (discussed in Chapter 20) or some kind of template so that the HTML can be updated independently of the servlet.

Also, although we now have methods that can easily be reimplemented to provide variations in the look and feel (as shown in Chapter 17, which focuses on XML), we haven't fully decoupled the logic. If we want the servlet to vary in its look and feel to different users, we could reintroduce logic into the display routines. In this case, it might be more appropriate to create another class hierarchy that controls the display and have the servlet call an instance of the display class, based on information stored in the session. We didn't do so here because we didn't want to complicate the example.

Especially in Web applications, decouple the application logic from the display logic.

Implementing application logic

We will briefly cover two more `ShoppingServlet` routines to give you an idea of how the Online Grocer's application logic can be implemented. To begin, look at the `login()` method:

```
public void login(ShoppingContext context)
     throws ServletException, IOException
 {
     String user = context.getParameter("USER");
     if (user == null) {
         showLoginPage(context, false, "Missing USER for METHOD=login");
         return;
     }
     String password = context.getParameter("PASSWORD");
     if (password == null) {
         showLoginPage(context, false, "Missing PASSWORD for METHOD=login");
         return;
     }
     int id = customers.getUserId(user, password);
     if (id >= 0) {
         context.login(id);
         showSearchPage(context);
     } else {
         showLoginPage(context, true, null);
     }
 }
```

First, we check the form inputs `USER` and `PASSWORD`. If either is missing, it's back to the Log In page. Checking the parameters against `null` protects us from the cases where our servlet is invoked incorrectly. If the user simply fails to enter the username or password, we get empty strings here, which will be handled by `getUserId()`. Next, we check the user/password combination against the user database. On success, we attach the user ID to the session and proceed. On failure, it's back to the Log In page. If we want, we can add more information for the missing username or password cases.

Finally, here's the search() method. This shows a pattern common to most of the routines:

```
public void search(ShoppingContext context)
    throws ServletException, IOException
{
    if (!context.hasUser()) {
        showLoginPage(context, false, "Missing USER for METHOD=search");
        return;
    }
    showSearchPage(context);
}
```

Because this routine expects the user to be logged in, we start by verifying that the session has a logged in user. If not, either it has timed out and we no longer know to whom we are talking (in which case the user must log in again), or a bad path was created and the user was allowed to proceed without logging in. When we are testing and not expecting timeouts, this represents a flow problem and provides the motivation for the last parameter to the showLoginPage() method.

Rather than show the rest of ShoppingServlet in detail, we will let you refer to the CD if you are interested. Hopefully, we have explained enough so that you can follow the routines we haven't discussed.

The flow chart in Figure 6-2 shows how ShoppingServlet satisfies the requirements specified in Chapter 4. In this flow chart, servlet entry points are represented by rectangles; these are the methods invoked by DispatchServlet. The pages that the routines produce (described in terms of the static pages built for the prototype in Chapter 5) are represented by rectangles with a cut-off edge. For example, the METHOD=home routine calls showLoginPage(), which is responsible for the page represented by PAGE1.HTM. Lines exiting these icons represent user actions (clicking links). Servlet or user decision points are represented by diamonds. The decision options available to the servlet (such as whether a log in is valid) or to the user (such as which link to click) are represented by lines branching out from each diamond. The routine called as a result of each decision is attached to each diamond.

Notice that the showLoginPage() method corresponds to two static pages: PAGE1.HTM and PAGE2.HTM. Also, you can see that showOrderPage() was accidentally left out of the prototype; we corrected this oversight here.

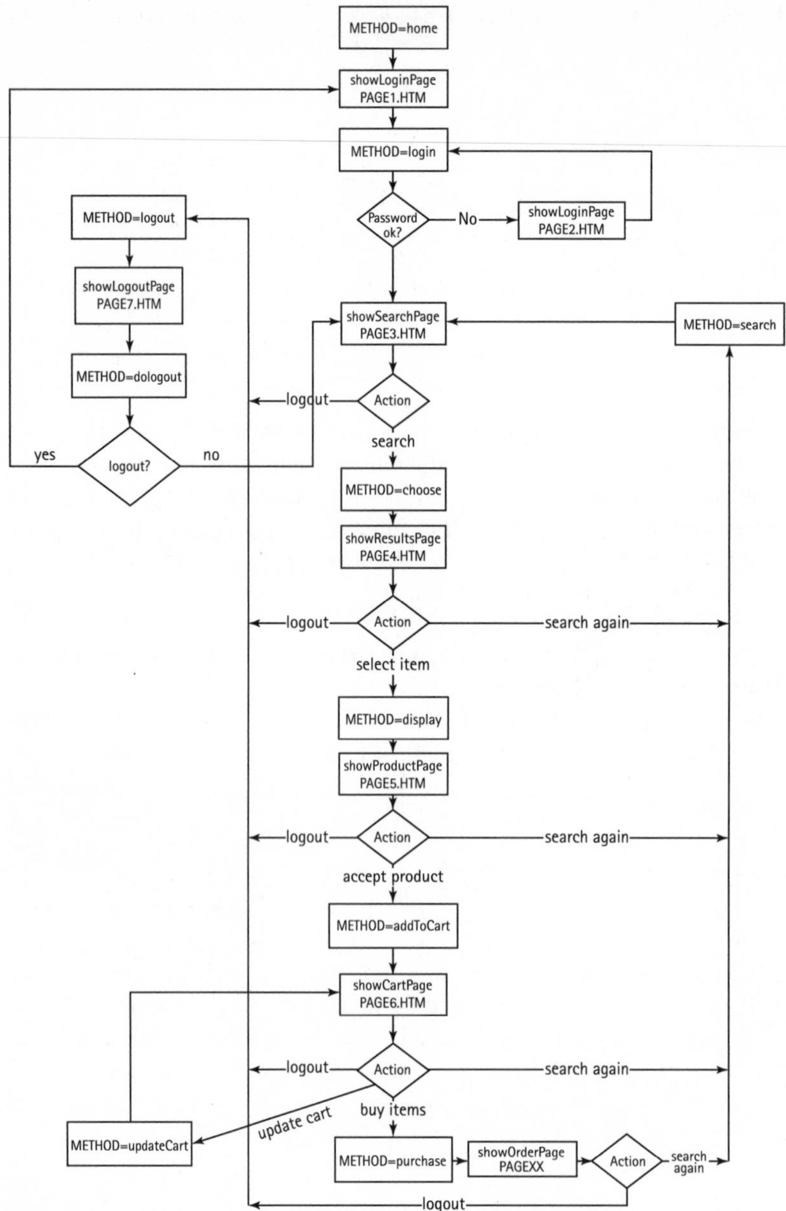

Figure 6-2: The ShoppingServlet method flow chart.

Developing the Data Framework

The last part of ShoppingServlet manages the data we are displaying and collecting. ShoppingServlet relies on external data for users, products, and shopping carts. Rather than create a database straight off the top, we simply define the interface of what ShoppingServlet requires and then specialize those classes to provide implementations as appropriate. This lets us switch the data logic independently of the server logic. In particular, we use this to create stubs for testing.

For a quick review of stubs, see the "Creating scaffolding and stubs" section of Chapter 9. If you are going to use stubs, build them into your design. If you fail to design for stubs, you are not likely to test your code when it comes time to do unit testing (also described in Chapter 9). If you do end up testing code that is not designed for stubs, you are likely to clutter your application with conditional logic or other testing-related code that will make the final application logic more difficult to understand and work with.

Developing the customer database

The customer database is the simplest interface. Its sole purpose is to validate user/password pairs. If we want to give detailed error messages (for example, invalid username versus invalid password), we need a beefier API. For present needs, though, this suits us fine. From a design point of view, this implies that a procedure independent of ShoppingServlet maintains customer information because ShoppingServlet cannot yet create accounts, delete accounts, or change passwords.

We will assume that customers need an active account to use the servlet and that all credit card or billing information is stored and handled by an independent business layer outside ShoppingServlet:

```
public abstract class CustomerDatabase {
    public abstract int getUserId(String user, String password);
}
```

If getUserId() returns -1, this means that the user/password pair is invalid. Otherwise, the returned value is a customer ID that uniquely identifies the person to whom we are talking. This is the number we store inside the session object.

With a lightweight abstract class such as this one, you could just as easily make CustomerDatabase a Java interface instead of a class. Unless you are providing some member variables or actual functionality, this is usually the preferred way to go. Sometimes people refer to stubs such as this as *mock objects*. For a detailed discussion of mock objects, refer to www.mockobjects.com.

Developing the product database

Next up is the ProductDatabase. First, we create a class to represent a single product and then create the database interface. We should make several important points here. First, by specifying an API that returns a Product object returning all the relevant fields for any given product, we are forcing any implementation to have all the information available. Even if we want to look up the description of only a single product ID, the database layer must access all the fields to return the appropriate details.

That's not entirely true, of course. The database layer could extend Product to perform lazy instantiation and to look up data only as Product itself is queried. This is perfectly valid, but if we intend that, we should make the Product class more lightweight and provide a default subclass to store the fields, as we have here.

The second point to note – especially in regard to products – is that the database implementation class doesn't have to interact with merely a single database (or any database at all). Product information can be dynamically retrieved from product suppliers. If the database is small relative to available memory, the complete database can be loaded once and cached in memory for really fast access:

```
public class Product {
    public int id;
    public String file;
    public String title;
    public String color;
    public boolean isFruit;
    public String description;

    ...
    public String getFile() {
        return "/images/" + file;
    }
}
```

The Product class is straightforward: it includes an integer ID to represent the product uniquely (like a barcode or SKU), a title (or product name), a color, whether it's a fruit, a longer description, and a filename for an image of the product. The getFile() method is a utility function to create a valid URL fragment from the base filename:

```
public abstract class ProductDatabase {
    // Returns a Vector<Product>
    public abstract Vector getMatches(
        boolean fruits, boolean vegetables,
        boolean green, boolean red, boolean yellow, boolean weird);
    public abstract Product get(int id);
}
```

The complete class is located on the CD.

The only functionality we want from the product database is the ability to find a list of available products matching some search criteria, as well as the ability to look up a single product. Note that with functions like getMatches() that return a Vector , what the Vector contains should always be documented (we generally do this using a C++ style notation such as Vector<Product>). This reminds future developers of how the code works and is rightly considered part of the interface, even though the language doesn't require it.

Future versions of Java will almost certainly support parameterized types; most of the proposals put forth so far use this same syntax. By documenting your containers in this fashion, you will eventually be able to migrate your code to use parameterized types by simply moving the comment into the declaration. One warning: If you use this notation inside Javadoc tags, you need to be careful because the text in those tags is assumed to be HTML, and the < and > characters are special characters in HTML. In this case, you might choose to write Vector<Product>, which is the equivalent HTML and produces nice Javadoc output, or simply sidestep the issue by writing Vector of Product.

Developing the shopping cart database

Last up are shopping carts, which list items a user has marked for purchase. We accumulate these until the user confirms the purchase. You might wonder why we need a database for these when they could easily be stored inside the convenient session object. There are a couple reasons:

- If the session times out, we don't want to lose the information. Taking items out of the user's cart is not good business.
- If the user logs out and comes back later, we want any old cart contents also to be retained.

We could keep one copy of the cart in the database for persistence and one in the session for speed. Some Web applications employ strategies such as this if the performance warrants it and sufficient memory resources are available.

The code for the shopping cart follows and is self-explanatory:

```
public abstract class CartDatabase {
    // Returns Vector<CartEntry>
    public abstract Vector getCart(int user);
    public abstract void add(int user, int item);
    public abstract void set(int user, int item, int quantity);
    public abstract void empty(int user);
}

class CartEntry {
    int id;
    int quantity;
    CartEntry(int id, int quantity) {
        this.id = id;
        this.quantity = quantity;
    }
    int getID() {
        return id;
    }
    int getQuantity() {
        return quantity;
    }
    void setQuantity(int quantity) {
        this.quantity = quantity;
    }
}
```

The complete class is located on the CD.

This completes the data abstraction layer. Note that before we can use these classes, we have to create some kind of concrete implementation.

Implementing stubs

To test this application without having to attach an actual database, we first create stubs for each of the databases we are using. The first stub provides the customer database that allows only one user (demo), whose password is password:

```
public class CustomerDatabaseStub extends CustomerDatabase {
    public int getUserId(String user, String password) {
        if (user.equals("demo") && password.equals("password"))
            return 0;
        return -1;
    }
}
```

The next stub represents the available products. We want enough data here to make the tests useful, so we store a static array of items and access them as a virtual database:

```
public class ProductDatabaseStub extends ProductDatabase {
    public static final String GREEN = "green";
    public static final String RED = "red";
    public static final String YELLOW = "yellow";
    public static final String WEIRD = "weird";

    public static final Product[] ALL = {
        new Product(0, "Apple", true, GREEN,
                    "apple_fruit_green.gif",
                    "Green apples are great for making caramel " +
                    "apples. The sour taste of the apple and the " +
                    "sweet taste of the caramel blend well " +
                    "together."),
        new Product(1, "Artichoke", false, GREEN,
                    "artichoke_veg_green.gif",
                    "Artichoke hearts are the tastiest part of " +
                    "the artichoke. When you eat the "+
                    "heart, it's love at first bite!"),
        ...
    };
    public Vector getMatches(boolean fruits, boolean vegetables,
                             boolean green, boolean red,
                             boolean yellow, boolean weird)
    {
        Vector v = new Vector();
        for (int i = 0; i < ALL.length; i++) {
            if (((fruits     && ALL[i].isFruit) ||
```

```
                    (vegetables && !ALL[i].isFruit)) &&
                    ((green  && ALL[i].color.equals(GREEN)) ||
                     (red    && ALL[i].color.equals(RED)) ||
                     (yellow && ALL[i].color.equals(YELLOW)) ||
                     (weird  && ALL[i].color.equals(WEIRD))))
                {
                    v.add(ALL[i]);
                }
            }
            return v;
        }
        public Product get(int id) {
            if (0 <= id && id < ALL.length)
                return ALL[id];
            return null;
        }
}
```

Because we use JDK 1.3, we use the `Vector.add()` method instead of the older `Vector.addElement()` method. If you want to compile these examples under JDK 1.2 or lower, you need to make any appropriate changes.

The last stub – the one that represents the user's shopping cart – is the most complicated. Although `CustomerDatabaseStub` supports only one user currently, we don't want to embed that assumption into the `CartDatabaseStub`. It should allow as many users as we can fit in memory so that if we later add users to the `CustomerDatabaseStub` or want to use the `CartDatabaseStub` with the other, "real" database implementations, we can do so reliably.

```
public class CartDatabaseStub extends CartDatabase {
    Hashtable carts; // Hashtable<Integer, Vector<CartEntry>>
    CartDatabaseStub() {
        carts = new Hashtable();
    }
    // Returns Vector<CartEntry>
    public Vector getCart(int user) {
        return (Vector) carts.get(new Integer(user));
    }
    public void add(int user, int item) {
        Integer userKey = new Integer(user);
        Vector v = (Vector) carts.get(userKey);
```

```
        if (v == null) {
            v = new Vector();
            carts.put(userKey, v);
        }
        Enumeration enum = v.elements();
        while (enum.hasMoreElements()) {
            CartEntry entry = (CartEntry) enum.nextElement();
            if (entry.getID() == item) {
                entry.setQuantity(entry.getQuantity()+1);
                return;
            }
        }
        v.add(new CartEntry(item, 1));
    }
    public void set(int user, int item, int quantity) {
        Integer userKey = new Integer(user);
        Vector v = (Vector) carts.get(userKey);
        if (v == null) {
            if (quantity == 0)
                return;
            v = new Vector();
            carts.put(userKey, v);
        }
        Enumeration enum = v.elements();
        while (enum.hasMoreElements()) {
            CartEntry entry = (CartEntry) enum.nextElement();
            if (entry.getID() == item) {
                if (quantity == 0) {
                    v.removeElement(entry);
                    if (v.isEmpty())
                        carts.remove(userKey);
                } else {
                    entry.setQuantity(quantity);
                }
                return;
            }
        }
        v.add(new CartEntry(item, quantity));
    }
    public void empty(int user) {
        carts.remove(new Integer(user));
    }
}
```

All the preceding stubs are located on the CD.

After we finish the stubs, we test them immediately. If we don't, we might end up digging through the application looking for bugs that are part of a defective testing harness.

Test your testing code.

For now, we will use the stubs. Later on, in Chapter 16, you learn about the JDBC connections when we discuss databases in detail.

Putting It All Together

We're almost there! All we need now are a few required static files as referenced by the servlet, and then we can start working with this Web application. We created a few images, available on the CD. Then, to start the whole process, we created an initial, static page that will be the beginning splash page, also available on the CD:

```
<HTML>
<HEAD>
<TITLE>Fruits and Vegetables</TITLE>
<LINK REL="stylesheet" TYPE="text/css" HREF="/fruits/fruits.css">
</HEAD>
<!-- broken link -->
<BODY BGCOLOR=#009900 BACKGROUND="fruits/background.gif">
<CENTER>
<A HREF="/servlet/fruits.ShoppingServlet">
```

```
<IMG SRC="/fruits/title.gif" ALT="Fruits & Vegetables" BORDER=0>
</A>
</CENTER>
</BODY>
</HTML>
```

If we don't want an extra splash page, we can add a redirect to the HTML:

```
<meta http-equiv="refresh"
     content="0; url=/servlet/fruits.ShoppingServlet">
```

If you use the HTML redirect, make sure that you consider users with browsers that do not support the `META` tag redirects and that you still use the static splash page in addition to the HTML redirect. In any case, you don't want users to have to remember a complicated URL such as this:

```
http://www.parasoft.com/servlet/fruits.ShoppingServlet
```

Not only is this hard to remember, it's also hard to type correctly!

You can also configure the Web server to redirect your initial URL automatically. For instance, to add an Online Grocer redirect to Apache, we can add a line like this to our `httpd.conf` file:

```
Redirect /index.html \
http://www.parasoft.com/servlet/fruits.ShoppingServlet
```

The specific details here vary, depending the Web server.

One last point before wrapping up our look at the Online Grocer application. This is just an example. It's not difficult to create a list of additional requirements for a real e-commerce application. In this case, we would want the server configured to use HTTPS (secure HTTP) because purchases are being made. We would also need a method to handle account maintenance, forgotten passwords, and actual billing – not to mention a real database of products, and so forth.

Summary

In this chapter, we explain our Java servlet implementation of the Online Grocer application. First, we review some issues relating to servlet development. Then, we describe the three main components of the application: the dispatch framework that provides an abstraction layer on top of the raw servlet API, the `ShoppingServlet` class that contains the application logic, and the data framework that manages the data the application displays and collects. Along the way, we illustrate several general principles that apply to any Web application, regardless of the implementation language.

In Part II, we use the Online Grocer application to discuss bulletproofing processes with some specific content.

Part II

Bulletproofing Practices

Chapter 7

Practicing Defensive Programming

IN THIS CHAPTER

- Validating user input
- Embedding debugging support
- Using defensive firewalls
- Using Design by Contract (DbC)

IN THIS CHAPTER, we discuss several defensive programming techniques you can use to bulletproof your code. Defensive programming is a fundamental error-prevention strategy. When you program defensively, you anticipate where failures can occur and then create an infrastructure that tests for errors, notifies you when anticipated failures occur, and performs damage-control actions you have specified – such as stopping program execution, redirecting users to a backup server, turning on debugging information you can use to diagnose the problem, and so on.

By applying defensive programming techniques, you can detect problems that might otherwise go unnoticed, prevent minor problems from growing into disasters, and save yourself a lot of debugging and maintenance time in the long run.

For instance, say that you have a stock trading system and you have built in to it an infrastructure that constantly checks the application's connection to the stock market. When this infrastructure detects a lost connection, it alters program execution so that users are brought to a page that explains the problem and directs them to the telephone trading system. The problem is detected immediately, and the damage control action ensures that your customers have an alternative way to perform their desired actions.

The specific defensive programming techniques discussed in this chapter share the same primary concept: Build debugging support into your code. This is one of the key principles introduced in Chapter 6.

Another dominant theme is the documenting (in a meaningful way) of how the code is supposed to work, in such a way that failures can be detected automatically and the appropriate damage-control efforts can be triggered. We discuss specific solutions in C++ and Java, but these techniques can be applied to a variety of languages, provided that the necessary language features and/or development tools are available.

Validating User Input

One of the largest sources of errors to any interactive program is invalid input. As the old saying goes, "Garbage in, garbage out." This expression is sometimes used to justify bad programming by placing blame on the user. After all, if users are not considerate enough to give us valid input, who are we to say what they want the program to do? In reality, bad input will be entered – even by well-intentioned users. Bulletproofing your code means preparing for all possible input.

We sometimes like to think of testing for invalid inputs as *monkey testing*. Pretend that a monkey is using your application, and consider how the monkey might interact with it. If your software can withstand the assault of a hungry monkey looking for bananas, it is probably robust enough for your users. This means never assuming, for example, that when a field requires a number, the user will only enter numbers.

There are basically two ways to check for invalid input: on the client and on the server. In the Online Grocer application described in Chapter 6, the user can enter arbitrary data in three forms:

- **The Log In page:** Here we check for empty usernames or passwords because these are required elements that cannot be left empty.
- **The Search page:** Here we verify that at least one check box is selected from each column. There's no point in allowing an empty search.
- **The Shopping Cart page:** Here we let the user type in values. We expect these values to be numbers 0 or higher.

Testing from the client side

Client-side testing means checking values in the user's browser before data is submitted to the server. If a problem occurs, the program can open a dialog box and alert the user. This way, the user can make corrections immediately, without waiting for a response from the server. In some cases, you can even disable the submission mechanism until the inputs are valid. This kind of testing prevents garbage values from ever entering your Web application.

The most common mechanism for doing client-side testing is JavaScript because most of today's browsers have at least some JavaScript support. JavaScript should not be confused with Java; the languages are completely different entities, although they do have similarities in syntax. Another option for a Microsoft-only environment is VBScript.

Whenever you use JavaScript in your HTML pages, you need to be keenly aware of the potential pitfalls. It's all too easy to write code that works here or there but fails to be truly portable. You can make your application completely unusable to people with browsers different from the ones you tested. Your best defense is to verify your JavaScript carefully against documented restrictions and to test thoroughly. In Chapter 8, we discuss some techniques and resources that will help you do this.

For an example of how client-side scripting can be done, consider how we might use it to validate input for our Online Grocer application's Log In page. Here's the form extracted from our Log In page:

```
<FORM METHOD=POST NAME=login
      ACTION="/servlet/fruits.ShoppingServlet">
  <TABLE BORDER=0 CELLPADDING=0 CELLSPACING=0>
    <TR>
    <TD ALIGN=CENTER VALIGN=MIDDLE HEIGHT=164 WIDTH=207
        BACKGROUND="/tomato.gif">
      <INPUT TYPE=TEXT NAME=USER VALUE="demo" SIZE=8><BR>
      <INPUT TYPE=PASSWORD NAME=PASSWORD SIZE=8><BR>
      <INPUT TYPE=HIDDEN NAME=METHOD VALUE=login>
      <INPUT TYPE=HIDDEN NAME=FRUITS VALUE=on>
      <INPUT TYPE=HIDDEN NAME=RED VALUE=red>
      <INPUT TYPE=HIDDEN NAME=YELLOW VALUE=yellow>
    </TD></TR>
    <TR><TD ALIGN=CENTER>
      <INPUT TYPE=IMAGE SRC="/login.gif" BORDER=0 NAME=Login><BR>
    </TD></TR>
  </TABLE>
</FORM>
```

To perform client-side checking, we would add the following code to our HTML page, which provides a function written in JavaScript:

```
<SCRIPT LANGUAGE="JavaScript">
function validate(form) {
    if (form.USER.value.length == 0) {
        alert("You must enter a valid username!");
        return false;
    }
    if (form.PASSWORD.value.length == 0) {
        alert("You must enter a valid password!");
        return false;
    }
    return true;
}
</SCRIPT>
```

In this code, we are verifying that there is at least one character for the username and password – we aren't checking whether they contain an invalid character or enforcing any additional restrictions. To use this check, we add a single attribute to the <FORM> tag:

```
<FORM METHOD=POST NAME=login
      ACTION="/servlet/fruits.ShoppingServlet"
      ONSUBMIT="return validate(this)">
```

This tells compliant browsers to call the `validate()` function before submitting the form, and if the function returns `false`, not to submit the form at all. Client-side scripting is extremely flexible, and this is only one brief illustration of how you can use it.

If you are using a lot of JavaScript code, it makes sense to include it in a separate file that can be referenced from many locations. This eliminates the need to duplicate your code in each file and helps the user's browser to cache the data and improve performance. You can include an external script using `SRC` attribute of the `<SCRIPT>` tag:

```
<SCRIPT SRC="file.js" LANGUAGE="JavaScript">
```

One file you might want to reuse is code that detects which browser is running and sets variables your other scripts can use to ensure portability. You can find examples of scripts like these and more at the sites listed in Appendix E.

Testing from the server side

Even if you have robust client-side tests, it's a good idea to include redundant checks in your server-side code. This covers you in case the client-side tests are somehow incomplete or the client-side code evolves over time and somehow the tests are removed. Also, some browsers might not support your client-side scripting, or the user might have disabled JavaScript support (perhaps in an attempt to get rid of annoying pop-up ads).

Implementing server-side checks is easy enough: Just validate the data as you would during client-side checks. The tricky part is deciding which page to return to the user. In the simplest case, you can send a page that basically says, "You entered something wrong. Go back and try again." Then the user has to click the Back button on the browser and try to figure out what went wrong.

If you are using the Back button as an error recovery mechanism, make sure that your pages are cooperating with browser caches in a positive way. If you tell the browser not to cache your page, the Back button has to generate a new request. In this case, the data the user enters will be lost. Depending on how much data was there, this may or may not be important. The other thing to note is that all `PASSWORD`-type input fields are reset, so your user will have to re-enter any passwords. This is done for security reasons so that if a user walks away from the browser, other people cannot click the Back button and access protected pages. Nevertheless, it can be an inconvenience to your users to try a shot-in-the-dark approach to find out why their page isn't loading. To a user, this process would go something like this: Fill out form, press Enter, nope, click Back, change data, re-enter password, nope, click Back, and so on.

A better approach – especially if the input is complicated or the cause of the failure is likely to be unapparent – is to return a page describing the specific problem (which fields are missing, which values are expected, and so on). You can still require the user to click the Back button after doing this. Another solution is to return the original page with the data, as well as markers indicating which values need to be changed. Then, all the user has to do is make the corrections directly and resubmit the page.

Embedding Debugging Support

Embedded debugging support breaks down into several categories:

- Code that detects errors
- Code that makes errors detectable
- Code that causes errors so that fault-handling can be verified

You could probably add some of your own refinements, but these are the ideas we are discussing.

Traditionally, while a piece of code is first being written, the developer spends considerable time writing diagnostic code to monitor the program execution. Typically, these pieces of code are removed after the initial debugging session. Although this is often appropriate for throwaway tests, we believe that there is value in creating a system for storing and maintaining debug information. Any such system must be relatively transparent to the developer to be useful. Overhead in terms of code complexity, execution time, and time spent understanding the code must be small. In fact, for most debugging information, the overhead should drop to zero after the application is deployed.

In C++, you can implement such a transparent system by adding conditional code such as the following:

```
#ifdef MONITOR_CODE
    printf("Reached point A");
#endif
```

This is a workable solution for some projects. The chief disadvantages are code clutter (especially if there is significant logic inside the `ifdef`) and the necessity of recompilation. To make this discussion more concrete, we provide a specific C++ implementation of a `Debug` support class we believe can help make robust applications. You can imagine this being used, for instance, in the context of a COM object or CGI library.

Working with the Debug class

The Debug class available on the CD offers the advantages of inserting diagnostic output in appropriate places in the code and adding manifold flexibility. The system presented here allows for the grouping of related pieces of information by name and places them under the control of an environment variable. In this manner, only the information relevant to the current debugging session is displayed, and the effort expended in generating this information is not wasted. If desired, such statements can be automatically disabled for the production system, using specially constructed classes for C++ programs and the preprocessor for C programs.

Consider a function that takes as an argument the name of an external program and is responsible for spawning it as a separate process and setting up a pipe so that the parent can control the child. For our purposes, we will set up a one-way communication channel; a more realistic example would set up a bidirectional pipe. The code might look something like this `OS::spawn()` method:

```
bool OS::spawn(string program, int & child_pid, int & channel)
{
    int to_child[2];

    if (pipe(to_child) < 0) {
        return false;
    }

    child_pid = fork();

    // Handle fork failure
    if (child_pid < 0)
        return false;

    // The parent process
    if (child_pid > 0) {
        close(to_child[0]);     // Close the unusable end of the pipe
        channel = to_child[1]; // Return the write side of the pipe
        return true;
    }

    // The child process
    close(to_child[1]);     // Close the unusable end of the pipe
    close(0);
    dup(to_child[0]);       // read-side -> stdin

    OS::execvp(program);    // Spawn the program

    exit(-1);               // If we get here, OS::execvp failed!
}
```

During the initial development of this code, it is very likely that the developer inserted code that generated appropriate messages as execution proceeded along the various stages of this code. These diagnostics might have included informational items such as the process ID of the parent and the child and the actual file descriptor number assigned by the system to this pipe. It is also very likely that the error-handling branches generated diagnostics as well, because knowing that the error-handling code was not executed gives good feedback about the correctness of the code.

However, the production system has no need for such verbose output, so the developer deleted all the carefully formatted and well thought-out diagnostics, leaving the preceding code.

Unfortunately, this effort will almost certainly be duplicated during a bug fix. The first time a developer experiences strange behavior while attempting to spawn an external utility, she will have to write diagnostic code very similar to the original (deleted) diagnostic code.

This problem can be solved with a facility that allows the diagnostics to reside permanently in the code, encourages the developers to maintain them, and can be selectively turned on whenever needed. This system should be effectively absent from the production system, although it might be useful to let select diagnostics remain available under a command-line switch or the setting of some environment variable for debugging.

Such a facility is encapsulated in the class `Debug`, shown next. At compile time, the symbol `DEBUG` determines which version of the code will be compiled. At runtime, individual categories of debugging information can be enabled by setting the environment variable `DEBUG_OPT` to a semicolon-delimited list of debug categories. The code is intentionally Spartan; you can extend it as appropriate for your application or reimplement the same concept in a different language.

The header file, which defines the interface, looks like this:

```
#ifdef DEBUG
class Debug
{
private:
    bool _active;
public:
    Debug(const char *);
    bool active() const { return _active; }
    void out(const char *file, long line,
             const char *, ...) const;
    static void trap();
};
#else
class Debug
{
public:
```

```
    Debug(const char *) {}
    static bool active() { return false; }
    static void out(const char *, ...) { }
};
#endif
```

As you can see, when the DEBUG symbol is not defined, the class Debug reduces to an empty implementation, which should allow the compiler to optimize away the code. The fully functional version will require linking against the Debug.cc source file, which provides an actual implementation (this file is available on the CD).

Adding diagnostics

Now we will revisit the OS::spawn() method and sprinkle some diagnostics. We instantiate an object of class Debug with the debugging category set to OS::spawn, and then we use this object to generate messages:

```
bool OS::spawn(string program, int & child_pid, int & channel)
{
    int to_child[2];
    Debug info("OS::spawn");        // Here is the Debug instance

    if (pipe(to_child) < 0) {
        info.out("OS::spawn: pipe() failed!");
        return false;
    }

    info.out("OS::spawn: ready to fork()");
    child_pid = fork();

    // Handle fork failure
    if (child_pid < 0) {
        info.out("OS::spawn: fork() failed!");
        return false;
    }

    // The parent process
    if (child_pid > 0) {
        info.out("OS::spawn: parent process: child_pid=%d", child_pid);

        close(to_child[0]);         // Close the unusable end of the pipe
        channel = to_child[1];      // Return the write side of the pipe

        return true;
    }
```

```
    // The child process
    close(to_child[1]);          // Close the unusable end of the pipe
    close(0);
    dup(to_child[0]);            // read end -> stdin

    info.out("OS::spawn: child process: calling OS::execvp");
    OS::execvp(program);         // Spawn the program

    exit(-1);                    // If we get here, OS::execvp failed!
}
```

This version of the code is much more feature-rich than the previous one. It is less likely that it will be modified during a debugging session because most of what it does can be observed and validated without even recompiling it. However, it can be made even more useful. A typical problem encountered with code that sets up communication channels with other processes is testing the overall robustness of the code. For example, if the child process dies and the parent attempts to write to the pipe, a `SIGPIPE` is generated by most Unix variants.

Using the `Debug` class, we can simulate this failure. Consider the following fragment:

```
// The child process
close(to_child[1]);     // Close the unusable end of the pipe
Debug fail("OS::spawn-fail");
if (fail.active()) {
    fail.out("OS::spawn: simulating execvp failure ...");
    close(to_child[0]);
    exit(-1);
}

close(0);
dup(to_child[0]); // Make the read end of the pipe our stdin
info.out("OS::spawn: child process: calling OS::execvp");
OS::execvp(program);     // Spawn the program
```

This lets us test how well the code behaves when this particular facility fails to perform as advertised. We just set the `DEBUG_OPT` environment variable to the value `OS::spawn-fail` and rerun the program.

The Apache Jakarta project has a much more detailed logging facility that supports Java (and hence servlets and JSP), known as `log4j`. Details and source are available at `jakarta.apache.org/log4j`.

Testing Your Testing Infrastructure

To ensure that your defensive programming infrastructure is going to detect the errors you want it to detect and respond appropriately, you test how it reacts to simulated problems. If you are using an improperly expressed or unduly restrictive infrastructure, you can do more harm than good.

Two main steps are involved in verifying your testing infrastructure. First, you develop test cases that check a variety of conditions that should trigger a response. Second, you verify whether the correct response was given. You should also make sure that the infrastructure does not trigger false alarms (also known as *false positives*) by testing it with a variety of conditions that should not trigger it and then checking whether your infrastructure falsely reported correct behavior as failure.

Using Defensive Firewalls

General debugging code is a good idea, and the `Debug` class we introduced creates a more formal way to manage debugging code in your program than simply inserting `print` statements. You can do something similar for your application.

A slightly more formal kind of debugging statement used in defensive programming is known as a *firewall*. Note that this is not related to the firewalls placed around Internet connections. The concept discussed here relates solely to code construction.

A firewall is a point in the logical flow of a program where the validity of logical constraints is checked. If a constraint specified in a firewall is satisfied, execution proceeds. If the constraint is violated, the firewall triggers, generates an appropriate error message, and possibly takes damage-control actions (such as redirecting users to a page explaining the problem or to a backup site) or diagnostic actions (such as turning on debugging information). If designed carefully, these firewalls serve the same purpose as physical firewalls: They can contain a dangerous fire and prevent it from causing a complete disaster.

Firewalls can be used to detect the following problems:

- Errors in the code containing the firewall (for example, a function that expects its integer argument to be strictly positive receives either zero or a negative number).
- Problems with a system that interacts with the code containing the firewall (for example, your stock trading application's connection to the stock exchange is broken).
- Incorrect implementation of the firewall (for example, it was improperly expressed or unduly restrictive). Even these messages are useful because they commonly indicate a flaw in the developer's thinking about the code.

In a sense, a firewall is live documentation that must be maintained and must never be allowed to get out of sync with the correct state of the program; it must always reflect the expectations of the designer. At first, most firewalls appear trivial and superfluous. However, experience with large projects shows that as software systems evolve and age, the implicit assumptions they make on their environment are more likely to be violated. Even the original designer of a piece of code can have a hard time reconstructing what constitutes proper use of that code.

Establishing design goals

So far, we have established that firewalls have three very important purposes:

- They alert you to errors.
- They perform damage control when errors occur.
- They document your code.

Because firewalls perform so many vital functions, it is well worth your time to design them carefully as you develop your code.

The ideal system for validating a software system's internal consistency would automatically generate firewalls based on the surrounding code. Unfortunately, such a system is still outside the realm of the currently feasible, and the burden of implementing and maintaining the consistency checks rests mainly with the developer. In any case, some assumptions simply aren't deducible from the code alone.

A practical alternative is to provide a method by which expressing the system invariants is simple and easy to learn and has very high return value in exchange for a negligible overhead, both in system performance and developer productivity.

Firewalls should not alter the execution flow of a program unless they are triggered. Firewalls should have either no effect or a negligible effect on the performance of the production version. The system should be simple to learn and maintain so that its use is effortless. The constraint validation should consist of simple checks that generally avoid allocating large memory blocks or calling expensive routines. Such testing is almost certainly useful but is beyond the scope of firewalls.

As with the preceding debugging example, we will show a concrete class that implements the concept. You can think about how this can apply to your application, regardless of language.

Introducing the Firewall class

One of the simplest cases of firewalls is to validate that the parameters passed to a function satisfy trivial constraints. For example, if a function assumes that a pointer argument is non-null and the required check is deemed an unacceptable performance penalty for the production system, the check can be implemented as a firewall. Even where your code handles a bad input value and adapts successfully, you can insert a firewall to indicate that the Application Programming Interface (API) was used improperly. Note that this `Firewall` class, like the `Debug` class earlier, can be compiled away into nothingness. As a result, it's not an appropriate solution for implementing recovery under expected failure conditions. The main goal is to identify unexpected failures, places in the code where things should always be okay.

Suppose that you are implementing a doubly linked circular list in terms of a `ListNode` class. `ListNode`s have two pointers to other `ListNode`s, the `_next` and `_prev` fields, and a few convenience functions.

The `ListNode` class might look like the following:

```
class ListNode
{
public:
    ListNode() : _prev(this), _next(this) {}
    void join(ListNode *);

// Other methods follow ...

// Implementation
private:
    ListNode * _prev;
    ListNode * _next;
};
```

The method `join()` takes a pointer to another `ListNode` and arranges the `ListNode` pointers so that the new node is inserted after it:

```
// join: insert newNode after me
// Assumes that newNode is not null
void ListNode::join(ListNode * newNode)
{
    newNode->_prev = this;
    newNode->_next = _next;
    _next->_prev = newNode;
    _next = newNode;
}
```

This piece of code dereferences two different pointers without checking them for validity. The rationale is simple. The parameter `newNode` is not allowed to be null, by design; a comment right above the implementation states this requirement very clearly. This implies that the first two lines in the method `join()` are safe. Also, recall that this node is supposed to be part of a circular list, so _next and _prev always point to other valid ListNodes.

The fundamental flaw in this argument is that these constraints are largely in the mind of the implementers of this class or, at best, are partially reflected in the overall design of the software system. Unfortunately, the comments surrounding a piece of code are tossed out by the preprocessor and do not turn into executable statements. In practice, it is easy to imagine how either or both of these assumptions could be violated.

The preceding code can be modified to check incorrect usage by using the assert macro provided by C++. The assert macro takes a boolean expression as an argument. It can be used to define the correct state of your program at specific locations within the code. If the expression evaluates to true, execution resumes with the statement that follows. If the expression is false, an error message is sent to stderr, and the program is forced to terminate. On Unix systems, a core file is generated, which, in turn, allows you to pinpoint the reason for the assertion failure. The runtime check can be removed by merely recompiling the code with the symbol NDEBUG defined on the compiler command line, eliminating the runtime overhead for the production system (the details might vary for your compiler). A more conscientious developer could use this facility and improve the preceding code as follows:

```
void ListNode::join(ListNode * newNode)
{
    // Enforce a non-null newNode
    assert(newNode != 0);

    newNode->_prev = this;
    newNode->_next = _next;

    // Verify that my next pointer is non-null
    assert(_next != 0);

    _next->_prev = newNode;
    _next = newNode;
}
```

Note that the two kinds of checks, although they look similar, are verifying different aspects of the code. The first one checks a parameter, which means that you are validating the usage of your method. The second one checks an internal variable; if this one is invalid, it means that the code somewhere else was incorrect. Thus, the second assertion is checking for internal consistency instead of correct calling.

The assert macro succeeds very well in satisfying our design goals. It enforces the assumptions made by the designer, and its effect on the performance is small for the test version and nonexistent for the production system. It suffers from the following drawbacks:

- **It treats all constraint violations uniformly.** It halts the program, making it less likely to be used as often as possible.
- **It is limited to evaluating simple boolean expressions.** Checks that must be evaluated in discrete steps require more mucking about in the code.

The class `Firewall` proposed next addresses both these drawbacks. This class provides a static method, `assert`, that is a direct replacement of the `assert` macro. Using `Firewall`, we would rewrite the preceding code as follows:

```
void ListNode::join(ListNode * newNode)
{
    // Enforce a non-null newNode
    Firewall::assert(
        newNode != 0,
        __HERE__,
        "node 0x%081x: appending null node", this
        );

    // Verify that my _next pointer is non-null
    Firewall::assert(
        _next != 0,
        __HERE__,
        "node 0x%081x: null _next pointer", this
        );

    // Append newNode
    newNode->_prev = this;
    newNode->_next = _next;
    _next->_prev = newNode;
    _next = newNode;
}
```

This code is more verbose, but the functionality achieved is correspondingly higher. The static method `Firewall::assert()` takes a variable number of arguments. The first is an expression that should evaluate to a boolean. The second, `__HERE__`, is a preprocessor macro that acts as shorthand for the `__FILE__` and `__LINE__` macros, providing the filename and line where the firewall is located. The third and following arguments represent a `printf`-style format string used to generate a message at runtime. The subsequent arguments (if any) obey the same rules as the arguments to `printf()`. In this example, we have printed the address of the offending node to assist in tracking down the problem with the debugger.

For more complex constraint validation, the `Firewall` class offers the method `active()`, which evaluates to `true` when firewalls are enabled. Also, the method `hit()` provides an unconditional firewall. Examples of both are shown here, where we rewrite `join()` to include a check that this node is, indeed, part of a doubly linked list:

```
void ListNode::join(ListNode * newNode)
{
    // Check assumptions
    if (Firewall::active()) {
        // Check _next pointer
        if (!_next) {
            Firewall::hit(
                __HERE__, "node 0x%08lx: null _next pointer", this
            );
        }

        // Check _prev pointer
        if (!_prev) {
            Firewall::hit(
                __HERE__, "node 0x%08lx: null _prev pointer", this
            );
        }

        // Validate next link
        if (_next->_prev != this) {
            Firewall::hit(
                __HERE__, "node 0x%08lx: corrupt _next link", this
            );
        }

        // Validate _prev link
        if (_prev->_next != this) {
            Firewall::hit(
                __HERE__, "node 0x%08lx: corrupt _prev link", this
            );
        }

        // Check newNode
        if (!newNode) {
            Firewall::hit(
                __HERE__, "node 0x%08lx: null argument to join", this
            );
        }
    }
```

```
    // Append newNode
    newNode->_prev = this;
    newNode->_next = _next;
    _next->_prev = newNode;
    _next = newNode;
}
```

In addition to the methods presented here, `Firewall` provides a lot of support for interactive use during a debugging session. For example, each method that generates a firewall hit calls the method `Firewall::trap()` so that there is a convenient location for a break point. Firewalls can be enabled or disabled from the debugger by assigning the class static `Firewall::_active` variable.

Implementing Firewall

The implementation of the class `Firewall` is very straightforward. If the symbol `FIREWALL` is not defined either in some header file or on the compiler command line, the class `Firewall` collapses into trivial inline functions that should be completely thrown away during the compiler's optimizing phase. This is the same design you saw in the `Debug` class earlier:

```
#ifdef FIREWALL
class Firewall
{
private:
    static bool _active;
    static bool _fatal;
    static void _init();
public:
    static bool active() { return _active; }
    static void trap();
    static void hit(const char *file, long line,
                    const char *fmt = "", ...);
    static void assert(bool cond,
                       const char *file, long line,
                       const char *fmt = "", ...);
};
#else
class Firewall
{
public:
    static bool active() { return false; }
    static void hit(const char *, ...) { }
    static void assert(bool, ...) { }
};
#endif
```

Aspect-Oriented Programming

One interesting programming methodology that can be applied to defensive programming is Aspect-Oriented Programming. In this methodology, you can create a new type of module called an *Aspect*. Aspects allow you to write modules that can be mixed in to your program, using special tools.

If you create your debugging routines as modules, you can isolate your debugging code from your mainline code and optionally build it in to your product whenever you like.

The main Web page discussing Aspect-Oriented Programming is `aosd.net`. You can find implementations that extend many popular languages to support Aspects. For a specific implementation of Aspects in Java, visit the AspectJ page at `aspectj.org`.

The actual implementations of the `Firewall` methods are in the `Firewall.cc` file available on the CD.

To enable firewalls in a program that has been appropriately compiled, just set the `FIREWALL` environment variable to `on`. This causes each firewall to generate output with `printf()`. You can modify the code to implement different actions. Alternatively, if you set the `FIREWALL` environment variable to `fatal`, each firewall calls the `exit()` function after generating output, terminating your program.

If you want to use the `Debug` or `Firewall` classes in your own programs, you can copy them from the CD and build them in to your own projects. However, remember, the important point is not the implementation but rather the concept of defensive programming.

Using Design by Contract

A more formal implementation of the firewall concept is Design by Contract (DbC). DbC was designed to create a contract between a piece of code and its caller; this contract specifies what the callee expects and what the caller can expect. The main idea behind DbC is that any piece of code in any language carries implicit contracts. The simplest example of an implicit contract in Java is a method to which you are not supposed to pass `null`. If this contract is not met, a `NullPointerException` occurs. In this case, the built-in checking of Java creates a kind of default firewall, a warning that something is wrong. However, there's no indication of whether the error is in the caller or the callee. An explicit DbC clause would clarify that callers are not supposed to pass `null`.

Another example of code with an implicit contract is a component whose specification states that it returns only positive values. If it occasionally returns negative values and the consumer of this component is expecting the functionality described in the specification (only positive values returned), the consumer can end up with a critical problem.

DbC originated in the Eiffel programming language, where classes are components that cooperate through the use of a contract that defines the obligations and benefits for each class. Formal DbC is not yet "officially" a part of most programming languages, including Java. However, there have been several recent efforts to graft parts of DbC onto Java and other object-oriented languages.

For an excellent introduction to DbC and a description of how it can be applied to Eiffel, see "Building bug-free O-O software: An Introduction to Design by Contract" at `www.eiffel.com/doc/manuals/technology/contract/page.html`.

Implementations of DbC vary in languages other than Eiffel, but the different implementations currently available do share some common traits. Typically, DbC is implemented by expressing the code's implicit contracts in terms of assertions. Three types of conditions commonly used to create contracts are

- **Preconditions:** To express conditions that must hold true before a method can execute
- **Postconditions:** To express conditions that must hold true after a method completes
- **Invariants:** To express conditions that must hold true any time a client can invoke an object's method

The contracts clearly document what each method requires and what it is required to do. This makes it possible to verify whether methods are used as expected and whether they deliver the results expected by other parts of the system. Additional conditions might be applicable to different programming languages. In Java, for instance, you can create a `Vector` that is intended to hold only `CartEntry` objects. The language, however, has no support for this notion; we express it in our sample code (`CartDatabase.java`) by means of the following comment:

```
// Returns Vector<CartEntry>
public abstract Vector getCart(int user);
```

This is our promise that `getCart` will return a `Vector` containing nothing but `CartEntry` objects. In C++, we would use a parameterized container. Therefore, a

DbC clause would be unnecessary to promise something already enforced by the language.

Third-party tools that support DbC generally have you incorporate specification information into comment tags and then instrument the code with a special compiler to create `assert`-like expressions out of the contract keywords. When the instrumented code is run, contract violations are typically sent to a monitor or logged to a file. The degree of program interference varies. You can often choose between *nonintrusive* monitoring (problems are reported, but program execution is not affected), having the program throw an exception when a contract is violated, or hand-coding custom actions.

For the rest of this section, we focus on how to implement DbC in Java with the Jcontract and Jtest products introduced in Chapter 4 and located on the CD. As usual, the same ideas apply to other solutions; these principles can also be implemented as firewalls.

Implementing Design by Contract in Java

In Java, DbC contracts are typically added to the code via Javadoc comments. A simple example of a contract that can be used with Jcontract is

```
public class ShoppingCart
{
    /**
     * @pre item != null
     * @post $result > 0
     */
    public int add(Item item) {
        _items.addElement(item);
        _totalCost += item.getPrice();
        return _totalCost;
    }
    private int _totalCost = 0;
    private Vector _items = new Vector();
}
```

The contract contains the following conditions:

- A precondition (`@pre item != null`) specifying that the item to be added to the shopping cart may not be `null`
- A postcondition (`@post $result > 0`) specifying that the value returned by the method is always greater than 0

Preconditions and postconditions can be thought of as sophisticated assertions. *Preconditions* are conditions that the method's client must satisfy before the method can execute; a violation of a precondition indicates a problem with the caller (the caller is misusing the method). *Postconditions* are conditions that the implementer of the class guarantees will always be satisfied after a method completes; a postcondition violation indicates a problem with the method's implementation.

Table 7-1 shows additional contract elements used by Jcontract. Some of these elements are standard Javadoc tags; others are not.

TABLE 7-1 MORE POSSIBLE CONTRACT ELEMENTS

Element	Purpose
`@invariant`	Specifies conditions (similar to postconditions) that apply to all the methods in the class. An invariant violation indicates a problem with the class's implementation.
`@assert`	Specifies boolean expressions about the state of the software. Each `@assert` expression is executed at the point in the program where the `@assert` tag is located. An assertion violation indicates a problem in the method implementation.
`@exception`	Specifies that the code is expected to throw a certain exception.
`@concurrency`	Specifies the concurrency mode in which the method can be called. If your method is not threadsafe, you can specify this using `@concurrency sequential`.
`@verbose`	Specifies verbose statements in the code.

The general syntax for a Jcontract comment is

```
DbcContract:
      DbcTag DbcCode
    | @concurrency { concurrent | guarded | sequential }

DbcTag:
      @invariant
    | @pre
    | @post

DbcCode:
      BooleanExpression
    | '(' BooleanExpression ')'
    | '(' BooleanExpression ',' MessageExpression ')'
    | CodeBlock
```

```
    | $none

MessageExpression:
      Expression
```

The preceding syntax description follows the common practice of using BNF (Backus-Naur Form) notation. If you are unfamiliar with this notation, you can get more details from "The Free Online Dictionary of Computing" (also known as FOLDOC) at `www.foldoc.org`, edited by Denis Howe.

Usually, any Java code can be used in the DbC code with the following restriction: The code should not have side effects. That is, it should not have assignments or invoke methods with side effects. Jcontract allows special expressions to be used in your contracts, in addition to Java code. For instance, earlier we used the expression `$result` to refer to the return value in a postcondition. You can find a complete list of allowed expressions and their meanings in the Jcontract User's Guide.

The greatest obstacle to implementing DbC is the effort required to create the contracts. If you are serious about implementing DbC, you need some way to check that the code is accurately and thoroughly documented with contracts. Fortunately, because DbC contracts are written in a standardized format, you can automatically check their implementation.

One way to automate this process is to use Jtest's static analysis feature to guide you through the process of adding DbC contracts. When you let Jtest statically analyze the `.java` file on which you are working, Jtest can apply a special set of coding standards that determine whether any DbC contracts are missing. You can decide whether you want to require precondition, postcondition, or invariant tags on `public`, `protected`, `package`, or `private` classes. When Jtest finds a missing contract, it reports which type of contract is missing and where each contract should be added. For example, if you decide that all `public` methods should have `@post` conditions, Jtest identifies `public` methods that lack `@post` conditions and indicates where these contracts should be added. If you have methods that legitimately have no contracts, you can indicate this with the special `$none` expression.

One situation you might encounter when implementing DbC is the tendency to overspecify contracts. In the `ShoppingCart` example, for instance, we require that `add()` always return a positive number. This seems like a simple enough contract. However, it implies other requirements: `Item.getPrice()` must always return a positive number, and carts cannot handle negative items. A case for nonpositive-priced items might be freebies or coupons. Negative quantities of items can be useful when you want to use `ShoppingCart` to handle returns. In these cases, you have to update the contract. You should not consider these cases failures of DbC. Rather, they illuminate an evolving sense of how the code is intended to function.

When you have a system for making sure that DbC contracts are implemented correctly, you will start noticing one of the primary benefits of using DbC: the time and effort saved by having accessible, readable documentation. Because the specification information is included in the code itself, you can rest assured that the specification will never be lost. Also, because DbC contracts are a structured, concise style of documentation, teams that use DbC have a much easier time understanding one another's documentation. This reduces the number of errors that stem from misunderstandings, increases productivity, and makes it easier to share code among projects.

USING DESIGN BY CONTRACT FOR UNIT TESTING

DbC can be used to prevent and detect errors throughout the development process. In fact, DbC can help you bulletproof your software as early as the unit-testing phase we introduce in Chapter 1 and describe in detail in Chapter 8. If your class is set up so that DbC contracts are checked (for example, after it has been instrumented with a DbC compiler), simply run your unit test cases as normal, and see whether any contracts are violated. Violations can surface as exceptions, entries in a log file, or messages in a GUI, depending on your DbC implementation. If you find inputs that cause contracts to fail, you should review the contract and the code, decide which one is causing the problem, and then fix the problem. For example, if one of your test cases reveals that a method fails to satisfy a postcondition when it is given a valid input, you fix the method so that it returns the correct value.

You can automate this black box (functionality) testing procedure with Jtest. As you create code, you incorporate specification information into it, using the DbC keywords explained earlier. Next, you compile your class as normal and tell Jtest to test it. Jtest then automatically performs the following DbC-related tasks, in addition to its normal white box (construction) testing, black box testing, regression testing, and static analysis tasks:

1. Instruments the code's specification information and recompiles the class with extra bytecodes that describe the contracts
2. Examines the class under test
3. Examines the code's contracts
4. Checks whether the class is missing necessary DbC comment tags
5. Designs inputs that test the functionality specified in the contract (and that meet the specified preconditions)
6. Executes the class under test with those inputs
7. Verifies whether the expected outcome was achieved, by determining the expected outcome based on contract information and comparing the expected outcome with the actual outcome

8. Suppresses any exception documented in the contract
9. Reports results

For a more detailed description of how Jtest uses DbC information, see Chapter 19.

USING DESIGN BY CONTRACT FOR SYSTEM TESTING

DbC information can also be used to prevent and detect problems at runtime, when it can check for contract violations as you exercise the system with your test cases or when the system is actually being used. This testing can expose instances where the system misuses a class or component, as well as instances where complex system interactions cause problems not apparent at the unit level.

The general procedure for checking contracts at runtime is similar to that used to check contracts at the unit level. Make the class's contracts testable (for example, by instrumenting the code with a DbC-enabled compiler), and then integrate that class into the system. If contract violations occur, they are reported as exceptions, log file entries, or GUI messages (depending on your implementation).

One way to automate this procedure in Java is to use the Jcontract tool included in the CD. When you have thoroughly tested a class or component and are ready to integrate it into the system, recompile it with Jcontract by simply calling Jcontract's `dbc_javac` compiler instead of `javac`. For example, to instrument and compile `Example.java`, you would enter the following command:

```
dbc_javac Example.java
```

Jcontract then instruments the code's specification information and recompiles the class with extra bytecodes describing how the class is supposed to work and be used.

Next, integrate the instrumented class into the system, and run the system. As the system runs, the class's contracts are checked and violations are reported . For example, if a component's DbC specification says that a particular method requires positive integer inputs, Jcontract reports a violation if the system passes that method any negative inputs. By default, contract violations are reported in the Jcontract monitor. This monitor displays the nature of each violation, as well as stack trace information.

You can customize Jcontract's degree of program interference to suit your needs. By default, Jcontract uses a nonintrusive runtime handler that reports violations but does not alter program execution. You can also choose a runtime handler that throws an exception when a violation occurs, choose a runtime handler that logs violations in a file, or create a customized runtime handler specially tailored to your needs.

Jcontract also adapts to your needs by letting you select which contract conditions you want it to instrument. This way, you can optimize program performance by having Jcontract focus on the conditions that are most important at your current stage of the development process. For example, after a well-tested class is integrated into an application, you might want to instrument and check only preconditions that verify whether the application uses the class correctly. This is an example of the earlier notion that testing code should be configurable to have a low impact if you expect it to be used throughout the lifetime of an application.

For a brief example of how Jcontract can be used to test components, see Chapter 19.

Adding contracts to the Online Grocer ShoppingServlet

The Online Grocer's `ShoppingServlet` (introduced in Chapter 6) contains many routines with assumptions about their caller. For instance, the `doUpdateCart()` method is expecting to be called from a form with certain fields set. We can do this by adding the following contract:

```
/**
  * Respond to a form update
  *
  * @pre context.hasUser() && hasValidParameters(context)
  */
 public void doUpdateCart(ShoppingContext context)
     throws ServletException, IOException
```

Here, the checks are too verbose to squeeze into a comment, so we add the function `hasValidParameters()`:

```
private boolean hasValidParameters(ShoppingContext context)
{
    int ct = 0;
    Enumeration enum = context.getParameterNames();
    while (enum.hasMoreElements()) {
        String name = enum.nextElement().toString();
        // Check for unexpected arguments
        if (name.startsWith("ITEM_")) {
            ct++;
        } else if (name.equals("METHOD")) {
```

```
            // Expected argument
        } else if (name.equals("UPDATE")) {
            // Expected argument
        } else {
            return false;
        }
    }
    // Make sure at least one cart item is present
    return ct > 0;
}
```

Now we can use Jcontract to build these checks into the servlet whenever we want. We must make sure that we choose an appropriate action for any detected errors – probably logging them to a file, because we don't want them on the Web pages we generate.

Note that many implementation choices are available: for example, how thoroughly to check arguments, whether to recover gracefully or forcefully, and whether to include checks in the final version of the application. Juggling these options is a delicate balancing act that requires practice and experience.

Summary

In this chapter, we discuss several defensive programming techniques that help you prevent errors, catch errors as early as possible, and contain the amount of damage that errors can cause. The more you use these techniques, the less time you spend debugging and performing maintenance. We recognize that there is a natural aversion to writing more code than seems to be necessary at the time. However, this extra code is a good investment in the future of the code and the development process. After this code is added, you can turn it on and find bugs quickly – even bugs of which you were not aware. If you do not practice defensive programming, you will have to add extra error-trapping code when you find a bug, or you will have more bugs that elude your testing and make their way to the released version of the program. As a result, you're likely to end up writing more code and having a less reliable application. It is much more effective to anticipate problems and deal with them as you go.

Chapter 8

Enforcing Coding Standards

IN THIS CHAPTER

- Understanding the importance of error prevention and coding standards
- Establishing coding standards for your Web application
- Working out the logistics of coding standard enforcement
- Enforcing coding standards on the Online Grocer application

IN CHAPTER 1, we briefly introduce the concept of coding standards. In this chapter, we discuss these standards more specifically and focus on how they assist in Web development.

Understanding the Importance of Error Prevention and Coding Standards

Before discussing how specific coding standards help you prevent errors, we're going to take a step back and explain why coding standards are so valuable. The reason is that error *prevention* is a much more effective and efficient strategy than error *detection*. Consider the benefits that the automobile industry gained by shifting its focus to error prevention.

During the 1970s, automobile manufacturers realized that many cars they produced had defects. To eliminate these defects, they assigned people to inspect the cars right off the assembly line and to diagnose any problems, fixing each defect one by one. Eventually, some automobile manufacturers realized that focusing on individual errors after they occur is inefficient. Major resources were being consumed, and what's worse, no general improvement was seen.

These manufacturers decided to take a new approach: Focus on preventing errors. The first step in doing this was to re-envision the problem as the *process* that allows bugs to be introduced. Each time they found a problem at the end of the assembly line, they didn't just fix it. They analyzed the problem and determined at which station in the assembly line it was introduced. Next, they examined the practices and procedures used in that station and devised ways to reduce the probability of that problem's being introduced there. For example, sometimes they rearranged the tools to prevent employees from accidentally using the incorrect tool. Sometimes they changed the procedures to make complicated processes less confusing. The more they did this, the fewer defects they found at the end of the assembly line, and the less time and money they wasted chasing after individual defects. They improved their process and, as result, produced better products faster and cheaper.

The automobile industry's initial approach to solving quality problems is much like the current practice in today's software industry: Ignore bugs during implementation, and try to chase after them one by one while debugging at the end of the development process. If you follow the automobile industry's lead and shift your focus from error detection to error prevention, you gain the same benefit: the ability to produce more reliable products in less time with fewer resources As the automobile industry discovered, the key to increasing quality and conserving resources is to improve the process so that it reduces the chance of errors being introduced in the first place. Most of this book discusses ways you can do this. One of the key ways to remove dangerous practices is to enforce coding standards.

Coding standards are language-specific rules that, if followed, significantly reduce the opportunity for you to introduce errors into an application. Coding standards should be implemented in all languages, including Java, Visual Basic, C/C++, Python, and HTML. Writing clean code is vital to your entire Web application's performance because your programs drive the back end and are constantly reused. Any problem with your programs' performance or functionality can slow down or crash your entire application.

Our aim in this chapter is to describe what coding standards are, how they streamline the development process, and how you can implement them as efficiently and painlessly as possible. We focus on HTML, CSS, JavaScript, Java, and C++ coding standards because these are among the most frequently used languages in Web development. Even if you are using other languages, you should have enough background to start creating your own coding standards after reading this chapter.

Implementing coding standards consistently pays off for individual developers and entire development teams. The benefits last not only throughout a project but also throughout the subsequent projects that use the code developed in the initial project. When you consistently apply coding standards in the construction phase of software development, you achieve the following benefits:

- Faster development time
- Increased product quality
- Increased code portability
- Increased code maintainability

- Increased code modifiability
- Increased code reusability
- Increased team (and personal) productivity
- Increased programming expertise
- Easier ISO 9000 certification

Establishing Coding Standards for Browser-Dependent Languages

Many problems that users experience when working with an application on their browser are difficult to expose in a test environment. As mentioned in Chapter 3, various browsers render code and handle nonstandard code differently. As a result, users can experience problems you never notice during traditional testing. For example, certain users might not be able to submit forms or view content you intended to display in a table, but other users experience no problems with that same functionality.

You simply cannot expose such problems if your only testing procedure is to look at your pages from a browser, and manually examining all facets of every possible dynamic page on every available browser would be a grueling and endless process. A more effective method is to check whether your code adheres to the appropriate language specification and avoids language elements not implemented consistently across browsers. The best way to do this is to enforce HTML, CSS, and JavaScript coding standards; these standards ensure that your code does not contain nonstandard or poorly implemented elements. By enforcing coding standards, you dramatically improve the chances of your code's functioning correctly for most potential users, without having to test how your code performs on each and every available browser, device, and configuration.

We start our discussion of this group of coding standards by looking at HTML. HTML is the most popular language for static and output pages sent to the client's browser and is the foundation on which CSS and JavaScript build.

Establishing coding standards for HTML

HTML, which stands for *Hypertext Markup Language*, has become the common language of the Web, used in some form by almost every Web site. As a language, it was designed to be simple enough for the average person to create by hand. One consequence of this is the wide variety of allowable syntax. Virtually any text file can be interpreted as HTML! Unlike other languages, required tags are merely optional, fields can be created or ignored willy-nilly, and quotes are optional. On the whole, browsers do their best to cope and have added their own, often incompatible, features to the language. As a result, many HTML authors don't even know the difference between good HTML and bad HTML. Coding standards serve as a tool for helping all HTML developers create good HTML.

By checking whether the code sent to your users' browsers adheres to HTML coding standards, you prevent the following types of problems:

- **Nonportable code.** For example, enforcing coding standards that identify ALIGN values that operate only in Netscape Navigator or Internet Explorer prevents code from being rendered in a random manner on browsers that do not support the nonportable tags.
- **Data input errors that corrupt data between the user form and the program on the server.** For example, enforcing a coding standard that identifies any BUTTON, INPUT TYPE=BUTTON, INPUT TYPE=CHECKBOX, or INPUT TYPE=RADIO tag that was contained within a FORM tag but did not contain a VALUE attribute prevents form submission errors.
- **Dynamic content errors.** For example, enforcing a coding standard that identifies any PARAM tag that is not nested within an APPLET or OBJECT tag prevents problems passing parameters to the specified applet or object.
- **Navigation-related errors that prevent visitors from arriving where the link should lead.** For example, enforcing a coding standard that identifies any A HREF statement that does not contain a clickable element prevents instances in which a user has no way to follow an intended navigation link.
- **Performance issues that can slow down your Web application.** For example, enforcing coding standards that identify empty or unnecessary tags reduces the time required for a browser to render each page.
- **Presentation errors that affect a page's appearance.** For example, enforcing a coding standard that identifies any TR tag that is not properly nested in a TABLE tag prevents tables from being rendered incorrectly or incompletely.
- **Security errors that affect data protection for those relying on client/server certificates to prove identity.** For example, enforcing a coding standard that identifies KEYGEN tags that are not nested within FORM tags ensures the key's privacy.

For a more detailed example of how HTML coding standards prevent errors, look at what happens when code does not follow the coding standard "OPTION must be nested within SELECT":

```
<HTML>
<HEAD><TITLE>Test Page</TITLE></HEAD>
<BODY>
<FORM ACTION="www.parasoft.com" METHOD=GET>
```

```
<SELECT NAME=MENU SIZE=3 MULTIPLE>
<OPTION>This is option 1
<OPTION>This is option 2
</SELECT>
<OPTION>This is option 3
</FORM>
</BODY></HTML>
```

When this code is rendered on the browser, it looks like the Web page shown in Figure 8-1.

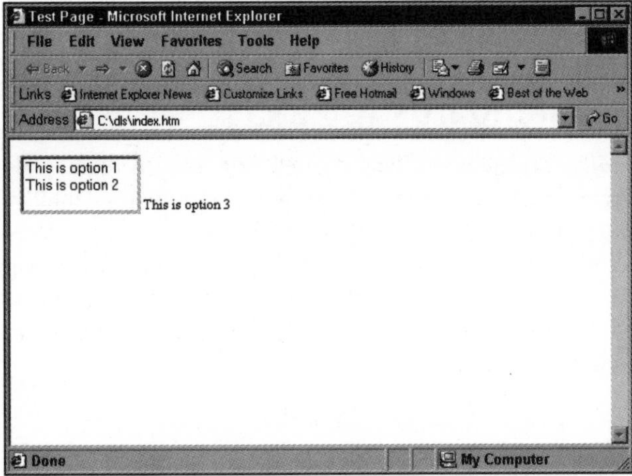

Figure 8-1: Code that does not follow HTML coding standards.

As you can see, the final `<OPTION>` tag should be nested between the `<SELECT>` and `</SELECT>` tags. Otherwise, the text that follows the `<OPTION>` tag will not be listed as an option in the menu that the developer has created with the `<SELECT>` and `</SELECT>` tags. Instead, the text `This is option 3` will be printed outside the menu, and users will be unable to select it.

A good start for HTML coding standards is an understanding of the established HTML standards from W3C (The World Wide Web Consortium). You can find an overwhelming amount of information at `www.w3.org`. At the time of this writing, the current HTML standard is 4.01, but most browsers have their own idea about what "standard" HTML means. One helpful resource that attempts to document the state of HTML across different browsers is Ron Woodall's *The Compendium of HTML Elements* at `htmlcompendium.org`.

Another useful specification is XHTML, which reformulates HTML in XML. If you choose to use XHTML, you can apply XML validators to verify correct code. There are three variants of XHTML, depending on how strict you want to be. You might find XHTML too constraining for your liking, but it definitely helps control errors.

We discuss XML in more detail in Chapter 17.

You can find a number of HTML checkers on the Web. For some examples, see `validator.w3.org`. Also, the tools you are already using to create your HTML might have integrated HTML checking. The important thing is making sure that you apply your standards consistently and set up a way to verify the code as you develop it and after it has been deployed. Later in this chapter, you will see an example of how to use the WebKing tool on the CD to check the HTML code in the Online Grocer application.

Establishing coding standards for CSS

CSS, which stands for *Cascading Style Sheets*, was created as a way to reuse style information from multiple HTML documents and thus allow greater customizability at many levels. CSS was designed to help with the goal of decoupling content from presentation. In the older model, your HTML becomes cluttered with formatting information. In the newer model, formatting information moves to an external style sheet, and the content becomes cleanly separated. The strictest version of XHTML is designed to enforce this separation.

USING CSS

There are three different ways to include CSS in your Web application. First, you can use inline CSS expressions with the `STYLE` attribute supported by many HTML elements:

```
<P STYLE="color: red">Hello</P>
```

Second, you can use the `<STYLE>` HTML tag to inline a section of CSS in to your HTML document:

```
<STYLE TYPE="text/css">
P {
    color: red
}
</STYLE>
<P>Hello</P>
```

Finally, you can store the CSS contents in a separate file, typically ending with `.css`, and include a reference to that file from your HTML:

```
<LINK REL="STYLESHEET" TYPE="text/css" HREF="test.css">
<P>Hello</P>
```

In this case, the file `test.css` would look like this:

```
P {
   color: red
}
```

This last method has the advantage of storing your styles in a single location, so you can give all your pages the same look and feel without duplicating code. Also, if you use the same style sheet often, browsers will generally have it available in their cache, which reduces downloading time. Note that you can also use JavaScript to set your styles, but this is not recommended because JavaScript styles are not nearly as portable as CSS.

It is important to realize in how many contexts CSS can occur, because that defines how you should enforce your coding standards. To be comprehensive, you have to enforce your standards consistently across all relevant contexts.

Currently, there are two official versions of CSS: CSS1 and CSS2. CSS1 is the original standard, which was later extended to become CSS2. Many features of CSS2 apply to audio and visual media and are not yet widely implemented. A third version, CSS3, is currently under development.

For more information specifically about CSS, see *Cascading Style Sheets, Designing for the Web* by Hakon Wium Lie and Bert Bos, or *Cascading Style Sheets: The Definitive Guide* by Eric A. Meyer.

DECIDING WHICH RULES TO USE

Because different browsers offer varied degrees of support for CSS, the best way to ensure that your styles will be effectively rendered on all possible browsers is to use standard CSS elements in the way they are designed to be used. The most effective way to verify that you are using standard CSS is to enforce CSS coding standards.

For example, say that you use the `PRE` tag to indicate text that a user should enter at a command prompt. However, the CSS entry that describes how to render text in `PRE` tags contains a nonstandard `font-family` element. Rather than write it as

```
PRE {
      font-family: monospace;
      font-size: 8pt
```

```
}
```

you accidentally omit a hyphen and write

```
PRE {
        fontfamily: monospace;
        font-size: 8pt
}
```

The text in the PRE tag might not be rendered differently than the regular text, so users would not be able to determine which text should be entered at the prompt. This problem can be avoided by enforcing a coding standard that identifies non-standard font-family elements.

Another common problem arises from specifying colors. CSS is particularly flexible when it comes to choosing colors. You can use names or several formats for specifying specific RGB values (combinations of Red, Green, and Blue). For instance, Lime, #00FF00, #0F0, RGB(0,255,0), and RGB(0%,100%,0%) all represent the same shade of green. This flexibility means that you have to be careful in how you restrict your use of colors to make sure that you are checking all the appropriate cases.

Although you can specify numerous colors, this doesn't mean that your customers can see any color you choose. Even ignoring black and white devices, such as some PDAs, not all computers are capable of displaying an arbitrary number of colors. The CSS specification defines 16 colors that correspond to the VGA palette. If you work with colors, you might want to use the Browser-Safe Palette created by Lynda Weinman, which shows the 216 colors you can reasonably expect to work on machines with at least 256 colors (these correspond to the overlap between Windows and Macintosh system colors).

Lynda Weinman's Browser-Safe Palette is available at www.lynda.com/hex.html.

A reasonable rule might be this: All colors should come from the 216-color palette and use only the #RRGGBB notation so that there is no possibility of undefined names. If you want to allow some names, you can make a list of color names you allow and can make sure that only those names are used. This is a case in which spell-checking names is useful because it can be hard for tests to know when an element is not the color the designer intended, and a simple typo can cause the browsers to (silently!) ignore your code.

As with HTML, there is no single standard you can apply to decide what is correct CSS. You can find the official specifications for CSS at w3c.org, but as usual, browser implementers have their own twist on how things should work. When you are determining which coding standards to enforce, you must decide which features you will and will not use. In addition to the common coding standards (that is, rules that lead you to write syntactically valid code), you can create rules to enforce your own policies. For example, you can disallow features added in CSS2 but not currently supported by most browsers.

As you enforce CSS coding standards, be aware of the problems that can arise from the language's built-in forward compatibility. So that old browsers can continue to function when new features are added (for instance, CSS3), complying browsers must ignore invalid CSS (within certain guidelines). This virtually guarantees that typos will be silently ignored and hence undetected. Therefore, you need some kind of tool or validation procedure directed specifically at finding these problems. Part of enforcing CSS coding standards must necessarily be the reporting of nonconforming constructs, even though this will not support future standards (the coding standard enforcement technology you use will have to be modified to support the new features).

If you want to try validating your CSS, browse to `jigsaw.w3.org/css-validator/validator-uri.html`, and enter the URL of a page that references the CSS. The validator will generate a page with the validation errors.

The benefits of this validator and the free HTML validator referenced in the HTML section are the cost and the possible access you might have to the validator's source code and authors. The disadvantages of free validators are that they might not be as comprehensive as commercial tools, might not meet your needs, and probably don't offer customer support in the business sense. In addition, they generally don't allow you to add custom rules. Moreover, some validators (such as the one just mentioned) can only test code available online.

Establishing coding standards for JavaScript

JavaScript is the most common client-side scripting language used on the Web today. By *client-side*, we mean that the scripts are executing on your customers' Web browsers, not on the server machine. This means that your code has to work in their environment, not yours. The issues involving JavaScript can seem more complicated than necessary. To understand JavaScript as it applies to Web applications, you must understand two different pieces: JavaScript as a programming language and the DOM (Document Object Model), which describes a portable interface to common Web elements.

REVIEWING THE JAVASCRIPT LANGUAGE

The JavaScript language is a simple scripting language inspired by Java but appropriately considered an altogether different language. It's sometimes referred to as *ECMAScript*, the official name for the language standard. ECMA, the European Computer Manufacturer's Association, is an international standards organization. Its home page is `www.ecma.ch`, and this is where you can find the ECMAScript standard, known as *ECMA-262*. Note that this standard lags rather far behind the functionality provided by current browsers.

Like other scripting languages, JavaScript defers largely to dynamic checking and allows a wide variety of messy code to function without visible error. For instance, you can assign a value to a field that does not exist. Rather than complain, the language simply creates the new field and assigns the variable. Similarly, accessing nonexisting fields gives you an undefined value instead of causing a runtime error.

For example, the following code displays the string `undefined` but does not otherwise alert you that you might have done something wrong:

```
document.foo = 'a';
alert(document.fooo);
```

REVIEWING THE DOM

The JavaScript language alone does not provide the necessary tools for creating dynamic HTML. To have sufficient functionality, you must also be able to access various elements relating to the browser and your documents. The interface is the *DOM*, which is a script-visible representation of the browser's state (typically the browser, windows, and HTML content). It defines the features you can access and the control you have over them. In some respects, the DOM functions as a standard library of components for Web-based JavaScript. The official DOM standards are available from W3C at `www.w3.org/DOM/`. Again, there is a difference between the interface described by the official standard and the actual interfaces as implemented by your users' browsers.

In our experience, one of the most common nuisances on the Web is the dreaded `A Runtime Error has occurred` message. Most often, this message arises from problems with the way the JavaScript code uses the DOM. Different browser developers have extended the interface in mutually incompatible ways, as well as developing different versions of the language.

For instance, from Internet Explorer, you can dynamically rewrite parts of the current HTML by assigning to the `innerHTML` property. If you use a version of the DOM that is not compatible with the user's browser, you can very well cause runtime errors by evaluating `undefined` values. To some degree, this can be dealt with at runtime by carefully writing your scripts to query the browser, for instance, using the `navigator.userAgent` property. However, the amazing variety of browsers makes writing a truly robust check very difficult. Most browsers claim to be some flavor of Mozilla (the `userAgent` name for Netscape) to support pages written to run only under Netscape. Here's how one version of Netscape identifies itself:

```
Mozilla/4.75 [en] (Windows NT 5.0; U)
```

Internet Explorer running on the same machine identifies itself as follows:

```
Mozilla/4.0 (compatible; MSIE 5.5; Windows NT 5.0)
```

The actual browser is MSIE 5.5 (meaning *Microsoft Internet Explorer 5.5*), but it wants to look like Mozilla/4.0 to JavaScript programs.

If you are developing JavaScript to work with the userAgent property, having a list of what values you might expect can be helpful. On the CD, we have included a file, useragents.txt, containing most of the userAgent values that occurred on one of our sites. This file is not comprehensive but is a good start for understanding which kinds of values might be used by different clients.

USING JAVASCRIPT

Now that you have some idea of what JavaScript is and why it causes so many problems, you can learn how it is used in Web applications and look at some simple ideas for coding standards.

As with CSS, you can embed JavaScript into your HTML pages in many ways. There are two main ways to handle large amounts of code. In the first method, you embed it directly via the <SCRIPT> tag, as follows. Notice the comments for backwards compatibility, as discussed in Chapter 3.

```
<SCRIPT TYPE="text/javascript" LANGUAGE="JavaScript">
<!--
function hello() {
    alert("Hello")
}
// -->
</SCRIPT>
```

In the second method, as with CSS, you store the same code in a separate file:

```
<SCRIPT TYPE="text/javascript" LANGUAGE="JavaScript"
SRC="test.js"></SCRIPT>
```

In this case, test.js would look like this:

```
function hello() {
    alert("Hello")
}
```

In both these cases, the JavaScript is executed while the page is loading into the browser. If appropriate, storing the script externally can improve the performance of your application because of browser caching.

You can also use JavaScript to react to certain user events. The simplest way is to use special `javascript` URLs – for instance:

```
<A HREF="javascript:alert('Hello')">Click here</A>
```

Commonly, you also use HTML attributes that support scripting special events – for instance:

```
<BUTTON TYPE="BUTTON" ONCLICK="alert('Hello')">Click here</BUTTON>
```

Any coding standards you decide to enforce on your JavaScript code should be applied equally in all contexts where JavaScript can occur. It is all too easy to overlook JavaScript that is deeply embedded inside HTML – especially if you are checking code manually.

DECIDING WHICH RULES TO USE

As you can see, JavaScript can fail in many ways. Your best defenses against these problems are thorough testing and coding standard enforcement. JavaScript coding standards prevent you from writing nonportable and error-prone code. For example, you can prevent scripting errors by enforcing a JavaScript coding standard that says not to use JavaScript keywords (such as `export`, `import`, `catch`, `class`, `const`, `extends`, and so on) as identifiers for variables or functions. This coding standard would identify code such as

```
var export = 20
```

For another example, you can prevent instability and infinite loops by enforcing a JavaScript coding standard that identifies any possible inconsistency between a `for` loop's increment statement and condition statement. This coding standard would identify code such as

```
for (x=0; x>0; x++) {
    // loop body
}
```

Many of the ideas we discuss in the next section apply equally well to your JavaScript code.

Two of our favorite references for working with JavaScript are *JavaScript: The Definitive Guide* by David Flanagan and *Dynamic HTML* by Danny Goodman. The latter book is especially helpful in trying to determine what is supported with different versions of Netscape and Internet Explorer.

Establishing General Coding Standards for Imperative Languages

Imperative programming languages are all the languages that include variables and statements to execute commands, for instance, JavaScript, Java, and C++. Because these languages have many similar elements, we can effectively discuss coding standards that cross the language barrier. To provide concrete examples, we will present code written in Java. However, the key element here is not the specific language being shown, but the principle being illustrated.

Code written in any language must be clear and readable. People should be able to determine its function at a glance. The following examples show several instances of how following coding standards can help maintain clarity and readability.

Some standards represent conventions of various development teams, and others are hard and fast rules. Some of these are amenable to automatic testing, and others might require manual code reviews. Which standards work best for you depends on your team and project.

Remember that rules are guidelines to produce better code, not necessarily strict requirements to be followed slavishly.

Choosing clear, meaningful variable names

Anytime you are writing code and choosing names for your variables, you want to make sure that you and other developers will have an easy time reading and working with your code. The names you choose are for the benefit of the reader, not the compiler (or interpreter).

Code should be as easy to read and understand as possible because it is merely a language representing real-life functions and processes. Anyone who looks at the code even months after it's been written should be able to determine its function at a glance. Later in the development process, when it is time to check code for errors, you have to be able to debug the algorithm and easily determine whether the logic is correct. This process runs much more smoothly if your code's variable names are connected to real life.

In the short term, the quickest and easiest method to name a variable is to make up an abbreviation for it. You save a few keystrokes every time you use a variable during the coding process, and you can assign abbreviations that have a particular meaning to you. You could write your code as follows:

```
public class ba
{
    private int bal;
    public void dep(int i) {
        bal += i;
    }
    public void wit(int i) {
        bal -= i;
    }
    public int get() {
        return bal;
    }
}
```

However, this solution is inadequate because in the long run, it severely hampers the code's readability and reusability for other developers. Any medium-size program written this way is very difficult to understand; at a glance, no one can tell what the code does, because it is just code. An abbreviation such as `ba` does not necessarily tell the reader that the code is dealing with a bank account. Such abbreviations have meaning only to you, and even you might forget what the abbreviations mean over time.

To determine the function of this code, other developers will have to figure out what each abbreviated variable name stands for. Their minds will be constantly forced to translate `ba` into `BankAccount` and `dep` into `deposit` at the same time they are supposedly checking the code's functionality.

You can prevent this extra work by having your group follow a more reasonable naming convention: Connect variable names to their real-life function. You can then focus on one problem at a time, which is the key to successful error prevention. The human brain is far more accurate when it compartmentalizes tasks, and accuracy is of utmost importance in preventing errors. With clearly written code, you can check the logic of the code and focus on real problems.

The preceding code's purpose is much clearer when rewritten as follows:

```
public class BankAccount
{
    private int balance;
    public void deposit(int amount) {
```

```
        balance += amount;
    }
    public void withdraw(int amount) {
        balance -= amount;
    }
    public int getBalance() {
        return balance;
    }
}
```

As you can see from this example, applying real-life experience and intuition to code checking is easier when variable names are connected to real-life functions. Intuition is important in checking code, for the same reason that it is important in understanding mathematics. Students who have trouble with algebra in high school often lack the ability to connect equations to real life. To them, algebra is a meaningless jumble of numbers and letters, and the process of solving a problem remains a mystery. However, when students learn to connect the problems to real life, they often show a marked improvement in their ability to reach a correct answer. They are using intuition and applying life experience to problems. Applying intuition is also essential to testing the logic of an algorithm.

In addition, naming variables in this way has lasting benefits for the productivity of your development group. Developers who join the group later will not waste time being confused by abbreviations that don't follow a particular pattern. The few extra seconds you spend using standard naming conventions today saves hours of extra work for you and your development group later in the development cycle.

In the long run, you might even find meaningful variable names more convenient than abbreviations because they help you avoid the confusion of having to assign and remember abbreviations for a long list of variables. You save yourself the trouble of improvising to find a different abbreviation for each variable. Developers generally know that they should follow naming conventions, but they fail to do so because they mistakenly think that using abbreviations is easier.

Because the second code example uses the names `BankAccount`, `deposit`, `withdrawal`, and `balance`, it is clear that this code is meant to add and subtract money from a bank account and hold the current balance. With good variable names in place, it is much easier to apply life experience as you check code. Nearly everyone has had the experience of depositing to and withdrawing from a bank account. This experience is invaluable in determining whether a program that performs these functions is working correctly.

Use clear, meaningful variable names connected to real-life functions.

Establishing Additional Naming Conventions

At ParaSoft, developers use the following naming conventions for variables, in addition to the convention just described:

- Variables start with lowercase and use mixed case for multiple words, for instance, `someVariable`.
- Classes start with uppercase and use mixed case, for instance, `SomeClassName`.
- Constants use all uppercase with underbars, for instance, `static final int MY_CONSTANT = 1;`.

Whereas the preceding convention pertains to the name itself, these deal with the format in which the name is written.

Steve McConnell's *Code Complete* dedicates an entire chapter (Chapter 9) to the subject of naming variables. This book is filled with useful ideas regarding code construction and includes examples from many programming languages.

Using proper indentation

One way of making code clear to any developers or testers that need to read it is to follow a standard pattern of indentation. The indentation clarifies how certain parts of the code correspond to other parts of the code. The following segment is an example of poorly indented code:

```
public class DanglingElse {
    public int map(int i) {
        if (i > 0)
            if (i > 10)
                return 10;
        else
            return -1;
        return 0;
    }
}
```

In this case, it looks as though the `else` statement refers to the first `if` statement. However, it really is associated with the inner `if` statement. If this code used different indentation, it would still have the same meaning to the compiler but would probably be more understandable to the reader. Don't worry yet about missing braces; these are covered in the next section.

Use indentation to make code clear and readable.

Using braces to show intent

Although proper indentation would make the code in the preceding example clearer, this code would be even clearer if it made proper use of braces. *Braces* are the curly scoping marks ({}) that give the compiler (and people) very necessary information about how parts of the code correspond to one another.

The developer who wrote the preceding code intended for it to return `-1` whenever `i` is less than or equal to `0`. The indentation in the code suggests that the desired outcome will indeed occur. Because the first `if` is indented at the same level as `else`, it appears that the code will return `-1` in any case where `i` is not greater than `0`. However, this code will actually return `-1` whenever `i` is less than or equal to `10`.

Braces instruct the compiler to associate the statements differently. When you write a segment of code that contains several `if` statements, use braces to make sure that the compiler associates statements the way you intended. When you fail to use braces with `else` statements, you are said to have created a *dangling* `else` statement.

The Importance of Indentation

Although the example here uses Java and the same principle applies equally to C++ and many other modern languages, one language that completely sidesteps this issue is Python. In Python, indentation determines nesting instead of brackets. Thus, you cannot create an indentation that looks different from how the program will be executed.

Discussing this feature in *Programming Python*, by Mark Lutz, Guido van Rossum, the creator of Python, writes

> Perhaps Python's most controversial feature is its use of indentation for statement grouping. . . . It is one of the language's features that is dearest to my heart. It makes Python code more readable in two ways. First, the use of indentation reduces visual clutter and makes programs shorter, thus reducing the attention span needed to take in a basic unit of code. Second, it allows the programmer less freedom in formatting, thereby enabling a more uniform style, which makes it easier to read someone else's code.

The following code uses braces and avoids dangling `else` statements:

```
public class DanglingElse {
    public int map(int i) {
        if (i > 0) {
            if (i > 10)
                return 10;
        } else {
            return -1;
        }
        return 0;
    }
}
```

Braces eliminate problems because they make your code explicit. Whenever you have `else` statements, use braces to specify the proper order of operations.

Avoid dangling `else` statements.

Using parentheses to show intent

Rules concerning proper use of marks such as braces or parentheses might seem trivial, but they apply to many important areas of your code. For example, the way you use parentheses determines the order of evaluation for expressions. In much the same way you follow an order of operations when solving algebraic equations, imperative languages first evaluate any expressions enclosed in parentheses. Whenever you are unsure of your order of evaluation, use parentheses to mark any expressions you want the compiler/interpreter to evaluate first. The following example illustrates the dangers of incorrectly used parentheses:

```
public class NeedsParentheses {
    public static void main(String args[]) {
        System.err.println("2 + 9 = " + 2 + 9);
    }
}
```

The developer intended this code to print *11*. Much to the developer's surprise, however, it prints *29* as the answer. The outcome of the program will be drastically wrong because the developer neglected to use parentheses properly.

If the developer had enclosed the second `2 + 9` in parentheses, that section of the code would be interpreted as an integer operation, which was the desired effect.

2 + 9 would be a simple integer addition. Furthermore, 2 + 9 would be calculated before the rest of the computations are performed. Without the parentheses, however, both +s following that string are treated as string concatenations because "2 + 9 = " is a string. The 2 and the 9 are converted to two strings independently and are printed side by side as *29*, providing a wildly inaccurate answer to a simple computation.

Use parentheses to clear up ambiguities.

Some developers argue that parentheses are necessary only if the code in question is not parsed properly without them. Certainly, adding parentheses around every operator can introduce clutter into your code. However, it is important to remember that most developers do not know or remember all the intricate details about operator precedence. Readable code should be immediately understandable by all your developers, not just the ones with experience writing compilers!

A good rule of thumb is to add parentheses any time the parsing is not obvious. A definition of *obvious* has to be specific to your organization.

Monitoring conditional statements

Many developers do not monitor the contents of their conditional statements (for example, if, do, and while). Errors in conditional statements are easy to overlook when you are checking your code. The following example illustrates the possible dangers of conditional statements:

```
public class IncorrectCondition {
    private int k = 10;
    void method(boolean val) {
        if (val = true) {
            k += 1;
        }
    }
}
```

The developer who wrote this code was trying to compare val to true, but wrote the code incorrectly. Because there is only one = between val and true, the expression inside the if condition represents an assignment. When this code is executed, k will always be added, regardless of what the value is. To make a comparison, you must use == instead of =. This error is an easy one to catch automatically but causes major problems when undetected.

Avoid assignment inside conditional statements.

One trick that some developers have adopted is to place any appropriate constant on the left side of a comparison expression. Then most languages refuse to parse the problematic code, and the error is detected early.

Another coding standard applicable to this particular situation is to mark all parameters to your methods as constant. In Java, you would use the `final` keyword, and in C++ you would use the `const` keyword. In this case, the incorrect code would fail to compile because you cannot assign values to `val` if it has been marked as constant. If you apply this rule frequently to your Java code, remember that `final` parameters and local variables are copied into any anonymous objects you create inside a method, so you can have unwanted overhead.

Using default labels to show intent

Developers who are unsure about how to use the `default` label often choose to omit the label from their code rather than wrestle with it. The results can be severe:

```
public class MissingDefault
{
    private int a = 0;
    void method(int i) {
        switch(i) {
        case 1:
            a = 10;
            break;
        case 2:
        case 3:
            a = 20;
            break;
        }  // missing default label
    }
}
```

If an unexpected value is presented here, the value is passed right through the code. It does not matter whether the value is correct.

To avoid this problem, provide a `default` label for every `switch` statement. If you are unsure of what to use as a `default` label, simply write

```
default:
    throw new IllegalArgumentException();
```

If the prospect of introducing undeclared runtime exceptions troubles you, this is a good place to add defensive firewalls, as explained in Chapter 7.

If you know that your default action is to do nothing, you write an empty case. This indicates to the reader that the case is intentionally empty, not simply forgotten:

```
default:
    break;
```

Provide a `default` label for each `switch` statement.

Using break statements

The following segment of code presents an example similar to the preceding one. Here it is clear that there is a missing `break` statement after `case 1` because the code assigns the value `10` to `a`, only to reassign it to `20` in the next statement.

```
public class MissingBreak
{
    private int a = 0;
    void method(int i) {
        switch(i) {
        case 1:
            a = 10;
        case 2: case 3:
            a = 20;
        default:
            a = 40;
        }
    }
}
```

There should be a `break` after each case, as displayed here:

```
case 1:
    a = 10;
    break;
```

Without these break statements, the code falls right through the case statements. It does not matter which case you are in; you automatically fall right through to the default. Fixing this problem is as simple as making sure that each case statement is followed by break.

Follow case statements with break.

In some instances, you legitimately want to allow certain cases to flow together. This represents a special exception to the rule and has to be documented as such. For instance, you could do this by using a comment such as

```
// fall through
```

It is important to document exceptions, so that the reader of your code doesn't have to spend extra time determining your intent. Even when you think that it's obvious that two cases are meant to flow together, you should not assume that the reader will understand this as easily as you do.

Applying coding standards to object-oriented programming

This section applies only to object-oriented (OO) programming languages such as Java and C++. If you have developers who are only used to procedural programming (that is, C or many scripting languages), they often lack training in creating clean object-oriented designs. Coding standards can help these developers quickly learn basic principles of OO programming and leverage the benefits of the language.

OO programming can help make code reusable, easily maintainable, and better organized. However, there are a number of pitfalls – for example:

```
public class BankAccount {
    public int balance;
}
```

The class BankAccount is used to represent a bank account, but the variable used to represent the balance has been made public. Even though declaring the variable public is legal according to the Java language, it makes the code very difficult to modify and improve. This is because the principle of encapsulation has been violated. There is a safer way of writing the code and achieving the same effect:

```
public class BankAccount {
    private int balance;
```

```
    public int getBalance() {
        return balance;
    }
    public void setBalance(int balance) {
        this.balance = balance;
    }
}
```

Here, the `balance` variable is declared `private`, and `public` methods are defined to access it. The code is now easier to maintain because you can change the `BankAccount` implementation without having to change any of the client code.

For example, we can make the `BankAccount` object threadsafe just by declaring the `getBalance()` and `setBalance()` methods synchronized. Note that none of the other methods that might be using `BankAccount` objects have to be modified in this case.

Declare instance variables as `private`.

Establishing Coding Standards for Specific Imperative Languages

Each programming language brings its own peculiarities and nuances to the development table. Insightful understanding into which language features are causing your development group the most problems can be your best beacon to creating appropriate coding standards.

Because our Online Grocer is implemented in Java, we focus mostly on Java.

Establishing coding standards for Java

Java is used in a wide variety of roles for Web development. Some of these include components such as EJBs (Enterprise JavaBeans), JSPs (JavaServer Pages), and servlets. Correct functioning of these components is vital to a robust Web application, especially when you get a significant number of hits. As mentioned at the beginning of this chapter, sloppily constructed code can slow down or crash your entire application.

To demonstrate the usefulness of Java-specific coding standards and get you started on developing your own set of Java coding standards, the following sections provide several examples of coding standards that help solve some common challenges of Java development.

The Java Virtual Machine

Although languages such as C++ use a compiler to generate binary code that targets a physical machine, the Java compiler generates bytecode that is, in turn, interpreted by a virtual machine. A *virtual machine* is an abstract design of a computer, defining the capabilities provided. The advantage of a virtual machine is the ability to run the same bytecode on any compatible implementation of the virtual machine. This is the source of Java's portability.

When we are talking about performance issues relative to the virtual machine, we mean understanding what's going on under the hood so that you write your code in a way that allows the virtual machine to perform smoothly. Some of these details can vary, depending on the specific virtual machine you are using, but most of the principles are basically the same. For example, the virtual machine specification requires a garbage collector to exist but does not detail which algorithms are used.

If you want to get into the nitty-gritty of the Java Virtual Machine, we recommend *The Java Virtual Machine Specification* by Tim Lindholm and Frank Yellin.

Two excellent references for Java coding guidelines are *Effective Java* by Joshua Bloch and *Practical Java* by Peter Haggar.

CALLING STATIC FUNCTIONS

As emphasized earlier, the clearer your code is, the more effective developers reading the code will be. This is another example of that principle. Consider the following segment of code, which shows two equivalent ways to invoke a static method. The first call to `getIt()` is misleading. Calling the method through the object can falsely convince the reader that we are dealing with a method that is not static. The second call, however, is not ambiguous. There is no way `getIt()` can be interpreted as anything other than a static method in the context `AClass.getIt()`, and, therefore, the reader will be in the proper mind-set to understand the code.

```
class AClass {
    static void getIt() {
    }
}

public class UsingStaticMethods {
    void method() {
        AClass object = new AClass();
```

```
        object.getIt(); // Works, but reader may make assumptions
        AClass.getIt(); // Better! getIt is clearly static
    }
}
```

This seems like a minor issue, but we have seen it result in confusion many times.

Call static functions through class references.

COMPARING STRINGS

Another mistake some Java developers make is to compare strings incorrectly. In this example, the developer intended to compare strings but ended up comparing references by using `if (s1 == s2)`. The way the code is written now, it merely says, "If `s1` and `s2` refer to the same instance of an object. . . ."

```
public class BadStringComparison {
    int combinedLength(String s1, String s2) {
        if (s1 == s2) {
            return 2 * s1.length();
        }
        return s1.length() + s2.length();
    }
}
```

To avoid this, use the `String.equals()` function.

Use the `String.compareTo()` or `String.equals()` function to compare strings.

APPLYING CODING STANDARDS TO IMPROVE PERFORMANCE

Coding standards can be used to prevent a wide variety of errors. The rest of our Java-specific examples show ways to use coding standards to improve the performance and reliability of your application.

The *speed* of your Web application is the time between the user's submitting a URL (typically by clicking in his browser) and receiving all the appropriate data back from your server. Apart from the connection speed, the most easily controlled part of that performance comes down to the code used to generate the response. For this reason, you want your code to perform as quickly as possible. Also, by ensuring that your code executes as efficiently as possible, you can handle numerous requests from each process.

Understanding the Java Virtual Machine (JVM) is important if you want to improve the performance of your code. Too often, developers force the JVM to do extra work, which adds overhead to any program. The key to understanding how to optimize Java code is to know what the JVM is doing behind the scenes.

For example, most Java programs make some use of the `String` object. `String` is an *immutable* object, which means that it can only be created and read, never modified. You should use the `String` class when you create strings that you do not think you will want to modify as you execute the program. If you do want to modify the strings you are creating, using the `String` class is inefficient. Consider the following code:

```
public class InefficientMakeMessage {
    public String getMessage(String[] words) {
        String message = "";

        for (int i = 0; i < words.length; i++)
            message += " " + words[i];

        return message;
    }
}
```

The preceding segment of code gets a new word every time it passes through the loop. It appears that we keep expanding the message string and that the message is being appended, but these appearances are deceiving. In fact, the old `String` message object is being discarded, and new memory is allocated every time the message is expanded. The old information from the message is copied to the new memory, and then a new character is added at the end. The new memory is one word longer than the old memory.

This code is deceptive if you don't understand how += is implemented. Because the `message` variable will correctly contain the appended values, you might think that the object was modified. Instead, a new string is being created each time += is called. We are creating extra work for the virtual machine because the garbage collector must clean up whatever memory is left behind. If we travel through the loop 1,000 times, the garbage collector has to identify and delete thousands of chunks of memory (multiple extra objects are created every time we go through the loop). These extra chunks of memory create significant overhead for the program.

We can eliminate these extra objects by using the `StringBuffer` class. Understanding the difference between `String` and `StringBuffer` is important. `StringBuffer` is a *mutable* object. Because it can be modified, `StringBuffer` can truly be appended, rather than give the appearance of being appended. You use `StringBuffer` in performance-critical sections of code, such as loops.

Outstanding Memory

Before further discussing methods of optimizing memory in Java, we should clarify the issue of *outstanding memory*. In any program that can dynamically allocate memory, you should understand how that memory is being used. Outstanding memory can be grouped into three categories: memory that is no longer accessible because there are no references to it (traditional *memory leaks*), memory that is accessible but no longer needed, and memory that is accessible and necessary for the program to execute.

Because of the manner in which Java is constructed, traditional memory leaks are not possible. Whereas programs written in C and C++ need to explicitly release memory after they are done with it, Java cleanup is handled by the garbage collector, which automatically recovers all memory that is not accessible.

Java developers who are confounded by programs that continuously increase their memory usage (so-called memory leaks in Java) are probably referring to the fact that if they have memory to which references exist, the garbage collector cannot get rid of the memory. No term is consistently used to define memory that is accessible but no longer necessary. For our purposes, we refer to this as *leftover memory*.

This problem occurs when variables in the program still refer to chunks of memory after they are done using it. They are essentially forgotten references. Typically, the developer isn't even aware that any references to the memory still exist, because in their mental model of the code, the task for which the memory was allocated is complete. The severity of the problem depends on how long the references stay in memory.

You should define `message` as a `StringBuffer` instead of a `String` when you expect to modify the value. Then you can use the method `append()` to modify the memory without creating new objects each time through the loop. In this case, you merely expand the existing memory without leaving behind a mess for the garbage collector. (Of course, the details are more complicated – `StringBuffers` might occasionally have to create new storage if the objects grow beyond their capacity.)

In the following example, we use `StringBuffer` to modify the string inside the loop:

```
public class MakeMessage {
    public String getMessage(String[] words) {
        StringBuffer message = new StringBuffer();

        for (int i = 0; i < words.length; i++) {
            message.append(' ');
            message.append(words[i]);
        }
```

```
        return message.toString();
    }
}
```

Here the append() method is used to add to the buffer. Every time we travel through the loop, we are extending the memory as we are growing the buffer. This way, we do not force the garbage collector to work harder. When we test the preceding two methods with arrays of 1,000 words, the first implementation creates 4,997 objects (on our configuration), and the second creates only 14 objects.

Performance-critical situations such as loops call for StringBuffer.

Use StringBuffer instead of String for nonconstant strings.

APPLYING CODING STANDARDS TO USE MEMORY EFFECTIVELY

If your Java components are using lots of memory, your computer will begin to overload. As more users work your application, you must make sure that you do not exceed your computer's capacity. This is even more critical with components that are, generally, started and then run for a very long time without being restarted Even a very gradual increase in utilized resources can eventually prove fatal (and difficult to debug). The previous example shows how creating many small objects negatively affects performance. The issue here is to avoid holding on to too much memory and get rid of chunks of memory that are no longer needed.

In the following example, we call the function makeSplashImage(). Assume that it creates a large set of objects and returns a reference that holds these objects in memory. Next, we send the memory reference (big_splash_image) to the displayMomentarily() function, which uses the memory to display an image. After the image is displayed, the memory is no longer needed in the program:

```
public class GUI {
    public static void main(String[] args) {
        Graphics big_splash_image = makeSplashImage();
        displayMomentarily(big_splash_image);

        while (moreUserInput())
            process();
    }
}
```

However, the reference big_splash_image has not been nulled, so the Java garbage collector cannot get rid of this memory until the function main() finishes.

This leftover memory will be unavailable to anything running inside the `process()` method. If you want to avoid leaving unwanted references in your Java programs, you must null these references as soon as you no longer need them. The change is simple:

```
public class GUI {
    public static void main(String[] args) {
        Graphics big_splash_image = makeSplashImage();
        displayMomentarily(big_splash_image);
        big_splash_image = null;
        while (moreUserInput())
            process();
    }
}
```

As another example, a Java servlet might create a new thread to manage connections to your database. In this case, you would likely have startup code, which might hold references to memory after it was done using it. If this thread object held on to the memory anyway, you would never be able to reuse that memory in the application.

Memory issues are common when temporary variables are used in Java. When you forget to assign your temporary variables to `null`, you end up with leftover memory, which adversely affects performance. This situation can occur in loops that are using large amounts of memory. Leftover memory problems are magnified when you use member variables for temporary results, because, at the latest, local variables are cleared automatically when the function returns.

As soon as they are no longer needed, nullify any temporary references to objects taking large amounts of memory.

APPLYING CODING STANDARDS TO HANDLE EXTERNAL RESOURCES

Java components frequently act as bridges to external resources, such as open files, database connections, sockets, and so forth. Your chances of leaking external resources (or *any* resource) tend to increase as the number of users and the execution time increase. Say that you are caching database connections that expire after 30 minutes. If you happen to be leaking open connections, the connections will pile up. If you don't have many users, the connections will eventually be closed by the timeout, so you will never know that a problem occurred. However, when you get a larger number of users, you will suddenly start running out of connections, even though you thought that you were managing the resource appropriately. If your application keeps temporary files open until it exits, normal testing – which can last a few minutes or run overnight – won't show any problems. If you run for a month, though, you can end up with enough temporary files to overflow your file system, and then your application will crash. This problem can be prevented with coding standards.

When you program in Java, you need to be aware that many layers of code are working underneath you. Although you are dealing mainly with a high-level language performing complex functions, the layers of code underneath that language are performing a host of other functions. These layers behave differently, depending on what you do to the code at the upper level.

The lower layers of your code are vital to the proper functioning of your application. They are the behind-the-scenes workers that make high-level functionality possible. Ignore these hidden layers, and they will most likely cause problems in your application.

One lower layer of your code you really cannot afford to ignore is your communication with external resources. If you open an external resource, you must close it as soon as you finish using it. The following coding example deals specifically with file inputs, which are just one type of external resource. However, the lesson from this example applies to all interactions with any external resources. This code looks as though it makes a clean exit:

```
public class ReadFile {
    public String read(String path)
        throws IOException
    {
        FileInputStream file = new FileInputStream(path);
        String contents = readFile(file);
        file.close();
        return contents;
    }
    ...
}
```

Again, this code is deceptive: It seems to run well but does not actually guarantee that the `close()` method will be invoked. If any errors cause exceptions before the call to `close()`, control will be transferred to a different part of the program. In the example, if the method `readFile()` throws an exception, control is transferred out of the method `read()`, and the file is not closed. Luckily, the standard IO classes attempt to close resources when they are garbage-collected, so you might get away with code like this. However, your code will be more reliable if you do not rely on classes to clean up after themselves – not only do you not know whether the resource is actually closed, but also the JVM specification does not require that the cleanup methods will even be called.

Any time there are exceptions that might affect external resource usage, you should stop to consider whether your resources are being properly released. If you

Using Lint

Programmers who cut their teeth on Unix and C might be familiar with the *lint* tool. Lint was a program that analyzed C code for a variety of portability and standard violations, many of which were quite serious. Because early C compilers didn't do a whole lot of checking and the language allowed all sorts of erroneous statements, this was a useful tool. Many detractors disliked the typically voluminous output, however, which often required sifting through hundreds of errors to find the "gems" indicating real problems. You could exert some control over the errors by adding comments to your code with special tags that the lint tool recognized.

For more information on lint, refer to *Checking C Programs with Lint* by Ian F. Darwin.

merely handle the exception, you face the strong possibility of a resource leak. In other words, you will run out of resources at some point, which means that you will not be able to open files or sockets and will not have access to the database. To put it another way, you have a finite amount of resources. Leaking resources strains these limited capabilities, causing your program to think that your resources are still in use when, in fact, they are not.

If your code throws exceptions when you use external resources, write a `finally` block. The `finally` block is always executed, regardless of whether you exit your code through exceptions or normal execution. When you use the `finally` block, you are guaranteed that your code will clean up after you by closing all your external resources.

The following code is an example of how to clean up in the `finally` block rather than in the original code:

```
public class ReadFile {
    public String read(String path)
        throws IOException
    {
         FileInputStream file = null;
         try {
            return readFile(file);
        } finally {
            if (file != null)
                file.close();
        }
    }
    ...
}
```

Now, we will be able to close the external resources and exit the method safely. We will also be able to open the external resources next time we need to use them. Using the `finally` block guarantees that we will not leak resources here.

When you are dealing with external resources, write a `finally` block to clean up.

Creating a sample C++ coding standard

C++ has its own peculiarities, including the requirement that developers manage their memory usage explicitly. This is one of the ugliest sources of failure in C++ programs. Luckily, you can address this issue to some degree with coding standards. The chief rule in managing memory is to know which object owns each piece of memory and to make sure that it accepts responsibility for cleaning up that memory.

Here is one example of C++ code that could be improved with coding standards:

```
class SomeObject {
private:
    char *cptr;
public:
    SomeObject(char *x) {
        cptr = strdup(x);    // ignore null case for this example
    }
    virtual ~SomeObject( ) {
        free(cptr);
    }
};
```

The developer has written a class containing a pointer member but has not defined a copy constructor. The compiler will copy the class using a default copy constructor, and the pointer will be copied to a new class. The outcome will be correct only if the developer did not intend to create a new memory location. Failing to define a copy constructor is a very complicated logical error, and the best way to expose this kind of error is to enforce coding standards. Coding standards remind you to write a copy constructor in cases like these.

As suggested earlier, the best way to write leak-free C++ code is to maintain a consistent idea of ownership. In this case, because `SomeObject` creates the memory and frees the memory in its destructor, the intent that `SomeObject` owns the memory is clear. Therefore, two different instances of `SomeObject` should not point to the same address, because two different objects cannot own the same memory. Thinking about things in this way is useful when writing or reviewing code that relies on pointers.

If you work with C++, we highly recommend Scott Meyers' books *Effective C++* and *More Effective C++*. These books cover a wide variety of techniques for solving common C++ problems. Many of these techniques can form a basis for coding standards.

Establishing Custom Coding Standards

In addition to enforcing industry-standard coding standards for each language, you can also create and enforce custom coding standards that prevent problems unique to your coding style, your team, or a certain project. For example, if you find that when you write Java or JavaScript code, you repeatedly use an inefficient or error-prone construct, you could create and enforce a coding standard to identify (and help you avoid) that construct, even if it's perfectly legal from the language's point of view. You can also use custom coding standards to establish a standard way of naming classes. For example, you could write a custom coding standard that says, "Begin instance field names with a signature based on their type," like the sometimes popular Hungarian Notation used by Microsoft (`msdn.microsoft.com/library/techart/hunganotat.htm`).

In the section "Enforcing Coding Standards on the Online Grocer Application," we provide a step-by-step example of how to create two simple custom coding standards: a Java naming convention and an HTML coding rule.

Working Out the Logistics of Coding Standard Enforcement

The best way to enforce coding standards is to use a technology that does so automatically. You can enforce coding standards during code reviews, but automatic enforcement is much more thorough and less time-consuming than manual enforcement. Automatic enforcement therefore increases the likelihood that you will introduce fewer bugs into your code from the beginning of a project. It also allows your code reviews to focus on more interesting tasks that cannot be automated.

The purpose of code reviews is to exchange ideas about how the code is written and to establish a standard group interpretation of the code. The most effective code reviews focus on tasks that cannot be automated. During these reviews, developers should be given the opportunity to explain their code to one another. Often, simply explaining the code exposes problems that could later lead to errors. When the group members discuss the code, their discussion should focus on important issues such as algorithms, object-oriented programming, and class design.

However, many code reviews do not do this; often, code reviews are dry, boring, and mechanical. That's why many developers hate them. For code reviews to be effective, they have to be fun and create ideas. Very often, code reviews deteriorate to focusing on enforcing coding standards. When this occurs, groups usually decide that code reviews are not valuable, drop code reviews from their development process, and lose the potential benefits that can stem from a correctly implemented code review.

If you decide to implement standards automatically, you must select or develop a technology that helps you do so. The best technology for the task enforces widely recognized coding standards (including complex ones) and groups these standards according to the severity of their violations. The technology should also be configurable and customizable. It's helpful if you can suppress the reporting of individual coding standards or groups of standards that do not apply to the current project. Also, aim for a technology that provides a way to design and implement additional standards that you or your team considers important in reducing the opportunity for introducing errors into a project.

Although we recommend automatically enforcing code standards as appropriate, we're not so foolish as to believe that all coding standards can be easily automated. In addition, many companies' standards documents include *guidelines*: general recommendations that are not as strict as rules. If your set of coding standards includes rules or guidelines that you cannot automate, you should try to keep these rules or guidelines in mind during pair programming or code reviews.

After you select an enforcement method, you can start implementing and enforcing coding standards. One way to implement coding standards is to divide standards into several groups, based on the severity of the violations, and then implement each group incrementally, starting with the group whose violations are most severe. Deciding which errors fall into which category requires a rule-by-rule analysis relative to your project. The following three examples illustrate coding standards of varying severity.

Standards in the severe category

The *severe* category includes standards whose violations have the most severe repercussions for the application. Enforcing these standards is critical, and any violations of these standards must be corrected before code can be checked into the code repository.

One example of a Java coding standard that falls into this category is "Reuse `DataSources` for JDBC connections." This standard identifies code that does not, but should, reuse `DataSource` objects for JDBC connections. A `javax.sql.DataSource` is obtained from WebSphere Application Server through a Java Naming and Directory Interface (JNDI) lookup; this operation has a high overhead. If you acquire a `javax.sql.DataSource` for each SQL access, you severely detract from the performance and scalability of the application.

Standards in the moderate category

The *moderate* category includes standards whose violations have a moderate effect on the application. One standard that belongs in this category is "Release `HttpSession` variables when finished." `HttpSession` objects live inside the WebSphere servlet engine until one of the following occurs:

- The application explicitly and programmatically releases it using the `HttpSession.invalidate()` method.
- WebSphere Application Server destroys the allocated `HttpSession` when it expires (by default, after 30 minutes).

WebSphere Application Server can maintain only a certain number of `HttpSessions` in memory. When this limit is reached, it serializes and swaps the allocated `HttpSession` to disk. In a high-volume system, the cost of serializing many abandoned `HttpSessions` can be quite high.

In this case, we have classified the error as only moderate because we expect that the timeouts will handle our current traffic requirements. If we expected that the timeouts were not capable of keeping our site functional, this would need to be upgraded to the severe category.

Standards in the informational category

The *informational* category of standards violations includes standards whose violations do not have an immediate effect on the application. Frequently, these are minor issues that depend on your local organization. For example, naming standards are often included in this category.

Enforcing Coding Standards on the Online Grocer Application

Now we're going to demonstrate how we use Jtest and WebKing (both introduced in Chapter 4) to enforce coding standards on the Online Grocer application's servlet, static pages, and dynamic pages.

Jtest, WebKing, and the code for the Online Grocer application are located on the CD.

Enforcing Java coding standards on the Online Grocer servlet

First, you will see how we use Jtest to enforce Java coding standards automatically on one of the Online Grocer class files. Jtest automatically enforces coding standards, as well as automating unit-level white box, black box, and regression testing.

In Chapter 9, we describe how to use Jtest to perform unit testing, including white box (construction) testing, black box (functionality) testing, and regression testing.

During static analysis, Jtest automatically enforces more than 250 coding standards, including many covered in this chapter. This enables you to enforce coding standards without consuming valuable code review time. Jtest statically analyzes each class by parsing the `.java` source and applying a comprehensive set of Java coding standards to it. After analysis is complete, Jtest alerts you to any coding standard violations.

Jtest divides its coding standards into descriptive categories, including

- Object-oriented programming
- Unused code
- Initialization
- Naming conventions
- Javadoc comments
- Portability
- Optimization
- Garbage collection
- Threads and synchronization
- Enterprise JavaBeans
- Class metrics
- Project metrics
- Design by Contract
- Internationalization
- Security
- Servlets

USING JTEST TO ENFORCE JAVA STANDARDS

To start the automatic coding standard enforcement, we configure Jtest to enforce all the coding standards it contains, indicate the file we want it to analyze (here, the `ShoppingServlet` class), and then click the Start button.

For this example, we enabled all of Jtest's rules, using the procedure described in the "Customizing Jtest's Coding Standard Enforcement Feature" section. However, this is a matter of preference, not a necessary step. As a result, we received a number of violation messages that did not apply to our current situation.

As Figure 8-2 shows, Jtest finds a number of coding standard violations in the sample class.

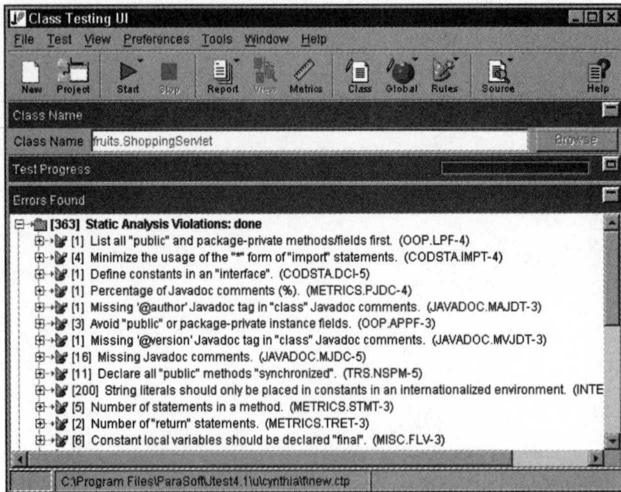

Figure 8-2: Coding standard violations found by Jtest.

To give you an example of how to work with Jtest's static analysis results, we will take a look at the violation of the coding standard "Reserve 'StringBuffer' capacity." Figure 8-3 shows the details Jtest provides for this violation after we expand the node that lists the violation. This detail contains the line where the violation occurs.

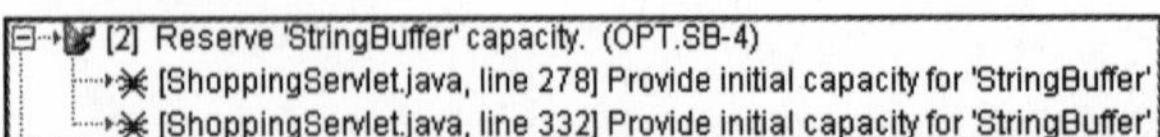

Figure 8-3: A violation of the "Reserve 'StringBuffer' capacity" coding standard.

If we double-click the node with the line number, Jtest opens a Source Viewer that highlights the code responsible for the violation. Figure 8-4 shows this Source Viewer.

This information reveals that the code does not specify the initial size of `StringBuffer`. As a result, this code could lead to performance problems. `StringBuffer` allocates only a 16-character buffer by default. If that capacity is exceeded, the `StringBuffer` class allocates a longer array and copies the contents to the new array. If we specify the initial size, all those allocations, copies, and garbage collections are avoided, and the code is optimized.

To specify the initial size, we simply replace the line

```
StringBuffer choices = new StringBuffer();
```

with

```
StringBuffer choices = new StringBuffer(128);
```

If this servlet is used again and again in the application, this optimization can have a significant effect on overall application performance.

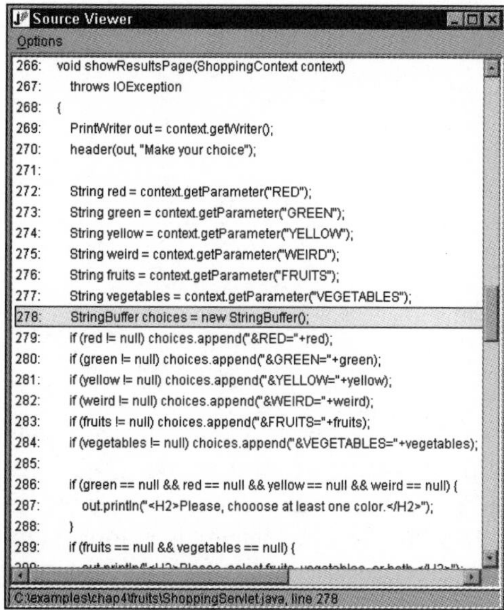

Figure 8-4: The violating code.

To invoke an editor from Jtest, right-click the result node that contains the line number where the violation occurs. Then choose Edit Source from the shortcut menu. Jtest opens the file in the editor specified in the Jtest preferences.

CUSTOMIZING JTEST'S CODING STANDARD ENFORCEMENT FEATURE

If you want to check for only the most critical coding standards or disable certain categories of coding standards, you can easily do so by changing the options in Jtest's test parameters. For example, if you do not develop EJBs and do not want to enforce coding standards related to EJBs, you simply disable the EJB coding standard category, as shown in Figure 8-5.

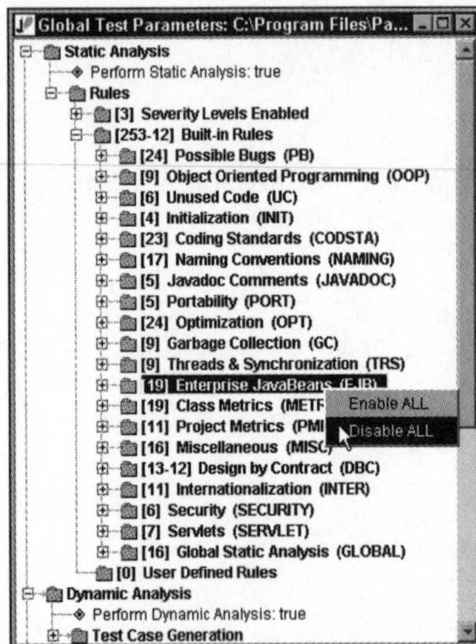

Figure 8-5: Disabling all rules of a certain descriptive category.

Alternatively, say that Jtest finds many coding standard violations in your code and you cannot possibly fix them all at once. Configure Jtest so that it enforces only the most critical coding standards by disabling rule severity categories, as shown in Figure 8-6. Then, as you clean up your code, incrementally enforce more and more categories of coding standards.

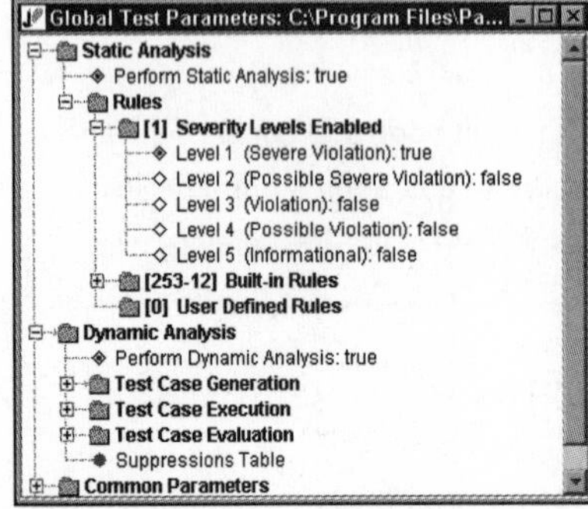

Figure 8-6: Disabling all but the most critical coding standards.

What Is RuleWizard?

RuleWizard is a graphical user interface for expressing patterns you want to detect in code or structured data. RuleWizard is included in the WebKing, Jtest, SOAPtest, and DataRecon tools available on the CD. It is also available in equivalent ParaSoft C/C++ development tools.

In RuleWizard, a *rule* is a graphical representation of a pattern you do not (or do) want to appear in your code. Rules are generally composed of the following elements:

- **Nodes:** The basic building blocks of rules. Nodes can be tags, elements, expressions, variables, constants, functions, or even statements. The nodes available for rule construction depend on the language for which you are building a rule and are displayed in a dictionary node tab on the left of the GUI.
- **Node Properties:** Programming elements or concepts about the node, and/or conditions between nodes. Right-clicking a node in the Rules/Results panel opens a shortcut menu that displays the commands available for that particular node.
- **Output:** The message that is reported each time the pattern in the given rule is detected. A rule's output is represented in the Rules/Results panel with a short arrow pointing down.
- **Rule Properties:** The properties of the rule, including the author and category.

A basic rule consists of only a parent node, output, and properties. More complex rules consist of a parent node, nodes with commands or sets of conditions between those nodes, output, and properties.

Each rule is expressed in terms of a "dictionary" that represents information about the type of data to be processed. The dictionary is an XML file that describes the nodes and node properties available for that type of data. The type of data is typically a programming language. Standard dictionaries are available for HTML, JavaScript, XML, CSS, Java, and so on. In addition, RuleWizard provides a mechanism for creating a dictionary that is specific to a particular XML-based language (such as WML, XHTML, or XSLT) or a custom dictionary based on selected XML files.

RuleWizard provides two main methods for writing and customizing rules:

- A unique point-and-click method in which you create a graphical representation describing the pattern you want the rule to identify
- The Auto-Create method in which RuleWizard creates a rule that checks for the pattern represented in a snippet of code you provide

CREATING AND ENFORCING CUSTOM CODING STANDARDS IN JTEST

You can also use Jtest's RuleWizard feature to create and enforce coding standards that identify problems unique to your coding style, your team, or a certain project. To give you an idea of how RuleWizard works, we will walk you through an example of how to create the following Java naming convention: "Begin the name of instance fields with a lowercase letter."

The first step in constructing a rule is to open RuleWizard. To open the version of RuleWizard found in Jtest, right-click the Rules toolbar button, and choose Launch RuleWizard from the shortcut menu.

Whenever you create a rule using the point-and-click method, the first thing you do is right-click the node that you want to be your rule's main subject. Then you choose Create Rule from the shortcut menu. To start composing this rule, open Declarations→Variables, right-click the `Field` node, and choose Create Rule from the shortcut menu.

After you choose Create Rule, you see the `Field` parent rule node in the right pane of the GUI, as shown in Figure 8-7. You now have the basic building block for a rule about fields.

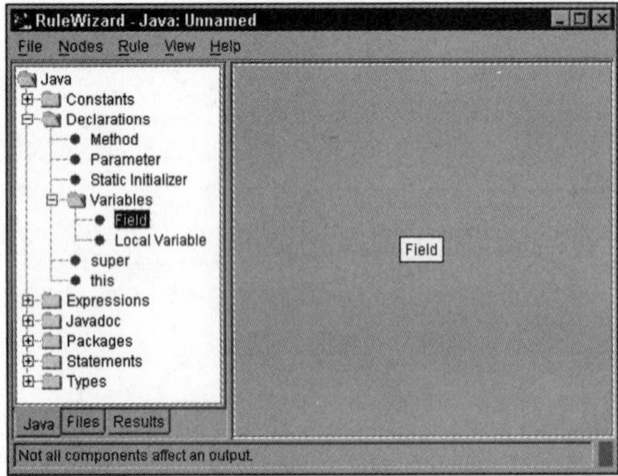

Figure 8-7: The first step in creating your naming convention rule.

To specify that you want this rule to check instance (nonstatic) fields, first add the IsStatic property by right-clicking the `Field` rule node and choosing IsStatic from the shortcut menu that opens. This says to check whether the field is static, but you want to check nonstatic fields. You can modify this rule to identify nonstatic fields by right-clicking the `IsStatic` node and choosing Toggle. This changes the rule condition to mean "if an instance variable is present."

Next, you specify that this rule will be about naming conventions by right-clicking the `Field` rule node and choosing Name from the shortcut menu. A `Name` rule node with the content `none` is now attached to your parent rule node, as shown in Figure 8-8.

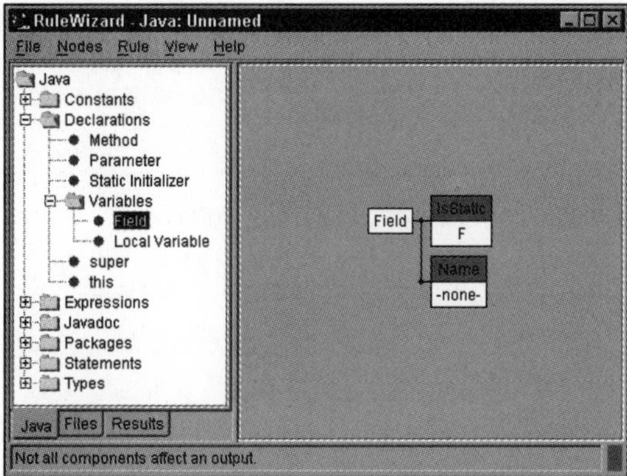

Figure 8-8: The evolving naming convention rule.

To continue developing the rule, right-click the `Name` rule node and choose Modify from the shortcut menu. The Modify String window opens. In this window's Regexp field, specify the value Jtest should look for in the name of the instance variable. In this example, you want the Name value to begin with a lowercase letter. Thus, you enter the regular expression `^[a-z]` in the Regexp field and check the Negate check box. The ^ indicates the beginning of an expression, and the `[a-z]` matches any lowercase letter. After you type this value and check the Negate check box, click OK.

Finally, you specify the text Jtest should print when this pattern is detected. The first step in doing this is to right-click the parent rule node (here, the `Field` rule node) and choose Create Output from the shortcut menu. This action invokes the Customize Output window, where you enter the message you want Jtest to deliver when this rule is violated. In this example, you could enter **`Invalid field name: $name`**. When this message is reported by Jtest, `$name` will be replaced by the actual name of the field.

After you click OK, your rule resembles the rule shown in Figure 8-9.

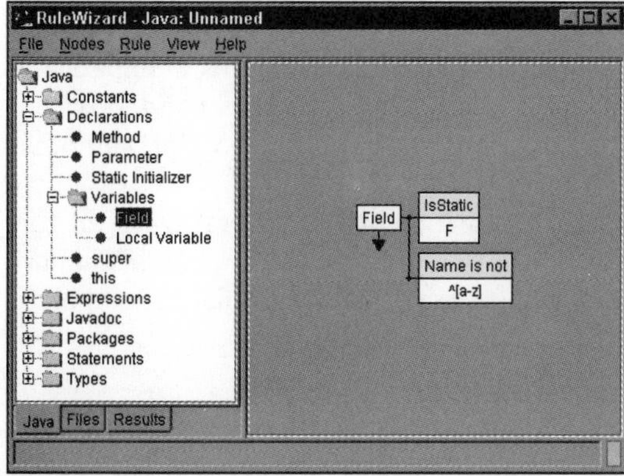

Figure 8-9: The final naming convention rule.

This rule tells Jtest to report the specified error message when an instance variable's name does not begin with a lowercase letter. The rule is now complete. After you customize this rule's properties and save it, Jtest enforces it automatically.

For complete instructions on using Jtest's version of RuleWizard, see the RuleWizard User's Guide. To access this, choose Help→View in the RuleWizard GUI.

Enforcing Web coding standards on the Online Grocer pages

HTML, CSS, and JavaScript coding standards are just as easy to enforce as Java coding standards. However, when your Web application is dynamic, you can't enforce coding standards on your dynamic pages until you are able to exercise at least part of your application on a browser.

For now, we describe the steps we use to enforce HTML and CSS coding standards on the Online Grocer application that we have already deployed.

If you want to follow along on your own system or apply this procedure to your own application, you must be able to exercise some of the application on a browser and create what we call a *client-side project file*. If you decided to follow our recommendation in the "Creating an Infrastructure for Testing Early and Often" sidebar in Chapter 6, whatever part of the application you are working on is already effectively deployed. You can also deploy an application using the instructions given in Chapter 10 or in any other manner that works for you and your team. Chapter 11 provides the instructions for creating a client-side project file.

In this example, we demonstrate how to check coding standards automatically with WebKing's CodeWizard tool. This tool is a coding standards validation tool that applies more than 200 coding standards for CSS, HTML, JavaScript, and other Web-related languages.

Like most WebKing tools, CodeWizard can be applied in several ways. In this section, we discuss how to apply it to files in the Project tree. You can also apply CodeWizard to different paths through the application or have virtual users apply it as they perform load testing.

For information on applying tools to paths and having virtual users apply tools, see Chapter 13.

USING WEBKING TO ENFORCE WEB CODING STANDARDS

After we create a client-side project and load the first few pages of our deployed application into WebKing (we load only a few pages to keep the examples as simple as possible), the WebKing Project tree contains nodes representing the loaded resources. To enforce HTML, CSS, and JavaScript coding standards on these files, we select the root Project tree node and click the CodeWizard button.

To enforce coding standards on a single page, locate and select the node representing that page in WebKing's Project tree. Then click the CodeWizard button.

CodeWizard detects the violations shown in Figure 8-10.

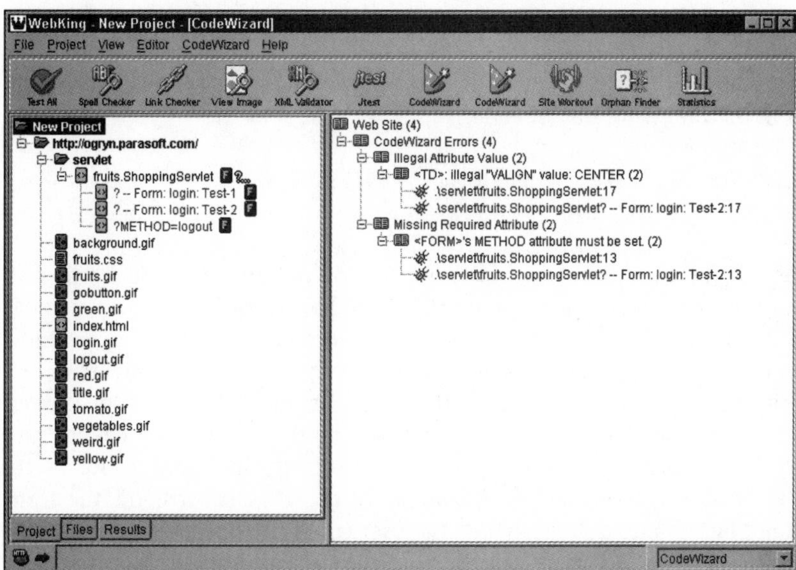

Figure 8-10: CodeWizard results from the Online Grocer's pages.

If you want to change the format in which results are listed, right-click the right panel of the WebKing GUI, and choose View → <your preferred option> from the shortcut menu. For a description of available options, see the WebKing User's Guide.

These results reveal two main problems:

- An illegal `VALIGN` value (`CENTER`)
- A `FORM` without a `METHOD` attribute

To view the source code responsible for a violation, you right-click the node containing the line number where the violation occurred, and choose Edit from the shortcut menu. WebKing then opens the file in the text editor you selected (or in its default text editor if you have not yet indicated your preferred text editor).

If you are viewing results in tree format, you have to expand that violation's branch to see the line number where the violation occurs.

When we open the source code for the `VALIGN` violation, we see that this problem occurs in the following line of code:

```
<TD ALIGN=CENTER VALIGN=CENTER HEIGHT=164 WIDTH=207
    BACKGROUND="/tomato.gif">
```

This problem generally is not critical to application functionality. Most browsers simply ignore a value they do not understand, and they use the default vertical alignment. However, browsers do not have a standard way of ignoring invalid tags. Although most current desktop browsers would simply render the contents of the table cell with the illegal `VALIGN` value in the default manner, there is no guarantee that other current browsers or future browsers will do the same. If, by chance, the illegal `VALIGN` attribute prevents a browser from correctly interpreting the `INPUT TYPE` tags embedded within the `TD` tag containing the `VALIGN` attribute, the form data might not be submitted properly and the user could have problems logging in. It is unlikely that this would occur (at least, with the current group of browsers), but when you work with unsupported tags, elements, attributes, and so on, you can never predict what will happen. Why take chances? If you identify and fix all your nonstandard HTML, CSS, and JavaScript code, you can rest assured that the pages that reach your users will work correctly on almost any current and future browser.

The second violation found (the FORM missing a METHOD) is more likely than the first to lead to problems. If a FORM does not have a METHOD attribute, users on certain browsers might not be able to submit it properly. In our case, the browser defaults to using the GET method, which is the general behavior of most browsers. This means that the username and password entered are tacked on to the URL and sent as plain text. As a result, anyone who has access to that URL can easily see the user's username and password because this information is stored in the server's access log and in the user's browser's history and even displayed in the browser window as the current URL. To fix this important security breach, we add METHOD=POST to the code generated by the servlet. (Note that this is only partial security because we aren't using HTTPS. Nevertheless, it's much better than allowing the arguments to be sent as part of the URL.)

You might decide that you never want to use METHOD=GET on your application, because of the security implications. If so, you can implement this rule as a custom coding standard and check it automatically.

CUSTOMIZING WEBKING'S CODING STANDARD ENFORCEMENT FEATURE

By default, WebKing enforces a select set of its available coding standards. If you want to disable some of the rules enforced by default, enable some of the rules that are not enforced by default, or add custom coding standards to the default CodeWizard Enforcer, perform the following steps:

1. Right-click the CodeWizard button, and choose Configure CodeWizard from the shortcut menu. The CodeWizard panel opens, as shown in Figure 8-11. Each loaded rule set, rule category or header, and rule will be represented in a tree structure. You can determine whether rules are listed by header or by category with the Sort by: Headers or Categories option.
2. (Optional) To enforce a rule that is not loaded (for example, to add a custom coding standard to the main CodeWizard tool rather than create a separate CodeWizard Enforcer for it), click Add Rule. Then use the file chooser to specify the rule you want to add.
3. Check the Rules tree check boxes of all rule sets, rule headers or categories, and individual rules you want CodeWizard to enforce. Clear the check boxes of those you do not want to enforce.
4. Save your modified configuration by clicking Save Rule Set.

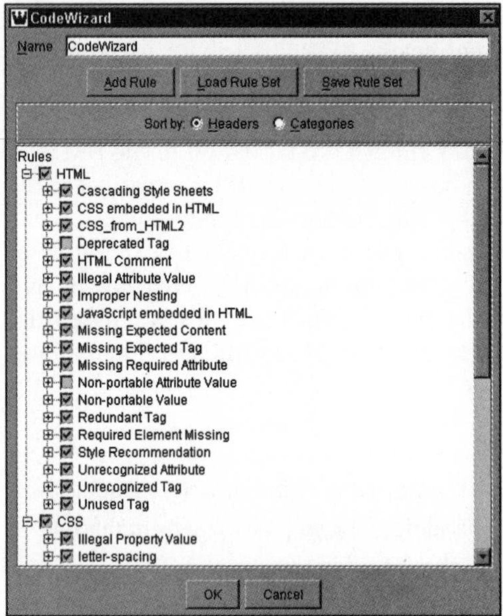

Figure 8-11: Customizing which rules WebKing enforces.

CREATING AND ENFORCING CUSTOM CODING STANDARDS IN WEBKING

Like Jtest, WebKing includes RuleWizard so that you can create and enforce custom coding standards, or "rules." To give you an idea of how this feature can be applied to HTML coding rules, we will demonstrate how to create the custom coding standard "Never use `FONT`." Although `FONT` is a perfectly legal tag, we do not want it used on our application because we plan to control all of our font presentation issues with a central CSS file. Also, if you are planning on transitioning to strict XHTML, you will eventually have to remove your `FONT` tags anyway because they are not allowed in strict XHTML.

To create the this simple rule using RuleWizard's Auto-Create feature, you do the following:

1. Open RuleWizard's HTML dictionary by choosing CodeWizard → Show Dictionary → HTML.
2. Open the Auto-Create dialog box by right-clicking the unused area of the HTML dictionary (on the left side of the GUI) and choosing Auto-Create Rules from the shortcut menu.
3. Enter `<FONT>` in the Auto-Create dialog box. From this tag, RuleWizard creates the rule shown in Figure 8-12.

   As is, this rule says to report an error if the `FONT` tag occurs – exactly what you want to check for.

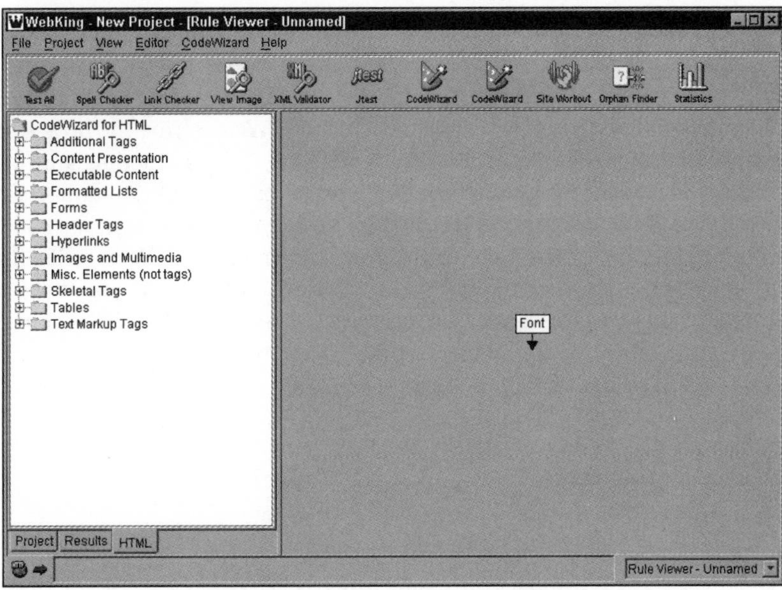

Figure 8-12: A rule that identifies any use of the FONT tag.

4. Customize the output message by right-clicking the output arrow, choosing Modify from the shortcut menu, and entering your message in the dialog box that opens.
5. Save the rule in any directory you choose.
6. Add this rule to the standard CodeWizard tool as described in the section "Customizing WebKing's Coding Standard Enforcement Feature."

You can also create a wide variety of CSS and JavaScript coding rules, as well as HTML-based rules that check page contents, in this same manner. In Chapter 12, we discuss in detail rules that check page contents. Note that you don't have to use WebKing to write rules for your application. We have examples that use Python, but you can also write them in any language that lets you analyze your target language (HTML, CSS, and so on).

The rules developed in this chapter are available on the CD.

Summary

In this chapter, we explain why error prevention is an effective way to improve application quality and reduce development time. We describe the how and why of applying coding standards to C++, Java, HTML, CSS, JavaScript, and other languages. We also offer practical tips on integrating coding standard enforcement into your development process. Finally, we show you how to enforce coding standards on the Online Grocer application's servlets and pages. We describe the significance of several errors found and explain ways to fix the problematic code.

The next chapter covers unit testing, which is another effective way to improve application quality and reduce development time.

Chapter 9

Performing Unit Testing

IN THIS CHAPTER

- Defining unit testing
- Understanding the benefits of unit testing
- Performing unit testing – an overview
- Performing unit testing on the Online Grocer's servlets
- Integrating unit testing into your development process

IN CHAPTER 8, you learned how the software industry can benefit by adopting the automobile industry's error-prevention focus. In this chapter, we discuss another automobile industry practice that can benefit the software industry: unit testing.

In software, unit testing involves testing each of the application's units independently as soon as they are built. The units tested are the smallest possible units. In Web applications, a *unit* can be a class from a servlet or an EJB, a function from a CGI, or a single page created by the interaction of a servlet and related classes.

For an example of why unit testing is such a valuable practice, take another brief look at the automobile industry. Decades ago, the manufacturers did not test the parts of the car until after the entire car was assembled. When the car was drivable, they took it to a rally and drove it tens of thousands of miles. After the race was over, they disassembled the car and examined how each unit (such as the shocks, the brakes, and so forth) performed, and they tried to determine ways to improve each unit. This method of testing was expensive and time-consuming.

Now the automobile industry has adopted an improved testing process. The manufacturers test each unit on its own before integrating it into the car. For example, if they want to test a shock, they build a machine that directly stresses the shock. After the machine exercises the shock for a few days, they examine how the shock performed. This practice ensures before assembly that each part works properly and is well constructed. After the car is assembled, it's run in rallies to test how the parts work together and to measure the car's overall performance. By following this procedure, the manufacturer produces higher quality cars faster and cheaper. In other words, through the practice of unit testing, the quality and efficiency of the production process is improved.

Again, the software industry lags behind the automobile industry. Unit testing is not commonly part of most software development processes and is rarely a part of most Web development processes. This is a shame. Web applications tend to contain more complex and disparate units than traditional software applications, so performing unit testing on Web applications is more difficult and also more critical than on traditional applications.

Throughout this chapter, we discuss efficient ways to perform unit testing on Web applications. We begin by defining unit testing and explaining how and why to perform unit testing on the classes that make up programs such as servlets, EJBs, CGIs, and the like. In the last part of the chapter, we demonstrate how we applied several unit-testing strategies to perform unit testing on classes we developed for the Online Grocer application. We use Java examples throughout this chapter, but you can apply the practices described here to units developed in any language.

Defining Unit Testing

Many developers think that unit testing means module testing. In other words, developers think that they are performing unit testing when they take a *module* – a subprogram that is part of a larger application – and test it. As we explain in Chapter 15, module testing is important and should certainly be performed. However, it is not the same as unit testing.

Unit testing means testing the smallest possible unit of an application. In Java development, unit testing involves testing a class as soon as it is compiled. This is the process we cover in this chapter. In Web development, unit testing also involves testing a single page as soon as it can be viewed and exercised. We call the process of testing a Web application by deploying it and then testing the pages it produces *Web box testing*. Chapters 10 through 14 explain the additional steps involved in Web box testing.

Understanding the Benefits of Unit Testing

Unit testing dramatically improves software quality by helping you detect errors at the stage where it is easiest and most cost-effective to find and fix errors. Because unit testing brings you much closer to the errors, it helps you detect errors that application-level testing does not always find. Take a closer look at Figures 9-1 and 9-2 (which you saw in Chapter 1) to see how unit testing does this.

Figure 9-1 shows a model of testing an application containing many units. The application is represented by the large oval, and the units it contains are represented by the smaller ovals. External arrows indicate inputs. Starred regions show potential errors.

To find errors in this model, you modify inputs so that interactions between units force some units to hit the potential errors. This is incredibly difficult. Imagine standing at a pool table, with a set of billiard balls in a triangle at the middle of the table, and having to use a cue ball to move the triangle's center ball into a particular pocket – with one stroke. This is how difficult it can be to design an input that finds an error within an application. As a result, if you rely only on application testing, you might never reach many of your application's units, let alone uncover the errors they contain.

As Figure 9-2 illustrates, testing at the unit level offers a more effective way to find errors. When you test one unit apart from all other units, reaching potential errors is much easier because you are much closer to those errors. The difficulty of reaching the potential errors when the unit is tested independently is comparable to the difficulty of hitting one billiard ball into a particular pocket with a single stroke.

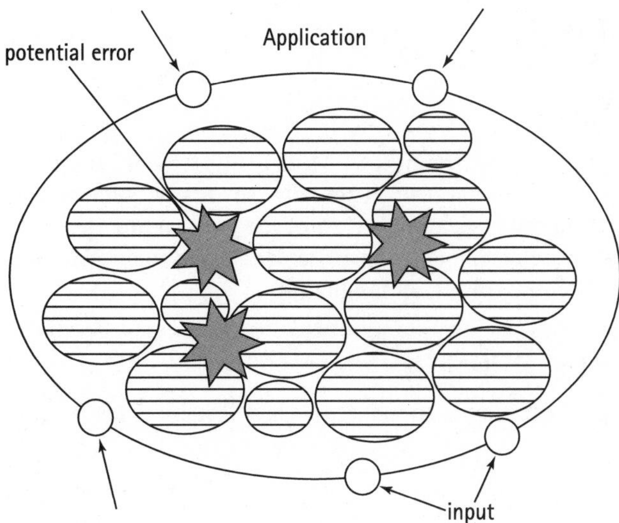

Figure 9-1: Application testing.

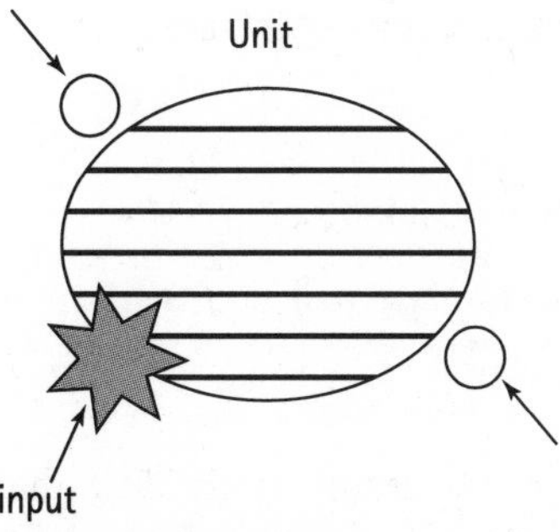

Figure 9-2: Unit testing.

Also, unit testing facilitates error detection by preventing bugs from spawning more bugs, which relieves you from having to wade through problem after problem to remedy what began as a single, simple error. As mentioned in Chapter 1, because new code builds on and interacts with existing code, if you leave a bug in your code, chances are that it will lead to additional bugs. If you delay testing until the later stages of development, you will probably have more bugs to fix, spend more time finding and fixing each bug, and change more code in order to remove each bug. If you test as you go, you can find and fix each bug more easily and minimize the chances of bugs spawning more bugs. The result: improved application reliability, as well as a significant reduction in debugging time and cost.

Performing Unit Testing – An Overview

Although it is incredibly valuable, unit testing can be difficult, tedious, and time-consuming if performed manually because it entails so many cumbersome processes. The following section provides an overview of the general processes that performing unit testing involves. Remember that we are using Java to provide concrete examples, but these concepts apply to all languages.

Creating scaffolding and stubs

The first step in performing unit testing is to make the class testable. This requires two main actions:

- Designing scaffolding that will run the class
- Designing stubs that return values for any external resources referenced by the class under test but not currently available or accessible

Creating *scaffolding* involves creating a new class or classes that are used only to test the original class. Scaffolding should include the following features:

- A standard way to specify setup and cleanup
- A method for selecting individual tests or all available tests
- A means of analyzing output for expected (or unexpected) results
- A standard form of failure reporting

Several modifications or rewrites may be required to design scaffolding that tests the class thoroughly and accurately. After the scaffolding is created, you must examine it carefully to ensure that it does not contain any errors. An error in the scaffolding can sabotage the test, but because you cannot test a class in isolation (the original problem), you cannot test the scaffolding, either.

If your class references any external resources (such as external files, databases, and CORBA objects) that are not yet available or accessible, you must create *stubs* that return values similar to those the external resource can return. When creating these stubs, you have to choose stub return values that test the class's functionality and provide thorough coverage of the class.

One advantage of the stub is that it provides a nice place for the software firewalls or DbC practices discussed in Chapter 7. For instance, we can write code to verify that `setStatus()` is passed only acceptable values. Most libraries do not provide exhaustive parameter checking, so this can be a helpful tool for making your code rock solid.

After the class is testable, you design and execute the necessary test cases. Ideally, you test the class's construction (perform white box testing), test its functionality (perform black box testing), and perform regression testing with each modification to ensure that changes did not affect the class's integrity. These three techniques are described in detail in the sections that follow.

Exposing crash-causing errors with white box testing

White box testing validates that your code has been constructed correctly. To perform white box testing, you design and execute test inputs derived from the class's internal structure to find out whether there are possible class usages that will make the class crash (in Java, this is equivalent to throwing an uncaught runtime exception), as well as coding defects that might make the code more error-prone. The success of white box testing hinges on the test inputs' capability to cover the class's methods as fully as possible and to find inputs that cause uncaught runtime exceptions.

Preventing and detecting construction problems as early as possible is particularly critical if your environment is hiding exceptions. In many languages, an illegal program operation usually results in the program's sudden termination and is therefore easily detected. Web applications often contain such errors and continue to run. For example, Java servlet engines will catch exceptions thrown by your servlet, and continue to handle new requests. Although this contributes to the application's robustness, it means that unexpected exceptions can be easily overlooked. Some developers dismiss such problems as irrelevant – if the program is still running, they reason, what's the problem? Unfortunately, these kinds of failures can contribute to hard-to-diagnose errors. The reason for this is that your program can enter an inconsistent state if you didn't plan for the possibility of the exception occurring.

By testing your units, you see these exceptions and can take the necessary precautions. All such exceptions should be caught by your scaffolding. One simple example is the `Integer.parseInt()` method. This method takes a string and returns the integer value of that string. However, if the string does not represent an integer, the method throws a `NumberFormatException`. Because this exception extends `RuntimeException`, you do not have to write special code to handle this exception. Therefore, you are likely to forget to handle the case in which the string does not represent an integer, and your code will be ill-prepared to handle this case.

White box testing is a critical step in ensuring both class and application quality, but because of the difficulty involved in performing it manually, people usually skip it or perform it less precisely than necessary. Effectively performing white box testing requires that someone determine exactly which test cases are necessary to fully exercise the class under test. This is very difficult to do manually. In our experience, typical test suites commonly exercise only 30 percent of the source code being tested; the remaining 70 percent is never executed. One reason that so little code is tested is the difficulty of writing test cases that test infrequently executed paths or extreme conditions. Achieving the scope of coverage required for effective white box testing mandates that a significant number of paths be executed. For example, in a typical 10,000-line program, there are approximately 100 million possible paths. Manually generating input that would exercise all those paths is infeasible and effectively impossible.

Exposing functionality problems with black box testing

Black box testing checks that a class behaves according to specification. As important as it is to ensure that a class is constructed strongly, it is *vital* to ensure that a class does what it is supposed to do and that all parts of the specification have been fulfilled. To perform black box testing, you create a set of input/outcome relationships that test whether the class's specifications are correctly implemented. At least one test case should be created for each entry in the specification document. Preferably, these test cases test the various boundary conditions for each entry. After the test suite is ready, you execute the test cases and verify whether the correct outcomes are generated.

Maintaining integrity with regression testing

Performing precise regression testing is another necessary step in guaranteeing software quality and reliability. *Regression testing* — testing modified code under the exact same set of inputs and test parameters used in previous test runs — is the only way to ensure that modifications did not introduce new errors into the class or to check whether modifications successfully eliminated existing errors. Every time a class is modified or used in a new environment, regression testing should be used to check the class's integrity. Ideally, you perform regression testing at least nightly to ensure that errors are detected and fixed as soon as possible.

White and Black Box Testing

The terms *white box testing* and *black box testing* refer more to the intent or thinking behind the testing than to the actual testing technique used. In each case, the term refers to your code metaphorically as a box. In white box testing, you are allowed to open the box and look inside when you create your tests. This means that you can try to find boundary conditions in the code and verify whether your tests have exercised all the paths in your code.

In black box testing, the box is painted black and sealed shut. All you can see are which inputs go into the box and which outputs come out. The idea behind this testing is to test by using the specification and the interface only.

Both ways of thinking are productive and useful and can provide insight into the different kinds of tests you need to create to exercise your code sufficiently. White box testing can also be referred to as *structural* or *construction testing*, and black box testing sometimes goes by names such as *behavioral* or *functionality testing*.

A related, but less common term, is *Web box testing*. The idea here is to include the Web server and necessary pieces into the box analogy, emphasizing that the code is being tested with extra Web infrastructure involved. In this usage, it is also implied that the testing is not happening on the actual server but in an isolated sandbox.

Performing Unit Testing on the Online Grocer's Servlets

As you can probably see by now (and will definitely see after reading the manual unit-testing example in the next section), unit testing can consume a fair amount of time, effort, and resources if performed manually. That's why it is rarely performed as often or as thoroughly as it should be. Automatic unit-testing tools such as Jtest, the Java unit-testing tool included on the CD, make unit testing practical by automating the processes involved.

In this section, we demonstrate three ways to perform unit testing, using classes from the Online Grocer application as examples. We start by describing manual unit testing. Next, we show how the JUnit testing framework can improve the manual testing process and then conclude by covering how Jtest can automate almost all of the required steps.

Performing manual unit testing

Because thorough manual testing requires a lot of detail, we cover only the simplest parts here, pointing out directions you can take to extend these ideas for your own classes.

In Chapter 6, we created a simple framework for writing servlets. The primary class in that framework is `DispatchServlet`. Here we follow through on our earlier promise to show how we can test this class. Because `DispatchServlet` is abstract, it cannot be directly instantiated for testing. This is okay because we need to add a few extra functions for testing anyway. First, we make a simple `ExampleServet`, and then we create two test harnesses that show ways to exercise the code. These establish the foundation for our manual tests:

```
public class ExampleServlet extends DispatchServlet
{
    public ExampleServlet() {
        super("hello");
    }
    public void hello(DispatchContext context) throws IOException
    {
        PrintWriter writer = context.getWriter();
        writer.println("<B>Hi!</B>");
    }
}
```

`ExampleServet` is available on the CD.

`ExampleServlet` has only one method, `hello()`, which is also the default method. Hence, any use of the `METHOD` parameter except `METHOD=hello` should cause an error. First, we test basic functionality to make sure that `hello()` works and that improper `METHOD`s are handled according to the design. Typically, the first testing pass involves testing the servlet as a ***standalone*** unit (no Web server). This requires extra supporting material to handle the role normally done by the servlet engine. This extra code is the ***scaffolding***, or ***harness***. Code to disable dependencies on the engine is a ***stub***.

The first step in building scaffolding is to create a class that contains the method `main()`, which is where any Java program begins executing. Without the method `main()`, there is no way to execute the class.

Next, we place some calls to exercise `ExampleServlet` in the `main()` method. This process is only the beginning; the class is usually more complicated than it appears. It might be necessary to set up some preconditions and postconditions that help ensure that the characteristics of the code remain the same before and after this code is executed. Preconditions and postconditions must be set by hand.

The following code is the basic code implementing the simple tests. Because the main entry point from the servlet engine is `doGet()`, this is the method where we begin testing. To call this method, we need a valid HttpServletRequest and HttpServletResponse. Because these are interfaces, we cannot create instances of them to pass (and passing null won't exercise the code properly). Hence, we need to create stubs for them, using the TestRequest and TestResponse classes, which will simulate the appropriate behavior. Here's the basic test harness:

```
public class TestHarness {
    public static void main(String[] args) {
        ExampleServlet servlet = new ExampleServlet();
        try {
            // Test 1
            TestRequest req = new TestRequest();
            TestResponse res = new TestResponse();
            servlet.doGet(req, res);
            String response = res.getResponse();
            System.out.println("Response: " + response);

            // Test 2
            req = new TestRequest() {
                public String getParameter(String name) {
                    if (name.equals("METHOD"))
                        return "undefined";
                    return null;
                }
            };
            res = new TestResponse();
            servlet.doGet(req, res);
            response = res.getResponse();
            System.out.println("Response: " + response);
        } catch (Exception e) {
            System.out.println("Tests failed");
            e.printStackTrace();
        }
    }
}
```

Next, we need to work on the TestRequest and TestResponse classes. We have to provide at least some implementation for every method in order to get the code to compile. Because our goal is to exercise ExampleServlet, we need to implement only enough functionality to reach that goal. Determining exactly what is and isn't necessary can be a tricky process. Because this example is so simple, we can get away with just implementing getMethod() and getWriter() and providing simple default return values for everything else.

If you plan on reusing stubs for all your servlets, you would want to add many more cases and throw exceptions anywhere you haven't implemented a working emulation. That way, you would be notified whenever you need to add functionality to your stubs to improve testing. These exceptions should extend `RuntimeException` so that you don't need to modify the method's signatures.

Here are the `TestRequest` and `TestResponse` classes:

```
public class TestRequest implements HttpServletRequest {
    public TestRequest() {
    }
    // Methods required by ServletRequest
    public int getContentLength() { return -1; }
    public String getContentType() { return null; }
    public String getProtocol() { return null; }
    public String getScheme() { return null; }
    public String getServerName() { return null; }
    public int getServerPort() { return 0; }
    public String getRemoteAddr() { return null; }
    public String getRemoteHost() { return null; }
    public String getRealPath(String path) { return null; }
    public ServletInputStream getInputStream() { return null; }
    public String getParameter(String name) { return null; }
    public String[] getParameterValues(String name) { return null; }
    public Enumeration getParameterNames() { return null; }
    public Object getAttribute(String name) { return null; }
    public BufferedReader getReader() { return null; }
    public String getCharacterEncoding() { return null; }
    // Methods required by HttpServletRequest
    public Cookie[] getCookies() { return null; }
    public String getMethod() { return "GET"; }
    public String getRequestURI() { return null; }
    public String getServletPath() { return null; }
    public String getPathInfo() { return null; }
    public String getPathTranslated() { return null; }
    public String getQueryString() { return null; }
    public String getRemoteUser() { return null; }
    public String getAuthType() { return null; }
    public String getHeader(String name) { return null; }
    public int getIntHeader(String name) { return -1; }
    public long getDateHeader(String name) { return 0; }
    public Enumeration getHeaderNames() { return null; }
```

```
    public HttpSession getSession(boolean create) { return null; }
    public String getRequestedSessionId() { return null; }
    public boolean isRequestedSessionIdValid() { return false; }
    public boolean isRequestedSessionIdFromCookie() { return false; }
    public boolean isRequestedSessionIdFromUrl() { return false; }
}

public class TestResponse implements HttpServletResponse {
    ByteArrayOutputStream buffer;
    PrintWriter writer;
    public TestResponse() {
        buffer = new ByteArrayOutputStream();
        writer = new PrintWriter(buffer);
    }
    // Interface for ServletResponse
    public void setContentLength(int len) { }
    public void setContentType(String type) { }
    public ServletOutputStream getOutputStream() { return null; }
    public PrintWriter getWriter() { return writer;}
    public String getCharacterEncoding() { return null;}
    // Interface for HttpServletResponse
    public void addCookie(Cookie cookie) { }
    public boolean containsHeader(String name) { return false; }
    public void setStatus(int sc, String message) {}
    public void setStatus(int sc) {}
    public void setHeader(String name, String value) {}
    public void setIntHeader(String name, int value) {}
    public void setDateHeader(String name, long date) {}
    public void sendError(int sc, String message) {}
    public void sendError(int sc) {}
    public void sendRedirect(String location) {}
    public String encodeUrl(String url) { return null; }
    public String encodeRedirectUrl(String url) { return null; }
    // Methods for testing
    public String getResponse() {
        writer.close();
        return buffer.toString();
    }
}
```

Executing `java fruits.TestHarness` produces output like the following:

```
Response: <B>Hi!</B>

Response: <P>Caught java.lang.NoSuchMethodException</P>
```

```
<PRE>
java.lang.NoSuchMethodException
	at java.lang.Class.getMethod0(Native Method)
	at java.lang.Class.getMethod(Unknown Source)
	at fruits.DispatchServlet.doInteraction(DispatchServlet.java:45)
	at fruits.DispatchServlet.doGet(DispatchServlet.java:23)
	at fruits.TestHarness.main(TestHarness.java:25)
</PRE>
```

This shows the text that the servlet would generate for these two test cases. In this case, this is the behavior we are looking for, so the code passes the tests. Naturally, you could add many other tests to make sure that you exercised all the important functionality.

If you wanted to perform regression testing, you could save this output to a file named something like `control.txt`. Whenever you wanted to verify that the code is still working, you would run the test again and compare the results to the `control.txt` file. This could be done automatically, using a tool such as `diff`, and would therefore require no human intervention unless an error is detected. It could even be integrated into your automated regular builds.

Later in this chapter, we show how to use JUnit to programmatically verify that the results are correct.

In more complicated examples, you would probably also add code to your test harness to verify that the output is matching whatever constraints are appropriate. For instance, you might want to parse the HTML and make sure that it is well formed. (The preceding examples are HTML fragments, and you would probably want to make sure that you are delivering full HTML documents, with appropriate `HTML`, `HEAD`, `BODY` tags, and so forth.) That would be equivalent to writing a full-featured testing tool! In later chapters of this section, we show you how you can use WebKing to perform this type of testing automatically after the servlet is deployed to a Web server.

Additionally, you could extend `TestRequest` and `TestResponse` to be configurable through the constructor or other additional methods. This way, you wouldn't need to extend them with inline classes, as we do in this example. Finally, you could extend `TestHarness` to read parameters from an external file so that you can accumulate a large number of test cases without continually modifying your code.

As you can see, this is quite a task, and this example is trivial. With real programs, robust, manual unit testing is a real chore. As mentioned earlier, unit testing is beneficial because it enables you to test your code much more thoroughly than you could with other testing techniques. However, if you have to perform all these steps manually, it generally is not practical to integrate unit testing into compressed Web development schedules.

The good news is that scaffolding and stubs can often be reused by many of your tests. When you start writing unit tests, you might find that you have to write a lot of support code and possibly redesign some routines or classes that did not provide a clean enough interface for your tests. Over time, it becomes easier to write unit tests because you have created enough structure to allow new tests to be added without creating a lot of extra code.

After you test your class as a unit, you might want to verify that it integrates well into the servlet engines (plays nicely with others). Here's a different test harness, which calls `ExampleServlet` via an HTTP connection.

If you do this, make sure that you've set up the class to be accessible from your Web server and that the code is using the correct URL to do so — in this case, we used `www.sample.com/ExampleServlet`.

```
public class TestHarness2 {
    public static String testURL(URL url) throws IOException
    {
        URLConnection c = url.openConnection();
        InputStream in = c.getInputStream();
        ByteArrayOutputStream out = new ByteArrayOutputStream();
        int b;
        while ((b = in.read()) != -1) {
            out.write(b);
        }
        return out.toString();
    }
    public static void main(String[] args) {
        try {
            // Test 1
            String response = testURL(new URL(
                "http://www.sample.com/ExampleServlet"));
            System.out.println("Response: " + response);

            // Test 2
            response = testURL(new URL(
                "http://www.sample.com/ExampleServlet?METHOD=undefined"));
            System.out.println("Response: " + response);

        } catch (Exception e) {
            System.out.println("Tests failed");
```

```
            e.printStackTrace();
        }
    }
}
```

All the preceding test classes are available on the CD.

This test case is equivalent to TestHarness but uses a completely different technique to work the code. Notice that you don't have to write any stubs for this sample because the servlet engine is invoking the code in the normal execution environment. This kind of harness could be written equally well in other languages, for instance, Python or Perl.

Here's some sample output from this test harness:

```
Response: <B>Hi!</B>

Response: <P>Caught java.lang.NoSuchMethodException: undefined</P>
<PRE>
java.lang.NoSuchMethodException: undefined
        at java.lang.Class.getMethod0(Native Method)
        at java.lang.Class.getMethod(Class.java:854)
        at fruits.DispatchServlet.doInteraction(DispatchServlet.java:45)
        at fruits.DispatchServlet.doGet(DispatchServlet.java:23)
        at javax.servlet.http.HttpServlet.service(HttpServlet.java:499)
        at javax.servlet.http.HttpServlet.service(HttpServlet.java:588)
        at org.apache.jserv.JServConnection.processRequest(JServConnection.java)
        at org.apache.jserv.JServConnection.run(JServConnection.java)
        at java.lang.Thread.run(Thread.java:479)
</PRE>
```

Notice that the output is almost identical to that from TestHarness, with some minor differences in the exception printout. In particular, the stack traces are different, as you would expect. Here, if you were using diff to compare output, it would complain that they are different, even though in terms of correct behavior, they are the same. This is one of the hazards of using diff for automatic testing – make sure that what you are diffing is appropriate.

Performing unit testing with JUnit

The unit testing process is simpler when performed with JUnit for Java, one popular (and free) unit-testing framework. This framework, available at junit.org, provides an easy way to collect and work with manually written tests like the one we just showed. If you write your tests within the JUnit framework, Jtest will automatically recognize them during automatic testing.

To build tests into the JUnit framework, first create a class that extends `junit.framework.TestCase`. For the tests we create, we generally use the original class name with an extra *Test* tacked on; to test `ExampleServlet` with JUnit, we create a class named `ExampleServletTest`. To access any package-visible methods or fields from our test, we make sure that the test class is contained in the same Java package as our original class.

Kent Beck, one of the early promoters of XP, has written a paper about testing frameworks, available at `www.xprogramming.com/testfram.htm`. In this paper, he establishes a general framework for creating unit tests for your own code. The ideas from this paper have been implemented in frameworks for a large variety of languages. You can download versions for most languages from `www.xprogramming.com/software.htm`. Naturally, the frameworks are more useful or better developed for some languages than for others.

Each `public` method that starts with the word *test* is used to build up our test suite. JUnit uses Java's reflection to collect these tests automatically. Other languages' frameworks might require users to collect the tests manually.

Here's the class we created for the JUnit test:

```
package fruits;

import java.io.*;
import javax.servlet.*;
import junit.framework.*;

public class ExampleServletTest extends TestCase {
    ExampleServlet servlet;
    public ExampleServletTest(String name) {
        super(name);
    }
    protected void setUp() {
        // Common initialization can go here
        servlet = new ExampleServlet();
    }
    protected void tearDown() {
        // Common clean-up can go here
    }
```

```
    public static Test suite() {
        return new TestSuite(ExampleServletTest.class);
    }
    public static void main(String[] args) {
        junit.textui.TestRunner.run(suite());
    }
    public void test1() throws ServletException, IOException {
        TestRequest req = new TestRequest();
        TestResponse res = new TestResponse();
        servlet.doGet(req, res);
        assertEquals("<B>Hi!</B>", res.getResponse().trim());
    }
    public void test2() throws ServletException, IOException {
        TestRequest req = new TestRequest() {
            public String getParameter(String name) {
                if (name.equals("METHOD"))
                    return "undefined";
                return null;
            }
        };
        TestResponse res = new TestResponse();
        servlet.doGet(req, res);
        assertTrue(res.getResponse().indexOf(
"Caught java.lang.NoSuchMethodException") >= 0);
    }
}
```

The `ExampleServletTest` class is available on the CD.

The `setUp()` and `tearDown()` methods are called automatically before and after each test. This allows the tests to share common code. Because all the tests are running in the same framework, it's important to avoid modifying global state that could affect other tests.

The `suite()` method creates an instance of the `TestSuite` class that describes all the available tests. The version we are calling here will use reflection on the `ExampleServletTest` class to create the suite automatically.

The `main()` method lets us run tests in text mode simply by invoking our class from the command line.

Finally, our two tests are contained in the methods `test1()` and `test2()`. In general, you want more descriptive names for tests that you yourself write. Here we have added checks that verify appropriate responses rather than just print the results. These checks are in the `assertEquals()` and `assertTrue()` methods, which trigger failures if the appropriate conditions are not met. In addition, any thrown exceptions trigger errors, which are caught by the framework.

We can run our tests by either running **`java fruits.ExampleServletTest`** from the command line or by starting the JUnit GUI with the command **`java junit.swingui.TestRunner`**. To use the GUI approach, we then have to enter the class name and click the Run button. The results look like Figure 9-3.

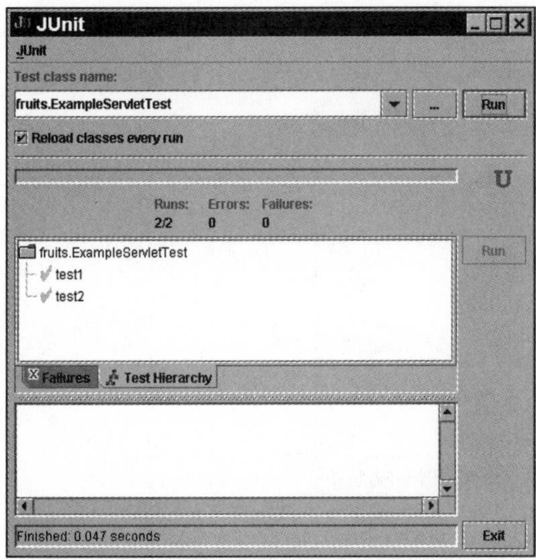

Figure 9-3: JUnit test results for ExampleServletTest.

A green bar indicates that all the tests were successful. If the tests were not successful, JUnit would display the errors in the bottom GUI panel.

One minor defect in the JUnit GUI at the time this book was written is that tests involving native code might not work properly unless you close and restart the GUI between executions.

Performing unit testing with Jtest

Next, we describe what the unit testing process entails when we use Jtest. First, we demonstrate how we use Jtest to test the `DispatchServlet` class automatically. Then we provide an additional example using the `ShoppingServlet` class.

TESTING DISPATCHSERVLET IN AUTOMATIC MODE

Jtest can start testing a class as soon as you have compiled it. You do not have to build additional code to create harnesses, scaffolding, or stubs or even create test cases. Jtest does this automatically. In fact, we don't need the `ExampleServlet` class – Jtest can even test abstract classes. To test the `DispatchServlet` class in Jtest, we simply load it into Jtest and click Start, as shown in Figure 9-4.

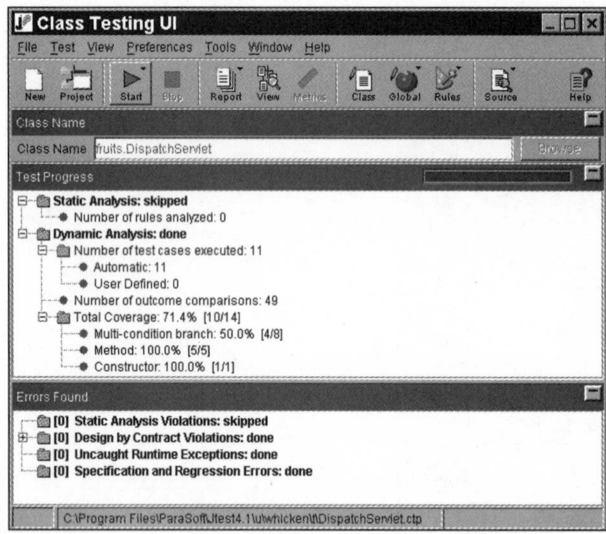

Figure 9-4: Testing DispatchServlet automatically with Jtest.

Jtest then examines the code under test and automatically designs and executes inputs to test it thoroughly. If necessary, Jtest also creates stubs for references to external resources. In this case, Jtest designs 11 test cases that achieve 71.4 percent coverage of the class.

If this class contained Design by Contract (DbC) comments describing its intended functionality, Jtest would automatically verify whether this functionality was implemented correctly. For an example of how this is done, see Chapter 19. For a review of DbC, see Chapter 7.

The Test Cases window, shown in Figure 9-5, displays the test cases and stubs that Jtest designed automatically. Automatically generated test cases are contained within the Automatic Test Cases branch. Jtest created two test cases that tested the `DispatchServlet()` method, three that tested the `doGet()` method, two that tested the `doPost()` method, and four others. It also automatically created stubs for many of the test cases. Each automatically created stub is marked with an empty box icon in the Test Case Input branch. The value listed in the node containing the empty box icon indicates the method and the action that is specified by the stub. In this example, Jtest creates stubs for the `HttpServletRequest` and `HttpServletResponse` classes, so we do not have to create them (as we do when performing manual unit testing or when testing with JUnit).

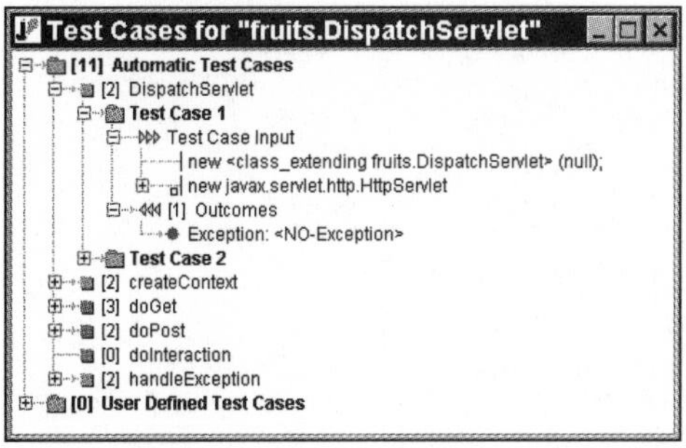

Figure 9-5: Test cases Jtest created for DispatchServlet.

Basically, Jtest enables us to test the class as soon as it is compiled – without requiring any additional work. It relieves us from having to create a harness, complete the `TestRequest` and `TestResponse` classes, and create test cases.

TESTING DISPATCHSERVLET WITH SPECIFIC USER-DEFINED TEST CASES

If we want to check the specific test cases we used in the preceding examples, we can specify them in a Test Class. A *Test Class* is a class used to specify test cases that Jtest should use to test the class. You can also specify Jtest test cases by adding method inputs, but Test Classes offer the most flexibility in developing test cases. You can use Test Classes to

- Use objects as inputs for static and instance methods.
- Test a calling sequence and check the state of the object, using asserts.
- Create complicated test cases that depend on a specific calling sequence.
- Validate the state of an object.

JUnit tests can be used as Test Classes in Jtest without any additional work. In this case, if we call our Test Class `DispatchServletTest`, it will be automatically run by Jtest whenever we test `DispatchServlet`, as long as the files are contained in the same directory. If you are not using JUnit, Jtest provides its own framework, so you can choose how to implement your tests. Here's an example using Jtest's framework – note that we have to use the `ExampleServlet` again because we are writing Java code that needs to compile. The following Test Class contains the two user-defined test cases we want to run:

```
package fruits;

import javax.servlet.http.*;

public class DispatchServletTest extends jtest.TestClass
{
    public static void test1()
        throws Exception
    {
        ExampleServlet servlet = new ExampleServlet();
        TestRequest req = new TestRequest();
        TestResponse res = new TestResponse();
        servlet.doGet(req, res);
        String response = res.getResponse();
        assert("Found: " + response,
               response.equals("<B>Hi!</B>\n"));
    }

    public static void test2()
        throws Exception
    {
        ExampleServlet servlet = new ExampleServlet();
        TestRequest req = new TestRequest() {
            public String getParameter(String name) {
                if (name.equals("METHOD"))
                    return "undefined";
                return null;
            }
        };
        TestResponse res = new TestResponse();
        servlet.doGet(req, res);
        String response = res.getResponse();
        assert("Found: " + response,
               response.startsWith(
                   "<P>Caught java.lang.NoSuchMethodException"));
    }
}
```

The `DispatchServletTest` class is available on the CD.

Like the JUnit example earlier in this chapter, these tests indicate failures either through the `assert()` method or by throwing exceptions.

To run the test cases specified in this Test Class, we replay the preceding Jtest test by clicking Start again. Jtest recognizes that a Test Class was added to the directory containing the class under test, and Jtest executes the test cases described in that Test Class. As Figure 9-6 illustrates, Jtest finds that these test cases produced the correct outcomes. If you run this example, you will see that the coverage has increased to 78.5 percent.

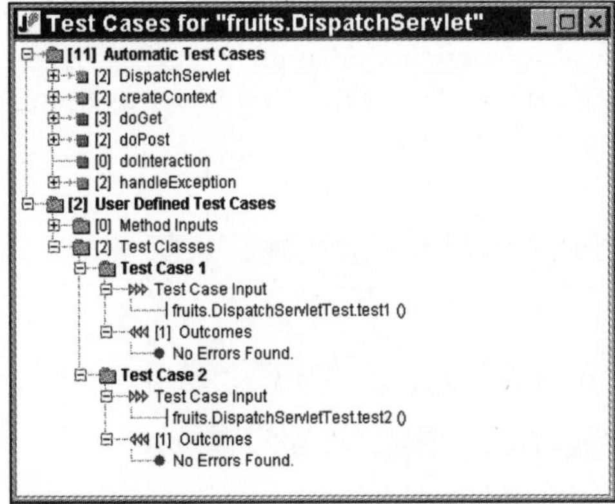

Figure 9-6: The result of our user-defined test cases for DispatchServlet.

All the unit testing techniques described in the section verify that the specified functionality worked correctly. The automatic one just did it much faster, with a lot less work. The manually written tests required just as much work in either case.

TESTING SHOPPINGSERVLET IN AUTOMATIC MODE

For a second example of testing with Jtest, look at how we perform automatic testing on another servlet, the `ShoppingServlet` class. When we test this class in Jtest without adding user-defined test cases, Jtest automatically creates and executes 53 test cases and a number of stubs. Figure 9-7 shows the distribution of these test cases.

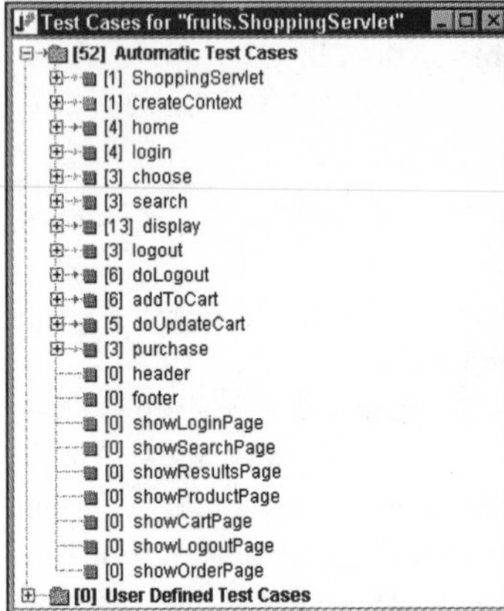

Figure 9-7: The distribution of test cases Jtest created for ShoppingServlet

These test cases achieve 64.5 percent coverage of the class. Moreover, one of the test cases Jtest developed to test the `display()` method also uncovers a problem with the class: It allows a `NumberFormatException` to occur. Jtest alerts us to this problem with the error message displayed in Figure 9-8.

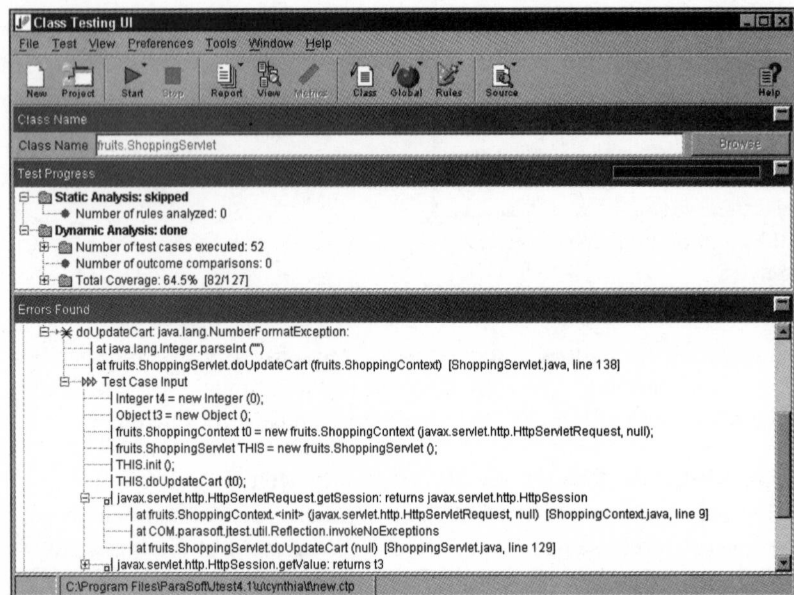

Figure 9-8: A problem Jtest found in ShoppingServlet.

The file and line information reveals that the problem occurred at line 138. To examine this code, we double-click the node containing the file and line information.

The source code, with the responsible line highlighted, is then opened in Jtest's Source Viewer (shown in Figure 9-9). If you look at the code above this line, you will see the problem. When a user tries to update an item quantity in the shopping cart and does not enter a valid number in the Item Number field, the `ShoppingServlet` class throws a `NumberFormatException`. However, we never validate the user input to check for negative numbers or nonnumbers.

For an example of code that can be added to solve this problem, see Appendix B.

Source Viewer

Options

```
public void doUpdateCart(ShoppingContext context)
   throws ServletException, IOException
{
   if (!context.hasUser()) {
      showLoginPage(context, false, "Missing USER for METHOD=doUpdateCart")
      return;
   }
   int user = context.getUser();
   Enumeration enum = context.getParameterNames();
   while (enum.hasMoreElements()) {
      String name = enum.nextElement().toString();
      if (name.startsWith("ITEM_")) {
         int item = Integer.parseInt(name.substring(5));
         int quantity = context.getInteger(name, 0);
         carts.set(user, item, quantity);
      }
   }
   showCartPage(context);
}
public void purchase(ShoppingContext context)
   throws ServletException, IOException
{
   if (!context.hasUser()) {
      showLoginPage(context, false, "Missing USER for METHOD=purchase");
```

C:\dls\demo\fruits\ShoppingServlet.java, line 138

Figure 9-9: The source of the problem.

Jtest can also be used to automate regression testing at the class level. This means that you can run test suites that monitor your code's integrity as soon as you have written a single class. Jtest remembers the outcomes from previous runs, compares them every time the class is tested, and reports errors when an outcome changes. If you do specify the correct outcomes, Jtest uses those values as a reference when running regression tests.

Integrating Unit Testing into Your Development Process

As you can see, the most feasible way to integrate unit testing into the compressed development schedules characteristic of Web development is to automate as much of it as possible. As soon as you complete and compile a unit, test the unit and fix all detected errors before checking the code into the source code repository. You can also integrate your unit testing into your automated regular builds if your unit-testing method can be run in batch mode. After unit testing is integrated into automated regular builds, all appropriate tests can automatically be rerun every night so that you can immediately determine whether modifications caused any undesired functionality changes or introduced any new unit-level problems.

Summary

This chapter covers unit testing. We explain how unit testing helps you to improve testing efficiency and keep your errors under control. We describe what unit testing entails: creating scaffolding and any necessary stubs, creating test cases that check code construction and code functionality, and devising a way to replay these test cases and easily determine when an error has occurred. Finally, we demonstrate several methods for performing unit testing, using classes from our demo Online Grocer application as examples.

Ideally, after performing unit testing on a part of your application, you deploy it and then start testing it via an HTTP connection. Chapter 10 explains the deployment process, and Chapters 11 through 14 explain the techniques you can use to test whatever part(s) of your application you deploy.

Chapter 10

Deploying Your Application

IN THIS CHAPTER

- Determining your deployment needs
- Leveraging deployment
- Creating a deployment process
- Automating deployment using WebKing

DEPLOYMENT IS THE PROCESS OF COPYING your application to a location where it will be exercised. In the simple case of traditional programming (where the application is a single executable file), the only step in deploying the application is to copy it where you want it to go. Deploying modern non-Web applications often requires moving complicated directory structures and can necessitate system-level configuration (for example, configuring Registry keys under Microsoft Windows). Web applications, as usual, are generally more complicated to deploy because they interact with the Web server and often other resources.

Many Web developers think of deployment only in terms of the final, user-accessible application. In this chapter, we discuss a variety of deployment possibilities. These different possibilities provide greater flexibility and power in where, when, and how you deploy, and they facilitate testing and bulletproofing. Deployment need not mean copying the entire application; it also applies to modules and even single pages within an application.

A location where your application, or part of your application, is deployed can also be referred to as a *staging area*. We introduce staging areas in Chapter 2 and describe how to create a staging area for a prototype application in Chapter 5. In the present chapter, we take a closer look at the purpose of deployment and staging areas and then focus on how to deploy your application (servlets, CGIs, and so on) to different staging areas. We pay particular attention to the notions of a personal staging area for development and a shared staging area for testing. By performing the practices described in this chapter, you can not only make your final application available to your end users but also establish an infrastructure that enables you to perform the client-side testing practices discussed in the remainder of Part II as early as possible.

You should strive to create a flexible deployment process so that from a single procedure, you can create, update, and maintain all staging areas you are using. This ensures that you don't duplicate mistakes or overlook changes in different staging areas.

Determining Your Deployment Needs

As discussed in Chapter 2, the general purpose of a staging area is to provide an area where a Web application can be tested before it goes live. There are two general types of staging areas: personal and shared. This chapter expands this notion so that you can determine exactly which staging areas are appropriate for your specific Web application. In fact, the final destination of your Web application can also be considered a staging area because the process for deploying the final application should be similar to the one you use for your testing staging areas (if it's not, your tests aren't testing the same application that will be on the final server). The terms *publishing* and *staging* can be used interchangeably with *deploying* in this context.

The most general definition of a staging area is any location where a well-defined subset of your application will be stored. Your source files should always live in a central, well-defined location so that all team members can always find the most current, official versions of your original components. Staging areas can properly be thought of as any place to which those files are copied for purposes of testing, development, and releasing to customers.

Choosing your staging areas

The number of staging areas you need depends on your project size, team size, and application requirements. Some staging areas are temporary ad hoc areas that belong to individuals and are used for developing the application. Other staging areas are formal shared areas that impose more restrictions on how much an individual is allowed to modify (or corrupt) the application. First, you will become acquainted with the general considerations in setting up staging areas; consider the questions raised in the following sections with respect to your application and organization. Then you will take a detailed look at the two most common types of staging areas, personal and shared.

WHAT IS THE AREA'S PURPOSE?

Generally, staging areas are used for one or more of three purposes: development, testing, and actual usage by the end user. We believe that the final staging area should not be the one you use for development and testing. However, in a small project, you might be able to do most of your testing on your development area. If you have a large project, you can dedicate special staging areas to testing key parts of your project. For example, you can have a special staging area for testing database performance and interactions. Developers can take turns working in this area as it relates to their changes. This is probably more efficient in terms of resources than giving each developer a copy of the entire database – especially if the database is large or requires special hardware.

IS THE AREA STORED LOCALLY OR REMOTELY?

Each area should be stored in an appropriate location. Generally, personal staging areas should be located on the developer's machine (stored *locally*). This guarantees that each developer can have his own server running without conflicting with other servers from other developers. It also gives the developer fast access to server configurations, files, and so forth.

Shared staging areas must be remote to at least some of the team members, although the file system can be mounted locally.

The choice of storage area is especially relevant to deployment because it dictates which methods are allowed. Locally stored areas or remote areas mounted locally can be deployed by simply copying files. Commonly, you deploy remote staging areas by using the FTP protocol. You can also configure HTTP servers to support deployment, using the HTTP `POST` method or a newer technique such as WebDAV.

WebDAV (Web-Based Distributed Authoring and Versioning) is a set of extensions to HTTP. These extensions allow multiple users to collaboratively manage and develop files located on remote Web servers. If your staging area is set up in this way, you need a deployment process that understands the WebDAV extensions. For more information about WevDAV, see `webdav.org`.

HOW MANY PEOPLE WILL BE USING THE AREA?

Will the staging area in question be owned and used exclusively by one person, or will multiple people be working together? We believe strongly in the benefit of personal staging areas, where appropriate, so that people developing the Web site can work without fear of interfering with others. This accelerates the development process by keeping people out of one another's way.

If multiple people are sharing a single staging area, make sure that everyone using the area knows the rules of that staging area and cooperates fully. If one user is developing or testing a module while someone else is changing it, both users will have poor results and can end up corrupting the application. In the worst case, some of these changes can even end up being checked in and stored in the master archive.

Often, you use a shared area for integration testing or to share limited resources such as databases.

IS THE APPLICATION FULLY OR PARTIALLY DEPLOYED?

Naturally, the final application should be fully deployed, but any other staging area can consist of only a well-defined subsection of functionality. Typically, the entire application is not needed to perform many testing methods. Moreover, during development, when the application isn't even finished, the application can be only partially deployed.

IS THE APPLICATION USING REAL OR STUBBED COMPONENTS?

Are the deployed components the real ones or special-purpose stubs specific to the task at hand? For instance, you can share a special debugging database server among many personal staging areas if the resources to set it up are not available to all developers. (In this case, you must take measures to ensure that the developers do not clobber one another.)

If you are using stubbed components, your deployment procedure should describe which components go to which staging areas. You must ensure that your stubs do not end up as part of the final application!

ARE THERE SPECIAL CONSIDERATIONS?

Vast multitudes of possibilities for special staging areas exist. Here we can only hint at a few of them, but we're sure that you can come up with many more, with a little creativity. Special considerations can affect any of the previously discussed issues. Some of the scenarios include

- Your application is deployed to different sites with different languages, so internationalization issues apply during deployment.
- Your application is automatically customized to different markets or designs.
- Your application is bundled onto a CD. In addition to normal deployment issues, you must make sure that everything works in this context. For example, you might need to add some extra files that describe how the CD is laid out, and so on.
- Your application is bundled into a zip file. This is a common way to create a deliverable snapshot for sites without dynamic elements. You can also

create a scenario in which the dynamic content is removed from the application as part of deploying to the zip file.

Even though you generally think about deploying from a local disk onto a remote Web server, this is not set in stone. For example, if your application pulls certain content from a related site, you would want to deploy from one Web server onto another one. Alternatively, you can make a zip file by deploying from a remote Web server onto your local disk. The possibilities are endless.

Understanding personal staging areas

The idea of the personal staging area is similar to the older concept of the *sandbox*. A sandbox is an environment in which one developer can work without affecting other developers' work. It enables the developer to see the results of his or her work and to experiment without worrying about affecting a fellow developer's part of the project.

A personal staging area provides Web developers with the same benefits. Basically, the staging area is a Web server that allows you to test your own code without affecting other developers' work. Typically, the Web server sits on the machine where you work; it can be the Apache Web Server, the Microsoft Web server (IIS), or another Web server. As you work with the code, you deploy it to this machine and test it.

Your personal staging area should include all application pieces related to the application module on which you are working. For example, if your module interfaces with a database, you would have a database in your staging area. This database can be a small-scale copy of the actual database the application will use, but it has to be the same type of database, with a similar configuration, similar operation, and some of the same data. Likewise, if the application interfaces with a legacy system, but the modules you are working on have nothing to do with the legacy system, you do not need any type of legacy system in your personal staging area.

Access to the shared source code repository is a critical element for successfully maintaining personal staging areas. This repository allows you to get copies of the necessary files, work on the copies without affecting other developers, and then test your modifications before checking the code back into the source code repository and making the modifications available to the entire development team. If all code is subjected to the appropriate tests and reviews before it is added to the repository, you can be confident that any code in the source code repository is clean and well tested. Keeping the source code repository clean is a critical step in controlling bugs. If buggy and/or error-prone code is added to the source code repository, there's a good chance that bugs will be introduced into the application as this code is modified and built on. If the code in the source code repository is correct and understandable, this chance is significantly lower.

We recommend that you establish a personal staging area and start testing your application as soon as you can exercise any part of it from a browser. By performing this testing as early as possible, you save yourself much time and work in the long run. Because critical Web problems are often the result of design or implementation flaws, fixing these problems frequently requires rewriting the problematic code. If you delay testing until the end of the development process, your problem is likely to be widespread, and you will have to rewrite a lot of code to remedy it. However, if you thoroughly test each servlet, bean, or other part of your application immediately after it is written, you can spot and resolve critical flaws before they become widespread. Essentially, you can prevent many problems that are difficult and costly to fix. This translates to fewer errors that elude testing, less time spent on testing and debugging, and faster time to market.

If you followed our recommendation in Chapter 6 to configure your development area to serve as a testing area, you can think of that area as your primary staging area. However, it's still important to deploy eventually to a staging area so that you can test and perfect your deployment procedure.

After a logical unit of the application (for example, a servlet, CGI, or set of programs) is tested on the personal staging area (using the testing techniques discussed in the remainder of Part II) and any errors are fixed, this site unit is checked into the source code repository, and information about deploying and testing that code can be added to the project file, introduced in Chapter 2. Note that the site unit does not have to be your entire application. The important thing is that it is a functioning part of your application that you can feasibly exercise and test.

Understanding shared staging areas

After the site unit on the personal staging area is deemed acceptable, it can be deployed to the shared staging area – the area where all the modules on which the developers are working are integrated into a single application. Figure 10-1 displays how code flows from the developers' machines to the shared staging area and then again to the actual deployment area.

This shared staging area should contain all the same pieces that the application will contain. In other words, if the application will work with an Oracle database and a legacy system, this staging area should contain a copy of both the Oracle database and the legacy system. The deployment area can have stronger machines, more complete databases, and so on. However, the application components on the shared staging area and the deployment area should have the same basic functionality so that your shared staging area accurately represents your deployment area. If it does not, you might find problems on your application that did not surface on your staging area.

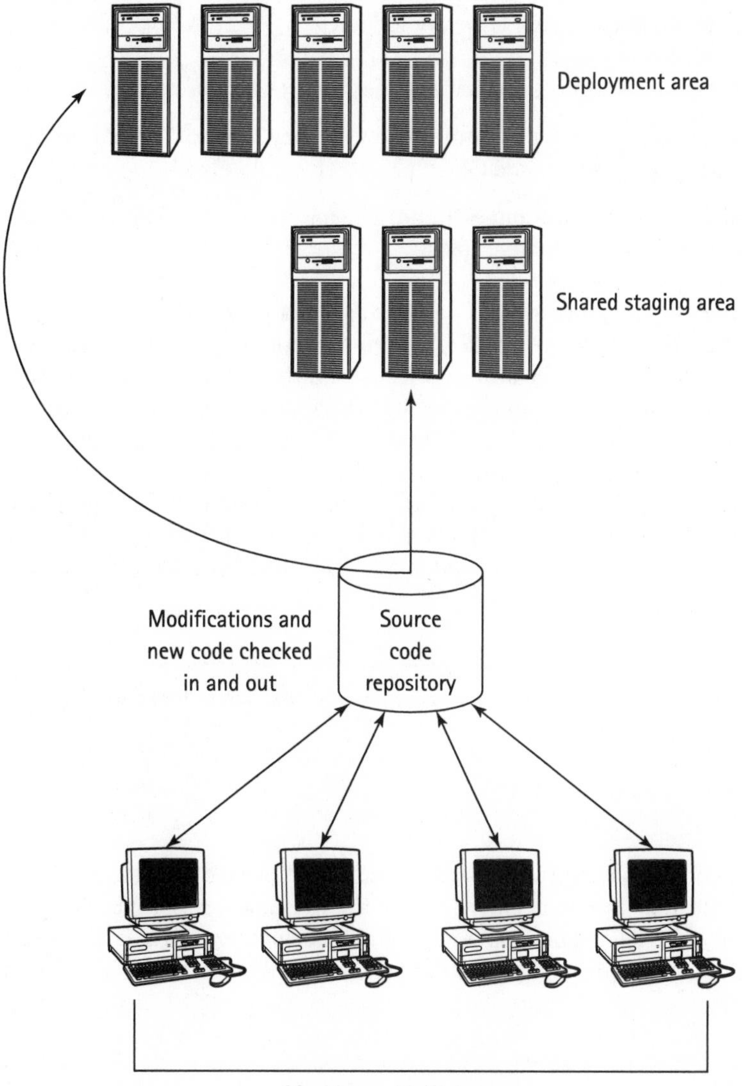

Figure 10-1: The flow of code across multiple staging areas.

Sometimes you do not have enough of the correct resources to make the shared staging area a functional copy of the final deployed application. In this case, you must judiciously choose between using stubs and sharing resources with the actual server. Naturally, extreme caution is necessary.

Assembling a shared staging area is more complicated than assembling a personal staging area. It can involve initializing databases, transforming XML files, and similar operations. This process typically includes

- Changing the directories to which application files are transferred
- Changing database-related operations so that they work off one or more shared databases instead of each developer's local database
- Performing initializations and setting up daemons (for example, to create the capability to talk to phone lines)

If your deployment procedure requires any transformations (for example, if you have an application that plugs in to different Web sites and has to assume the host Web site's look and feel), you perform and test the transformations on a staging area. We recommend that you establish one staging area for each version of your application. For example, if you are transforming XML to HTML for one audience (people who are accessing the application using Web browsers) and transforming it to WML for another (people who are accessing the application via cell phones), you create one shared staging area for the HTML version and another for the WML version. You do not make an application available to users until you have thoroughly tested every type of output it can create.

Chapter 17 discusses ways to transform pages to different looks and feels using XML.

After the code on the shared staging area is thoroughly tested and any problems repaired, the application can be deployed to the final, usable destination. The procedure for deploying the application to the final deployment area is the same process for deploying it to the shared staging area, except that different destination targets are used.

Chapter 15 discusses techniques for testing code on the shared staging area.

Leveraging Deployment

After you determine your deployment needs, you establish the process you will use for each of your deployment areas. Many decisions are already made for you, based on the requirements you laid out in the preceding section. One point to emphasize again is that if you are deploying to multiple locations, you want to share as much of the deployment process as possible. As long as you are creating a formal process, you might as well consider how to maximize your payoff.

Although the main purpose of deployment is to copy your application from one place to another, you can leverage much more benefit than simply moving bytes. When code is transferred from one area to another, you have the opportunity to introduce additional steps. With a well-defined process, you can satisfy many goals at once. This is necessary for a bulletproof application.

Establishing gates

The first principle related to deployment is the notion of a *gate* introduced in Chapter 2. A gate is a set of conditions or requirements that must be met before progressing to the next stage. One use for gates is to ensure that code checked in to the source code repository meets certain quality standards. Another use is to ensure that files failing to meet your standards are not deployed.

Gates can be implemented as a succession of boolean filters: At each step, you apply a condition, or filter. If the condition is satisfied (for example, the specified test is passed with zero errors), you proceed to the next filter. If the condition is not met, the deployment process is aborted. Only when all filters have been satisfied can deployment proceed.

The kinds of filters you use as part of your deployment process depends on your application. If your application uses Java, you can use Jtest as a filter to ensure that your Java programs adhere to Java coding rules and pass unit tests. If you write Web programs in C or C++, you can set up a filter to check whether the code follows C/C++ coding rules. If you are developing in C/C++ and are concerned about memory corruption (which is a particularly critical issue when applications work with CORBA or other object brokers), you can set up a C/C++ runtime error-detection tool as a filter.

If you decide to use filters, we recommend that you test your files as you develop them, in addition to testing them as part of the deployment process. The goal is not to move testing to the deployment stage but to guarantee that bad files are not deployed. In the case of products like Jtest, you generally run the program you want to use as a filter in interactive mode, customize the test parameters as needed, and then save the customized test parameters so that they can be invoked from the command line. This enables you to automate testing during the deployment procedure.

Running additional commands

In addition to running filters, you can attach a variety of commands to your deployment process to drive actions such as these:

- To compile programs
- To transfer files to the correct directory of a Web server
- To modify databases
- To initialize objects
- To change file permissions

For instance, you can run a command that automatically creates a site index from the current data so that you can deploy a current index. Depending on what you are doing and how you are doing it, you can run commands before or after the actual copying takes place.

Supporting multiple staging areas

If you are using a single deployment process to support multiple staging areas, your process has to be flexible enough to accommodate any differences between the target destinations. At minimum, this means different file locations. At the other extreme, you can have staging areas that represent vastly different views of the application, some with stubs, others with some functionality removed or localized, and so forth.

A common need is to indicate whether each file belongs to a specific staging area. You can also execute filters or additional commands differently, depending on which staging area you are working with. For instance, you can temporarily relax some filters when you are publishing to a development area, but never for the final published application.

All necessary differences have to be parameterized and documented so that everyone involved understands what's going on.

Creating a Deployment Process

The worst case of manually deploying your application is to copy all the files by hand – either by dragging and dropping your files or by invoking some FTP application and individually specifying which files and directories go where. If you're forced into this situation, the key to success is to develop detailed documentation about what goes where; this will help you repeat the same installation later on. Filters and additional commands can be implemented as to-do lists that the person doing the copying has to follow. Generally, to attain some robustness and repeatability, you set up a more automatic procedure.

Using makefiles is a more common practice and significantly better than the manual deployment. *Makefiles* are text files used to describe transfers and transformations. This is a good solution for some projects because makefiles are well understood by many developers (especially on Unix) and are likely to be retained by successive developers. You can use parameters and variables to control customization upon deployment and even set up filters and additional commands, as described in the preceding section. Makefiles can also be set up to copy only files that have changed, instead of redeploying the entire application. This greatly speeds up minor updates to the final site. However, along with these many benefits come significant drawbacks. Makefile syntax can be arcane and hard to understand if anyone other than the developers has to make changes. Also, if you are publishing to or from remote directories, you lose much of the power because makefiles operate best on local file systems (you can overcome some of this by combining makefiles with scripting techniques).

Perhaps the most common deployment solution is to use a jumble of scripts or batch files, along with some written notes about gotchas that came up in past deployments. Many scripting languages can be used to create custom deployment scripts, including Perl, Python, PC Batch files, and Unix-style csh scripts. One interesting tool for automating deployment is Expect, a tool that uses the Tcl language to automate interactive applications such as Telnet, FTP, and so forth. This lets you write scripts that run on remote machines so that you can run commands that need to be invoked on remote staging areas.

You can download Expect from `expect.nist.gov`. If you plan on using Expect, you need to become familiar with the Tcl programming language on which Expect is built. Tcl is currently hosted at `scriptics.com`.

If you would like to learn more about Expect, we recommend *Exploring Expect: A Tcl-Based Toolkit for Automating Interactive Programs* by Don Libes.

One technique that allows you to use simple scripting – even if your target destination is on a remote server – is to have the script or makefile bundle all the necessary pieces into a single zip or tar archive. After that archive is created, you manually FTP and extract it on the Web server as a separate step (in some cases, this extraction step can be scripted). This is clearly not as desirable as automating the entire process but is probably more reliable than transferring the files individually.

If you use custom scripts to deploy your application, you must make sure that they are well documented and are checked in to your source control system. To support deployment to multiple locations, you might have to use parameters or configuration files to remove hard-coded assumptions about any individual staging area. There also might be dependencies relating to the machine from which the application is being deployed; these might depend on the details of your source control system.

A step past manual coding of deployment is to use a tool that bundles all the necessary actions into a single interface. You will learn how to use WebKing to do this in the next section.

Automating Deployment Using WebKing

If you use WebKing to deploy your site unit, you can establish a deployment infrastructure that enables you to re-create or update your staging area on demand with a click of a button (or automatically, as part of an automated nightly build). WebKing also records all essential deployment information in a file so that it can easily be passed on to QA, the Webmaster, other developers looking to create a similar deployment infrastructure, and so on. The WebKing documentation refers to the entire process as *publishing*, which takes files from a source location and places them at a target location. You can specify any number of source locations or target locations, as well as types of targets.

The rest of this section shows how to deploy part or all of your application with WebKing, using our deployment of the Online Grocer application as an example. In this case, the source is stored locally, and we are deploying to a Web server installed on the same machine. If we were installing onto a remote machine, the only step that would change is how you specify the destination, by using FTP instead of simple file copying.

Adding program files to the Project tree

The first step in deploying a site unit (for example, a servlet, CGI, or set of programs) is to add the source files for that unit to the WebKing Project tree and project file. If you have not already created a WebKing project file containing your existing static HTML and image files, see Chapter 5 or the WebKing User's Guide for instructions. If you already have a project file, open it by choosing Project→Open Site/Project and then selecting the appropriate project file. To open a project file, choose the file with the `.wkj` extension, not the one with the `.site` extension.

Often your directory contents and structure change between the prototype phase and the initial deployment. For example, we added and rearranged some files in our Online Grocer source directories to develop the application and make the files easier to work with. In such instances, you can prompt WebKing to update its Project tree by choosing Project→Refresh.

After you open a project file, we recommend that you create a separate site within the project that contains the source files for the program(s) you want to deploy and test. This is not necessary, but it makes the deployment procedure significantly simpler.

To create a new site for your program source files, do the following:

1. Right-click the project node in the Project tree (the name of this node is either *New Project* or the name you assigned to this project). Then choose Add New Site from the shortcut menu (see Figure 10-2). The Site Properties panel opens.

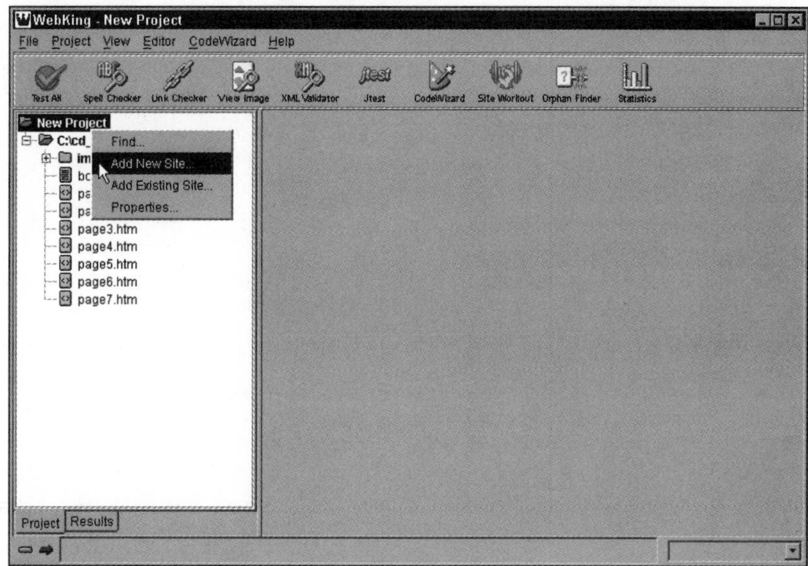

Figure 10-2: Adding a new site to the project file.

If you do not see the Add New Site option, you have not created or opened a project (`.wkj`) file.

2. Indicate the location of your program source files in the Source tab. Figure 10-3 shows the settings we use to deploy the Online Grocer's programs. For details on specifying source location(s), see the "Creating a Project File with WebKing" section in Chapter 5, or see the WebKing User's Guide.

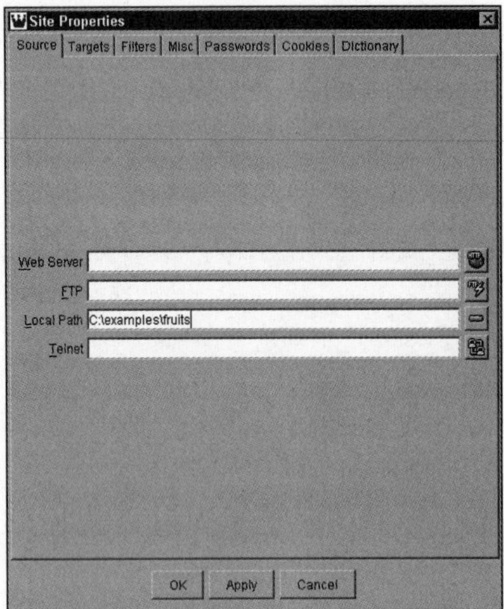

Figure 10-3: The Site Properties panel parameters used to add Online Grocer program files.

WebKing adds the specified files to the Project tree. You can then rename the different sites in your Project tree by doing the following:

1. Right-click the node that represents the site name, and choose Site Properties from the shortcut menu that opens. The Site Properties panel opens.
2. Open the Site Properties panel's Misc tab, and enter a new name for the site in the Name field.

Figure 10-4 shows the updated and relabeled Online Grocer Project tree.

If you have additional source files that exist in other locations, add them now, using indirect links. This is necessary if your application is not collected all in one place before deployment. For information on adding a file using indirect links, see the WebKing User's Guide.

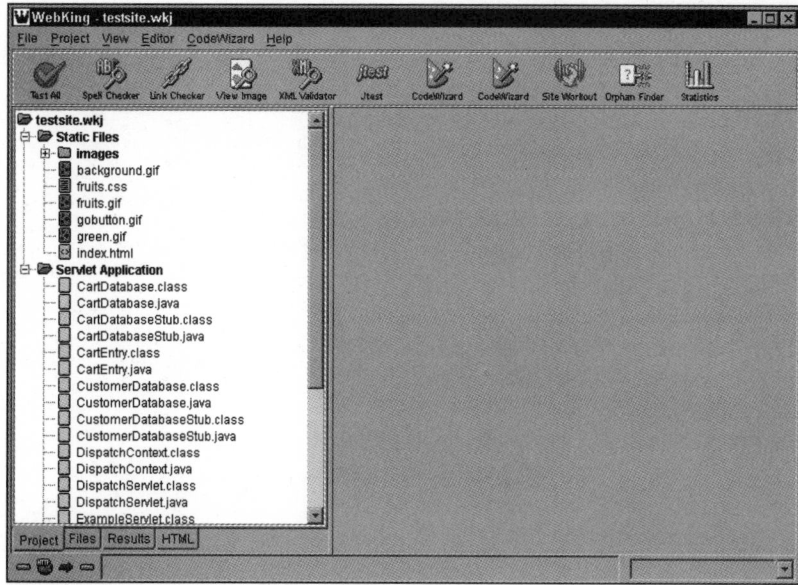

Figure 10-4: The Online Grocer Project tree after we added program files.

Indicating a new target

The first deployment instruction to enter is the one that tells WebKing to transfer the compiled files in your source directories to the appropriate area of your Web server (for example, a `servlet` directory or a `cgi-bin` directory).

The first step is to indicate the target directory for this new site that contains your program source files. WebKing uses the term *target* to refer to both staging areas and specific locations within staging areas.

To specify a target for the new site, do the following:

1. In the Project tree, right-click the node that represents the new site, and choose Site Properties from the shortcut menu. The Site Properties panel opens. Working with the Online Grocer project, we right-clicked the Servlet Application Project tree node to invoke this menu.

2. In the Site Properties panel's Targets tab, enter the location of your deployment target. We specified that we want the Online Grocer program files deployed to `C:\website\servlets`, as shown in Figure 10-5.

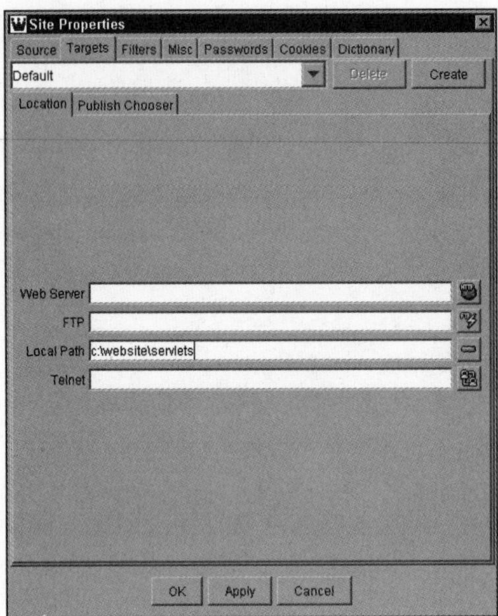

Figure 10-5: The parameters used to specify the Online Grocer servlet target.

WebKing is then configured to transfer the program files to the listed target.

If you do not want the directory structure on your target to mirror the directory structure on your Project tree, you can have WebKing rename and/or reorganize directories and files as part of the deployment process. For example, say that you have three program source directories that need to be published within the same directory on your Web server. You can perform this operation in WebKing with alternative deployment directories. For instructions, see the WebKing User's Guide.

Preventing the deployment of source files

Next, you want to prevent WebKing from transferring your programs' source files (for example, files with `.java`, `.c`, and `.cpp` extensions) to the Web server. There is generally no reason to have your source files on nondevelopment staging areas, including the final destination.

To prevent the deployment of your source files, do the following:

1. In the Project tree, right-click the node that represents the site containing the files you want to block, and choose Site Properties from the shortcut menu. The Site Properties panel opens.

2. In the Site Properties panel's Targets tab, select your current deployment target. You probably haven't configured any additional targets at this point, so you don't need to choose anything.
3. In the Targets tab's Publish Chooser tab, indicate which files you do not want to deploy (for the Online Grocer project, we did not want to deploy the `.java` files). To indicate that you do not want to deploy a file, right-click that file's node, and choose Do Not Publish Page from the shortcut menu, as shown in Figure 10-6. A red Do Not Publish icon is placed to the right of any file that will not be deployed.

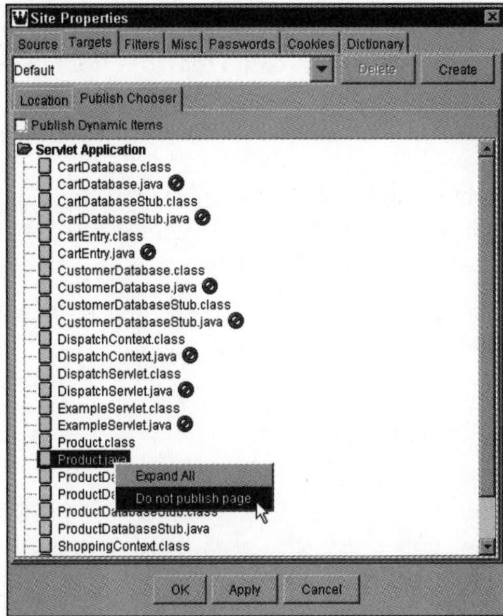

Figure 10-6: Indicating which source files should not be deployed.

WebKing is then configured to deploy only the appropriate files. Your next step is to configure WebKing to create the compiled files that you want to deploy.

Adding deployment commands

After the source files are added to the Project tree and you have configured your first deployment target, you have the option to tell WebKing to perform additional steps whenever you deploy your application. This information is communicated via publishing commands. WebKing recognizes two types of publishing commands:

- **Pre-publish commands:** Executed *before* source files are published to the target

- **Post-publish commands:** Executed *after* source files are published to the target

WebKing's publishing commands let you configure WebKing to automate virtually any imaginable operation. This functionality enables WebKing to behave like an automated, enhanced makefile. The interface for adding publishing commands is as flexible as possible to enable you to automate any deployment procedure you need to perform.

To add any deployment operation to your deployment infrastructure, do the following:

1. To create a publishing command for a *single* directory or file, right-click the directory or file in the Project tree, choose Properties from the shortcut menu, and click the Publish tab.

   or

   To create a publishing command for *all or most* files in a site, right-click the site's node directory or file in the Project tree, choose Site Properties from the shortcut menu, and click the Filters tab.

2. Click + in the Publish commands area. The Pre/Post-Publish Command window opens (see Figure 10-7).

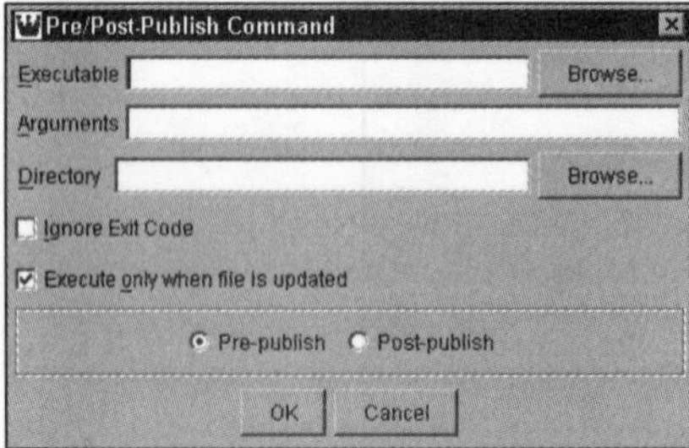

Figure 10-7: The Pre/Post-Publish Command window.

3. Enter information for your pre-publish or post-publish command in the appropriate fields:

   a. **Executable:** Enter or browse to the executable that you want to invoke this command.

   b. **Arguments:** Enter the arguments you want to pass to the executable.

   c. **Directory:** Enter or browse to the directory containing the files to which this command should be applied.

d. **Ignore Exit Code:** Many programs return a special exit code when they are done running. Generally, a nonzero exit code indicates that an error of some sort occurred, and WebKing aborts publishing if a nonzero exit code is detected. Choose this option if you want WebKing to disregard the exit code of the invoked program.

e. **Execute only when file is updated:** Choose this option if you want this command executed only when the associated file is updated. If you use a command that applies to multiple files, you generally do not select this option because it depends only on the file to which the command is attached.

f. **Pre-publish/post-publish:** This indicates when you want the command executed.

The command is then added to the list of commands, as shown in Figure 10-8. Pre-publish commands are displayed in the upper half of the window; post-publish commands are displayed in the lower half.

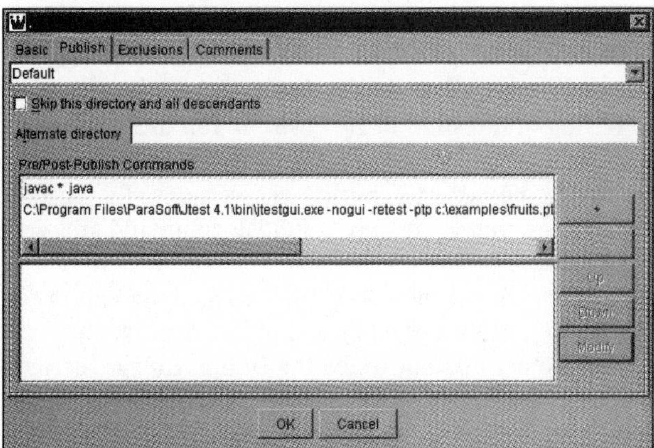

Figure 10-8: A list of pre- and post-publish commands.

All specified commands will be executed automatically every time your application is deployed or every time the application is deployed *and* the associated file is updated (depending on how the command was configured). Commands are executed in the order in which they are listed. To rearrange the order of the commands, select the command that you want to move up or down, and click Up or Down. To modify a command, select the command from the list of commands, and click Modify.

The first publishing command you enter is typically the one that compiles your programs. We generally make this a pre-publish command because we like to compile the programs before the main application deployment. This way, we can test the files before they are deployed and abort the deployment if any problems are found.

To compile the Online Grocer .java source files, we invoke the javac executable and pass *.java to compile all the files in the C:\examples\fruits directory. After following the preceding steps for creating a publishing command, we get the command displayed in Figure 10-9. After we close this window, a publishing command icon is shown next to the Servlet Application Project tree node to indicate that a command is attached.

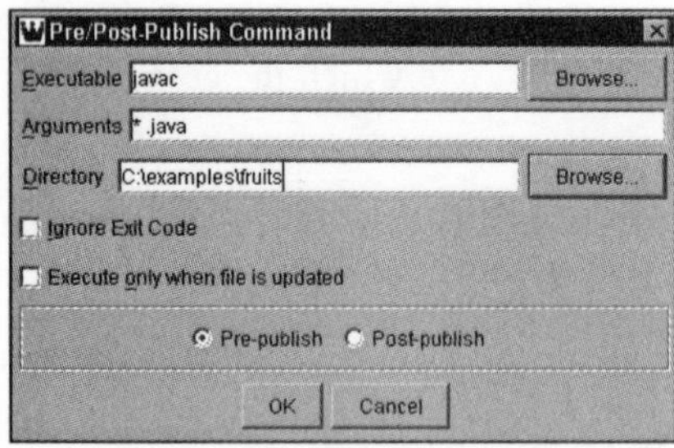

Figure 10-9: The command used to compile .java files.

Setting up gates

At this point, WebKing should be configured to deploy your site unit to a staging area so that you can start exercising and testing it. However, if you are truly committed to bulletproofing your application, you must take one more step before deploying the application: Configure boolean filters that act as gates. To set up a boolean filter that tests your programs, you create a pre-publish command and verify the exit code.

For the Online Grocer application, we use Jtest as a filter so that we can check for coding standard violations, as well as unit-level errors, before deployment.

We have already set up a Jtest project file that tested the Online Grocer servlets; this project file is named fruits.ptp and is located in our c:\examples directory. Figure 10-10 displays the completed command we use to apply this Jtest test as a boolean filter.

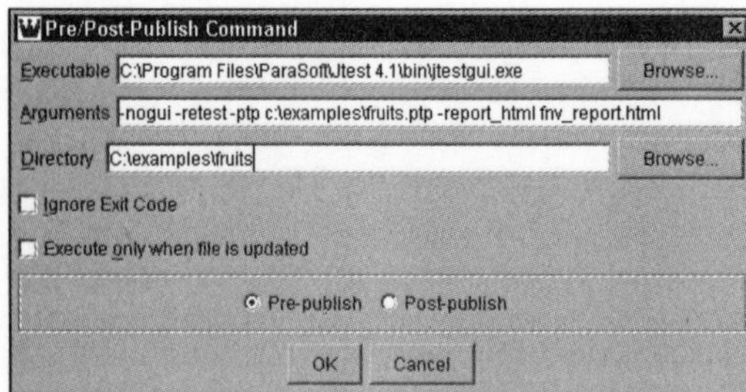

Figure 10-10: The command use to set up Jtest as a boolean filter.

The command we are executing is

```
C:\Program Files\ParaSoft\Jtest 4.1\bin\jtestgui.exe -nogui -retest \
-ptp c:\examples\fruits.ptp -report_html fnv_report.html
```

This command tells Jtest to run the tests saved in `c:\examples\fruits.ptp` in *batch mode* (in other words, without opening a GUI). The `-retest` flag says to retest all classes (even classes previously tested by Jtest). The `-report_html fnv_report.html` flag tells Jtest to create an HTML format report of results and save that report as `fnv_report.html` in the source directory, `C:\examples\fruits`.

For your commands to work properly, it is critical that the compilation command is executed before the filter command that tests the compiled class files. If your commands are not listed in the correct order, rearrange them, using the Up and Down buttons in the Properties panel.

Deploying the application

At this point, WebKing should be configured to perform all operations required to compile and test your source files and (if the files pass the requisite tests) to deploy the selected site unit on your personal staging area. The only step left is to start the actual deployment. To deploy an application, you do the following:

1. Choose Project→Publish. The Publish panel opens. Figure 10-11 shows the Publish panel for the Online Grocer project.

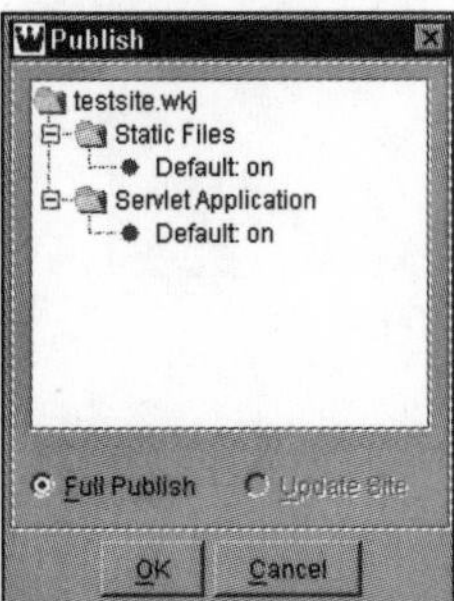

Figure 10-11: The Publish panel.

2. Select the site(s) you want WebKing to deploy. The deployment setting node beneath the name of each site indicates whether the site will be

deployed. To change the setting, right-click the node and choose Toggle Off (if you do not want to publish a site) or Toggle On (if you do).

3. Indicate whether you want WebKing to perform a full publish or to update the application, by selecting one of the buttons at the bottom of the panel.

WebKing then performs the specified deployment operations. For example, when we deploy the Online Grocer project, WebKing compiles our `.java` files and runs the specified Jtest test. The Jtest pre-publish command we describe in the "Setting Up Gates" section configures WebKing to only deploy the servlet files if Jtest does not find any errors in the specified files.

We purposefully left errors in the Online Grocer files to demonstrate how WebKing behaves when a boolean filter fails. After WebKing invoked Jtest to test the files, Jtest ran its tests and sent result information to WebKing. Because Jtest found errors in the files, WebKing aborted the deployment and opened a dialog box alerting us to the problem. We looked at the brief summary of Jtest results in the WebKing Results panel (shown in Figure 10-12) and decided to look at Jtest's report file (saved in `C:\examples\fruits`) to determine which problems Jtest found.

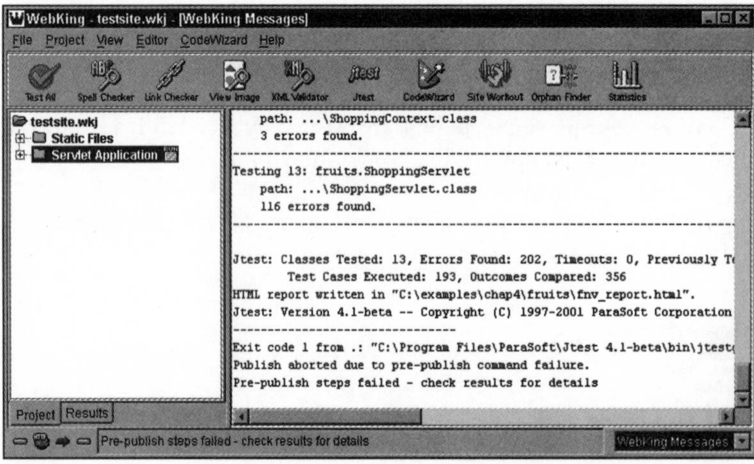

Figure 10-12: How WebKing indicates a failed Jtest boolean filter.

We reviewed the Jtest results, fixed the problems that needed to be fixed, and configured Jtest to suppress the handful of problems that weren't really relevant to the project at hand. Next, we resaved the Jtest parameters file (so that the information about what to suppress can be used the next time WebKing invokes Jtest) and tried to deploy the application again. This time, the deployment succeeded and the appropriate files were created and placed in the appropriate places on our personal staging server.

Summary

In this chapter, we discuss how to select staging areas appropriate to your project and to set up a deployment procedure. We also show how to create an automatic deployment infrastructure for parts of your application or for your entire application. We cover how to add source files to your project file and then configure WebKing to compile them and transfer the correct compiled files to the appropriate target locations. We also look at how to set up boolean filters to help you ensure that files containing errors are not deployed.

In the remaining chapters in Part II, we discuss methods of testing the parts of the application you have deployed. We start by showing you how to test the most basic functionality and then move to progressively more detailed tests. By checking each application part's most fundamental problems as early as possible, you save yourself from spending hours fine-tuning a program only to find out later that it has fundamental functionality problems and needs to be completely rewritten.

Chapter 11

Finding Flow Problems – Broken Links and More

IN THIS CHAPTER

- Understanding client-side failures
- Understanding server-side failures
- Understanding logical errors
- Detecting flow problems manually
- Detecting flow problems automatically

IF YOU WANT TO TEST your most fundamental functionality first, we recommend that you begin by testing whether your programs return the pages the user requests. If your programs do not, you have a serious functionality problem. The severity of the problem depends on the importance of the affected functionality and the frequency with which it can be accessed. For example, a rarely accessed broken link to a Meet the Webmaster page is much less problematic than a log in program that always leads to an error page. However, even the most insignificant broken link will eventually be discovered by users and threaten to damage your company's reputation.

In this chapter, we divide all flow problems into three categories. The first category is *client-side failures*. This category includes all errors caused by the client, including broken links. Generally, of course, the broken link is because the application displayed a broken link to the user, but because the immediate origin of the error is the user's browser, it falls into the client-side failure category. The next category is *server-side failures*, problems that arise within the Web server context. This category includes exceptions thrown inside the servlet, unavailable resources, and the like. The final category is *logical errors*, which occur when the application generates pages and links without any client or server failures, but the pages do not follow the paths intended by the developers. These problems generally indicate errors in the application.

The culprit can be anything from an elusive problem in your program or database to a simple typo or HTML coding error. No matter what causes the problem, finding and fixing it early is much easier. That's why we constantly stress the importance of testing each logical chunk of your application as soon as possible. If you delay your testing until later in the development process, you can reuse problematic code and build on it before you realize that you have a problem. If so, a simple one-minute, one-line change can blossom into a month-long debugging and/or rewriting nightmare.

One surefire way to avoid such nightmares is to check each page for flow-related problems as soon as possible. In other words, test each static page as soon as it is developed, and test each dynamic page as soon you can access it via an HTTP connection. At this point, we will focus on determining whether the part of the application deployed in Chapter 10 returns the correct output pages. You might encounter some expected broken links if your application is not complete. For now, you can safely ignore these problems, as long you replay your existing tests each time you add a new element to the staging area. This practice requires extreme caution; if you become accustomed to ignoring certain broken links, you might overlook them in your final application.

Understanding Client-Side Failures

Client-side failures include all failures initiated on the client side, which, in Web applications, means in the user's browser. Generally, this category covers bad URLs, failure to send proper authorization when necessary, and so forth. It's important to understand how many client-side failures can occur. A thorough knowledge of the kinds of errors you are looking for is essential to developing an adequately detailed testing strategy. If your notion of a bad link is limited to a URL that causes the server to generate a `Page Not Found` response, you probably won't check for all the necessary kinds of errors. The HTTP standard defines 18 status codes for client errors:

```
400 Bad Request
401 Unauthorized
402 Payment Required
403 Forbidden
404 Not Found
405 Method Not Allowed
406 Not Acceptable
407 Proxy Authentication Required
408 Request Timeout
409 Conflict
410 Gone
411 Length Required
412 Precondition Failed
413 Request Entity Too Large
414 Request-URI Too Long
```

```
415 Unsupported Media Type
416 Requested Range Not Satisfiable
417 Expectation Failed
```

You can get specific details on each of these errors from the HTTP standard itself, available as RFC2616 at `www.w3.org/Protocols/rfc2616/rfc2616.html`, but the names themselves give you some idea of the things that can go wrong. What most people consider typical failures are classified as 404 (`Not Found`).

Other kinds of broken links can properly be considered client-side failures even if they do not cause an HTTP failure. The simplest example is a URL specifying an anchor that either does not exist or is defined multiple times in the loaded page. The intent of the developer is not consistent with the page being tested, so the application should be corrected. These kinds of errors are easy to catch automatically but hard to catch by hand because it is often not apparent that an anchor is involved. For instance, if you have a long page with a footnote at the bottom and you want to link to the footnote, you might have a URL such as `/fruits/manual.html#note`. The intent is for the user to see the footnote. However, if `manual.html` does not have a `note` anchor (perhaps it was misspelled or deleted by someone who didn't realize that it was being used), the user will be taken to the top of the long page instead and never see the footnote.

Another consideration is the context in which the link is used. Some contexts are simpler to debug than others. For instance, `<A>` links on which the user can click are generally the case that is tested most often. Other links are not as obvious and are therefore easier to neglect. For instance, broken `<IMG>` links behave differently on different browsers. Some browsers display a special image representing the missing one, and other browsers just leave a blank space. If the image is small or in an out-of-the-way place, it can easily be overlooked by testers. Broken `<BACKGROUND>` images are universally ignored by the browsers we've used. The only way to notice this problem is to know what the background should look like and to observe when it is incorrect. Missing sound files (and other similar files) are equally difficult to check. Another case to consider is JavaScript that loads URLs. One common action is to replace certain images when the mouse hovers over the icon. Testing this requires a very thorough effort, as well as knowledge of the page's construction.

Depending on your choice of Web servers and your target audience, you might want to configure your final application to generate a better response to broken URLs than the default behavior of the user's browser. For instance, Figure 11-1 displays what your users might see when encountering a standard 404 error using Internet Explorer.

A better response would be to record the failure and where it came from so that you can have someone look at it ASAP. Then notify the user that you are aware of the problem and working on it. Figure 11-2 shows the page that performs this function for the Online Grocer application.

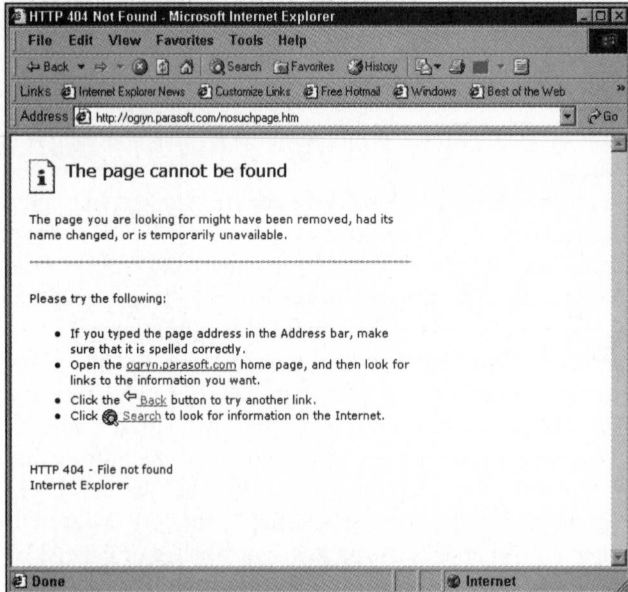

Figure 11-1: A standard 404 error.

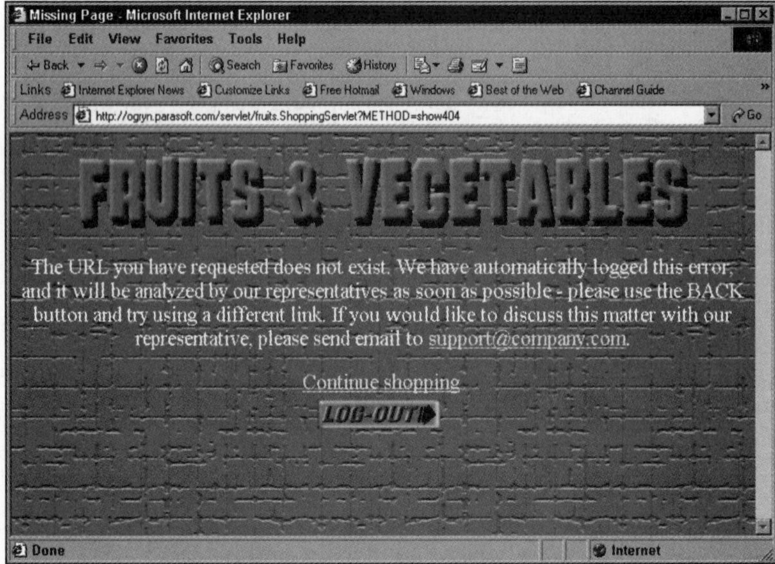

Figure 11-2: The Online Grocer's customized broken link page.

To configure the Online Grocer to use this page for unexpected URLs, we first add the following methods to the `ShoppingServlet` class:

```
public void show404(ShoppingContext context)
    throws ServletException, IOException
{
    show404Page(context);
}

void show404Page(ShoppingContext context)
    throws IOException
{
    PrintWriter out = context.getWriter();

    header(out, "Missing Page");
    out.println("<P>The URL you have requested does not exist.  We have ");
    out.println("automatically logged this error, and it will be analyzed ");
    out.println("by our representatives as soon as possible - please use ");
    out.println("the BACK button and try using a different link.</P>");
    out.println("<P>If you would like to discuss this matter with our ");
    out.println("representative, please send email to ");
    out.println("<A HREF=mailto:support@company.com>");
    out.println("support@company.com</A>.</P>");
    out.println("<A HREF=\""+SERVLET+"?METHOD=search\">");
    out.println("Continue shopping</A><BR>");
    out.println("<A HREF=\""+SERVLET+"?METHOD=logout\">");
    out.println("<IMG SRC=\"/logout.gif\" ALT=\"Logout\" BORDER=0></A>");
    footer(out);
}
```

As with the rest of the servlet, we decouple the entry point, `show404()`, from the routine that displays the actual HTML, `show404Page()`. Then we can change the generated responses independently from the application logic. Because our Web server is logging all URLs, we don't write any specific code in `show404()` to log these errors. Depending on your setup, you can write these errors to a file, store them in a database, or e-mail them to your Webmaster (keeping in mind that you don't want to swamp your e-mail with repeated errors – you can set it up to send only new, not previously seen, errors). You can also take advantage of the Referer property sometimes available in the HTTP header to indicate which page the users came from. This information helps you quickly identify the cause of the broken link. If you do this, be sure to check the Referer property, not Referrer property – the HTTP standard requires this spelling.

To configure our Apache server to use our new error page, we simply add the following code to the `httpd.conf` configuration file:

```
ErrorDocument 404 \
http://ogryn.parasoft.com/servlet/fruits.ShoppingServlet?METHOD=show404
```

Test your error page! This means checking its links, spelling, and the like. If your application is clean and has no bad links, you should specifically try bad URLs so that you are prepared for the unexpected.

Make sure that you, your testers, and your testing applications *know that this page represents an error*. If you reach this page during normal application activity, you have a bug that needs to be fixed. If your testers are not paying attention, they won't realize that this page is a problem because it looks like the rest of the application. Automatic tools have an even harder time recognizing that this page indicates a problem because they don't actually read the page. You will soon learn more about this when we show you how to use WebKing to find broken links, later in the chapter.

Understanding Server-Side Failures

Server-side failures are problems that originate on the Web server. This category includes problems with the server configuration, errors in your application, and missing or unavailable resources. Returning to the HTTP standard, you find six status codes representing server failures:

```
500 Internal Server Error
501 Not Implemented
502 Bad Gateway
503 Service Unavailable
504 Gateway Timeout
505 HTTP Version Not Supported
```

Server-side failures can introduce a variety of problems beyond these error messages. Say that you have a C++ CGI program that generates a response page. If your program crashes halfway through, the user might see only half the page in the browser. If the page is long, it might not be obvious that the page isn't complete. In the case of the Online Grocer's `ShoppingServlet`, if an exception is generated by the code, a server-side error occurs. One way to handle this more neatly is to catch the exception in the servlet and generate an appropriate response. For the Online Grocer application, we've bundled all this handling into one canned response, but a real application handles different errors in various ways.

It's important to your error recovery that you don't send half-prepared data to your end users. If your application has any chance of crashing while generating the response, you must generally write the response to a separate buffer and then send the response to the user only when the response is fully generated. The Online Grocer application does not do this. However, it does decouple the basic logic from the response generation, which at least minimizes the possibility of error. A fully robust application needs a more careful implementation to handle unexpected errors (such as memory failures on the server).

Server-side failures can generate ugly response pages, just like client-side failures. Figure 11-3 shows a page you can get from Apache if you haven't configured your servlets correctly; this particular one is classified as a 500, or `Internal Server Error`.

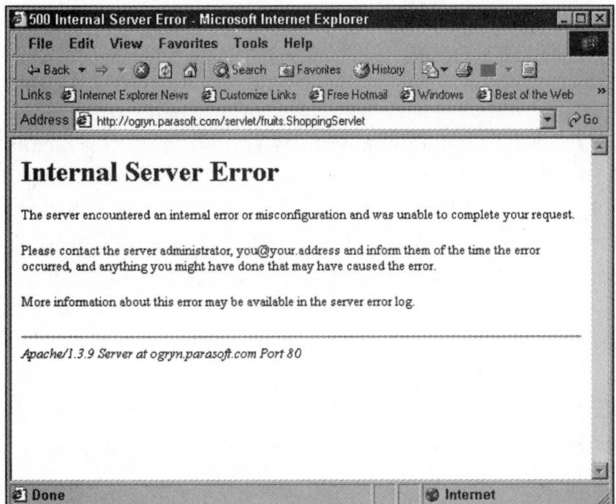

Figure 11-3: A standard 500 error.

As with the client-side errors discussed in the previous section, you might want to put a nicer face on this message for your end users. Because the technique is the same, we will not repeat the details here.

Understanding Logical Errors

In addition to client-side and server-side failures, there is a wide variety of flow-related problems best categorized as logical errors. With logical errors, you have URLs that return valid pages, but either the pages are not the correct ones or they do not have the correct side effects. These errors result from links to the incorrect page, dynamic links with incorrect arguments, and forms with bad parameters. Logical errors do not cause an HTTP failure but do contribute to the incorrect flow of your application.

Logical errors are, by nature, more application-specific than either client-side or server-side errors. For this reason, automatic tools are generally of limited use in detecting logical errors (the automatic tool has no clue that something has gone wrong). If, however, you have a tool that is configurable to test application-specific logic, you can devise tests that are appropriate for detecting these kinds of errors.

Chapter 12 discusses content verification, a technique for exposing logical errors in your application.

In addition to the pages the user sees, sometimes your application will generate side effects. For instance, after the user indicates that the groceries should be purchased, several actions have to be triggered, such as debiting the credit card, adding an order to the database, and updating available inventory. Thorough testing means verifying that these side effects are actually occurring. A user sitting in front of a Web browser cannot tell. Luckily, side effects are generally easier to detect automatically than other kinds of logic errors. You usually know where you anticipate side effects, and you can create test cases within your tool to query the appropriate resources and verify the side effects after the prerequisite pages have been loaded.

Chapter 16, where we discuss databases, includes examples of code that produces side effects and strategies for verifying side effects.

Detecting Flow Problems – An Overview

Now that you have a good idea of the kinds of errors you are looking for, you can examine some of the methods to detect these errors. Basically, there are two main ways to detect flow problems. The first way is to browse through the application and watch for pages that do not return the expected content and other broken links. The second way is to use an automatic tool to detect broken links and flag the error pages that are returned when a program fails.

To begin the discussion of testing practices, we will look at how to perform a quick check on the individual pages your application produces. Then we will move on to more detailed and thorough testing methods, such as creating and testing various paths to the output pages and performing load testing. We begin with the fastest and easiest methods because we want to help you start testing as soon as possible. If the most fundamental aspects of your application have problems, you must start fixing those problems immediately. If, for example, you invest time creating detailed load-testing scenarios and fine-tuning your servlet's performance and then find that the servlet does not function correctly, you might have to rewrite the servlet. As a result, you waste the effort you spent fine-tuning the original broken code.

What's even more critical than performing these tests in the suggested order is to test your application piece by piece. If you wait until you complete the majority of your sizable application before you start performing the most basic tests, you might end up discovering a major functionality problem and have to rewrite the entire application at the last minute before the expected release or update. If you thoroughly test each piece of the application as soon as it is available, you can rest assured that what you have done so far is correct and solid, in and of itself.

Finding Flow Problems Manually

To find flow problems manually, you click through the required elements and note which ones work and which do not. To find problems related to broken links, you follow all available links on every page. To determine whether a server-side failure occurs, you manually invoke the dynamic page by clicking links, setting the necessary input parameters and state variables, submitting forms, and so on. Obviously, this can be tedious and time-consuming. It can also be unreliable if you do not have an effective way to track what you have checked and what you have not.

See Chapter 13 for a more complete discussion of what is involved in invoking pages that require certain state variables to be set.

If you check for flow problems on a page-by-page basis, the task is considerably more manageable. If you test each page individually, as soon as it is available, your tests have a much better chance of covering all available links and reaching all dynamic pages. However, this work does add up as the application grows and you test more and more pages. Also, this method inevitably consumes a large amount of resources that could be better used on projects requiring human intelligence, such as developing a new application unit or complex test case scenarios.

If you have to rely on manual testing, you should develop checklists that are used rigorously. This is the only defense against the many weaknesses of manual testing. When you test manually, beware of the following:

- **Links that are not visible or not immediately visible.** For example, look for scripted links, background images, sounds, and the like.
- **Links that only *seem* to work.** You can solve part of this problem by disabling caching during manual testing so that you are actually testing the server.

- **All newly added links.** Any static checklist inevitably becomes out of sync with the application.

If your application uses clickable images, you have to verify that each clickable region leads to the correct destination and that the clickable regions are mapped properly to the image. When you access the application from the client side, it can be difficult to determine (and thus test) all the regions that have been defined by the HTML.

If your application uses forms, thorough manual testing means testing all permutations of all items on the form. In the case of the Online Grocer application, for instance, the Main Search page has three check boxes for product type and three check boxes for color. This alone yields 2^6 options: 64!

Although manual testing is not the recommended solution for robust link checking, it is a good technique for catching logical errors. There is no substitute for having users sit down and work through your application. This is the only way to find out whether the application provides a good user experience, and it's your last resort against errors your testing procedure fails to catch.

Finding Flow Problems Automatically

By testing automatically, you can perform your initial tests more efficiently and thoroughly, as well as easily repeat your tests to verify whether application changes (program modifications, file additions and deletions, and so on) introduce new errors or solve previously existing errors. Many free and commercial tools and services are designed to attack the problem of broken links.

The majority of the following examples focus on how to find flow problems with WebKing. Although some of this information is specific to WebKing, most of the ideas and techniques apply to any automatic link-testing solution you implement. Using WebKing is an effective way to target your flow-related problems because WebKing automatically

- Invokes dynamic pages and checks the links they contain
- Exposes a wide variety of link problems, including problems that occur only on certain browsers
- Flags failures by watching for an error page to occur – even if you have multiple customized error pages

Creating a client-side testing project

Tests for broken links (as well as all the other types of testing discussed in Chapters 12 through 14) are *client-side tests*: tests that check the application through an HTTP connection. Before you start testing your application from the client side, we recommend that you create a new project file that contains all your client-side testing information. It is possible to perform all your tests from the server-side testing file with which you have been working up to this point, but your testing is more efficient if you have different project files for different types of testing: your project files become more focused and, thus, easier to work with. Moreover, it is easier to share project files. Each team member checks out from source control only the specific project file related to the stage of development or testing he or she is performing.

We describe the basic process of creating a new WebKing project in Chapter 5 when we show you how to create a project file for your prototype. However, this process is now slightly different because you are loading dynamic programs, not just static files.

To create a client-side testing file, you create a new project and add a site that accesses your application from your staging server. These are the steps in detail:

1. Choose Project → New Project. A New Project node is added to WebKing's Project tree.
2. Right-click the New Project node in the Project tree, and choose Add New Site from the shortcut menu. The Add New Site to Project panel opens.
3. Enter the name of your application's base URL in the Source tab's Web server field. For example, we entered `http://ogryn.parasoft.com` to access the Online Grocer on a machine within our firewall (see Figure 11-4).

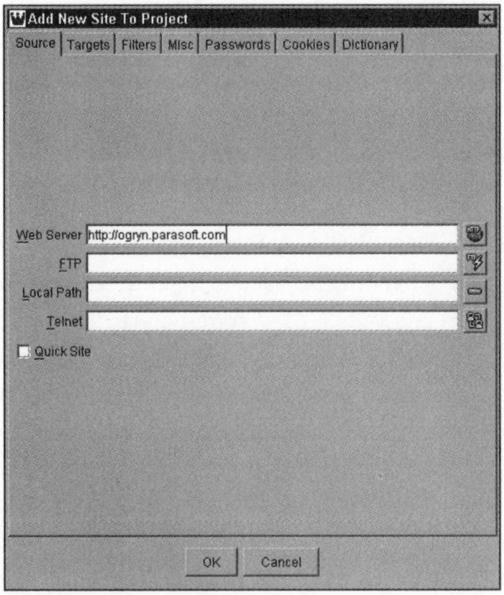

Figure 11-4: Completing the Add New Site to Project panel for a client-side project.

4. Click the HTTP button to the right of the Web server field, and set the following parameters in the HTTP Configuration dialog box that opens (see Figure 11-5):
   - Default Pages: *
   - CGI Directory and Log Directory: Blank
   - Obey Robot Restrictions: Off
   - Pass Cookies: On
   - Invoke CGI for All Arguments: On
   - Scan Forms with Default Input: Off
   - Fill Active Inputs Manually: On
   - Case Insensitive Server: Depends on your server

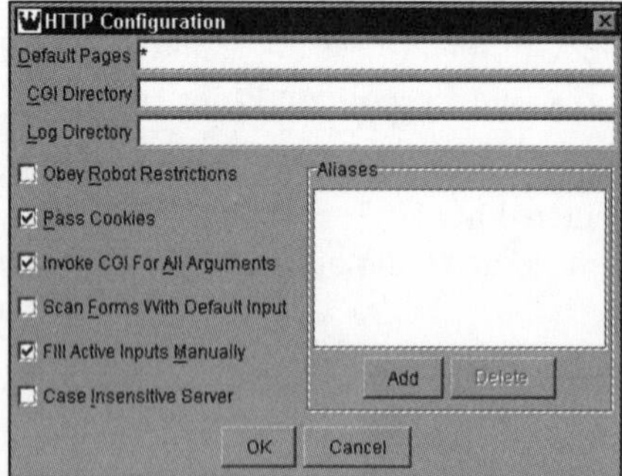

Figure 11-5: Completing the HTTP Configuration dialog box for a client-side project.

The Case Insensitive Server option is used by WebKing to determine whether filenames with different case really represent the same file. For instance, do `index.html` and `Index.html` correspond to the same page? If you are using a Windows Web server, these do represent the same page; on other platforms, they generally do not. In the interest of maintaining clean links and to enable you to switch servers if you later decide to, we recommend not using the Case Insensitive Server option. This way, if you refer the to same file using different cases, you will see multiple nodes in the Project tree and will be able to ensure that your application uses filenames consistently. The only time we recommend using this option is when you need to test an existing site that does not use case consistently.

WebKing then loads the application from the indicated Web server. When we created a client-side project for the Online Grocer application, WebKing opened a dialog box representing the Log In page (shown in Figure 11-6). This is one example of the dialog boxes you use to enter specific inputs for pages that allow form inputs (the specific contents depend on the contents in the related form). To keep our examples as simple as possible, we focus on the results of two preliminary test cases for the Online Grocer Log In page: one with a valid username and password and one with a valid username but an incorrect password. In this example, we are using `demo` as a username and `password` as the password (for security reasons, the password is displayed as a sequence of asterisks). The `METHOD`, `FRUITS`, `RED`, and `YELLOW` values are hidden inputs on the form, which you can see here but cannot modify. The `x=115, y=1` text indicates where we clicked on the image to submit the form – this is how you click on different areas of an image if they represented distinct, useful tests.

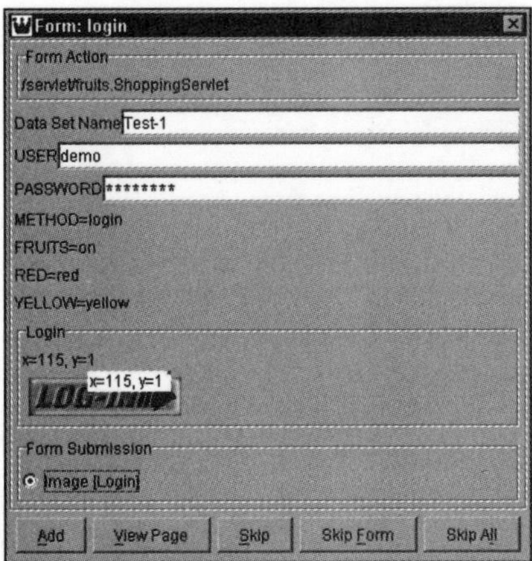

Figure 11-6: Adding a test case for the Online Grocer Log In page.

After creating our test cases, we indicate that we want to ignore the other forms for the time being by clicking the Skip All button in the next form dialog box that appears.

Figure 11-7 shows the Project tree produced after WebKing's initial client-side load of the Online Grocer application. The nodes representing dynamic pages are rendered in red text underneath the `servlet` node.

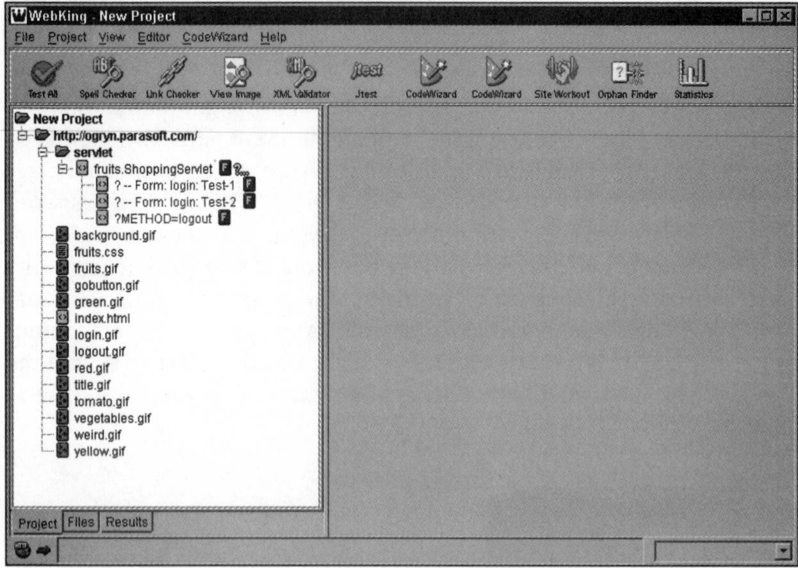

Figure 11-7: The Online Grocer's client-side testing Project tree.

WebKing's Statistics tool indicates that we have loaded the following files and directories:

```
Total Directories: 2
Total Files: 15
    Pages: 2
    Images: 12
    Other: 1

Other Content:
    Cookies: 1 (might depend on expiration)

File Extensions (excludes directories)
    css: 1
    gif: 12
    html: 1
    ShoppingServlet: 1

Content Types (excludes directories)
    image/gif: 12
    text/css: 1
    text/html: 2
```

Detecting standard broken links

You can use WebKing's Link Checker tool to automatically detect *standard* broken links (broken links that are not covered up by a special error page you developed). WebKing can check links in both dynamic and static pages. WebKing not only determines when the specified URL cannot be invoked but also alerts you to a variety of link format errors that work on most – but not all – browsers. These include

- URLs that contain a newline character
- URLs that contain the incorrect slash (\ instead of /)
- Empty URLs (`<A HREF="">`)
- URLs that contain a space character
- URLs that contain more than one # character
- URLs with extra slashes (`<A HREF="http:///www.parasoft.com">`)

If your application contains any of these iffy types of URLs, users with stringent browsers (such as browsers in PDAs or other Internet appliances) might not be able to access application features that work fine in your test environment.

To learn how the Link Checker tool works, consider the procedure we use to apply it to the Online Grocer application. At this point, our client-side Project tree contains a static splash page, the supporting files (images), and the following pages generated by the `ShoppingServlet` class that drives most of the Online Grocer's functionality:

- A Log In page
- A Main Search page (delivered after a successful log in)
- A Log In Failed page (delivered after a failed log in)
- A Log Out page

Chapters 4–6 describe all these files. The static splash page is represented by the `index.html` node; the dynamically generated pages are represented in the `servlet` directory.

The Project tree does not contain all the files used in the Online Grocer application because, for simplicity's sake, we did not exercise any forms past the initial login form. Thoroughly exercising these other pages requires creating paths. We will test the pages loaded so far and wait until we have specified paths to test the remainder of the pages.

The best way to test a page that requires specific inputs and state is to specify the click path required to invoke the desired instance of the page and test the version of the page that will be invoked after the specified path is actually traversed.

For information on specifying a path to a page, see Chapter 13. After you create a path to the page, you can apply the Link Checker tool to the path (as described in Chapter 13).

To check whether any of the currently loaded pages contain broken links, we select the root Project tree node and click the Link Checker button. This tells WebKing to run the Link Checker tool on all appropriate files in the Project tree. If we wanted to test only a single file, we would select that file's Project tree node and click the Link Checker button.

WebKing checks the available links and reports the results, shown in Figure 11-8.

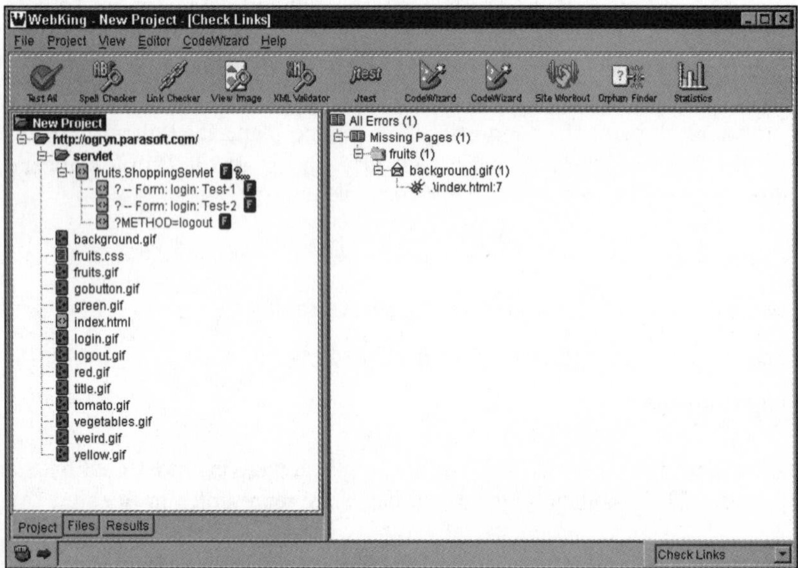

Figure 11-8: Check Links results from the Online Grocer.

By default, WebKing does not check *external* links (links to a Web site not contained in the current project — for example, a site with a different host name from the current site's host name) to improve the speed of your testing. Also, it is not polite to continually access other people's Web sites when you are testing your own application. You should occasionally verify your external links because these sites might come and go, but it is important to acknowledge that you are using others' resources and to be considerate.

To configure WebKing to check external links, right-click the Check Links button, choose Configure Check Links from the shortcut menu, and select the Check External Links option in the Configure Check Links panel.

From these results, we can determine that the link from the first page to the servlet-created second page worked correctly. This is the key functionality we wanted to test at this point. Another problem occurred, though: `index.html`'s link to the background image was broken, so the background did not appear on `index.html`. To learn more about this problem, we right-click the error message and choose Edit to open the source code in our selected editor. A quick look at the code reveals the problem:

```
<BODY BGCOLOR=#009900 BACKGROUND="fruits/background.gif">
```

The link points to `"fruits/background.gif"`, but because both the `index.html` and `background.gif` files sit in the root directory, that line of code should be written as

```
<BODY BGCOLOR=#009900 BACKGROUND="background.gif">
```

A General Strategy for Fixing Problems Found

Here are steps you can follow to fix most problems uncovered during client-side testing:

1. Determine the file that is the root of the problem. Is it a static file? a program file that creates an HTML page?
2. Determine how this file interacts with the rest of the system. Does it work with a database? other programs? a legacy system? components?
3. Apply a specialized tool that enables you to focus on the type of problem. For example, if you find that the problematic file accesses a database, apply a tool that lets you closely monitor database access. If you find a problem in an isolated servlet, use a Java testing tool to exercise the servlet thoroughly. If you find a problem with a file that accesses CORBA, use a tool made specifically for testing CORBA to try to pinpoint the problem.
4. Fix the problem before it has the opportunity to spawn more problems. Then continue your testing.

For detailed information on exploring results, see the WebKing User's Guide.

Detecting error pages

If your server is configured to generate errors under failure conditions, you must test for any occurrences of your error pages. Sample error pages include special pages to make client-side and server-side failures more user-friendly (as shown earlier in this chapter), as well as pages generated by your application under failure conditions (for example, if the database you are using becomes inaccessible). If we are running tests on the Online Grocer application using only valid usernames and passwords, the page reporting a failed log in is also an error page we would want to detect and report.

Because these pages are the actual content returned by the server, you generally cannot detect these problems with link-checking tools. Even worse, testing the page only once and assuming that it will always be correct is insufficient; the page might

Masking Your Errors

On most Web applications, the system is configured to display a standard error page when an error occurs. Rather than send users an obvious error page, some applications automatically route users who encounter problems to a special page that acts like an exception handler but doesn't look like one. For example, you can set it up so that whenever an error occurs, users see a page that says, `Server is busy - please try again later`. When users see this page, they do not get details of the crash or exception that has occurred. Instead, they assume that your application is overloaded and/or temporarily short on bandwidth. In other words, they won't know whether you have a buggy application or your application is experiencing problems beyond your control.

If you feel the need to employ such tactics, you can still track problems by checking when this page is reached. If necessary, you can store detailed information as comments in the HTML that you can automatically detect. However, in our experience using the Web, you should not expect your users to be fooled. Sites that are frequently unavailable are rightly regarded as buggy, regardless of the cause.

Nice error messages, regardless of how informative they are, cannot compensate for a buggy application. The main purpose of error pages is to provide a final safety net for unexpected errors, as well as to help you find critical problems during testing so that you can target and fix major problems before the application is available to users. When your application is live, your error page won't save you from major problems.

fail only occasionally. Fortunately, you can detect these problems by keeping track of when your error pages are reached. As long as you know some distinguishing pattern contained in each error page, you can create and enforce a rule that searches for matches of that pattern. The ideal pattern is a phrase or an HTML fragment that occurs in your error page but does not exist in any other pages on your application. By creating a rule that identifies this pattern, you can find critical flow problems even when they are not technically broken links and fix these problems so that users do not end up reaching this error page.

Using the WebKing tool is the easiest method for creating and enforcing rules. You can have it automatically construct a rule foundation based on a pattern you enter. Then you can modify the automatically created rule until it fully expresses the pattern you want WebKing to search for and identify. You can also create these rules with Python. Later in this chapter, we show you how to create a sample rule using both WebKing and Python. Before we delve into the logistics of designing rules, we will introduce the Online Grocer error page that the sample rules need to detect.

Because we want to test the servlet as soon as possible, we create a very basic error page to be invoked when a server-side problem occurs. At this point in the development process, our users are Web developers, so we want the error page to deliver a plain page with a message describing the specific problem that occurred. For our Java servlet, we can print the information stored in the exception, including the stack trace where the error occurred. A sample page contains the following information:

```
Caught java.lang.NoSuchMethodException: undefined

java.lang.NoSuchMethodException: undefined
      at java.lang.Class.getMethod0(Native Method)
      at java.lang.Class.getMethod(Class.java:854)
      at book.DispatchServlet.doInteraction(DispatchServlet.java:45)
      at book.DispatchServlet.doGet(DispatchServlet.java:23)
      at javax.servlet.http.HttpServlet.service(HttpServlet.java:499)
      at javax.servlet.http.HttpServlet.service(HttpServlet.java:588)
      at org.apache.jserv.JServConnection.processRequest(JServConnection.java)
      at org.apache.jserv.JServConnection.run(JServConnection.java)
      at java.lang.Thread.run(Thread.java:479)
```

Clearly, this page is not appropriate for the final deployed application; the typical end user won't understand what this page means and will only be confused by it. Later in the development process, we will replace this debugging page with a more user-friendly error page directed toward our end users. This step is easy to overlook, though. Because the final application should never generate this page under normal conditions, it's conceivable that simple testing will not remind us that this page needs to be updated. One simple way to solve this problem is to generate a special URL that always triggers the failure page and add this URL to the test suite. If we still want detailed information available from the error page but don't want users to have to look at it, we will put it inside an HTML comment in the page. Then it is available when needed but otherwise out of the way.

The first step in determining whether and when this basic error page is reached is to design a rule that identifies the error page. We decide to search for the pattern of any text phrase that reads `Caught <something> Exception`. This pattern is sure to appear on all error pages but not on any of our regular application pages. Moreover, this pattern is general enough that it will match the error pages produced for different types and instances of exceptions. If we decide to look for an overly specific phrase (such as `Caught java.lang.NumberFormatException: 1`), the rule will identify only one specific instance of that error and not provide the comprehensive testing for which we are aiming.

To satisfy these requirements, we will develop a rule that searches for `Caught.*Exception`, a string that uses regular expressions to represent a general phrase. The period represents any single character, and the asterisk matches 0 or more occurrences of the preceding character. Together, these two characters indicate any combination of any characters. By placing these characters in the middle of the phrase, we express that we want to match any phrase that has the word *Caught*, any combination of other characters, and the word *Exception*.

You make your rules general by using regular expressions instead of exact phrases. As we discuss in detail in Chapter 12, general rules are especially useful for checking elements on dynamic pages that are always slightly different. For tips on using regular expressions, see Appendix D.

DETECTING ERROR PAGES WITH PYTHON

If you have some way to access a page's contents, you can script any rules you like, using the language of your choice. Here the preceding rule is implemented in Python, assuming that the file contents have been stored locally and the filename is passed as an argument. By using an XML parser within Python, you can access the parsed XHTML contents:

```
import xml.dom.minidom
import sys
import re

document = xml.dom.minidom.parse(sys.argv[1])

elements = document.getElementsByTagName('P')
for tag in elements:
    c = tag.childNodes
    if len(c) == 1 and c[0].nodeType == xml.dom.Node.TEXT_NODE:
```

```
s = c[0].data
if re.compile("^Caught .*Exception$").match(s):
    print s
    sys.exit(1)
```

This rule is available on the CD-ROM as `rule.py`. You can run this rule for yourself from the CD by executing `python rule.py error.html`.

This method of detecting error pages is restrictive for several reasons:

- You must be able to access and store many instances of your dynamic pages for testing.
- You must work within the confines of your scripting language and libraries. In this case, the parser we used requires the HTML to be parseable as XHTML (well formed with respect to beginning and ending tags, and so forth).
- You must have expertise in the scripting language being used, as well as in how to find the problems. Often, the initial code needs to be tweaked and adjusted to perform well on actual examples. Additionally, when you want to modify your rules in response to changes on your application, you must enlist the help of some of your most experienced developers.

If you already have a Python framework for testing your code and you choose or create a more fault-tolerant HTML parser, this solution might be workable for you. Chapter 14 has a simple sample framework into which you can plug this rule. Even here, though, it will likely become unwieldy as you accumulate rules over time.

DETECTING ERROR PAGES WITH WEBKING

To create this same rule in WebKing (using the RuleWizard feature), you perform the following steps:

1. Open the HTML RuleWizard dictionary by choosing CodeWizard → Show Dictionary → HTML. A dictionary of available rule subjects is displayed in the left side of the WebKing GUI.
2. Right-click the unused area of the HTML tab, and choose Auto-Create Rules from the shortcut menu. The RuleWizard Automatic Creation window opens.
3. Enter the piece of code that is unique to the error page in the RuleWizard Automatic Creation window. For this example, enter **Caught**

IllegalArgumentException in the window. WebKing then creates the basic rule pattern shown in Figure 11-9.

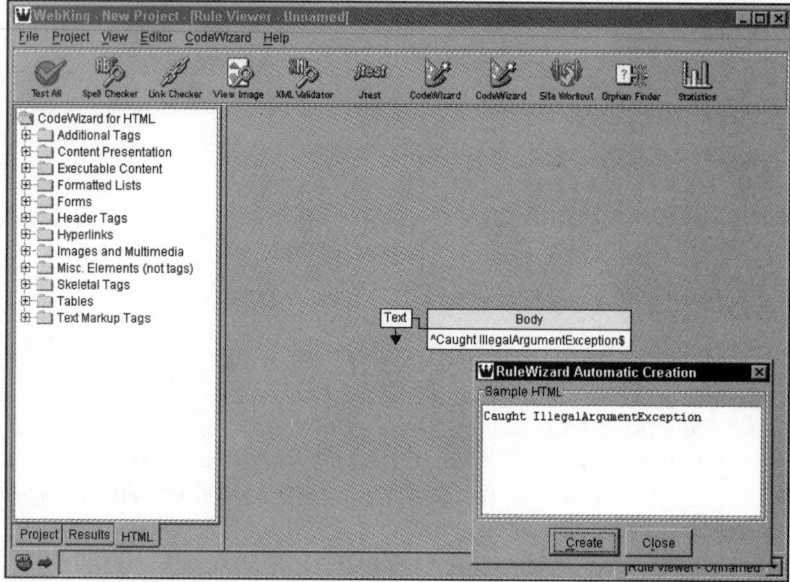

Figure 11-9: The automatically created exception rule structure.

The expression in this rule matches a specific exception, but you want to match any exception.

4. Modify this rule so that it matches *any* exception, by right-clicking the `Body` node, choosing Modify, and modifying the expression so that it reads **Caught.*Exception**. This modified rule identifies any variation of the error message that will be displayed if the servlet throws an exception.

5. Customize the output message.

   a. Right-click the output arrow, and choose Modify from the shortcut menu. The Customize Output window opens.

   b. In the Customize Output window, replace the existing text with the message you want reported when this page is reached. In this example, enter the text **Error page has been reached: exception occurred.** This way, whenever this rule is violated, you (or whoever else inherits this test case) will know exactly which problem occurred.

6. Customize the rule's properties.

   a. Right-click the unused area of the right panel, and choose Properties from the shortcut menu. The Properties panel opens.

b. In the Properties panel's CodeWizard tab, replace the text in the Header field with a message describing this rule's general type of violation (for example, enter **Exception Found**).

7. Save the rule by right-clicking the unused area of the right panel, choosing Save As from the shortcut menu, and specifying where you want to save this rule.

Figure 11-10 shows the final rule.

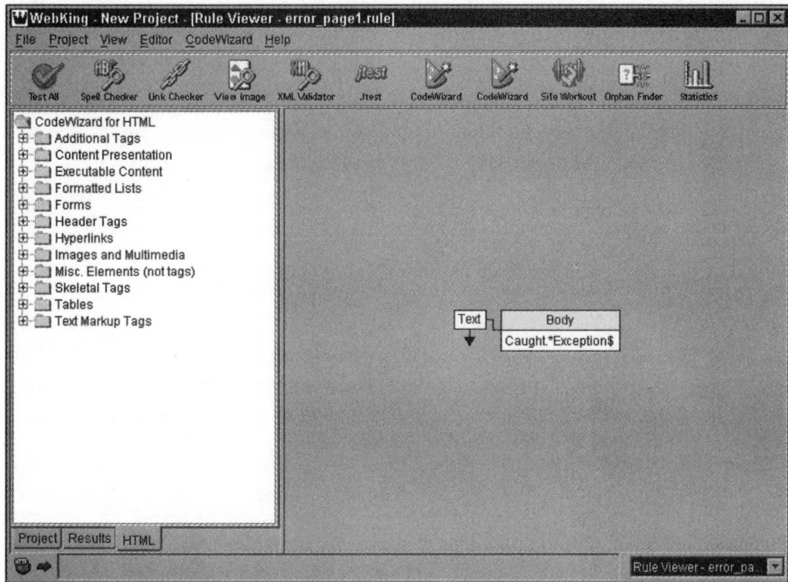

Figure 11-10: The completed exception rule.

This rule is available on the CD-ROM as `error_page1.rule`.

The rules you create with RuleWizard are enforced by WebKing's CodeWizard tool. This tool's fundamental purpose – checking coding standards – is discussed in Chapter 8. Here, you will focus on how to use it to enforce the RuleWizard rule you just created.

Before you can apply a rule, you must create a new CodeWizard Enforcer for it or add it to an existing CodeWizard Enforcer. A *CodeWizard Enforcer* is a tool that checks either a set of rules or a single rule. You create a new CodeWizard Enforcer that checks this rule by choosing CodeWizard → Create Enforcer and selecting this rule from the file chooser.

All CodeWizard buttons use the same icon. To determine which button is associated with which rule or rule set, place your cursor over the button. A popup menu containing the button's name opens.

To apply this rule to the Online Grocer application, we select the root Project tree node and click the correct CodeWizard Enforcer button. When WebKing enforces this rule, it checks whether each file contains a string that has the word *Caught*, any combination of other characters, and the word *Exception*. If this pattern is found, WebKing reports the specified violation message. In this case, no matches are found, so we know that the `ShoppingServlet` is at least able to create these first few application pages without crashing. After we create paths through the other pages this servlet can produce, we apply this rule again. Chapter 13 describes how we do this and what is discovered.

To test our rule fully, we would create at least one case where the error page was created, to make sure that we are correctly flagging the error page. One way to do this is to create a hidden method in the `ShoppingServlet` class, say `simulateError()`, which would always throw an exception. Then we could add a link to our servlet with the argument `METHOD=simulateError` and verify that our rule detected the resulting page.

For complete information on using RuleWizard, see the documentation available by choosing CodeWizard → RuleWizard Documentation in the WebKing GUI.

Summary

In this chapter, we describe the three causes of flow problems: client-side failures, server-side failures, and logical errors. In each case, you must think about all the things that can go wrong and must test for those conditions — a thorough understanding of the possible errors is necessary if you want to ensure that your testing is complete. We also show how to create error pages to put a presentable front on some of the common problems that occur. Finally, we cover how to detect the various kinds of errors, including application-specific rules for custom errors, and present a brief strategy for finding the cause of problems found. In Chapter 12, we present more information on creating application-specific rules to find logical errors. We show how to validate side effects which modify a database in Chapter 16.

Chapter 12

Verifying Content

IN THIS CHAPTER

- Checking spelling
- Checking applets
- Verifying requirements

IF YOU WANT A TRULY BULLETPROOF application, you should not only check that the pages flow as expected but also carefully verify that all available pages function correctly and contain the required elements. In this chapter, we look at some additional client-side testing techniques you can use to verify the contents of the pages sent to the clients' browsers (by *contents* we mean everything in the page's source code – from HTML tags, to JavaScript code, to images, to the text that will be rendered in the browser). Some of the tests we discuss are application-independent, including spelling and applet validation. Others are more application-specific (for example, tests that verify whether pages contain the required messages or GUI elements).

Checking for Misspelled Words

Misspelled words can prevent even the most well-designed application (and the company it represents) from appearing accurate, intelligent, and thorough. Nevertheless, many Web applications are filled with typos. Naturally, many kinds of typos slip through even the most thorough spell checker (for example, *feat* instead of *feet*). In this case, we're primarily addressing obviously misspelled words. Why are so many otherwise carefully built Web applications riddled with incorrectly spelled words? Mostly because of the lack of effective ways to verify spelling.

Checking spelling with traditional spell checkers and scripts

If you are writing static pages using a GUI, you quite often have an option to check spelling. In this case, there is no excuse for typos. On the other hand, if you are using a text editor or your pages are dynamically generated, you need a tool that can read HTML files and find spelling errors. Many people are understandably turned off when spell-checking the following code:

```
<P>This is a sample <a href="foo.html">link</a>.</p>
```

HTML-ignorant editors report that href and foo (or foo.html, depending on the tool) are misspelled. Checking a real page results in so many tags and words next to tags being reported incorrectly that most developers in this situation either avoid spell-checking altogether or spell-check but fail to catch real errors because they are obscured by so many false errors.

Another option is to try to convert your documents to text and spell-check those text files. This is an effective process, but painful if you convert your files one by one. You might be able to automate this process using command-line tools supporting *PYX*—a special syntax developed by the XML community to allow streaming Unix-like commands. Here's the PYX equivalent of the preceding HTML sample; lines beginning with a hyphen (-) represent the text we want to spell-check:

```
(p
-This is a sample
(a
Ahref foo.html
-link
)a
-.
)p
-\n
```

Here's how you can use one of the Python scripts available on www.pyxie.org to automate the process:

```
python html2pyx.py foo.html | grep "^-" > foo.txt
ispell foo.txt
```

Needless to say, this is a solution that can be appreciated only by a developer. Using any of these conversion techniques, though, you will still miss typos like this one:

```
<img src="image.gif" alt="hydden">
```

Because ALT attributes are displayed if the image is unavailable or is on a browser that does not support images or has images disabled, the text should be spell-checked. This kind of error is also easy for your human testers to miss because they might not even see the text unless they are running in the correct environment. The PYX output for this sample looks like this:

```
(img
Asrc image.gif
```

```
Aalt hydden
-\n
```

You could extend the preceding Python command to find lines beginning with `Aalt` and also spell-check those attributes. You would also add any other pieces you wanted to spell-check, including `ALT` attributes from other tags.

You can find `html2pyx.py` and several HTML examples on the CD.

A final spelling-related problem we have encountered is the high incidence of jargon or special terminology on many Web pages. Typically, spell checkers let you ignore words that are correct but are simply not in the dictionary you are checking against. It's nice to be able to mark such words as being specific to a page or a site, if appropriate. Then you don't clutter your dictionary with special-purpose words that don't necessarily apply globally.

What is necessary to solve these problems is a fully HTML-aware tool that can grab the HTML pages directly from your Web application (so that they can be checked even if dynamically generated). WebKing happens to fit this description neatly. WebKing can grab static and dynamic pages, and its spell checker understands HTML tags, so it does not erroneously report HTML tags and words adjacent to tags as misspelled. It is even able to spot spelling errors that appear only when the code is rendered (for example, `an<B>error</B>`). As a result, this spell checker makes it easier for you to focus on finding and fixing the real spelling errors on your application.

Checking spelling with WebKing

WebKing checks spelling with its Spell Checker tool. To learn how the Spell Checker tool works, consider the procedure we use to apply it to the Online Grocer application.

To check whether any of the pages currently in the Project tree contain misspelled words, we select the root Project tree node and click the Spell Checker button. This tells WebKing to run the Spell Checker tool on all appropriate files in the Project tree. If we wanted to test only a single file, we would select that file's Project tree node and click the Spell Checker button.

WebKing then checks spelling of files that contain text and reports the results, shown in Figure 12-1.

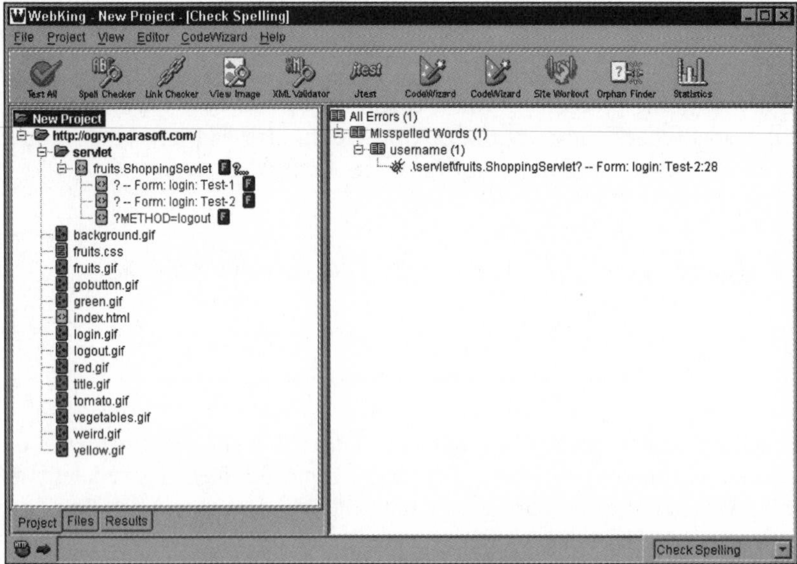

Figure 12-1: Check Spelling results from the Online Grocer application.

The results reveal that the Spell Checker did not recognize the word *username* and reported it as misspelled. Before deciding what action to take with this message, we have to decide whether we want to allow the term *username* in our application or change it to *user name*. If we choose the former option, we need to add the word *username* to one of WebKing's dictionaries so that WebKing does not report this word as misspelled in future tests. If we choose the latter option, we need to edit the servlet code responsible for producing this phrase so that it will print *user name* instead of *username*.

WebKing has three types of dictionaries: User, Site, and Page.

User dictionaries contain words you want WebKing to accept on any page that you test with WebKing. There is one User dictionary for each WebKing user.

Site dictionaries contain words you want WebKing to accept on any page from the current WebKing site. There is one Site dictionary per site, so you can have multiple Site dictionaries per project.

Page dictionaries contain words that are acceptable only on the current page. You can have a different Page dictionary for every appropriate node (HTML, XML, and so on) in the Project tree.

Detecting Spelling Problems at the Source

If your application generates a large number of pages on-the-fly, you can often be proactive about looking for spelling errors. For instance, if you are pulling strings from a database like the one the Online Grocer application uses, you should try to run a spell checker against your database. You can do this either with a database-aware spell checker or by exporting your database to a file and spell-checking that file.

If you are using ASP or JSP, you might be able to fall back on the convert-to-text and spell check approach if you can find a tool that will perform the necessary conversion. Although tedious, this approach is definitely better than skipping spell-checking altogether. Really advanced tools might be able to pull strings from Java or C/C++ programs and check them. However, this would tend to report many false positives because not all strings used in programs represent complete strings that are shown to users.

We will allow *username* on our application, so we need to add the word to our Site dictionary. Here is the general procedure for adding words to a dictionary:

1. In the Results panel, right-click the message related to the appropriate misspelled word message. A shortcut menu opens.
2. Choose Add <word> to dictionary from the shortcut menu, and choose the command associated with the dictionary to which you want to add this word.

The selected word is automatically added to the specified dictionary, and the error is removed from the Results panel.

By default, WebKing's Spell Checker is not *case-sensitive*. In other words, if you add *ParaSoft* to a dictionary, it will not report *Parasoft* or *parasoft* as misspelled. If you would prefer the Spell Checker to be case-sensitive, right-click the Spell Checker button, choose Configure Check Spelling from the shortcut menu, and select the Case Sensitive option in the dialog box that opens.

You can also import or manually add words to a dictionary, as well as configure WebKing to check the spelling of languages other than English. WebKing can use any word list or dictionary compatible with ispell. For details on performing these tasks, refer to the Check Spelling section of the WebKing User's Guide.

The International Ispell page is located at `fmg-www.cs.ucla.edu/fmg-members/geoff/ispell.html`. This is where you can download ispell, as well as dictionaries for many languages.

Testing Applets

Well-designed and reliable applets can enhance application appeal and functionality. However, many applets are not well designed or reliable – especially many of the third-party applets freely available on the Web. One way to test applets is to write and execute test cases for them. These test cases, like all your test cases, should test both critical functionality and a wide variety of unexpected but possible inputs. Another way is to use WebKing's Jtest applet tester. This tool performs automatic white-box testing on Java applets. In other words, when the Jtest applet tester finds an applet, it examines the applet and creates and executes test cases designed to exercise the applet as thoroughly as possible to see how it handles a wide variety of expected and unexpected inputs.

For a detailed discussion of white box testing, see Chapter 9.

To use the Jtest applet tester feature to test the applets on a single page, locate and select the node representing that page in WebKing's Project tree, and click the Jtest button. To test all files in the Project tree at once, select the root node of the Project tree, and click the Jtest button. When WebKing sees an `APPLET` tag, it finds the class file referenced in the tag and sends that file to Jtest.

Each test produces a report containing the following information:

- Test statistics
- Each exception found (including the stack trace and arguments used to uncover the exception)
- Coverage data
- Annotated source code for all user classes accessed

This report is displayed in the right side of the WebKing GUI.

To use WebKing's Jtest applet tester, you need the Jtest tool installed on your system.

Verifying Requirements

Beyond the usual checks that apply to most applications lies a whole host of design and functionality requirements that can be checked only with application-specific knowledge. This includes the logical errors mentioned in Chapter 11 and anything else that affects whether the users see what the designers intended. For example, do your pages contain the correct buttons, images, and links? Are these elements presented properly? Do the correct messages appear when and where they should? Do the correct forms appear in the correct pages? Does each form contain the correct options? Does each form submit the correct default elements?

Checking these requirements can be quite a feat, especially if your application's pages change frequently according to user, time, preferences, and other variables. Not only must you determine how to test (and retest) every requirement, but you must also figure out a way to deal with the constant changes. The pages containing the required elements often change according to variables such as user and time, and sometimes the required elements themselves change as these variables change.

There are three main ways to check these application-specific requirements:

- Check each element manually.
- Use a record/playback tool to check for changes in required elements.
- Use rules to check for the presence of required elements.

The remainder of this chapter discusses how you can use these methods to check whether your requirements are implemented, as well as whether your requirements are still satisfied as your application evolves. We will briefly introduce the first two methods and then focus closely on the last method. We are focusing primarily on the rules method because we strongly believe that it is the most thorough, flexible, and efficient way to check requirements in Web applications.

Building a black-box (functionality) test suite

When you test requirements, you are essentially testing your application's functionality. You can create a *black-box (functionality) test suite* – a set of tests that check whether your application performs according to specification – using any of the methods discussed in the remainder of this chapter. Here are some general tips on creating a black-box test suite that apply to all the methods we introduce.

START EARLY AND WORK INCREMENTALLY. We recommend that each time you complete a new program or module that can create output pages, you deploy the program or module, check whether the pages it produces flow as expected, and then create and run test cases that check the required elements in each page it can produce. This way, you are creating test cases while the site unit's code and intended functionality are fresh in your mind, and you are alerted to functionality problems before you start fine-tuning this site unit or start developing another. QA can later extend the set of rules you develop, as necessary.

DESIGN YOUR TESTS SO THAT A MESSAGE IS REPORTED ONLY IF AN ERROR OCCURS. For example, if you want to require a certain greeting, you should configure your test case so that it reports an error message if the greeting is incorrect (or missing), but it does not report any message if the greeting appears correctly. This way, you do not have to sort through unnecessary messages, and you can easily determine whether your test suite passes or fails, by checking whether any messages were reported. Also, if you set up the test suite in this way, you can require that the application pass this test suite before it can be deployed. For details on setting up such a boolean filter, see Chapter 10.

DESIGN AT LEAST ONE TEST CASE FOR EACH REQUIREMENT INCLUDED IN THE SPECIFICATION. Ideally, you should check each requirement under a wide variety of conditions. For example, if you are checking whether a personalized greeting appears in a configurable welcome page, you should test whether the greeting appears correctly for users with a variety of name formats (one-word names, two-word names, three-word names, names with a combination of letters and numbers, names with abbreviations, names with periods, and so on), as well as a wide variety of different configurations (pages with different colors, different layouts, different categories, and so on). As explained in detail in Chapter 13, dynamic pages can appear differently (and contain different problems) each time they are invoked. To test the requirements in a page thoroughly, you have to test a large number of possible instances of that page.

GROUP YOUR TESTS SO THAT THEY CAN BE RUN AS A SET. Preferably, you should configure this test suite so that it can be run automatically each night and you can have the results available in the morning. This way, you receive immediate notification when an application modification breaks previously correct functionality, and you can fix the problem while the revision is still fresh in your mind.

Before the first test suite run (and after any significant application or test suite modifications), give your tests a few trial runs so that you can quickly identify and deal with any false positives that occur.

False positives should be handled immediately. If you allow them to remain in your test suite, you and your team members can become desensitized to errors and so accustomed to ignoring these false positives that critical errors will be lost in the sea of false positives.

NEVER GIVE UP – EVEN IF THE TEST SUITE PRODUCES AN OVERWHELMING NUMBER OF ERRORS. Tackle the problems incrementally. Work on cleaning up the most critical type of problem or application area, and then move to the next, then the next, and so on. Of course, the best way to avoid overwhelming results is to follow our first tip: Start early and work incrementally.

Verifying requirements manually

One way to check your requirements is to manually examine the application pages as rendered in a browser or to look at the source code for each file. However, this method is extremely time-consuming and error-prone.

First, you have to invoke each page you want to test. As explained in Chapter 13, this alone is a tedious process. Next, you must check all the required items. If the item you are checking is displayed in the page itself, you can look at the item in the browser and record whether the item met the specification. While checking each requirement, you have to account for browser variations, browser configurations, system variations, and so on. Because the early rapid development of browsers outpaced standards development, most browsers do not strictly conform to standards. As a result, elements that look fine on one browser might not even appear on another.

If the requirement you want to check is something that does not appear in the page (for example, a requirement as to what hidden inputs a form should submit), you have to open the page's source code, search for that element in the file, and record whether it appears correctly.

To ensure that the requirements are met under all circumstances, you need to create a wide variety of expected and unexpected paths to each page and repeat the tests. If a page can be produced in 50 ways, you cannot check the elements in one instance and assume that they will work the same way in the other 49 possible instances.

For a more detailed discussion about why it's so important to create and test a wide variety of paths, see Chapter 13.

Unfortunately, each time the application changes, you must reinvoke every instance of each page you tested and recheck each required element on each page. This can take more time than developing the application.

Verifying requirements with record/playback tools

Record/playback tools are tools frequently used for *regression testing* (making sure that errors are not introduced into an already functioning application). Basically, they let you click through as many pages on your application as you like and take digital pictures of how the pages look; this is the recording stage. Later, you can have the playback stage re-create the same pages and compare the digital pictures, reporting any serious differences. Exact details beyond this depend on the specific tool you are using.

These tools provide an easy and effective way to check whether your pages remain exactly the same. For example, if you want to test that every button, word, image, and so on in a single click path always remains the same, these tools are very beneficial.

However, these tools' strength can also be their limitation if your application is very dynamic and/or modified frequently. If your application changes with time (for example, as new items become available or as situations change), these tools cannot test your specifications without reporting false positives for items that are supposed to change. Moreover, you have no reliable way of verifying requirements involving items that change on a regular basis. For example, suppose that one of your pages is required to contain a calendar that highlights the current date. If your application is working correctly, the calendar changes every day, and an error is reported any time a calendar does not match the one in your control case. You get false errors (false positives) every day except for the day you created the test case.

Another drawback of this method is that unless the tool is storing HTML source code, it can check only elements that appear in the browser. If you want to check requirements apparent at the code level (for example, a requirement as to what hidden inputs a form should submit), you have to test them using an alternative method.

If you do decide that one of these tools can help you reach your requirements testing goals, choose a product that is compatible with your development environment and suits the needs of your testing procedure. Make sure that you can run your tests automatically and that the results are easy to understand and use. We don't generally recommend record/playback tools for Web applications because they are, by nature, dynamic and constantly changing, which is not a good fit for this kind of checking.

Verifying requirements with application-specific rules

The third, and recommended, way to check your requirements is to create and enforce general rules describing the required elements in terms of the code patterns that create the required elements. Such rules overcome the problems with the preceding two methods.

The first and foremost advantage of the rules method is that rules are flexible, so you can create rules that are as general or specific as the situation requires. For example, you can use general rules to check whether a calendar always highlights the current date or if a `Current Local Temperature` message appears in the correct location. Also, you can use specific rules to check for the exact width of a table or the presence of an exact phrase or image. You can even use rules to check whether the application writes the correct information to the database.

We discuss this database verification technique in detail in Chapter 16.

Even if the element you want to check changes according to time, user, and other variables, you can use a single rule to check multiple instances of the element. You can rest assured that your tests will not report false positives for items that are changing as intended. For example, if your application's welcome page is required to contain a message welcoming each user by name, you can create a rule to check this functionality requirement. This rule could describe the required greeting phrase in its most basic and general elements (a phrase that begins with the word *Welcome*, followed by a space character, followed by any string that might represent a name). This rule is general enough to accept any possible username but specific enough to report problems such as missing names caused by database access problems (which might produce a greeting such as `Hello`) or spacing problems in the servlet code (which might produce a greeting such as `HelloJohn`). You can then use this rule to check whether a wide variety of welcome pages contain the correct type of greeting.

The second advantage of rules is that they describe the required elements in terms of the code. As a result, they are more accurate than GUI-level checks, they are not sensitive to browser variations, and they are able to check elements that are not apparent in the page displayed on the browser. For example, you can check whether a form submits the correct hidden inputs or has the correct action. It would be tedious to check these requirements manually, and it is impossible to check these requirements with most record/playback tools.

The third advantage of rules is that they are repeatable and extensible. After you create a rule, you can apply it to a single file, all files, or files in selected click paths, with a simple script or with the click of a button. Even if the application is modified, you can still check your requirements without any additional work. As long as the rule describes the specification in general terms, you do not need to modify the rule unless you change the requirement itself. For example, say that you have an image named `logout.gif` that is required to link to `/servlet/some.Servlet?METHOD=logout`. If you create a general rule that checks this functionality and later modify the `logout.gif` image, you do not have to change the rule to check whether the modified page still implements the requirement correctly. Manual testing has to be repeated from scratch each time an element is modified, and record/playback scripts have to be rerecorded (or at least updated) each time an element involved in the test is modified.

As shown in Chapter 11, you can write rules in any sufficiently powerful language, including Python. For now, we will focus on the ideas of the rules rather than the implementation, so we will use WebKing's RuleWizard.

Creating a Testing Infrastructure

In Chapters 6 and 7, we discuss how it pays to plan ahead when you are developing your application. If you know ahead of time what you will be testing for and how you will be testing, you can design your project around making that testing easy.

For instance, it is sometimes appropriate to bury, in your HTML files, hidden messages designed to support your verification techniques. You do this by including HTML comments wherever is appropriate. These comments should contain information that is helpful for your testing but not intended for your end users. Because this information will be available to anyone who views the HTML source, it's not a good idea to have these comments include sensitive information (such as the home phone number of the support person responsible for the file).

CREATING AND ENFORCING APPLICATION-SPECIFIC RULES WITH WEBKING

WebKing's RuleWizard feature provides an easy way to identify specific patterns in your code. RuleWizard is most often used to find patterns that you do not want to appear in your code (in other words, patterns that represent errors or violations). However, it can also be used to check for the presence of patterns that you always want to appear in your code, or even more complex rules. You can create rules that search for an exact pattern (such as an exact phrase within a specific table cell), or you can use regular expressions to have RuleWizard search for general patterns (such as the phrase *Welcome <some_combination_of letters>!* or *Today is <valid month name> <valid date>, <valid year>*).

By creating a rule for each requirement listed in the specification, you can not only establish a reliable method for checking whether the requirement is satisfied in the initial test but also create a regression test suite you can use to check whether application modifications affect any of the requirements.

Before you start creating rules, you should refer to your specification to see which elements and functionality are required for each page. Does the specification require certain form pages to contain submit buttons? certain graphical elements, such as company logos? a certain message, such as a personalized greeting? As you decide on which elements to describe in rules, remember, you can create rules that apply to specific pages, rules that apply to all pages, rules that apply to all pages with a certain title, link, word, and so on. Your rules can be as general or specific as your requirements.

If you are using RuleWizard to create your rule, you can choose from three available rule-creation options:

- In RuleWizard's Auto-Create dialog box, enter code representing the element you want to check for. Then let RuleWizard's Auto-Create feature automatically construct your rule.

- Customize one of the template rules included with WebKing.
- Create your rule from scratch by pointing, clicking, and entering values in dialog boxes.

In this chapter, we look at how to customize template rules included in the WebKing installation. These template rules are described in the WebKing User's Guide. Experimenting with these template rules is a good way to familiarize yourself with how RuleWizard works and what valid rules look like.

WebKing's Auto-Create feature works best for creating rules that identify specific HTML patterns. These patterns can be either patterns that you want to find or patterns that you want to verify are not present. For information on using the Auto-Create feature, see Chapters 8 and 11.

For information on building a rule from scratch, see the RuleWizard User's Guide. To access this User's Guide, choose CodeWizard → RuleWizard Documentation in the WebKing GUI.

No matter how you create rules, you can introduce flexibility into the rule by using regular expressions to describe specific elements (such as particular usernames or dates) in terms of their most basic and general elements. For example, the username element could be described as any combination of eight or fewer letters, and the date element could be described as a string that starts with *January, February, March*, and so on, followed by a space, followed by any number between 1 and 31. For a quick guide to using regular expressions, see Appendix D.

To give you an idea of how to customize a template rule, we will walk you through an example. For the sake of this example, assume that you want to verify whether the Online Grocer's Log In page always contains a login form with the correct `ACTION` attribute. You can check this functionality by developing a rule that checks whether all pages with ***Login*** in the `TITLE` tag contain a form named ***login*** with the `ACTION` attribute `/servlet/fruits.ShoppingServlet`.

To create this rule, you perform the following steps:

1. Open the template rule by choosing CodeWizard → Edit Rule and then choosing the NoForm.rule (in `<webking_installation_dir>/templates`) from the file chooser. The rule opens in the right WebKing panel, as shown in Figure 12-2.

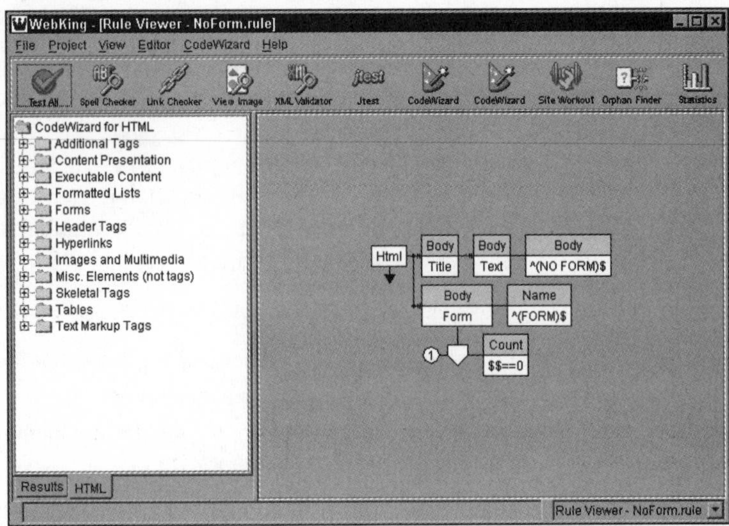

Figure 12-2: The NoForm template rule.

As is, this rule checks whether a page with certain `TITLE` text contains the specified form. You want to check for not only the correct form but also the correct form `ACTION`, so you have to add some conditions to this rule, as well as modify the existing fields.

2. Specify the text that appears in the `TITLE` tag of the pages that should contain the link.

   a. Right-click the node associated with the content of the `TITLE` text (here, the top-right node), and choose Modify from the shortcut menu. The Modify String window opens.

   b. In the Modify String window, replace the existing text with a word or phrase that identifies all the pages that you want to contain a certain link. For this example, you want to enter **^Login$**. (^ indicates that the rule should look for a string that begins exactly like the next character; `$` indicates that the rule should look for a string that ends exactly like the preceding character. Together, these characters tell the rule to look for an exact match of the embedded string.) Figure 12-3 shows what the modified rule branch should look like. This branch now specifies that you want to look for pages whose `TITLE` contains the exact string `Login`.

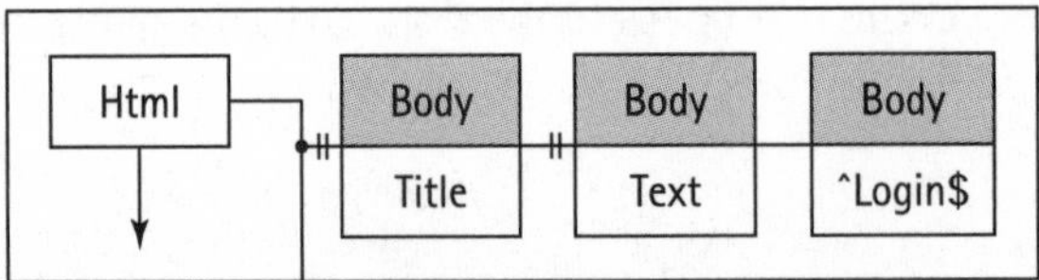

Figure 12-3: Specifying the TITLE text that identifies our Log In page.

3. Specify the name of the form that you want each page titled *Login* to include.

   a. Right-click the node associated with the form name (here, the middle-right node), and choose Modify from the shortcut menu. The Modify String window opens.

   b. In the Modify String window, replace the existing text with the name of the form you want to check. For this example, you want to enter **^login$**. Figure 12-4 shows what the modified rule branch should look like. This branch now specifies that you want to check for the presence of a form named *login*.

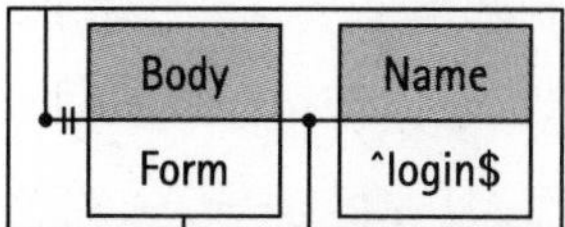

Figure 12-4: Specifying the form name that identifies our login form.

4. Specify that you want the rule to check whether the login form contains the correct `ACTION`.

   a. Right-click the `Body/Form` node, and choose Action from the shortcut menu. An `Action` node is added to the rule, which represents the URL named by the `ACTION` attribute.

   b. Right-click the `Action` node, and choose Filename from the shortcut menu. An empty `Filename` node is then added to the rule.

   c. Right-click the `Filename` node, and enter **/servlet/fruits.ShoppingServlet** (the required form `ACTION`) in the Modify String dialog box that opens. This specifies which URL filename the form's `ACTION` should reference.

5. Customize the output message.

   a. Right-click the output arrow, and choose Modify from the shortcut menu. The Customize Output window opens.

   b. In the Customize Output window, replace the existing text with **Log In page does not contain login form.**

6. Customize the rule's properties.

   a. Right-click the unused area of the right panel, and choose Properties from the shortcut menu. The Properties panel opens.

   b. In the Properties panel's CodeWizard tab, replace the text in the Header field with a message describing this rule's general type of violation. For example, you could enter **Form Elements.**

7. Save the rule by right-clicking the unused area of the right panel, choosing Save As from the shortcut menu, and specifying a new name and (optional) location for this rule.

The rule is now complete; it says, "If you find a page with *Login* in the title, count the number of forms that are named *login* and have the `ACTION /servlet/fruits.ShoppingServlet`; if the count is 0, report an error." In other words, "Report an error if any page titled *Login* does not contain a form named *login* that has the `ACTION /servlet/fruits.ShoppingServlet`." Figure 12-5 shows the final rule structure.

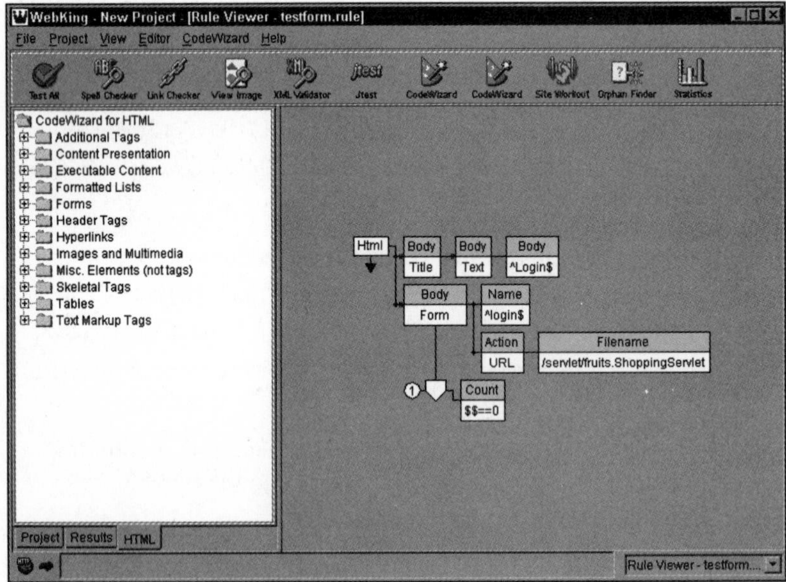

Figure 12-5: The completed "Login form" rule.

This rule is available on the CD as `testform.rule`.

If this were your own application, you would probably want to create more rules to check this page's basic requirements. For example, you could create a rule that checks for the presence of the correct text fields, a rule that checks for the presence of the correct hidden inputs, and a rule that checks for the presence of the Fruits and Vegetables logo.

We could combine all the rules relating to the form into one large form rule, or we could break some of our existing rules (such as the `testform.rule`) into at least two rules. The scope of the rule is a matter of personal preference. Creating larger rules can be more efficient than creating many tight, specific rules. However, because specific rules have more specific error messages, violation messages for specific rules tend to be easier to interpret than violation messages for more encompassing rules. Smaller rules are also easier to update or delete independently as your specifications and your understanding of the application evolve.

To enforce a rule or set of rules created with RuleWizard, you create a CodeWizard Enforcer for each rule or set of rules and specify which files or paths you want each enforcer to check. The process for creating and applying a CodeWizard Enforcer for these rules is the same as for the error page rule discussed in Chapter 11.

You can also tie specific rules to a single page or a specific instance of a single page. For example, if you want to check whether a servlet delivers the correct `Login failed, please try again` message whenever a user enters invalid log in information, you can create a rule that checks for the presence of that message and then configure WebKing so that it always tests whether the page returned after a failed log in contains this message. For details on how to configure such a test, see Chapter 13.

DECIDING WHICH RULES TO CREATE

After you become familiar with your preferred rule-creation method, you can create rules that check virtually any code-related or page-related requirement. Here are some examples.

Rules that check functionality. The purpose of these rules is to check that general functionality is implemented correctly and consistently. For example, you can use these rules to

- Check whether a form has the correct action, input fields, hidden inputs, option values, and so on.
- Check whether a link appears on the correct pages and points to the correct URL.

Testing Your Rules

We recommend that you test each rule you design before you use it to test application functionality. After all, if the rule does not work as expected, it can't help you determine whether your application works as expected.

One way to test whether the rule reports errors correctly is to test whether it identifies known violations and does not report false positives when the requirements are met. You can do this by creating a simple static HTML file that contains several variations of the element you want to test and then using this file as your test case. Ideally, this file should have several instances of a correct element and several instances of an incorrect element.

You can apply your rules to this test file without adding the file to your Project tree. Just enable WebKing's File Viewer by choosing View → Show File Viewer, locate and select your test file in the Files tab added to the left side of the WebKing GUI, and click the appropriate CodeWizard button.

These tests also serve as excellent documentation for what you were trying to achieve and as regression tests against future changes. We recommend storing these test cases under source control, along with the rule and any available rule documentation. This way, you have the information available when you return to the rule or when another developer needs to understand or modify the rule.

Rules that check layout and presentation. The purpose of these rules is to check that a page is configured properly and contains the correct elements. For example, you can use these rules to

- Check whether a table contains the correct dimensions.
- Check whether the correct images appear in the correct location.
- Check whether images exceed a required width.

Rules that check text. The purpose of these rules is to check that a page contains the correct text information. For example, you can use these rules to

- Check whether the correct message appears after a successful or unsuccessful log in.
- Check whether a greeting appears.
- Check whether a price falls above or below an acceptable range.

Rules that help you identify obsolete elements. Because Web application specifications tend to change quite rapidly to keep up with new technologies, market demands, and customer requests, you will probably modify your specification as you develop your application. When you do modify the specification, you can create rules that identify elements from the old specification. This serves two purposes. Initially, the rules will identify all the pages that need to be changed; this will help you implement the new specification as rapidly as possible. Later, the rules will identify any possible regressions. For instance, imagine that one of your content developers returns from vacation unaware of the changed specification and adds an old-style page to your application. The custom rule would tell him that he has to convert the page to the new standard. This type of rule is an example of a very application-specific rule. It might not even be appropriate over a long period of time. You might use such a rule only while making the change and then discard it. However, because rules are so easy to create and apply, it is still useful to create rules solely for the purpose of performing ad hoc queries. You could use these rules to

- Find all files that reference a discontinued product or outdated feature.
- Find all files that use an outdated image.

Summary

In this chapter, we review a number of ways to verify that the content of the pages generated by your application is correct. Many application-independent techniques are available, including spell-checking and applet validation. In addition, you can create application-specific tests that help to ensure that your specification is implemented properly and to detect logic errors, as discussed in Chapter 11. You need not limit your testing to the ideas described in this chapter or book. With some thought, you can add many useful checks to your test suites.

Every time you find a defect in your application, review whether any of your testing techniques should have found this defect. If so, determine why they did not, and take corrective action (improving either the tests or your procedures in running the tests). If you do not have any tests that could have found the error, spend some time thinking about ways you could automatically do this. As you develop tests, remember that there are no concrete guidelines regarding their scope, generality, and so on. As long as your tests work for your application, they are good and useful.

Chapter 13

Creating and Testing Paths

IN THIS CHAPTER

- Defining paths
- Determining which paths to use
- Finding an efficient way to specify and test paths
- Specifying critical paths
- Testing critical paths
- Creating and testing random paths

WHEN YOU ARE WORKING WITH WEB APPLICATIONS, change is one of the few things you can count on. Pages change according to user preferences, variables, time, inputs, and so on. For example, an e-commerce application's shopping cart page can be created a thousand times a day and be created differently each time it is invoked.

If you want to make sure that the pages your users encounter work correctly, you must create and test the specific instances of the pages that your users are likely to see when they use your application. However, this can be challenging. Specific state and input variables are required in order to invoke certain pages. For example, if you want to invoke and test a check out page, you must first set the username and password variables and have at least one item added to a shopping cart. If you want to test the pages returned for both valid and invalid log ins, you must set the inputs necessary to create those pages.

One way to invoke such a page is to traverse a path similar to the one the user might take to reach it. If you click the same links and enter the same inputs as your users most likely will, you should receive an instance of the page that is similar to the one the users will encounter. To select a specific potential user path, you need a mechanism to record your paths. This can be as simple as a printed checklist specifying which actions to take at each step of the path.

Ideally, testing involves creating two types of paths: the most critical paths through your application and a wide variety of paths through your application. We discuss the first type of paths in the beginning of this chapter and the second type of paths in the latter part. We describe how to create and test your most critical and popular paths first because they represent your application's most fundamental functionality. If this functionality does not work, your users will frequently have problems with the application, and you will have to deal with quite a negative backlash. Because you can cover so much important ground by testing these paths, if you could test only one small part of your application, we would recommend that you test the functionality represented in these paths.

Defining Paths

Intuitively, paths are easy to understand. Open a browser, start clicking away, and you have traversed a path. Millions of people do it all the time. To test your application thoroughly, however, you must occasionally break paths down into more detail. For instance, loading the first splash page of the Online Grocer application into your Web browser seems like one event but actually causes four accesses to our Web server:

```
GET /
GET /fruits.css
GET /title.gif
GET /background.gif
```

The first access retrieves the HTML page `index.html`, which is our default page. The second file, `fruits.css`, is the style sheet used by `index.html`. The `title.gif` file is our splash image, and `background.gif` is the background image used to texture the page. Depending on the browser, the browser settings, and the user's cache, any specific load of this page can load all four of these or just a subset.

If an application uses frames or JavaScript, its Web server might receive a very large number of requests that all correspond to a single step of a path. When we refer to loading pages or URLs from paths, we generally mean all the associated files, as well as the initial one that triggered the multiple loads.

Determining Which Paths to Use

To maximize your testing effort, make sure that you test your critical paths before you start testing possible, but not as common, paths. The more carefully you decide which paths to record and test, the more you will get out of these tests. Also, if you do shotgun testing first, there might be a temptation to neglect critical path testing under the assumption that "it's already covered." By testing critical paths first, you help control this tendency.

Basically, testing critical paths involves recording and testing the paths that represent the use cases described in your specification document and the most popular paths through your application. These two types of paths should be the same. If not, you have a problem. If your intended functionality has changed, you need to update your specification document. If your application does not implement the desired functionality, try to pinpoint the reason and consider your options.

When you specify and test paths that represent the most vital functionality, you can rest assured that you have thoroughly tested the part of the application that will be used the most frequently.

Finding an Efficient Way to Specify and Test Paths

Two main difficulties are involved in invoking the precise dynamic page you want to view and/or test: passing the appropriate parameters to the program that creates each dynamic page and setting the program's internal state variables as they would be set if a user had actually taken the specified path through the application.

For example, let's assume that you want to test your application's credit card–processing functionality. To test this functionality, you not only have to give the program inputs indicating payment type, credit card type, and credit card number but also have to set the program's internal variables in such a way that the program has a username and password and has some items in the shopping cart. If you did not have all these variables set, you would be invoking (and testing) a page other than the one your users could encounter, and you might miss a critical problem.

One option is to modify your application to provide test harnesses or stubs that enable you to reach such pages directly. Although that testing is well and good, it cannot substitute for integration testing or testing the application in the context the user will be using.

One of the most basic methods for specifying and testing paths is to write down all the paths on a piece of paper and check them off as you test them by hand. You could invoke the desired pages without using paths at all, by manually setting the appropriate variables, but this process is tedious and error-prone. The alternative is to click through all the prerequisite pages manually. This is more likely to generate the correct page but is even more tedious and still susceptible to human error. Moreover, if you set variables using either of these two methods, you have to repeat the entire process every time you want to view or test the page you created. These manual methods of invoking pages are usually impractical. As a result, developers who practice these methods generally do not have ample time to view and test their dynamic pages as often or thoroughly as they would like. You can save considerable time by automating this process. In Chapter 14, we show how to use a scripting language to simulate user paths in the context of load testing. Those same ideas can be applied here, but the implementation is tedious.

Here, we discuss how to test paths using WebKing, which takes care of the low-level details for you. If you use WebKing to specify the paths to the pages you want to test, WebKing saves this path information so that you can invoke and test any page in the path – exactly as it would appear within the given path – with the click of a button. This makes it much easier to retest the page (for example, each time you modify the program and want to see how the changes affect the output page).

Specifying Critical Paths

Before you start specifying your paths in WebKing, make sure that your application is accessible from a Web server. We recommend that you open the client-side testing project file (discussed in Chapter 11) and add your path-related information and test cases to this file.

Specifying critical paths involves two main tasks:

- Creating a default set of paths
- Extending the default paths until they represent the paths representing the user actions or specific page instances you want to test

Creating a default set of paths

To create a default set of paths, press F4. WebKing opens the Path tab and generates a default set of paths in the Path tree. Each level of the tree represents one step in a possible path. Multiple branches can stem from a single path node because multiple links can be followed from a single page. Because the same page (or multiple instances of the same page) can be accessed at various points in various paths, the same general page can be represented multiple times in this tree.

It is not necessary to specify an anchor here (as you did when creating paths in Chapter 5). When WebKing loads an application from a Web server, it automatically selects the initial page as your anchor. If you have multiple entry points to your application, however, you can indicate multiple anchors. These are used later as starting points for creating new paths.

Specifying the appropriate path

You can specify paths by using the WebKing Path Creator browser or the Path tree's shortcut menus. Whichever method you use, the basic strategy is the same: Extend one of the paths in the Path tree until it represents the user action or specific page instance you want to test.

USING THE PATH CREATOR BROWSER

The Path Creator browser lets you create paths by browsing a Web site as you normally would. WebKing monitors your actions and records them from a user's point-of-view. At the time this book was written, this feature was supported using only Microsoft Windows and Internet Explorer.

To specify a path with the Path Creator browser, you do the following:

1. Right-click the root Path tree node, and choose Expand Using Browser→ While Browsing from the shortcut menu. The root page opens in the WebKing Path Creator browser.
2. In the browser, specify your path by clicking links and completing and submitting forms where necessary. When you are done indicating a path, close the browser window.

When you choose Expand Using Browsing, you can have the nodes added to the Path tree as you are browsing or after you are browsing. The WebKing User's Guide explains the difference between these options in detail. As a general rule of thumb, start by using the While Browsing option. If this does not work on your application, switch to the After Browsing option.

USING PATH TREE SHORTCUT MENUS

To specify a path using Path tree shortcut menus, you do the following:

1. Right-click the Path tree node that represents the path step you want to extend.
2. If you want to add a file that does not require filling out a form, here is what you do:
   a. Choose Expand Links from the shortcut menu to add a linked page to the path. A dialog box containing the names of URLs to which the selected page links opens (see Figure 13-1). URLs not yet included in any path are selected by default.

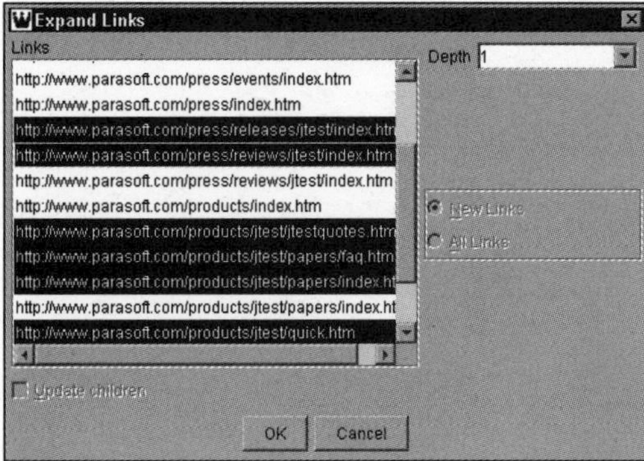

Figure 13-1: The Expand Links dialog box lists available links.

b. Select the URL(s) representing the pages you want to add to the path.

c. Determine how many layers of links you want to expand, by entering a value in the Depth field. If you enter 1, WebKing adds only the selected links (set A) to your Path tree. If you enter 2, WebKing adds the selected links (set A) and the pages to which set A links (set B). If you enter 3, WebKing adds the selected links (set A), the set of pages to which set A links (set B), and the pages to which set B links (set C). Whenever you choose a depth of 2 or higher, you also need to indicate whether you want WebKing to expand all links found or only the new links (links not yet included in the Path tree).

d. If the pages whose links you are expanding invoke children pages, indicate whether you want WebKing to rescan those children pages for new links, by checking or clearing the Update Children option.

3. If you want to add a page that requires filling out a form, here is what you do:

a. Choose Add Form Test → <name of form>. For example, to add the page created after you submit specific inputs for the `test` form, you would choose Add Form Test → test. After you choose this option, a form dialog box like the one shown in Figure 13-2 opens. The options in this dialog box represent the options in the form itself.

b. To add an existing JavaScript action, select the code for that action in the upper window, and click the Add button to copy that script to the lower window. To add your own scripting actions, click the New button, and type any JavaScript you want. Because you can choose in which window or frame context the code will be evaluated, you can refer to DOM elements as necessary. You can add any combination of existing and custom script elements into a single test case, as appropriate for your application.

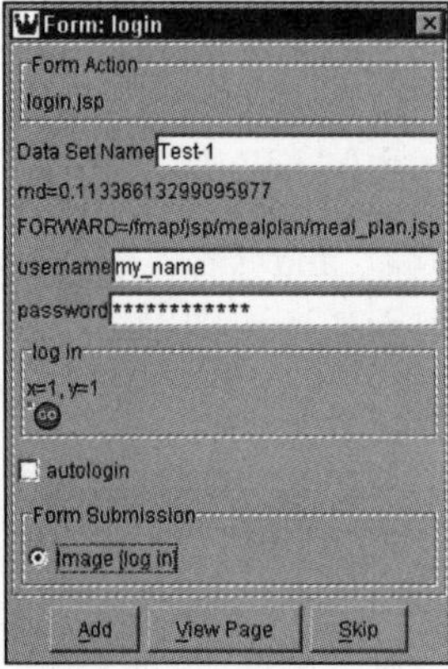

Figure 13-2: Entering form inputs in the form dialog box.

4. Repeat this process of adding nodes to the Path tree until this tree represents the paths and pages you want to test.

ADDING DISCONNECTED PAGES

Sometimes you cannot add certain path steps by expanding links or entering form inputs. For example, a certain frame configuration might prevent you from expanding a particular link, or you might want to specify a path that mimics a user following a series of links and entering a URL in the browser's address bar. In these types of situations, you can manually add path nodes to your Path tree.

To manually add a path node to your Path tree, you do the following:

1. Right-click the path node from which you want the new node to follow.
2. Choose Add Path from the shortcut menu. The Add New Link dialog box opens (see Figure 13-3).

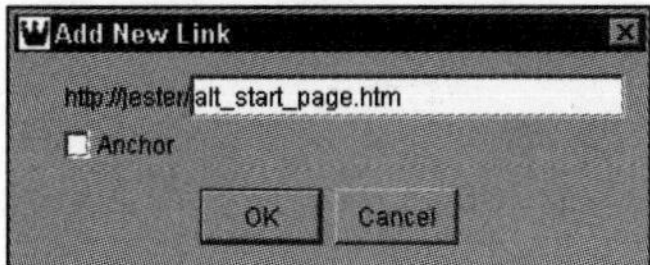

Figure 13-3: Adding a disconnected page to the path.

3. Complete the text field so that it expresses the complete URL of the path node you want to add.
4. (Optional) If you want to make this file an anchor (for example, to indicate that it is an entryway into your application), select Anchor.

Specifying the Online Grocer's Critical Paths

For an example of how these concepts can be applied, consider how we specify paths through our Online Grocer application. The first paths we create for the Online Grocer application are two paths representing the two use cases included in our specification (described in Chapter 4). As you recall, we recorded these same two paths for our prototype application in Chapter 5. We can use these paths as a model for the new paths we create through the now dynamic application.

We record both the use cases by clicking links and submitting forms in WebKing's Path Creator browser. When we are done recording these two paths, our Path tree displays these paths, as shown in Figure 13-4.

As you can see, the Path tree represents at least one instance of each critical application page. This means that we can now test our application's most critical functionality.

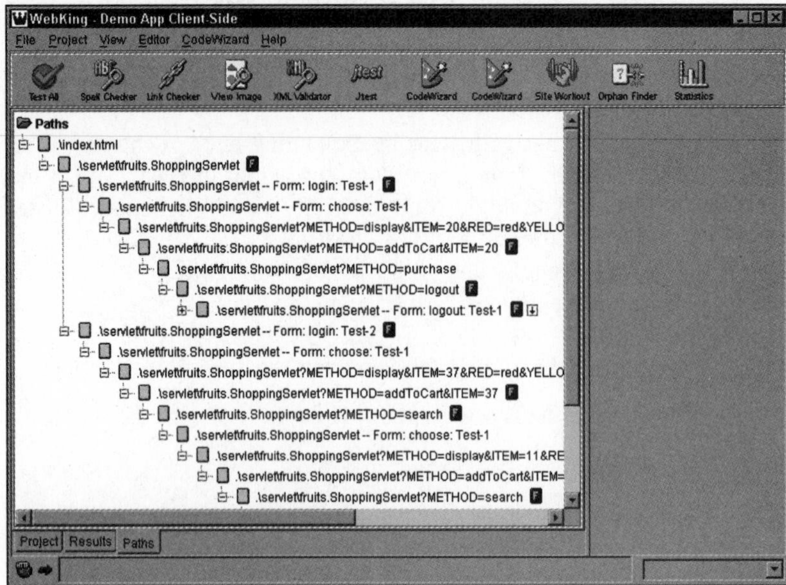

Figure 13-4: The paths that represent our two main use cases.

Testing Critical Paths

With WebKing, you can test critical paths in two ways: using tools explicitly and using virtual users (via the Site Workout feature). If you want to apply multiple tools to all pages in the paths, we recommend that you initially use the Test All feature because it requires the least amount of setup and lets you easily apply a set of tools to all or selected paths. If you have a tool that can be used only on a particular path page (such as a CodeWizard Enforcer for a rule that checks whether the page returned for a failed log in displays the correct message) and you want to associate that tool permanently with the path page for which it is designed, we recommend that you use virtual users to connect the appropriate tool to the appropriate page.

Testing your paths with Test All

WebKing's Test All feature lets you apply a customizable group of testing tools to all pages and files in the Path tree or Project tree.

To apply a group of tools to one or more path segments, you perform the following steps:

1. Click the Test All button when the Path tab is visible. The Configure Test All dialog box opens.
2. In the Configure Test All dialog box, specify which tools you want WebKing to use, and click Go. You can choose from the following tools:

- **Check Links:** Finds broken links (discussed in Chapter 11).
- **CodeWizard:** Finds nonportable and incorrect HTML, CSS, and JavaScript code (discussed in Chapter 8).
- **Test Spelling:** Finds misspelled words (discussed in Chapter 12).
- **Validate XML:** Checks whether XML is well formed and valid (discussed in Chapter 17).
- **Any CodeWizard Enforcer you have added:** Checks the rules that this enforcer is configured to enforce. Functionality depends on the nature of the included rule(s). Custom rules can do anything from finding programs that crash, to spotting missing GUI elements, to helping you prevent your most common coding mistakes (discussed in Chapters 8, 11, and 12).
- **Any tool you have added to WebKing:** Depends on tool functionality. Instructions for adding a tool are in Chapter 5.

After you click Go, WebKing applies all requested tests to all paths in the Path tree and displays a brief summary of test results in the Results panel. You can access individual error messages by either of two ways:

- Choose a specific test (for example, CodeWizard), using the View Selector in the bottom-right side of the status bar.
- Click the appropriate node in the Results tab in the left side of the WebKing GUI.

Testing the Online Grocer Application's critical paths

For an example of how to apply the preceding concepts, consider how we test the Online Grocer application's critical paths. First, to quickly test the Online Grocer's most critical functionality, we open the Path tab and click the Test All button. This invokes the Test All tool that runs multiple WebKing tools (or external tools integrated into WebKing) with the click of a button. For this test, we configure Test All to apply the tools introduced in the previous chapters:

- Link Checker
- CodeWizard
- The CodeWizard Enforcers created for our custom rules
- Spell Checker

As Figure 13-5 shows, these tests expose several new errors.

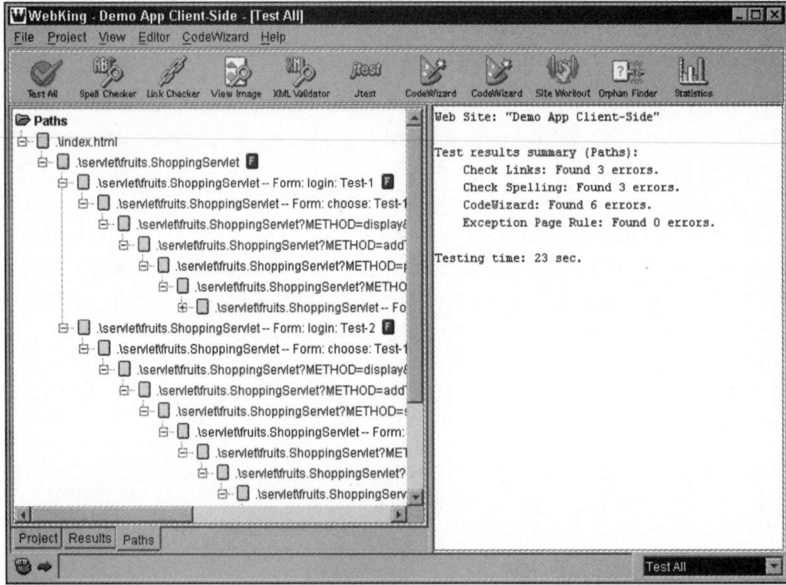

Figure 13-5: Errors found in our first path test.

The detailed Link Checker results shown in Figure 13-6 reveal that several log out buttons do not lead to the Log Out page as they should.

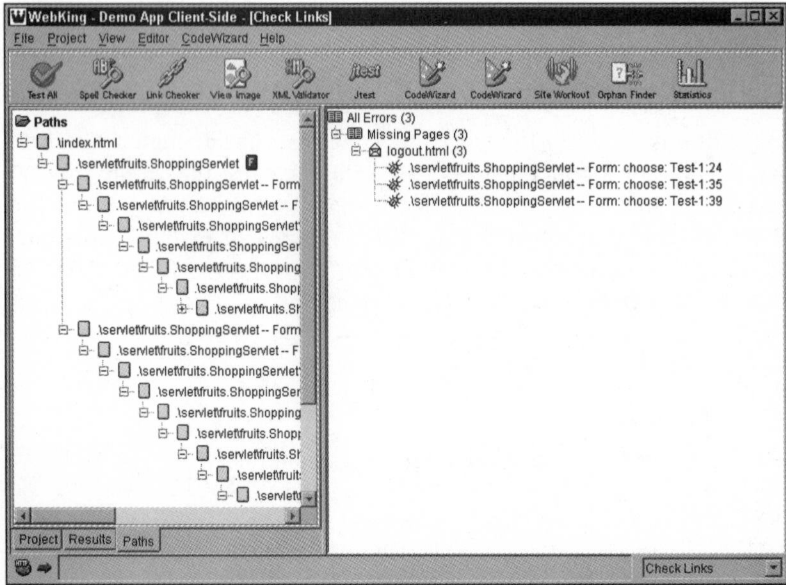

Figure 13-6: Broken links to the Log Out page.

To explore this problem, we open the responsible file's source code in WebKing's editor and quickly recognize the problem: When `ShoppingServlet` creates the Search Results page, the code it generates contains a broken link to the Log Out page. It points to `/logout.html` (a page that does not exist on the Web server) instead of `/servlet/fruits.ShoppingServlet?METHOD=logout`.

This test also reveals some new spelling errors and a CodeWizard error: a violation of the rule requiring that `FORM`'s method attribute must be `POST` or `GET`. We described this rule in Chapter 8 when discussing the coding standard violations we found in the initial few pages of this application.

After fixing the problems found in the two most critical paths, we decided to create additional test cases to verify some of the other functionality described in our specification from Chapter 4. We describe the most interesting tests in the following sections.

CHECKING THE APPLICATION FLOW

For an example of how to test the application flow, consider how we verify whether the flow detailed in the specification is actually implemented. Assume that we want to test whether pages 4, 5, 6, and 7 link to the Main Search page. To do this, we try to extend the current paths, using options available in the Path tree's shortcut menu. We right-click the `.\servlet\fruits.ShoppingServletForm: choose: Test-1` node representing page 4 (the Search Results page), choose Expand Links from the shortcut menu, and try to add the `http://ogryn.parasoft.com/servlet/fruits.ShoppingServlet?Method=search...` link leading to the Main Search page. However, this URL is not included in the list of available links (shown in Figure 13-7).

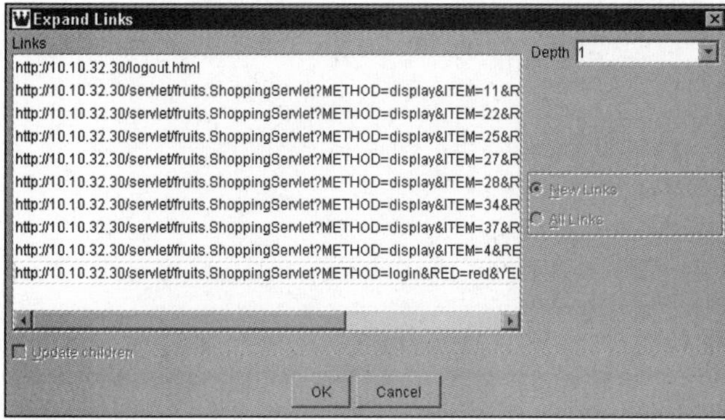

Figure 13-7: A list of available links that does not include the link we want to add.

We explore this apparent problem by having WebKing display page 4 as it would appear in the specified path and by checking this functionality manually. When we click the Make Another Choice link, the application incorrectly brings us to the

Log In page, not the Main Search page. This type of problem is difficult to find automatically because the link leads to a valid page, but not the correct page. As discussed in Chapter 11, the best way to test for these types of logical flow problems is to create and enforce rules that check whether a certain text or image link leads to the correct page.

To develop a test that automatically verifies whether the Make Another Choice link opens the correct page, we use RuleWizard's Auto-Create feature to design a rule that checks whether any `A HREF` statement containing the phrase ***Make another choice*** links to an incorrect file (any URL that doesn't match `/servlet/fruits.ShoppingServlet?METHOD=search.*`). The rule we created is displayed in Figure 13-8 and is available on the CD as `choicetest.rule`.

Before adding this test to the test suite, we check whether it works as expected by running it on the page with the error we want the rule to identify. The test finds the error, so we add it to our test suite, fix the `ShoppingServlet` code responsible for this error, and replay the test to verify that our changes solved the problem.

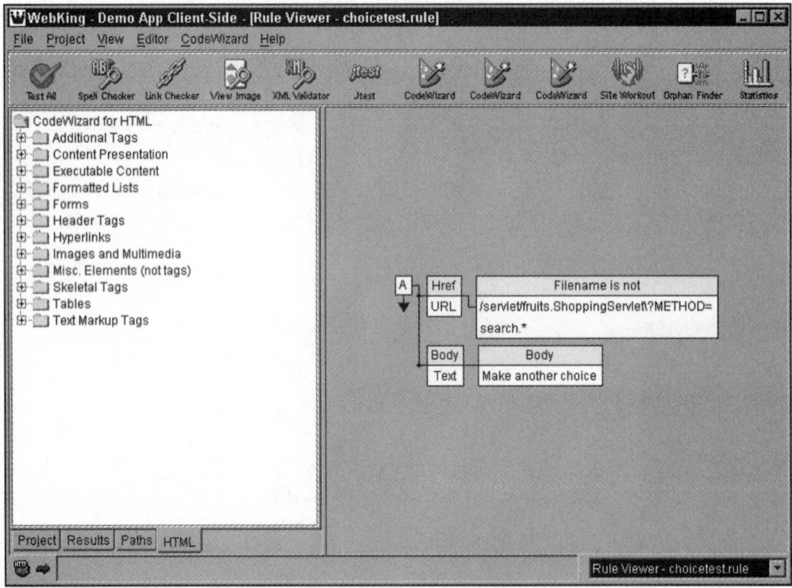

Figure 13-8: A rule that checks our Make Another Choice link.

CHECKING APPLICATION CONTENTS

For an example of how to check some of the contents detailed in an application's specification, consider how we verify whether the Log In Failed page produces the correct message.

First, we create a path representing the page created after an incorrect username and/or password is entered in the Log In page. We browse the page (shown in Figure 13-9) as it would appear in the path and determine that it works correctly.

Figure 13-9: The correct Log In Failed page.

To ensure that this functionality continues to work as expected, we create a regression test case for this functionality by developing a rule that checks for the presence of the message that should be delivered upon an unsuccessful log in. The rule we create (shown in Figure 13-10 and included on the CD as `log_in_failed.rule`) basically says, "If the file does not contain text that reads *Please re-enter your username and password*, report an error." This rule provides a way to easily check whether future application modifications introduce a problem into this functionality.

Because this rule applies only to a specific page – the page that the servlet returns after a user submits an incorrect username or password – it would be pointless to apply it to *all* pages in the Path tree. To avoid unnecessary testing and false positives, we don't apply it using the Test All feature. Instead, we select the Path tree node representing this file and click the toolbar button that enforces this rule.

Later in this chapter, you learn how to associate a rule permanently with a particular instance of a page.

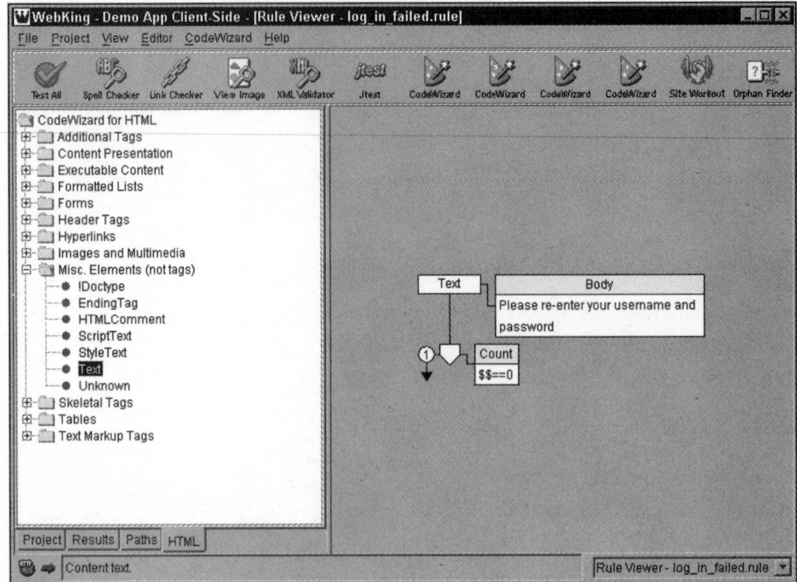

Figure 13-10: A rule that checks our log in failed message.

CHECKING FOR SERVER-SIDE ERRORS

For an example of how to check for server-side errors, consider how we verify our Shopping Cart page's update functionality. First, we use the Add Form Test option to record a path that represents a user updating the Shopping Cart quantity with a normal item quantity (such as 10 or 2). After the new return page is added to the Path tree, we use the Test All button to reapply the general tests we ran previously. No problems are found.

To ensure that we are testing this functionality thoroughly, we decide to also test how it handles abnormal inputs. To do this, we add another path node that represents a user adding strange but possible inputs (see Figure 13-11).

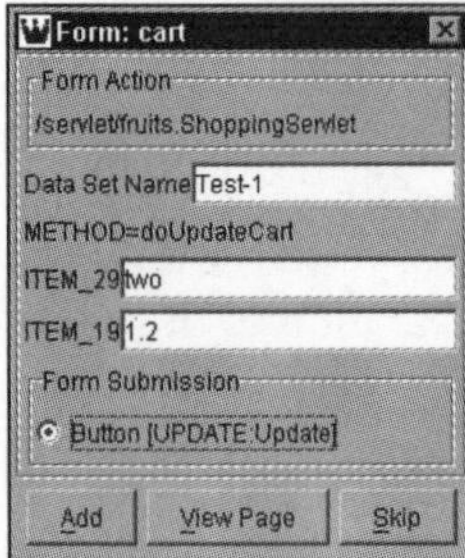

Figure 13-11: Testing the Shopping Cart page's update form.

A page for this new test is then added to the Path tree. We check the result of the test by having the Test All feature apply the standard tools and all our existing general custom rules (including the ones we described in earlier chapters). As Figure 13-12 shows, the error page rule that identifies exceptions was violated in this test.

We discuss the purpose and logistics of creating the error page rule (`error_page1.rule`) in Chapter 11.

This reveals that the servlet crashes when a string input is submitted in the update form. When looking at the `ShoppingServlet` code, we find that even though the code requires an integer for this parameter, the code never checks this input's type and thus allows types of inputs (such as strings) that cause the `ShoppingServlet` class to throw an exception.

To fix this problem, we add some data verification logic to the `doUpdateCart()` method inside the `ShoppingServlet` class. This code checks for negative numbers or nonnumbers (which are caught as `NumberFormatExceptions`).

```
// First pass, validate the user-entered data
boolean isOK = true;
Enumeration enum = context.getParameterNames();
while (enum.hasMoreElements()) {
    String name = enum.nextElement().toString();
    if (name.startsWith("ITEM_")) {
        try {
            int quantity = context.getInteger(name, 0);
            if (quantity < 0) {
                isOK = false;
            }
        } catch (NumberFormatException e) {
            isOK = false;
        }
    }
}
if (!isOK) {
    showErrorPage(context);
    return;
}
```

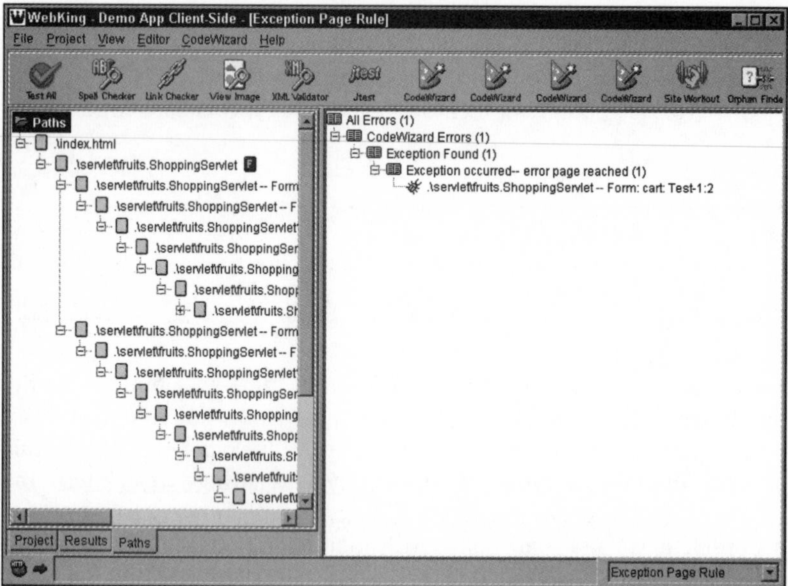

Figure 13-12: WebKing determined that our exception page was reached.

If we had wanted, this would have been a good place to disallow ridiculously large numbers, such as 1,000,000 bananas.

To handle these conditions, we add a page to explain to the user that her input is not correct. This is implemented by the `showErrorPage()` method.

```
void showErrorPage(ShoppingContext context)
    throws IOException
{
    PrintWriter out = context.getWriter();

    Vector cart = carts.getCart(context.getUser());
    header(out, "Invalid Changes");
    out.println(
        "<p>The changes you've made are invalid. Please go back and make sure ");
    out.println(
        "all fields have valid numbers greater than or equal to zero.</p>");
```

```
    out.println("<A HREF=\""+SERVLET+"?METHOD=search\">");
    out.println("Cancel changes</A><BR>");
    out.println("<A HREF=\""+SERVLET+"?METHOD=logout\">");
    out.println("<IMG SRC=\"/logout.gif\" ALT=\"Logout\" BORDER=0></A>");
    footer(out);
}
```

For a full-featured commercial application, we would want to give users more information about exactly what went wrong, so that they would not have to scratch their heads trying to figure it out. Also, if this were a real application, we would want to update the application specification and associated documentation to include the new paths.

Testing your paths with virtual users

An alternative way to test paths is to have virtual users apply selected tools as they traverse paths. Virtual users' fundamental purpose is to perform load testing, but they can also be used to test your critical paths or traverse and test a variety of paths through your application (as described later in this chapter). They are especially useful if you have created a test that can be applied only to a specific path page (such as the Log In Failed rule we describe earlier in this chapter). This section provides a brief overview of how to use WebKing's virtual users to test paths.

For a more detailed and comprehensive discussion of virtual users, see Chapter 14.

After you record critical paths, you can configure virtual users to follow and test certain path segments, complete paths, or groups of paths. The behavior of each virtual user is determined by a *user profile*, a description of the paths the virtual user will traverse, its browsing tendencies, the tests it performs, and so forth.

Here are the steps to create user profiles that tell virtual users to run selected tools on certain paths:

1. Open the Site Workout panel by clicking Site Workout. The Site Workout Panel opens (see Figure 13-13).
2. Select the Default User in the User Profiles area of the Site Workout panel, and click Configure. The User Profile panel for this user profile opens (see Figure 13-14).

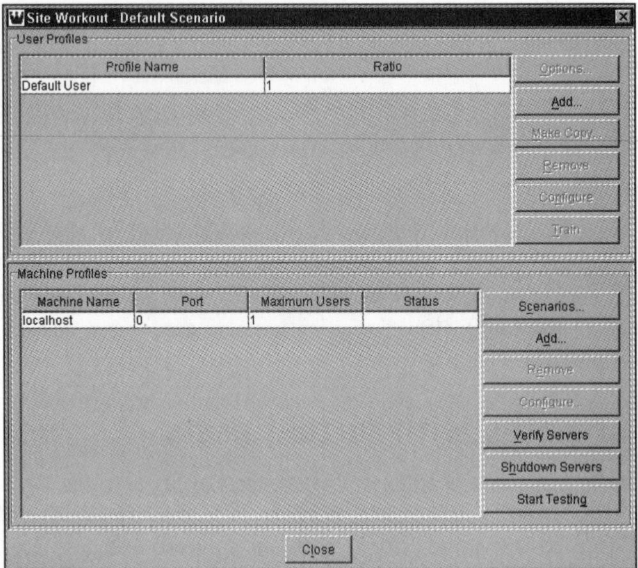

Figure 13-13: The Site Workout panel.

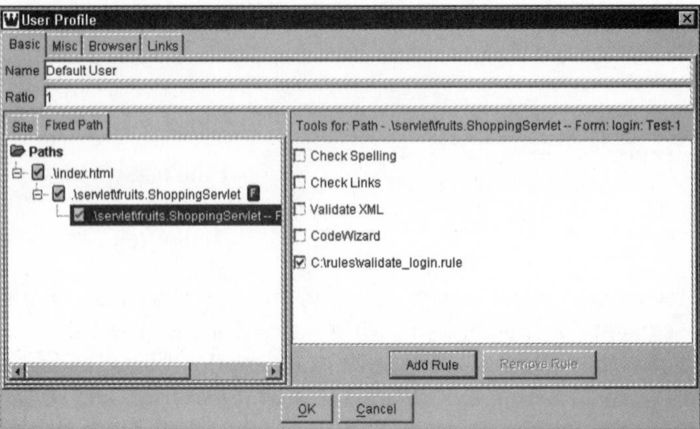

Figure 13-14: Configuring a user profile to apply a rule to a specific path page.

3. Enter a name that identifies this virtual user in the Name field of the User Profile panel's Basic tab. For example, you could enter **Path to failed log in.**

4. Add one or more paths in the Fixed Path subtab.

   - To add a path, go to the Fixed Path subtab, right-click the final node of a path or path segment you want to add, and choose Use Test from the shortcut menu. Red check marks indicate items that will be tested, and blue check marks indicate items that are parents to items that will be tested. This makes it easy to see which paths are involved.

- If you want to ensure that a particular path is traversed and tested, add only one path to the user profile. (You can create other profiles for additional paths.) If you want WebKing to choose from many different instances of a similar path on each test (for example, several paths that involve the same pages but use a different username and password), add all these tests to this user profile.

You can expand the Path tree by right-clicking the unused area of the Fixed Path subtab and choosing Expand All from the shortcut menu.

5. Indicate which tools you want to apply to which pages or paths.
   - If you want to apply a tool to all path pages, select the Fixed Path node, and select the tool that you want to apply to all paths in the right side of the Basic tab.
   - If you want to apply a tool to only one path page, select the Fixed Path node representing that path page, and check the check box that represents the tool you want to apply to that page (refer to Figure 13-14). Check boxes for tools that have already been applied to all paths are grayed out.
6. Set Max number of loops to 1 from the Misc subtab.
   - Because this is not load testing (yet), you set the maximum number of loops to 1. This tells Site Workout to use, exactly once, each path you have marked and then finish. If you use the Unlimited option, Site Workout continually chooses from the available paths randomly and keeps testing until you explicitly stop the test.
7. Disable Image and Sound links from the Links subtab.
   - Again, because this is not load testing, there is no advantage to loading image and sound files at this point. They just slow down the testing. Naturally, if you have dynamic images or sounds, this would not be true, so you would leave these on.
8. Click OK to close the User Profile panel.
9. Configure any additional user profiles by repeating steps 2–8.
10. Click Start Testing when you are done adding user profiles and want to execute the tests.

WebKing then creates a virtual user, based on one of the available user profiles. Whenever the virtual user reaches the end of its path, WebKing automatically creates a new virtual user, based on one of the profiles available in the User Profile panel. If you set the maximum number of loops to 1 for all your user profiles, WebKing uses all the paths you set up, once, and then it terminates and displays the results.

If at least one user profile does not have a fixed number of loops, WebKing keeps creating virtual users until you click Stop Testing in the Site Workout panel. If all your user profiles have an unlimited numbers of loops, all your user profiles will eventually be used, as long as you allow the test to run for an ample period of time – even if you have, for instance, one virtual user and 20 user profiles. This configuration is better suited to load testing because it's not clear when you need to click Stop Testing to cover your test cases completely and more tests will be run (and rerun) than are strictly necessary at this point.

In either case, after the test is finished, you can view test results in WebKing's Results panel. Results for the tests you configured WebKing to perform (for example, Check Links, CodeWizard) are available via the View Selector or Results tab.

WebKing's virtual users can be used to perform much more complex tasks than those described here. For a detailed description of virtual users, see Chapter 14.

Testing the Online Grocer's critical paths with virtual users

Now, we will describe how we used the preceding virtual user techniques in our Online Grocer testing efforts. Earlier in this chapter, we created a rule to check whether the Online Grocer application's log in functionality delivers the correct log in failed message when it is given an invalid username and/or password. If we apply this page-specific tool to all path pages, we get many false positives. The rule reports an error for any page not containing the *Please re-enter your username and password* phrase, but we only care whether the appropriate page – the one delivered after incorrect log in parameters are submitted – contains this message.

There are two main ways to deal with this problem. One solution is to use Test All to perform only the general application tests and then apply the page-specific test by selecting the Path tree node representing the Log In Failed page and clicking the toolbar button that enforces the appropriate rule. However, we want to make sure that we do not forget to perform this test, and we want to be able to automate this entire testing procedure as part of our automated regular build. We can accomplish both these goals by creating a user profile that would have the virtual user traverse this path and apply the rule only to the Log In Failed page.

The first step in doing this is to open the Site Workout panel and create a user profile that will follow the existing path to the Log In Failed page. We then select the node representing that page and check the check box associated with this rule. The settings we used to do this are shown in Figure 13-14.

To run the test, we close the User Profile panel and click Start Testing. After the test is complete, we look at the results and see the expected result: No errors (we had already determined that this page displayed the correct response). At this point, we save our project file so that we can easily restore and replay this test case in the future.

There are two separate parts to this test: (1) which rule to run and (2) on which file to run the rule. This means that we can change parts 1 and 2 independently. For instance, if we later create another page that should generate the same text, we can also attach our rule to that page. On the other hand, if we decide that the message should change slightly, all we have to do is edit our rule. We don't need to change the files to which the rule is attached. This decoupling enables our tests to adapt easily as the application evolves over time.

Creating and Testing Random Paths

By now, you should have recorded and tested the most critical paths through your unit or application – but you're not done yet! The next step is to add and test a wide variety of additional paths through the application. First, we will explain why it's important to create and test additional paths. Then, we will demonstrate how you can use WebKing to automatically create the number and range of paths that are vital to thorough, successful testing.

It is of utmost importance to ensure that the most critical paths through your application work as expected. If the most basic and popular functionality does not work, avoiding unhappy customers and negative backlash will be difficult. However, if you want to ensure that users do not encounter problems when they stray from these critical paths (as users inevitably do), you must also create and test a wide variety of paths through your application.

Every path through a Web application can create different pages, and each page can have different problems. Consider the number and variety of shopping cart pages a large e-commerce application generates in a day or the different number of itineraries an airline application creates. If you test only one or two instances of each page, you cannot be certain that other instances of the same page do not contain serious problems. For example, an output page can look fine when arrived at through most application paths but can appear blank when arrived at via an unexpected path. The best way to ensure that your users do not encounter these strange errors is to exhaustively create and test random paths through each application unit and across the entire application.

You can create additional paths by hand, as you created the paths representing your most critical and popular user paths. However, because each Web application contains so many potential paths, manually recording a sufficient number of realistic paths through an average-size application to expose all its problems would be virtually impossible and incredibly tedious. Fortunately, you can use WebKing to create virtual users that traverse the necessary number and variety of paths for you.

Virtual users can either automatically create paths or traverse fixed paths that you specify. So far, we have been using only fixed paths. This section focuses on how to configure virtual users to create random paths automatically.

Configuring virtual users to create paths

To set up a path-creating virtual user, you perform the following steps:

1. Click Site Workout. The Site Workout panel opens.
2. Click Add to open a User Profile panel in which you can create a new profile.
3. Enter a name that identifies this virtual user in the Name field of the User Profile panel's Basic tab. Generally, this name should describe any distinguishing properties of the virtual user.
4. (Optional) Indicate the page where you want the virtual user to start creating paths, by right-clicking the node that represents that page in the Site subtab and choosing Start Pages from the shortcut menu. A green circle is added to the right of any node that represents a page designated as a start page.
5. (Optional) Indicate the tools you want the virtual users to apply to the pages they reach. To select a tool, select the root Site subtab node, then click the tool's check box on the right side of the Basic tab.
6. (Optional) Customize the virtual user's general browsing tendencies by setting the parameters in the User Profile Misc tab (see Figure 13-15). Options that influence path-creating virtual users include
   - **Chance of exit:** Determines the virtual user's tendency to exit the application.
   - **Chance of back button:** Determines the virtual user's tendency to click the Back button.
   - **Max number of clicks:** Determines the maximum number of clicks included in a single virtual user's path. (When a virtual user is done creating a path, WebKing creates a new virtual user based on a different user profile.)
   - **Average delay:** Determines the virtual user's average delay between clicks.

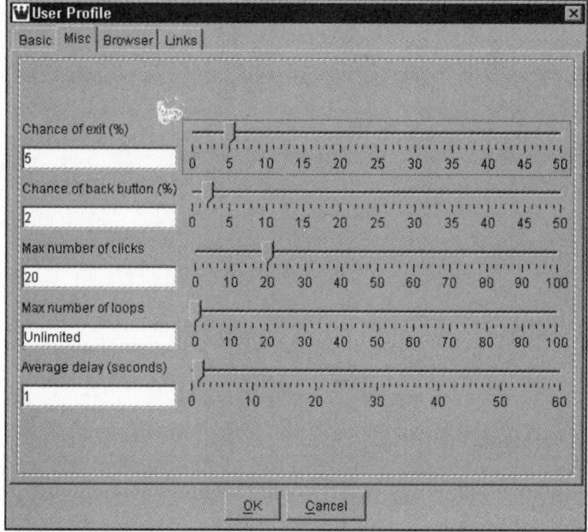

Figure 13-15: Customizing virtual user browsing tendencies.

7. (Optional) Customize the browser the virtual user will be emulating, by modifying the Browser tab settings (see Figure 13-16).

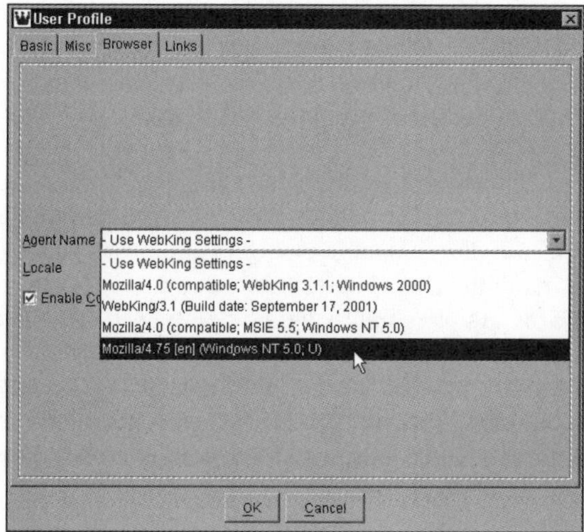

Figure 13-16: Customizing virtual user browser settings.

8. (Optional) Customize the virtual user's tendency to follow certain types of links, by modifying the Links tab's load frequency settings for specific types of links (listed in the top portion of the Links tab shown in Figure 13-17) or general categories of links (listed in the lower portion of the tab).

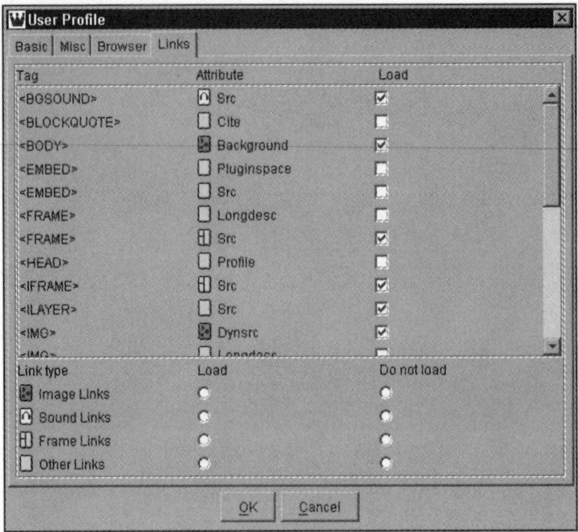

Figure 13-17: Customizing the links virtual users will follow.

Preventing virtual users from accessing certain files

Sometimes you don't want virtual users to access certain files as they create paths. For example, you might want to prevent virtual users from repeatedly traversing paths that place undue stress on your server or from accessing files that remove cookies (such as log out pages). If you prevent virtual users from traversing these types of files, you can perform multiple tests on that part of the application without logging in multiple times.

To prevent WebKing from accessing a certain file as it creates paths, right-click that file's Site tab node in the User Profile panel's Basic tab, and choose Restricted Pages from the shortcut menu. For example, when testing the Online Grocer application we have the random virtual users avoid the `/servlet/fruits.ShoppingServlet?METHOD=logout` page and leave that testing to our fixed paths. This makes the random testing more efficient because almost all our pages link to the Log Out page and our virtual users will tend to terminate testing prematurely if this page is accessed. We could then test the Log Out page by creating one profile that is allowed to log out wherever it chooses and assign this profile a relatively small distribution.

Training virtual users

If your application uses forms (as the Online Grocer application does), the virtual users have to know how to complete them. They can randomly test forms as a monkey would, by banging on the keyboard. However, this is appropriate only for some forms (for instance, random inputs for a login form would help you verify how bad inputs are handled, but are unlikely to log in your virtual users). By spending a few minutes telling virtual users how to handle the various types of forms on your application (that is, "training" virtual users), you can teach them how to behave when they encounter forms in subsequent test runs.

Here are the steps to train virtual users:

1. Open the Site Workout panel by clicking Site Workout.
2. In the User Profiles area of the Site Workout panel, select the user profile you want to train, and click Train. WebKing then starts running a test with this user profile and opens a form dialog box when the virtual user encounters a form. The dialog box that it opens looks like the one shown in Figure 13-18.

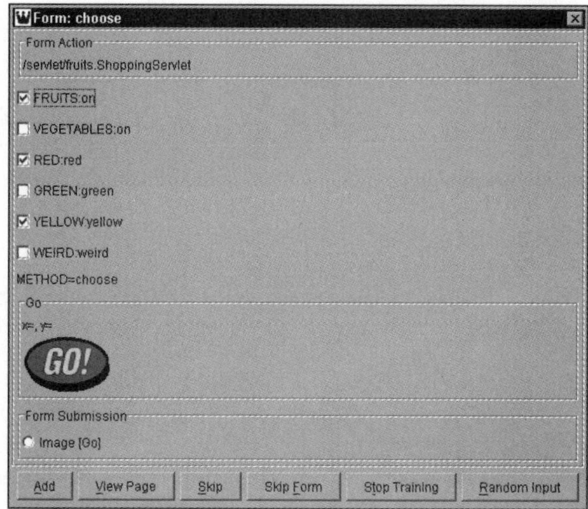

Figure 13-18: Training virtual users how to complete forms.

3. In the form dialog box, indicate how you want a virtual user who adopts this user profile to handle this form.
   - If you want this user profile to generate new inputs for all fields of that form every time it encounters that form, click Random Input.
   - If you want this user profile to use specific inputs when it encounters this form, enter those inputs in the appropriate fields and click Add.
   - If you want this ignore this form for now, click Skip.
   - If you do not want to add any more tests to this form, click Skip Form.
   - If you do not want to add any more tests to any form, click Stop Training.

4. Continue indicating how you want each form or form type handled until you reach all forms or want to stop training the selected user profile.
5. When you want to stop training this user profile, click Stop Training in the Site Workout panel. This is unnecessary if you click Stop Training from the form dialog.

The next time a virtual user adopts this profile, the specified forms are handled in the manner you determined. Any forms that you did not train the virtual user on will be ignored by that virtual user.

Random inputs are especially helpful in testing pages like the Online Grocer's Product Search page. Virtual users using random inputs eventually try all combinations of check boxes that might lead to different paths through the application. This kind of exhaustive testing is very tedious to do by hand.

Running the test

To run the test, open the Site Workout panel by clicking the Site Workout button, and then click the Start Testing button. This is exactly the same procedure used to run fixed paths, but in this case, the virtual users keep running until you explicitly tell them to stop. Note that you can run the fixed paths and random paths together or separately by setting the ratio of user profiles. To run random tests only, set all the fixed path profiles to have a ratio of 0.

When you start the Site Workout, virtual users automatically choose and traverse paths through your application. Whenever the virtual user reaches the end of its path, WebKing automatically creates a new virtual user based on the available user profile settings. A given random path is terminated under any of the following conditions:

- The Chance of Exit parameter as specified in the user profile forces the virtual user to exit the application.
- A page marked as a stop page has been reached.
- The maximum number of clicks as specified on the user profile has been reached.

The current test run continues until you click Stop Testing. After the test is finished, you can view results for the tests you configured WebKing to perform (for example, Check Links, CodeWizard) by selecting the appropriate type of result from the View Selector or Results tab.

Before you proceed, make sure that you save the user profiles you have created, by resaving your project file. If you do not, you will have to reconfigure them all from scratch when you want to have virtual users create and test paths based on the behavior described in these profiles.

Creating additional paths through the Online Grocer application

For an example of how these ideas can be applied, consider how we use WebKing to automatically create random paths through the Online Grocer application.

First, we create two user profiles:

- A demo user to log in as demo and randomly walk through most forms on the application, ignoring the Log Out page
- A cookie-less user to simulate users who come to our application but do not have cookies enabled

With some effort, we could come up with other interesting profiles. For instance, we could make sure that we have one profile with delays long enough that the `HTTPSessions` stored inside our Java servlet will expire.

As noted in Chapter 6, we have written our application so that most unexpected conditions in the servlet cause the initial Log In page to be displayed. When we reach this path from an unexpected condition, we add a special comment to the HTML, describing what happened:

```
<!-- Error: some message -->
```

We then create a rule to find this pattern and a CodeWizard Enforcer that checks this rule. To configure our desired tests, we set both our user profiles to test all pages found with this rule, the error page rule, the standard CodeWizard rules, and the spell checker.

We run these tests by clicking Start Testing. The results reveal that our new custom rule identified a problem:

```
Missing USER for METHOD=choose
```

After looking into this, we realize that users without cookies seem to log in but are immediately bounced out of the application after the Search page. This behavior isn't very friendly, so we change the servlet to let cookie-less users know that our application requires cookies. To do this, we add the following check to the `login()` function:

```
if (context.isNew()) {
    showCookiesRequiredPage(context);
    return;
}
```

We also add an accompanying new page:

```
/**
 * Our error page -- happens if user tries to log in
 * without cookies
 */
void showCookiesRequiredPage(ShoppingContext context)
    throws IOException
{
    PrintWriter out = context.getWriter();
    header(out, "This Site Requires Cookies");
    out.println("<p>This site requires a browser that has cookies enabled.</p>");
    footer(out);
}
```

If this were a real application, we would also update our design documents and specifications to note the new path.

Our tests also expose several spelling errors in our database of product descriptions. These can be difficult to find but, fortunately, are easy to fix.

The virtual users are randomly generating paths, so it can pay to let them run for a long time because they eventually generate numerous paths. Because many duplicated tests are also run, WebKing filters out duplicated error messages so that you see only a list of unique errors at the end of the test. We recommend letting Site Workout run overnight or over a weekend. This way, you can thoroughly test your application without influencing your productivity.

Summary

Path testing is one of the best tools for testing the overall construction of your Web application. It encompasses integration testing, construction testing, and many kinds of page validation. Whether you do it manually from a checklist, write scripts using a scripting language, or automate the whole task using tools, you should strive for the most complete possible coverage of your application.

Chapter 14

Performing Load Testing

IN THIS CHAPTER

- ◆ Understanding the importance of load testing
- ◆ Configuring virtual users
- ◆ Setting up scenarios
- ◆ Running tests and interpreting the results
- ◆ Leveraging load testing
- ◆ Using Python for load testing
- ◆ Using WebKing for load testing

IF YOU HAVE BEEN FOLLOWING the general practices described in this book, by the time you have a *functioning* Web application (meaning that you can interact with it as the user does), you will have tested all your parts individually, both for performance and reliability and as integrated components. You should have reasonable confidence in the correctness of your application. However, you're not through testing yet!

If, on the other hand, you have skipped out on early aspects of testing, this is your last best place to catch problems before your customers do. Problems uncovered during load testing are often the most difficult to locate and expensive to fix, but solving them is absolutely critical to constructing a bulletproof Web application. As we have said before, you don't have to wait until your application is 100-percent complete to begin load testing (or any testing, for that matter). As long as your Web application can be used as the customer would use it, you can begin right away. A good process makes your early testing efforts reusable on the final, completed application (or, as is more common, on a constantly evolving application).

We begin our discussion of load testing by looking at its general purpose. In earlier chapters, we discussed ways to create paths and exercise an application, but this was system testing, not load testing. *System testing* verifies whether the unit or application under test performs according to a specification. *Load testing*, on the other hand, goes one step further. It verifies whether that correct behavior persists when many users are exercising the application simultaneously. More than any specific testing technique, the difference in focus is what distinguishes the two practices.

Understanding the Importance of Load Testing

When developing a non-Web application, many software companies test by having teams of testers and beta testers exercise the application. If the application performs decently, it gets the gold stamp of approval and is passed on to unsuspecting customers. Although this approach is commonly used, it is riddled with opportunities for incomplete, shoddy testing. More importantly, it's even less effective for Web applications than standard ones. This is because normal applications have only one user at a time and generally don't stay loaded for long periods of time. (Operating systems and client/server systems are, naturally, exceptions to this rule, but they can hardly be considered normal applications.)

Your Web application might be perfectly well behaved when running with a few careful users who know what they are doing. However, introduce a large number of users with incompatible systems, inevitable network delays, and applications that run for months without restarting, and suddenly your seemingly perfect code mysteriously fails. Some large Web sites are saddled with applications requiring constant reinitialization. Rather than fix the source of the problem, the people working on these applications spend time and effort supporting multiple, fault-tolerant servers that can restart applications when they hang or consume too many resources and redirect users to other servers still currently running. When users access applications with such problems, they often have to resubmit URLs to receive a valid or correct response.

An initial investment in making sure that your application can handle the expected load is better than engineering workarounds for buggy software!

We need to make a key point before going into the details of load testing: No matter how hard you try, there will be a limit to what your application can support. No server or set of servers can handle an infinite load. That's why in load testing, perhaps more so than in other domains of testing, it's critical to know up front what your goals are. How many users do you want to support simultaneously? How much data do you expect to handle? Are you going to use multiple servers to distribute the load? (If so, you had better think of that early in the development process because you will probably need to have your application distribute user state appropriately.) Do you have a method to increase the scalability of your application if it becomes more successful than you planned? Can you cope with short periods of overactivity (due to a mention in a news article, for instance)?

If you don't know what your goals are, you will not be able to determine when you have performed sufficient load testing. Also, if your application evolves over time, your load testing has to continue and evolve with the application. Each time your application changes, make sure that your load-testing requirements are updated appropriately and that new features are examined for their possible effect on the performance and scalability of your application.

Configuring Virtual Users

Because typically you cannot effectively get enough people to sit down and load-test your application (and even if you could afford this, it wouldn't meet all the requirements we're about to discuss), you're forced to create *virtual users:* computer-controlled testers that pretend to be users exercising your application from a browser. Whether these virtual users come from an off-the-shelf package or are carefully custom scripted, you have to make sure that they cover the necessary requirements for properly load-testing your application. The first issue at hand is this: If a virtual user mimics a human using your application, what kinds of things should it support to be adequate? We cover only the basic items here. Because we don't have working artificial intelligences yet, your virtual users will necessarily implement relatively simple models. As you test your application, you will probably be able to think of ways to bring your virtual users closer to actual user behavior.

You can combine both worlds by having some actual users exercise your application concurrently with virtual users, thus adding more unexpected possibilities to an otherwise predictable test. Naturally, you wouldn't want to add this many variables until your load tests were being passed cleanly on their own.

Addressing technical issues

To emulate real user behavior, you need to learn about your current or potential users' browsers and configure your tests accordingly. Because users interact with your Web application using a Web browser, some of the most basic questions are related to the browser – for example:

- What browsers are your users using?
- Which versions?
- On which platforms are the browsers running?

Unless you are writing an application for a very limited audience, your virtual users should test as wide a variety of browsers as possible. Virtual users representing users with browsers you don't support should access your application under load testing. If your server is creating different content for different browsers, exercising all appropriate combinations is especially critical.

If you have access to a running Web application with appropriate logging, you can get a rough idea of which browsers (and other Internet applications, such as search engines) are accessing your application. You will be surprised at the amazing variety of tools being used to access your application, even though the majority are typically different versions of Internet Explorer and Netscape. When you have this information, you can create a random set of profiles to test your application while pretending to be those various browsers and tools.

Because your virtual users are computer controlled, they will generally be unable to interact with the real browsers you want to test. Some tools can drive real browsers, but this usually limits you to a small subset of testable browsers, and also restricts the types of tests you can perform. Therefore, your virtual users should be capable of emulating different browsers as required by your tests. The most basic way to make your virtual users pretend to be using different browsers is to set the User-Agent field on their HTTP requests, which triggers any different behaviors from the server. This might be sufficient for simple applications but not for complex ones – especially ones relying on a large amount of JavaScript. Ideally, your virtual browsers will act as much as possible like the browser they are emulating. This means emulating the following things:

- The order in which images and frames are loaded
- How the JavaScript is evaluated (and any resulting side-effect loads)
- Whether multiple downloads occur simultaneously and with which protocol

Because the range of possible browsers is large and undocumented, you can only approximate these behaviors. Take advantage of any known dependencies in your application, and make sure that you are at least testing those.

After you identify a specific virtual browser for each virtual user, there are still issues related to how the browser has been configured. You can enable or disable a wide variety of features that affect how the client interacts with your application. These settings include, but are not limited to,

- Whether to cache files and how much cache space is available
- Whether to support scripting
- Which language(s) the browser prefers (this is critical if you are supporting multiple languages, for example, English and French)
- Whether to use cookies (or allow users to disable cookies)

Each virtual browser should have its own cache, cookies, passwords, and so forth, as appropriate.

Finally, your virtual browsers will be running on virtual computers somewhere, so at a bare minimum, you must decide the connection speed each virtual computer will use to access your application for realistic testing.

Selecting paths

After you have a virtual browser configured, you decide how the virtual user will interact with it. The absolute simplest implementation of a virtual user is a script requesting a number of URLs, one after another. The key consideration in this mode is which paths to use for load testing. An excellent start is to use any test cases that have already been set up for verifying the validity of your application. Test cases covering both critical paths and basic features are good starting points to make sure that your application is being exercised while under load. At this point, you probably already have test data for completing any relevant forms or other key features. Why not reuse this data for load testing?

Another way to create load-testing test cases is to analyze your log file for common paths and mimic the common paths you find. If your application is already live, a tool that automatically creates paths based on your log files would be helpful in setting up these kinds of tests.

The danger with using any set of fixed paths is the possibility of missing some important paths. Any reasonably large application has an infinite combination of paths, due to your lack of control over how the user enters and navigates the application.

Chapter 13 discusses the wide variety of potential paths and suggests ways to achieve the necessary coverage.

Chapter 15 reviews several methods for gleaning path information from a live application.

Simulating human behavior

More realistic (and useful) testing accounts for more complexities of user interaction. A higher-level model would load a URL and all accompanying data (images, frames, scripts, sound files) using a cache model and execute JavaScript as appropriate (including ongoing timers). Then, the virtual user would look at the page for a while (sometimes referred to as *think time*), choose a link to follow, and trigger the specified action. The process would continue until the user gives up and quits the virtual browser. Figure 14-1 shows a sample flow chart for this kind of virtual user. Handwritten scripts can emulate this behavior but are unlikely to find subtle complications if they are just issuing `GET` requests. For example, JavaScript dependencies or race conditions require detailed analysis of the results returned from the Web server.

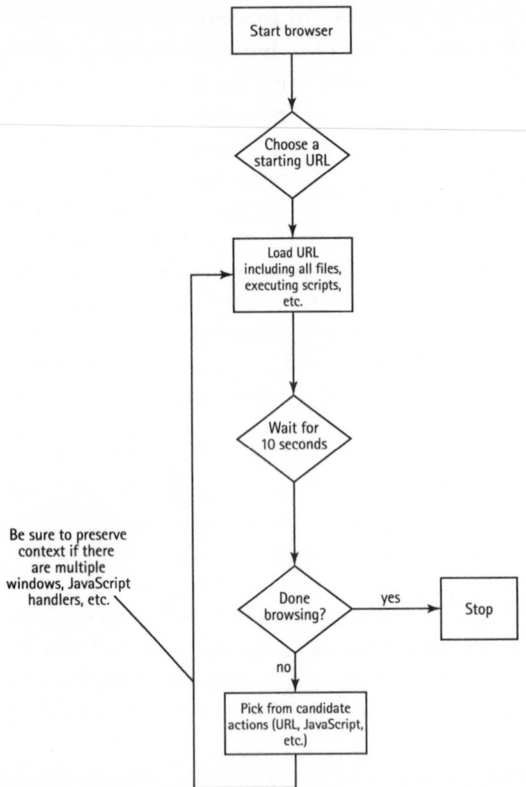

Figure 14-1: A sample flow chart for a simple virtual user.

If you wait for a constant period of time, your tests will not be very realistic and can cause "waves" of access. It is much better to use randomly distributed patterns more typical of real usage. You can also include very large wait times every now and then to cover bathroom breaks, lunch hours, and weekends when the virtual browser is left running and the user returns expecting things to work. If your application implements a timeout on any application data, make sure that you occasionally include at least some virtual users that wait longer than this time to verify how the situation is handled.

In this simple model, there's also the issue of how you choose which links to follow. You have many choices and can create endless permutations. For example, you can

- Randomly choose from all available links (and scripted, dynamic actions).
- Choose links near the top of the page more often than those near the bottom.
- Choose historically popular links more often than less popular ones (mirroring actual measured behavior more accurately).

Of course, real users don't always constrain themselves to these options. In addition to following links, they can visit old URLs from their browser's history, type in new ones they have written down on a piece of paper, use the Back and Forward buttons in rapid succession, and close and create new windows. A user might click on a visible link before the rest of your data is finished loading (causing possible server confusion), or your application might get loaded in a subframe from some other site that points to your application. If you use frames, it's possible that your code was not designed for these situations and will fail in unusual ways. (If you care about this problem, it's better to force a top-level frame to be created for your application.)

Many browsers contain options to open links in a new window. If you rely on JavaScript or frames, this is something you should definitely test. Lately, we've seen a good amount of online advertisements that break under these conditions.

In addition, your virtual users should be able to interact with any live elements of your pages, including JavaScript actions, forms, applets, multimedia presentations, and so forth. For instance, entering a particular value into some form element can have a side effect of generating a new URL elsewhere on the page. Unless your virtual users can sniff out these links on their own, you will have to remember to add them as fixed paths.

Comparing fixed paths and random paths

If you consider fixed paths and simulated users walking random paths as competing solutions for load testing, you might be tempted to ask which one is better. Take a look at the pros and cons of each.

If you use only fixed paths, you must invest a lot of initial effort to set up your tests. You have to analyze which paths are important, decide how many are enough, and make sure that your scripts are flexible enough to handle changing URLs (for example, passing cookies or session IDs as URL parameters). Of course, you already need to do much of this work to test your application independent of load testing. If you use your critical paths, you will be sure to cover at least your most fundamental and popular functionality.

If you use only random path walkers, you test more combinations of paths and eventually hit paths you overlooked from your fixed test cases. As your application evolves, random walkers still do a good job of working all the different features. On the down side, your testing is only as good as your walking algorithms. Any features not supported by your walkers are not tested. (For instance, your random walkers might not be able to fill out forms in meaningful ways.)

We have found the best practice to be a combination of both: Use fixed paths to guarantee coverage of core functionality, and add random walkers to cover other possibilities.

For a more general discussion of fixed paths and random paths, see Chapter 13.

Setting Up Scenarios

A virtual user describes how a single user will interact with your Web application. A *scenario* describes how many virtual users will combine to create an actual load to test your application. Your scenarios should vary according to the specific goals of a given test run. A complete load-testing solution includes a variety of scenarios to provide better coverage.

Testing for capacity

One of the most basic kinds of scenarios is *capacity testing*. This type of testing starts with a small number of users and gradually increases the number of users until your application fails to meet the minimum acceptable performance criteria. This gives you a quick estimate of how many users your application will likely be able to support. Note that the usefulness of this estimate depends on the accuracy of your virtual user modeling. If you test only on your intranet, you might not be accounting for limited bandwidth on your connection to the outside world. Similarly, if your virtual users aren't consuming resources in ways typical to your eventual customers, you won't see the full effects of multiple users.

Testing for endurance

Endurance testing involves establishing some kind of reasonable load and letting it run for a very long time. Keeping the load reasonably heavy typically helps you detect any failure situations sooner. The longer you run the test, the better. If you're serious about endurance testing, it's best to run the test overnight or over the weekend. After the tests have run a long time, pay careful attention to whether resources are still being used effectively and whether performance has degraded at all. Some situations result in slow degradation over time, and others cause no apparent problems until some critical threshold is reached and the application rapidly falls to unacceptable levels (or crashes altogether).

Testing for robustness

Spike testing is one form of robustness testing designed to evaluate how your application will handle a sudden influx of traffic. This influx can stem from different causes. For example, a spike can occur if your application is mentioned in a prominent location or if an advertising campaign returns greater results than expected. Another type of spike condition is a denial-of-service attack, in which a malicious third party attempts to swamp your service with more requests than it can handle. To simulate this kind of scenario, you start out with a reasonable load and then suddenly increase activity. For the best results, experiment with the parameters that control how fast the spike hits and how long it lasts.

In addition, you should determine (and test) how your server should respond to spike conditions. After a certain threshold, should new users simply be denied service or be taken to an alternative static server? Do you want to require that existing users continue to function acceptably, with only new users suffering? What kinds of failures are handled? If your application crashes, do you have a recovery plan? Possible recovery plans include

- Having backup servers take over
- Automatically restarting the server
- Notifying a human user to fix the problem

These plans need to be prepared and tested before any such failures affect your actual application.

When preparing scenarios, you can also take advantage of any inside information you have about how your application functions. If certain kinds of requests consume more resources, try to set up scenarios aimed at swamping that resource. This is another kind of white box testing that helps you prepare for possible Web disasters.

For a review of the general concept of white box testing, see Chapter 9.

Testing expected usage

In addition to special scenarios targeted at answering specific questions, you create scenarios that mimic expected usage. If you have statistics from an already running application, you can base your scenarios on this history. For instance, Web usage often peaks during the day. Some applications see a jump in activity during their users' lunch hour. If your application has a large international audience, you might see different peaks at different times.

When you have an expected usage scenario, you should scale it to create the same usage pattern but with a heavier load. This helps to verify that your application can handle local peaks in activity. If you can handle twice the maximum expected number of users with no difficulty, you should be prepared to deploy your application (especially if you have a plan for growth when your application starts evolving and becoming more popular).

Running the Tests and Interpreting the Results

With the groundwork of virtual browsers, users, and scenarios completed, you're ready to start performing load testing on your application! Whether you are using custom scripts or other tools, you should be able to choose which test or tests to run and see the effect they have on your application.

The value of your load tests increases dramatically with the amount of information they can provide you while running. If the only information you have is whether the application has crashed, you can determine whether your application will crash, but nothing else. The kinds of things to look for are described in the following sections.

Analyzing performance

At a minimum, you need to see how your application is performing as the testing proceeds (or after it is finished). Are users receiving responses within the acceptable minimum time? Remember, the Web is a wide-open marketplace. If your application is not performing within a user's expectations, the user can generally go somewhere else. Ideally, you configure your tests to report when performance becomes unacceptable so that you can immediately determine when something is wrong.

Analyzing scalability

Scalable applications use resources in such a fashion that as the number of users (or amount of data) increases, the application does not experience unsupportable, non-linear growth. As you are running your scenarios, keep your eye on the following things:

- The amount of memory the server is using
- The amount of disk space required for temporary files
- Whether the database is growing in a controlled fashion, based on the number of users and amount of data

If you have a load-balancing solution implemented, make sure that the workload is, in fact, being distributed in an even mode according to whatever algorithms are in place. If so, you should also test the effect of adding and removing servers while the tests are running, to make sure that you can do this on the production application while actual customers are working.

Testing correct behavior

Even if your application is performing adequately and scaling properly, you can experience problems that cause user failures. For instance, maybe a servlet starts throwing exceptions after the load increases and, instead of a nicely formatted HTML page, users get a page explaining that some mysterious error has occurred, in technical detail they can't understand. As you test, be aware that some parts of dynamic pages fail only under certain loads. For example, generated URLs could become incorrect if more than 256 users are logged in simultaneously. Unless your load testing efforts include a detailed analysis of the information the server returns during testing, these kinds of errors are not going to be caught, even with a fully detailed set of virtual users and scenarios. That's why it's important to include some basic validation and error checking during load testing. This necessarily slows down your load testing, but if that's a concern, you can run some tests with validation and some without (depending on the specific aspect of your application you are testing at that moment).

Tracking down the problem

When a problem exists, you want as much information as possible about what triggered the problem. For example, it is good to know the URL being requested, the history of requests leading up to it, and what else (generally) was going on at the same time. If the problem (whatever it is) can be easily reproduced, there's a good chance you can identify which component of the system is failing and pass the information to the appropriate person responsible. When the component has been repaired (or redesigned to handle the necessary workload), the tests should be repeated to verify correct behavior.

Leveraging Load Testing

When you have a load-testing framework in place, you can also test other aspects of your application. This section details a few of the options and brings up some miscellaneous points to consider as you are managing your own Web application.

Real Web applications are dynamic. In addition to changing in response to user requests, they change over time as the functionality provided is improved and customers' needs are met with new features. This means that you need a procedure to update a working application. Whether you choose to redirect all users to a static URL during the update or implement some sophisticated algorithm, test the selected procedure under a load to verify that you can perform these updates according to your plan even while users are trying to access your application.

After your application is deployed and in use, keep your eye on any problems that could develop in actual conditions. You can automate this by using some of your load tests on the actual application. For instance, you can run a few random users every hour and verify performance or run critical paths every few minutes. When a failure is detected, you want the Webmaster or other appropriate people notified immediately. An automatic solution can be configured to send email or dial a pager when preset conditions fail. We discuss such monitoring efforts in more detail in Chapter 15.

If you choose to perform load testing on your actual server, you should arrange to do so in a way that does not affect any usage data you are logging. Otherwise, when you are analyzing your users' behavior, you will obscure their actual patterns with artificial ones you introduced as part of your checking.

Using Python for Load Testing

In this section, you will learn how to load-test your application using customized scripts written in Python. Many of the same ideas and considerations apply to any technique you choose to implement for load testing. To keep our example concrete, we use basic load-testing scripts to simulate virtual users testing our Online Grocer application. You can adapt and apply these scripts to your own situation and needs.

All the files and scripts shown in this section are available on the CD.

The absolute simplest implementation of a virtual user is a script that requests a number of URLs, one after another. Here's a sample script that does just that:

LoadTest-1.py

```
#!/usr/bin/python
import time
import urllib

urls = open('urls.txt').readlines()
for url in urls:
    url = url.strip()
    t0 = time.time()
    page = urllib.urlopen(url)
    page.readlines()
    t1 = time.time()
    print 'Reading ' + url + ' took', t1-t0, 'second(s)'
```

This script assumes that a file named `urls.txt` is in the current working directory and that this file has a list of URLs to request (one URL per line). If you change `page.readlines()` to `print page.readlines()`, it prints the contents of the responses.

You can also add validation code to verify the contents of the server responses. Chapter 17 contains an example of how to write such code for XML.

A sample `urls.txt` file based on loading the Online Grocer Splash page might look like this:

```
http://www.parasoft.com/fruits/index.html
http://www.parasoft.com/fruits/fruits.css
http://www.parasoft.com/fruits/fruits/background.gif
```

Here is the output from running the script:

```
>python LoadTest.py
Reading http://www.parasoft.com/fruits/index.html took 0.0780 second(s)
Reading http://www.parasoft.com/fruits/fruits.css took 0.0 second(s)
Reading http://www.parasoft.com/fruits/fruits/background.gif took 0.0159 second(s)
```

Each URL sequence simulates a user walking a path through the application. If you are using this method, you also need to be able to submit forms and do anything else necessary to simulate the correct traffic.

At this point, we have a general idea of how we will proceed, so we try to follow a real path through the Online Grocer application. First, we determine which URLs are going to be loaded. Rather than try to figure out the full sequence of loads required by following a flow chart, we decide to restart our Web server with an empty log file and then manually walk a path in which we are interested. This way, when we are done, we can copy the server's log file, which should correspond to the path we walked.

To walk the desired path, we log in, search for red and yellow fruits, add bananas to our cart, search for green vegetables, add bell peppers to our cart, change the cart to contain 0 bananas and 2 bell peppers, purchase the cart, and log out. The resulting log file from our Web server shows 48 accesses to complete this transaction. Log file formats typically vary according to server configuration; our logged accesses look like this:

```
access.log
10.10.32.30 - - [22/May/2001:13:18:00 -0700] \
    "GET /fruits HTTP/1.1" 301 323
10.10.32.30 - - [22/May/2001:13:18:00 -0700] \
    "GET /fruits/ HTTP/1.1" 304 -
10.10.32.30 - - [22/May/2001:13:18:00 -0700] \
    "GET /fruits/fruits.css HTTP/1.1" 304 -
10.10.32.30 - - [22/May/2001:13:18:00 -0700] \
    "GET /fruits/fruits/background.gif HTTP/1.1" 404 308
```

```
10.10.32.30 - - [22/May/2001:13:18:01 -0700] \
    "GET /servlet/fruits.ShoppingServlet HTTP/1.1" 200 1161
```

Next, we translate this file to the `urls.txt` format so that our Python script can create the same path. When we do so, we notice that we don't have any support for using HTTP `POST` or for simulating the user's think time. Another problem: The time we are printing is per URL instead of per user action. To fix these problems, we modify the `urls.txt` format as follows and name the new file `load.txt`:

```
GET /fruits/
GET /fruits/fruits.css
GET /fruits/fruits/background.gif
WAIT 10
POST /servlet/fruits.ShoppingServlet METHOD=choose&FRUITS=on&RED=red&YELLOW=yellow
GET /fruits/images/banana_fruit_yellow.gif
GET /fruits/fruits.css
GET /fruits/images/lemon_fruit_yellow.gif
GET /fruits/images/cherry_fruit_red.gif
GET /fruits/images/mango_fruit_yellow.gif
GET /fruits/images/orange_fruit_yellow.gif
GET /fruits/images/pineapple_fruit_yellow.gif
GET /fruits/images/pomegranate_fruit_red.gif
GET /fruits/images/redpear_fruit_red.gif
GET /fruits/images/strawberry_fruit_red.gif
WAIT 10
```

The paths have been abbreviated here to better illustrate the key differences. The file on the disk contains full URLs for each `GET` and `POST`.

In this case, we execute three `GET`s followed by a `WAIT` for 10 seconds to represent the first page. Then, we execute a `POST` with accompanying `GET`s, followed by another `WAIT` to represent the second page.

A key point is that the translation from `access.log` to `load.txt` was done by hand, and because some information was missing in `access.log`, we had to add that by hand, also. For instance, we had to add the breaks that represent pages to the user and the arguments that were passed to `POST`.

Whenever you modify a script manually, there's a chance you might introduce errors. If you make manual modifications, make sure that you review the revised script carefully.

Also, because the `LoadTest` script might have a lot of output that we want to analyze, we will change the program to generate XML output. Finally, we will change the program to accept multiple path files on the command line and randomly walk different ones until we kill the process. This way, we can start bunches of these programs to create loads on our server.

For a discussion of XML, see Chapter 17.

Here's the modified version of `LoadTest` that supports our new requirements:

LoadTest-2.py

```
#!/usr/bin/python

import random
import sys
import time
import urllib

def usePath(path):
    print '<LoadAnalysis path="' + path + '">'
    t0 = time.time()
    urls = open(path).readlines()
    for url in urls:
        cmd = url.split()
        if cmd[0] == 'GET':
            page = urllib.urlopen(cmd[1])
            page.readlines()
        elif cmd[0] == 'POST':
           page = urllib.urlopen(cmd[1], cmd[2])
           page.readlines()
        elif cmd[0] == 'WAIT':
            t1 = time.time()
            print '    <Load time="' + str(t1-t0).strip() + '"/>'
            time.sleep(float(cmd[1]))
           t0 = time.time()
    print '</LoadAnalysis>'

while 1:
    index = random.random()*(len(sys.argv) - 1)
    usePath(sys.argv[int(index) + 1])
```

Here is a sample of the new output:

```
>python LoadTest-2.py load.txt
<LoadAnalysis path="load.txt">
    <Load time="0.0319999456406"/>
    <Load time="0.0150001049042"/>
</LoadAnalysis>
```

So far so good. However, careful analysis of the servlet indicates that, although it seems to be working, the user never actually gets logged in! The reason is that our code still doesn't support cookies, so no sessions were created. Because our Python load tester doesn't look at the output, it can't identify such problems. Adding enough cookie support to handle `ShoppingServlet` is straightforward. We added this support in `LoadTest-3.py`. The main change is inside the code that handles `GET` and `POST` requests, which now looks like this:

```
request = urllib2.Request(cmd[1])
if cookie != '':
    request.add_header('Cookie', cookie)
page = urllib2.urlopen(request)
 info = page.info()
 if info.has_key('Set-Cookie'):
    cookie = page.info()['Set-Cookie']
page.readlines()
```

This code doesn't handle multiple cookies, but they aren't required for this application, so we're okay.

If you look at `LoadTest-3.py` on the CD, you will see that we also added some commands for debugging path creation, as well as more documentation for our path. We also fixed a broken link that `LoadTest-2.py` failed to report (`fruits/fruits/background.gif`). The final output (using the new `load2.txt` instead of `load.txt`) now looks like this:

```
<LoadAnalysis path="load2.txt">
    <Load action="Go To Splash Page" time="0.18799996376"/>
    <Load action="Go To Log In Page" time="0.0149999856949"/>
    <Load action="Log In As Demo" time="0.328000068665"/>
    <Load action="Choose Red & Yellow Fruits" time="2.46899998188"/>
    <Load action="Click On Bananas" time="0.0159999132156"/>
    <Load action="Add Bananas To Cart" time="0.0150001049042"/>
    <Load action="Search For More" time="0.0159999132156"/>
    <Load action="Choose Green Vegetables" time="2.26499998569"/>
    <Load action="Click On Bell Peppers" time="0.0160000324249"/>
    <Load action="Add Bell Peppers To Cart" time="0.0149999856949"/>
```

```
    <Load action="Modify Amounts In Cart" time="0.0319999456406"/>
    <Load action="Purchase Items In Cart" time="0.0150001049042"/>
    <Load action="Log Out" time="0.0159999132156"/>
</LoadAnalysis>
```

The results show that our search request (`Choose Red & Yellow Fruits`) has the slowest response time (by far). Without digging into the details, we can't tell whether this is because our servlet is slow or because we are displaying lots of images the user needs to load. In this case, we could comment out the image requests from `load2.txt` and rerun our tests to get just the time spent processing the search itself.

This gets us much closer to our goal of performing realistic load testing. So far, this script has completely ignored our specification of the virtual browser, except that when we created our path originally, the caching algorithms of our browser controlled which files were loaded (you can see this in `access.log`, if you're interested). In fact, in this case, we forgot to flush the browser cache before creating our initial `access.log`, so some of the loads are completely missing. Another weakness is that we're not doing much error checking; `fruits/fruits/background.gif` returned a 404 (which means that the page was not found), but our first script kept running along silently. The final script fails on 404s, but not in a pleasant way.

`LoadTest-3.py` is now becoming complicated, and it's still making many assumptions but not doing much checking. With some work, it could be refactored, cleaned up, and extended.

Rather than create an enormous script tailored to our Online Grocer application, we will move on to an example using WebKing, which does much of this work for us.

Our choice of Python is completely arbitrary. The CD includes an equivalent version of `LoadTest-3` written in Perl (`LoadTest-3.pl`). If you want to use this version, you need to have a version of Perl installed with the `HTTP` and `Time::HiRes` modules loaded. Except for the language details, the code looks quite similar, with the same benefits and drawbacks.

Using WebKing for Load Testing

This section explains how to use WebKing to bring the concepts of load testing to life on the Online Grocer application. The main advantage of WebKing is that the virtual users are already written for you, and you can also leverage all the tests you have already created, as well as perform comprehensive system testing simultaneously with the load testing. We introduce WebKing's virtual user feature briefly in Chapter 13. Here we go over the information in more detail, specifically from a load-testing point of view.

The first step, naturally, is to start up WebKing and load the appropriate project file. You will be testing your application as a client would, so you load a client-side testing project as described in Chapter 11. Load testing is controlled by the Site Workout feature. You can access this feature by clicking the Site Workout toolbar button shown in Figure 14-2.

Figure 14-2: The Site Workout button.

This opens the Site Workout control panel, shown in Figure 14-3.

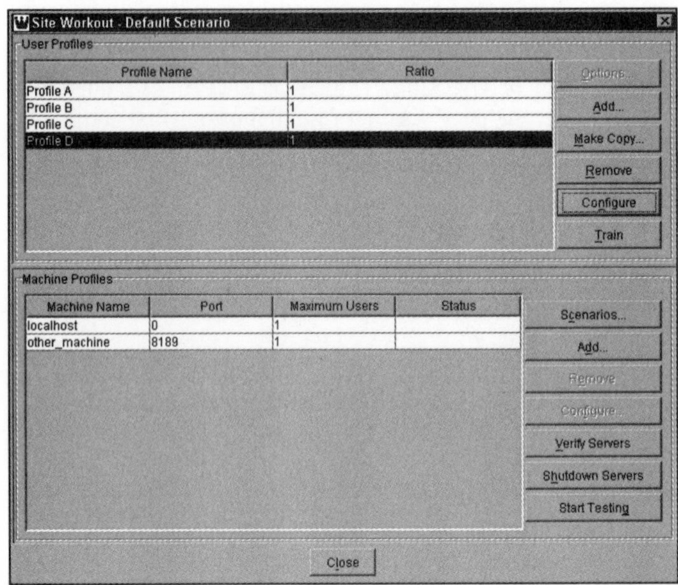

Figure 14-3: The Site Workout control panel.

The top half of the control panel, the User Profiles area, lets you configure new and existing virtual users. The lower half, the Machine Profiles area, lets you control how the virtual users are distributed across your network to generate the desired load. We will cover each aspect in turn.

Creating user profiles

You can create as many unique user profiles as you want by clicking the Add button and specifying profiles in the User Profile dialog box that opens (see Figure 14-4).

The Ratio parameter lets you control the distributions of created profiles. For instance, if you want twice as many Profile Bs as Profile As, you give Profile B a ratio of 2 and Profile A a ratio of 1. This extends to as many profiles as you want to support. Specific scenarios can exert more control over the distribution of profiles, as explained later in this section.

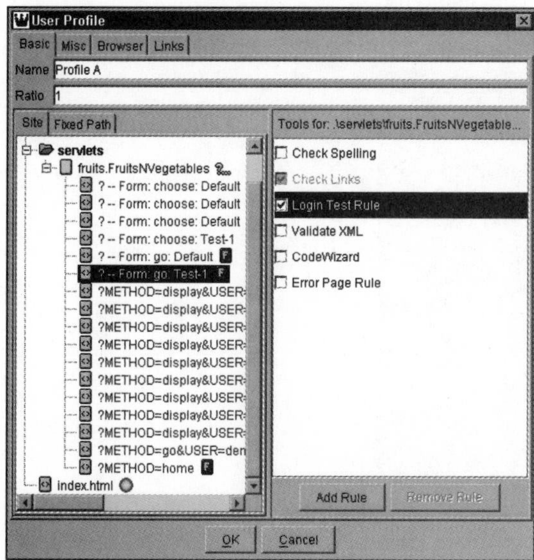

Figure 14-4: The User Profile panel.

A user profile can run in one of two modes: random paths or fixed paths. If you want to use random paths, no additional configuration is required. If you want to select fixed paths, you add them to your Path tree, as detailed in Chapter 13. Then, from the User Profile panel's Basic tab, select the Fixed Path subtab, right-click any paths you want that profile to use, and select Use Test. Red check marks indicate items that will be tested, and blue check marks indicate items that are parents to items being tested. This makes it easy to see which paths will be tested and which will not.

If you are using fixed paths, the load tester generates error messages when the virtual user cannot follow fixed paths for any reason (for instance, the link it's supposed to follow doesn't exist). This helps you identify subtle errors that occur only under a load. The Python testing code, for instance, never checked whether the requests being made were feasible. If, for some reason, a link being followed did not appear when expected, the scripted load tester would incorrectly continue to traverse a path that no longer existed.

When we use virtual users to test paths through the Online Grocer application, we also take advantage of WebKing's capability to attach tools to run on various pages. It's important not to forget this capability during load testing. Some of the common failures that occur under load can be detected only if you are validating the contents of the pages as you are testing. This is particularly important because the process has been automated – no human is going to be checking all the pages retrieved from the server.

The Misc tab of the User Profile dialog box (shown in Figure 14-5) lets you control certain aspects of the virtual users' behavior.

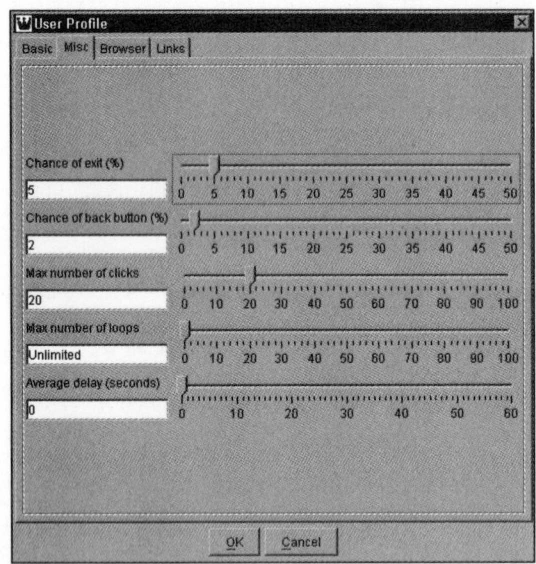

Figure 14-5: The Misc view of the User Profile panel.

If you recall the basic flow of our virtual users (refer to Figure 14-1), each virtual user emulates a real user accessing the application and clicking links from a browser. The options supported here are

- **Chance of exit:** What is the chance that the user will decide to leave your application after looking at each page (for example, by exiting the browser or going to another site)? When a virtual user exits your application, WebKing automatically creates a new virtual user if the maximum number of loops has not been exceeded. The chance of exit option applies only to random paths because fixed paths always terminate at the last page of the path.
- **Chance of Back button:** What is the chance of the user clicking the Back button rather than clicking a link? If your application does not support the Back button, you can disable this. This option applies only to random

paths. You can specifically choose to use the Back button from fixed paths when and where you like.

- **Max number of clicks:** How far will the user dig into your application before giving up? This lets you impose an upper limit on the number of clicks a virtual user will follow. If you have the chance of exit set above 0, you can set the maximum number of clicks to unlimited (which is represented by 0 on the line graph) and let the user go as far as the random walk takes him. If you do not have any chance of exit, the only way your virtual users will give up is by reaching the maximum number of clicks. This option applies only to random paths.
- **Max number of loops:** How often is this virtual user used during a given session of load testing? If you have profiles that are checking only key functionality and you don't want them running over and over during load testing, you can configure this option so that they are used only a few times. Commonly, you set the limit to 1, meaning "Run each test case once." If N is the value entered and you are using random paths, the virtual user will create N random paths. If you are using fixed paths, it will use each fixed path N times.
- **Average delay (seconds):** How long will the user read your page before deciding what to do next? This represents the user's think time. The value you select here is just the average delay; to create a more realistic load, WebKing varies the delays within the specified range. A reasonable think time for many applications is 15 seconds. Average delay applies to fixed and random paths.

If your average delay is large, you can run more virtual users from a single host computer because your bandwidth is not in as high demand. While some users are "thinking," other users will be sending requests. If you set your average delay to 0, your virtual users will be pushing the pipe as hard as they can. In this case, you cannot support as many simultaneous virtual users per machine.

If you are utilizing the full capacity of your machine, the load as defined by the number of accesses will be equivalent. In one case, though, you will be simulating more users than the other. For example, if you have 10 virtual users who each access 1 page per second, the load is 10 hits per second. If you have 1 virtual user who accesses 10 pages per second, the load is still 10 hits per second. The load is the same in both cases, but the events being simulated are different. Understanding how your application works is key to creating the ideal load-testing scenario.

The Browser and Links tabs of the User Profile dialog let you control certain aspects of the virtual browser. From the Browser tab, you choose the User-Agent representing the browser you want to emulate. You can enter one of your own or choose one from the available list. WebKing adapts its JavaScript support to match the DOM of the User-Agent you specify. You can also choose a Locale, which corresponds to the language the virtual browser requests. Some applications, for instance, dispatch different content to English speakers and French speakers. If you want a user to prefer French, you use `fr` as its locale. (Locales are explained in more detail in the WebKing documentation.) You can also control whether cookies are enabled. This is useful because some browsers do not support cookies, and even browsers that do support cookies allow users disable them.

From the Links tab shown in Figure 14-6, you choose which types of objects are loaded. If, for instance, you want to emulate a text-only view, you disable image and sound links. This makes the test run faster because less data is transferred as the virtual user traverses your application.

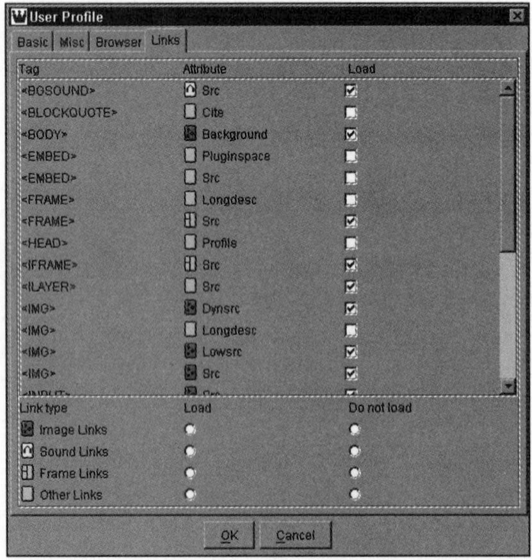

Figure 14-6: The Links view of the User Profile panel.

To learn more about ways to customize the behavior of virtual users and virtual browsers, see the WebKing User's Guide.

Specifying machine profiles

So far, we have discussed ways to set up one virtual user at a time. If you want to generate a load, you have to use many virtual users simultaneously in some cooperative fashion.

The simplest case is to use the machine on which you are running WebKing to test your application. This machine is referred to by the generic name *localhost.* You set the basic options for this machine in the Machine Profiles dialog box (shown in Figure 14-7). To reach this dialog box, highlight the localhost entry in the Site Workout Control panel, and click the Configure button. When you are working with the local machine, the port option does not apply and is disabled. The only option you can specify is Maximum Users (how many users to use simultaneously). You can also use the Maximum Users field to control how many concurrent threads are running. The WebKing User's Guide has full details on how to do this. The best values for Maximum Users depend on your Average Delay.

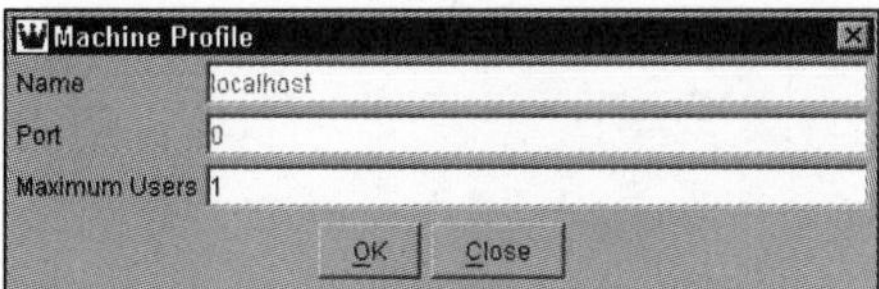

Figure 14-7: The Machine Profile dialog box.

If you are generating a serious load, you will probably need to employ more than one machine. Depending on how many users you want, what their think time is, and how much analysis you are doing, you might have to get many machines cooperating. You do this by setting up WebKing servers that will respond to testing requests from a master WebKing.

By setting the machine profiles, you can specify which machines you will use and through which ports they will communicate. You can even control machines in remote locations from a central WebKing to create a more diverse load. Each machine uses two port numbers to communicate with the master WebKing: the one you specify in the Machine Profile dialog box and the port number immediately following it. You can disable usage of some machines by setting the maximum number of users to 0 for those machines. We recommend referring to the WebKing User's Guide for more details when you are ready to test on multiple machines.

Running your tests

Whatever configuration you are using, you start the test by clicking the Start Testing button. WebKing then begins creating a load on your server and collecting the results. The total load of your test is the sum of the load generated by all machines doing the testing. While the tests are running, you get an overview of how your application is performing. This overview is displayed as a performance graph, shown in Figure 14-8.

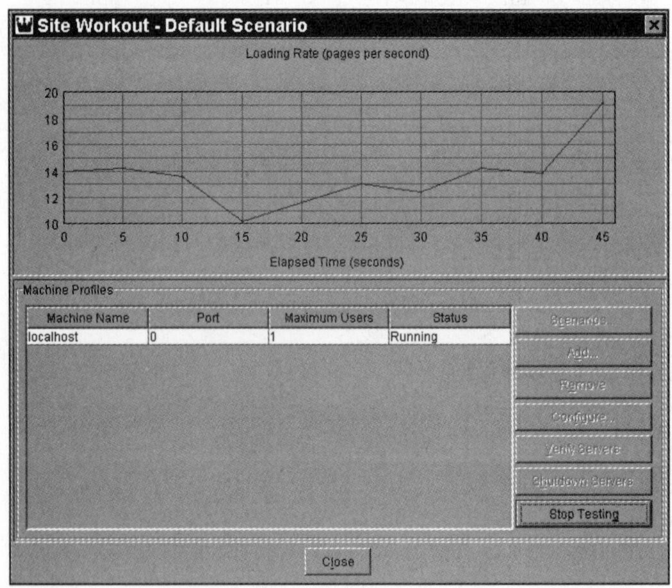

Figure 14-8: A sample performance graph.

The top graph shows how many pages are being loaded per second per machine. Because we are testing a steady-state load, we would expect performance to remain mostly level. If, over a period of time, the performance gradually degrades, you might have a resource leak. Possibly, memory is being allocated and not freed, or sessions are not timing out properly. This corresponds roughly to an endurance-testing scenario (described in the section "Setting Up Scenarios"). In this graph, our steady load is approximately 14 pages per second (this includes top-level clicks, so each page can include many CSS pages, scripts, images, and so on).

If the number of accesses is significantly lower than you expect, you are probably not saturating your machine. Whenever you have a low number of Maximum Users and a high Average Delay, WebKing spends most of its time waiting for the virtual users to do something.

After the tests are done, WebKing generates a report, such as that shown in Figure 14-9, describing the results in some detail. You can look at min/max and average load time, either by individual URL or by file.

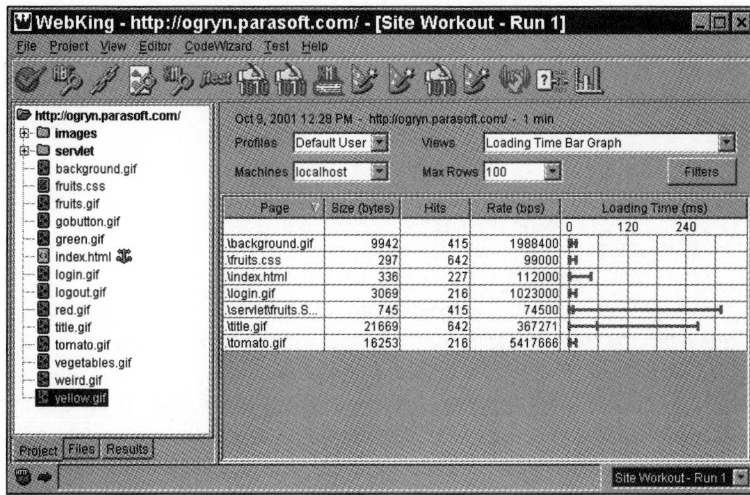

Figure 14-9: A sample load testing report.

By choosing the Test Information view, you get a summary of the test runs in text format. Here's an example of such a summary for one of our Online Grocer load tests:

```
Project:            http://ogryn.parasoft.com/fruits/
Started:            May 22, 2001 12:39:12 PM
Finished:           May 22, 2001 12:41:30 PM
Total hits:         3757
Total size:         27285 kbytes
Average load time:  31 ms

Machines
    localhost: * (1 user)

Errors
    Check Links: 1 error

---------------
Scenario: Default Scenario
```

```
Profiles
    Default User
      Type:                     Random path
      Ratio:                    1
      Chance of exit:           10 %
      Chance of back button:    10 %
      Max number of clicks:     20
      Number of loops:          Unlimited
      Average delay:            15 sec
```

Creating your own scenarios

So far, we have tested immediately after setting up profiles and machines. Because WebKing gives you a default profile (random) and machine (the current one), you can begin testing with no additional effort beyond creating a project file. This default scenario is steady-state usage, with no expiration. This is appropriate for initial testing and can be acceptable for endurance testing if the load is adequate. However, for more detailed tests, you should create custom scenarios. You do this from the Scenarios panel, shown in Figure 14-10. To access this panel, click the Scenario button in the Site Workout panel.

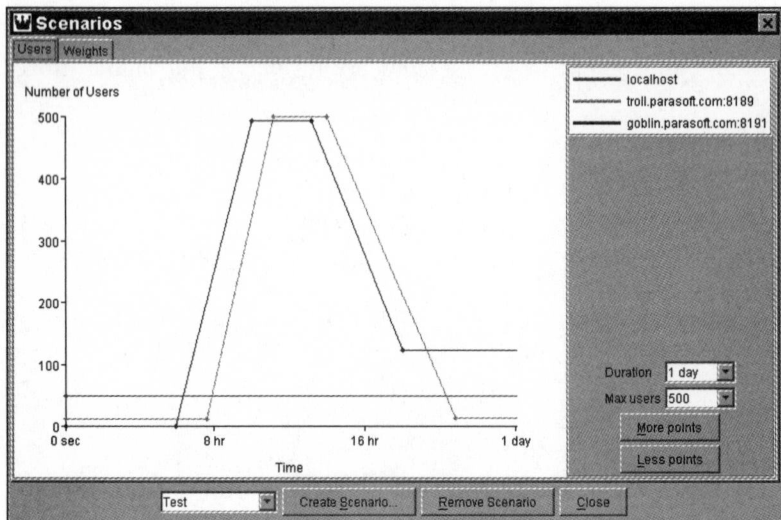

Figure 14-10: The Scenarios panel with users.

The Users tab lets you control how many users you want per machine over time. You can choose the period of your scenario using the Duration box. For example, to test the Online Grocer application, we choose to run for an entire day (24 hours).

The localhost will keep a relatively steady load of 50 users. The machine named *troll* will start with 10 users, spike up to 500 users after 8 hours, and return to 10 users after 21 hours. The machine named *goblin* will start with zero virtual users, spike up to 490 users after 7 hours, and move to a steady 120 users after 18 hours. At the end, our total load should be 180 users. Depending on how much traffic we expect our site to handle, this could represent either a spike test designed to tax our resources or simply a daily ebb and flow.

The Weights tab of this same panel lets you control how your user profiles are distributed over time and available machines. A pie chart illustrates how profiles will be distributed at any given point in time. This ability to create scenarios enables you to perform more selective kinds of testing. Generally, however, you generate the most common scenarios just by controlling the number of users.

Summary

Load testing is a critical aspect of testing for all Web applications. As with other kinds of testing, the more you put into it, the more you get out of it. More comprehensive types of loads yield more reliable applications. One technique that will help you achieve comprehensive load is using both fixed and random paths as test cases; another complementary technique is to enlist the help of virtual users that can serve as an army of workers, automatically exercising a wide array of options. In addition, you can design specific scenarios to test different aspects of your application. Ideally, these scenarios include capacity testing, endurance testing, spike testing, and expected usage testing. You can use many techniques to implement load testing, including scripting and specialized load-testing tools, such as WebKing.

Chapter 15

Performing Application-Level Testing

IN THIS CHAPTER

- Defining unit, module, and application testing
- Understanding application testing concerns and practices
- Ensuring continued functionality and performance
- Updating the application

THIS CHAPTER CONCLUDES PART II, a discussion of bulletproofing during development. In this chapter, we briefly explain how unit testing, module testing, and application testing are related and then review the key concepts in Part II, with an eye towards the final application. Finally, we cover several issues of maintaining and developing a Web application that already has an established user base.

Often, people have different ideas about how much time should be spent on various aspects of development. In *The Mythical Man-Month*, author Fred Brooks provides this rule of thumb for how to divide your time among various software tasks:

- Spend one-third of the project time on planning.
- Spend one-sixth of the project time on coding.
- Spend one-quarter of the project time on component and early system testing.
- Spend one-quarter of the project time on system testing, with all components in hand.

What this means is that even if you have been testing your units all along, as we recommend, you should not gloss over your final system testing – that is, application testing. Although each component has been individually tested, applicationwide testing still needs to confirm that each piece – wherever it lives – is performing correctly in the application environment. Early testing helps you reach your goals sooner but cannot replace application testing. Application testing does require substantial time on any reasonably sized application. Unfortunately, this is often where resources fail to be available because of compressed time-to-market requirements.

Defining Unit, Module, and Application Testing

Viewed from a distance, there isn't much difference between testing your application at the unit, module, or application level. Certainly, the application is just a special case of a module encompassing all the units. As Figure 15-1 illustrates, there is a continuum of testing from small-scale to large-scale.

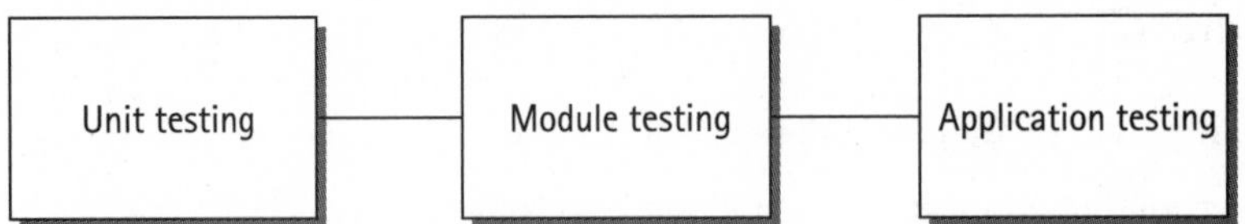

Figure 15-1: The testing continuum.

In its purest form, *unit testing* means testing the smallest functional unit of an application. In a procedural language, this means testing a single function. In an object-oriented language, this means testing a single class. When you group several units into a meaningful subset of your application, this is considered a *module*, whether or not the language you are using has a notion corresponding to the module. For instance, Java has the notion of packages. An entire package can be considered a module for testing purposes, but you can also combine subsets of different packages to create a functional, testable model. At the far right of the spectrum, you have *application testing*, which involves all the units and modules from your application.

One generalization that applies has to do with the distinction between white box and black box testing. During white box testing, you create tests based on the details of your source code. During black box testing, you primarily concentrate on the interface to your code, or your specification. With respect to the testing continuum, unit testing tends to include more white box testing, and the farther you move towards application testing, the more you generally concentrate on specification and requirements instead of code details. As a result, application testing typically includes more black box testing than white box testing.

For a detailed discussion of unit testing, as well as a review of white box testing and black box testing, see Chapter 9.

If your application is a component or a Web service designed to be used by others, definitions become even fuzzier. For your purposes, the component or service *is* the application. For those using your service, you are merely an external module. However, because you are dealing with a continuum, there's no point quibbling over semantics.

You can perform application-level testing as soon as your application is in place. Note that you can begin application testing as soon as you have the *skeleton* of a complete system – you do not have to (and should not!) wait until your application is feature-complete to begin application-level testing. Feature-poor but working applications are good places to begin testing.

Understanding Application Testing Concerns and Practices

Having good answers to the following questions is critical to the success of your application testing:

- Are you testing everything that needs to be tested to ensure that the application functions correctly? Not everything that needs to be tested is apparent (for example, resource usage problems and other behind-the-scenes functionality problems), so you must think hard about this before planning your testing strategy.
- How do you know when you have performed enough testing? How will you gauge coverage – by tests created? tests executed? paths covered? pages tested? Moreover, how will you determine whether you are thoroughly exercising and testing the interactions between your application's parts (servlets, server, databases, components, and so on)?

This section addresses several important issues to consider while designing and performing application testing. This discussion should give you some idea of how to answer the preceding questions for your own application.

Testing at the GUI level

The goal of testing is, of course, to find any kind of error that can occur while your application is being executed. Many of these errors have immediate, user-visible consequences (such as page load failures or ASP error messages). Others silently affect the performance of your application and the integrity of your data and/or server hardware and trigger impossible-to-trace failures further down the road. This section concentrates on analyzing errors visible from the client/browser. We refer to these errors as *GUI-level* errors.

Because various problems can surface after the application's parts are integrated, it's important to develop GUI-level tests that cover interactions between the application's parts, within any new parts, and so on. Basically, you test any interaction or feature that has not been tested yet. If you want to be entirely confident in your application's capability to function correctly, aim to test any kind of output the user might see. For instance, many applications automatically generate e-mail under certain conditions or create resources meant to be downloaded and used with other software (songs, movies, and the like). The output from these actions should be tested along with every other form submission, reload, and so on.

Ideally, your application-level GUI testing should involve replaying and extending the tests discussed throughout Part II. The procedures for applying these tests at the application level are basically the same as those for applying them at the unit level. The only real difference is the number of paths and pages to which they are applied. If you (or other team members) have been developing and saving test cases for each unit, extending the current test cases for application testing should not be much of a chore, as long as your testing methods are automated and extensible. Simply extend the available paths so that they test necessary additional paths throughout the application, and apply the available test cases to the appropriate paths and pages. If your paths contain nonstandard types of application features (for example, automatic e-mail generation) that have not been tested yet, decide which standards are appropriate, and take measures to guarantee the validity of all these items.

Configuring DNS

When setting up your server, it's a good idea to make sure that people can easily access your domain. DNS (*Domain Name System*) records are typically set for the Web server to be some machine like `www.parasoft.com`. However, people often hear and see URLs without the `www`, such as simply `parasoft.com`. For such a URL to work, you must have the proper DNS records setup.

This configuration information goes into the DNS db file in the form of an `A` record. For example, the `www.parasoft.com` record (assuming that our address is `10.10.1.1`) will be

```
www                     IN      A       10.10.1.1
```

or

```
www.parasoft.com        IN      A       10.10.1.1
```

In addition, you need to add a new `A` record for the domain by itself. This is done by adding

```
parasoft.com.           IN      A       10.10.1.1
```

Notice that there is a trailing dot (`.`) after the `parasoft.com`. Without that dot, this won't work. Also notice that `parasoft.com` is set up to be the same address as `www.parasoft.com`.

Before the Web, it was common to make the domain record (`parasoft.com`) match the mail server. This enabled easy mail access without knowing the mail server for a domain. For instance, you could send mail to `info@parasoft.com` instead of `info@mail.parasoft.com`. This is really just an old legacy behavior — the same effect for mail is achieved properly by having the correct MX (*Mail Exchanger*) records set up for your domain. If you make sure that you have a record for your mail server, you should be fine. For example, if your mail server is `10.10.1.2`, you would have

```
                        IN      MX    10 mail.parasoft.com
```

and

```
mail                    IN      A        10.10.1.2
```

This way, you can have all your mail go to your domain name (for example, `parasoft.com`), and Web traffic can also access that same domain. This makes it easier to refer to your URL in ads, on the phone, and so forth.

Details like this are typically the responsibility of your system administrator. However, if you are in charge of a Web project, you should assume responsibility for testing that the customer can access your site with any URLs you deem appropriate. If they can't, you can let your system administrator know that work has to be done on her side.

For more information about DNS, see *DNS and BIND* by Paul Albitz and Cricket Liu.

Detecting runtime errors

Errors that are not immediately visible to the user (or, in this case, the tester) are more difficult to detect. The good news is that many techniques are available that automatically find large classes of runtime errors.

The simplest technique to find inconsistencies at runtime that might not otherwise be visible is to insert checks into your program that verify assumptions the code is making. For example, if you assume that the user isn't logged in twice and there's a way to check this from the code, adding that check would be a good idea. Often these kinds of checks are called *dynamic assertions* or *defensive firewalls.*

For a more detailed discussion of defensive firewalls and other methods of building debugging support into your code, see Chapter 7.

A more sophisticated approach is to use language-specific practices and technologies to identify undesirable runtime states. If you're using C/C++ for your CGIs or dynamically loaded server modules, you can use a tool such as ParaSoft's Insure++ to verify that C/C++ code is not abusing memory or violating common practices of coding in those languages. If you're using Java, you can use Jtest, a similar tool with added support for Java's exception-handling mechanisms, and Jcontract, a tool that combines the best parts of firewalls and runtime testing to further guarantee that your code is always working smoothly.

Even if you have a good system for detecting runtime problems, you have to verify that you're getting good coverage of your program's executable space. After all, the best checks in the world can't find bugs in code that doesn't get exercised.

Monitoring test case coverage

When running automatic test suites, there is a danger in assuming that the test suites have adequately exercised your new application. As new functionality and subsystems are brought online, new test cases need to be added to exercise these features. In addition, you must constantly be on the lookout for aspects of the application that have not yet been exercised. This includes looking at the following issues:

- **Code coverage for servlets, CGIs, and similar programs.** How much of the applications have been covered?
- **Comprehensive site walking.** Have all unique URLs been visited?
- **Functional testing.** Have all features been fully exercised? Are the failure paths properly protected?

You can apply different types of tools to determine how comprehensively different aspects of your application are being exercised.

Monitoring performance and memory usage

Performance analysis can be broken down by subsystem and must be considered at each level. Memory usage must also be considered at all levels but is particularly important to monitor on the server side.

Performance and memory monitoring is especially important in conjunction with load testing. Luckily, when you have a good test suite, you have an excellent basis to build scenarios for load testing. In addition to exercising common paths and expected usage, you must consider unexpected usage and the traffic patterns and volume that could occur if you face a denial of service attack or a sudden unexpected surge in traffic, which might result from your application being mentioned on a popular site.

While tests are underway, check all machines involved to see how loaded they are, how much memory is in use, and how much disk space is available. This checking is especially critical if a machine uses the disk for caching or storing program state. You should have adequate resources to perform smoothly under even the highest expected load.

Ensuring Continued Functionality and Performance

Unless you are a contractor and your contract has ended, your job is not finished after your application has been deployed to a production staging area and you have actual usage on an ongoing basis. If you want to ensure that the application continues to function smoothly, you must watch for ongoing stability, common user patterns, and continuing scalability.

Checking the evolving application with regression testing

Comprehensively testing your application can be an expensive proposition. One reason people do not perform comprehensive testing is their inability to repeat the tests at a later point. Hence, comprehensive testing at four points during development would cost four times more than merely testing once at the end (in this naive model). This is why automating tests is so important: Your tests can be reused and applied as often as practical (ideally, nightly or weekly).

During development you should constantly be analyzing and maintaining old tests, at both the unit and application levels. Diligence in this effort significantly improves your error detection and prevention without consuming too much of your time. One of the greatest killers of well-intentioned test suites is the failure to plan for growth. A useful and reusable test suite has to allow for additional tests to be added cleanly, so that anyone can understand why they are added and what they are testing. Your tests should be documented well enough to minimize duplicate test cases and to support test case modifications as the application changes.

As the application evolves, some tests naturally begin to fail – because they no longer apply, because the method or path being tested has changed, or because the check was too restrictive. As soon as a test fails, someone should analyze the failure and determine the category into which it falls. The appropriate remedy should be taken, and the suites should be returned to a clean state.

The payoff for carefully maintaining a regression test suite is that it helps you detect the subtle effects that can result from application modifications – including design consequences overlooked by the developer. By catching these early, you can prevent bad designs from being propagated so densely into the code that they are difficult and costly to remove. This is another reason test suites should be comprehensive enough to include the seldom visited corners of your application.

We haven't spent a lot of time discussing bug tracking, although this is clearly an important part of any ongoing development process. Different development groups employ widely different bug-tracking strategies, with lots of people using homegrown solutions.

Currently, we use the Bugzilla tracking program available for free at `bugzilla.mozilla.org`. This program can effectively manage a good amount of detail, and uses a convenient Web-based interface.

Monitoring your production application

You can detect existing problems, stop glitches from developing into disasters, and improve the quality of your continued testing efforts by performing *monitoring:* watching how the live application responds to actual user traffic and/or generated traffic that mimics actual user traffic. Most monitoring activities fall into one of the following two categories: performance monitoring and usage monitoring.

PERFORMING PERFORMANCE MONITORING

Basically, *performance monitoring* involves checking for degradation in the application's performance as it is actually running. Performance monitoring is essential if your application performs critical functions and a performance degradation or failure would cause serious repercussions for your customers and/or company.

Assuming that you already performed load testing on each site unit and on the entire application before it went live, you should have some idea of how your application will perform under certain types and loads of user traffic. However, after the application goes live, a variety of problems can occur. Your application can receive more traffic than you anticipated (and tested). Performance can suffer when the database is filled to a certain limit. Some of your servers can fail – and so on, and so on. As any Web system administrator knows, the possibilities for failure are virtually endless. That's why it's important to monitor regularly how the application performs under actual usage conditions.

The most thorough monitoring efforts include two varieties of performance monitoring:

- Monitoring from inside the Web site
- Monitoring from various points throughout the world

MONITORING PERFORMANCE INTERNALLY By monitoring performance from inside the Web site, you can determine where problems within your system are causing performance to lag can then take steps to prevent critical situations. This type of monitoring is typically performed by a monitoring tool attached to your Web site somewhere before its network connection to the outside world. The tool measures the period that elapses from the time a packet first enters your Web site to the time the Web site returns a response. This includes the time it takes to pass through your Web server, application servers, databases, legacy systems, and so on. Figure 15-2 shows one possible instance of this path.

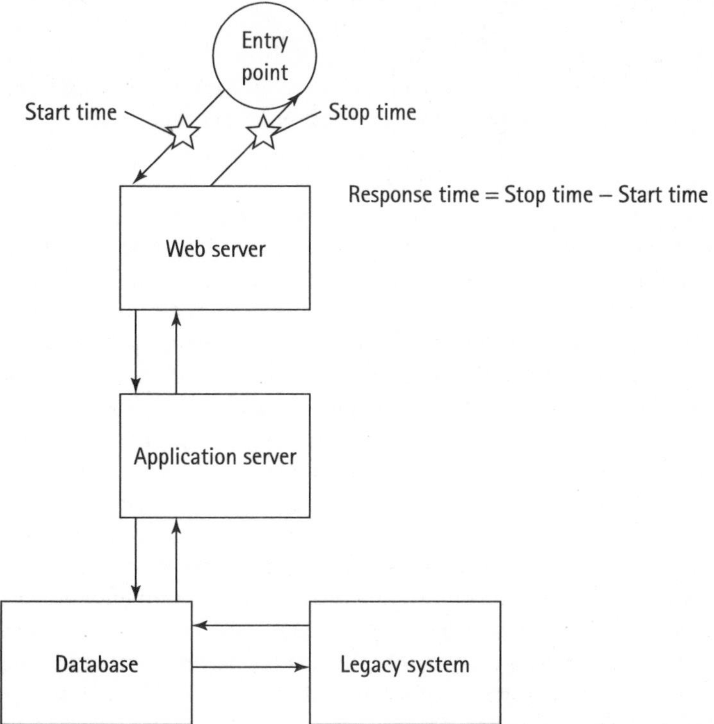

Figure 15-2: The packet path measured by internal performance monitoring.

If performance is critical to your application, you should move beyond simply recording performance rates and configure your monitoring system so that the appropriate actions are taken if performance problems are detected. For example, you could decide that 20 seconds is the maximum tolerable response time and configure the system to notify your system administrator any time that the monitoring tool sees packets taking more than 20 seconds to pass through your site. This way, you can start acting on problems before they turn into full-fledged disasters.

MONITORING PERFORMANCE REMOTELY If you have the resources to do so, we recommend that you also monitor total performance: the period that elapses between the time the client sends a request and the time the client receives a response. By testing total performance, you can determine how factors outside your site are affecting the user's experience. Even if your monitoring efforts reveal that the packets travel through your site at lightning-fast speeds, some (or all) of your users can be experiencing performance problems because of bottlenecks between their browser and your Web servers. For example, their ISP's system might be slowing them down. Their connection to their ISP might be slowing them down. Users in certain geographical areas might have severe performance problems, or you might not have adequate bandwidth leading to and from your servers.

One way to determine what kind of performance your various users are experiencing is to set up (or gain access to) remote clients throughout the world that have built-in monitoring systems. Have each client generate traffic to your site. Then the monitoring device attached to each client can measure the time it takes for each packet to travel from that client to your site, through your site, and back to that client.

When you perform usage monitoring (discussed later in this chapter), you learn the geographical distribution of your users. If you use this information to distribute your remote client/monitoring systems in such a way that they represent your actual users, you can increase your tests' capability to predict accurately the performance your actual users will experience. You can also use this user profile information to determine the severity of problems specific to a certain geographical location. For example, if you learned that performance is slow for users in Asia and you knew that 40 percent of your users are in Asia, you would take immediate steps to remedy the problem. However, if only 0.5 percent of your users are in Asia, you might not invest large amounts of time, effort, and money in improving the connection to Asia.

RELIEVING BOTTLENECKS There is a tendency in the industry to throw an application together as soon as possible, spend exorbitant amounts of money monitoring the application to detect difficulties, and purchase expensive hardware to try to remedy those problems. Unfortunately, you usually cannot purchase a satisfying user experience. Even if you perform sophisticated monitoring and use cutting-edge load balancers and the like, your users can still perceive your application as slow. Why? Because the last mile is often what determines the user's experience of your application. If a user has a slow modem or slow ISP and your site has animations on the home page, you could have the best hardware available and your user would still perceive your application as slow.

By *last mile*, we mean the distance between your Web server and the client's browser.

When you learn that users are experiencing your site at less than optimal speeds, your first response should not be to upgrade your hardware. Before you make any purchases, take a close look at your application's design and code. Does it contain animations or large graphics that are not essential to the goals of your application? Do the HTML pages sent to the user's browser contain unnecessary tags and excessive whitespace? Do you use absolute links where you could use relative links? Although these things might seem trivial in the scope of a complex Web application with a sophisticated setup, they can make a difference in the last mile and can have a significant effect on whether your users have pleasant experiences on your application or tire of waiting for the browser to render pages and browse to your competitor's site.

If your monitoring efforts determine that the problem lies somewhere within your Web application, take a close look at your application's parts. If you have not already done so, now is the time to perform load testing on each unit to determine whether a design flaw (such as an inefficient method of accessing the database) is slowing down your application. Also, check whether your code follows coding standards designed to prevent performance problems.

For information on load testing, see Chapter 14. For information on coding standards, see Chapter 8.

The Relationship between Load Testing and Performance Monitoring

From a technical perspective, load testing and performance monitoring are quite similar. The primary activity involved in both processes is checking the response rates of packets. With the correct equipment and configuration, both processes can measure response times within the Web site or roundtrip response times to requests generated from remote locations. Because of these innate similarities, often the same technologies can be used for load testing and monitoring.

The main differences between these two techniques are purpose and scope. The purpose of monitoring is to gauge how your application responds to realistic types and levels of user traffic. The goal of load testing is to test how your application responds to your anticipated maximum load. As a result, load testing often involves sending a larger volume of requests to the Web site, running a wider variety of test cases, and checking for functionality problems, as well as slow response rates.

If you want to check that your application performs well under actual conditions and know that it can still support your maximum anticipated load as it evolves, perform regular (for example, weekly) load testing and constant performance monitoring when your application is live. This way, you can not only spot actual problems but also learn what problems might occur. Then you can take steps to prevent them from affecting your actual users.

PERFORMING USAGE MONITORING

Usage monitoring typically involves gathering and analyzing information such as

- **User profile information.** What ISPs are users using? Where are they located? What types of browsers are they using?
- **Navigation information.** What are the most popular paths through your site? How long do users spend on various pages? What is the last page most users access before they exit the site?
- **Feedback on content and campaigns.** Which pages are most popular? Which are the least popular? How many unique visitors have reached special URLs referenced in advertisement, direct mail campaigns, and so on?

Usage monitoring is not essential to keeping your site up and running, but it can help you improve your users' experience on your site and the quality of your testing. We are going to focus on how you can use the user profile and navigation information to improve the quality and scope of your testing efforts. However, note that usage monitoring has a host of additional benefits. For example, it can help you to do the following:

- Measure the success of advertising and marketing campaigns.
- Improve application appeal and usability.
- Evaluate the effect of application changes.
- Estimate your Web application's ROI.
- Detect and respond to changing user interests.

In our discussion of path creation and load testing (in Chapters 13 and 14, respectively), we suggest that you base your test cases on anticipated user behavior (if the application is not yet live) or actual user behavior (after the application is live). Usage monitoring gives you the necessary feedback to make sure that your test cases are testing the most popular paths through your application and that the virtual users you have created to perform tests are an accurate representation of your actual users. As mentioned in Chapter 13, every different path through a Web application can produce different pages, and each instance of each page can contain different errors. This means that if the paths you are testing are not the same paths your users are taking, your tests can be missing errors that surface in very popular pages. You can prevent this situation by monitoring who is using your application and where they are going and then modifying your paths and virtual user profiles accordingly.

For example, if you find that you have a large number of users from text-only browsers such as Lynx, have virtual users experience and test the application as these users do. If you find that you are not testing the most popular paths through your application, create test cases that follow those popular paths and check whether the pages in these paths flow as expected, contain coding errors or misspelled words, contain required GUI and text elements, and so on.

Gathering information about user profiles and behavior requires either reading log file entries or monitoring packet movement through your site. If you are performing performance monitoring, you are already performing one of these practices in order to gauge your application's response time. To produce usage information, you perform additional analysis of the same information. If you are gathering this information from log files, you should learn how your Web server maintains log files and make sure that you are recording all the information you are likely to use. You can change the log file format anytime you like, but you can never go back and collect data that you didn't record.

Updating the Application

If your Web application will be changing frequently, you want a procedure in place to allow easy updates. One common solution is to have daily content updates automatically deployed onto running sites. If you are using WebKing, this can be automated easily by using WebKing in a command-line, scripted mode. You can run the following command to cause WebKing to add updates incrementally to an existing application:

```
webking my.wkj -cmd "publish"
```

Under Windows NT/2000, you could use the `at` program to schedule this command to run automatically at midnight every night. Under Unix, you would probably set up a `cron` job that works the same way.

The benefit of this automation is the security of knowing that the updates will occur smoothly and automatically, without human intervention. The drawbacks are these:

- Most automatic procedures include at least a slim chance of failure. You need a procedure to detect problems when they occur and to allow for speedy human intervention to remedy the problem.
- Because this command depends on the contents of the project file, you need to be absolutely certain that only valid content is available from those files. Boolean filters, as explained in Chapter 10, can protect against this, but anyone working with the project file should be made aware that automatic updates are occurring.

If you decide to implement this automatic publishing, you might want to establish a process for creating different project files that contain new content and for marking content available for publication. If you are managing a large amount of content, you can mark various pieces for publication on different dates. With

WebKing, you can do this by maintaining a different project file for each day's contents. The idea is to always take an earlier project file, rename it to use the new date, and add content new for that day to that file. Then you would have a succession of project files such as this:

```
my-12jan2001.wkj
my-13jan2001.wkj
my-14jan2001.wkj
```

In a system like this, you would probably require that new material be added only to the most recent project file.

When WebKing publishes a project, it can create a log file showing which files were updated. This file serves as a modification history and can help point to possible problems when something goes wrong. For example, if the application stops working on January 15, you know that something published from the `my-14jan2000.wkj` file (either a new file or a modified one) is responsible. By reverting to the `my-13jan2000.wkj` file and performing a full publish, you might be able to restore a working site (assuming that you can actually publish the same versions of all files that were used in that version).

If you are using different versions of the same files, either you want a process that tightly integrates with your source control system, or you need to create different directories or files to represent the different versions of your content. If you perform frequent updates, you might want to make sure that your publishing process is fully reversible by archiving older versions of each file you update.

Summary

Web applications are among the hardest to test of all development projects because of their distributed nature. You need to test the various components – generally using widely different technologies – and all their interactions across multiple, potentially incompatible architectures. Good practices and useful technologies are your best defense against inadequate testing. The practices covered in Part II of this book will help you in your quest to create bulletproof applications.

In Part III, which comprises the rest of the book, we cover specific details regarding select areas of Web application development. Each chapter focuses on details of a specific technology and how general principles are specialized with respect to that technology.

Part III

Other Technologies

Chapter 16

Bulletproofing Databases

IN THIS CHAPTER

- Designing your database
- Implementing your database
- Monitoring and testing your database
- Maintaining your database

THIS CHAPTER DISCUSSES WAYS to bulletproof databases (in particular, relational databases, which add a set of well-defined capabilities to a database system). The database is a common component of many significant Web applications. Like other application components, it can potentially introduce problems into the application's overall functionality and reliability. It also has the potential to confuse, corrupt, misuse, or overwrite vital data. Throughout this chapter, we discuss methods for preventing these problems from occurring in the first place, as well as strategies for rooting out flaws and errors that have already been introduced. Along the way, we introduce ways that you can use Python, WebKing, and DataRecon (available on the CD) to verify database design and structure, validate data, and monitor a live database to ensure that it continues to run smoothly.

You have many database servers from which to choose; two common choices are Oracle and MySQL. If you want to experiment with databases but don't have a database server, MySQL is a popular open-source database server available for most platforms. You can download this product from `mysql.com`.

Designing Your Database

We define a *database* as a set of tables, fields, indices, stored procedures, and so on, that constitute permanent information storage for a Web application. We are *not* referring to the Database Management System (DBMS) software itself. Most applications work with a database through a variety of abstraction layers. The most common abstraction is SQL (Structured Query Language). *SQL* is a database query language supported by virtually every database provider in existence and is what you and your team members will likely use to interact with your database.

With this in mind, the first step in developing a bulletproof database is to think carefully about your database structure. You can prevent many development and maintenance problems by carefully planning how the information will be distributed into tables (if you are using the relational model) and then stored in a database, as well as by accounting for physical and technological constraints and performance issues. It can be tempting for database structure designers to take a pure, theoretical approach – especially with the relational model, which has a good background in mathematics. Distributing information into too many tables – however elegant from a theoretical point of view – can result in very ineffective data retrieval. If your application uses a large number of join operations to fetch useful and frequently needed information, it can slow down the entire system.

Choosing proper indices

Proper indexing is an important factor in designing your database structure. Indexing facilitates random access to required records. For example, without an index, a table with 100,000 records requires, on average, scanning 50,000 records before the required one is found. As a consequence, many disc read operations have to be performed. Disc access is a slow operation; it takes milliseconds to access given data on disc. Compared to modern CPU speeds, this is an eternity. With a binary search (the basis for many indexing techniques), the number of required disc block reads is proportional to the logarithm of table size, which, in this case, is approximately 17. This is significantly faster. Naturally, the actual number varies, depending on the indexing technique used. It is far beyond the scope of this chapter to discuss all indexing issues. You can, however, follow simple indexing guidelines to improve the overall performance of Web applications that access a database. Here are some possible guidelines:

- **Small tables almost never need indices.** Often, the entire table is entirely cached in memory. Even if it isn't, the performance is probably acceptable. In this case, using indexed access can hurt performance more than help.
- **Larger tables should be indexed based on their join operations.** When you have a table large enough to be of concern, determine all the join operations your application will perform. *Join operations* connect two or more tables by comparing the values of a given field. As a rule of thumb, tables involved in join operations should be indexed according to the fields that constitute the join conditions.
- **Tables that are frequently searched based on one or more fields should definitely be indexed.** For example, your application might search a user database by log in name during each log in action. If the user database is large, indexing by log in name can speed up the log in task.

- **Tables that store persistent information about application activities (for example, a table with customer purchase history) should be indexed by date fields.** Marketing and research teams often use this data as the basis for their statistical reports, and they typically need to make reports for specific time ranges (for example, reports of sales per month, sales per quarter, and so on). If you index by the date field, you significantly reduce the amount of records that have to be analyzed, thereby improving the performance of those reports. In one system we were using, marketing analysis was actually dominating database performance, so this consideration can indeed make a difference.

If you over-index, you might slow down your application rather than speed it up. Indexing has a price. Inserting new records, deleting records, and updating records require additional operations to keep your indexes in sync with your data. This requires additional disc access. Writing to the hard drive is an even more expensive operation than reading from it — especially if your database software tries to make integrity-safe writes (so if a crash occurs, no partially committed writes are left in a database). Tables indexed too heavily, especially when frequently updated, can slow operations so much that you lose the performance gain from the fast data access the added indices allow. Every index also consumes some space in the database storage area. It is not uncommon for the overall table size to be smaller than the summary index's size. Depending on your database target size, this might or might not be an important factor to consider when planning for indexing.

Considering data size and scalability

You can save yourself a lot of work (and pain) in the long run if, before setting up the initial database for a Web application, you determine the space and performance requirements and plan accordingly. Insufficient scalability is a common cause of database problems. If you have not planned appropriately, your seemingly flawless system can fall apart overnight if it is faced with unanticipated heavy usage.

During the design phase, it's critical to consider how your system will grow over time. We recommend that you generously estimate the average and peak number of users and volume of data. As a general rule, it's a good idea to plan to accommodate at least twice the amount of expected users and data. Also, make sure that you have a plan for scaling up the system as necessary (for example, by adding more servers, more memory, more discs, and so on), and consider how you will respond to error conditions. Ideally, you will handle problems gracefully and leave users with a good impression rather than drive them to the competitor. Note that this response depends largely on the server, not on your application.

Scalability should be viewed as a software issue as well as a hardware issue. In fact, scalability problems are often the result of software issues (such as inefficient means of accessing and processing data). For example, say that you have two applications that are identical, except that Application A's database uses proper indices and Application B's database does not. Application A will be faster than Application B — even if Application A runs on an average server and Application B runs on a top-of-the-line server.

Ensuring data integrity

Data integrity refers to ensuring that your database contents are not corrupted. Data integrity is absolutely critical to your application. After all, if you aren't expecting to be able to use and retrieve the data, why gather it at all? There are many potential problems, but much can be done to protect your valuable data – even as early as the design phase. A well-designed database denies bogus data, protects referential integrity, understands relationships between tables, and knows what kind of data is in what fields and how it should be formatted. Bad data should just slide off its surface, as rain slides off a rain slicker. Note that this does not relieve you from checking for bad data in the client. It's just your last-ditch effort to prevent any problems.

When you structure the data intelligently, data validation is easier, and validation schemes are portable and much easier to understand. Just as object-oriented programming ties together code and data, a good design ties together the data structure and integrity requirements.

The first way you can preserve data integrity is to perform data normalization. Many good texts are available on data normalization; several are listed in Appendix E. In a nutshell, *data normalization* is the process of making sure that data is protected by removing redundant and repetitive data, separating unrelated data, and controlling the number and type of relationships. This is especially important in databases containing both one-to-many and many-to-many relationships.

Data normalization typically includes the following steps:

- Eliminate repeating groups (first normal form).
- Eliminate redundant data (second normal form).
- Eliminate columns that are not related to the key pieces of data being stored (third normal form). In other words, make sure that your tables represent relatively tightly coupled data and move unrelated data to a different table. This prevents update/delete idiosyncrasies, especially for groups that come and go, such as users from a particular company.
- Isolate independent multiple relationships (fourth normal form).

Another key to data integrity is to make sure that the data types for the fields suit the type of data you expect to be storing. For example, phone numbers are rarely stored as numerical data because they have the formatting information of hyphens, parentheses, extension numbers, and so on. Determining appropriate data types before a lot of data goes into the system saves time-consuming, difficult, and costly reworking of the data structure. Make sure that numeric fields are wide enough to store the largest numbers you foresee being used there. For example, age can always be three digits: No one lives to be 1,000 years old, but many people do live to be 100.

The amount of data each field contains also affects data integrity. A common pitfall is to put multiple pieces of data in a single field (for example, storing a person's complete name in a single field). Even if you do not currently use an operation that accesses only first names, you might in the future. Rather than ask when you would need such separation, you should consider whether you have a compelling reason to store two or more pieces of data in the same field – even though doing so makes it very difficult to pull them apart later. In an extreme example, if you want good name data, you use six fields:

```
Salutation / Title (Mr, Mrs, Dr, etc)
First name
Preferred name (Nicknames and so forth. For example, Bob for Robert)
Middle name (or initial)
Last name
Suffix (Jr, Sr, II, III, etc.)
```

You can also improve data integrity by designing your database so that it is somewhat self-documenting. One way to do this is to add two tables to your database: one for storing information about the tables themselves and one for storing information about the fields. In the Tables table, you add a table name for each table you use and use a notes field to record what is stored in each table, as well as any additional information you want to record (for example, expected size, expected usage patterns, author, and so on). In the Fields table, you add a table name (to establish the relationship with the Tables table) and the name of each field, notes for each field, related fields, and so on. In this way, you can easily create a report of the data structure in your system, no matter what database you are using. You also have an easier time working on the database throughout development because the purpose of each table or field is clear. In the long run, the extra work involved in documenting is well worth the maintenance benefits. Because the overhead of these additional tables is small, you can maintain this information even on your production database.

If you are documenting your database in this way, you can also record the expected values for each table or field so that it is clear which data each table or field should contain and is obvious if the wrong type of data is used. For example, if you have an age field, you list that the expected data for that field is a number greater than or equal to 0 and less than 200. If you are working only with young adults, you specify that age should be greater than 12 and less than 20. This information lets you implement simple tests that verify your system's data integrity and ensure that bogus data is never used.

You can also check data integrity by performing tests in the code itself or in the forms, as discussed in Chapter 7. Each method has its pros and cons. The one that is right for your situation depends on your needs. The method you use to check data integrity is not important; you can achieve the desired effect with any method.

Understanding data redundancy

Data redundancy is often perceived as undesirable – in fact, we said so in the preceding section. However, it is useful in certain situations. On the one hand, it can lead to data inconsistency. If you keep the same information in two separate tables, there's a good chance that the two versions will vary because your application updates one table but not the other. On the other hand, redundancy can increase efficiency. Duplicate information can relieve you from having to perform extra retrieval or join operations. This information can also be useful when an error occurs and data is damaged. In other words, it can be used as a backup to help rescue information. Data loss and corruption might not occur often, but they will occur on occasion. Negotiating between possible data inconsistency and potential efficiency gains is one of the challenges involved in designing a database.

Other types of data redundancy are also helpful in creating robust, enterprise Web applications. One type is a redundant mass storage system such as a RAID (Redundant Array of Independent Discs). A RAID distributes information writes over several discs in such a way that no data will be lost if one of the discs fails. This is very low-level data redundancy. A good RAID has very little effect on efficiency and allows you to replace a malfunctioning disc without interrupting the system's operation.

A similar type of data redundancy is file system journaling. Journaling file systems maintain extra information that allows recovery from operating system crashes (such as power failures) without having inconsistent data. One disadvantage of this method is that it does not save you from hardware disc failures. Another is that very few file systems have journaling capability.

Making backup copies also creates data redundancy. Its sole purpose is to prevent data from being lost in a serious crisis. We hope that you already have some kind of backup system in place for your Web application. You should consider whether your databases can cooperate with your other backups or whether they require a special procedure of their own. This is especially important for enterprise applications, where robustness and reliability are key issues.

Another instance of data redundancy is the use of redundant servers for reporting purposes. Even top-performing DBMSs have their limitations. At some point, when the number of clients increases, a DBMS will hit its limit. That's why it's important not to overload your primary server by using it to create time-consuming and resource-costly statistical and marketing reports. These reports can be performed on a backup server – especially if the reports do not have to be created in real time and a one-day delay is acceptable.

Implementing best practices and standards

As you are designing your database, you can improve its quality by following certain best practices and implementing standards where appropriate. One best practice is to use descriptive names for tables and fields. If you do this, it is easy to tell at a glance which data is stored in a particular field or table. This saves time during development and makes it easier for developers to work with different databases. Also, creating reports from the database information becomes easier. The people creating the reports usually aren't involved in the design of the database, so understandable, descriptive table and field names help them perform their job more efficiently and accurately. Carefully chosen table and field names are also beneficial if the database is developed by one party and used by another.

Other best practices for database design help you handle application programming language constraints and DBMS limitations. In either case, establishing and following conventions regarding database design helps you speed up overall application development, avoid known pitfalls, and improve the experience for anyone working on or using the application. Conventions and standards represent the lessons learned from practical development experience. If you don't follow conventions and standards, you often end up repeating the same mistakes again and again.

The following are examples of the types of standards you can apply to ensure that mistakes are not repeated and that the lessons learned from them are not forgotten. These standards are not a prescription for a good database. Rather, they are a set of guidelines you can use as a general foundation for developing standards suited to your project's unique needs.

- Avoid using different names for the same logical data in different tables. For example, say that you create a USERS table with a field named ID. If you later refer to this field from a CURRENT_CARTS table, you will have to change its name to prevent the user identifier from being confused with the cart identifier. If you do change the user identifier name, the same data will have different field names in different tables. This could also be confusing.
- Use informative names, not meaningless abbreviations. For example, use *description* instead of *desc*. Although *desc* might seem clear at the time of creation, when the database grows and developers come and go, it might not be clear and could lead to confusion, wasted time, and errors. Note

that this rule does not make sense in every situation. For example, there is no value in naming a field *Product_description* if it is going to exist only in the PRODUCTS table; *description* would work just fine in this case.

- The size of a character variable should be a multiple of 4. In many cases, character arrays representing character variables in computer memory are aligned to 4, so keeping this explicit is generally a good idea.
- Integer identifier types should have a size of 9. This is the maximum size that can be represented as a 32-bit `int` type (although it doesn't cover the entire range). Using smaller sizes for identifier data generally does not improve performance, so we don't recommend it. If your data naturally has a smaller number of digits (for example, age or year of birth), that would qualify as an exception because there is a meaningful notion behind the limit. Using larger sizes does not make sense because the larger sizes cannot be represented easily. Whenever possible, it is better to use the `int` type in your program code and `NUMERIC(9)` in your database because doing so improves performance.
- Avoid the type `LONG` in Oracle databases. Using this type is very tempting because it allows you to store large amounts of text without worrying about overflows. However, the `LONG` type is difficult to search, and even if you do not need to search a particular field at the current time, you might want to do so in the future as your application and users' needs evolve. Implementing a flexible solution from the beginning is much easier than trying to change it later. Notice that we violate this rule in the next example. These are guidelines, not commandments.
- Minimize the number of fields in each table. A table with too many fields usually indicates a bad logical design. For example, it can indicate that the table contains a hidden structure that would be better if split into smaller, more directed tables.

Some additional rules to consider as you design the database include

- Use creation date fields for fast-growing tables to facilitate maintenance.
- Use the primary/secondary key mechanism carefully so that it does not cause problems when you remove obsolete records.

Following the preceding two rules during the design phase prevents performance bottlenecks from occurring later on. We explain exactly how these issues benefit performance in the "Keeping database size under control" section later in this chapter.

Choosing a layout for the Online Grocer database

Now you will see how we designed the Online Grocer application's database. Here's the initial table layout we chose to satisfy our requirements. In developing this table, we tried to apply most – but not all – of the recommendations we have covered so far.

```
Table 1: USERS
Username:              VARCHAR2(16)
Password:              VARCHAR2(16)
User_id:               NUMERIC(9)

Table 2: PRODUCTS
Product_name:          VARCHAR2(64)
Product_image:         VARCHAR2(256)
Product_description: LONG
Product_cost:          NUMERIC(9)
Product_id:            NUMERIC(9)
Product_kind:          NUMERIC(3)
Product_color:         VARCHAR2(16)

Table 3: CARTS
Creation_date:         DATE
User_id:               NUMERIC(9)
Cart_cost:             NUMERIC(9)
Cart_quantity:         NUMERIC(6)
Cart_id:               NUMERIC(9)

Table 4: CART_ITEMS
Cart_id:               NUMERIC(9)
Product_id:            NUMERIC(9)
Item_cost:             NUMERIC(9)
Item_quantity:         NUMERIC(6)

Table 5: CURRENT_CARTS
Cart_id:               NUMERIC(9)
User_id:               NUMERIC(9)
```

Most of the fields should be self-explanatory. As a result, it's easy to identify data that appears to be redundant. This example contains two cases of data redundancy, each demonstrating a different reason for using data redundancy.

The first case of data redundancy is having a cost field in the CART_ITEMS table (Item_cost) even though it already exists in the PRODUCTS table (Product_cost). Every cart item refers to some product from the PRODUCTS table by means of the

Product_id identifier. As a result, duplicating the cost field seems to be redundant because this information is available in the product definition. However, even though prices can (and probably will) change over time, we might want to freeze an item's price after a user adds it to the shopping cart. If so, we need two separate fields for the two prices. Duplicating product cost in the CART_ITEMS table also allows us to keep statistical information about each transaction. If purchase information changed whenever product prices changed, it would be impossible to track who paid what for each item.

The second case of data redundancy is having Cart_cost and Cart_quantity in the CARTS table. Both fields hold information that can easily be deduced from the CART_ITEMS table (the former by summarizing the cost of the contents and the latter by counting records for a given cart). However, there are three reasons to duplicate this information:

- **To increase our control over data integrity.** By checking whether values stored in the CARTS and CART_ITEMS tables match, we can verify whether the application is storing purchase information correctly.
- **To expedite and facilitate report creation.** If we want to learn which customers purchase the most, it is easier to look in the CARTS table than the CART_ITEMS table because the former usually has far fewer records. For the same reason, reports that calculate the average number of items in a cart, average item cost of items in a cart, and so on, are easier to create and faster to execute with data from the CARTS table than from the CARTS_ITEMS table.
- **To help keep the database size under control.** Even though it might be nice to have a record of all data we ever collected, this is not always feasible. Often, old records (such as old products and customers) need to be removed to conserve space. For example, say we decide to delete old records from the CART_ITEMS table. We could then keep records from the CARTS table and use these records for statistical purposes.

Performing preliminary tests

After you create your basic database structure, you can start testing it – even before you write a single line of application code. Here you will see how we use the DataRecon program provided on the CD to perform some fundamental tests on the Online Grocer database. DataRecon is an automated database verification and monitoring tool. It provides you with an easy way to verify database integrity and application-database interactions.

Early in the database development process, you can use DataRecon to view and verify the database's structure and contents. Any time you want to check what a table contains, you simply drag the node representing it into DataRecon's report viewer; SQL is not necessary. You can also use DataRecon to create rules regarding database structure, format, contents, and so on.

For example, say that we want to access the preceding tables with DataRecon. First, we specify which data source we want to view and how to connect to it (as shown in Figure 16-1).

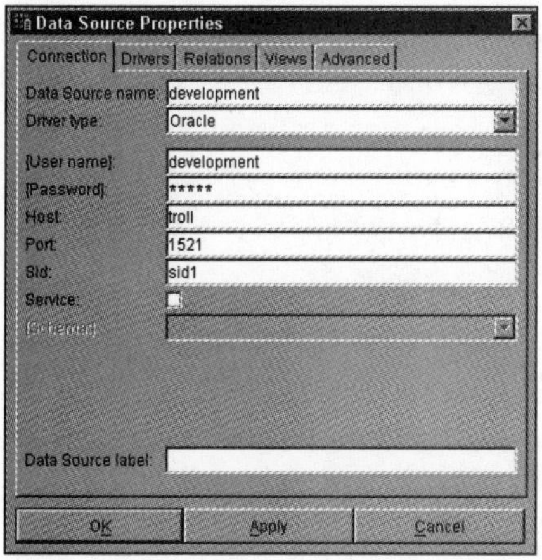

Figure 16-1: Configuring DataRecon to connect to the Online Grocer database.

DataRecon then connects to and reads from the database. It creates a new data source and represents it as a tree displaying the data source's tables and fields. We can easily create a simple report and view which data is being stored in the database, by dragging and dropping tables or fields from the left side of the GUI (as shown in Figure 16-2). For complete information about DataRecon's reporting capabilities, refer to the DataRecon User's Guide.

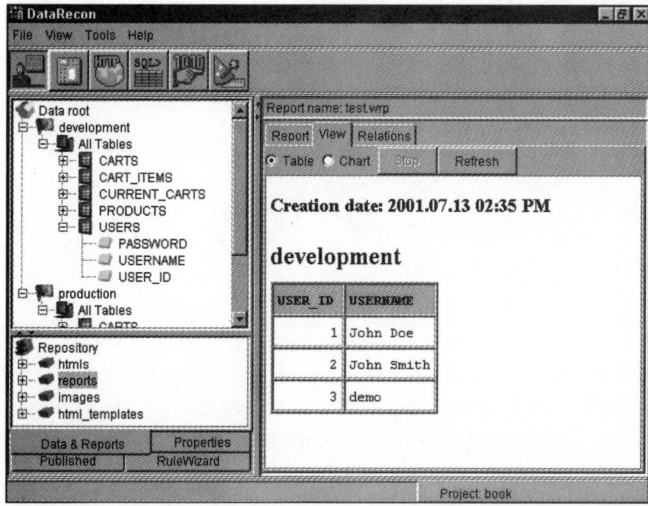

Figure 16-2: Using DataRecon to view database records.

You can also use DataRecon to create rules that validate your database structure. For example, assume that we want to check that fields of `VARCHAR` JDBC type have sizes that are multiples of 4.

JDBC types are standardized database field types, but actual types vary from one DBMS vendor to another. JDBC drivers map actual types to JDBC types. Because DataRecon uses JDBC drivers to connect to databases, it can only be used to create rules based on JDBC types instead of actual types. In most cases, however, JDBC types are either equivalent to actual types or very similar.

The first step in implementing this test is to use DataRecon's RuleWizard to create a rule that describes the pattern we do not want to allow in our database (fields of `VARCHAR` JDBC type whose sizes are not multiples of 4). Figure 16-3 shows the complete rule. Note that we use the regular expression `$$ % 4 != 0` to represent *is not a multiple of 4*. Here, `$$` represents the `Length` value, and the remainder of the expression is similar to Java or C syntax.

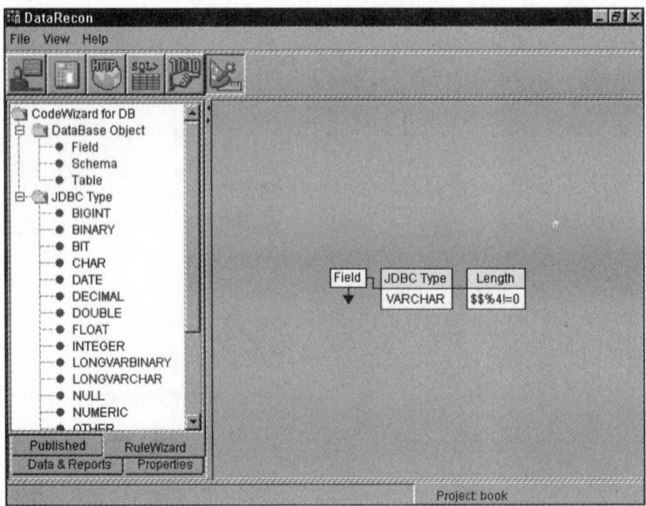

Figure 16-3: A rule that checks whether fields of VARCHAR JDBC type have sizes that are multiples of 4.

Next, we configure DataRecon to implement this rule by adding this test as the first entry in our test suite. We can then play the test and watch the results. By saving this and future tests, we create a regression test suite that allows us to quickly verify the integrity of our data as the database ages and evolves. This initial rule just checks our table design.

You could also implement similar guidelines using a Python script, as discussed in Chapter 11.

Implementing Your Database

After you design your database, the next step is writing the code necessary to interact with it. At this point, you need to be aware of the many problems that can arise with respect to how an application interacts with a database management system. This way, you can take proactive steps to prevent such problems and detect any existing problems as soon as possible. In this section, we discuss these issues in the context of our implementation of the Online Grocer database.

Choosing a connection management strategy

The first step in implementing our Online Grocer database was to connect to the application by extending our abstract `Database` classes with concrete implementations that use JDBC to access our actual database. (The original Online Grocer application used stubs to hide the database details). Before we developed the first class that provided real database access via JDBC, we had to decide on our policy regarding connection management. The simplest way seemed to be to open a connection whenever it was necessary and close it when it was no longer needed. This was not the most convenient way, though. In the Online Grocer application, we have three classes that will use database connections. Distributing connection details throughout the code is not a good idea. Encapsulating connection management details in a single class is much better, for at least two reasons:

- If you decide to connect to a different database, you can change connection details in one place rather than in multiple places.
- You can implement connection pooling so that several connections can be used at once but the total number of connections to a database can be controlled. In the Online Grocer application, we are using a very simple connection management strategy, but if we encapsulate connection management details into one class, we can easily adopt a more elaborate strategy in the future.

Implementing a connection pool

We created the `ConnectionManager` class to encapsulate our connection management policy. This class is meant to be instantiated only once, regardless of the other code or number of threads (in design patterns terminology, this is referred to as a *singleton*). This is necessary if we really want to control resource usage (connections).

This class contains two methods, `getConnection()` and `reclaimConnection()`, that are intended to be used by our other classes. Both are synchronized so that only one thread executes on either of them at the same time. This is necessary to make sure that the same connection is not assigned to two threads because of race conditions. However, this also makes these methods prone to bottlenecks, so we need to be careful implementing and using them.

The `getConnection()` method from the `ConnectionManager` class (shown in the following code excerpt) first checks whether we have any connections available for reuse. If so, we can return one of those connections immediately, and we're done. Otherwise, we need to allocate a new connection.

In this system, connections are never closed — they are only reused. This means that the resource requirement is that you must have enough resources available to handle the maximum expected load. A more complicated system would, ideally, close connections if a large number of them were not being used over a long period of time.

The `ConnectionManager`'s `reclaimConnection()` method simply puts the connection back on the list of available connections. It is the caller's responsibility to ensure that every connection returned from `getConnection()` is either closed or re-added to the `ConnectionManager` by calling `reclaimConnection()`. If `reclaimConnection()` is called, the connection should not be closed.

```
synchronized Connection getConnection() throws SQLException
{
    if (connections.empty()) {
        return createConnection();
    }
    return (Connection) connections.pop();
}

synchronized void reclaimConnection(Connection connection)
{
    connections.push(connection);
}
```

Actual connections are created in the `createConnection()` method. The driver manager creates the connection using the driver and connection parameters, including the database URL (which points to an appropriate database instance), a username, and a password required to access the database. In the Online Grocer application, we used the JDBC-to-ODBC bridge driver and connected to an ODBC database named *fruits*. No authorization was required.

A ready-to-use MS Access database is available on the CD. You can connect to this database using a JDBC-ODBC driver (using Microsoft Windows). A JDBC-ODBC driver is provided by Sun Microsystems bundled with the Java 2 SDK or JRE, so you shouldn't have any problems with driver class availability. All you do to connect to this database is create an ODBC data source that points to the provided file and is named *fruits*. Details on how to do this are provided on the CD.

Here's the code from `ConnectionManager` that is responsible for creating a new connection – the initialization parameters are hardcoded in the source code for this simple example:

```
private Connection createConnection() throws SQLException
{
    Connection connection = DriverManager.getConnection(DBURL, LOGIN, PASSWORD);
    connection.setAutoCommit(true);
    return connection;
}
```

Accessing the database using JDBC

When we had our connection management set, we could create the first JDBC extension to our `Database` classes. The simplest class to extend is `CustomerDatabase`. We had to provide only one method, `getUserId()`, which authorizes a user with a password and returns the user's identifier upon success and `-1` upon failure. The class name of this JDBC extension is `CustomerDatabaseJDBC`, and the implementation of our one method looks like this:

```
public int getUserId(String user, String password)
{
    ConnectionManager manager = ConnectionManager.getInstance();

    Connection connection = null;
    PreparedStatement selectStatement = null;
    ResultSet resultSet = null;

    try {
        connection = manager.getConnection();
        selectStatement = connection.prepareStatement(
            "SELECT User_id FROM USERS WHERE Username = ? AND Password = ?");
```

```
            selectStatement.setString(1, user);
            selectStatement.setString(2, password);

            resultSet = selectStatement.executeQuery();

            if (resultSet.next())
                return resultSet.getInt(1);
        } catch (SQLException exception) {
            log(exception);
        } finally {
            if (resultSet != null) {
                try {
                    resultSet.close();
                } catch (SQLException ex) {
                    log(ex);
                }
            }
            if (selectStatement != null) {
                try {
                    selectStatement.close();
                } catch (SQLException ex) {
                    log(ex);
                }
            }
            if (connection != null)
                manager.reclaimConnection(connection);
        }
        return -1;
    }
```

First, we get the handler to the `ConnectionManager` instance in a way that is typical for a singleton pattern. Next, we request a connection. After the connection is obtained, the real work begins. We are using two JDBC classes: `PreparedStatement` and `ResultSet`. We declare variables to hold instances of these classes before our `try...catch` blocks; this allows us to refer to them from the `finally` clause, where we can perform any necessary cleaning and reclaim the connection. This technique is very convenient. After the cleaning code is placed in the `finally` section, we no longer have to worry about catching all the possible exceptions (such as `NullPointerException`) to close the opened statements or result sets. We can even place the return statement inside the `try` clause, and the `finally` section will still be executed before returning from the function. Any exceptions we catch are passed to the `log()` method, which provides a hook for monitoring our application. In this case, we just print an error message that should be logged by the server.

Comparing PreparedStatement and Statement

We generally prefer using `PreparedStatement` over just `Statement`. In the preceding implementation method, we could build a complete SQL query string and call the `executeQuery(String)` method of the `Statement` class. This would save us two extra lines of code. In a simple and portable query, this is not bad.

However, SQL query parameters are often a source of errors — especially if you need to connect to various databases from different vendors. For example, if you are passing a string argument such as `username = argument`, enclosing the argument within apostrophes is important. To construct such a query, you could write

```
"SELECT User_id FROM USERS WHERE Username = '" + user +
    "' AND password = '" + password + "'";
```

So far so good. The problems begin when the username or password contains an apostrophe. Suddenly, the SQL sentence is invalid, and the "working" application with "tested" code does not work for some users.

`PreparedStatement` takes care of details such as special characters in string arguments. It also helps with date fields. Different databases use different date formats within SQL sentences. Rather than try to determine which format works with each database, you can leave the problem of cross-database differences to JDBC drivers and use `PreparedStatement`.

The first statement within the `try` section creates a `PreparedStatement` object via an SQL sentence. The next two statements set parameters for the SQL sentence's `WHERE` clause. Then, the `executeQuery()` method is invoked; this actually executes the completed SQL sentence.

After executing the query, we get a `ResultSet` object. We can use this object to iterate over all the results from our query. In our case, we expect one record at most, so we make only one iteration in an `if` block. As a result, if another record with the same log in and password but different identifier exists, it will be ignored. If we did have multiple user identifiers with the same username and password, this would represent a logical error in our database. There's nothing we could do about such a situation during log in. Instead, whoever creates new user identifiers has to be responsible for guaranteeing unique mappings between usernames and user identifiers.

Next, we reach the `finally` section. We already mentioned that this section is supposed to close opened statements and/or result sets and reclaim the connection to the connection manager. Checking that both the result set and the statement are not `null` is also important. Because we don't know at which stage the section was entered, we cannot assume that the statement and result set were created.

The other methods in our `Database` access classes (`CustomerDatabaseJDBC`, `CartDatabaseJDBC`, and `ProductsDatabaseJDBC`) are similar to the one described in this section. They follow the same pattern: Establish a connection, perform the necessary tasks, and then reclaim the connection. Connections are established only on the entry points and are passed as arguments to private routines, so we do not have to continually access the `ConnectionManager`.

The complete JDBC example is available on the CD. Note that although you can run this example, not all the details have been fully implemented (for instance, our redundant field `Cart_quantity` is not maintained).

Keeping the database size under control

When many transactions are stored during normal application operation, the database tends to grow very rapidly. Tables can accumulate millions of records and occupy gigabytes of disc space. Operations on such large tables (even those using indices) require many disc block reads, thus causing performance bottlenecks.

An obvious strategy for preventing these problems is to remove obsolete records. However, in many cases, you do not want to lose the opportunity to access historical data (for example, to make annual comparisons). Simply deleting the obsolete information won't suit your purposes – you need to archive it.

One possible way to archive old information is to back up the database regularly. This can prevent data loss, but the large size of most databases prevents this from being an efficient option. A better archiving strategy is to design the database so that there is a simple yet accurate way to move old data from a primary database to a secondary database.

In the Online Grocer example, the tables whose size we most need to watch are CARTS, CART_ITEMS, and CURRENT_CARTS. The first two tables store records about all carts created by Online Grocer users. CURRENT_CARTS indicates which carts are the most recent ones (in other words, the ones users see as current when accessing the Online Grocer). Removing old CARTS records is relatively easy, thanks to the Creation_date field. This lets us, for example, completely remove all carts created a year ago or move these carts to a secondary archival database.

Things become more complicated with the CURRENT_CARTS table. This table does not have a Creation_date field. As a result, no record in this table can be removed until the corresponding CARTS record is removed. Because this table's records are smaller than the CARTS table's records, this approach helps keep the database size under control. On the other hand, we might want to clean the CURRENT_CARTS table more frequently because product offers change over time and a half-year-old cart might contain outdated prices. We had to decide whether we wanted to duplicate creation date information in the CURRENT_CARTS table and have an easy way of deleting invalid records or keep this information only in the CARTS table and have a more difficult time developing SQL statements to remove the unwanted data.

There are several reasons for clearing a products database like the one used for the Online Grocer application. One obvious reason is to remove discontinued products so that users cannot order them. However, it is not always a good idea to delete these items. If the CART_ITEMS table could keep records that refer to discontinued products, deleting products and all referring records would leave carts in an inconsistent state. Some records in a given cart would be removed, and others would stay. On the other hand, leaving carts untouched would require you to give up the foreign/primary key mechanism (when you delete an item with a foreign key dependency, you invalidate the other item, so the database has to delete the associated items as well to maintain consistency). This also might not be desirable. Consistent deleting of entire carts that reference discontinued products is also not helpful because it removes purchase information and prevents you from keeping complete statistics about purchase history.

One way to clean obsolete records is to add an additional field named *Inactive* indicating that a given product should not show up as a catalog item in our Online Grocer store. It is also good to add a Deactivation_date field that keeps track of when a given product is made inactive. If we implemented this approach, our table structure would be as follows:

```
Table 2: PRODUCTS
Product_name:          VARCHAR(64)
Product_image:         VARCHAR(256)
Product_description:   LONG
Product_cost:          NUMERIC(9) // price * 100
Inactive:              NUMERIC(1)
Deactivation_date:     DATE
Product_id:            NUMERIC(9)
```

This increases the size of records in this table but allows for much easier and more accurate maintenance. Records remain in the database for statistical purposes, but users will be unable to see or purchase inactive items.

This simple example shows that maintaining database size and information is an issue that must be addressed properly at the design phase. If it is not, you will waste a lot of time and effort developing workarounds in the long run.

Ensuring data integrity

Earlier, we discussed data integrity with respect to designing your database. The same issues of integrity apply when implementing your application logic. Maintaining data integrity is just as important as making sure that only valid data is added to your database in the first place. Whether incorrect data is entered into the system or correct data later becomes incorrect, you end up with the same result: incorrect data. As discussed earlier, some issues can be accounted for in the design phase, but others must be implemented in the application logic.

One significant factor to consider while implementing a database is that records are persistent and errors in them usually do not surface immediately. Often, your application can run for weeks before someone notices an error in certain aspects of your data logging. For example, if you are storing invoices, the system might seem to run fine even if some invoices are not recorded completely and some items are missing. Invoices are usually printed as they are being created. If a printout was made from data in application memory instead of data stored in a database, neither the customer nor the person issuing the invoice would notice that a problem occurred. The summary report (usually based on totals stored in a main invoice record) would also appear fine. However, after a while (possibly months later), someone might notice a discrepancy when trying to create a report of which items were actually sold. If this error is found late in (or after) the development process, fixing it could be a long, involved process.

The worst thing about these kinds of errors is that the corrupted data is usually nonrecoverable. After you fix your application, the old data is still wrong. The repair can prevent you from introducing new errors but cannot correct all the errors already made. That's why it's so important to start worrying about data integrity as early as possible and to continue doing so after deployment.

USING TRANSACTIONS

Modern DBMSs provide the concept of a transaction to ensure data integrity. A *transaction* is a set of operations that are either performed as a whole or entirely discarded. A good example is storing a sales invoice in a database. An invoice typically has one record that describes general things such as creation date, sale date, total, tax due, customer reference, and so on. Also, an invoice contains separate records that describe each item sold, using details such as item, amount sold, actual price, discount, and so on. Each invoice must be stored as a whole. If it is not, you are likely to end up with inconsistencies (for example, an inconsistency between the total items and the summarized items). Because transactions can help you ensure that the invoice is stored as a whole, they can help you avoid such inconsistencies. Another situation in which transactions are helpful is fund transfers. Transactions help you ensure that money is not removed from one account unless it is successfully added to the other.

If transactions are so useful in ensuring data consistency, why should we worry about it? Transactions are beneficial only if they are used properly. It's a developer's responsibility to start the transaction, perform all required reads and writes while the transaction is open, and then commit it or *roll it back* (undo a transaction in progress) if necessary. Failure to do so can easily result in inconsistent records, despite having a transactional DBMS. Moreover, failure to localize a single transaction within the code (for example, distributing it among 10–20 objects) can cause records to be created after the transaction to which they logically belong has already been committed. Such situations can be difficult to detect because everything appears fine in normal operation (without many concurrent reads and writes). The real trouble starts when something goes wrong or conflicts arise.

It is also important to remember that transactions can take a toll on the DBMS. Depending on a transaction's implementation, an open transaction that changes a given record might lock this record from other updates until the transaction is completed. This can cause deadlocks if the transactions are not immediately committed. Extremely large transactions can not only cause deadlocks but also cause the DBMS to run out of rollback space and inhibit its capability to perform any required rollbacks.

A detailed discussion of transaction details is beyond the scope of this book. We can offer you the following tip, though: Treat transactions as you would any other resource. The more localized they are, the easier they are to maintain. In addition, the smaller they are, the less they tax the DBMS.

If your application makes several related changes to your database at once, you should combine all the updates into a single transaction. By doing so, you can safely abort your changes when any errors occur during the update. An example of a transaction can be found in the `createCart()` method of the `CartDatabaseJDBC` class. This is a private method that creates a new empty cart. Two records are inserted into two tables: CARTS and CURRENT_CARTS. If performed in this order, this operation is not particularly vulnerable to unexpected crashes. In the worst case, it leaves a cart that will never be used. If this operation were performed in the reverse order, we might end up with a record in CURRENT_CARTS referring to a nonexistent cart. Using transactions (as long as they are supported by an underlying database) assures us that either both records are committed or no record is committed. That's how properly used transactions help keep a database in consistent state. Here's the source code to handle our transaction:

```
private int createCart(Connection connection, int userId)
    throws SQLException
{
    int cartId = getNextId(connection);

    Boolean isOk = false;
    PreparedStatement statementCart = null;
    PreparedStatement statementCurCart = null;
```

```
        boolean bAutoCommit = true;
        try {
            bAutoCommit = connection.getAutoCommit();
            connection.setAutoCommit(false);

            statementCart = connection.prepareStatement(
                "INSERT INTO CARTS (Cart_id, User_id, Creation_date, " +
                "Cart_quantity, Cart_cost) VALUES (?, ?, ?, 0, 0)");

            statementCart.setInt(1, cartId);
            statementCart.setInt(2, userId);

            Calendar cal = Calendar.getInstance();
            java.util.Date date = cal.getTime();
            statementCart.setDate(3, new java.sql.Date(date.getTime()));

            statementCart.executeUpdate();

            statementCurCart = connection.prepareStatement(
               "INSERT INTO CURRENT_CARTS (Cart_id, User_id) VALUES (?, ?)");

            statementCurCart.setInt(1, cartId);
            statementCurCart.setInt(2, userId);

            statementCurCart.executeUpdate();

            connection.commit();
            isOk = true;
            return cartId;
        } finally {
            if (!isOk) {
                try {
                    connection.rollback();
                } catch (SQLException ex) {
                    log(ex);
                }
            }
            close(statementCart);
            close(statementCurCart);
            try {
                connection.setAutoCommit(bAutoCommit);
            } catch (SQLException ex) {
                log(ex);
            }
        }
    }
```

To begin a transaction, we disable the auto-commit feature at the beginning of the `try` body and invoke `commit()` at the end of it. Otherwise, every executed statement would be committed immediately (and we want to have everything committed at once, at the end). To handle unexpected problems, we invoke `rollback()` whenever an exception is thrown. In any case, we re-enable the auto-commit feature when we are done, because our `ConnectionManager` will be reusing the connection. The `close()` method is shorthand for the code shown earlier that only closes the statements if they are non-null, and logs any exceptions that occur as a result.

USING VALIDATION

Your application should verify the correctness of any values that will be stored in your database. It is particularly important to verify data your users provide. For instance, if you store social security numbers, you should verify that you have a valid number before you store it in the database. Even if you can't exhaustively check the data, implement whatever checks you can perform. For example, in our PRODUCTS table, we could spell-check each description as it is added to the database.

USING IDENTIFIERS

Many database designs use *identifiers*, additional fields used to uniquely identify pieces of data. Identifiers allow you to refer to a particular record in a well-defined way. They also make it easier to refer to records in one table from records in another table. In the Online Grocer application, we use identifiers in the USERS, PRODUCTS, CARTS, and CART_ITEMS tables. These identifiers make it easier to refer to the records in the CARTS table from the CART_ITEMS table, and vice versa.

Because identifiers are used to uniquely identify data in a table, you must guarantee that your identifiers are unique in order to preserve your data integrity. Failure to implement correct algorithms or failure to plan for sufficiently large identifiers can destroy valuable information as your program's invariants become compromised.

Our identifiers are implemented as integers, which can be conveniently used in both DBMSs and software applications. When working with integer identifiers, you need to remember that an integer in memory can represent only a finite set of numbers. The allowable size for an integer depends on the DBMS itself and is thus vendor-specific.

Another thing to consider is how integer numbers behave in an application. If you decide to represent identifiers as integer types in a 32-bit environment, those identifiers cannot be larger than 2147483647. When an identifier reaches the maximum value and is increased by 1, it suddenly becomes –2147483648. The type of unsigned integer allows a maximum value of 4294967295. After incrementing one more time, it suddenly becomes equal to 0, which leads to unpredictable behavior. (This is caused by the way integers are represented – if you have all bits set [`FFFFFFFF`] and add 1, the bits are reset [`00000000`]).

On the other hand, creating arbitrarily large identifiers may not be feasible because you need to represent them somehow. You could use 64-bit long integers, but this causes performance degradation on 32-bit systems because CPUs have to perform extra work to deal with 64-bit numbers. Also, not every language has 64-bit integers. In that case, you could use a string variable of some size for the identifier, but operations on strings are generally slower than operations on integers. A third solution is to create your own type to represent very large identifiers (for example, split into two integers), but this requires implementing comparison operators and will also slow down operations. The bottom line is that if you do not anticipate very large numbers, developing elaborate solutions simply might not pay off.

It is important to understand how many distinct identifiers will be required during the application lifetime and to adjust sizes according to these predictions. We will assume that in the Online Grocer application there will be 30,000 distinct daily visits that will generate 30,000 unique carts. Every cart will have, on average, 20 items. This gives us 600,000 identifiers generated every day. During a year, this ends up being 219,000,000 identifiers. Even if the load does not grow from year to year, the Online Grocer will begin to have trouble after nine years if we use the `int` type in the program code or after 19 years if we use unsigned `int` types. This isn't bad, but it's not the kind of reasoning that helps us sleep well at night.

One possible solution for this problem and similar situations is to recycle identifiers. Because all that is required of identifiers is that they remain unique for a certain time period, you can eventually recycle old identifiers. As long as the ratio with which you use identifiers does not rise dramatically, starting over at 1 after a maximum limit has been reached is another possible way to keep the number of identifiers manageable. In this case, you just need to guarantee that any individual identifier does not end up with two simultaneous meanings. Another way to achieve this result is to recalculate your identifiers occasionally, particularly after you have cleaned out old values.

If you decide to recycle old identifiers, you should always verify that the identifiers you want to reuse no longer exist in your system.

Monitoring and Testing Your Database

Now that we have an actual database environment, we can take a more detailed look at some monitoring and testing options with respect to the Online Grocer application. As data enters your system, the possibility of corruption, unexpected data, or invalid data types always exists. If you want to keep constant tabs on the quality and validity of data, you should implement an ongoing process of database monitoring.

Monitoring your database with DataRecon

To demonstrate how to monitor database contents with DataRecon, we will describe how to create a test that checks the growth of the CART_ITEMS table (potentially the fastest-growing table in the Online Grocer application) by reporting an error if any of this table's cart item identifiers are greater than 1,000,000,000.

The first step in creating this test is to create a report in DataRecon's report editor that displays only cart item identifiers exceeding our limit. First, we open the report editor and drag the node representing the Cart_id field (from the CART_ITEMS table) to the report editor workspace. A rectangle representing the field is then added to the report editor workspace, and we can view this field's records by simply selecting the View tab. Next, we filter out any record with a Cart_id less than 1,000,000,000 by placing a simple condition on the type of data DataRecon should display for that field (as shown in Figure 16-4) and returning to the View tab. Next, we remove the execution time value from the report because execution time is not relevant to what we want to check.

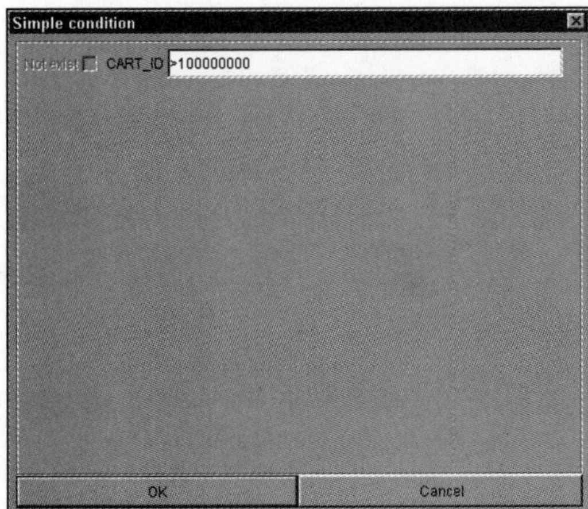

Figure 16-4: Filtering out records with Cart_id under 1,000,000,000.

The next step is to create a test that automatically verifies whether the database follows our rule. First, we create a control case by having DataRecon record the result of the preceding report (a table which contains zero records that satisfy this condition). Next, we configure a test that will prompt DataRecon to generate a current report of Cart_id values that are more than 1,000,000,000 and compare this report to the control case. If the test reveals that the current CART_ITEMS table contains identifiers larger than 1,000,000,000, an error is reported. If all is well, DataRecon reports that the tests succeeded (as shown in Figure 16-5).

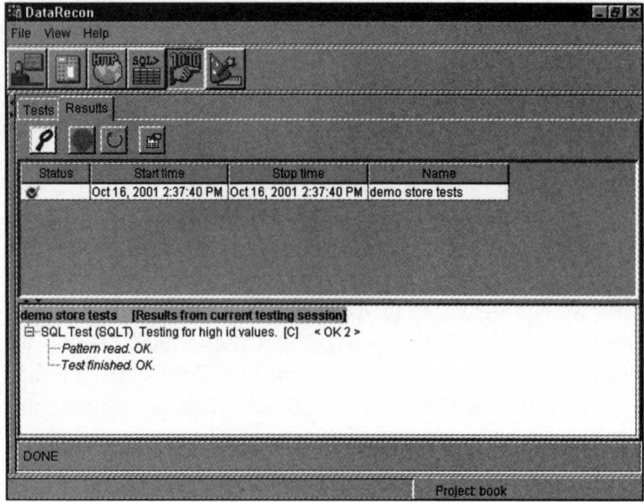

Figure 16-5: A successful test outcome.

You can use this same strategy to create tests that check for data integrity among different tables, unexpected values recorded in the database, and so on. It's all just a matter of creating a report that represents the desired results, recording a control case, and running the tests.

Verifying your database during path testing

As we have said, if your application is modifying a database, you might want to include a database validation procedure in your path testing. Basically, this involves modifying the path to include extra checks for your database. You can do this with any path-testing procedure. First, we will show some simple Python code to validate your database and then demonstrate how this can be integrated into WebKing.

The concept of paths and techniques to specify test paths are discussed in detail in Chapter 13.

USING PYTHON

Scripting database access is generally easy. However, because the database connection layer is not 100-percent standardized across vendors, the exact solution you use will depend on your database. This example uses the ODBC support available in Python to access a database available under Microsoft Windows.

```
import dbi, odbc
import sys, fpformat

try:
    s = odbc.odbc('database/user/password')
    cur = s.cursor();
    sql = 'select "Total Price" from DEMOTABLE'
    sql += ' where productid=\'#GA302293\''
    cur.execute(sql)
    rec = cur.fetchall()
    print '<TotalPrices>'
    for price in rec:
         print '  <Item price="'+
                fpformat.fix(price[0],2).strip()+'"/>'
    print '</TotalPrices>'
except NameError,e:
    print 'error ', e, 'undefined'
```

The general strategy used here is to connect to the ODBC source, using the `odbc.odbc()` function, and then execute any arbitrary SQL statements using the `execute()` function. After you have the results, you can write whatever code you like to check the data. Instead of checking the results, this particular script creates an XML representation of the output that looks like the following:

```
<TotalPrices>
  <Item price="29.90"/>
  <Item price="30.90"/>
  <Item price="63.80"/>
  <Item price="98.70"/>
  <Item price="33.90"/>
  <Item price="34.90"/>
  <Item price="215.40"/>
  <Item price="258.30"/>
  <Item price="38.90"/>
  <Item price="79.80"/>
  <Item price="40.90"/>
</TotalPrices>
```

If you are using the Python scripts from Chapter 14 for your load testing, you can insert code like this to allow database checks during path traversal. In this case, you would want to write additional code to check the values returned from the database. Here we have generated XML output, so we can easily plug our results into WebKing.

USING WEBKING

After creating paths using WebKing, it's easy to attach database checks. Because we want to find errors automatically, without requiring a human to examine the output of our script every time it runs, we use RuleWizard to create a custom rule and have WebKing enforce it automatically. In this case, we want to verify that all our prices are below $300 (this means a price of 30000 because our prices are stored in cents). First, we save the sample Python script output to a file, `prices.xml`. Then, from WebKing, we choose CodeWizard→Create XML Dictionary and select prices.xml. This creates a custom dictionary of nodes based on the contents of `prices.xml`. We name the dictionary `prices.cwd`.

At this point, we have an easy way to create our rule ("Find all `Item` elements with a `price` attribute greater than 30000"). We can easily modify this rule to find all sorts of patterns; the use of XML makes this particularly clean.

The next step is to create a tool in WebKing that combines our Python script with our RuleWizard rule. First, we create a tool by selecting File→Customize Preferences and clicking the New button on the Tools panel. Next, we select External Tool and click OK. For the executable, we select the Python interpreter and pass our script as the argument. We decide to name our tool *Dump Prices*. Because we want to see what text the command produces during our debugging process, we enable the Keep Output option.

Next, we right-click the Tools tab node representing the Dump Prices tool, choose Add Output→New Output→Rule Enforcer from the shortcut menu, and attach the XML rule. From this point forward, whenever we run the Dump Prices tool, WebKing will pull the requested data from our database, run the XML rule, and print any appropriate messages.

To test our new tool, we go to the Path tab, select the item that represents the file modifying the database, and click the button for our Dump Prices tool. Output messages are shown in the GUI's right pane.

We could modify our RuleWizard rule to print the actual output so that we can verify whether the rule is working correctly.

The final step is to configure the Site Workout feature to use our rule. From the Fixed Path subtab in the User Profile panel's Basic tab, we select the part of the path that modifies the database and check the box next to the Dump Prices tool. From this point forward, whenever we run Site Workout, WebKing automatically checks whether the database contents meet our criteria (no prices over $300) after the path that modifies the database has been executed.

See Chapter 13 for instructions on applying a tool to specific parts of a path.

USING DATARECON AND WEBKING

If you don't want to customize scripts to access your database, you can use DataRecon to generate and publish HTML report pages representing the records you want to check and then use HTML rules to verify the records.

Monitoring Performance

When discussing design, we recommended that you anticipate load and design your database accordingly. After the database is up and running, you should check whether it handles your anticipated peak and average load.

To verify that the database can handle realistic loads, scale up the system to typical usage levels, and test its performance. Is data delivered in a timely fashion? Does it deliver good average performance?

Next, test the system under expected maximum peak conditions. Again, verify whether the system is operating at acceptable levels. It can't always be blazingly fast, but it shouldn't be so slow that it drives users away. Also, check whether your application responds appropriately to error conditions. All database errors should be handled as gracefully as possible, and not cause total application failure.

To be confident in your database's scalability, we recommend that you test the following conditions:

- Average usage
- Peak usage
- Expected number of users (then double it and check again)
- Expected volume of data (then double it and check again)

The first step in doing this with DataRecon is to create a report representing the records you want to check and to place that report on a Web server. Next, you create a WebKing path representing the path required to write the data to the database. Then, you add a link to the DataRecon HTML report as the final node in that path.

If this report is deployed on the same server as your Web application, you can add the link to the DataRecon HTML report using WebKing's Add Link feature. If not, you might have to add an additional site to your project in order to add this link. Chapters 5 and 10 describe this procedure.

The next step is to create a rule that verifies whether the correct data is written to the database. Then, you create a CodeWizard Enforcer for that rule in the normal manner. Finally, you set up a virtual user to test this path and apply the appropriate rule to the appropriate page.

Depending on how you create your tests, the relevant database records might have to be cleaned before each path is executed. If necessary, you can configure WebKing to execute your tests in a given order, as explained in the WebKing User's Guide.

You could repeat this process to check different test cases. For example, you could check whether different types of inputs were written to the database correctly or whether the data was written consistently when you took a different path to the program that performed the write.

Maintaining Your Database

When you have a functioning Web application, you will be working with your database on an ongoing basis (checking performance, running reports, and so forth). A database's design is important to its success, but a good design will not help if the application-database interaction does not continue to work as expected. That's why monitoring is so critical. If application problems cause incorrect records to be entered in the database but you do not discover the problem immediately, the resulting cost of data loss can be extremely high.

In this section, we discuss two common problems that arise as the database evolves: updating a live database and making sure that the database and application remain in sync.

Updating your database

Data in a database has various purposes. Some data acts as definitions or dictionaries, and other data serves as live records. For example, in the Online Grocer, the PRODUCTS table containing items serves as a dictionary or catalog of what's available, and the CARTS, CART_ITEMS, and CURRENT_CARTS tables are *live* records, meaning that they are frequently updated.

If the database design takes the data's purpose into account, transfers and updates are generally much easier. For example, say that we want the contents of our PRODUCTS table to be developed by a third party and transferred to the live application upon completion. If our database is designed well, such transfers should be simple.

One basic update technique is to delete all the old contents of the definitional tables and replace them with new contents. However, this approach has two main problems. The first problem is that if you use primary/foreign keys, you might not be able to freely delete records to which other parts of the database refer. Before you delete the records, you must make sure that all references to them are removed or modified. If you are not modifying the key, the only safe way to make changes is to change the record contents. Another problem is related to the complexity of your definitional data. If your definitional information is distributed across many tables or, even worse, across tables related to one another by primary/foreign keys, updating it all could be a complicated process.

Another possible update technique is to divide definitional data and operational data into separate logical databases. Such an approach has two main benefits. The first is that it enables you to easily update definitional data using a full import without having to worry about keeping operational data intact. The second benefit is that it enables you to distribute data into physically different databases, as well as logically different databases. This, in turn, improves scalability.

By *definitional data* we mean constant, unchanging data. By *operational data*, we mean dynamic, variable data.

This separation approach is not free from drawbacks. Data, when separated, might be inconsistent. For example, after a product catalog is updated, it might turn out that the operational database contains some records referring to deleted items. The application should be prepared for such situations (for example, by silently deleting references, if possible, or by displaying `record not available` messages). Also, when data is separated, the application has to maintain more connections to increased numbers of databases. If you're processing a large number of concurrent users, this can impede your performance. You can try to open and close connections so that only one connection is open at once, but doing so can be time-consuming.

In the Online Grocer application, we can separate the PRODUCTS table into a distinct logical (or physical) database and then update the live server by performing the following steps:

1. Export the new database to a file.
2. Stop the server.

We strongly recommend that you make a backup before deleting any data.

3. Delete the old products database.
4. Import the new database from the file so that the new database takes the place of the old one.
5. Restart the server.
6. Perform acceptance tests on the updated database to make sure that everything is functioning correctly.

Acceptance tests are minimal functionality tests. In such tests, you do not investigate all possible variations. Rather, you check for basic functionality. In this situation, acceptance tests are not for testing the application itself (we assume that it must be tested before the update begins) but to make sure that the update process was performed correctly. A flawed update process usually manifests itself in some functionality not working.

Keeping your database and application in sync

Database structures rarely remain the same throughout the development process. This is especially true in Web development, which lends itself more to an iterative development process than a waterfall model. New versions of your application, with new features, are developed every two to three months, and many new features require you to store new information in your database. This means that the new application version needs not only a new database structure but also new definitional data.

For a discussion of the waterfall and iterative development processes, see Chapter 1.

If you are using one database for development and a different database for your application, be careful that they do not become out of sync as you make modifications. One way to do this is to have DataRecon automatically check the consistency of the database structures. For example, say that we want to determine whether the Online Grocer's development and production databases differ. First, we add a new Database Structure Test to our DataRecon test suite, specify how to connect to the development database, and indicate that we want DataRecon to create an XML file containing a detailed description of the development database's objects. When we play the test, DataRecon creates an XML file that represents the current structure of the database – this establishes our control case. Next, we configure DataRecon to compare the production database structure with the control (development) database structure. We can then run this test automatically to quickly determine whether the two databases have become out of sync and can add it to our regression test suite so that we can constantly monitor the consistency of these two databases.

Summary

Databases are useful for developing Web applications. In general, databases are not as flexible as other parts of your code. When you begin collecting data, you won't want to make frequent changes to your database layout because doing so can affect the surrounding code significantly and invalidate data you have already collected. Hence, investing effort in designing and documenting your database structure in the early stages of development pays off in the long run.

When your database is up and running, make sure that you have tools to analyze its performance, ensure its integrity, and verify that it interacts correctly with your code. This chapter introduces several ways to do just that.

Chapter 17

Bulletproofing XML

IN THIS CHAPTER

- ◆ Understanding XML
- ◆ Determining when to use XML
- ◆ Using XML
- ◆ Using XML in the Online Grocer application
- ◆ Verifying XML

THE EXTENSIBLE MARKUP LANGUAGE (XML) is a family of technologies that describe structured data. XML has received much press recently as the cure-all for every problem related to Web application development. A reminder of Fred Brooks's 1986 observation that "there is no silver bullet" is applicable here. This chapter looks at the technology behind the hype. Although XML is not a panacea, it does offer attractive features that, when used properly, can support the goal of producing a bulletproof Web application.

This chapter focuses primarily on two questions: When does using XML positively contribute to the goal of a bulletproof Web application? and When using XML, which techniques can be employed to ensure that the use of XML contributes to the Web application's robustness rather than to its fragility? Assuming that you are interested in producing robust Web applications, these questions can be rephrased: When and why should I use XML? and How should I use XML? Before addressing these questions, it is helpful to review what XML is.

Understanding XML

XML is a family of technologies defined by recommendations from the World Wide Web Consortium (W3C). The W3C describes XML as "the universal format for structured documents and data on the Web." That's a general description – what does it mean? Here are some key points about XML.

First, XML describes *structured data* (data organized in a definite pattern). Structure refers to components and relationships between the components.

Second, the term *XML* means different things in different contexts. Sometimes it refers to an entire family of technologies. Other times it refers to a syntax of elements, attributes, and documents for serializing information. The W3C has a large collection of XML-related activities and recommendations. Some of these are official W3C recommendations, and others are works in progress. They cover technologies such as the following:

XForms	XHTML	XLink
XML	XML Base	XML Encryption
XML Protocol	XML Query	XML Schema
XPath	XPointer	XSL and XSLT

Recommendations and works in progress from the W3C can be found at `www.w3.org`.

Third, XML can be considered in terms of both documents and data. A *document-centric view* emphasizes the angle bracket–dominated syntax and focuses on XML as a text document that can be edited with a text editor. A *data-centric view* considers XML a serialization format for data that will be generated and parsed automatically and will generally not be viewed or manipulated directly by humans.

There are both similarities and differences between XML and HTML. Both technologies have tags (or elements) and attributes as a result of efforts to simplify the Standard Generalized Markup Language (SGML), which is an international standard for the description of marked-up electronic text. XML differs from HTML in that HTML mixes content and presentation whereas XML is specifically for representing content. However, technologies such as Cascading Style Sheets (CSS), the eXtensible Stylesheet Language (XSL), and the eXtensible Hypertext Markup Language (XHTML) enable presentation to be applied to XML.

For a simple example of XML, we will return to the Online Grocer application introduced in Chapter 4. Previously, the product information was assumed to be stored in a database, queried through a Java class, and then encoded into HTML. However, if we wanted to exchange our product list with our business partners over the Web, we could generate XML documents that look something like this:

```
<?xml version="1.0" encoding="US-ASCII"?>
<ProductList>
```

```
  <Product color="green" file="apple_fruit_green.gif" id="0" isFruit="true">
    Green apples are great for making caramel apples. The sour taste
    of the apple and the sweet taste of the caramel blend well together.
  </Product>
  <Product color="green" file="artichoke_veg_green.gif" id="1" isFruit="false">
    Artichoke hearts are the tastiest part of the artichoke. When you
    eat the heart, it's love at first bite!
  </Product>
  <Product color="green" file="asparagus_veg_green.gif" id="2" isFruit="false">
    Asparagus is easy to cook.
  </Product>
  <Product color="green" file="avocado_fruit_green.gif" id="3" isFruit="true">
    Avocados are the main ingredient in guacamole.
  </Product>
  <Product color="yellow" file="banana_fruit_yellow.gif" id="4" isFruit="true">
    Smart monkeys eat bananas. Are you smart?
  </Product>
</ProductList>
```

Even without going into detail about what each node means, two points are apparent: XML is readable, and XML is not *that* readable. Keep this in mind when working with XML and when deciding between XML and alternative technologies.

This example and others in this chapter are available on the CD.

Determining When to Use XML

Now that you have a basic understanding of XML, you will learn how it can be used and review issues to consider when determining whether XML is a good fit for a given problem.

A recurring theme throughout this book is that detecting errors early is better than catching them late and that preventing errors from being introduced is better yet. An implication of this maxim is that preventing errors in the design stage is preferable to doing so in the code construction phase. It is easy to say that producing a bulletproof application is a design requirement, but often it is not obvious how design decisions will affect the quality of the final product.

Because the decision to use XML is more an architectural decision than a code construction detail, it is important to consider its effect on flexibility, simplicity, and performance during the design phase. Making careful decisions at this time will improve the overall quality and robustness of the application.

Comparing XML to other technologies

Technologies are not chosen in a vacuum. Whenever you are trying to decide whether to use XML for an application, it is helpful to consider the alternatives to XML for that particular application.

One technology to which XML is often compared is HTML. The argument goes that XML is like HTML but separates content from presentation, enabling content reuse, whereas HTML's inlining of content within presentation formatting tags discourages reuse. There is truth in this idea but also a danger of oversimplification. In practice, XML is not used today as a strict replacement of HTML but rather as an intermediary format that works in conjunction with HTML. Currently, almost all pages on the Web are in HTML by the time they reach the browser. Therefore, it is more appropriate to compare HTML to the combination of XML and HTML. When the options are explained in this way, the pros and cons are clearer. Using XML as an intermediary format has the benefits of increased flexibility and greater code reuse because one XML document can be transformed into multiple display formats. On the other hand, creating HTML directly without XML has the benefit of simplicity. Whether the extra flexibility offered by the XML is worth the extra complexity depends on the application.

One XML technology that is appropriate to compare directly with HTML is XHTML. XHTML is a reformulation of HTML that is consistent with XML grammar. If you are using XML in your Web application, you should consider producing your final pages in XHTML.

The XHTML recommendation is found at `www.w3.org/MarkUp`.

XML can also be an alternative to technologies that have nothing to do with HTML. Consider the problem of sharing data between two applications. In the context of the Online Grocer application, there might be opportunities to partner with other online vendors. Exchanging information about produce availability and prices would be crucial to such a partnership. How can this data be exchanged? One solution is to design a protocol specifically for exchanging the produce information and have all the vendors implement this protocol. Basically, this is the approach that Electronic Data Interchange (EDI) has taken. This approach can work if the companies involved are so large and powerful that they can dictate that all their partners purchase compatible EDI systems to do business with them. However, this is not a very attractive solution for companies that do not have this luxury.

A variation on this approach is to create a protocol that relies on common denominators among partners. For example, if all partners are implementing their services in Java, serializing information as Java objects is a potential option. However, there are two problems with this approach. A barrier of entry exists for potential partners not using Java. Also, each of the partners cannot easily switch to a different architecture as different considerations arise.

XML offers a solution that requires neither expensive investment in EDI systems nor a tight coupling between the architectures of partners' systems. Instead, document types can be established for XML, which specifies the elements, attributes, and data types that are acceptable. Each partner can use a standard XML parser to parse the data – even if one partner is running Java on a Sparc station, another is running Visual Basic on Windows 2000, and a third is running Perl on Linux. Free and commercial XML parsers are available for all mainstream programming languages.

The Apache project provides free, open-source XML parsers in Java, C++, and Perl. You can download them at `xml.apache.org`.

Balancing flexibility and simplicity

When deciding which technology to use for your application, consider your application's anticipated lifetime. Potential changes that can occur during the lifetime of your application should be anticipated and accounted for. This does not mean that every application must be written to include every feature that could be useful in the future. Rather, it means anticipating the categories of change that might occur and designing flexibility into your solution. This enables you to make significant changes without redesigning your whole system.

The goal of flexibility can make XML solutions more attractive than many of the alternatives. As already discussed, many other solutions can reasonably be implemented, but they do not all provide the same flexibility as XML. The longer the life cycle of your application and the more changes you anticipate, the more important this consideration becomes.

Another key design goal is simplicity. Whereas flexibility has more of a future focus, simplicity has benefits that are realized immediately. Simplicity of design improves the quality of your solution in a number of ways. Consider the following advantages that a simple design has over a complex design:

- It is easier to communicate to all members of the team.
- It is less likely to have subtle design flaws.
- It is often implemented and debugged more quickly.
- It is easier to maintain because it is easier to understand.

Note that the first three benefits can be realized almost immediately, whereas the last one extends into the future. Although simplicity can be thought of as bulletproofing for the short term, it does not necessarily imply shortsightedness.

In some situations, using XML is the ideal way to achieve simplicity, but in others, it can complicate more than it simplifies. For example, compared to an EDI system, a small XML document for exchanging information is relatively simple. On the other hand, consider the problem of setting up your Web application so that it can be reconfigured and deployed in different ways without being recompiled. If the configuration options are complex and interrelated, XML might be a good choice. However, if the configuration involves a simple list of boolean values that can be true or false, a plain-text file listing the options and their values would be a simpler solution.

Different applications require different design goals, but flexibility and simplicity are important goals for any application.

Good designs are not achieved by blindly applying supposedly infallible rules, but rather by recognizing the pros and cons of several feasible approaches and selecting the solution that best fits the given problem. If you have thought of only one solution to a complex problem, you probably don't understand the problem well enough to think of the best solution. When a design fits a problem space well, flexibility and simplicity are often achieved simultaneously.

Considering performance

Performance can be critical in Web applications. However, we have observed that a common mistake is to apply optimizations prematurely in the development process. This leads to unnecessary compromises in flexibility and simplicity. For example, when multiple operations are performed concurrently, optimizing the nonbottleneck operations does not improve the overall system performance, which is constrained by the bottleneck operation. In this case, it would be premature to optimize before determining where the bottlenecks are. Also, optimizing components in isolation can, in some cases, diminish the overall system performance.

A simple rule of thumb to prevent premature optimizations is this: Do not forfeit simplicity and flexibility for performance unless you have measured the difference in performance and determined that it is worth the trade-off. Here is a corollary: If the performance difference is not worth measuring, the performance gain does not warrant overriding the goals of simplicity and flexibility.

Applying this principle to decisions involving when and where to use XML means first evaluating the options in terms of simplicity and flexibility. If, based on these considerations, XML is the best choice, measure performance, and determine whether XML will work within your performance goals. XML is verbose and generally not as efficient as binary representations. However, this does not necessarily affect the Web application noticeably if provisions are taken to minimize the effect of the verbose representation. (For example, communication protocols such as HTTP 1.1 can compress data on-the-fly, minimizing the effect of over-the-wire verbosity.)

Using XML

After deciding to use XML, you must determine *how* you should use it. In this section, we take a more detailed look at how to use XML.

Parsing XML

There are two primary approaches to parsing XML: the Document Object Model (DOM) and the Simple API for XML (SAX). Each describes a different set of interfaces for accessing and manipulating XML data programmatically. Note that both approaches are language-independent interfaces. Implementations for both sets of interfaces are available in most common programming languages.

Using a DOM parser involves parsing a document to create a document object. This document object can be queried and manipulated in terms of its constituent nodes, which are elements, attributes, and so on. It is a tree-based representation that is easy to understand if you view an XML file as a tree structure. This approach works well if you want to manipulate the tree structure directly. However, depending on how the data is being used, this approach can have performance disadvantages. For example, even if an application is interested only in the value of an attribute of the document's root node, it must parse the entire document before it can determine the attribute's value. Also, depending on the implementation, each document that is parsed can consume significant memory resources.

The official W3C DOM describes a document object model for XML and HTML documents. This includes some interfaces that are specific to either XML or HTML. In Chapter 8, we introduce DOM in the context of Web browsers, focusing on JavaScript accessing HTML documents. In this chapter, DOM refers to the API for accessing XML documents.

The SAX is a set of streaming interfaces that deconstructs the information in an XML document into a linear sequence of method calls. Using the SAX parser involves specifying an object or objects to receive callbacks as the XML document is parsed. Unlike the DOM parsers, the SAX parser does not produce a document object that can be traversed and, therefore, does not make provisions for manipulating the XML document as a tree structure. Instead, the objects receiving the callbacks are responsible for storing any information that is needed after the parsing is complete. This approach works well when reading an XML document in a context where only specific information is relevant and other information can be ignored. It also works well for converting an XML document into a more application-specific representation

Be wary of oversimplifications such as "SAX is better than DOM." Instead, recognize that both approaches have merits and that the best choice depends on the problem at hand.

Specifying XML-based languages

XML is a *meta-markup* language. This means that it provides mechanisms for defining languages that are implemented in XML. Many members of the XML family of technologies referred to earlier fall in this category. There are two basic mechanisms for defining these languages: Document Type Definition (DTD) and XML Schema.

The DTD is the original mechanism specified in the XML 1.0 W3C recommendation. The syntax derives from SGML. Here is a sample DTD that can be used to define a document type corresponding to the XML product list introduced in the beginning of this chapter:

```
<!-- ProductList DTD -->
<!ELEMENT ProductList (Product)*>
<!ELEMENT Product (#PCDATA)>
<!ATTLIST Product color (red|green|yellow|weird) #REQUIRED
                  file CDATA #REQUIRED
                  id CDATA #REQUIRED
                  isFruit (true|false) 'true'>
```

To reference this DTD from an XML file, begin the XML file with the following lines:

```
<?xml version="1.0" encoding="US-ASCII"?>
<!DOCTYPE ProductList PUBLIC "-//OnlineGrocer//ProductList//EN"
"ProductList.dtd">
```

DTDs provide mechanisms for expressing which elements are allowed and what the composition of each element can be. Legal attributes can be defined per element type, and legal attribute values can be defined per attribute.

However, DTDs have some shortcomings. They do not provide the capability to extend types, they do not have provisions for namespaces, and competency in DTD writing requires learning a syntax that seems obscure to those outside the SGML world.

XML namespaces are a provision for defining a scope for which names apply in XML documents. This allows you to combine elements and attributes from multiple sources without introducing naming conflicts.

To address these issues, XML schemas were introduced. Like DTDs, schemas define a set of legal elements, attributes, and attribute values. However, schemas are namespace-aware and are more type-oriented than DTDs. Also, schemas themselves are an XML-based language, so learning schemas does not require learning a new syntax. Here is a schema representation for the product list:

```
<!-- ProductList Schema -->
<xsd:schema xmlns:xsd="http://www.w3.org/2001/XMLSchema">
 <xsd:element name="ProductList">
  <xsd:complexType>
   <xsd:sequence>
    <xsd:element ref="Product" minOccurs="0" maxOccurs="unbounded"/>
   </xsd:sequence>
  </xsd:complexType>
 </xsd:element>
 <xsd:element name="Product">
  <xsd:complexType>
   <xsd:simpleContent>
    <xsd:extension base="xsd:string">
     <xsd:attribute name="color" use="required">
      <xsd:simpleType>
       <xsd:restriction base="xsd:string">
        <xsd:enumeration value="red"/>
        <xsd:enumeration value="green"/>
        <xsd:enumeration value="yellow"/>
        <xsd:enumeration value="weird"/>
       </xsd:restriction>
      </xsd:simpleType>
     </xsd:attribute>
     <xsd:attribute name="file" type="xsd:string" use="required"/>
     <xsd:attribute name="id" type="xsd:nonNegativeInteger" use="required"/>
     <xsd:attribute name="isFruit" type="xsd:boolean" default="true"/>
    </xsd:extension>
   </xsd:simpleContent>
  </xsd:complexType>
 </xsd:element>
</xsd:schema>
```

To reference this schema from an XML file, you specify the `noNamespaceSchemaLocation` attribute in the `ProductList` element like this:

```
<ProductList xmlns:xsi="http://www.w3.org/2001/XMLSchema-instance"
  xsi:noNamespaceSchemaLocation="ProductList.xsd">
```

Note that the flexibility and expressiveness of schemas comes at the cost of increased complexity and verbosity.

Validating XML

XML that is written to conform to an XML-based language can be checked for correctness on multiple levels. The first (and least stringent) level is that the XML be well formed. An XML document is said to be *well formed* when it conforms to the grammar specified in the XML recommendation. See the recommendation for an official definition of *well-formedness*, which basically includes constraints such as the following:

- There is exactly one root element.
- Every element has a closing tag and an opening tag, or else it is a single empty element.
- Attribute values are quoted.
- No attribute may appear more than once in the same element.

Well-formedness constraints verify that a document is parsable XML. An additional constraint that can be imposed is verifying whether the XML is valid. Originally, *valid* meant that the XML was well formed, specified a DTD, and conformed to that DTD. Later, the concept of *schema-valid* was introduced, meaning that the document is well formed and conforms to a schema. Now, documents that conform to either a DTD or a schema are commonly described as valid.

The good news is that checking for both well-formedness and validity can be performed automatically by validating XML parsers. This means that by defining a DTD or schema, you can use a validating parser to confirm that documents conform to the language you have defined. This concept is simple but quite powerful because it lets you use tools to detect errors automatically that you (or your customers!) would otherwise have to find the hard way.

Using XML in the Online Grocer Application

To discuss XML in more detail, we will turn to the Online Grocer application. Suppose that we would like to make the functionality of this Web application available to wireless devices such as cell phones. This section looks at several technologies that would be appropriate to this task, including Wireless Markup Language (WML) and eXtensible Stylesheet Language Transformations (XSLT).

Using the Wireless Markup Language (WML)

WML is an XML-based language designed to express content to a wireless device. The small screen size and the low bandwidth normally available on cell phones and pagers do not readily lend themselves to HTML. WML is designed to meet the same need as HTML but is specifically targeted to wireless devices. WML generally provides a slightly higher level of abstraction of the user interface than does HTML. This allows (at least in theory) a single WML page to work with a wide range of wireless devices.

WML is critical to our efforts to make our Online Grocer application accessible to wireless devices. We will generate equivalent WML for each HTML page in the original application. For example, the original HTML Main Search page that allows users to select products based on type and color looks like this:

```
<HTML>
  <HEAD>
    <TITLE>Welcome</TITLE>
    <LINK REL="stylesheet" TYPE="text/css" HREF="/fruits/fruits.css">
  </HEAD>
  <BODY BGCOLOR=#009900 BACKGROUND="/fruits/background.gif">
    <CENTER>
      <TABLE BORDER=0 CELLPADDING=0 CELLSPACING=0>
        <TR><TD ALIGN=CENTER>
          <IMG SRC="/fruits/title.gif" ALT="Fruits & Vegetables">
        </TD></TR>
        <TR><TD HEIGHT=20></TD></TR>
        <TR><TD ALIGN=CENTER>
          <FORM NAME=choose METHOD=POST
ACTION="/servlet/fruits.ShoppingServlet">
          <TABLE BORDER=0 CELLPADDING=5 CELLSPACING=0>
          <TR><TD VALIGN=TOP>
            <INPUT TYPE=CHECKBOX NAME=FRUITS VALUE=on CHECKED>
            <IMG SRC="/fruits/fruits.gif" ALT="Fruits" ALIGN=middle><BR>
            <INPUT TYPE=CHECKBOX NAME=VEGETABLES VALUE=on>
            <IMG SRC="/fruits/vegetables.gif" ALT="Fruits" ALIGN=middle><BR>
          </TD><TD VALIGN=TOP>
            <INPUT TYPE=CHECKBOX NAME=RED VALUE=red CHECKED>
            <IMG SRC="/fruits/red.gif" ALT="Red" ALIGN=middle><BR>
            <INPUT TYPE=CHECKBOX NAME=GREEN VALUE=green>
            <IMG SRC="/fruits/green.gif" ALT="Green" ALIGN=middle><BR>
            <INPUT TYPE=CHECKBOX NAME=YELLOW VALUE=yellow CHECKED>
```

```
          <IMG SRC="/fruits/yellow.gif" ALT="Yellow/Orange" ALIGN=middle><BR>
          <INPUT TYPE=CHECKBOX NAME=WEIRD VALUE=weird>
          <IMG SRC="/fruits/weird.gif" ALT="Weird" ALIGN=middle><BR>
        </TD></TR>
        </TABLE>
        <INPUT TYPE=HIDDEN NAME=METHOD VALUE=choose><BR>
        <INPUT TYPE=IMAGE SRC="/fruits/gobutton.gif" BORDER=0 NAME=Go><BR>
        </FORM>
        <HR>
        <A HREF="/servlet/fruits.ShoppingServlet?METHOD=logout">
        <IMG SRC="/fruits/logout.gif" ALT="Logout" BORDER=0></A>
      </TD></TR>
    </TABLE>
  </CENTER>
 </BODY>
</HTML>
```

When this code is rendered in a traditional browser, it looks something like the page shown in Figure 17-1.

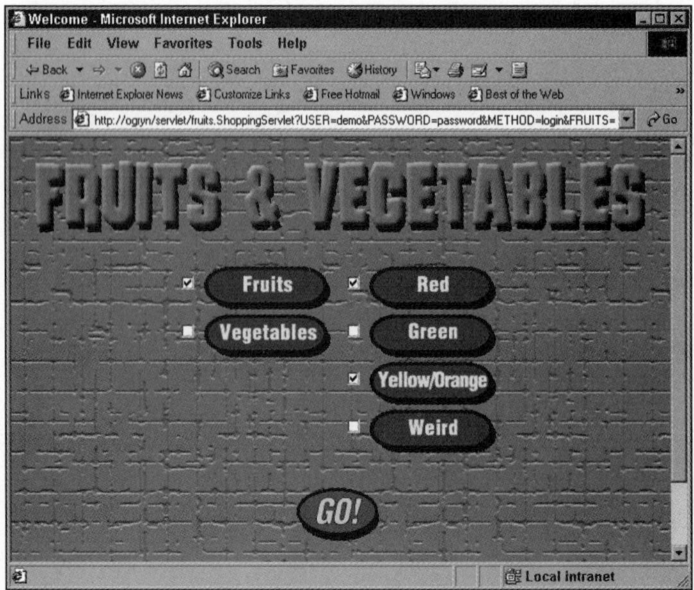

Figure 17-1: The Main Search page rendered in a traditional browser.

We would like to create a version of this content in WML that would be appropriate for cell phones. Here is one possible implementation:

```
<?xml version="1.0" encoding="US-ASCII"?>
<!DOCTYPE wml PUBLIC "-//PHONE.COM//DTD WML 1.1//EN"
  "http://www.phone.com/dtd/wml11.dtd">
<wml>
    <card title="Fruits and Vegetables">
        <do label="Go" type="accept">
            <go method="get" href="/servlet/fruits.ShoppingServlet/">
                <postfield name="METHOD" value="choose"/>
                <postfield name="Types" value="$Types"/>
                <postfield name="Colors" value="$Colors"/>
            </go>
        </do>
        <do label="Log Out" type="reset">
            <exit/>
        </do>
        <p mode="nowrap">
            <b>Select Types</b>
            <select name="Types" multiple="true" title="Types">
                <option value="Fruits">Fruits</option>
                <option value="Vegetables">Vegetables</option>
            </select>
        </p>
        <p mode="nowrap">
            <b>Select Colors</b>
            <select name="Colors" multiple="true" title="Colors">
                <option value="Red">Red</option>
                <option value="Green">Green</option>
                <option value="Yellow/Orange">Yellow/Orange</option>
                <option value="Weird">Weird</option>
            </select>
        </p>
    </card>
</wml>
```

When rendered on a WML-enabled device, this code might produce results like those shown in Figure 17-2.

How can files like this be checked? One way is to gather all the mobile devices you anticipate might be used to access this application and to test the file on every one of those devices. Ultimately, testing with actual devices is necessary because, in the real world, implementations do not always match their specifications. An easier test is to view the WML in a WML browser emulator from the machine on which the WML was created. However, even before you view the WML through a browser, you can perform a simple check by running the WML through an XML validator to confirm validity. This method is easier because it does not require an emulator. Moreover, it can catch errors that the emulator does not. For example, the emulator might accept nonportable proprietary extensions of WML or might just ignore elements or attributes it does not understand. An XML validator faithfully reports these cases as errors because the document does not conform to the DTD.

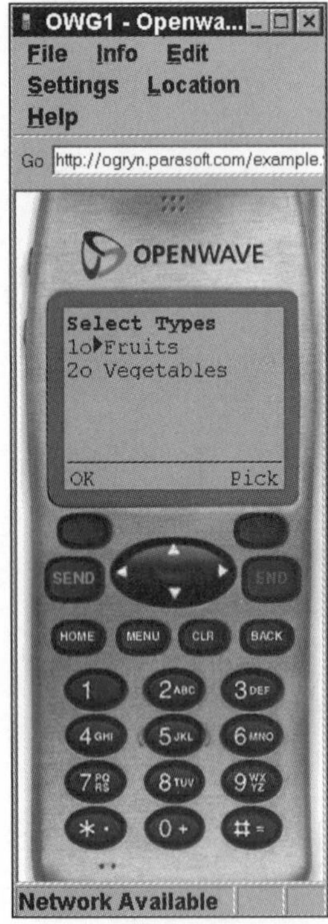

Image of the Openwave Simulator courtesy of Openwave Systems Inc.

Figure 17-2: The Main Search page rendered on a WML-enabled device.

Take another look at the HTML page and the equivalent WML page. Except for the names of the product types and colors, the two pages do not have much in common. The product types and colors will be determined at runtime by a lookup to a database, so these pages will need to be generated dynamically. However, this implies that for each page generated, we need code to generate both an HTML version and a WML version. Furthermore, if the look and feel of either the WML or HTML version changes, we must change the code that generates these pages. This code will tend to be difficult to maintain because we have so many variables contributing to the logic.

Also, we now have both content and presentation tied up in the servlet code that dynamically generates the HTML and WML. How can we decouple the content and presentation? One way is through the use of eXtensible Stylesheet Language Transformations (XSLT), the transformation language used by XSL.

Using eXtensible Stylesheet Language Transformations (XSLT)

XSLT is an XML-based language used for describing transformations you can apply to XML documents to convert them from one document type to another. The transformed document can be a modified version of the same document type, a different document type in XML, or HTML, or even an arbitrary text format.

Why is this important? Recall that separating content from presentation was one of the motivations for using XML rather than embedding content inside HTML. However, information intended for display in a browser still requires instructions for presentation. XSL provides a way to describe the presentation of an XML document.

Returning to the Online Grocer application, we can factor out the content that is present in the HTML and the WML representations by having the servlet generate an XML page containing this content. We then have one XSL that translates from the XML to HTML and another XSL that translates from the XML to WML. When the server receives a request, it generates the XML file and applies the appropriate XSL transformation, depending on whether the request comes from an HTML-accepting client or a WML-accepting client.

Here is one example of XML that can be generated by the servlet as the basis for the Online Grocer application's Main Search page:

```
<?xml version="1.0" encoding="US-ASCII"?>
<page title="Fruits and Vegetables">
  <MultiSelect title="Types" minimum="1">
    <option value="Fruits" image="/fruits/fruits.gif" default="true"/>
    <option value="Vegetables" image="/fruits/vegetables.gif" default="false"/>
  </MultiSelect>
  <MultiSelect title="Colors" minimum="1">
    <option value="Red" image="/fruits/red.gif" default="true"/>
    <option value="Green" image="/fruits/green.gif" default="false"/>
    <option value="Yellow/Orange" image="/fruits/yellow.gif" default="true"/>
    <option value="Weird" image="/fruits/weird.gif" default="false"/>
  </MultiSelect>
  <GoButton name="Go" image="/fruits/gobutton.gif"/>
  <LogoutButton name="Log Out" image="/fruits/logout.gif"/>
</page>
```

Here, both the types and the colors are represented by `MultiSelect` elements, which have child `option` elements. Note that there are many alternative representations. For example, each color choice could be represented by a `Color` element.

Also, some information must be in the XML file because it comes from the database, but other information can go in either the XML file or the XSL transformations.

Here is the `main_wml.xsl` file that transforms the preceding XML into WML:

```
<xsl:stylesheet xmlns:xsl="http://www.w3.org/1999/XSL/Transform" version="1.0">
  <xsl:output method="xml" version="1.0" encoding="US-ASCII"
   omit-xml-declaration="no" doctype-public="-//PHONE.COM//DTD WML 1.1//EN"
   doctype-system="http://www.phone.com/dtd/wml11.dtd" indent="yes"/>
 <xsl:template match="page">
   <wml>
    <card title="{@title}">
      <do type="accept" label="{/page/GoButton/@name}">
       <go href="/servlet/fruits.ShoppingServlet/" method="post">
        <postfield name="METHOD" value="choose"/>
        <xsl:for-each select="MultiSelect">
         <postfield name="{@title}" value="${@title}"/>
        </xsl:for-each>
       </go>
      </do>
      <do type="reset" label="{/page/LogoutButton/@name}">
       <exit/>
      </do>
      <xsl:for-each select="MultiSelect">
       <p mode="nowrap">
       <b>Select <xsl:value-of select="@title"/></b>
       <select title="{@title}" multiple="true" name="{@title}">
        <xsl:for-each select="option">
         <option value="{@value}">
          <xsl:value-of select="@value"/>
         </option>
        </xsl:for-each>
       </select>
       </p>
      </xsl:for-each>
    </card>
   </wml>
 </xsl:template>
</xsl:stylesheet>
```

Similarly, here is the `main_html.xsl` file that transforms the XML into XHTML.

```
<?xml version="1.0" encoding="US-ASCII"?>
<xsl:stylesheet xmlns:xsl="http://www.w3.org/1999/XSL/Transform" version="1.0">
  <xsl:output method="xml" version="1.0" encoding="US-ASCII"
   omit-xml-declaration="no" doctype-public="-//W3C//DTD XHTML 1.0 Strict//EN"
   doctype-system="DTD/xhtml1-strict.dtd" indent="yes"/>
```

```
<xsl:template match="page">
  <html>
   <title><xsl:value-of select="@title"/></title>
   <body bgcolor="#009900" background="/fruits/background.gif">
    <center>
      <table border="0" cellpadding="0" cellspacing="0">
       <tr><td align="CENTER">
         <IMG SRC="/fruits/title.gif" ALT="{@title}"/>
       </td></tr>
       <tr><td height="20"></td></tr>
       <tr><td align="CENTER">
       <form name="choose" method="POST"
             action="/servlet/fruits.ShoppingServlet">
         <table border="0" cellpadding="5" cellspacing="0">
         <tr>
          <xsl:for-each select="MultiSelect">
           <td valign="TOP">
            <xsl:for-each select="option">
             <input type="CHECKBOX" value="on" checked="{@default}"/>
             <img src="{@image}" alt="{@value}" align="middle"/><br/>
            </xsl:for-each>
           </td>
          </xsl:for-each>
         </tr></table>
         <input type="HIDDEN" name="METHOD" value="choose"/><br/>
         <input type="IMAGE" src="{/page/GoButton/@image}" border="0"
           name="{/page/GoButton/@name}"/><br/>
       </form>
      <hr/>
      <a href="/servlet/fruits.ShoppingServlet?METHOD=logout">
      <img src="{/page/LogoutButton/@image}" alt="{/page/LogoutButton/@name}"
        border="0"/></a>
      </td></tr>
      </table>
    </center>
   </body>
  </html>
 </xsl:template>
</xsl:stylesheet>
```

Applying this XSL transformation to the XML output from the servlet results in the following XHTML:

```
<?xml version="1.0" encoding="US-ASCII"?>
<!DOCTYPE html PUBLIC "-//W3C//DTD XHTML 1.0 Strict//EN" "DTD/xhtml1-strict.dtd">
<html>
```

```
<title>Fruits and Vegetables</title>
<body background="/fruits/background.gif" bgcolor="#009900">
 <center>
  <table cellspacing="0" cellpadding="0" border="0">
   <tr>
    <td align="CENTER">
     <IMG ALT="Fruits and Vegetables" SRC="/fruits/title.gif" />
    </td>
   </tr>
   <tr>
    <td height="20" />
   </tr>
   <tr>
    <td align="CENTER">
     <form action="/servlet/fruits.ShoppingServlet" method="POST" name="choose">
      <table cellspacing="0" cellpadding="5" border="0">
       <tr>
        <td valign="TOP">
         <input checked="true" value="on" type="CHECKBOX" />
         <img align="middle" alt="Fruits" src="/fruits/fruits.gif" />
         <br />
         <input checked="false" value="on" type="CHECKBOX" />
         <img align="middle" alt="Vegetables" src="/fruits/vegetables.gif" />
         <br />
        </td>
        <td valign="TOP">
         <input checked="true" value="on" type="CHECKBOX" />
         <img align="middle" alt="Red" src="/fruits/red.gif" />
         <br />
         <input checked="false" value="on" type="CHECKBOX" />
         <img align="middle" alt="Green" src="/fruits/green.gif" />
         <br />
         <input checked="true" value="on" type="CHECKBOX" />
         <img align="middle" alt="Yellow/Orange" src="/fruits/yellow.gif" />
         <br />
         <input checked="false" value="on" type="CHECKBOX" />
         <img align="middle" alt="Weird" src="/fruits/weird.gif" />
         <br />
        </td>
       </tr>
      </table>
      <input value="choose" name="METHOD" type="HIDDEN" />
      <br />
      <input name="Go" border="0" src="/fruits/gobutton.gif" type="IMAGE" />
      <br />
```

```
      </form>
      <hr />
      <a href="/servlet/fruits.ShoppingServlet?METHOD=logout">
       <img border="0" alt="Log Out" src="/fruits/logout.gif" />
      </a>
     </td>
    </tr>
   </table>
  </center>
 </body>
</html>
```

Evaluating XSLT

Now that you have seen a concrete example of how XML, XSLT, WML, and XHTML can be used together, let us reconsider some of the design decisions involving XSLT. First, it is helpful to realize that some technologies are required and others are optional. If you need to deliver content to multiple wireless devices, you must serve WML. However, XSLT is very much an optional technology. Both the WML and the XHTML could have been generated directly from the servlet. This is true not only for this specific case, but also in general. Using XSLT is just one way you can transform XML documents from one type to another. Another way is to write code in any language that can parse, manipulate, and serialize the DOM tree.

Recently, it has become popular to speak as though XSLT is clearly the right way to transform one XML document into another type of XML document. We suggest that this is an oversimplification. In bulletproofing your Web application, both approaches have benefits.

The XSLT approach has the benefit of using a language specifically designed for transforming XML documents. Also, because XSL itself is XML, the processing tools used for XML files (including validating parsers, editors, and even other XSLTs) can be applied to XSL documents.

On the other hand, XSLT is a completely new language to learn and is applicable only to transforming XML documents. When developers use languages with which they are familiar, they not only are more efficient but also tend to make fewer errors. Thus, if developers are already proficient in a general-purpose language such as Python, Perl, or Java, they can probably code the transformation faster and better if they use languages with which they are already familiar.

The point is not that XSL is bad or that other languages are better. The point is that you need to recognize what your options are and that each option has pros and cons that you must weigh to make an intelligent decision.

Verifying XML

In this section, we examine bulletproofing techniques that apply to XML. The techniques we discuss include detecting and preventing errors, performing custom verification with scripts or rules, and verifying data.

Detecting and preventing errors

If you use XML in your Web application, you must consider how to detect and prevent errors in XML. Error detection should be performed at several levels. In general, each XML document should

- Be well formed.
- Be valid.
- Comply with group standards.
- Comply with application-specific rules.

Note that the first two items test conformance to universal standards and the latter two test conformance to a standard that is more limited in scope. We will examine the first two in some detail and return to the latter two in our discussion of custom verification.

Checking for well-formedness and validity are, in some ways, straightforward: Any validating XML parser can perform these tests. However, in many cases the XML does not exist as a static document that resides in the source code repository. Instead, it is dynamically generated by the Web application itself. This adds an interesting wrinkle to the task of validating the XML. One solution is to incorporate validating code into the server so that the XML is validated when it is generated. This has the advantage of ensuring that an error will be detected immediately. Because this check happens on-the-fly, it lets you make provisions for any problems that do occur (for example, canceling pending transactions as appropriate).

The problem with this approach is that performance is critical in most Web applications, so validating XML every time it is generated is undesirable. If the code generating the XML is deterministic, validating each document that is generated is overkill. Instead, it is sufficient to perform offline testing on generated documents that represent sufficient coverage of the XML-generating code.

For an example of how you can check for well-formedness and validity, consider how we perform these checks on the new version of the Online Grocer application. This version of the application now generates two types of pages for each path in the application: one page in XHTML and one page in WML. We want to check that each XHTML page and each WML page are valid XML, and we decide to use scripts to perform this task.

In Chapter 14, we briefly explore what is required to exercise paths in a Python script. This approach can be extended to validate XML pages.

Here is the script we use to validate the Online Grocer's XML code. This script requests a sequence of URLs that are listed in a separate file. For each URL, it makes a connection and validates the contents of the page found at that URL. Finally, it summarizes the results.

ValidatePages.py

```
#!/bin/python
import urllib
import xml.sax

class ErrorReporter(xml.sax.handler.ErrorHandler):
   def error(self, exception):
       print 'Error in ' + url + ': ', exception
       raise exception
   def fatalError(self, exception):
       print 'Fatal error in ' + url + ': ', exception
       raise exception
   def warning(self, exception):
       print 'Warning in ' + url + ': ', exception

urls = open('urls.txt').readlines()
ran = 0
failed = 0
for url in urls:
    url = url.strip()
    print 'Validating ' + url
    page = urllib.urlopen(url)
    ran = ran + 1
    try:
        xml.sax.parse(page, xml.sax.handler.ContentHandler(), ErrorReporter())
    except (xml.sax.SAXException):
        failed = failed + 1
print failed, 'out of', ran, 'pages failed.'
```

If `urls.txt` contains the following lines,

```
http://soaptest.parasoft.com/GetEmployeeService.wsdl
http://www.w3.org/TR/xhtml1
http://www.foodmagic.com
http://soaptest.parasoft.com/GetPIService.wsdl
http://www.parasoft.com
```

running the script yields the following results:

```
> python ValidatePages.py
Validating http://soaptest.parasoft.com/GetEmployeeService.wsdl
Validating http://www.w3.org/TR/xhtml1
Validating http://www.foodmagic.com
Fatal error in http://www.foodmagic.com:  <unknown>:2:17: not well-formed
Validating http://soaptest.parasoft.com/GetPIService.wsdl
Validating http://www.parasoft.com
Fatal error in http://www.parasoft.com:  <unknown>:16:2: mismatched tag
2 out of 5 pages failed.
```

Here, two of the five pages fail because they contain HTML and our script expects XML. As you saw in Chapter 14, this approach becomes much more complex for applications that are primarily dynamic because available URLs change, depending on the context. Also, the use of `GET` or `POST`, cookies, user agents, and so on, must be taken into account. In Chapter 13, you saw how WebKing can be used to test paths for dynamic applications. WebKing includes an XML validator, so the same approach can be used to validate the XHTML and WML pages, as well as any other XML pages from our Web application. Simply run the XML validator on the Project or Path tree, or enable the XML validator in the user profile configurations used in the Site Workout feature.

Performing custom verification with scripts

Validating XML is helpful but not sufficient. Valid XML is guaranteed to conform to the DTD or schema, but often we like to impose additional conditions before deeming a particular document correct. For example, say that we have determined that a significant portion of our target customer base is using SuperBrand cell phones. SuperBrand cell phones have the unfortunate trait of not supporting the `multiple` attribute of the `select` element in WML. As a result, every `select` element in a WML card displayed on a SuperBrand cell phone allows only a single option selection, regardless of whether the `multiple` attribute is set to `true` or `false`. We certainly hope that SuperBrand gets its act together and fixes this. However, in the meantime, we have an existing customer base that will be very unhappy if it can't use our application.

We could address this issue by creating an internal rule for our development team that says not to generate any WML with `select` elements that have the `multiple` attribute set to `true`. However, we want to enforce this rule automatically so that we can save time and be absolutely certain that no violating code is passed on to our customers.

Our XML validator can check this rule only if we introduce a different DTD that is like the WML DTD but disallows `multiple="true"`. This is not only ugly but also ineffective: We can't deliver our WML to customers if it references a DTD that their phones are not prepared to deal with. We could develop another XSLT that removes the reference to our custom DTD and replaces it with the regular WML DTD. This works but is an ugly solution – it requires performing an extra XSL transformation and tweaking the WML DTD, which might reference other DTDs. If you decide to modify the DTD, you have to perform extra work and might inadvertently introduce incompatibility with the original DTD. A final drawback of this approach: In some scenarios (such as when the conformance requirement is one that is not expressible in a DTD), it will not work at all.

A better approach is to leave the DTD alone and perform additional checks through a separate mechanism that is not tied to validation. One way to do this is through scripting. The following Python script defines a function that tests a WML page to see whether it will work on SuperBrand cell phones:

SuperBrand.py:

```
#!/bin/python
import urllib
import xml.sax

class MultipleFinder(xml.sax.handler.ContentHandler):
   def __init__(self, url):
       self.url = url
   def startElement(self, name, attrs):
       if name=='select':
           if attrs.get('multiple') == 'true':
               raise xml.sax.SAXException(
                   '<select> must not have multiple="true" in '
                   + self.url)

def isOkWml(url):
    wml = urllib.urlopen(url)
    try:
        xml.sax.parse(wml, MultipleFinder(url))
    except xml.sax.SAXException, msg:
        print msg
        return 0
    return 1
```

In this example, we use a SAX parser instead of a DOM parser because we do not need to store a full representation of the parse tree.

Calling `isOkWml()` for a URL that points to a WML page with the offending attribute value will result in both a message printed and a return value of 0, which indicates that the URL is not okay. Here is the modified `ValidatePages.py` file that calls `isOkWml()` from `SuperBrand.py`:

ValidatePages.py

```
#!/bin/python
import urllib
import xml.sax
import SuperBrand

class ErrorReporter(xml.sax.handler.ErrorHandler):
   def error(self, exception):
       print 'Error in ' + url + ': ', exception
       raise exception
   def fatalError(self, exception):
       print 'Fatal error in ' + url + ': ', exception
       raise exception
   def warning(self, exception):
       print 'Warning in ' + url + ': ', exception

urls = open('urls.txt').readlines()
ran = 0
failed = 0
for url in urls:
    url = url.strip()
    print 'Validating ' + url
    page = urllib.urlopen(url)
    ran = ran + 1
    try:
        xml.sax.parse(page, xml.sax.handler.ContentHandler(),
           ErrorReporter())
        if not SuperBrand.isOkWml(url):
           failed = failed + 1
    except (xml.sax.SAXException):
        failed = failed + 1
print failed, 'out of', ran, 'pages failed.'
```

Of course, this has the same shortcomings as our original script in that it does not lend itself to very dynamic applications where the URLs we would like to test are in flux, nor does it take into account `GET` versus `POST`, cookies, or user agents. Also, the more of these checks we add, the larger and more complex our testing scripts become, until creating and maintaining the scripts themselves constitutes a significant endeavor.

Performing custom verification with rules

Another way to check whether our code follows the SuperBrand rule is to express the rule with WebKing's RuleWizard and enforce it with WebKing's CodeWizard. The first step in building this rule is to open the WML dictionary containing the elements we will use to construct the rule. Figure 17-3 shows what the WML dictionary looks like in WebKing.

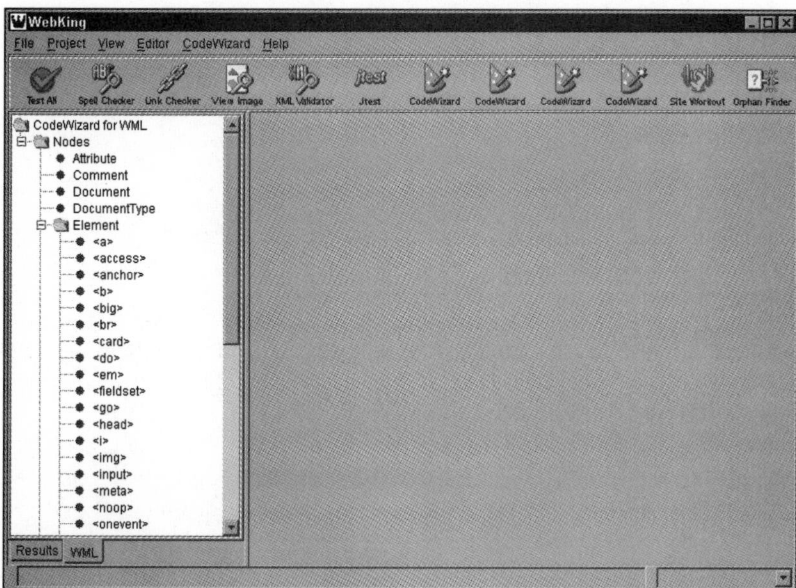

Figure 17-3: WebKing's WML dictionary.

Note that the nodes, or basic building blocks of the rule, are the basic building blocks of WML. Each element and attribute that is legal in WML is included in the dictionary because the dictionary is generated from the WML DTD.

We can now use this dictionary to express graphically a rule that detects WML that we know will not work with SuperBrand cell phones. This involves choosing a start node from the dictionary on the left (in this case, the `<select>` element) and modifying this node by choosing the option for `@multiple`, meaning the `multiple` attribute. (The @ character is used to designate an attribute in XML languages such as XPath and XSLT, as well as in RuleWizard.) We select `true` for the `multiple` attribute because we want to be notified when this attribute is `true`. Finally, we specify an output message. Figure 17-4 shows the complete rule and the output message.

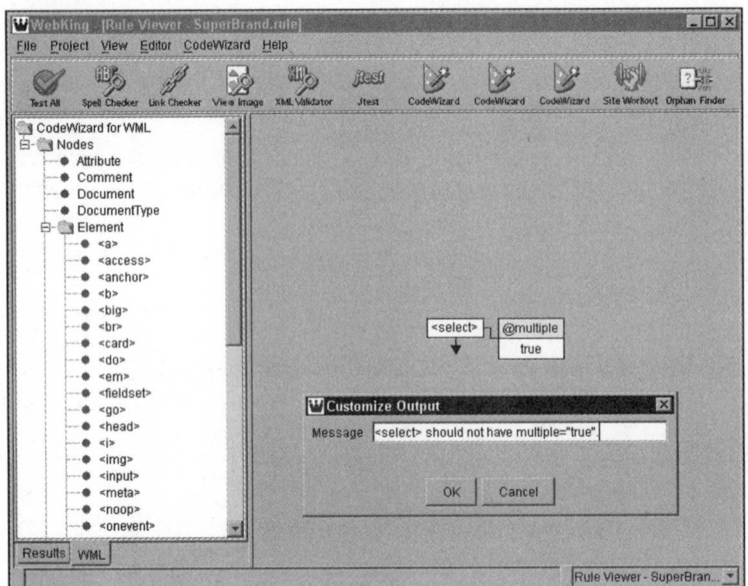

Figure 17-4: Our custom SuperBrand rule.

Next, we create a CodeWizard Enforcer that will represent this rule, and we then apply this CodeWizard Enforcer to this version of our Web application. Here is the sample output:

```
examples\chapter17\example.wml  18  <select> should not have multiple="true".
examples\chapter17\example.wml  26  <select> should not have multiple="true".
```

Because RuleWizard allows you to express patterns in terms of nodes in the dictionaries and because you can create dictionaries for any type of XML document, you can use RuleWizard to find patterns and enforce constraints on XML files and generated XML documents. This provides the higher-level checking that goes beyond simply validating the XML and enforces application-specific rules and team-specific coding standards. By automating the verification process at each level, you can increase your confidence that the Web application's usage of XML is consistently correct.

Looking beyond the code – Verifying data

Because XML provides a way to express structured data as well as code, it is helpful to think about bulletproofing XML as involving data verification. Data verification is a higher-level type of integrity check. Coding errors can be context-insensitive. For example, a memory overwrite is a coding error regardless of what the function is intended to do. The correctness of data, however, is inherently context-sensitive because data without a context is meaningless. It is important to recognize that verifying data necessarily requires application-specific checks. This means extra work compared to lower-level verification, but the payoff is that you ensure data integrity. The more data-driven your Web application is, the more essential data integrity becomes.

Verifying other XML languages

The principles and techniques presented in this chapter apply to any XML language. This section provides a brief sampling of several XML languages to explore what data and code verification can look like in various contexts. The intention is not to provide a comprehensive study but to give you a feel for how the principles of verifying data and code integrity can be applied to a variety of contexts.

SYNCHRONIZED MULTIMEDIA INTEGRATION LANGUAGE (SMIL)

SMIL (pronounced "smile") is an XML-based language designed for publishing multimedia presentations on the Web. A SMIL presentation is composed of elements of various media types, including streaming audio, streaming video, images, and text.

Some elements in SMIL contain a `repeatCount` attribute that indicates how many times that element should be repeated. A sample verification rule for SMIL requires that the `repeatCount` attribute must not be negative. Note that although negative values do not make sense, they are not explicitly prohibited. Figure 17-5 shows a RuleWizard rule that identifies any elements that have a negative value for the `repeatCount` attribute.

Figure 17-5: A rule requiring that the repeatCount attribute not be negative.

SCALABLE VECTOR GRAPHICS (SVG)

SVG is an XML-based language for describing 2D graphics. In addition to vector graphics, which consist of straight lines and curves, SVG supports images and text.

SVG also includes facilities for grouping, styling, and transforming objects. Animation can be achieved through dynamic manipulation of the DOM.

According to the SVG DTD, each `svg` element can contain 0 or one `title` element and 0 or one `desc` element. However, it is likely that many SVG authors will always want to have both a `title` and a `desc` element defined for a `svg` because the `title` enables the display program to show a ToolTip and the `desc` is useful for search engines. Thus, we can easily envision two similar rules:

Each `svg` element should have a `title`.

Each `svg` element should have a `desc`.

Figures 17-6 and 17-7 show the graphical representations of these rules in RuleWizard. The first rule, shown in Figure 17-6, can be understood as follows: "For each `svg` element, in the body of the element, collect all the direct children that have the tag name `title`. Count up the number of elements collected. If the count equals 0, the rule is violated."

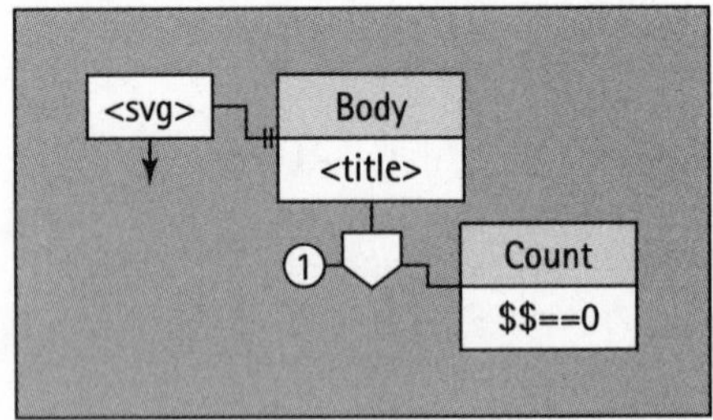

Figure 17-6: A rule requiring that every <svg> element have a <title> element.

The second rule, shown in Figure 17-7, works the same way but searches for `desc` instead of `title`.

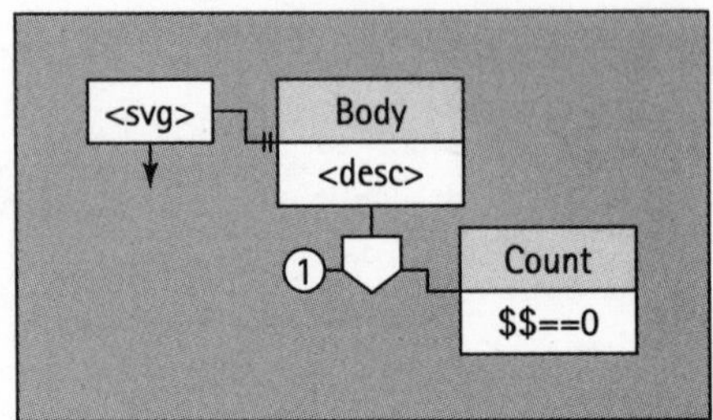

Figure 17-7: A rule requiring that every <svg> element have a <desc> element.

MATHEMATICAL MARKUP LANGUAGE (MATHML)

MathML is an XML-based language for describing mathematical notation and capturing both its structure and content. MathML is intended to provide a standard way for communicating mathematics on the Web.

The Decreasing Order Rule is an example of an application-specific rule for MathML. This rule states that polynomial expressions' terms should be listed in decreasing order. The first equation follows this rule; the second one does not:

$x^2 + 3x - 4 = 0$

$3x + x^2 - 4 = 0$

This rule is more complicated than previous ones because it requires interpreting text as numerical values and performing quantitative comparisons. However, it is still within the expressive capability of RuleWizard. Figure 17-8 shows the RuleWizard rule that expresses this guideline.

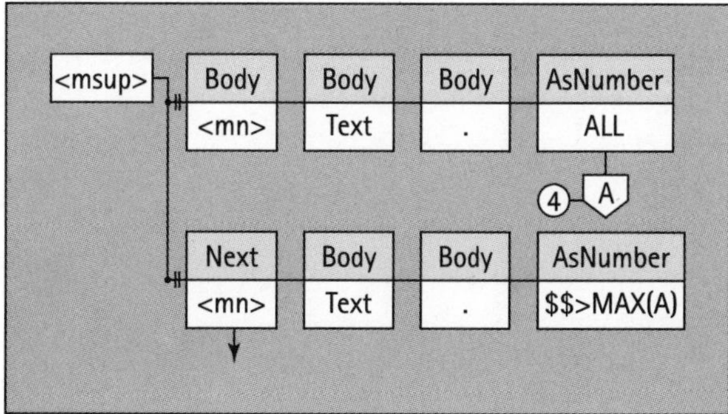

Figure 17-8: The Decreasing Order Rule.

The rule's `AsNumber` components convert the string to a number and the `$$ > MAX(A)` expression means ***this number is greater than the maximum number contained in collector A.***

Some rules require more sophisticated logic than simple conditional expressions. In these cases, rules can be augmented with scripting. WebKing supports user methods written in Java, Python, and JavaScript.

SIMPLE OBJECT ACCESS PROTOCOL (SOAP)

SOAP is an XML-based language used as a wire protocol for Web services. It includes facilities for Remote Procedure Calls (RPC). We take a closer look at SOAP in the next chapter.

Summary

XML, when used appropriately, is an effective technology for creating bulletproof Web applications. Leveraging XML requires weighing design tradeoffs to determine which technology is the best fit for the problem, as well as utilizing tools and techniques that verify correctness at each level of the implementation. All XML languages conform to the common XML syntax, so tools and techniques for code and data verification can usually be reused across multiple XML languages. Because XML skills apply to multiple languages, learning to use XML effectively is well worth the effort.

Chapter 18

Bulletproofing Web Services

IN THIS CHAPTER

- Understanding Web services
- Implementing your Web service
- Testing your Web service
- Testing SOAP services with SOAPtest
- Testing SOAP clients with SOAPtest

WEB SERVICE IS A TERM that has emerged to describe a software module deployed on the Web and intended for use as a component of one or more applications distributed across the Internet. This chapter introduces Web services and focuses on how to ensure that these services are robust.

Understanding Web Services

This section looks at the anatomy of a Web service. An obvious prerequisite for understanding how to develop robust Web services is a clear understanding of what a Web service entails!

A Web service inherently exists as part of a larger system. It is the servicing of these other components that gives Web services their name. Thus, a primary consideration in the design of a Web service is the protocols that will be used to communicate with other components of the system.

The first relevant protocol is the *transport layer*, which is typically HTTP or HTTPS. In fact, using HTTP as the transport layer is a defining characteristic of a Web service. Other transport protocols, such as Java's Remote Method Invocation (RMI), CORBA's Internet Inter-Orb Protocol (IIOP), or DCOM's Distributed Computing Environment Remote Procedure Call (DCE RPC) can enable distributed applications, but such applications are not considered Web services because they are not deployed on the Web.

The second important protocol is the *packaging layer*. This defines how content is wrapped up into messages that are sent over the transport layer. The emerging standard in this arena is *Simple Object Access Protocol (SOAP).* SOAP is implemented in XML and relies heavily on XML namespaces and XML schemas to define document types that describe messages. SOAP describes a simple request/response mechanism for Remote Procedure Calls (RPC), illustrated in Figure 18-1.

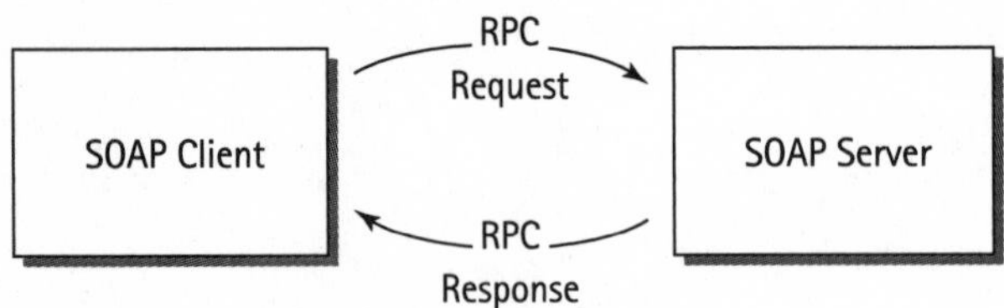

Figure 18-1: A SOAP Remote Procedure Call.

Another technology relevant to the current discussion is the *Web Services Description Language (WSDL).* This language, also implemented in XML, is used to describe the types of requests accepted by a particular Web service. It is used to communicate meta-information about the Web service and, as such, is not strictly necessary for invoking the Web service itself.

For example, consider a Web service that provides information about employees. It contains a method named `getEmployee()`, which takes a last name as an argument and returns information about all employees with that last name. Here is a WSDL for such a service:

GetEmployeeService.wsdl

```
<?xml version="1.0"?>
<definitions name="GetEmployeeService"
 targetNamespace="http://soaptest.parasoft.com/GetEmployeeService.wsdl"
 xmlns:tns="http://soaptest.parasoft.com/GetEmployeeService.wsdl"
 xmlns:xsd="http://www.w3.org/1999/XMLSchema"
 xmlns:soap="http://schemas.xmlsoap.org/wsdl/soap/"
 xmlns="http://schemas.xmlsoap.org/wsdl/">
 <message name="GetEmployeeServiceRequest">
  <part name="LastName" type="xsd:string"/>
 </message>
 <message name="GetEmployeeServiceResponse">
  <part name="return" type="xsd:string"/>
 </message>
 <portType name="GetEmployeePortType">
  <operation name="getEmployee">
   <input message="tns:GetEmployeeServiceRequest" name="GetEmployee"/>
   <output message="tns:GetEmployeeServiceResponse"
    name="GetEmployeeServiceResponse"/>
  </operation>
 </portType>
```

```
 <binding name="GetEmployeeBinding" type="tns:GetEmployeePortType">
  <soap:binding style="rpc" transport="http://schemas.xmlsoap.org/soap/http"/>
   <operation name="getEmployee">
   <soap:operation soapAction=""/>
   <input>
    <soap:body use="encoded" namespace="urn:EmployeeQuery"
     encodingStyle="http://schemas.xmlsoap.org/soap/encoding/"/>
   </input>
   <output>
    <soap:body use="encoded" namespace="urn:EmployeeQuery"
     encodingStyle="http://schemas.xmlsoap.org/soap/encoding/"/>
   </output>
  </operation>
 </binding>
 <service name="GetEmployeeService">
  <documentation>Get Personnel files</documentation>
   <port name="GetEmployeePort" binding="tns:GetEmployeeBinding">
    <soap:address
location="http://soaptest.parasoft.com/soap/servlet/rpcrouter"/>
   </port>
 </service>
</definitions>
```

This file is available on the CD, as are the scripts, rule-related files, and XML-related files referenced in this chapter.

The main point here is that WSDL provides a standard way to describe services in the form of parsable XML. Here is a sample request that conforms to the interface specified in the preceding WSDL.

```
POST /soap/servlet/rpcrouter HTTP/1.0
Host: soaptest.parasoft.com
Content-Type: text/xml; charset=utf-8
Content-Length: 466
SOAPAction: ""

<?xml version='1.0' encoding='UTF-8'?>
<SOAP-ENV:Envelope xmlns:SOAP-ENV="http://schemas.xmlsoap.org/soap/envelope/"
 xmlns:xsi="http://www.w3.org/1999/XMLSchema-instance"
 xmlns:xsd="http://www.w3.org/1999/XMLSchema">
 <SOAP-ENV:Body>
  <ns1:getEmployee xmlns:ns1="urn:EmployeeQuery"
```

```
    SOAP-ENV:encodingStyle="http://schemas.xmlsoap.org/soap/encoding/">
    <LastName xsi:type="xsd:string">Skywalker</LastName>
   </ns1:getEmployee>
  </SOAP-ENV:Body>
</SOAP-ENV:Envelope>
```

The first six lines are the HTTP header. The rest is the SOAP envelope of the RPC request, which requests information on all employees with the last name *Skywalker*. Here is a response:

```
HTTP/1.1 200 OK
Date: Mon, 15 Oct 2001 15:47:33 GMT
Server: Apache/1.3.14 (Unix)  (Red-Hat/Linux) mod_jk
Content-Length: 466
Set-Cookie2: JSESSIONID=lohllwlxml;Version=1;Discard;Path="/soap"
Set-Cookie: JSESSIONID=lohllwlxml;Path=/soap
Servlet-Engine: Tomcat Web Server/3.2.1 (JSP 1.1; Servlet 2.2; Java 1.3.0; Linux
2.2.5-15 i386; java.vendor=Sun Microsystems Inc.)
Connection: close
Content-Type: text/xml; charset=utf-8

<?xml version='1.0' encoding='UTF-8'?>
<SOAP-ENV:Envelope xmlns:SOAP-ENV="http://schemas.xmlsoap.org/soap/envelope/"
 xmlns:xsi="http://www.w3.org/1999/XMLSchema-instance"
 xmlns:xsd="http://www.w3.org/1999/XMLSchema">
 <SOAP-ENV:Body>
  <ns1:getEmployeeResponse xmlns:ns1="/soap/servlet/rpcrouter"
   SOAP-ENV:encodingStyle="http://schemas.xmlsoap.org/soap/encoding/">
   <return xsi:type="xsd:string">&lt;?xml version=&quot;1.0&quot;
    encoding=&quot;US-ASCII&quot;?&gt; &lt;EmployeeQuery&gt;
    &lt;Employee lastName=&quot;Skywalker&quot; firstInit=&quot;G&quot;
    middleInit =&quot;V&quot; employeeID = &quot;19435755334443375007228б&quot;
    age=&quot;29&quot; gender=&quot;Male&quot;
    college=&quot;YU&quot; major=&quot;Engineering&quot; degree=&quot;B.S.&quot;
    experience=&quot;7&quot; salary=&quot;85000&quot;/&gt;
    &lt;/EmployeeQuery&gt;</return>
  </ns1:getEmployeeResponse>
 </SOAP-ENV:Body>
</SOAP-ENV:Envelope>
```

Again, the first few lines are the HTTP header, and the rest is the SOAP envelope. In this case, the response contains an embedded XML file. Because the SOAP response envelope itself is in XML, the body of the response uses escape characters to refer to the angle brackets and double quotes.

SOAP specifications can be found in the XML Protocol section of the W3C: `www.w3.org/2000/xp/`. The WSDL recommendation can be found at `www.w3.org/TR/wsdl`.

SOAP has also been incorporated as the messaging protocol for ebXML, a set of specifications with a broader goal of enabling a modular business framework. For more information on ebXML, see `www.ebxml.org`.

Implementing Your Web Service

Although it's possible to write an entire Web service implementation from scratch, a better approach is to reuse common components to perform the common functions. In particular, you will most likely use a standard Web server such as Apache or Microsoft's IIS to transport your service over HTTP. Also, you will likely use a SOAP server to interface directly with the Web server, to provide a higher-level API for serializing data from the implementation language into SOAP primitives and to construct messages.

Your actual service can be implemented in any number of languages. In fact, one of the design goals of Web services in general and SOAP in particular is to abstract users of the Web service from the details of the particular implementation language chosen. The choice of the SOAP server, however, is largely influenced by – if not determined by – the choice of both the implementation language and the Web server. For example, developing a service in Java and using Apache Web server lends itself to using Apache SOAP as the SOAP server. Likewise, those implementing a service in Visual Basic and deploying on Microsoft's IIS should check out Microsoft's SOAP Toolkit. The details of deployment vary from server to server, but the basic stages of development and deployment are the same.

Testing Your Web Service

As soon as you begin implementing your service, begin testing it. It is important to test each Web service you develop as an independent module. If you test each Web service in isolation from the rest of your application, you can be confident that the system being developed is really a loosely coupled collection of robust services that are flexible enough that individual services can evolve without requiring changes in other services. Neglecting this testing can result in a large, brittle, monolithic application that happens to be distributed across the Internet (which makes it even more difficult to debug!).

For a service to be tested as an independent module, it needs a specification (either formal or informal) describing the assumptions that the service makes about the world, the operations it provides, and the intended state of the world following its operations. Thinking about each service as an independent entity with its own specification will help you determine how to test your services.

Using a testing client

To most effectively test your Web service in isolation, you use a client specifically designed for testing Web services. A designated testing client enables you to test your service throughout the development cycle, even if other portions of your Web application are not yet operational. The client must have the capability to invoke methods from the Web service via the supported protocols. In the case of testing a SOAP service over HTTP, this means that the client must be able to initiate an HTTP connection to the correct address, formulate a SOAP request message, send it over the HTTP connection, and receive the response. The response must then be analyzed for correctness, either by inspection or by running the response through some other processing that verifies conformance to a specification. This verification can be as simple as performing a text comparison with the expected response or as complex as extracting specific information from an XML document and performing application-specific checks.

The ease of writing this type of client depends partially on the technologies chosen to implement the client. You obviously do not want to implement the HTTP protocol and write an XML parser from scratch just to create a testing client! A better approach is to use a scripting language such as Python. Scripting languages have traditionally been popular for testing purposes because they are quick to develop in, they often provide high-level functionality, and some of the scalability shortcomings of scripting languages are less critical for simple testing applications than for full-scale application development. The following section explores this approach in some detail.

Because the testing client is different from the production client, it can reveal hidden assumptions and interoperability issues that might otherwise arise much later. Unveiling these assumptions early allows them to be addressed early rather than be propagated throughout the application.

Creating a Python testing client

Writing a Python testing client for a specific SOAP service first requires the general capability to invoke SOAP services from Python code. As of this writing, this capability is not built in to Python itself, although there is discussion of this changing in the near future. However, Python modules with this functionality are available for download. This example uses SOAPpy, an open-source development project available for download at `sourceforge.net/projects/pywebsvcs`. The following code illustrates that invoking a SOAP service through this module is quite simple:

employee.py

```
#!/usr/bin/python
import sys
import SOAP

server = SOAP.SOAPProxy(
        "http://soaptest.parasoft.com/soap/servlet/rpcrouter",
        namespace='urn:EmployeeQuery')
print server.getEmployee(LastName='Skywalker')
```

This script invokes the employee Web service described earlier. The service allows queries by last name and returns the results in the form of an XML document. Running the preceding script by typing **python employee.py** produces the following output:

```
<?xml version="1.0" encoding="US-ASCII"?>
<EmployeeQuery>
<Employee lastName="Skywalker" firstInit="W" middleInit ="O"
  age="72" gender="Male"
  college="QU" major="Physics" degree="Ph.D."
  experience="13" salary="118831"/>
 <Employee lastName="Skywalker" firstInit="P" middleInit ="V"
  age="36" gender="Female"
  college="VU" major="Engineering" degree="B.S."
  experience="10" salary="61023"/>
 <Employee lastName="Skywalker" firstInit="K" middleInit ="R"
  age="25" gender="Female"
  college="HU" major="Computer Science" degree="B.S."
  experience="6" salary="41568"/>
</EmployeeQuery>
```

This approach works very well for running a simple test. Of course, this yields only a single result for a single input parameter. The script can be expanded to support multiple inputs and multiple outputs as follows:

employee2.py

```
#!/usr/bin/python
import sys
import SOAP
import os

server = SOAP.SOAPProxy(
        "http://soaptest.parasoft.com/soap/servlet/rpcrouter",
        namespace='urn:EmployeeQuery')
lastNames = [ 'Ackbar', 'Fett', 'Kenobi', 'Skywalker', 'Solo', 'Palpatine' ]
```

```
for name in lastNames:
   result = open('CurrentResults/' + name + '.xml', 'w')
   result.write(server.getEmployee(LastName=name))
```

Because multiple outputs are generated, the preceding script writes each output to a different file so that the outputs don't run together. The filename is chosen based on the last name used for the query. Each file is created in a directory named `CurrentResults`, which contains the files `Ackbar.xml`, `Fett.xml`, `Kenobi.xml`, `Palpatine.xml`, `Skywalker.xml`, and `Solo.xml` after the script has been run. These files can then be examined for correctness. However, we are starting to get enough results that examining them by hand is becoming tedious and error-prone.

VERIFYING THE RESPONSES

To work more efficiently, we would like to be able to easily run a large number of tests and receive a summary that reports which tests succeeded and which failed. In addition, we would like to be able to see details about the tests that failed. To do this, we need to formalize our definition of success and failure in the context of the Web service. Here are sample scenarios that would qualify for an intuitive notion of failure:

- The attempt to open a socket to the URL of the SOAP service fails. This indicates a network problem or an incorrect URL or IP address.
- The SOAP service returns a fault, such as `<Fault SOAP-ENV:Server: service 'urn:EmployeeQuery' unknown>`. This indicates an error caused by the server or by the client, depending on the type of fault.
- The SOAP service responds and does not return a fault, but the responding message is not readable by the client, because of an interoperability issue. For example, either the server or the client (or both!) might not resolve XML namespaces in accordance to the standard.
- A response is received but not in the expected format. For example, the response is in an incorrect XML format or some other arbitrary text format. This type of error can be detected by validating XML via a DTD or XML schema.
- A response is received in the format expected, but the data contained is incorrect – for example, when we request records for *Fett* but receive records for *Kenobi.*

Note that the symptoms of the first three problems are independent of any particular SOAP service because they fail at the levels of the HTTP protocol and the SOAP protocol, which are consistent across SOAP services. The fourth and fifth problems can also arise in any SOAP service, but the details and, therefore, the detection of them are necessarily application-specific. For example, a different SOAP service might accept a ticker symbol and return a stock quote. In this scenario, an expected response (SOAP envelope omitted for clarity) might be

```
16.87
```

and the actual response might be

```
AMZN:  16.87
```

or perhaps

```
<Quote symbol="AMZN" value="16.87"/>
```

This is an example of receiving a response in an unexpected format. The details of checking for this type of error depend on the specific service because different services can have different response types. Likewise, the service might return an incorrect quote, but any code checking the validity of the quote will necessarily be different from code detecting that Kenobi records are incorrectly returned from a Fett query in the employee service.

Each of the potential failure types exhibits different symptoms when encountered in our Python script. The first three problems typically throw Python exceptions and crash the script. A more robust version of the script will then have to catch these exceptions, record them as test failures, and continue testing. The format can be verified by parsing the response with a validating XML parser. Detecting incorrect results in the correct format is the most application-specific test. It generally requires writing code that parses the XML and tests for constraints. In the case of the incorrect last name from the employee service, the code has to check that the `lastName` attribute of each `Employee` element matches the last name specified for that particular query. Note that another approach for detecting this particular error would be to apply an XSLT that returns the elements that don't fit the specified query. For example, the following XSL outputs `Different last names!` when applied to an XML document containing employees with more than one unique last name:

```
<?xml version="1.0"?>
<stylesheet version="1.0" xmlns="http://www.w3.org/1999/XSL/Transform">
<output method="text"/>
<template match="/EmployeeQuery">
 <variable name="uniqueLastNames"
  select="Employee[not(@lastName=following::Employee/@lastName)]"/>
  <if test="count($uniqueLastNames)>1">
   <message>Different last names!</message>
  </if>
</template>
</stylesheet>
```

Applying this XSL transformation to SOAP RPC responses from the `getEmployee()` service will detect any responses that contain more than one unique last name.

PUTTING IT ALL TOGETHER

The following Python script flags these errors and moves the list of employees to a separate file:

employee3.py

```
#!/usr/bin/python
import sys
import SOAP
import os
import socket
import xml.parsers.expat

def startElement(elementName, attrs):
    if elementName == 'Employee':
        last = attrs['lastName']
        if last != name and not last in badLastNames:
           badLastNames.append(last)

server = SOAP.SOAPProxy(
       "http://soaptest.parasoft.com/soap/servlet/rpcrouter",
        namespace='urn:EmployeeQuery')
lastNames = open('lastNames.txt').readlines()
ran = 0
failed = 0
for name in lastNames:
   name = name.strip()
   try:
       print 'Processing ' + name
       ran += 1
       result = open('CurrentResults/' + name + '.xml', 'w+')
       result.write(server.getEmployee(LastName=name))
       parser = xml.parsers.expat.ParserCreate()
       parser.StartElementHandler = startElement
       result.flush()
       result.seek(0)
       badLastNames = []
       parser.Parse(result.read())
       if len(badLastNames) > 0:
          failed += 1
          for bad in badLastNames:
             print 'Incorrect last name: '+bad+' (expected '+name+').'
```

```
    except:
        failed += 1
        print name + ' failed: ', sys.exc_info()[1]
print "Summary: ", failed, " of ", ran, " tests failed."
percent = 100*(ran-failed)/ran
print "Success rate is " + str(percent).strip() + "%."
```

Running the script yields this output:

```
> python testEmployees.py
Processing Ackbar
Processing Fett
Incorrect last name: Chewbacca (expected Fett).
Processing Kenobi
Processing Skywalker
Processing Solo
Processing Palpatine
Summary:  1  of  6  tests failed.
Success rate is 83%.
```

The functionality of our test script has increased significantly. However, what started out as a couple lines has already grown enough that those unfamiliar with Python might feel squeamish. It is clear that as we continue to add functionality to our module testing, our script will continue to grow in size and complexity. If we anticipate that the testing solution will become large, we might consider switching to a nonscripting language, which tends to scale better. However, this will in some ways exacerbate the problem, because the code size will at least double if the preceding code is implemented in either C++ or Java. Either language would also require third-party modules for both the SOAP client protocol and the XML parsing. If you choose this option, you will soon find that significant development efforts are spent creating testing tools rather than focusing on developing the Web service.

Testing SOAP Services with SOAPtest

Another way to perform these tests is to use SOAPtest, a testing tool for Web services. SOAPtest automates the testing of Web services that use SOAP as a wire protocol and HTTP or HTTPS as a transport protocol. It provides an easy interface for exercising Web services, performing black box testing, and testing SOAP clients. In addition, it can be used to confirm the responses to SOAP RPC calls with features such as fault detection, textual comparisons, XML validation by DTDs or XML schemas and RuleWizard, which provides a way to find complex patterns in XML. Responses requiring application-specific verification such as business logic validation are supported through scripting. SOAPtest also performs regression testing of

Web services, including the automatic creation of regression test controls from SOAP RPC responses. It includes a built-in XSLT processor, XML parser, and editor.

SOAPtest is available on the CD.

The first step in testing your Web service with SOAPtest is to create a test suite. The test suite defines all the tests you intend to perform on your service. The SOAPtest GUI includes a Test menu containing the option Create Test Suite. Selecting this option causes a tree-view graphical representation of the new test suite to appear on the left side of the GUI. Right-clicking the test suite node provides a menu for adding tests to the test suite. Each test has an associated tool and an associated input. Available tools include SOAP RPC, XSLT, Validate XML, RuleEnforcer, and so on. Method tools can also be used script your own actions.

A SOAP RPC test involves sending a request, receiving the response, and verifying the response by applying other tools. Creating a SOAP RPC test requires selecting the SOAP RPC tool and specifying the call information. SOAPtest includes automatic serializers, enabling you simply to complete values in a GUI, as shown in Figure 18-2. Specify the URL to a WSDL to enable SOAPtest to extract information such as the RPC Router, the methods contained in the service, and the target URIs and signatures of each method. Next, specify the parameter values. Repeat this process for as many test cases as you want. Then right-click the test suite node, and select Run to run the tests. This prompts SOAPtest to run the tests, automatically check for the first three types of errors on the list from the "Verifying the Responses" section of this chapter, and report a summary of the test results.

Testing for the last two types of errors requires only minor modifications to the test suite. To automatically create a regression test control based on existing outputs, right-click the node representing a single test or the node representing the entire test suite, and choose Create Regression Control from the shortcut menu. SOAPtest then adds a Diff tool to all selected tests. Each time this tool is used, it compares the results of the control test to the current test run.

As you saw in Chapter 17, searching for patterns to detect problems in XML is often useful. Any SOAP service that returns XML data, such as the employee service, can use the same techniques to find application-specific errors. Also, because the SOAP response itself is expressed in XML, this technique is applicable to any SOAP message, even if the value of the response is not in XML. In SOAPtest, as in WebKing, RuleWizard helps you find patterns by providing you with a way to express complex patterns graphically in the form of rules. After such rules are created, CodeWizard Enforcers can be added to tests. Each CodeWizard Enforcer detects the patterns specified by one or more rules.

Rules can be used to express a pattern that should never appear in the output (and identify files containing that unwanted pattern). For example, in the case of the `getEmployee()` service, the number of distinct last names should never be more than one. This rule can be expressed in RuleWizard, as shown in Figure 18-3.

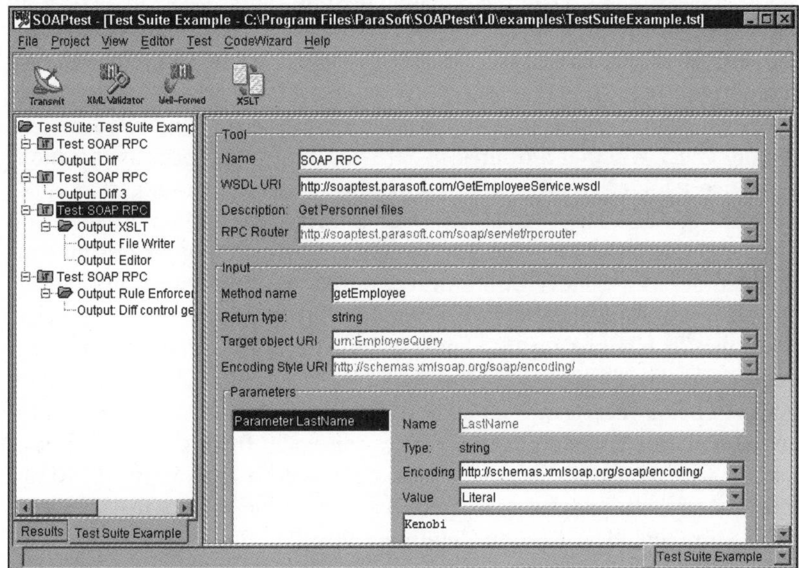

Figure 18-2: Testing a SOAP RPC in SOAPtest.

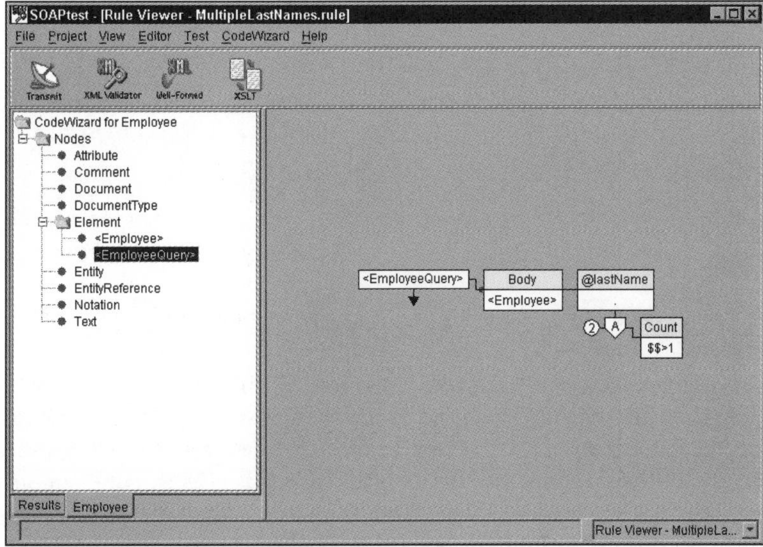

Figure 18-3: Using RuleWizard to write the MultipleLastNames rule.

This rule says to find `EmployeeQuery` elements containing a child `Employee` element that has a `lastName` attribute. It collects all the unique `lastName` attribute values into the collector A and, if the count is greater than 1, reports an error message. For example, if the rule is run on a document containing three employees, all with the last name *Skywalker*, it does not report an error because there is only one unique last name. If two are named *Skywalker* and one is named *Vader*, however, it does report an error.

A rule can also express a pattern that you want to ensure remains in your code. To automatically check whether a desired pattern continues to appear as the application and service evolve, create a rule expressing that pattern, add that rule's CodeWizard Enforcer to a test, and then add a Diff tool to that CodeWizard Enforcer. The same effect can be achieved automatically by adding regression controls to any test that has a CodeWizard Enforcer output. Chaining tools in this way enables you to develop sophisticated tests without writing scripts.

Having said that, sometimes writing code is still required for performing verification. For example, you cannot express a RuleWizard rule that checks whether a given output matches a record in a database. For these types of very application-specific checks, you can plug in custom verification code. In this particular case, you can specify a method that queries a database to verify the output. SOAPtest then invokes this method, passing the object it receives from the SOAP RPC call. The method's return value is used to determine whether the test has passed or failed. Having built-in tools for the common cases and the ability to plug in code makes the simple tasks easy while keeping the complex tasks possible. Incorporating usage of such tools into the development process is an important part of developing reliable services.

Load testing is also an important step for ensuring robust Web services. At the time of this writing, the version of SOAPtest supporting load testing is not yet released. For the latest version of SOAPtest, visit `www.parasoft.com`.

Testing SOAP Clients with SOAPtest

In addition to working as a client to test Web services, SOAPtest can be used as a server to test clients. When SOAPtest is used in this way, it serves as a platform on which Web services are deployed. This is helpful for a couple reasons. First, testing the client on the production service can have undesirable side effects. For example, if the service is provided by a financial institution and the functionality includes account transfers, it is certainly not recommended to test and debug clients by making transfers on real accounts! One solution is to have a development service and a production service and to test and debug the clients with the development service. This is a nice option when it is available, but when the service is provided by a third party, the production service is often the only one available. In that case, you need to deploy a service to test your client. A second reason for deploying a service in SOAPtest is that the same verification tools used to test RPC responses can be used to verify RPC requests.

As an example, consider the manipulation of items in the shopping cart in our Online Grocer application. Normally, the shopping cart would be manipulated via the Web interface. However, manipulating the application programmatically might also be desirable. For instance, say that our Online Grocer forges a partnership with another online service and that other service wants to purchase items for their customers. This is a business opportunity for the Online Grocer to gain some extra purchases from its partner's customers. It is also a business opportunity for the partner if the Online Grocer provides a commission for each purchase that comes through this means. However, this type of tight integration requires that the partner be able to place orders programmatically. Services required could include

- `addItemToCart()`: Adds a specified item to a specified cart
- `disposeCart()`: Deletes a specified cart
- `getCartItems()`: Returns the items in a specified cart
- `getCartTotal()`: Returns the total cost for a specified cart
- `getCartsByUserId()`: Returns all carts for a specified user
- `getNewCart()`: Creates a new cart for a specified user
- `purchaseCart()`: Purchases a specified cart

Deploying these services in SOAPtest is simple. First, we choose View→Show Web Services. A Web Services tab appears in the left window of the GUI. We select the Web Services root node within the Web Services tab and set the port number to the port on which we want to publish these services. Now, we can add services and define methods for SOAP RPC calls.

For example, to add the `getCartTotal()` service, we right-click the main Web Services node and select Add Output→Web Service. A node labeled `undefined method` is added to the Web Services tree. After we select the new service by clicking it, a method parameters panel appears in the right frame of the SOAPtest GUI. Here we can determine how SOAPtest unmarshalls parameters and marshalls return values. If we select Automatically, SOAPtest will unmarshall parameters and marshall return values for us. In this case, the function signature should exactly match the RPC method that will be requested. If we select Manually, we ourselves can unmarshall the parameters and marshall the return values. We choose the automatic marshalling option here for simplicity.

Marshalling refers to the process of converting values from a programming language representation to XML. *Unmarshalling* describes the reverse process.

Methods in SOAPtest may be implemented in Java, Python, or JavaScript. Here is a simple implementation of the `getCartTotal()` method in Python:

```
def getCartTotal(cart_id):
    return 12345
```

The input parameter `cart_id` is ignored, and the constant total of $123.45 is hardcoded. (We are returning an integer for the amount in cents to avoid any potential rounding errors.) Despite its simplicity, this two-line function provides the beginning of client verification.

Next, we start the service by right-clicking the root node and selecting Start Server. Then we invoke the client and confirm that it sends the request and receives the response. We could add more checks by running tools on the requests.

To view the incoming requests in our browser, we right-click the service node and select Add Output→Server Request→Existing Output→Browser.

If you choose a browser as an output, you will see the SOAP envelope each time the client sends a request. To search for patterns in these requests, add a new CodeWizard Enforcer tool. In addition to performing checks, this provides an easy means for debugging any problems in the client.

To perform more sophisticated tests on this client, we need a more sophisticated implementation of the service. If we wanted to, we could implement the full service in SOAPtest. The following example fleshes out `getCartTotal()` by querying a database that contains the actual cart data:

```
from java.sql import *
from oracle.jdbc.driver import *

def getCartTotal(cart_id):
  sql = "select SUM(item_cost) from cart_items where cart_id='"
  sql += str(cart_id) + "'"
  rs = executeQuery(sql)
  if rs.next():
    return rs.getInt(1)
  return -1;
```

```
def executeQuery(query):
  return getConnection().createStatement().executeQuery(query)

def getConnection():
  DriverManager.registerDriver(OracleDriver())
  url = 'jdbc:oracle:thin:@jester.parasoft.com:1521:fruits'
  return DriverManager.getConnection(url, 'demo', 'demo')
```

Another option is to use SOAPtest as a wrapper around an existing Web service. In this case, SOAPtest functions as a proxy that performs additional checks on the requests and responses to perform whatever verification is appropriate for your particular application.

Summary

The way that testing Web services relates to bulletproofing Web applications depends on the role that Web services play in your application. Your Web application may include SOAP servers, SOAP clients, or both. Regardless of the configuration, testing early and often is key to success. Of particular importance are a testing client, which enables module testing of the service, and a testing server, which enables module testing of the client. In this chapter, we explain how automated tools in general – and SOAPtest in particular – can facilitate module testing by providing a flexible framework that applies both standard and customizable verifications to SOAP RPC requests and responses without requiring the development of a comprehensive testing client. Applying these tools and techniques is an important part of creating a Web service that is reliable and robust.

Chapter 19

Bulletproofing Components

IN THIS CHAPTER

- ◆ Creating bulletproof interfaces
- ◆ Implementing bulletproof components
- ◆ Applying unit testing to components
- ◆ Performing client testing
- ◆ Applying system testing to components

AS EXPLAINED IN CHAPTER 15, a *module* is a group of units (for example, classes in Java) that can be built in one language or multiple languages. A module can be a group of classes that manages a shopping cart, manages customer relations, updates inventory, and so on. A *component* is a specific type of module. In other words, all components are modules, but not all modules are components. In this chapter, we restrict ourselves to components that run on a specialized application server (such as WebLogic from BEA, WebSphere from IBM, and so on). Components like these allow your Web application to take advantage of features provided by the server, including object persistence and scalability. Such components have two unique traits that distinguish them from other modules.

First, to interact with the application server, each component has an interface describing how to initialize it, what preconditions that application must meet before it runs, and so forth. The application using the component can interact with the components only through this interface. Therefore, it is critical that the component has a clear, complete interface and that the component behaves in the way the interface suggests.

Second, because the component is so closely tied to the application server and because the application server typically assumes some of the functions normally left to the program, the component must follow certain restrictions. These restrictions depend on the technology being used or the specific application server. In addition, after the component is running, it should be tested as it runs on the application server.

Enterprise JavaBeans (EJB) are one specific technology for building distributed components. The EJB architecture is a server-side technology (specified by Sun Microsystems) that allows you to write components in Java. These components can be deployed on any compatible EJB server. Often, these components are used to implement the business logic of a Web application. EJB components are also referred to as *enterprise beans.* An EJB server provides scalability, transaction handling, and multi-user security. You can use EJBs to simplify handling the complex issues inherent in distributed applications. Because the core functionality is handled by the EJB server, you are free to concentrate on the business logic you are trying to implement.

This chapter covers strategies for overcoming the challenges associated with EJB development and use. Similar notions to those introduced in this chapter also apply to distributed components implemented using other technologies. To keep the discussion generic, we frequently refer to *components* instead of the more specific terms *EJBs* and *enterprise beans.*

The bulletproofing strategies you should use depend on your relationship to the component. If you are developing an original component, focus on strategies that help you create a functional, usable component. Basically, you want to do everything possible to ensure that the component is correct, that it will work in a variety of environments, and that its specifications and limitations are clear. In particular, you should

- Ensure that the component follows any necessary restrictions.
- Include specification and usage information in the component's public interface.
- Thoroughly test each component's functionality and construction at the unit level.
- Perform client testing of the component as it sits on the application server.

If you are using a component to add functionality to your Web application, focus on strategies related to the communication between the component and the application server. When you integrate a component into your Web application, you should read its specification and usage information (unless you wrote it), integrate it into your system, and perform system testing. If you are both developing and using components, you must perform the tasks appropriate to both roles.

When describing how we tested our sample components, we refer to the Design by Contract (DbC) technique introduced in Chapter 7. You might want to review that material to better understand how we tested our code.

Creating Bulletproof Interfaces

Because the interface is typically the Web application's only window into the functionality of a component, the interface should clearly describe and enforce the component's requirements and functionality. Such an interface decreases the chances that the application will use the component incorrectly and encounter problems. One way to ensure that the interface is used correctly is to document the public interfaces using a standardized format such as DbC. If you do this, your contracts can be used while your component is running on the application server, and any requirements can be strictly enforced.

Documenting the component's functionality with DbC not only makes the component easier to use but also easier to test. When code contains contracts, you can use development tools to automatically create test cases that verify each unit's functionality. In addition, when the component's contracts are processed in such a way that they are automatically checked at runtime, client and system tests become much more effective. As the component executes, it automatically notifies you whenever it is used incorrectly or fails to satisfy the expected conditions. This testing technique is discussed in more detail later in this chapter.

For an example of how DbC can be added to components, look at the simple `AccountEJB` sample class located on the CD. This class contains the business methods for the bean and all the methods that do the actual work. The class's contracts describe the expected arguments and the specification. For instance, the following contracts specify that the `id` argument cannot be `null` and that the initial balance when creating an account cannot be negative. The conditions have been implemented separately so that when you get a violation, you know exactly which check failed. The method declaration looks like this:

```
/** @pre id != null */
/** @pre balance >= 0 */
public String ejbCreate(String id, int balance)
    throws CreateException
```

The following contract for the `deposit()` method specifies that the `amount` argument cannot be negative and that `amount` must be added to the account balance:

```
/** @pre amount >= 0 */
/** @post getBalance() == $pre (int, getBalance()) + amount */
public void deposit(int amount)
```

The `getBalance()` method contains an `@post` contract in the following code specifying that the method will always return a nonnegative value. Therefore, the component client (your Web application) can always assume that this method returns a nonnegative value.

```
/** @post $result >= 0 */
public int getBalance () {
```

Implementing Bulletproof Components

After you have a well-defined interface, you can concentrate on producing a correct implementation. You must make sure that your EJB meets the requirements common to all EJBs, satisfies any contracts you have created, and is portable, fast, and secure.

As with any aspect of Web application development, it's wise to enforce coding standards designed to prevent problems unique to your specific solution, as well as the basic set of coding standards for the language you are using. Certain restrictions are recommended for EJB development. EJBs that do not adhere to these restrictions might work only on certain servers, or they might not work at all. If you want to ensure that your component will work wherever you want to run it, taking extra precautions during development is important.

The rest of this section lists sample coding standards for you to consider while developing EJBs. These standards are largely based on recommendations made in Sanjay Mahapatra's "Programming Restrictions on EJB" in *JavaWorld*, August 2000.

For a discussion of coding standard enforcement methods, see Chapter 8.

Fundamental EJB requirements

The first thing you do is to make sure that your code adheres to the requirements common to all EJBs. Some fundamental requirements based on the official Enterprise JavaBeans Developer's Guide are

- A bean class should be declared as `public`.
- A bean class cannot be declared as `abstract`.
- A bean class cannot be declared as `final`.
- A bean class must not define the `finalize()` method.
- Finder methods cannot be `final` or `static`, and they must be `public`.
- A finder method's `return` type must be the primary key or a collection of primary keys.

- A bean class should implement one or more `ejbCreate()` methods.
- `ejbCreate()` must be `public` and cannot be `static` or `final`.
- A `SessionBean`'s `ejbCreate()` method's `return` type must be `void`.
- An `EntityBean` class should implement one or more `ejbPostCreate()` methods.
- `ejbPostCreate()` must be `public`, and it cannot be `static` or `final`.
- An `ejbPostCreate()` method's `return` type must be `void`.

The Enterprise JavaBeans Developer's Guide is available at this site: `web2.java.sun.com/j2ee/j2sdkee/techdocs/guides/ejb/html/DevGuideTOC.html`.

Portability guidelines

Portability guidelines help guarantee that your bean does not depend on any specific server, giving you vendor independence. Some portability guidelines are

- Do not use AWT functionality for keyboard input/display output. This restriction exists because server-side business components are meant to provide business functionality that excludes user interfaces and keyboard I/O functionality.
- Do not use file access/`java.io` operations. EJB business components are meant to use resource managers such as JDBC (instead of file system APIs) to store and retrieve application data. Also, deployment tools provide the facility for storing environment-entry elements into the deployment descriptor, so that EJB components can perform environment-entry lookups in a standardized manner via the environment-naming context. Thus, the need to use file system–based property files is mostly eliminated.
- Do not listen to or accept socket connections or use a socket for multicast. EJB components are not meant to provide network socket server functionality. However, the architecture lets EJB components act as socket clients for RMI clients and thus communicate with code outside the container's managed environment.
- Do not start, stop, or manage threads in any way. This restriction eliminates the possibility of conflicts with the EJB container's responsibilities of managing locking, threading, and concurrency issues.

Optimization guidelines

Optimization guidelines help your beans cooperate with the server to optimize performance and scalability. Some optimization guidelines are

- Do not use `static`, non`final` fields. Declaring all `static` fields as `final` ensures consistent runtime semantics so that EJB containers have the flexibility to distribute instances across multiple JVMs.
- Do not use thread synchronization primitives to synchronize multiple-instance execution. By avoiding this feature, you allow the EJB container flexibility to distribute instances across multiple JVMs.
- Avoid accessing EJB entity beans from client or servlet code. It is better to wrap and access EJB entity beans in EJB session beans because this satisfies two performance concerns:
  - Reduce the number of remote method calls. When the client application accesses the entity bean directly, each getter method is a remote call. A wrapping session bean can access the entity bean locally and collect the data in a structure, which it returns by value.
  - Provide an outer transaction context for the EJB entity bean. An entity bean synchronizes its state with its underlying data store at the completion of each transaction. When the client application accesses the entity bean directly, each getter method becomes a complete transaction. A store and load follow each method. When the session bean wraps the entity bean to provide an outer transaction context, the entity bean synchronizes its state when the outer session bean reaches a transaction boundary.

Security guidelines

Security guidelines are recommendations that prevent your running bean from introducing security holes. Some security guidelines are

- Do not use the Reflection API to query classes that are not otherwise accessible to the EJB component because of Java's security rates. This restriction enforces Java platform security.
- Do not attempt to create or obtain a class loader, set or create a new security manager, stop the JVM, or change the input, output, or error streams. This restriction enforces security and maintains the EJB container's capability to manage the runtime environment.
- Do not set the socket factory used by the URL's `ServerSocket`, `Socket`, or stream handler. By avoiding this feature, you also enforce security and maintain the EJB container's capability to manage the runtime environment.

- Do not read or write a file descriptor directly. This restriction plugs potential security holes.
- Do not obtain security policy information for a particular code source. This restriction plugs potential security holes.
- Do not load native libraries. This restriction plugs potential security holes.
- Do not access packages and classes that the usual rules of Java make unavailable. This restriction plugs potential security holes.
- Do not access or modify security configuration objects (`Policy`, `Security`, `Provider`, `Signer`, and `Identity`). This restriction plugs potential security holes.
- Do not use the subclass and object substitution features of the Java Serialization protocol. This restriction plugs potential security holes.
- Do not pass the `this` reference as an argument or return the `this` reference as a result. This restriction plugs potential security holes.

Applying Unit Testing to Components

A component is really a collection of units and can therefore benefit greatly from unit testing. Testing both the interface and the implementation is critical. If the component does not perform according to specification, your Web application will be unable to perform correctly. Moreover, if the unit is not constructed strongly enough to handle a wide variety of possible inputs, it might not work as well in other environments as it works in your testing environment. Again, the result is a difficult or impossible-to-use component.

See Chapter 9 for a detailed discussion of unit testing.

Performing unit testing for EJB classes is more or less the same as performing unit testing for other classes. The only additional step you have to perform is defining extra stubs for method calls that require interactions with the application server.

Rather than repeat the unit testing information introduced in Chapter 9, we will show you an example of how to use Jtest to perform unit testing on an EJB class in a way that leverages the DbC contracts that we recommend you include in every component's public interface.

Using Jtest, you can automatically test your EJB classes in isolation – without defining extra stubs for method calls that require interactions with the application server.

Jtest can also be used to check whether EJBs follow the necessary restrictions.

For an example of how Jtest works with EJBs, take a look at how we use Jtest to test the `AccountEJB` class described earlier in this chapter.

We start by testing in completely automatic testing mode. To start the test, we just tell Jtest which class to test and click the Start button. Jtest then creates stubs for calls to the database, automatically generates the life cycle calls necessary for an entity bean (`setEntityContext()`, `ejbCreate()`, and `ejbPostCreate()`), and creates and executes 44 test cases, which achieve 96.5 percent coverage. The Test Cases window displayed in Figure 19-1 shows the distribution of test cases generated.

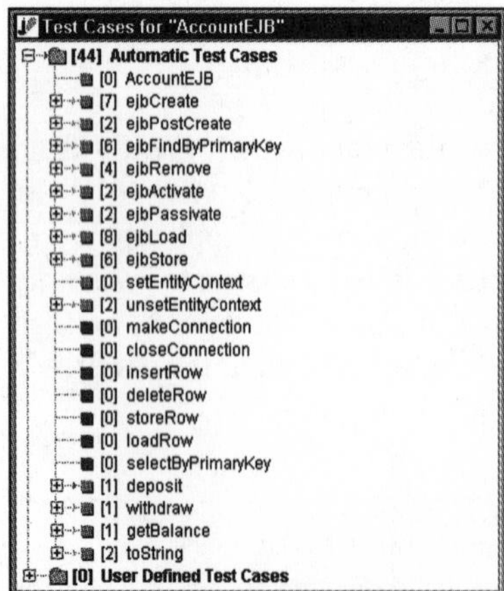

Figure 19-1: Test cases automatically created for Account EJB.

When Jtest created these test cases, it checked the `@post` contracts we included in the code. To see how this works, take a look at the `deposit()` method:

```
/** @pre amount >= 0 */
/** @post getBalance() == $pre (int, getBalance()) + amount */
public void deposit(int amount)
{
    _balance -= amount;  // BUG: should be "+="
}
```

This method contains a postcondition contract specifying that `amount` should be added to the account balance. This method also contains a simple error we added for demonstration purposes: It subtracts `amount` instead of adding it.

This method is so simple that the postcondition is probably inappropriate. You should have unit tests that verify that the function is performing correctly, and if you do, the postcondition doesn't really add anything in this case. This illustrates that there are many nuances in deciding where and how to apply contracts.

On the other hand, if you expect that this method will be overridden by a subclass later on, you might want a contract such as this one to force your children to behave correctly. Because contracts are inherited, you can impose requirements on classes that might later be added to the system.

Jtest created a test case to check this postcondition contract, automatically uncovered the problem, and reported the error message shown in Figure 19-2.

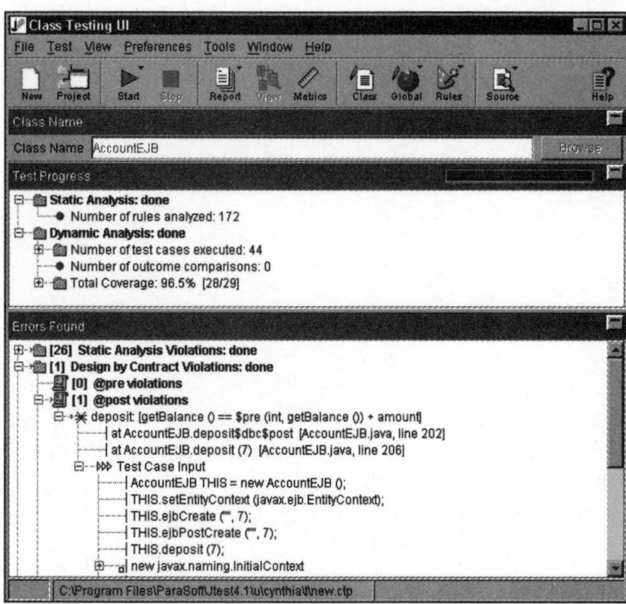

Figure 19-2: A functionality problem is detected.

As you can see in Figure 19-3, the automatically generated test case that exposed this error created an account with the balance 7 and deposited 7 into it.

Instead of 14, the resulting balance was incorrectly 0 (as shown in the `THIS.toString()` outcome).

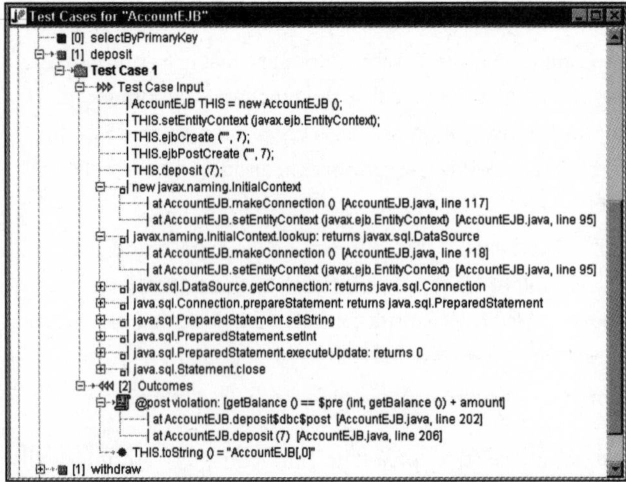

Figure 19-3: An automatically generated test case that exposed the functionality problem.

The DbC contract information we entered was also used to determine which test cases to avoid. When a class includes DbC contracts, Jtest generates only test cases that satisfy the `@pre` contracts. In the preceding example, Jtest did not generate test cases with a null `id` or a negative `balance` for `ejbCreate()` because this method contains the following contracts:

```
/** @pre id != null */
/** @pre balance >= 0 */
public String ejbCreate(String id, int balance)
    throws CreateException
```

The automatic test cases are saved by Jtest and can be reused at any time. As this class evolves, we can rerun these test cases each time we modify the class, by opening the correct test parameters file and clicking the Start button.

Now, assume that we had planned to run the following test cases:

Test Case 1

1. Create an account with `id John` and balance `200`.
2. Deposit `100` into the account.
3. Verify that the resulting balance is `300`.

Test Case 2

1. Create an account with id Mary and balance 100.
2. Attempt to withdraw 200 from the account.
3. Verify that an InsufficientFundsException is thrown.

The first test case we planned on running is very similar to one of the automatic test cases. If we wanted, we could skip this manual test case and just use the automatic one in its place. For now, we will include it as a contrast to the automatic method. The first step to implementing our additional test cases is to create a Test Class, located on the CD as AccountEJBTest.java.

For a review of Test Classes, see Chapter 9.

Next, we need to create a concrete instance of the Account interface, which we call AccountImpl, and then define stubs for the method calls that would require interactions with the application server. In cases like this, the simplest way to write stubs is to return a pure stub object for the call to InitialContext.lookup(). We do this by calling the makeStubObject() method inherited from jtest. TestClass. Whenever a pure stub object is referenced, Jtest automatically develops stubs for any method calls to it. As a result, we only have to worry about creating a user-defined stub for that first stub call, and Jtest will automatically develop the additional stubs that are needed. For example, here's one of the stubs Jtest developed to run the first test case:

```
Auto-Stub: javax.sql.DataSource.getConnection: returns java.sql.Connection
    at AccountEJB.makeConnection ()  [AccountEJB.java, line 114]
    at AccountEJB.setEntityContext (null)  [AccountEJB.java, line 88]
    at AccountImpl.<init> ("John", 200)  [AccountEJBTest.java, line 69]
    at AccountEJBTest.testCase1 ()  [AccountEJBTest.java, line 14]
```

When we run the test, Jtest uses the DbC contracts as it checks these test cases. For example, the testCase1() method exposes the bug in the deposit() method, verifying that our manual test is detecting the same error as the corresponding automatic test:

```
AccountEJBTest.testCase1: @post: \
        [getBalance() == $pre (int, getBalance()) + amount]
    at AccountEJB.deposit$dbc$post  [AccountEJB.java, line 207]
    at AccountEJB.deposit (100)  [AccountEJB.java, line 212]
```

```
    at AccountImpl.deposit (100)  [AccountEJBTest.java, line 74]
    at AccountEJBTest.testCase1 ()  [AccountEJBTest.java, line 16]
```

The @pre contracts we added are also used: Jtest reports an error whenever we try to execute a test case with invalid input. For example, assume that we have Jtest run the following user-defined test case:

```
public static void testNegativeDeposit()
    throws Exception
{
    Account account = new AccountImpl("Bad", 300);

    account.deposit(-100);  // bad input
    int balance = account.getBalance();

    assert(balance == 200, "test case BadInput");
}
```

Jtest finds the following error:

```
AccountEJBTest.testNegativeDeposit: @pre: [amount >= 0]
    at AccountEJB.deposit$dbc$pre  [AccountEJB.java, line 206]
    at AccountEJB.deposit (-100)  [AccountEJB.java, line 210]
    at AccountImpl.deposit (-100) [AccountEJBTest.java, line 92]
    at AccountEJBTest.testNegativeDeposit ()[AccountEJBTest.java, line 43]
```

Because the bug here is in the calling code, the goal of this test case is to verify that our contracts are correctly implemented.

Performing Client Testing

Producing bulletproof EJBs involves a type of testing that is not relevant to non-component classes: client testing. The purpose of client testing is to test directly how the EJB behaves on the application server. Unit testing does not cover this because it tests the individual EJB units independently on your development machine. Like client testing, system testing (discussed later in this chapter) involves testing the EJB on the application server. However, it is difficult to call the EJB directly at the system level, and system testing depends greatly on the running environment for its execution.

Client testing entails directly invoking the EJB on the application server, sending direct RMI calls to the EJB as it runs on the application server, receiving the EJB's response, and checking whether the response is correct. This process can be performed manually or automatically. We will demonstrate how we performed it manually, so that you can see the basic steps involved.

To set up this type of testing, you must make sure that the application server is up and running and that the bean is loaded into the application server.

For our simple example, assume that we want to perform client testing on the sample `AccountEJB` we have been using throughout this chapter. First, we package it and deploy it on an application server. Next, we write the following client class to check the two test cases described earlier in this chapter:

```
public class ManualClientTesting
{
    public static void testCase1()
        throws Exception
    {
        Context context = new InitialContext();
        Object objref = context.lookup("MyAccount");

        AccountHome home = (AccountHome) PortableRemoteObject.narrow(
              objref, AccountHome.class);

        Account account = home.create("John", 200);
        account.deposit(100);
        int balance = account.getBalance();

        assert(balance == 300, "test case 1");
    }
    public static void testCase2()
        throws Exception
    {
        Context context = new InitialContext();
        Object objref = context.lookup("MyAccount");

        AccountHome home = (AccountHome) PortableRemoteObject.narrow(
              objref, AccountHome.class);

        Account account = home.create("Mary", 100);
        InsufficientFundsException exception = null;
```

```
        try {
            account.withdraw(200);
        } catch (InsufficientFundsException ex) {
            exception = ex;
        }
        assert(exception != null, "test case 2");
    }
    private static void assert(boolean success, String message)
    {
        System.out.println(message + ": " + (success ? "passed" : "FAILED"));
    }
    public static void main(String[] args)
        throws Exception
    {
        testCase1();
        testCase2();
    }
}
```

This class connects to the application server running the `Account` bean, creates the account object inside the server, applies the `deposit()` and `withdraw()` methods to it, and then checks that the result values are the expected ones. Notice how `testCase2()` is designed to verify that the component throws the correct exception when it is passed an invalid argument.

When we run this class, we receive the following output:

```
$ java AccountClient
test case 1: passed
test case 2: passed
```

You can automate some of the client-testing process with Jtest or other tools designed specifically for testing components. You can also automate parts of the client-testing process by adding DbC contracts to your code and then compiling your component's code in such a way that the contracts are automatically checked at runtime. If any of your test cases violate the conditions expressed in the code's contracts, errors are reported in the manner specified by your DbC implementation. The next section provides more information on using DbC for error-detection purposes.

Applying System Testing to Components

If you are using an application server, you should perform system testing as soon as you integrate the component into your system. This ensures that it is used correctly and that system interactions don't cause the component to have problems. Like most bulletproofing practices, this type of testing can be performed manually or automatically.

To perform system testing manually, you first compile every application source and then deploy the entire application to the application server. The client feeds the application inputs and returns outputs. `System.out.println()` statements can be used in the client to check return values from the bean. If the outputs from the client are not correct, a problem exists in either the bean or the client.

If the author of the component has used DbC contracts to document the component's public interface, as well as a tool (such as Jcontract) that has instrumented these contracts so that they can be checked at runtime, system testing can be very simple. You integrate the instrumented version of the component into your system and then run your system using your normal test suite. Your test suite should test all facets of the application – including its interactions with databases and other business logic components – to ensure that a wide range of possible interactions and uses are tested.

As the component's contracts are checked at runtime, you are alerted when any of the following problems occur:

- **The rest of the system uses the instrumented classes incorrectly.** For example, the contract says that a method requires positive inputs, but part of the system passed it negative inputs.
- **The instrumented classes' interactions with the rest of the system lead to functionality problems.** For example, a certain chain of reactions causes an assertion to fail or a method to return a value that violates its postcondition.

For an example of how this works, consider how we test `AccountEJB` at the system level. At this point, the `AccountEJB` class already contains DbC contracts and has been compiled with Jcontract's compiler. All we do is integrate the class into the system and run our test suite. As the system executes, we are automatically notified when the `AccountEJB` class is used incorrectly or does not function as expected. When running tests in this mode, it is best to configure Jcontract to report DbC violations by throwing exceptions specific to the type of contract that is violated. When contracts are violated, you can then zero in on the problem by using the stack trace information in the report of results.

For example, when the `deposit()` method is called with a negative `amount`, the `@pre` contract is violated, and the component throws the following `jcontract.PreException` at runtime:

```
jcontract.PreException: @pre: [amount >= 0]
    at AccountEJB.deposit$dbc$pre  [AccountEJB.java, line 206]
    at AccountEJB.deposit (-100)  [AccountEJB.java, line 210]
    at AccountImpl.deposit (-100)  [AccountEJBTest.java, line 92]
    at AccountEJBTest.testNegativeDeposit () [AccountEJBTest.java, line 43]
```

When an `@post` contract is violated, the component throws a `jcontract.PostException`. For example, when the `deposit()` method is called with a valid input, the `@pre` contract is not violated, but the `@post` contract generates the following exception:

```
jcontract.PostException: @post: \
        [getBalance() == $pre (int, getBalance()) + amount]
    at AccountEJB.deposit$dbc$post  [AccountEJB.java, line 207]
    at AccountEJB.deposit (1000)  [AccountEJB.java, line 212]
    at AccountImpl.deposit (1000)  [AccountEJBTest.java, line 74]
    at AccountEJBTest.testCase1 ()  [AccountEJBTest.java, line 16]
```

Summary

If you are creating components, make sure that each component you produce is clearly documented, works as you claim it does, and is robust enough to work well in the various environments where it might be used. If you are developing an application that uses distributed components, start performing frequent and thorough system testing as soon as you integrate it into your system. This helps you verify that the component works as advertised and that it functions smoothly within the context of your system. Problems inevitably surface when you integrate distributed components into a complex Web application. If you perform system testing on a staging area, you can catch many of these problems before your application goes live. More problems are also likely to surface when actual users start accessing your system in ways your test cases did not anticipate. You can control the damage of these problems by frequently checking whether problems are reported during the first few days the system is live and by making sure that you have adequate resources on hand to deal with any problems that might arise.

Chapter 20

Bulletproofing JSP

IN THIS CHAPTER

- Exploring server-side scripting
- Applying coding standards to embedded code
- Implementing the Online Grocer application using JSP

THIS CHAPTER COVERS WAYS to bulletproof JSP (JavaServer Pages) and related server-side scripting technologies. We start by taking a quick look at the basic technologies and discussing ways to apply coding standards to code that is part HTML and part something else (Java, VBScript, and so on). We finish by describing an implementation of the Online Grocer application using JSP and by discussing several bulletproofing issues related to this implementation. Although our examples focus on JSP, the pitfalls and practices we discuss apply to most server-side scripting languages.

Even if you aren't using these technologies, we recommend getting at least a rudimentary understanding of the ideas and techniques involved because they can give you ideas for issues involving your own particular development project. The field of server-side scripting is currently undergoing rapid changes and is something you might want to include in future projects.

Exploring Server-Side Scripting

Server-side scripting includes a wide variety of similar technologies that can be invoked by your Web server. When a request is made of the Web server, the selected technology finds the indicated resource (file), invokes any commands on the page, and returns the result. The common feature of the server-side scripting options discussed in this chapter is the capability to combine your script and your HTML into a single file. This differentiates these technologies from traditional CGI programs or servlets.

The general goal of server-side scripting technologies is to allow rapid development of dynamically generated pages. To do this, you simply create a page with an extension that matches the technology (`.asp`, `.jsp`, `.php`) and thus tells the server which scripting engine to invoke. Write your HTML as usual, and whenever you want to include dynamic elements, you can add the relevant code directly into your document. This flexibility and ease of use are key factors in the ongoing success of server-side scripting.

Another goal sought by many server-side scripting advocates is separation of the user interface (the HTML) from the content generation (the business logic). This frees designers to do what they do best (create interfaces) and enables developers to concentrate on what they do best (implement logic). One example of this separation is the creation of JSP tag libraries, which let you create custom tags to represent pieces of code. This helps to maintain a clean separation of presentation and implementation.

Because server-side scripting places your code and your HTML in the same file, it is very easy to intertwine your user interface with your application logic. In our experience, this makes your application harder to debug and modify over time.

To give you a better idea of what server-side scripting entails, we're going to give you a quick overview of three technologies – ASP, PHP, and JSP – before we cover coding standards and discuss our JSP implementation of the Online Grocer application. Note that the three solutions we discuss here do not cover all the server-side scripting possibilities, but they represent some of the most common ones.

Introducing ASP

ASP stands for *Active Server Pages*. This is the server-side scripting solution provided by Microsoft. It is available to any application using IIS, and there are also alternative ASP implementations for other servers. By default, ASP pages use VBScript (a version of Visual Basic) to script the dynamic pages, but you can also use other languages, including JavaScript, Python, Ruby, and PerlScript. You choose the language by including a line such as the following at the top of your ASP file:

```
<%@ LANGUAGE = Jscript %>
```

ASP scripting elements are embedded inside `<%` and `%>` tags, like this:

```
<p>The time is now: <%=Time()%></p>
```

When the page is processed by the Web server and sent to the client, the embedded scripts are evaluated, and only the resulting HTML is sent to the client. In this case, the special <%= notation means to take the result of the script and store it in the document. Therefore, the user will see the current time displayed on the page. Each time this page is requested, the code will be reevaluated so that the time displayed is always current.

Introducing PHP

PHP is shorthand for *PHP: Hypertext Preprocessor* (the acronym is recursive). PHP is an open-source server-side scripting solution originally created by Rasmus Lerdorf. Although PHP is used most commonly with the Apache server, it can run equally well on a number of other servers, including the most common ones. By default, PHP tags look like this:

```
<?php echo "Hello"; ?>
```

Like ASP, you can also configure PHP to accept tags (<% %>). The scripting language itself borrows syntax from C, Java, and Perl and mixes this borrowed syntax with PHP-specific features. PHP is especially popular in combination with databases – database connectivity is a strong point of the language.

You can find out more about PHP (and download free binaries) at php.net or zend.com.

Introducing JSP

JSP stands for *JavaServer Pages*. This is the scripting solution provided by Sun Microsystems. JSP supports Java and is built on top of Java servlets. Most Web servers can be made to support JSP with the addition of the appropriate configuration and a servlet engine. Commonly, JSP servers compile JSPs into equivalent servlets when they are first accessed, and then subsequent accesses are served by already compiled servlets.

Simple JSP tags look just like ASP tags (<% %>). Here's a sample JSP snippet:

```
<p>The time is now: <%= new java.util.Date() %></p>
```

JSP is particularly feature-rich and allows you to create custom tags (or use third-party tag libraries) to simplify your code. Unfortunately, we don't have enough space in this chapter to get into many of the interesting details.

An excellent book to get you started with JSP is *Professional JSP*, 2nd Edition. When you are ready for more information, we recommend *Advanced JavaServer Pages* by David Geary.

Turning your pages inside out

If you compare a typical CGI program or servlet to any of these server-scripting solutions, you will see that they're two sides of the same coin. For example, Table 20-1 illustrates the similarities between the `showLoginPage()` method of the `ShoppingServlet` class and `home.jsp`, a JSP implementation of the same functionality (this file is described in more detail later in this chapter).

In the Servlet column of this table, we have HTML embedded in Java; in the JSP column on the facing page, we have Java embedded in HTML. What's going on in both is basically the same. The nice thing about the JSP version is that anyone who understands HTML can easily change that aspect of the page without worrying about the implementation details.

Applying Coding Standards to Embedded Code

The family of technologies similar to JSP shares the common feature of embedding a programming language into HTML documents. (Some of these technologies are more flexible. For example, you can create JSP documents that combine Java with XML.) From a coding-standard point of view, this essentially creates a unique, new language to think about.

The most important coding standard we recommend for server-side scripting — regardless of the implementation — is to strive always to make the source look like HTML. By keeping the code simple and clean, you enable nonprogrammers to help develop that part of your application. This way, area specialists can concentrate on what they know best, rather than waste time worrying about messing up the code.

As a corollary, it should be clear that you want to minimize the amount of non-HTML code appearing on your pages. Not only does this additional code make the pages look less like HTML, but it also might indicate that you haven't adequately isolated your business logic from your presentation. JSP, in particular, makes this easy by allowing you to hide code in beans or behind custom tags.

Server Side Includes

Server Side Includes (also referred to as *SSI*) are a less powerful form of server-side scripting than the examples given earlier. Files using this technology often use the `.shtml` extension. Rather than defining new tags, SSI embeds server directives inside HTML comments; for example:

```
<!--#include virtual="/cgibin/example.pl" -->
```

The `<!-- -->` is the usual HTML comment marker. The particular directive tells the server to run the `/cgibin/example.pl` program and embed the results into the current document at the position where the comment occurs.

SSI also includes support for defining and using variables, executing shell commands, and conditionally including HTML fragments. If you are familiar with C or C++, you'll be right at home with the following syntax:

```
<!--#if expr="${InternetExplorer}" -->
Internet Explorer specific code goes here
<!--#else -->
Code for other platforms goes here
<!--#endif -->
```

A sample SSI coding standard could check that comments which contain # directives do not include any space between the `<!--` and #. If this guideline is not followed, the server will ignore the directives and treat them as regular HTML comments. Another coding standard could check that only `.shtml` files contain SSI directives. Following this guideline would prohibit you from including directives in `.html` files, where they generally would not be processed.

For SSI examples and information on configuring Apache to use SSI, visit the Apache SSI tutorial at `httpd.apache.org/docs/howto/ssi.html`.

One popular development tool for server-side scripting is ColdFusion. ColdFusion uses ColdFusion Markup Language (CFML) as the original source language. CFML looks much like HTML or XML, and integrates cleanly with those languages. You can often recognize sites using ColdFusion because their files use the `.cfm` extension. For more information about ColdFusion, visit `www.coldfusion.com`, or read *Programming ColdFusion* by Rob Brooks-Bilson *or Professional Cold Fusion 5.0* by Simon Horwith, et al.

TABLE 20-1 COMPARING SERVLETS AND JSP

Servlet

```
void showLoginPage(ShoppingContext context, boolean complain, String error)
  throws IOException
{
  PrintWriter out = context.getWriter();
```

```
  header(out, "Login");
```

```
  out.println("<FORM NAME=login ACTION=\""+SERVLET+"\" METHOD=post>");
  out.println("<TABLE BORDER=0 CELLPADDING=0 CELLSPACING=0>");
  out.println("<TR><TD ALIGN=CENTER VALIGN=MIDDLE " +
          "HEIGHT=164 WIDTH=207 BACKGROUND=\"/tomato.gif\">");
  out.println("<INPUT TYPE=TEXT NAME=USER VALUE=\"demo\" SIZE=8><BR>");
  out.println("<INPUT TYPE=PASSWORD NAME=PASSWORD SIZE=8><BR>");
  out.println("<INPUT TYPE=HIDDEN NAME=METHOD VALUE=login>");
  out.println("<INPUT TYPE=HIDDEN NAME=FRUITS VALUE=on>");
  out.println("<INPUT TYPE=HIDDEN NAME=RED VALUE=red>");
  out.println("<INPUT TYPE=HIDDEN NAME=YELLOW VALUE=yellow>");
  out.println("</TD></TR><TR><TD ALIGN=CENTER>");
  out.println("<INPUT TYPE=IMAGE SRC=\"/login.gif\" " +
          "BORDER=0 NAME=Login><BR>");
  out.println("</TD></TR></TABLE>");
  out.println("</FORM>");
```

```
  if (complain)
    out.println("<P><B>Please re-enter your " +
            "username and password.</B></P>");
  // Mark the page as improper, so we can detect site errors!
  if (error != null)
    out.println("<!-- Error: " + error +" -->");
```

```
  footer(out);
}
```

JSP
```<%@ page import="fruits.*" %>```   ```<jsp:useBean id="error" scope="session" class="fruits.ErrorBean"/>```

```
<jsp:include page="header.jsf" flush="true">
  <jsp:param name="title" value="Login" />
</jsp:include>
```

```
<FORM NAME=login ACTION=login.jsp METHOD=post>
<TABLE BORDER=0 CELLPADDING=0 CELLSPACING=0>
  <TR><TD ALIGN=CENTER VALIGN=MIDDLE
        HEIGHT=164 WIDTH=207 BACKGROUND="tomato.gif">
    <INPUT TYPE=TEXT NAME=USER VALUE=demo SIZE=8><BR>
    <INPUT TYPE=PASSWORD NAME=PASSWORD SIZE=8><BR>
    <INPUT TYPE=HIDDEN NAME=METHOD VALUE=login>
  </TD></TR>
  <TR><TD ALIGN=CENTER>
    <INPUT TYPE=IMAGE SRC="login.gif" BORDER=0 NAME=Login><BR>
  </TD></TR>
</TABLE>
</FORM>
```

```
<%
if (error.isError()) {
   String message = error.getMessage();
%>
<P><B><%= message %></B></P>
<%
   error.reset();
}
%>
```

```
<jsp:include page="footer.jsf" flush="true"/>
```

Applying language-specific coding guidelines to files that contain different types of code (for example, Java and HTML) is tricky. For instance, in our JSP examples, we have Java buried inside `<% %>` comments and HTML fragments with Java around them. If you are equipped to enforce Java and HTML coding standards, the odds are that your routines will fail if you apply them directly to your source `.jsp` file. It usually is not valid HTML and certainly is not a valid `.java` file. Only after the page has been evaluated is the document required to be properly formed HTML. For instance, some tags might be generated by the embedded language, so tags in the original JSP won't match up until the document has been evaluated. (Two examples of this are the JSP Online Grocer's `header.jsf` and `footer.jsf` files that move part of the HTML to separate implementation files. We cover this in more detail in the next section.) Even humans trying to enforce coding standards can have a difficult time following the pages – especially if the pages are not well written.

One solution is to try to separate the parts of your JSP file into their component pieces. If you can do this, you can run all your Java and HTML coding standards on the resulting files. Tomcat, for instance, creates `.java` files for each JSP page whenever they are first evaluated. When you force your JSP engine to evaluate a given `.jsp` file and create a servlet implementation of the `.jsp` file, you effectively remove the Java from the HTML (more accurately, you replace the Java-inside-HTML version with an HTML-inside-Java version). If you know where your JSP server stores these files, you can run your coding rules on the generated `.java` files that correspond to the original JSP files.

You might need to adjust your rules to account for the automatically generated code created by the server. There's no point in reporting violations in parts of the code that do not correspond directly to your JSP, because that's not part of the code you can control.

The HTML side is more straightforward. Although the original JSP (or ASP or related technologies) file is not valid HTML, the generated page definitely should be. After your coding standards are configured to run via an HTTP connection, you can easily grab instantiated versions of your pages and validate them as usual. All our earlier discussions about dynamic HTML apply here.

Another option is to create and enforce custom JSP coding standards. If your server-side scripting solution doesn't have a way to separate your language elements from your HTML, this might be the only way to check those elements automatically. A full discussion of how to do this is beyond the scope of this book and might require specialized coding. However, because JSP (and ASP, PHP, and so on) follow the same general syntax as HTML, you should be able to create custom rules that interact with your page at that level. Although the general HTML rules might not apply until after the page is evaluated, this might be the best method if you want rules that look at the original code. Many JSP developers are also leaning towards making the JSP valid as XML; in this case, you could apply any XML tools you have.

For a simple example, we will show you how we use WebKing's HTML RuleWizard to implement a guideline saying that all our included JSP files should use the `.jsf` extension. The JavaServer Pages specification recommends not using `.jsp` for include files to avoid ambiguity between full JSP files and fragments, so this is a case of taking a general principle and making it more specific for our purposes. The tags we want to identify look like this but reference pages with names not ending in `.jsf`:

```
<jsp:include page="footer.jsf" flush="true"/>
```

To create the rule, we enter the preceding text into RuleWizard's Automatic Rule Creation dialog and tweak the resulting rule to produce the final results, shown in Figure 20-1. In terms of the WebKing HTML dictionary, `jsp:include` is an `Unknown` tag. Our rule has to scan for all `Unknown` tags, choose those that match `jsp:include`, find the `page` attribute, and check whether that value ends with `.jsf`. If the `jsp:include`'s `page` attribute does not end with `.jsf`, the rule should report a violation.

The `.jsf` extension rule is available on the CD as `jsf.rule`.

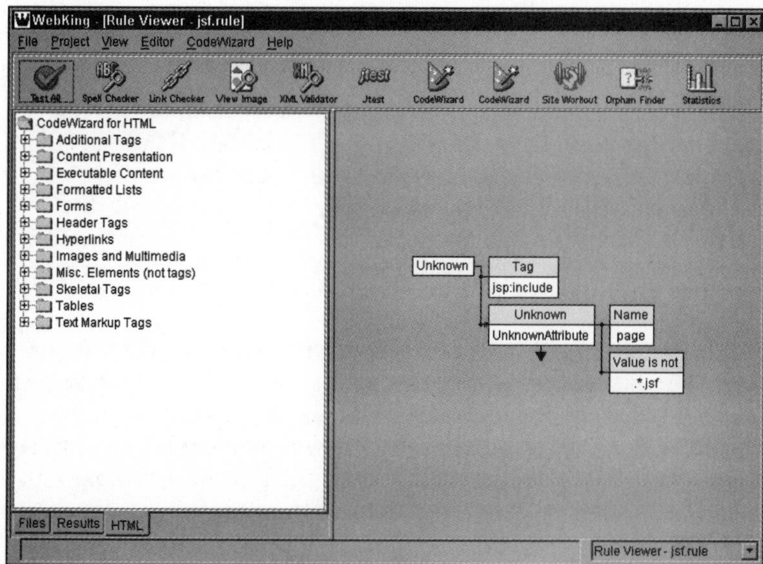

Figure 20-1: The .jsf extension rule.

To run this rule on a `.jsp` file, we have to tell WebKing to treat JSP files temporarily as HTML files (see the WebKing User's Guide for information on how to do this) and follow the usual process of creating an enforcer. Because our actual application doesn't violate this rule, we modified `home.jsp` to refer to `header.jsp` and `footer.jsp` instead of the actual `.jsf` files so that we could verify that our rule was implemented correctly. When we run this rule on the modified `home.jsp` file, we get the following output, confirming that our rule functions as expected:

```
[home.jsp:5] Included files should have .jsf extension: "header.jsp"
[home.jsp:38] Included files should have .jsf extension: "footer.jsp"
```

Changing this rule to use `.jspf` instead of `.jsf` or simply to reject `.jsp` extensions is a simple matter of changing the regular expression used by the rule.

Implementing the Online Grocer Application Using JSP

As mentioned in Chapter 6, the `ShoppingServlet` class didn't do a good job of decoupling our presentation from our business logic. We did develop different display methods for each page, but if a Web designer came in to make changes, he or she would have to understand our Java and be able to rebuild the application. Now that we have introduced JSP, we can reimplement the Online Grocer application in a way that more fully decouples the code from the presentation. Note that you can do this many ways; this is just one example. The specific benefits we hope to achieve with this approach are

- Make it easier for the individual team members to focus on the parts of pages that most concern them. Because JSP files look like HTML files with extra tags, it is easy for designers to modify page layout, graphics, colors, and so on, without having any (or only very basic) knowledge about Java. On the other hand, developers can easily test application flow and logic by creating raw JSP files and leaving graphical design details for designers.
- Make the presentation and logic easier to understand. Clean JSP files present the HTML with very few other tags, so it is easy to look at the page and determine what the resulting page will look like. Moreover, the Java code should be free from statements about how to produce HTML code, so that it can focus entirely on the application logic. This increased code focus and clarity allow for faster development.
- Create a relatively simple way to change the application's look and feel (or even produce alternative sets of pages for different purposes) without having to change the application's logic. For example, we could produce

one set of pages for WML browsers, a different set for regular HTML browsers, and yet another set that uses XML – all without touching the actual logic implementing the application. In this scenario, the testing performed on one version's application logic would carry over to the other versions, reducing the number of bugs overall.

The JSP version of the Online Grocer uses the same flow as the servlet version. From the user's point of view, virtually no discernable difference exists between these versions, in both usability and look and feel. We also use the same support classes (namely `Product`, `ProductDatabase`, and so on). To be able to minimize the amount of code that appears in our JSP files, we use some simple beans. Here, *bean* is used in the sense of a reusable software component. We are not referring to the more complex Enterprise JavaBeans discussed in Chapter 19.

Although only a few pages of the JSP implementation of the Online Grocer application are shown in the text, the complete implementation is available on the CD.

In this implementation, we use the following JSPs to replace the indicated methods from the servlet version of the Online Grocer:

- `home.jsp`: Contains the login form. Replaces the `showLoginPage()` method in the `ShoppingServlet` class.
- `search.jsp`: Contains a form that allows users to search for produce. Replaces the `showSearchPage()` method.
- `search_results.jsp`: Displays the results that match the search criteria. Replaces the `showResultsPage()` method.
- `display.jsp`: Displays information about the selected product. Replaces the `showProductPage()` method.
- `cart.jsp`: Displays the shopping cart. Replaces the `showCartPage()` method.
- `purchase.jsp`: Displays information about the order submission. Replaces the `showOrderPage()` method.
- `logout.jsp`: Requests a confirmation before logging out the user. Replaces the `showLogoutPage()` method.

At this point, we're looking only at the part of our application that is shown on the client browser. All these methods contain the `show` prefix; this indicates that they are responsible solely for creating output. Two additional pages – `header.jsf` and `footer.jsf` – provide the look and feel for the preceding list of pages. Finally, there are a couple of `.jsp` files that implement only logic, with no display routines: `login.jsp` and `update_cart.jsp`.

Figure 20-2 shows the flow among all the JSP implementation's pages. When we start discussing specific JSPs, we will look at how the flow between the pages is implemented.

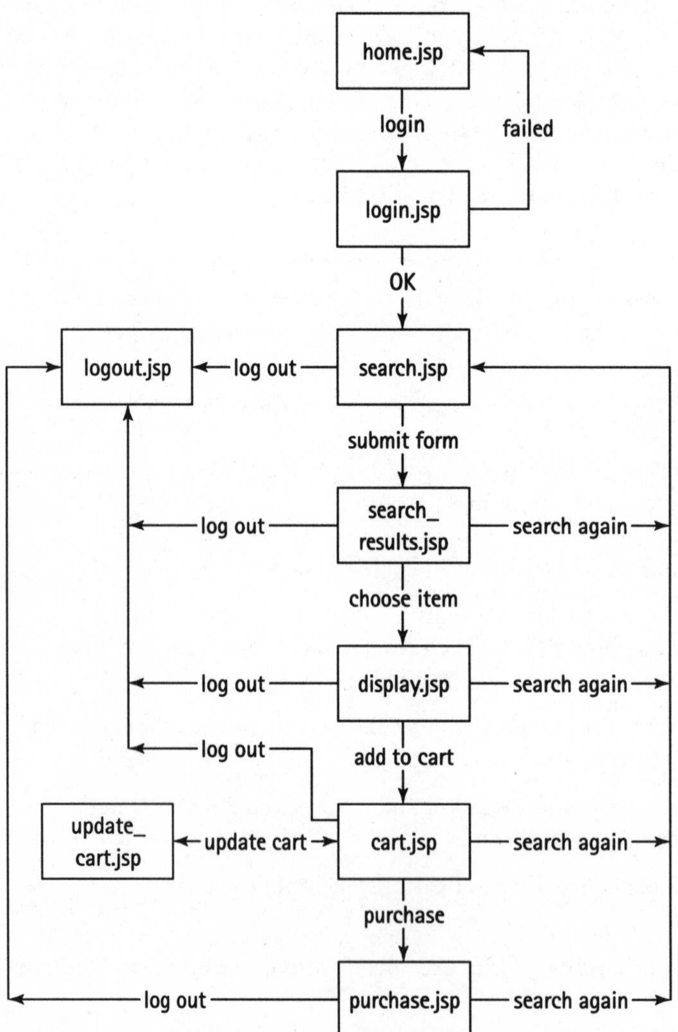

Figure 20-2: The JSP implementation's page flow.

Implementing a common header and footer

To begin exploring the JSP implementation, you will see how we implemented a page that contains no content but contains a common header and footer and all the look-and-feel elements such as the background, a title image, and an empty table layout ready to position contents. The files `header.jsf` and `footer.jsf` correspond to our `header()` and `footer()` methods in `ShoppingServlet`. Remember that these pages are fragments not meant to be invoked directly; they are to be included from other JSP files.

First, look at `header.jsf`, the file that establishes a common header for the other files:

```
<%
    String sTitle = new String("Fruits & Vegetables");
    String sSubTitle = request.getParameter("title");
    if (sSubTitle != null) {
       sTitle += " - " + sSubTitle;
    }
%>

<HTML>
<HEAD>
    <TITLE><%=sTitle%></TITLE>
    <META http-equiv=Content-Type content="text/html; charset=windows-1252">
    <LINK href="fruits.css" type=text/css rel=stylesheet>
</HEAD>

<BODY bgColor=#009900 background=background.gif>
<CENTER>
<TABLE cellSpacing=0 cellPadding=0 border=0>
  <TR>
    <TD align=center><IMG alt="Fruits &amp; Vegetables"
      src="title.gif"></TD></TR>
  <TR>
    <TD height=20></TD></TR>
  <TR>
    <TD align=center>
```

The first section of `header.jsf`, enclosed within `<%` and `%>` braces, reads a parameter `title`, which should be set by the including JSP file using the `<jsp:param>` tag, and creates a page title string. If the parameter is missing, we just use *Fruits & Vegetables* for the title.

It is a good practice to check whether the request object contains the expected parameters. Certain parameters can be available in some paths but not in others. However, if you're working with critical parameters or want to make sure that you are aware of problems that are occurring (for example, during the testing phase), you must do more than simply check for the presence of parameters and proceed as normal if they are not there. For example, if you are in the testing stage, you might want to test for parameters and then have the program throw an exception any time a parameter is missing. This way, you will be alerted to missing parameters (which are often difficult to detect because the program often seems to work correctly when some parameters are missing). One way to implement this practice is to use assertions or other defensive programming techniques.

The other technique to flag these cases is to embed HTML comments that can be detected automatically, using custom coding standards. In this case, you could add something like the following whenever `header.jsf` is called with no `title` parameter:

```
<!-- BUG: header.jsf called with no title parameter -->
```

For information on defensive programming, see Chapter 7.

If you do implement intrusive checks for testing purposes, make sure that you remove them before you deploy the actual application. At that point, the JSP should be built to handle any problems that occur. If possible, it should try to survive and handle the problem in such a way that the user is never aware of it. If recovery is impossible, it can deliver an explanatory message to the user and recommend contacting your support staff. If you use embedded comments, you might want to leave them in your final application, depending on your requirements.

After we determine the string we will use for our title, we open the `HTML` tag and the `HEAD` tag. In the `HEAD` tag, we establish a common style for all pages by pointing to the stylesheet file `fruits.css`. Next, we open the `BODY` tag and create a table that establishes the basic page framework (the actual page contents will be positioned in these table cells).

The `footer.jsf` file determines the closing tags that accompany the opening tags specified in `header.jsf`. This file establishes the following standard footer for all pages:

```
    </TD>
  </TR>
</TABLE>
</CENTER>
</BODY>
</HTML>
```

After these two files were completed, we created an empty JSP file with the standard look and feel (but no actual contents) by creating a new file with the following code:

```
<jsp:include page="header.jsf" flush="true">
   <jsp:param name="title" value="Empty page" />
```

```
</jsp:include>

<jsp:include page="footer.jsf" flush="true"/>
```

Note that we use the <jsp:include> tag in our empty page to include the header and footer contents we plan to use to standardize all pages. This is a very convenient way to establish a consistent look for an entire Web application, as long as you include it on every page that is going to produce visible output. The JSP Online Grocer application is a very simple application, so making it consistent is not all that difficult. When you are working with larger applications, it's a good idea to establish project-specific coding standards that cover standard headers, footers, error pages, and so on.

You can implement project-specific coding standards for JSP, ASP, and server-side scripting technologies by using RuleWizard, Python, or another technology to create and enforce rules, as described in Chapters 8, 11, and 12.

A final thing we would like to point out about this simple page is our use of relative links. This works for our purposes, but some applications are better off with configurable absolute links. Such links can be implemented as follows (where root_dir is a string with a configurable root path to our pages):

```
<LINK href="<%=root_dir%>/fruits.css" type=text/css rel=stylesheet>
```

It is sometimes beneficial to treat links to static elements (such as graphics or static HTML pages) differently than you treat links to JSPs. This helps you maintain application portability even if your Web application is mounted on various URLs. For example, one instance of an application can be mounted on http://<server1>//<application_instance1>/, and a second instance can be created and mounted on http://<server1>//<application_instance_2>/. If you have this scenario and are referring to your pages as follows, your links will not work for the second instance of the application:

```
<A HREF=/<application_instance_1>/jsp/some_jsp_page.jsp></A>
```

An added benefit of using separate, configurable paths to static elements is that you gain additional flexibility. Because your links are not relative, you can, for example, place the static elements on a separate server than your JSPs if you find that this configuration results in better performance.

Implementing the Log In page (home.jsp)

Our Log In page (home.jsp) contains our login form. When the user clicks the log in button, login.jsp checks whether the log in is valid and (depending on the result of that check) brings the user back to this page (which now contains an appropriate log in failed message) or to the Main Search page. Like the empty page created in the preceding section, this page uses the common header and footer to establish the standard look and feel. However, this page contains many more elements than that blank page:

```
<%@ page import="fruits.*" %>

<jsp:useBean id="error" scope="session" class="fruits.ErrorBean"/>

<jsp:include page="header.jsf" flush="true">
   <jsp:param name="title" value="Login" />
</jsp:include>


<FORM name=login action=login.jsp METHOD=post>
<TABLE cellSpacing=0 cellPadding=0 border=0>
    <TR>
      <TD vAlign=middle align=center width=207
          background=tomato.gif height=164>
      <INPUT size=8 value=demo name=USER><BR>
      <INPUT type=password size=8 name=PASSWORD><BR>
      <INPUT type=hidden value=login name=METHOD>
      </TD>
    </TR>
    <TR>
      <TD align=center>
      <INPUT type=image src="login.gif" border=0 name=Login><BR>
      </TD>
    </TR>
</TABLE>
</FORM>

<%
if (error.isError()) {
    String message = error.getMessage();
%>
<P><B><%= message %></B></P>
<%
    error.reset();
}
```

```
%>

<jsp:include page="footer.jsf" flush="true"/>
```

The first tag makes classes from the `fruits` package available to our Java code. This package contains all beans and helper classes we want to use from inside our JSP. The next tag refers to the first bean, which will be available as `error`. This bean has *session scope*, meaning that its lifetime duration is connected to session duration. All references to this bean within a single session will refer to the same instance of the `ErrorBean` class. We use this bean to pass error messages in the case of failed log ins, although this is not the only way to pass data between pages. We chose this method to illustrate beans' session scope and to avoid placing error messages inside requests.

The next lines of code in this file are responsible for including the common application heading. These are the same lines of code used to include this heading on the blank page.

After the heading is added, a form is opened. This form's `action` attribute has a value of `login.jsp`. This might seem odd at first glance if you are thinking of JSPs as traditional HTML pages. However, JSPs are usually compiled to servlets the first time they are accessed and, as you have seen in previous chapters, servlets can be referenced as form `action` attributes and act like CGI programs.

The rest of the form's elements are similar to those in the servlet version of this page. The last bit of code (before the include for the standard footer) is responsible for issuing any error messages found in `ErrorBean`. If the bean does not contain an error, no message is sent to the client.

The file `home.jsp` is a good, simple example of a page that can contain different contents. There are two basic versions of this page. If no error message is present, the standard contents (without an error message) are displayed. If an error message is present, the page contains the error message.

The JSP Online Grocer's `search_result.jsp` is a more complex example of a page that can contain different contents. Depending on query results, this page can contain any of the following:

- A message stating that no match was found
- One row of results
- More than one row of results

As you develop JSPs, be aware that the content of the resulting page, as well as navigation elements, might have to vary with application state (such as number of products found). For example, in a more advanced application than ours, a page similar to `search_result.jsp` could also display a limited group of results on each page and provide a way to navigate between the various results pages. One way to deal with situations like this is to use conditional statements in the JSPs. If you do, make sure that you thoroughly exercise and test each possible condition.

Creating beans

Before proceeding to the next sample page, let's talk about beans. *Beans*, in the context used here, are reusable components that serve as an interface between JSPs and the underlying application logic. Although it is quite common to insert some Java code into the page itself (as in our example), this code should be limited to reading request parameters, passing them to the appropriate beans, reading data from beans, and formatting the resulting page. Implementing business logic with beans outside the page is a good practice. In the JSP Online Grocer application, we use three basic beans that encapsulate logic:

- `UserBean`: Authorizes the user and provides information about the user if requested. This bean's scope is a session.
- `CatalogBean`: Provides information about available products and performs queries as required. This bean's scope is a page.
- `CartBean`: Manages the user's shopping cart. This bean's scope is a session.

We also have a helper bean named `ErrorBean`. We considered using one more bean – a bean that would have the scope of the application and provide all configuration details, such as paths to images, paths to JSPs, and paths to static pages – but we decided against it because our application is so small and simple.

The capability to use beans with different scopes is a very convenient and powerful feature provided by the JSP technology. However, beans do have weaknesses. Because a bean is a Java class, it can have the same problems as any other Java class. One particular problem you must watch for is application errors that cause beans to return unexpected values. For example, our `UserBean` might suddenly return a null username for a valid user. We do not currently include the username in our application's pages, but in the future we might want to use `Hello <%=username%>!` to add a personalized greeting at the top of each page. If we chose to implement this functionality, we would have to check whether the bean returns unexpected values, to prevent our application from delivering messages such as `Hello null!`. One way to prevent these problems is to take an approach like the one described for checking and handling parameters. In this case, you would want each JSP to deliver a message about the problem or try to recover from it. The strategy you choose depends on the feature's importance and your current development stage.

Implementing the log in functionality (login.jsp)

Next, look at `login.jsp`, the page that is executed when someone submits the login form on the Log In page:

```
<%@ page import="fruits.*" %>
```

```
<jsp:useBean id="error" scope="session" class="fruits.ErrorBean"/>
<jsp:useBean id="cart" scope="session" class="fruits.CartBean"/>
<jsp:useBean id="user" scope="session" class="fruits.UserBean"/>

<%
    user.logout();
    cart.reset();
    error.reset();
    String sUsername = request.getParameter("USER");
    String sPassword = request.getParameter("PASSWORD");
    user.login(sUsername, sPassword);
    if (user.isValid()) {
        cart.reset(user.getId());
        response.sendRedirect(
            response.encodeRedirectUrl("search.jsp?FRUITS=x&RED=x&YELLOW=x")
            );
    } else {
        error.setError("Invalid login, please try again.");
        response.sendRedirect(response.encodeRedirectUrl("home.jsp"));
    }
%>
```

This page contains no presentation (which is to say, it produces no HTML). First, it logs out the user and clears the cart. This is really not necessary. Although the cart is a session object, we also have a per-user distinction mechanism. However, we would rather be overly cautious than allow a simple mistake. After logging out the user and clearing the cart, this JSP tries to authorize the user by checking the `USER` and `PASSWORD` parameters from the HTTP request. If the `USER` and `PASSWORD` parameters are valid, it redirects flow to `search.jsp`. If these parameters are not valid, it creates an error message and redirects flow back to `home.jsp`. Notice that we only check for success or failure, but we could just as easily return error-specific pages to give the user more detail about what went wrong.

When you make flow control decisions (as we do with `login.jsp`), you can forward control to the desired location in two ways. If you understand how these two techniques work and how they differ, it is much easier to avoid common mistakes.

The first way to control flow is to use the `<jsp:forward>` tag. In this case, the redirect occurs entirely on the server. The server transfers control to another JSP, static document, CGI program, servlet, and so on, and stops the execution of additional code on the rest of the original page. Moreover, it does *not* notify the client that submitted the request, and the location field at the top of the client browser window will not reflect the new URL. The user's browser will be completely unaware of the redirect, which can occasionally cause obscure flow errors.

For example, say that we have a `save_new_user.jsp` file that is invoked by an `add user` form. This page adds the user to the database and then redirects flow to a welcome page that greets the new user. Sample code for this functionality might look as follows:

```
<jsp:useBean id="addUser" class="beans.AddUserBean"/>

<%
    try {
        addUser.createContext(request, response);
        addUser.saveUserInformation();
%>
        <jsp:forward page="welcome.jsp">
        </jsp:forward>
<%
    } finally {
        addUser.destroy();
    }
%>
```

After a user completes an `add user` form and clicks the Submit button, `save_new_user.jsp` is executed, and flow is transferred to another page. Everything works fine until the user clicks the Refresh button. From the user's point of view, it seems as though the Welcome page was refreshed. However, because the browser was not notified about the flow redirection, `save_new_user.jsp` will be executed one more time, and a duplicate user entry might be added into the database.

In this case, it would be better to use the second flow-control method: Use the `sendRedirect()` method of the `response` object (as we do in `login.jsp`):

```
<jsp:useBean id="addUser" class="beans.AddUserBean"/>

<%
    try {
        addUser.createContext(request, response);
        addUser.saveUserInformation();
        response.sendRedirect(response.encodeRedirectUrl("welcome.jsp"));
    } finally {
        addUser.destroy();
    }
%>
```

The `sendRedirect()` method forces the browser to redirect the request to another location. In this case, the page itself continues executing. If this is not the behavior you want, you should use an explicit `return` statement.

When you are using either of these methods, nothing should be sent to the client's browser before the redirect occurs. Although most current browsers behave correctly, older browsers are known to mix already sent code fragments with the page to which flow was redirected.

Implementing the Main Search page (search.jsp)

The final page to look at here is the Main Search page, `search.jsp`. This JSP is responsible for the first page a user sees after a successful log in:

```
<%@ page import="fruits.*" %>

<jsp:useBean id="user" scope="session" class="fruits.UserBean"/>
<%
    if (!user.isValid()) {
        response.sendRedirect(response.encodeRedirectUrl("home.jsp"));
        return;
    }
%>

<jsp:include page="header.jsf" flush="true">
   <jsp:param name="title" value="Welcome" />
</jsp:include>

<%
    String red = (request.getParameter("RED") != null) ? "CHECKED" : "";
    String green = (request.getParameter("GREEN") != null) ? "CHECKED" : "";
    String yellow = (request.getParameter("YELLOW") != null) ? "CHECKED" : "";
    String weird = (request.getParameter("WEIRD") != null) ? "CHECKED" : "";
    String fruits = (request.getParameter("FRUITS") != null) ? "CHECKED" : "";
    String vegetables =
        (request.getParameter("VEGETABLES") != null) ? "CHECKED" : "";
%>

<FORM name=choose action=search_results.jsp method=post>
<TABLE cellSpacing=0 cellPadding=5 border=0>
  <TR>
    <TD vAlign=top>
      <INPUT type=checkbox <%=fruits%> value=on name=FRUITS>
      <IMG alt=Fruits src="fruits.gif" align=middle><BR>
      <INPUT type=checkbox <%=vegetables%> value=on name=VEGETABLES>
      <IMG alt=Fruits src="vegetables.gif" align=middle><BR>
```

```
    </TD>
    <TD vAlign=top>
      <INPUT type=checkbox <%=red%> value=red name=RED>
      <IMG alt=Red src="red.gif" align=middle><BR>
      <INPUT type=checkbox <%=green%> value=green name=GREEN>
      <IMG alt=Green src="green.gif" align=middle><BR>
      <INPUT type=checkbox <%=yellow%> value=yellow name=YELLOW>
      <IMG alt=Yellow/Orange src="yellow.gif" align=middle><BR>
      <INPUT type=checkbox <%=weird%> value=weird name=WEIRD>
      <IMG alt=Weird src="weird.gif" align=middle><BR>
    </TD>
  </TR>
</TABLE>

<INPUT type=hidden value=choose name=METHOD><BR>
<INPUT type=image src="gobutton.gif" border=0 name=Go><BR>

</FORM>

<HR>
<A href="logout.jsp"><IMG alt=Logout src="logout.gif" border=0></A>

<jsp:include page="footer.jsf" flush="true"/>
```

This page includes extra code before the standard header. This extra code checks whether UserBean is in a *valid state* (that is, it checks whether it was authorized correctly). If it is not, control is immediately returned to home.jsp. Note that we use a return statement to avoid unnecessary – and most likely incorrect – execution of the rest of the page. Requiring code that checks user validity is another example of a project-specific coding standard that should be enforced on all pages except for home.jsp and login.jsp.

After the code that includes the header, we have code that checks the request parameters. Next, we create a search page with prechecked selections based on those parameters. Because request parameters are accessed by name, when request parameters are misspelled, null values can be processed instead of the expected values. Our page will handle any such null value as if the parameter was not set. It is very important to test pages with request parameters thoroughly, using the techniques described throughout Part II, if you want to make sure that you discover problems relating to misspelled parameters before your users do.

After the search form, an extra link is added to allow the user to log out.

The remaining JSPs in the Online Grocer application follow the same basic pattern as the pages we have already described. You can find the complete JSP version of the Online Grocer application on the CD. If you look at the beans we use, you will see that we are using the same Java classes that the servlet version uses (for example, `Product`, `ProductDatabase`, `CustomerDatabase`, `CartDatabase`, and so on). Thus, our JSPs are really just a different layer on top of the same abstraction. You can even choose between using the stubs introduced in Chapter 6 and the JDBC classes presented in Chapter 16.

Summary

Server-side scripting is a convenient technique for creating dynamic Web applications. As with any new technology, it introduces its own twists and turns to your development processes. Nevertheless, the same general principles still apply: defensive programming, coding standards, and thorough testing. You should strive to maintain your code so that readers who only understand HTML will be able to work with your files. Also, you must take extra care to keep your business logic isolated from the presentation. It's far too easy to slip something ugly into the code to meet a deadline, with the intent of removing it later. With diligent effort, however, you can implement bulletproof applications using server-side scripting.

Appendix A

What's on the CD-ROM?

THIS APPENDIX PROVIDES YOU with information about the contents of the CD that accompanies this book. For the latest and greatest information, please refer to the README file located at the root of the CD. This appendix covers

- System requirements
- Instructions for using the CD with Windows and Linux
- The contents of the CD
- Troubleshooting the CD-ROM

System Requirements

Make sure that your computer meets the minimum system requirements listed in this section. If your computer doesn't match up to most of these requirements, you might have a problem using the contents of the CD.

- *For Windows 9x, Windows 2000, Windows NT4 (with SP 4 or later), Windows Me, and Windows XP:*
  - A PC with a Pentium processor running at 120 Mhz or faster
  - At least 32MB of total RAM installed on your computer. For the best performance, we recommend at least 64MB
  - An ethernet network interface card (NIC) or modem with a speed of at least 28,800 bps
  - A CD-ROM drive
- *For Linux:*
  - A PC with a Pentium processor running at 90 Mhz or faster
  - At least 32MB of total RAM installed on your computer. For the best performance, we recommend at least 64MB
  - An ethernet network interface card (NIC) or modem with a speed of at least 28,800 bps
  - A CD-ROM drive

Using the CD with Windows

To install the items from the CD to your hard drive, follow these steps:

1. Insert the CD into your computer's CD-ROM drive.
2. A window appears, with the following options:
   - **Install:** Gives you the option to install the supplied software and/or the author-created samples on the CD-ROM
   - **Explore:** Allows you to view the contents of the CD-ROM in its directory structure
   - **eBook:** Allows you to view an electronic version of the book
   - **Links:** Opens a hyperlinked page of Web sites
   - **Exit:** Closes the AutoRun window

If you don't have AutoRun enabled or the AutoRun window does not appear, follow these steps to access the CD:

1. Click Start→Run.
2. In the dialog box that appears, type **d:\setup.exe.** (the letter *d* is the letter of your CD-ROM drive). This opens the AutoRun window.
3. Choose the Install, Explore, eBook, Links, or Exit option from the menu. (See step 2 in the preceding list for a description of these options.)

Using the CD with Linux

To install the items from the CD to your hard drive, follow these steps:

1. Log in as root.
2. Insert the CD into your computer's CD-ROM drive.
3. If your computer has Auto-Mount enabled, wait for the CD to mount. Otherwise, follow these steps:

   a. Command-line instructions:

   At the command prompt, type

   ```
   mount /dev/cdrom /mnt/cdrom
   ```

   This mounts the cdrom device to the `mnt/cdrom` directory. If your device has a different name, exchange `cdrom` with that device name — for instance, `cdrom1`.

b. Graphical instructions:

Right-click the CD-ROM icon on the desktop, and choose Mount CD-ROM from the selections. This mounts your CD-ROM.

4. Browse the CD and follow the individual installation instructions for the products listed in the next section.

5. To remove the CD from your CD-ROM drive, follow these steps:

a. Command-line instructions:

At the command prompt, type

```
umount /mnt/cdrom
```

b. Graphical instructions:

Right click the CD-ROM icon on the desktop, and choose UMount CD-ROM from the selections. This unmounts your CD-ROM.

What You'll Find

The CD contains source code examples, applications, and an electronic version of the book. Following is a summary of the contents of the CD-ROM arranged by category.

Sample Files

By *sample files*, we mean files to which we refer throughout the book, including scripts, rule files, and source files for the various implementations of our sample Online Grocer application. (Available files include the complete servlet implementation [with and without errors] and the complete JSP version.)

These files are collected in the `examples` directory, which is organized by chapter. We have included a brief `README` in each `examples` subdirectory. Consult this file for more information about a particular directory's contents.

Apache

Freeware version
Apache is a freely available Web server that is distributed under an open source license. Apache runs on most Windows and Unix operating systems. For more information about this program, visit `httpd.apache.org/`.

Pyxie

Open source
Pyxie is a freely available library for processing XML with the Python programming language. We use the `html2pyx.py` script in Chapter 12. For more information about this program, visit `pyxie.sourceforge.net/`.

Tomcat

Open source

Tomcat is a freely available servlet engine that supports servlets and JSPs. For more information about this program, visit `jakarta.apache.org/tomcat/`.

Additional resources

A file listing the resources mentioned in Appendix E, with hyperlinks to the files when possible, is included on the CD-ROM.

ParaSoft programs

Windows and Linux evaluation versions of the following programs are included on the CD-ROM. You can obtain free evaluation licenses for these tools by sending an e-mail to `license@parasoft.com` or by calling 1-888-305-0041. For more information about these programs, visit `www.parasoft.com`.

Some programs are available on additional platforms. To download free demo versions for other platforms, visit `www.parasoft.com`.

WEBKING

Evaluation version

WebKing is a comprehensive Web development, testing, and management tool that performs many of the practices involved in creating a bulletproof Web application. It exposes load, construction, functionality, presentation, content, and design problems by examining the application's dynamic and static pages. In addition, WebKing provides an infrastructure that can automatically compile, deploy, and test programs and scripts and verify the related output pages.

JTEST

Evaluation version

Jtest is a Java unit-testing tool that automatically tests any Java software – servlets, JSP, Enterprise JavaBeans (EJBs), or applets – at the class level without requiring the developer to write a test case, harness, or stub. Jtest automatically tests code construction (white box testing), tests code functionality (black box testing), and maintains code integrity (regression testing). In addition, Jtest checks whether code follows more than 240 Java coding standards, and it allows the creation and checking of any number of custom coding standards.

JCONTRACT

Evaluation version

Jcontract is a Java development tool that checks Design by Contract (DbC) format-specification information at runtime. It can be run independently of Jtest, but the two tools are complementary. After you use Jtest to test your class or component thoroughly at the unit level, use Jcontract to instrument and compile the DbC-commented code. Jcontract then monitors the application at runtime and performs the user-determined action when a contract is violated. Jcontract is particularly useful for determining whether an application misuses specific classes or components and for detecting system-level functionality problems.

SOAPTEST

Evaluation version

SOAPtest is a tool for testing Web services that use SOAP as a wire protocol and HTTP as a transport protocol. SOAPtest provides an easy interface for exercising Web services and testing their functionality. It can be used to confirm the responses to SOAP RPC calls with features such as fault detection, textual comparisons, and XML validation by DTDs or XML schemas. It can also be used to express and flag complex patterns in XML. In addition, SOAPtest lets users validate responses requiring application-specific verification (such as business logic validation) and performs regression testing of Web services.

DATARECON

Evaluation version

DataRecon is a database verification and monitoring tool that allows database design verification, data validation, structural verification, and regression testing. When you can use HTTP to reach the part of the application that accesses the databases, DataRecon can check whether the application writes the correct information to the database, reads the correct information from the database, and adds it to the Web page as expected.

The electronic version of this book

The complete (and searchable) text of this book is on the CD-ROM in Adobe's Portable Document Format (PDF), readable with a freeware version of Adobe Acrobat Reader (also included). For more information on Adobe Acrobat Reader, go to `www.adobe.com`.

Troubleshooting the CD-ROM

If you have difficulty installing or using the CD-ROM programs, try the following solutions:

- Download a new version of any program you are having trouble with (or download a version better suited for your system).
- Contact the company or organization responsible for the program with which you are having difficulty.

If you still have trouble with the CD, please call the Hungry Minds Customer Service phone number: 1-800-762-2974. Outside the United States, call 1-317-572-3994. Hungry Minds provides technical support only for installation and other general quality-control items. For technical support on the applications themselves, consult the program's vendor or author.

Appendix B

"Errors" in the Online Grocer Application

THE SERVLET IMPLEMENTATION of the Online Grocer application presented in Chapters 4–6 contains several intentional errors. This appendix briefly summarizes the errors and indicates where you can find a more detailed discussion in the book. A version of the application with all the corrections can be found on the CD in `examples/appendixb/fruits`. If you find any errors you think we overlooked, please e-mail us at `bulletproof@parasoft.com`.

ProductDatabaseStub.java

Our stubbed database contains 11 spelling mistakes. See Chapter 13, the section "Creating additional paths through the Online Grocer application."

ShoppingServlet.java

Our original servlet requires cookies but never checks whether the user's browser supports them. We extended the `login()` method to check for browsers that do not support cookies (see Chapter 13, the section "Creating additional paths through the Online Grocer application"). We also added a new display routine, `showCookiesRequiredPage()`:

```
if (context.isNew()) {
    showCookiesRequiredPage(context);
    return;
}
```

The `addToCart()` method is missing a check for a logged in user:

```
if (!context.hasUser()) {
    showLoginPage(context, false, "Missing USER for
METHOD=addToCart");
    return;
}
```

The doUpdateCart() method does not validate data entered by the user (see Chapter 13, the section "Checking for Server-Side Errors"). We added a new display routine, showErrorPage():

```
boolean isOK = true;
Enumeration enum = context.getParameterNames();
while (enum.hasMoreElements()) {
    String name = enum.nextElement().toString();
    if (name.startsWith("ITEM_")) {
        try {
            int quantity = context.getInteger(name, 0);
            if (quantity < 0) {
                isOK = false;
            }
        } catch (NumberFormatException e) {
            isOK = false;
        }
    }
}
if (!isOK) {
    showErrorPage(context);
    return;
}
```

The showLoginPage() method is missing METHOD=post from the generated form (see Chapter 8, the section "Using WebKing to Enforce Web Coding Standards").

The incorrect code is

```
out.println("<!-- FORM must have METHOD attribute set: POST or GET -
->");
out.println("<FORM NAME=login ACTION=\""+SERVLET+"\">");
```

The corrected code is

```
out.println("<FORM NAME=login METHOD=post ACTION=\""+SERVLET+"\">");
```

The showLoginPage() method uses VALIGN=CENTER instead of VALIGN=MIDDLE (see Chapter 8, the section "Using WebKing to Enforce Web Coding Standards").

The incorrect code is

```
out.println("\n<!-- CENTER: Illegal VALIGN attribute value: should
be MIDDLE -->");
out.println(
    "<TR><TD ALIGN=CENTER VALIGN=CENTER HEIGHT=164 WIDTH=207
BACKGROUND=\"/tomato.gif\">");
```

The corrected code is

```
out.println(
    "<TR><TD ALIGN=CENTER VALIGN=MIDDLE HEIGHT=164 WIDTH=207
BACKGROUND=\"/tomato.gif\">");
```

The showResultsPage() method had a typo (chooose instead of choose). See Chapter 13, the section "Creating additional paths through the Online Grocer application".

The incorrect code is

```
out.println("<H2>Please, chooose at least one color.</H2>");
```

The showResultsPage() method generates incorrect links.

The incorrect code is

```
// BUG: Points to login page instead of "search"
out.println("<A HREF=\""+SERVLET+"?METHOD=login"+
    choices.toString()+"\">Make another choice</A><BR>");
out.println("\n<!-- Missing Page: \"/logout.html\" -->");
out.println("<A HREF=\"/logout.html\">");
out.println("<IMG SRC=\"/logout.gif\" ALT=\"Logout\"
BORDER=0></A>");
```

The corrected code is

```
out.println("<A HREF=\""+SERVLET+"?METHOD=search"+
    choices.toString()+"\">Make another choice</A><BR>");
out.println("<A HREF=\""+SERVLET+"?METHOD=logout\">");
out.println("<IMG SRC=\"/logout.gif\" ALT=\"Logout\"
BORDER=0></A>");
```

The original servlet has no special code to handle incorrect URLs. We added the show404() and show404Page() methods to replace the generic page unavailable with our own message (see Chapter 11).

The original servlet displays debugging stack traces when internal errors occur (see Chapter 6, the section "Establishing uniform exception handling"). For the improved version of the site, we have overridden handleException() to produce more user-friendly output.

The overridden method is

```
/**
 * Our error page -- how to handle unexpected problems.
 * This version assumes that we never throw exceptions once
```

```
 * we've started creating the response page
 */
protected void handleException(HttpServletRequest req,
                               HttpServletResponse res,
                               Throwable t) {
    // Log error for analysis
    System.err.println("Error");
    t.printStackTrace();

    try {
        PrintWriter out = res.getWriter();
        header(out, "System Difficulties");
        out.println("<p>This site is currently experiencing
difficulties.  If you would");
        out.println("like immediate assistance, please contact ");
        out.println("<a
href=\"webmaster@example.com\">webmaster@example.com</a>.</p>");
        footer(out);
    } catch (IOException e) {
    }
}
```

index.html

Our static Splash page has a broken link (see Chapter 11).

The incorrect HTML is

```
<BODY BGCOLOR=#009900 BACKGROUND="fruits/background.gif">
```

The corrected HTML is

```
<BODY BGCOLOR=#009900 BACKGROUND="background.gif">
```

Appendix C

Installing and Starting WebKing

WEBKING IS CURRENTLY AVAILABLE for Windows and Unix. The CD included with this book includes version 3.1 for Windows and Linux. To be able to try this product, you must obtain an evaluation license from ParaSoft as described in this appendix. Note that this version of WebKing is included only for demonstration and evaluation purposes, so you can follow the examples in this book and try it out on your own applications. If you intend to continue using WebKing, you will need to purchase a license.

If you have misplaced your CD, you can download trial versions of WebKing at `www.parasoft.com`. If you would like a Solaris version, you can download it from this same location.

Windows System requirements include

- At least 64MB RAM (128MB recommended)
- JDK or JRE 1.3 or higher
- Windows NT 4.0, 2000, ME, or 9*x*

Linux system requirements include

- At least 64MB RAM (128MB recommended)
- JDK or JRE 1.3 or higher (If you are on Linux, you need a recent kernel (2.2.*xx*) and a glibc of 2.1.2 or higher to get this JDK version.)

Installing and Starting WebKing (Windows)

If you are working on Windows NT or Windows 2000, log in to Windows using an account with Administrator privileges before you install WebKing.

To install WebKing on a Windows machine, do the following:

1. In Windows Explorer, locate and double-click the WebKing31_Win32_jre131.exe installation file available in the CD's products directory.

2. Follow the on-screen installation directions.

After you complete the installation program, WebKing is installed on your machine.

After installation is complete, you can run WebKing by choosing Start→Programs→WebKing→WebKing.

Before you begin using WebKing, you must install a license by doing the following:

1. Start WebKing. The Password window opens.

2. Call 1-888-305-0041 or e-mail license@parasoft.com to receive your license. If you send e-mail, be sure to include the Machine Id that WebKing displays in the Password window and to mention that you received WebKing from this book.

3. In the Password window, enter your password and expiration date, and click OK.

Installing and Starting WebKing (Linux)

To install WebKing on a Linux machine, do the following:

1. If you haven't already done so, copy the WebKing31_UNIX.tar.gz installation file (from the CD's products directory) to the directory where you want to install WebKing (typically /usr/local).

2. Change directories to the directory where you are going to install WebKing (typically /usr/local).

3. Extract the necessary files by entering the following command at the prompt:

   ```
   tar -xvzf WebKing31_UNIX.tar.gz
   ```

   Entering the appropriate command creates a directory named webking/3.1 within your current directory and then extracts all WebKing files into this directory.

4. Edit the webking script to indicate the correct paths to your Java installation and your WebKing installation. This script (webking) is typically located in /usr/local/webking/3.1/.

The `WEBKING` variable should be set to the directory containing the script you are currently editing.

If your environment does not have a `$JAVA_HOME` variable, you must add it to the script. To do this, add the following line before the line containing the `JRE` variable:

```
JAVA_HOME=<path to JDK(typically /usr/local/jdk/)> ; export
JAVA_HOME
```

For example,

```
JAVA_HOME=/usr/local/jdk/ ; export JAVA_HOME
```

To run WebKing, change directories to the `webking/3.1` directory, and enter the following command at the prompt:

```
webking
```

Before you begin using WebKing, you must install a license by doing the following:

1. Start WebKing. The Password window opens.
2. Call 1-888-305-0041, or e-mail `license@parasoft.com` to receive your license. If you send e-mail, include the `Machine Id` that WebKing displays in the Password window, and mention that you received WebKing from this book.
3. In the Password window, enter your password and expiration date, and click OK.

Learning More

You can access the WebKing User's Guide by choosing Help→Online Documentation in the WebKing GUI or by clicking the F1 key when the WebKing GUI is open.

If you have any questions, comments, or feedback, please contact WebKing technical support at 1-888-305-0041.

Appendix D

Tips on Writing Rules

MANY OF THE TOOLS DISCUSSED in this book include RuleWizard, a feature that enables you to create graphical rules to enforce coding standards, or search for patterns in various kinds of files. In this appendix, we review the basic syntax supported by RuleWizard for creating *regular* expressions (used to test strings) and ***boolean*** expressions (used to test numbers).

Regular Expressions

Regular expressions are used to match strings. They are supported by many languages, including Perl and Python. RuleWizard's regular expressions are similar to those supported by Perl.

Here are some tips to keep in mind when working with regular expressions:

- The caret (^) indicates the beginning of a string in parentheses; the dollar sign ($) indicates the end of a string in parentheses. Thus, to get an exact match for a string, use the format `^(STRING)$`. For example, `^(soft)$` would flag only *soft*.
- Regular expression searches are case-sensitive by default.
- When using regular expressions, the backward slash (\) is an escape character you can use to match a period (`.`), an asterisk (*), or another character that has a nonliteral meaning.

Table D-1 lists the most common characters and metacharacters you can use in regular expressions.

Table D-1 REGULAR EXPRESSION CHARACTERS AND METACHARACTERS

Character/ Metacharacter	Matches	Examples
.	Exactly 1 non-null character.	`.at` matches *hat, cat, bat, fat,* etc., but not *at.*
		`w...ing` matches *webking* and *working* but not *what a king* or *wing.*
?	0 or 1 occurrences of the preceding character.	`j?test` matches either *jtest* or*test.*
*	0 or more occurrences of the preceding character.	`a*soft` matches *asoft* or *aaaaasoft.* `.*ing` matches *webking, waning, wing, what was that thing.*
+	1 or more occurrences of the preceding character.	`a+soft` matches *aaaaasoft* or *aaasoft* but not *asoft.*
[]	1 occurrence of any character inside the brackets; the caret (^) inverts the brackets metacharacter.	`[cpy]up` matches *cup, pup,* or *yup.* `rule0[1-4]` matches *rule01, rule02, rule03, rule04.*
		`[^ch]at` matches all 3-letter words ending with *at* except for *cat* and *hat.*
[A-Z]	Any uppercase letters from *A* to *Z.*	`[A-Z]` matches any uppercase letter from *A* to *Z.*
[a-z]	Any lowercase letters from *a* to *z.*	`[a-z]` matches any lowercase letter from *a* to *z.*
[0-9]	Any integer from 0 to 9.	`rule[0-9]` matches any expression beginning with *rule* and ending with an integer.
{}	Like *, but the string it matches must be of the length specified in the braces.	`a{2}` matches *aaa.* `a{3,}` matches at least 3 occurrences of the preceding character (*aaaaaa* or *aaaaaaaa* but not *aa*).
		`a {2,5}` matches 2–5 occurrences of the preceding character (*aaa* and *aaaaaa* but not *aa* or *aaaaaaaaaaaaaaaaa*).

<table>
<tr><th>Character/ Metacharacter</th><th>Matches</th><th>Examples</th></tr>
<tr><td>|</td><td>The string before the |, the string after the |, or both.</td><td><code>rulewizard|codewizard</code> matches rulewizard, codewizard, or both.</td></tr>
<tr><td>\d</td><td>Exactly 1 digit.</td><td></td></tr>
<tr><td>\D</td><td>Any 1 character except a digit.</td><td></td></tr>
<tr><td>\w</td><td>1 letter, 1 number, or the underscore character.</td><td></td></tr>
<tr><td>\W</td><td>Any 1 character except a letter, number, or underscore character.</td><td></td></tr>
<tr><td>\s</td><td>Exactly 1 character of whitespace (a space, tab, or newline).</td><td></td></tr>
<tr><td>\S</td><td>1 character that is not whitespace.</td><td></td></tr>
</table>

Boolean Expressions

Boolean expressions are used to match values; `$$` is used with expressions to indicate a variable. Table D-2 gives a few examples of valid expressions you can use.

TABLE D-2 SAMPLE EXPRESSIONS

Expression	Matches	Example
`$$==n`	A value equal to n.	`$$==1` matches values equal to 1.
`$$<n`	A value less than n.	`$$<100` matches values less than 100.
`$$>n`	A value greater than n.	`$$>100` matches values greater than 100.
`$$<=n`	A value less than or equal to n.	`$$<=550` matches values less than or equal to 550.
`$$>=n`	A value greater than or equal to n.	`$$=>1` matches values greater than or equal to 1.

Scripting Rules

If you are writing a rule that requires a more sophisticated check than a simple regular expression or boolean expression, you can combine the searching and checking of RuleWizard with custom scripts written in Java, Python, or JavaScript. Currently, this functionality is available only in WebKing and SOAPtest. For more information, consult the appropriate documentation.

Appendix E

Additional Resources

THIS APPENDIX LISTS RESOURCES mentioned in the book, as well as additional resources where you can find more information about topics covered in the book. Due to the dynamic nature of the Web, we can't guarantee that these URLs will all remain valid by the time you read this page.

An HTML file with links to the online resources is available on the CD.

General Web Development and Testing (Chapters 1–6 and Beyond)

Applets. `java.sun.com/applets/`.

Arnold, Ken, and James Gosling. Multithreaded Programming in Java. *Webtechniques* (October 1996). `www.webtechniques.com/archives/1996/10/gosling/`.

Baker, Scott. Applying Software Design Techniques to the Web. *Webtechniques* (August 2000). `www.webtechniques.com/archives/2000/08/baker/`.

Beazley, David. *Python Essential Reference*. New Riders Publishing. 2001 (ISBN 0735710910).

Beck, Kent. *Extreme Programming Explained: Embrace Change*. Addision-Wesley Publishing Company. 1999 (ISBN 0201616416).

Bentley, Jon Louis. *Programming Pearls*. Addison-Wesley Publishing Company. 1999 (ISBN 0201657880).

Bradenbaugh, Jerry. *JavaScript Application Cookbook*. O'Reilly & Associates. 1999 (ISBN 1565925777).

Brauchie, Richard. How to Test Cookies in a Stateful Web System. *Stickyminds.com* (October 15, 2001). `www.stickyminds.com`.

Concurrent Versions System. `www.cvshome.org`.

Cookie Central. `www.cookiecentral.com/fax`.

Cox, Brad. Web Applications as Java Servlets. *Dr. Dobb's Journal* (May 2001). `www.ddj.com/articles/2001/0105/0105i/0105i.htm`.

FastCGI. `www.fastcgi.com`.

Fielden, Tim. Gone in 60 Seconds: Web Application Development Accelerated. *Infoworld* (October 23, 2000). www.infoworld.com/articles/mt/xml/00/10/23/001023mtwebappdev.xml.

Flanagan, David. *JavaScript: The Definitive Guide.* O'Reilly & Associates. 1998 (ISBN 1565923928).

Floyd, Michael. Cascading Style Sheets: To Hell with Standards. *Webtechniques* (March 1999). www.webtechniques.com/archives/1999/03/beyo/.

Fournier, Roger. Build Better e-business Apps Faster. *Infoworld* (December 15, 2000). www.infoworld.com/articles/tc/xml/00/12/18/001218tcsystem.xml.

Fournier, Roger. *A Methodology for Client/Server and Web Application Development.* Prentice Hall. 1998 (ISBN 0135984262).

Fowler, Martin. The Agile Manifesto. *Software Development* (August 2001). www.sdmagazine.com/documents/s=844/sdm0108a/0108a.htm.

Fowler, Martin. The New Methodology. martinfowler.com/articles/newMethodology.html.

Fowler, Martin, Kent Beck, John Brant, William Opdyke, and Don Roberts. *Refactoring: Improving the Design of Existing Code.* Addison-Wesley Publishing Company. 1999 (ISBN 0201485672).

Free On-Line Dictionary of Computing. www.foldoc.org.

Gamma, Erich, Richard Helm, Ralph Johnson, and John Vlissides. *Design Patterns: Elements of Reusable Object-Oriented Software.* Addison-Wesley Publishing Company. 1995 (ISBN 0201633612).

Heinle, Nick, Bill Pena, Bill Penai, and Martin Webbi. *Designing with JavaScript, 2nd Edition: A Definitive Introduction (O'Reilly Web Studio).* O'Reilly & Associates. 2001 (ISBN 156592360X).

JavaScript Examples. www.js-examples.com.

The JavaScript Source. javascript.internet.com.

Jeffries, Ron, Ann Anderson, and Chet Hendrickson. *Extreme Programming Installed (The XP Series).* Addison-Wesley Publishing Company. 2000 (ISBN 0201708426).

Jones, Capers. *Programming Productivity.* McGraw-Hill Book Company. 1986 (ISBN 0070328110).

Jython. www.jython.org.

Kernighan, Brian, and Rob Pike. *The Practice of Programming.* Addison-Wesley Publishing Company. 1999 (ISBN 020161586X).

Lea, Doug. *Concurrent Programming in Java: Design Principles and Patterns.* Addison-Wesley Publishing Company. 1999 (ISBN 0201310090).

Lundh, Feedrik. *Python Standard Library.* O'Reilly & Associates. 2001 (ISBN 0596000960).

McConnell, Steve. *Rapid Development: Taming Wild Software Schedules.* Microsoft Press. 1996 (ISBN 1556159005).

McGregor, John. Taking Testing to the Extreme. *JOOP* (February 2001). www.joopmag.com/html/from_pages/article.asp?id=192&mon=2&yr=2001.

Maguire, Steve. *Debugging the Development Process.* Microsoft Press. 1994 (ISBN B00005R08G).

Maguire, Steve. *Writing Solid Code.* Microsoft Press. 1993 (ISBN 1556155514).

Manifesto for Agile Software Development. www.agileAlliance.org.

Morgan, Lisa. Aspirin for the Headache. *SD Times* (March 15, 2001). www.sdtimes.com/news/026/special1.htm.

Mosley, Daniel J. *Client Server Software Testing on the Desk Top and the Web.* Prentice Hall. 1999 (ISBN 01318388806).

Nguyen, Hung Quoc. *Testing Applications of the Web: Test Planning for Internet-Based Systems.* John Wiley & Sons. 2000 (ISBN 047139470X).

Nic's JavaScript Page. www.javascript-page.com.

Nyman, Noel. Using Monkey Test Tools. *Software Testing and Quality Engineering* (January/February 2000). www.stickyminds.com.

Ousterhout, John. Scripting: Higher Level Programming for the 21st Century. home.pacbell.net/ouster/scripting.html.

Persistent Client State HTTP Cookies. home.netscape.com/newsref/std/cookie_spec.html.

Python. www.python.org.

Reilly, David. How Do I Use Servlets for State and Session Management? *Dr. Dobb's Journal* (May 2000). www.ddj.com/articles/2000/0005/0005m/0005m.htm.

Splain, Steven, Stefan P. Jaskiel, and Alberto Savoia. *The Web Testing Handbook.* Software Quality Engineering Publishers. 2001 (ISBN 0970436300).

Stottlemyer, Diane. Automated Web Testing Toolkit: Expert Methods for Testing and Managing Web Applications. John Wiley & Sons. 2001 (ISBN 0471414352).

Strom, David. Why Is Web Development So Painful? *SD Times* (July 15, 2000). www.sdtimes.com/cols/webwatch_010.htm.

W3C. The World Wide Web Security FAQ. www.w3.org/Security/Faq/.

Whittaker, James. What Is Software Testing? And Why Is It So Hard? *IEEE Software* (January/February2000). www.computer.org/software/so2000/pdf/s1070.pdf.

Williams, Al. Born to Serve. *Webtechniques* (August 1998). www.webtechniques.com/archives/1998/08/java/.

Xprogramming.com. xprogramming.com.

Yourdon, Edward. *Decline and Fall of the American Programmer.* PTP Prentice Hall. 1993 (ISBN 013191958X).

Defensive Programming (Chapter 7)

AspectJ. aspectj.org.

Aspect-Oriented Software Development. aosd.net/.

Eldridge, Geoff. Java and Design by Contract. www.elj.com/eiffel/feature/dbc/java/ge/.

Interactive Software Engineering. Building Bug-Free O-O Software: An Introduction to Design by Contract. www.eiffel.com/doc/manuals/technology/contract/page.html.

Kolawa, Adam. Automating the Development Process. *Software Development* (July 2000). www.sdmagazine.com/documents/s=742/sdm0007c/0007c.htm.

Log4j. jakarta.apache.org/log4j.

Meyer, Bertrand. *Object-Oriented Software Construction, 2nd Edition.* Prentice Hall. 2000 (ISBN 0136291554).

Nic's JavaScript Page. www.javascript-page.com.

Payne, Jeffrey E., Michael A. Schatz, and Matthew N. Schmid. Implementing Assertions for Java. *Dr. Dobb's Journal* (January 1998). www.ddj.com/articles/1998/9801/9801d/9801d.htm.

Plessel, Todd. Design by Contract: A Missing Link in the Quest for Quality Software. www.elj.com/eiffel/dbc/.

Coding Standards (Chapter 8)

Anderson, Joel, and Chris Kunicki. More Real World Cross-Browser HTML Development. *Webtechniques* (August 2000). www.webtechniques.com/archives/2000/08/kunicki/.

Anderson, Joel, and Chris Kunicki. Real World Cross-Browser HTML Development. *Webtechniques* (May 2000). www.webtechniques.com/archives/2000/05/kunicki//.

Bloch, Joshua. *Effective Java Programming Language Guide.* Addison-Wesley Professional. 2001 (ISBN 0201310058).

Darwin, Ian F. *Checking Programs with Lint (1st Edition).* O'Reilly & Associates. 1998 (ISBN 0937175307).

ECMA. www.ecma.ch/.

Flanagan, David. *JavaScript: The Definitive Guide.* O'Reilly & Associates. 1998 (ISBN 1565923928).

Goodman, Danny. *Dynamic HTML: The Definitive Reference.* O'Reilly & Associates. 1998 (ISBN 1565924940).

Haggar, Peter. *Practical Java Programming Language Guide.* Addison-Wesley Publishing Company. 2000 (ISBN 0201616467).

Lemay, Laura. HTML Coding: Validating HTML Code. *Webtechniques* (April 1997). www.webtechniques.com/archives/1997/04/html/.

Lie, Hakon Wium, Bert Bos, and Robert Caillau. *Cascading Style Sheets, Designing for the Web.* Addison-Wesley Publishing Company. 1999 (ISBN 0201596253).

Lindholm, Tim, and Frank Yellin. *The Java Virtual Machine Specification.* Addison-Wesley Publishing Company. 1999 (ISBN 0201432943).

Lutz, Mark. *Programming Python.* O'Reilly & Associates. 2001 (ISBN 0596000855).

McConnell, Steve. *Code Complete: A Practical Handbook of Software Construction.* Microsoft Press. 1993 (ISBN 1556154844).

Meyer, Eric A. *Cascading Style Sheets: The Definitive Guide.* O'Reilly & Associates. 2000 (ISBN 1565926226).

Meyers, Scott. *Effective C++.* Addison-Wesley Publishing Company. 1992 (ISBN 0201924889).

Meyers, Scott. *More Effective C++*. Addison-Wesley Publishing Company. 1995 (ISBN 020163371X).

MSDN. Hungarian Notation. msdn.microsoft.com/library/techart/hunganotat.htm.

Nic's JavaScript Page. www.javascript-page.com.

Seltzer, Larry. Not on the Same Page. *Internet World* (June 15, 2000). www.internetworld.com/magazine.php?inc=061500/6.15internettech2.html.

W3C. www.w3.org.

W3C CSS Validation Service. jigsaw.w3.org/css-validator/validator-uri.html.

W3C. Document Object Model (DOM). www.w3.org/DOM/.

W3C HTML Validation Service. validator.w3.org.

Weinman, Lynda. The Browser-Safe Color Palette. www.lynda.com/hex.html.

Woodall, Ron. The Compendium of HTML Elements. htmlcompendium.org.

Unit Testing (Chapter 9)

Beck, Kent. Simple Smalltalk Testing: With Patterns. www.xprogramming.com/testfram.htm.

Cole, Oliver. White-Box Testing. *Dr. Dobb's Journal* (March 2000). www.ddj.com/articles/2000/0003/0003a/0003a.htm.

Junit.org. www.junt.org.

XP Software. www.xprogramming.com/software.htm.

Deployment (Chapter 10)

Expect Home Page. expect.nist.gov.

Libes, Don, and Tim O'Reilly. *Exploring Expect: A Tcl-Based Toolkit for Automating Interactive Programs*. O'Reilly & Associates. 1994 (ISBN 1565920902).

TCL Developer Xchange. scriptics.com.

WebDAV Resources. webdav.org.

Client-Side Testing (Chapters 11–14)

Hypertext Transfer Protocol (HTTP) 1.1. W3C Recommendation (June 1999). www.w3.org/Protocols/rfc2616/rfc2616.html.

International Ispell. fmg-www.cs.ucla.edu/fmg-members/geoff/ispell.html.

Lindsay, Philip. Design for Performance. *E-business Advisor* (November 2000). advisor.com/Articles.nsf/aid/LINDP01.

Pyxie. www.pyxie.org.

Raikow, David. Internet Stress. *Smart Partner* (April 30, 2001). www.zdnet.com/sp/stories/news/0,4538,2713965,00.html.

Savoia, Alberto. Trade Secrets from a Web Testing Expert. *STQE* (May 1, 2001). www.stickyminds.com.

Straathof, Jeff. Load Testing Intranet Application. *Webtechniques* (January 1997). www.webtechniques.com/archives/1997/01/straathof/.

Application-Level Testing (Chapter 15)

Albitz, Paul, and Cricket Liu. *DNS and BIND*. O'Reilly & Associates. 2001 (ISBN 0596001584).

Bugzilla. bugzilla.mozilla.org.

Brooks, Frederick. *The Mythical Man-Month, Essays on Software Engineering*. Addison-Wesley Publishing Company. 1995 (ISBN 0201835959).

Databases (Chapter 16)

Bowman, Judith, Sandra Emerson, and Marcy Darnovsky. *The Practical Sql Handbook: Using Structured Query Language*. Addison-Wesley Publishing Company. 1996 (ISBN 0201447878).

Carroll, Erin, and Andrew Wilson. Database Programming with JDBC. *Webtechniques* (October 1996). www.webtechniques.com/archives/1996/10/carroll/.

Date, C.J. An Introduction to Database Systems (7th Edition). Addison-Wesley Publishing Company. 1999 (ISBN 0201385902).

5 Rules of Data Normalization. www.datamodel.org/NormalizationRules.html.

Gilfillan, Ian. Database Normalization. wdvl.internet.com/Authoring/DB/Normalization.

Litt, Steve. Normalization. Troubleshooters.com. www.troubleshooters.com/codecorn/norm.htm.

MySQL. mysql.com.

North, Ken. The Ascendancy of Java Data Access. *Webtechniques* (August 1998). www.webtechniques.com/archives/1999/08/data/.

North, Ken. Building Web Databases. *Webtechniques* (September 1996). www.webtechniques.com/archives/1996/09/north/.

Scherer, Douglas, William Gaynor, Arlene Valentinsen, Sue Mavris, and Xerxes Cursetjee. *Oracle 8*i *Tips & Techniques*. McGraw-Hill Professional Publishing. 1999 (ISBN 0072121033).

Van Haecke, Bernard. *JDBC: Java Database Connectivity*. IDG Books Worldwide, Inc. 1997 (ISBN 0764531441).

XML (Chapter 17)

Apache XML Project. xml.apache.org/.

Box, Don, Aaron Skonnard, and John Lam. *Essential XML: Beyond MarkUp (The DevelopMentor Series).* Addison-Wesley Publishing Company. 2000 (ISBN 0201709147).

Brooks, Fred. *No Silver Bullet.* Information Processing 1986, The Proceedings of the IFIP Tenth World Computing Conference.

Extensible Markup Language (XML) 1.0 (Second Edition). W3C Recommendation (October 6, 2000). www.w3.org/TR/REC-xml.

Fischer, Peter. Migrating from HTML to XML. *Webtechniques* (July 2000). www.webtechniques.com/archives/2000/07/fischer/.

Floyd, Michael. Separating Body from Soul. *Webtechniques* (July 2000). www.webtechniques.com/archives/2000/07/floyd/.

Jones, Kevin. A Better Way for Web Development. *JavaPro* (August 2000). www.devx.com/upload/free/features/xml/2000/04fal00/kj0004/kj0004.asp.

Martin,Teresa. *The Project Cool Guide to XML for Web Designers.* John Wiley & Sons. 1990 (ISBN 047134401X).

Mathematical Markup Language (MathML) Version 2.0. W3C Recommendation (February 21, 2001). www.w3.org/TR/MathML2.

Scalable Vector Graphics (SVG) 1.0 Specification. W3C Candidate Recommendation (November 2, 2000). www.w3.org/TR/SVG/.

Synchronized Multimedia Integration Language (SMIL) 2.0 Specification. W3C Working Draft (March 1, 2001). www.w3.org/TR/smil20.

XML Schema Part 0: Primer. W3C Recommendation (May 2, 2001). www.w3.org/TR/xmlschema-0/.

XSL Transformations (XSLT) Version 1.0. W3C Recommendation (November 16, 1999). www.w3.org/TR/xslt.

Web Services (Chapter 18)

ebXML. www.ebxml.org/.

Project: Web Services for Python. sourceforge.net/projects/pywebsvcs.

St. Laurent, Simon, Ed Dumbill, and Joe Johnston. *Programming Web Services XML-RPC.* O'Reilly & Associates. 2001 (ISBN 0596001193).

Scribner, Kenn, and Mark Stiver Sams. *Understanding SOAP: The Authoritative Solution.* Sams. 2000 (ISBN 0672319225).

Snell, James, and Ken MacLeod. *Programming Web Applications with SOAP.* O'Reilly & Associates. 2000 (ISBN 0596000952).

Web Services Description Language (WSDL 1.1) Specification (March 15, 2001). www.w3.org/TR/wsdl.

XML Protocol Activity. www.w3.org/2000/xp/.

Components and EJB (Chapter 19)

Ambler, Scott W. Enterprise JavaBean Persistence 101. *Software Development* (August 2000). www.sdmagazine.com/documents/s=741/sdm0008i/.

Ambler, Scott W. Enterprise JavaBean Persistence 201. *Software Development* (October 2000). www.sdmagazine.com/documents/s=739/sdm0010j/.

Englander, Robert, and Mike Loukides. *Developing Java Beans.* O'Reilly & Associates. 1997 (ISBN 1565922891).

Java 2 Enterprise Edition JavaBeans Developer's Guide (v1.2.1). web2.java.sun.com/j2ee/j2sdkee/techdocs/guides/ejb/html/DevGuideTOC.html.

Mahapatra, Sanjay. Programming Restrictions on EJB. *JavaWorld* (August 2000). www.javaworld.com/javaworld/jw-08-2000/jw-0825-ejbrestrict.html.

Nygard, Michael, and Tracie Karsjens. Test Infect Your Enterprise JavaBeans. *JavaWorld* (May 2000). www.javaworld.com/javaworld/jw-05-2000/jw-0526-testinfect.html.

Spitzer, Tom, and Hakim, Jack. Delivering Enterprise JavaBeans. *Webtechniques* (May 1999). www.webtechniques.com/archives/1999/05/spitzer/.

Spitzer, Tom. Testing the Promise of Enterprise JavaBeans. *Webtechniques* (May 1999). www.webtechniques.com/archives/1999/05/spitzer-02/.

Stein, Lincoln. In Quest of Enterprise JavaBeans. *Webtechniques* (June 1999). www.webtechniques.com/archives/1999/06/webm/.

Server-Side Scripting and JSP (Chapter 20)

Brown, Simon, Robert Burdick, Jayson Falkner, Ben Galbraith, Rod Johnson, Larry Kim, Casey Kochmer, Thor Kristmundsson, and Sing Li. *Professional JSP, 2nd Edition.* Wrox Press Inc. 2001 (ISBN 1861004958).

Geary, David. *Advanced JavaServer Pages.* Prentice Hall PTR. 2001 (ISBN 0130307041).

Henry, Ethan. A Look Inside JavaServer Pages. *Webtechniques* (November 1999). www.webtechniques.com/archives/1999/11/note/.

Jones, Kevin. Putting Up a Good Front. *JavaPro* (March 2001). www.devx.com/upload/free/features/javapro/2001/01mar03/kj0103/kj0103.asp.

PHP. php.net.

Trachtman, Michael. Caffeinate Your HTML with a Shot of Java. *Webtechniques* (May 2000). www.webtechniques.com/archives/2000/05/trachtman/.

Tremblett, Paul. What Are Java Server Pages? *Dr. Dobb's Journal* (December 1999). www.ddj.com/articles/1999/9912/9912k/9912k.htm.

Williams, Al. Consistency with JSP. *Webtechniques* (July 2000). www.webtechniques.com/archives/2000/07/java/.

Williams, Al. Who Are You, Anyway? *Webtechniques* (July 2000). www.webtechniques.com/archives/2001/02/java/.

Yunjian, Duan, and Willie Wheeler. Serving XML with JavaServer Pages. *JavaPro* (August 2000). www.devx.com/upload/free/features/javapro/2000/08aug00/ww0008/ww0008.asp.

Zend. zend.com.

Index

A

B

D

E

F

G

N

O

T

continued

X

Y

Hungry Minds, Inc. End-User License Agreement

READ THIS. You should carefully read these terms and conditions before opening the software packet(s) included with this book ("Book"). This is a license agreement ("Agreement") between you and Hungry Minds, Inc. ("HMI"). By opening the accompanying software packet(s), you acknowledge that you have read and accept the following terms and conditions. If you do not agree and do not want to be bound by such terms and conditions, promptly return the Book and the unopened software packet(s) to the place you obtained them for a full refund.

1. **License Grant.** HMI grants to you (either an individual or entity) a nonexclusive license to use one copy of the enclosed software program(s) (collectively, the "Software") solely for your own personal or business purposes on a single computer (whether a standard computer or a workstation component of a multi-user network). The Software is in use on a computer when it is loaded into temporary memory (RAM) or installed into permanent memory (hard disk, CD-ROM, or other storage device). HMI reserves all rights not expressly granted herein.

2. **Ownership.** HMI is the owner of all right, title, and interest, including copyright, in and to the compilation of the Software recorded on the disk(s) or CD-ROM ("Software Media"). Copyright to the individual programs recorded on the Software Media is owned by the author or other authorized copyright owner of each program. Ownership of the Software and all proprietary rights relating thereto remain with HMI and its licensers.

3. **Restrictions On Use and Transfer.**

   (a) You may only (i) make one copy of the Software for backup or archival purposes, or (ii) transfer the Software to a single hard disk, provided that you keep the original for backup or archival purposes. You may not (i) rent or lease the Software, (ii) copy or reproduce the Software through a LAN or other network system or through any computer subscriber system or bulletin-board system, or (iii) modify, adapt, or create derivative works based on the Software.

   (b) You may not reverse engineer, decompile, or disassemble the Software. You may transfer the Software and user documentation on a permanent basis, provided that the transferee agrees to accept the terms and conditions of this Agreement and you retain no copies. If the Software is an update or has been updated, any transfer must include the most recent update and all prior versions.

4. **Restrictions on Use of Individual Programs.** You must follow the individual requirements and restrictions detailed for each individual program in the "What's on the CD-ROM?" appendix of this Book. These limitations are also contained in the individual license agreements recorded on the Software Media. These limitations may include a requirement that after using the program for a specified period of time, the user must pay a registration fee or discontinue use. By opening the Software packet(s), you will be agreeing to abide by the licenses and restrictions for these individual programs that are detailed in the "What's on the CD-ROM?" appendix and on the Software Media. None of the material on this Software Media or listed in this Book may ever be redistributed, in original or modified form, for commercial purposes.

5. **Limited Warranty.**

   (a) HMI warrants that the Software and Software Media are free from defects in materials and workmanship under normal use for a period of sixty (60) days from the date of purchase of this Book. If HMI receives notification within the warranty period of defects in materials or workmanship, HMI will replace the defective Software Media.

   (b) HMI AND THE AUTHOR OF THE BOOK DISCLAIM ALL OTHER WARRANTIES, EXPRESS OR IMPLIED, INCLUDING WITHOUT LIMITATION IMPLIED WARRANTIES OF MERCHANTABILITY AND FITNESS FOR A PARTICULAR PURPOSE, WITH RESPECT TO THE SOFTWARE, THE PROGRAMS, THE SOURCE CODE CONTAINED THEREIN, AND/OR THE TECHNIQUES DESCRIBED IN THIS BOOK. HMI DOES NOT WARRANT THAT THE FUNCTIONS CONTAINED IN THE SOFTWARE WILL MEET YOUR REQUIREMENTS OR THAT THE OPERATION OF THE SOFTWARE WILL BE ERROR FREE.

   (c) This limited warranty gives you specific legal rights, and you may have other rights that vary from jurisdiction to jurisdiction.

6. **Remedies.**

   (a) HMI's entire liability and your exclusive remedy for defects in materials and workmanship shall be limited to replacement of the Software Media, which may be returned to HMI with a copy of your receipt at the following address: Software Media Fulfillment Department, Attn.: *Bulletproofing Web Applications*, Hungry Minds, Inc., 10475 Crosspoint Blvd., Indianapolis, IN 46256, or call 1-800-762-2974. Please allow four to six weeks for delivery. This Limited Warranty is void if failure of the Software Media has resulted from accident, abuse, or misapplication. Any replacement Software Media will be warranted for the remainder of the original warranty period or thirty (30) days, whichever is longer.

(b) In no event shall HMI or the author be liable for any damages whatsoever (including without limitation damages for loss of business profits, business interruption, loss of business information, or any other pecuniary loss) arising from the use of or inability to use the Book or the Software, even if HMI has been advised of the possibility of such damages.

(c) Because some jurisdictions do not allow the exclusion or limitation of liability for consequential or incidental damages, the above limitation or exclusion may not apply to you.

7. **U.S. Government Restricted Rights.** Use, duplication, or disclosure of the Software for or on behalf of the United States of America, its agencies and/or instrumentalities (the "U.S. Government") is subject to restrictions as stated in paragraph (c)(1)(ii) of the Rights in Technical Data and Computer Software clause of DFARS 252.227-7013, or subparagraphs (c) (1) and (2) of the Commercial Computer Software - Restricted Rights clause at FAR 52.227-19, and in similar clauses in the NASA FAR supplement, as applicable.

8. **General.** This Agreement constitutes the entire understanding of the parties and revokes and supersedes all prior agreements, oral or written, between them and may not be modified or amended except in a writing signed by both parties hereto that specifically refers to this Agreement. This Agreement shall take precedence over any other documents that may be in conflict herewith. If any one or more provisions contained in this Agreement are held by any court or tribunal to be invalid, illegal, or otherwise unenforceable, each and every other provision shall remain in full force and effect.

Professional Mindware™

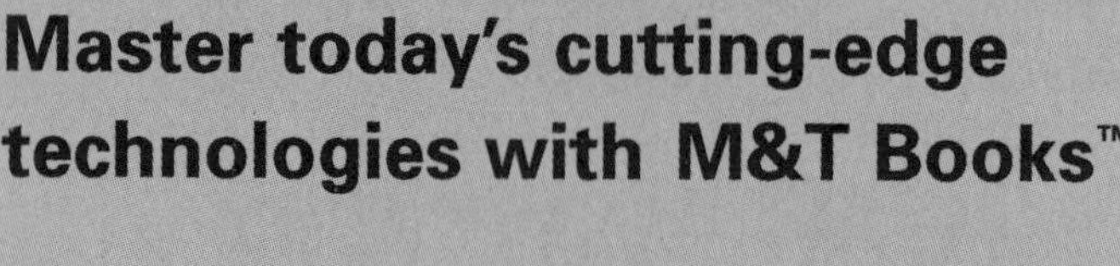

As an IT professional, you know you can count on M&T Books for authoritative coverage of today's hottest topics. From ASP+ to XML, just turn to M&T Books for the answers you need.

Written by top IT professionals, M&T Books delivers the tools you need to get the job done, whether you're a programmer, a Web developer, or a network administrator.

Open Source: The Unauthorized White Papers
408 pp • 0-7645-4660-0 • $19.99 U.S. • $29.99 Can.

XHTML™: Moving Toward XML
456 pp • 0-7645-4709-7 • $29.99 U.S. • 44.99 Can.

Cisco® IP Routing Handbook
552 pp • 0-7645-4695-3 • 29.99 U.S. • $44.99 Can.

Cross-Platform Perl, 2nd Edition
648 pp • 0-7645-4729-1 • 39.99 U.S. • $59.99 Can.

Linux® Rapid Application Development
648 pp • 0-7645-4740-2 • $39.99 U.S. • $59.99 Can.

XHTML In Plain English
750 pp • 0-7645-4743-7 • $19.99 U.S. • $29.99 Can.

XML In Plain English, 2nd Edition
750 pp • 0-7645-4744-5 • $19.99 U.S. • $29.99 Can.

The SuSE™ Linux® Server
600 pp • 0-7645-4765-8 • $39.99 U.S. • $59.99 Can.

Red Hat® Linux® Server, 2nd Edition
816 pp • 0-7645-4786-0 • $39.99 U.S. • $59.99 Can.

Java™ In Plain English, 3rd Edition
750 pp • 0-7645-3539-0 • $19.99 U.S. • $29.99 Can.

The Samba Book *(Available Spring '01)*
550 pp • 0-7645-4773-9 • $39.99 U.S. • $59.99 Can.

Managing Linux® Clusters *(Available Spring '01)*
xx pp • 0-7645-4763-1 • $24.99 U.S. • $37.99 Can

MySQL™/PHP Database Applications
(Available Spring '01)
504 pp • 0-7645-3537-4 • $39.99 U.S. • $59.99 Can.

Available wherever the very best technology books are sold.
For more information, visit us at www.mandtbooks.com

©2001 Hungry Minds, Inc. All rights resrved. M&TBooks, the M&T Books logo and Professional Mindware are trademarks of Hungry Minds. All other trademarks are property of their respective owners.